T0354745

Notable Americans with Slovak Roots

Books Authored or Edited by Miloslav Rechcigl, Jr.

Scholarly Publications:

American Jews with Czechoslovak Roots
Czechs Won't Get Lost in the World Let Alone in America
Beyond the Sea of Beer or Czech America as Few People Know It
Encyclopedia of Bohemian and Czech American Biography (3 vols.)
Czech It Out. Czech American Biography Sourcebook
Czech American Timetable. Chronology of Milestones
in the History of Czechs in America
Czech American Bibliography. A Comprehensive Listing
Czechmate. From Bohemian Paradise to American Haven. A Personal Memoir
On Behalf of their Homeland: Fifty Years of SVU
Czechs and Slovaks in America
Czech and Slovak American Archival Materials and their Preservation
Czechoslovak American Archivalia 2 vols.
Czech-American Historic Sites, Monuments, and Memorials
US Legislators with Czechoslovak Roots
Educators with Czechoslovak Roots
Deceased Members of the Czechoslovak Society of Arts and Sciences
Czechoslovak Society of Arts and Sciences Directory: 8 editions
The Czechoslovak Contribution to World Culture
Czechoslovakia Past and Present 2 vols.
Studies in Czechoslovak History 2 vols.

Scientific Monographs:

Nutrition and the World Food Problem
Comparative Animal Nutrition. Vol. 1. Carbohydrates,
Lipids, and Accessory Growth Factors
Comparative Animal Nutrition. Vol. 2 Nutrient Elements and Toxicants
Comparative Animal Nutrition. Vol. 3. Nitrogen,
Electrolytes, Water and Energy Metabolism
Comparative Animal Nutrition. Vol. 4. Physiology of Growth and Nutrition
Man, Food and Nutrition. Strategies and Technological Measures
for Alleviating the World Food Problem
World Food Problem: A Selective Bibliography of Reviews
Food, Nutrition and Health. A Multidisciplinary Treatise
Enzyme Synthesis and Degradation in Mammalian Systems
Microbodies and Related Particles

Handbook Series in Nutrition and Food: 18 vols.

Czech Publications:

Pro Vlast. Padesát let Společnosti pro vědy a umění
Postavy naší Ameriky

NOTABLE AMERICANS WITH SLOVAK ROOTS

Bibliography, Bio-Bibliography and Historiography

MILOSLAV RECHCIGL, JR.

SVU Scholar-in-Residence and Past President
Czechoslovak Society of Arts and Sciences (SVU)

With the assistance of Michael Kopanic, Jr.

2019

authorHOUSE®

AuthorHouse™
1663 Liberty Drive
Bloomington, IN 47403
www.authorhouse.com
Phone: 1 (800) 839-8640

Published by AuthorHouse 04/10/2019

ISBN: 978-1-5462-7320-2 (sc)
ISBN: 978-1-5462-7321-9 (hc)
ISBN: 978-1-5462-7319-6 (e)

Library of Congress Control Number: 2018914974

Print information available on the last page.

Any people depicted in stock imagery provided by Getty Images are models, and such images are being used for illustrative purposes only. Certain stock imagery © Getty Images.

This book is printed on acid-free paper.

Because of the dynamic nature of the Internet, any web addresses or links contained in this book may have changed since publication and may no longer be valid. The views expressed in this work are solely those of the author and do not necessarily reflect the views of the publisher, and the publisher hereby disclaims any responsibility for them.

In affection to my charming wife Eva,
loving children Jack and Karen,
adorable grandchildren Greg, Kevin, Lindsey, Kristin and Paul,
and dear daughter-in-law Nancy
and
in memory of my beloved parents.

FOREWORD

Slovaks gained their modern statehood only 25 years ago, although they lived in Central Europe for centuries. The history of Central Europe is inextricably linked to political, cultural and social-economic developments of Slovak people. Also, the reasons of vast Slovak emigration in the 19th and 20th centuries originate from the developments in Central Europe. The Austro-Hungarian Empire did not create any favorable conditions for ethnic groups living on its territory and in combination with the dire economic situation, political oppression and lack of basic social care forced hundreds of thousand Slovaks to leave their homeland for different parts of the world.

The United States became a primary destination for many Slovak emigrants for different reasons. The industrial revolution created many new job opportunities and let Slovak workers earn money abroad and provide for their families at home. Many Slovaks decided to leave their homeland for the United States in order to enjoy political and social freedom, equal opportunities and a better future for their children.

The history and strength of the United States has been shaped by active participation of many Slovak immigrants. They worked hard in mines and steel-mills, creating wealth and well-being in Pennsylvania, Cleveland, Illinois and other parts of the United States. Behind every personality in this book there are a number of family members who would save every penny to provide for a better future for their children and grandchildren.

Slovaks living in the United States never forgot about their homeland. They followed the developments in Austro-Hungarian Empire and showed solidarity with their compatriots. As soon as conditions for the creation of an independent state were in place, Slovak-Americans stepped forth and together with Czech-Americans signed the Cleveland and the Pittsburgh Agreements calling for the creation of Czechoslovakia. 75 years of Czechoslovakia and 25 years of Slovakia showed that the dream of our Slovak-American compatriots has been fulfilled. They dreamed of better lives for their children and grandchildren, so that they did not have to emigrate out of despair without the hope of returning to their homeland. They fought for better lives for Slovaks at home and they deserve our utmost gratitude.

This book is about Slovaks who made the United States and Slovakia famous. Their numbers, in just about every area of human endeavor, will surprise you. This has been a unique undertaking and I would like to cordially thank its author Mila Rechcigl for dedicating his professional and personal life to collecting, promoting and defending the Slovak heritage in the United States.

Peter Kmec
Foreign Policy Advisor to the Slovak Prime Minister
Former Ambassador of the Slovak Republic to the US

PREFACE

A s noted in one of my earlier papers,[1] Slovak Americans are well known for their cultural contributions in church-related activities, their ethnic press, their work in fraternal organizations and for sponsorship of various community events.[2] Less known are accomplishments of Slovak Americans in specific professions. This is particularly evident in the Slovak League's Bicentennial monograph, *Slovaks in America*,[3] one of a very few major publications on the subject, which focus mostly on religious aspects, devoting over 100 pages to Slovak parishes in America alone. As is true in in most other similar publications, the emphasis has been on Roman Catholicism, with limited attention to Slovak Protestants, and the exclusion of the Slovak American Jews. Although excellent historiographies, relating to the Slovaks in America, have been written by reputable scholars,[4] they cannot very well go beyond what has been written.

The purpose of this monograph is to correct some of these shortcomings. It is also apparent that some of the areas of Slovak bibliographical and historiographical literature are rather scanty, since so little has been written.

---

[1] Rechcigl, Miloslav, Jr., "Cultural Contributions of Americans with Roots in Slovakia," *Kosmas. Czechoslovak and Central European Journal*, 14, No. 1 (Fall 2000), pp. 95-106. See also Miloslav Rechcigl, Jr.'s monograph, *Beyond the Sea of Beer. History of Immigration of Bohemians and Czechs to the New World and their Contributions*. Bloomington, IN: AuthorHouse, 2017, pp. 767-778.

[2] Prior to the referenced publication, I had presented a paper at the SVU Conference in Kosice in 1995, on "On the Slovak Greats in America, about Whom Less Likely is Known," which was subsequently printed in the Slovak media (Part 1," *Forum*, October 1995, pp. 8-9; Part 2, *Ibid.*, November 1995, pp. 15-16.

[3] Krajsa, Joseph C., ed., *Slovaks in America*: A Bicentennial Study. Middletown, PA: The Slovak League of America, 1978. 494p.

[4] Stolarik, M. Mark, "From Field to Factory: The Historiography of the Slovak Immigration to the United States," *International Migration Review* 10, No. 1 (Spring 1976), pp. 81-102; Stolarik, M. Mark, "The Historiography of Slovak Immigration to the United States and Canada, 1976-1988," *Ethnic Forum* 8, No. 1 (1988), pp. 23-39; Kopanic, Michael, J., Jr., "The Slovak Community of Cleveland: Historiography and Sources," *Ethnic Forum*, 10, No. 1 / 2 (January 1990), pp. 83-97; Kusik, James P., *Recent Research on Slovak Americans: A Selective Bibliography*. Technical Report, Saint Xavier University, March 2017. 17p.

This is no reflection of the lack of work done by individual Slovak Americans in any one particular field. As the reader will find out, Slovak Americans have been involved in just about every field of human endeavor. It is for this reason why this compendium has been enlarged to also include biobibliographical literature, an area which has, so far, been neglected.

As for the definition what constitutes a *bona fide* a Slovak American, included are individuals with the roots in Slovakia, irrespective of their ethnicity or nationality, who were either born there or who descended from there.

To identify such individuals has not always been easy, particularly in the case of the first Slovak immigrants in the 19th century. They usually listed Hungary as their country of origin, without mentioning their Slovak ancestry. What makes it even more difficult was when they omitted listing the name of the village or town from which they came. Slovaks born during the era of the Czechoslovak Republic usually gave Czechoslovakia as the country of their birth, without specifying the location. So, for the sake of uniformity, we have marked all Slovaks of that era as being born in Czechoslovakia, abbreviated as Czech., while all other individuals born on the Slovak territory as being born in Slovakia. Some of these difficulties have been overcome by increased interest in genealogy which forces the individuals to research their ancestral past.

The monograph has been organized by subject areas and, generally, follows an outline as in my recent publication, *American Jews with Czechoslovak Roots*.[5] One of the novelties of the publication has been the inclusion of an archival material subsection which provides information relating to family papers in various archives, and the genealogical GENi subsection, an excellent source of family trees on specific families. Both sources also provide a wealth of reliable biographical information. Other than that, there is no one single resource, to which one could turn, except perhaps to Wikipedia, which needs to be doublechecked for reliability.

I wish to express my appreciation to a noted Slovak American historian, Michael Kopanic, for his comments and suggestions, and for kindly reviewing the draft manuscript.

---

[5] Rechcigl, Miloslav, Jr., *American Jews with Czechoslovak Roots*. Bloomington, IN: AuthorHouse, 2018.

Contents

Listings

LISTINGS

I. General References

A. BIBLIOGRAPHIES

Jerabek, Esther, *Czechs and Slovaks in North America: A Bibliography*. New York: SVU, 1976. 448 p.

Kona, Martha Mistina, Ph. D. Dissertations in Slovakiana in the Western World: Bibliography (including Master's Theses), Wilmette, IL.: K & K House; Martin : Matica slovenská, 1996.

Lacko, Michael, "Slovaks Abroad," in his *Slovak Bibliography Abroad 1945-1964*. Cleveland-Rome: Slovak Institute, 1966, pp. 207-244.

Lacko, Michael. "Slovaks Abroad," in his *Slovak Bibliography Abroad 1966-1975*. Cleveland-Rome: Slovak Institute, 1977, pp. 194-238.

Miller, Wayne C. "Slovak Americans: A Guide to the Slovak- American Experience," in: *A Comprehensive Bibliography for the Study of American Minorities*. New York: New York University Press, 1976, Vol. 1, pp. 637--643.

Rechcigl, Miloslav Jr., "A Classified Guide to Bibliographies Relating to Czech, Slovak, and Ruthenian Immigrants in America," *Kosmas* 7 (1988), pp. 189-212.

Rechcigl, Miloslav Jr.," Czechs, Slovaks and Ruthenians in the U.S.: A Selective Bibliography." *Czechoslovak and Central European Journal* 10, No. 1 (Summer 1991), pp. 82-132.

Rechcigl, Miloslav, Jr., Slovak Americans: A Selective Bibliography in English," in: *Czechs and Slovaks in America*. Boulder, CO: East European Monographs, 2005, pp. 27-34.

Rechcigl, Miloslav, Jr., *American Jews with Czechoslovak Roots. A Bibliography, Bio-Bibliography and Historiography*. Bloomington, IN: AuthorHouse, 2018. 388p.

České a slovenské knihy v exilu. Bibliografie 1948-1989. By Ludmila Šeflová. Praha: ČSDS, 2008. 550p.

"Slovaks," in: *The Peoples of Pennsylvania. An Annotated Bibliography of Resource Materials*. Compiled by David E. Washburn. Pittsburgh: University of Pittsburgh Press, 1981, pp. 189-205.

B. Archival Materials and Library Holdings

1. Surveys

Czech and Slovak American Archival Materials and their Presentation. Proceedings of the Working Conference, held at the Czech and Slovak Embassies in Washington, DC on November 22-23, 2003. Edited by Miloslav Rechcigl, Jr. Prague: Prague Edition Ltd., 2004. 166 p.

Rechcigl, Miloslav, Jr., *Czechoslovak American Archivalia.* Olomouc - Ostrava: Palacký University, 2004. 2 vols. 206p., 368 p.

Wynar, Lubomyr and Lois Butler, "Slovak American Resources," in his *Guide to Ethnic Museums, Libraries and Archives in the United States.* Kent, OH: Kent State University School of Library Science, 1978, pp. 281-186.

Rechcigl, Miloslav, Jr., *Czech And Slovak American Archival Materials and their Presentation.* Prague: Prague Edition, 2004. 166p.

Siemaszkiewicz, Wojciech, "Documenting the Efforts of the Home Countries: Poland, the Czech Republic, Slovakia and Émigré Collections in the United States of America," *Slavic & East European Information Resources,* Vol. 14, No. 4, Oct. 2013, pp. 227-233.

2. Specific Archives

a. Files of Organizations

"American Fund for Czechoslovak Refugees, (New York, NY) Records, in: Immigration history Research Center Archives, Minneapolis, MN. See - https://archives.lib.umn.edu/repositories/6/resources/3888

"Archives and Czechs and Slovaks Abroad," The University of Chicago Library. See - https://www.lib.uchicago.edu/e/su/slavic/acasa.html

"Archives of the Society for the History of Czechoslovak Jews, 1962-2010," in: Leo M Baeck Institute, New York, NY. See - http://digifindingaids.cjh.org/?pID=2956147

"Czech and Slovak Archive Collections," in: Czechoslovak Genealogical Society International. See - https://www.cgsi.org/news/2011/11/17/archive

"The Czech and Slovak Collections at the Library of Congress," in: Overviews of the Collections. See - https://www.loc.gov/rr/european/coll/czec.html

"Czech / Slovak American Collection, 1892-ongoing," in: Milwaukee Co. Historical Society. See: https://milwaukeehistory.net/czechslovak-american-collection-1892-ongoing/

"Czech Republic & Slovakia," in: Harvard University Research Guides. See - https://guides.library.harvard.edu/slavicstudies/czechrepublicslovakia

"Czechoslovak Society of Arts and Sciences Records SVU)," in: IHRC3006. See - https://archives.lib.umn.edu/repositories/6/resources/7706

"First Slovak Wreath of the Free Eagle Records," in: Historical Society of Pennsylvania, Philadelphia, PA. See - https://discover.hsp.org/Record/ead-3563/Description#tabnav

"Ladies Pennsylvania Slovak Catholic Union Records, 1905-1984," in: Research Library of the Balch Institute for Ethnic Studies, Philadelphia. See - http://www2.hsp.org/collections/Balch%20manuscript_guide/html/lpscu.html

"National Slovak Society of the United States of America (Pittsburgh, PA) Records," in: IHRC Archives, University of Minnesota, Minneapolis. See - https://archives.lib.umn.edu/repositories/6/resources/4299

"Pennsylvania Slovak Catholic Union Collection," in: The Historical Society of Pennsylvania, Philadelphia, Pa. See - http://fliphtml5.com/umov/ovue/basic

"Slovak American Collection of Printed Materials," in: IHRC Archives, University of Minnesota. See - https://archives.lib.umn.edu/repositories/6/search?q[]=Slovak+American+Collection+of+printed+materials.&op[]=&field[]=keyword&from_year[]=&to_year[]=&page=1813

"Slovak American Periodicals," IHRC Archives. See - https://www.lib.umn.edu/ihrca/periodicals/slovak

"Slovak Archives," in: University of Ottawa Library. See - https://uottawa.libguides.com/c.php?g=265223&p=1774099

"Slovak Manuscript Collections," in: The Research Library of the Balch Institute, Philadelphia, PA. See - http://www2.hsp.org/collections/Balch%20manuscript_guide/html/slovak.html

"Slovak Subject Collection 1944-2002," in: Hoover Institution. See - http://www.oac.cdlib.org/findaid/ark:/13030/tf0m3n97dv/?query=Slovak

"Slovak Institute and Reference Library - Personalities File." See - http://www.slovakinstitute.com/archives.htm

b. Files of Individuals

"Vojtech E. Andic Papers," in: IHRC Archives, University of Minnesota. See - https://archives.lib.umn.edu/repositories/6/resources/3937

"Bela Bartok Papers, 1941-1943," in: Columbia University, Rarebook & Manuscript Library. See - http://www.columbia.edu/cu/lweb/eresources/archives/rbml/Bartok/

"Edward J. Behuncik Papers," in: The Historical Society of Pennsylvania, Philadelphia. See - https://discover.hsp.org/Record/ead-MSS170

"Papers of Charles Belohlavek 1903-1983," in: Research Library of the Balch Institute for Ethnic Studies, Philadelphia. See - http://www2.hsp.org/collections/Balch%20manuscript_guide/html/belohlavek.ht

"Bettelheim Family Collection," in: US Holocaust Memorial Museum. See - https://collections.ushmm.org/search/catalog/irn553992

"Richard Pollak Collection of Bruno Bettelheim Research Materials 1863-2006," in: The University of Chicago Library - Special Collections Research Center. See - https://www.lib.uchicago.edu/e/scrc/findingaids/view.php?eadid=ICU.SPCL.POLLAKBETTELHEIM

"The George Blanda Collection," in: SCP Auctions. See - http://scpauctions.com/george-blanda/

"Art and History of Maurice Brown," in: Maurice Braun Gallery. See - http://www.mauricebraungallery.com/

"Cihuly Collection," in: Morean Arts Center. See - http://www.moreanartscenter.org/chihuly/

"Bela Csejtey Papers," in: Online Archive of California. See - https://oac.cdlib.org/findaid/ark:/13030/c8k35sdm/entire_text/

"Ján Denďúr Papers, 1898-1988," in: The Historical Society of Pennsylvania, Philadelphia. See - https://hsp.org/sites/default/files/mss/finding_aid_3032_dendur.pdf

"Alfred Diamant papers, 1950-2010, bulk 1960-1996," in: Indiana University Archives. See - http://webapp1.dlib.indiana.edu/findingaids/view?doc.view=entire_text&docId=InU-Ar-VAD3919

"Doránsky Family Fonds," in: Archives and Special Collections of the University of Ottawa Library. See - https://uottawa.libguides.com/ld.php?content_id=10658491

John T. Fiala Papers (1860-1871)," in: Missouri Historical Society Archives, St. Louis. See - http://mohistory.org/collections/item/resource:103165.

"Felix Frankfurter Papers, 1846-1966," in: Library of Congress. See - https://www.loc.gov/item/mm73047571/

"D. Carleton Gajdusek Papers,1918-2009," in: US National Library of Medicine, NIH. See - https://oculus.nlm.nih.gov/cgi/f/findaid/findaid-idx?c=nlmfindaid;idno=gajdusek565

"D. Carleton Gajdusek Papers, 1926 - 1997," in: University of California, San Diego Libraries. See - https://library.ucsd.edu/speccoll/findingaids/mss0421.html

"Gleiman Family Fonds," in: Archives and Special Collections of the University of Ottawa. Library. See - https://uottawa.libguides.com/ld.php?content_id=10658189

"Joseph Goldberger Papers, 1891-1949," in: University of North Carolina, Chapel Hill. See - https://finding-aids.lib.unc.edu/01641/

"Joseph Goldberger Papers," in: Vanderbilt University. Library. See - https://www.library.vanderbilt.edu/biomedical/sc_diglib/archColl/27.html

"Louis Grossmann Papers, 1896-1926," in: Jacob Rader Marcus Center of the American Jewish Archives. See - http://collections.americanjewisharchives.org/ms/ms0092/ms0092.html

"Andrew G. Grutka Papers," in: Calumet Regional Archives, CRA334, Indiana U Northwest. See - http://www.iun.edu/~cra/cra_records/cra334.shtml

"Štefan Hreha Fonds," in: Archives and Special Collections of the University of Ottawa Library. See - https://uottawa.libguides.com/ld.php?content_id=10658493

"Adolph Huebsch Papers. 1850-1884," in: The Jacob Rader Marcus Center of the American Jewish Archives. See - http://collections.americanjewisharchives.org/ms/ms0469/ms0469.html

"B.W. Huebsch Papers, 1893-1964," in: Library of congress. See - https://www.loc.gov/item/mm79050013/

"B. W. Huebsch Papers, 1909-1963," in: Columbia University Libraries Archival Collections. See - http://www.columbia.edu/cu/lweb/archival/collections/ldpd_4078918/

"Papers of Vladimir Hurban, 1917-1951," in: Research Library of the Balch Institute for Ethnic Studies, Philadelphia. See - http://www2.hsp.org/collections/Balch%20manuscript_guide/html/hurban.html

"Vladimir Hurban Papers," in: Historical Society of Pennsylvania (HSP), Philadelphia, PA. See - https://discover.hsp.org/Record/ead-MSS034

"Rose Schury Hurbanek Papers and Photographs 1925-1995," in: University of Pittsburgh Library System, PA. See - http://historicpittsburgh.org/islandora/object/pitt%3AUS-QQS-mss719/viewer

"Oszkár Jászi Papers, 1876-1979," in: Columbia University Libraries Archival Collections. See - http://www.columbia.edu/cu/lweb/archival/collections/ldpd_4078945/

"Yeshayahu Jelinek papers," in: IHRC Archives, University of Minnesota. See - https://archives.lib.umn.edu/repositories/6/resources/4038

"Rafael Joseffy Music and Personal Papers, 1812-1915," in: University of Illinois Archives. See - https://archives.library.illinois.edu/archon/?p=collections/controlcard&id=10646 -

"Alois Kaiser, 1840-1908), in: Milken Archive of Jewish Music. See - https://www.milkenarchive.org/artists/view/alois-kaiser/

"Ľudovit Kandra Fonds," in: Archives and Special Collections of the University of Ottawa Library. See - https://uottawa.libguides.com/ld.php?content_id=10657998

"George Alexander Kohut Papers. 1895-1965," in: The Jacob Rader Marcus Center of the American Jewish Archives. See - http://collections.americanjewisharchives.org/ms/ms0381/ms0381.html

"Tom T. Kovary family collection," in: US Holocaust Memorial Museum. See - https://portal.ehri-project.eu/units/us-005578-irn37744

"Eugene A. Kozlay Papers," in: Syracuse University Libraries, Special Collections. See - https://library.syr.edu/digital/guides/k/kozlay_ea.htm

"David Lefkowitz, Sr. Papers," in: American Jewish archives. See - http://collections.americanjewisharchives.org/ms/ms0195/ms0195.html

"David E. Lilienthal Papers 1900-1981," in: Princeton University Library. See - https://findingaids.princeton.edu/collections/MC148

"Jacob M. Lowy Collection," in: Library and Archives Canada. See - http://www.bac-lac.gc.ca/eng/lowy-collection/pages/lowy-collection.aspx

"Bernard Dov Marton Papers, 1914-1991, 1998" in: Yeshiva University Libraries. See - http://libfindaids.yu.edu:8082/xtf/view?docId=ead/bernardmarton/bernardmarton.xml;query=;brand=default

"Medlen Family Collection, 1905-1991)," PennState University Libraries. See - https://www.libraries.psu.edu/findingaids/CCHC7.htm

"Thomas M. Messer Papers, 1949-2010," in: Smithsonian. Archives of American Art. See - https://www.aaa.si.edu/collections/thomas-m-messer-papers-6570

"Jozef A. Mikuš Fonds," in: Archives and Special Collections of the University of Ottawa. See - https://uottawa.libguides.com/ld.php?content_id=10658000

"Rev. Kenneth Dexter Miller papers," in: IHRC Archives, University of Minnesota. See - https://archives.lib.umn.edu/repositories/6/resources/4324

"Peter Molčan Fonds," in: Archives and Special Collections of the University of Ottawa Library. https://uottawa.libguides.com/ld.php?content_id=10658272

"Mudry (Michael) Papers 1939-2000," in: Hoover Institution. See - http://www.oac.cdlib.org/findaid/ark:/13030/kt7580366n/?query=Slovak

"Ernest Nagel Papers 1930-1988," in: Columbia University. Rare Book & Manuscript Library - http://www.columbia.edu/cu/lweb/eresources/archives/rbml/Nagel/index.html

"Morris Newfield Papers," in: American Jewish Archives. See - http://collections.americanjewisharchives.org/ms/ms0045/ms0045.html

"Michael Novak Collection," in: University of Notre Dame Archives. See - http://archives.nd.edu/findaids/ead/xml/nvk.xml

"Michael Novak Papers," in: IHRC Archives, University of Minnesota, Minneapolis. See - https://archives.lib.umn.edu/repositories/6/resources/4309

"Stefan Osusky Papers," in: IHRC Archives, University of Minnesota, Minneapolis. See - https://archives.lib.umn.edu/repositories/6/resources/4438

"Jan Papanek Papers," in: Manuscripts and Archives Division, The New York Public Library, New York, NY. See - http://archives.nypl.org/mss/2334

"John Pastorak, Sermons," in: Archives & Special Collections, University of Nebraska–Lincoln Libraries. See - http://archivespec.unl.edu/findingaids/ms088-pastorak-unl.html

"Adam Podkrivacky Papers," in: Immigration History Research Centers Archives, Minneapolis, MN. See - https://archives.lib.umn.edu/repositories/6/resources/4465

"Papers of Justine Wise Polier, 1892-2015," in: Harvard University Library. See - http://oasis.lib.harvard.edu/oasis/deliver/~sch00238

"Andrej Potocky Fonds," in: Archives and Special Collections of the University of Ottawa Library. See - https://uottawa.libguides.com/ld.php?content_id=10658496

"The Max Reinhardt Archives & Library," in: Binghamton University Libraries. See - https://www.binghamton.edu/libraries/special-collections/researchandcollections/reinhardt.html

"Richard H. Rich Papers, 1902-1981," in: Emory University, Stuart A. Rose Manuscript, Archives, and Rare Book Library, Atlanta, GA

"Andrew Rolik Papers," in: IHRC Archives, University of Minnesota. See - https://archives.lib.umn.edu/repositories/6/resources/4513

"Greta L. Schreyer Papers, 1956-1979," in: Smithsonian Archives of American Art. See - https://www.aaa.si.edu/collections/greta-l-schreyer-papers-8571

"Tibor Serly Papers, 1905-1992," in: Columbia University Libraries Archival Collections. See - http://www.columbia.edu/cu/lweb/archival/collections/ldpd_5420150/

"Karol Sidor Papers," in: Hoover Institution. See - http://www.oac.cdlib.org/findaid/ark:/13030/c88w3jxt/?query=Slovak

"Papers of Klement Simoncic," in: Hoover Institution Archives. See - https://www.hoover.org/news/hoover-archives-acquires-papers-klement-simoncic

"Slabey, Andrew Paul Papers, 1917-1966," in: Historical Society of Pennsylvania (under Slovak) - See -http://www2.hsp.org/collections/Balch%20manuscript_guide/html/slovak.html

"Juraj Slávik Papers," in: Hoover Institution Archives, Stanford, CA. See - http://www.oac.cdlib.org/findaid/ark:/13030/kt6n39p6z0/entire_text/

"Anna M. Sotak Papers," in: Western Reserve Historical Society. See - http://ead.ohiolink.edu/xtf-ead/view?docId=ead/OCLWHi2431.xml;query=;brand=default

"Joseph Staško Fonds," in: Archives and Special Collections of the University of Ottawa. See - https://uottawa.libguides.com/ld.php?content_id=10658498

"Imrich Stolárik Fonds," in: Archives and Special Collections of the University of Ottawa. See - https://uottawa.libguides.com/ld.php?content_id=10658499

"Leo Szilard Papers," in: University of California Library, San Diego. See - https://library.ucsd.edu/dc/collection/bb0752385q

"Benjamin Szold Papers, 1855-1902," in: he Jacob Rader Marcus Center of the American Jewish Archives. See - http://collections.americanjewisharchives.org/ms/ms0265/ms0265.html

"Papers of Henrietta Szold, 1889-1960," in: Harvard University Library. See - http://oasis.lib.harvard.edu/oasis/deliver/~sch00935

"Jacob Weinberger Collection - MSS 105," in: Arizona Historical Foundation. See - http://www.ahfweb.org/download/Weinberger_MSS_105.pdf

"Jacob Weinberger Papers 1906-1974 MSS-380," in: Arizona Archives Online. http://www.azarchivesonline.org/xtf/view?docId=ead/asu/weinberger_j.xml;query=;brand=default

"Stephen Wise Papers, 1841-1978," in: American Jewish Historical Society Center for Jewish History. See - http://digifindingaids.cjh.org/?pID=365016

"Stephen S. Wise Collection. 1893-1969," in: The Jacob Rader Marcus Center of the American Jewish Archives. See - http://collections. americanjewisharchives.org/ms/ms0049/ms0049.html

"Ivan Zarobsky Papers, 1921 to 1955," in: University of Toledo Archives, MS Collection. See - http://www.utoledo.edu/library/canaday/findingaids1/UM_4.pdf

"Robert Zecker Collection" in: IHRC Archives, University of Minnesota. See - https://archives.lib.umn.edu/repositories/6/resources/7491

"Alexander von Zemplinsky Collection, 1887-1939," in: Library of Congress. See - http://memory.loc.gov/diglib/ihas/loc.natlib.scdb.200033894/default.html

"John Zubek Papers," in: University of Manitoba Libraries. See - http://www.umanitoba.ca/libraries/units/archives/collections/complete_holdings/ead/html/zubek.shtml

C. BIOGRAPHICAL COMPENDIA

"Biographies," in: *Panorama: A Historical Review of Czechs and Slovaks in the United States of America.* Cicero, IL: Czechoslovak National Council of America, 1970, pp. 187-313.

Droba, Daniel D., ed. *Czech and Slovak Leaders in Metropolitan Chicago.* Chicago: The Slavonic Club of the University of Chicago, 1934. 307p.

Kona, Martha M., *Slovak Americans and Canadians in American Catholic Who's Who, 1911-1981 and Slovak Ethnicity.* Wilmette, IL: K&K House, 1984. 101 p.

Paučo, Jozef, *Slovenski priekopnici v Amerike,* Cleveland: Prva Katolicka Slovenska Jednota, 1972.

"Personalities File" (comprising mostly Slovak Americans), in: Slovak Institute. See - http://www.slovakinstitute.com/archives.htm

Rechcigl, Eva and Miloslav Rechcigl Jr., *SVU Directory. History, Organization and Biographies of Members.* 7th ed. Washington, DC: SVU Press, 1992. 390 p.

Rechcigl, Miloslav, Jr., *Educators with Czechoslovak Roots.* A U.S. and Canadian Faculty Roster. Washington, DC: SVU Press, 1980.122p.

Rechcigl, Miloslav, Jr., *Deceased Members of the Czechoslovak Society of Arts and Sciences (SVU) (1957-2008).* Revised and enlarged edition. Washington, DC: SVU Press, 2008. 71p.

Rechcigl, Miloslav, Jr., *American Jews with Czechoslovak Roots. A Bibliography, Bio-Bibliography and Historiography.* Bloomington, IN: AuthorHouse, 2018. 388p.

Rechcigl, Miloslav, Jr., Eva Rechcigl and Jiri Eichler, *SVU Directory. Organization, Activities and Biographies of Members.* 8th ed. Washington, DC: SVU Press, 2003. 368 p.

Reichman, John J., "Biographies of Czechs and Slovaks in Illinois," in his *Czechoslovaks of Chicago.* Chicago: The Czechoslovak Historical society, 1937, pp. 67-107.

Štěrba, F. C., *Češi a Slováci v Latinské Americe.* (Přehled jejich kulturního přínosu). Washington-New York: SVU, 1962. 61p.

D. MEMOIRS (INCLUDING HOLOCAUST)

Alzo, Lisa A, *Three Slovak Women.*2nd ed. CreateSpace, 2011. 122p.

Amir, Giora, *A Simple Life.* CreateSpace, 2016. 302p.

Baca, John, *A Humble Beginning: My Life.* Allegra Print & Imagining, 2011. 644p.

Bachleba, Steven, *Portrait of an Immigrant*: The Odyssey of a Slovak Boy - Who Immigrated to America with his Family in 1939. CreateSpace, 2013. 178p.

Barak-Ressler, Aliza, *Cry Little Girl: A Tale of the Survival of a Family in Slovakia.* Yad Vashem Publications, 2003. 241p.

Bendik, Edward, Last *Train Out. Escaping Europe - December 1939.* The Author, 2018. 140p.

Bitton-Jackson, Livia, *Saving What Remains:* A Holocaust Survivor's Journey Home to Reclaim Her Ancestry. Lyons Press, 2009. 208p.

Bitton-Jackson, Livia, *My Bridges of Hope.* Simon Pulse, 2011. 384p.

Bodnar, John, "Coal Town Chronicles and Scholarly Books," in: *Ethnic Historians and the Mainstream: Shaping the Nation's Immigration Story.* Edited by David Gerber and Alan Kraut. Rutgers University Press, 2013, pp. 46-65.

Bruchac, Joseph, *Bowman's Store: A Journey to Myself.* Lee & Low Books, 2001. 320p.

Daluge, Agnes Lackovic, *Rosa's Miracle Mouse*: The True Story of a WWII Undercover Teenager. Authors Direct Books, 1999. 227p.

Dunai, Harry I., *Surviving in Silence: A Deaf Boy in the Holocaust, The Harry I. Dunai Story.* Washington, DC, Gallaudet University Press, 2002. 192p.

Eger, Edith Eva, *The Choice: Embrace the Possible.* Scribner, 2017. 304p.

Eisen, Max, *By Chance Alone.* A Remarkable True Story of Courage and Survival at Auschwitz. HarperCollins Publishers, 2016. 304p.

Folta, Richard C., *Of Bench and Bears: Alaska's Bear Hunting Judge*. 2nded. Great Northwest Publishing, 2002.

Gleiman, Lubomir, *From the Maelstrom*. Bloomington, IN: AuthorHouse, 2011.

Greenfield, Martin and Wynton Hall. Regnery History, 2016. 250p.

Jason, Sonya, *Icon of Spring*. Pittsburgh: University of Pittsburgh Press, 2004. 182p.

Jason, Sonya N., *Maria Gulovich, OSS Heroine of World War II:* The Schoolteacher Who Saved American Lives in Slovakia. Jefferson, NC: McFarland & Co., 2008. 286p.

Karas, Nicholas Stevensson, *Hunky: The Immigrant Experience*. Bloomington, IN: AuthorHouse, 2004. 580p.

Kedar-Kehat, Hani, My Nitra: A Family's Struggle to Survive in Slovakia. Yad Vashem Publications, 2015. 254p.

Kemeny, Esther, *On the Shores of Darkness*: The Memoir of Esther Kemeny. The Haller Company, 2003. 144p.

Knill, Iby, *Woman Without a Number*. Scratching Shed, 2010. 320p.

Knill, Iby, *The Woman with Nine Lives*. Scratching Shed Publishing Ltd, 2016. 208p.

Kocur, Richard D., *Jan Kocur - A Story of Slovak Pride, American Patriotism, & the Golden Age of the Slovak League of America*. Modra Publishing, 2009. 286p.

Kovaly, Heda and Erazim Kohak, *The Victors and the Vanquished*. New York: Horizon Press, 1973. 274p.

Kovaly, Heda, *Under a Cruel Star: A Life in Prague, 1941-1968*. New York: Holmes & Meier Publishers, 1997. 192p.

Kovaly, Heda Margolius, *Prague Farewell*. Lexington, MA: Plunkett Lake Press, 2010. 224p.

Kubicek, Peter, *Memories of Evil: Recalling a World War II Childhood*. BookBaby, 2012. 118p.

Lay-Dopyera, Margaret, *My Life as a Dopyera*. Eureka Woods Publications, 2000. 100p.

Levy, Alan, *So Many Heroes*. The Permanent Press, 2015. 421p.

Malie, Rita, *Goodbye America*. Jacksonville Beach, FL: High-Pitched Hum, Inc., 2007. 73p.

Margolius, Heda, *I Do not Want to Remember Auschwitz 1941 - Prague 1968*. London: Weidenfeld and Nicolson, 1973. 174p.

Palka, Jan, *My Slovakia, My Family*. Minneapolis, MN: Kirk House Publishers, 2012. 424p.

Peterik, Jim, *Through the Eye of the Tiger: The Rock 'n' Roll life of Survivor's Founding Member.* BenBella Books, 2014. 352p.

Pier, Andrew, O.S.B., *The Woodlands Above -- Mines Below.* Independence, OH: First Catholic Slovak Union, 1988.

Reichental, Tomi, *I Was Boy in Belsen.* O'Brien Press, 2016. 384p.

Resko, John Allen, *The Gates of Saint Charles. Testing the Waters of a Religious Vocation: A Memoir.* Bloomington, IN: iUniverse, Inc., 2009. 210p.

Rokicak, August, *Growing Up Slovak in America.* Xlibris, 2010. 108p.

Rombauer, Roderick. E. A History of Life. The Author, 1903; reprinted by Forgotten Books in 2018.

Ruzicka, Luba, *Luba's Travels.* "Travels of the Heart. CreateSpace, 2012.

Ryba, Anne Lucas, Humble Beginnings. Kearnery, NE: Morris-Publishing, 2000. 242p.

Sermer, Zuzana, *Survival Kit.* Azrieli Foundation, 2012. 192p.

Sherman, Judith H., *Say the Name: A Survivor's Tale in Prose and Poetry.* University of New Mexico Press, 2005. 199p.

Šimko, Vlado, *Z oboch strán železnej opony.* Lekárove spomienky. Bratislava: Petrus Publishers, 2016. 240p.

Sister Cecilia and William Brinkley, *The Deliverance of Sister Cecilia*: As Told to William Brinkley. Farrar & Straus & Young, 1954. 360p.

Slonim, Eva, *Gazing at the Stars: Memories of a Child Survivor.* Black. Inc., 2014. 198p.

Stolarik, Mark, *Where is My Home: Slovak Immigration to North America (1870-210).* Peter Lang AG, 2012. 392p.

Szapor, Judith, *The Hungarian Pocahontas: The Life and Times of Laura Polanyi Stricker, 1882-1959.* Bloomington, IN: East European Monographs, 2005. 200p.

Tomasov, Agnes, *From Generation to Generation.* Second Story Press, 2010. 256p.

Tomasov, Joseph, *From Loss to Liberation.* Azrieli Foundation, 2017. 208p.

Viest, Ivan, *An Immigrant's Story.* Bloomington, IN: Xlibris Corp., 2006. 550p.

Vilcek, Jan, *Love and Science: A Memoir.* Seven Stories Press, 2016. 272p.

Vrba, Rudolph, *I Escaped from Auschwitz.* Barricade Books, 2002. 447p.

Walko, Ann, *Eternal Memory.* Pittsburgh, PA: Sterling House Publisher, Inc., 1999. 182p.

Weiss, David, *Renaissance or Remembrance?* Jewish Life in My Two Ancestral Hometowns. Expert Promotions LLC, 2017. 104p.

Williams, David, *A Race to Freedom- The Mira Slovak Story.* America through Time, 2018. 400p.

D. INTERVIEWS - ORAL HISTORIES

Center for the Study of History and Memory, Whiting, IN, *Whiting Indiana: Generational Memory 1991-1993.* See - http://www.dlib.indiana.edu/reference/cshm/ohrc102.html

"Recording Voices & Documenting Memories of Czech & Slovak Americans," in: Oral Histories, National Czech and Slovak Museum and Library, Cedar Rapids, IA, See - https://www.ncsml.org/oral-histories/

E. HISTORIOGRAPHY

Bielek, František, "Slovak Emigration in the Years 1880-1939 and Problem Involved in Its Study," in: *Overseas Migration from East-Central and Southeastern Europe, 1880-1940.* Edited by Julianna Puskas. Budapest: Akademia Kiado, 1990, pp. 59-73.

Cincik, Joseph G. "A Study of Documents from Earliest Slovak-American Connections," *Slovenské noviny,* January 13, 1950.

Kona, M. M., *Ph.D. Dissertations in Slovakiana in the Western World.* Martin: Matica Slovenská, 1996.

Kopanic, Michael, J., Jr., "The Slovak Community of Cleveland: Historiography and Sources," *Ethnic Forum,* 10, No. 1 / 2 (January 1990), pp. 83-97.

Kovtun, George J., *A Czech and Slovak History. An American Bibliography.* Washington, DC: Library of Congress, 1996. 481 p.

Kusik, James P., Recent Research on Slovak Americans: A Selective Bibliography. Technical Report, Saint Xavier University, March 2017. 17p. See - https://www.researchgate.net/publication/315756241_Recent_Research_on_Slovak_Americans_A_Selective_Bibliography

Opatrný, Josef, "Nota introductoria," in: *Las Relaciones entre Europa Central y América Latina.* Contextos históricos. Praha: Universidad Carolina, 2017, pp. 7-16.

Polišenský, J., La emigración checoslovaca a América Latina 1680-1945. Problemas y fuentes," *Jahrbuch für Geschichte von Staat, Wirtschaft und Gesellschaft Lateinamerikas,* 13 (1976), pp. pp. 216-248.

Rechcigl, Miloslav, Jr., *American Jews with Czechoslovak Roots. A Bibliography, Bio-Bibliography and Historiography.* Bloomington, IN: AuthorHouse, 2018. 388p.

Stolarik, M. Mark, "From Field to Factory: The Historiography of the Slovak Immigration to the United States," *International Migration Review* 10, No. 1 (Spring 1976), pp. 81-102.

Stolarik, M. Mark, "The Historiography of Slovak Immigration to the United States and Canada, 1976-1988," *Ethnic Forum* 8, No. 1 (1988), pp. 23-39.

Stolarik. M. Mark, "Slovak Historians in Exile in North America, 1945-1992," Human Affairs (Bratislava), 6, No. 1 (1996), pp. 34-44.

F. Periodicals

Bakay-Záhorská, Michaela, and Zdena Kráľová. "Slovak Cultural Heritage in the USA–Periodicals." Thesis, Pedagogická Fakulta Univerzita Konštantína Filozofa v Nitre, 2015.

Bakay-Záhorská, Michaela, and Zdena Kráľová. "The Compatriot Magazine 'Jednota': A Mirror of Hundred-Year History of Slovak Immigrants in the USA." *XLinguae*, Vol. 8, No. 3 (2015), pp. 66–75.

Exilová periodika. Katalog periodik českého a slovenského exilu a krajanských tisků, vydávaných po roce 1945. By Lucie Formanová, Jiří Gruntorád, Michal Přibáň. Praha: Ježek, 2000. 504p.

"History of the Canadian Slovak," in: Kanadský Slovak. See - https://www.kanadskyslovak.ca/index.php/history

Olekšák, Peter, and Albert Kulla. "The Slovak Periodical Press: Historical Development, Current Content, New Forms of Access," *Slavic & East European Information Resources*, Vol.8, No. 2/3 (December 2007), pp. 21–29.

"Slovak American Periodicals," in: IHRC Archives. See - https://www.lib.umn.edu/ihrca/periodicals/slovak

"Zoznam novín a časopisov vydávaných v Amerike pre slovenských vysťahovalcov pred r. 1900" (List of newspapers and periodicals published in America for Slovak emigrants prior to 1900), *Slovo z Britskej Kolumbije*, 9, No. 2 (2016), pp. 6-7.:

G. DIRECTORIES - LISTS

American Czech and Slovak Telephone and Business Directory, 19451-1942 for Chicago and Suburbs. Chicago: Czech Publishing Co., 1941, 160p.

Biographical Directory of the Members of the Czechoslovak Society of Arts and Sciences. Compiled and edited by Eva Rechcigl and Miloslav Rechcigl, Jr. New York, and later, Washington, DC: SVU Press, 1966, 1968, 1972, 1983, 1988, 1992, 2003. 1-8 editions.

Deceased Members of the Czechoslovak Society of Arts and Sciences (SVU)(1957-2008). Revised and enlarged edition. Compiled by Miloslav Rechcigl, Jr. Washington, DC: SVU Press, 2008. 71p.

Educators with Czechoslovak Roots. A U.S. and Canadian Faculty Roster. Compiled by Miloslav Rechcigl, Jr. Washington, DC: SVU Press, 1980.122p.

Index of Czechoslovak Organizations in the United States. Chicago: Exhibit Committee of the Czechoslovak Group, 1933. 115p.

Necedov, John, Ed., *Slovak American Classified Directory: The Slovak Red Book.* New York: Slovak American Classified Directory, 1941. 56p.

"Personalities File" (comprising mostly Slovak Americans), in: Slovak Institute. See - http://www.slovakinstitute.com/archives.htm

Slovak American Hall of Fame. Notable Individuals Who Made a Difference (Revised 2). See - https://www.academia.edu/32446089/Slovak_American_Hall_of_Fame._Revised.doc

U.S. Legislators with Czechoslovak Roots. From Colonial Times to Present with Genealogical Lineages. Compiled by Miloslav Rechcigl, Jr. Washington, DC.: SVU Press, 1987. 65p.

H. DICTIONARIES

English Slovak Dictionary. Anglicko slovensky slovník. By Jan Šimko. Mundelein, IL: Bolchazy-Carducci Publishers, 1991. 1445p.

James, Henry, *The American (Webster's Slovak Thesaurus Edition).*Icon International, 2008. 426p.

Konus, Jozef J., *Slovak-English Phraseological Dictionary/Slovensko-Anglicky Frazeologicky Slovnik.* Passaic, NJ: Slovak Catholic Sokol, 1969.

Kovac, Edward, *Slovak and English Interpreter.* Scranton, PA: Obrana Press, 1951.

Kovac, Edward, Jr., *The Practical English-Slovak Slovak-English Dictionary.* K Enterprises, 1983.

Kovac, Jakub, *The Slovak Dictionary: A Concise English-Slovak Dictionary.* CreateSpace Independent Publishing Platform, 2018. 146p.
Lorinc, Sylvia Galova and Stephen R. Hoferka, Jr. Slovak Phrase Book. Pittsburgh: Lorhof, 1991
Malatinsky, Joseph P., *Slovak Handy Dictionary.* Hippocrene Books, 1995. 1999p.
Orbach, Christopher Leopold, *Slovak-American Interpreter: Nový Anglický Tlumocník pre Slovákov V Amerike...* Nabu Press, 2012. 194p.

I. HANDBOOKS

Nemecek, Paul M. *Czech and Slovak Research Handbook of Biographies and Organizations.* Western Springs, IL: P. M. Nemecek, c2003.
Schlyter, Daniel M. *A Handbook of Czechoslovak Genealogical Research.* Buffalo Grove, IL: Genun Publisher, 1985

J. LIBRARIES - MUSEUMS - ARCHIVES

Czech & Slovak Museum, Omaha, NE
Official Website: "Czech & Slovak Museum." See - http://czechandslovakmuseum.org/

Czechoslovak Heritage Museum, Cicero, IL
Official Website: "Czechoslovak Heritage Museum." See - http://czechoslovakmuseum.com/

Jankola Library & Slovak Museum, Danville, PA
Official Website: "Jankola Library & Slovak museum." See - http://jankolalibrary.sscm.org/slovakmuseum.html; http://jankolalibrary.sscm.org/index.html

National Czech & Slovak Museum & Library, Cedar Rapids, IA
Official Website: "National Czech & Slovak Museum & Library." See - https://www.ncsml.org/

National Slovak Society Heritage Museum, McMurray, PA
Official Website: "National Slovak Society Heritage Museum)." See - http://nsslife.org/museum/

Slovak Canadian Heritage Museum, Mississauga, Canada
Official Website: "Slovak Canadian Heritage Museum." See - http://www.slovakcanadianheritagemuseum.ca/

Slovak Heritage Museum, Cudahy, WI
See Society's Website - http://www.wisconsinslovakhistoricalsociety.org/about.html

Slovak Institute, Cleveland, OH
Official Website: "Welcome to Slovak Institute." See - http://www.slovakinstitute.com/ Historical: Jim Dubelko, "The Slovak Institute." See - https://clevelandhistorical.org/items/show/609

K. LINKS ON INTERNET

"Links," in: Slovak Treasures - and American Slovaks. See - http://www.slovakcooking.com/2010/blog/slovak-treasures/
Rechcigl, Miloslav, Jr., *Czechoslovak Americana on the Net*. A Comprehensive Systematic Guide to Internet Sites Relating to Immigrants in America from the Territory of Former Czechoslovakia, Including Bohemia, Moravia, Silesia, Slovakia, and Subcarpathian Ruthenia. In: academia. edu. See - https://www.academia.edu/11446096/Czechoslovak_Americana_on_the_Net._A_Comprehensive_Systematic_Guide_to_Internet_Sites_Relating_to_Immigrants_in_America_from_the_Territory_of_Former_Czechoslovakia_Including_Bohemia_Moravia_Silesia_Slovakia_and_Subcarpathian_Ruthenia
Rechcigl, Miloslav, Jr., *Czechoslovak Genealogy Sites on the Internet*. Rockville, MD: SVU, 1999.74p.

II. Slovak Heritage

A. GENERAL SURVEYS

1. Slovak History

Bolecek, B. V. and Irene Slamka, *The Slovak Encyclopaedia*. New York: Slovak Academy, 1981.

Drobna, Olga, Eduard Drobny, and Magdalena Gocnikova, *Slovakia: The Heart of Europe*. Wauconda, IL: Bolchazy-Carducci Publishers, 1996.

Dvorak, Pavel, *The Early History of Slovakia in Images*. Budmerice, Slovakia: Vydavateľstvo Rak Budmerice, 2006.

Filová, Danica, Marián Petričko and Ivan Klč, Eds., *One Thousand and Twenty Years of Young Slovakia*. Slovakia: Dušan Kutálek, 2014. 768p.

Fisher, Sharon, *Political Change in Post-Communist Slovakia and Croatia: From Nationalist to Europeanist*. New York: Palgrave Macmillan, 2006.

Henderson, Karen, *Slovakia: The Escape from Invisibility*. London: Routledge, 2002.

Kirschbaum, Joseph M., ed. *Slovakia in the 19th and 20th Centuries*. Proceedings of the Conference on Slovakia Held on June 17-18 in Toronto. Toronto: Slovak World Congress, 1973. 368p.

Kirschbaum, Stanislav J. and Anne C. R. Roman, eds. *Reflections on Slovak History*. Toronto: Slovak World Congress, 1987. 183p.

Kirschbaum, Stanislav, *A History of Slovakia: The Struggle for Survival*. New York: St. Martin's Press, 1995.

Lettrich, Jozef, *History of Modern Slovakia*. New York: Frederick & Praeger, 1955.

Mikula, Susan, *Slovakia: A Political History, 1918-1950*. Milwaukee: Marquette University Press, 1963.

Mikus, Joseph A., *Slovakia: A Political and Constitutional History with Documents*. Bratislava: *Slovak Academic* Press, 1995.

Oddo, Gilbert L., *Slovakia and Its People*. New York: Robert Speller & Sons, Publishers, 1960.

Parker, Andrew, *Slovakia History: Early History, The People's Origin, Culture and Environment*. CreateSpace Independent Publishing Platform, 2017. 182p.

Reich, Mikuláš, Dušan Kováč and Martin D. Brown, *Slovakia in History*. New York: Cambridge University Press, 2013. 434p.

Seton-Watson, Robert W., ed. *Slovakia Then and Now: A Political Survey*. London: G. Allen & Unwin; Prague: Orbis, 1931. 356p.

Slovak Academy of Sciences. Encyclopaedical Institute. *Slovakia and the Slovaks*. Bratislava: Goldpress Publishers, 1994.

Slovakia. A European Story. Edited by Miroslav Londák, Slavomír Michálek, Peter Weiss. Bratislava: Publishing House of the Slovak Academy of Sciences, 2016. 351p.

Slovakia and the Slovaks: A Concise Encyclopedia. Edited by Milan Strhan and David P. Daniel. Bratislava: Goldpress Publishers, 1994.

Špiesz, Anton and Dušan Čaplovič, *Illustrated Slovak History*. Edited by Ladislaus J.Bolchazy, with notes and summary by Michael J. Kopanic, Jr., Wauconda, IL: Bolchazy Carducci Publ., 2006.

Tybor, M. Martina, "Slovakia: Ancestral Homeland of Slovak Americans," in: *Slovaks in America. A Bicentennial Study*, pp. 89-98.

Ward, Thomas Klimek, *People of the Word: A Synopsis of Slovak History*. Martin: Matica Slovenská, 2000.

Yurchak, Peter P. *The Slovaks: Their History and Traditions*. Whiting, Indiana: Rev. John J. Lach, 1947.

2. Czechoslovakia

Bakke, Elizabeth. "Czechoslovakism in Slovak History," in: *Slovakia in History*. Edited by Mikuláš Teich, Dušan Kováč and Martin D. Brown. Cambridge: Cambridge University Press, 2011, pp. 247-268.

Bradley, John F. N. *Czechoslovakia: A Short History*. Edinburgh: Edinburgh University Press, 1971. 212p.

Busek, Vratislav, and Nicolas Spulber, eds., *Czechoslovakia*. New York: Praeger, 1957. 520p.

Johnson, Owen V., *Slovakia 1918–1938: Education and the Making of a Nation*. Boulder, CO: East European Monographs, 1985.

Čapek, Karel, et al., *At the Cross-Roads of Europe: A Historical Outline of the Democratic Idea in Czechoslovakia*. Prague: Pen Club, 1938. 275p.

Czerwinski, Edward J., and Jaroslaw Piekalkiewicz, Eds., *The Soviet Invasion of Czechoslovakia: Its Effects on Eastern Europe*. New York: Praeger, 1972. 210p.

Gruber, Josef, ed. *Czechoslovakia: A Survey of Economic and Social Conditions.* Translated from Czech manuscripts by Ales Broz, Stanislav V. Klima and Jiri J. Kral. New York: Macmillan, 1924. 256p.

Hajda, Jan, ed. *A Study of Contemporary Czechoslovakia.* Chicago: University of Chicago for the Human Relations Area Files, Inc., 1955. 637p.

Hoch, Karel, et al. *World Peace and Czechoslovakia, 1919-1934.* Introduction by Kamil Krofta. London, Maastricht, A. A. M. Stols, 1936. 121p.

Jelinek, Y., *The Lust for Power: Nationalism, Slovakia and the Communists, 1918-1948.* Boulder, CO, 1983.

Johnson, Owen, V., *Slovakia 1918–1938: Education and the Making of a Nation.* Boulder, CO: East European Monographs, 1985.

Kavka, František. *An Outline of Czechoslovak History.* Translated by Jarmila and Ian Milner. Prague: Orbis, 1960. 179p.

Kerner, Robert J., ed. *Czechoslovakia: Twenty Years of Independence.* Berkeley and Los Angeles: University of California Press, 1940. 504p.

Krofta, Kamil. *A Short History of Czechoslovakia.* New York: R. M. McBride & Co., 1934. 198p.

Kusin, Vladimir V., ed. The Czechoslovak Reform Movement, 1968. London: International Research Documents, 1973. 358p.

Mamatey, Victor S., and Radomír Luža, eds. *A History of the Czechoslovak Republic, 1918-1948.* Princeton, N.J.: Princeton University Press, 1973. 534p.

Maurice, Charles E. *Bohemia from the Earliest Times to the Foundation of the Czecho-Slovak Republic in 1918.* London: T. F. Unwin, 1922. 576p.

Polišenský, Josef V. *History of Czechoslovakia in Outline.* Prague: Sphinx Publishers,1948. 142p.

Rechcigl, Miloslav, Jr., Ed. *The Czechoslovak Contribution to World Culture.* The Hague: Mouton & Co., 1964. 682p.

Rechcigl, Miloslav, Jr., Ed. *Czechoslovakia Past and Present.* The Hague: Mouton & Co., 1968. 2 vols.

Rechcigl, Miloslav, Jr., Ed. *Studies in Czechoslovak History.* Meerut: Sadhna Prakashan, 1976. 2 vols.

Seton-Watson, R. W., *The New Slovakia.* Prague: Fr. Borovy, 1924.

Seton-Watson, R.W., *Slovakia Then and Now: A Political Survey.* London: George Allen & Unwin, 1931.

Seton-Watson, Robert W. *A History of the Czechs and Slovaks.* London, New York: Hutchinson, 1943. 413p.

Skilling, H. Gordon, ed., *Czechoslovakia 1918-88: Seventy Years from Independence.* New York: St. Martin's Press, 1991. 232p.

Stone, Norman, and Eduard Strouhal, eds., *Czechoslovakia: Crossroads and Crises, 1918-88*. New York: St. Martins' Press, 1989. 336p.

Sundaram, P. K., comp. *Whither Czechoslovakia?* Essays and Documents on Czechoslovak Crisis. New Delhi: Dawn Publishers, 1969. 188p.

Thomson, S. Harrison. *Czechoslovakia in European History*. 2nd ed. Princeton, N.J.: Princeton University Press, 1953. 485p.

Zartman, I. William, ed. *Czechoslovakia: Intervention and Impact*. New York: New York University Press, 1970. 127p.

Zinner, Paul E. *Communist Strategy and Tactics in Czechoslovakia, 1918-48*. New York: Praeger, 1963. 264p.

3. The Slovak Republic

Bartl, Julius et al., *Slovak History: Chronology & Lexicon*. Wauconda, IL: Bolchazy-Carducci Publishers, 2002.

Hacker, Paul, Slovakia on the Road to Independence. University Park, PA: Pennsylvania State University Press, 2010. 256p.

Henderson, Karen, *Slovakia: The Escape from Invisibility*. London: Routledge, 2002.

Jacobs, Michael, *Blue Guide: Czech and Slovak Republics*. London: A.&C. Black, 1999.

Humphrey, Rob, *The Rough Guide to the Czech and Slovak Republics*. New York: Rough Guides, 2006.

Junas, Lil, *My Slovakia: An American's View*. Martin, Slovakia: Vydavateľstvo Matice slovenskej, 2001.

Lazistan, Eugen, Fedor Mikovič, Ivan Kučma, and Anna Jurečková, *Slovakia: A Photographic Odyssey*. Wauconda, IL: Bolchazy-Carducci Publishers, 2001.

Leff, Carol Skalník, *The Czech and Slovak Republics: Nation versus State*. Boulder: Westview Press, 1997.

Mannová, Elena, *A Concise History of Slovakia*. Bratislava: Historický ústav SAV, 2000.

Spiesz, Anton, and Dusan Caplovic, *Illustrated Slovak History: A Struggle for Sovereignty in Central Europe*. Wauconda, IL: Bolchazy-Carducci Publishers, 2001.

Toma, Peter A. and Dušán Kováč, *Slovakia: From Samo to Dzurinda*. Stanford, CA: Hoover Institution Press, 2001. 432p.

B. Jewish Slovak Heritage

Dlugoborski, Waclav, Gila Fatran, Jehuda Bauer, Yeshayahu Jelinek, et al., *The Tragedy of the Jews of Slovakia: 1938-1945. Slovakia and the Final Solution of the Jewish Question*. Auschwitz-Birkenau State Museum, 2002. 319p

Berger, Natalia, ed. Where Cultures Meet: The Story of the Jews of Czechoslovakia. Tel Aviv: Beth Hatefutsoth, Nahum Goldmann Museum of the Jewish Diaspora: Ministry of Defence Pub. House, 1990. 222p.

Buchler, Yehoshua R., "The Jews of Slovakia: Some Historical and Social Aspects," *Review of the Society for the History of Czechoslovak Jews* 1 (1987), pp. 167-76.

Bútorová, Zora and Martin Bútora, "Wariness Towards Jews as an Expression of Post-Communist Panic: The Case of Slovakia," *Czechoslovak Sociological Review* 28 (August 1992), pp. 92–106.

Conway, John S., "The Churches, the Slovak State and the Jews 1939-1945," *The Slavonic and East European Review*. 52, No., 126 (January 1974), pp. 85–112.

Heitlinger, Alena, *In the Shadows of the Holocaust and Communism: Czech and Slovak Jews Since 1945*. New Brunswick: Transaction, 2011.

Hilberg, Raul (2003, "Slovakia," *The Destruction of the European Jews*, Volume 2 (2003), pp. 766–792.

Jelinek, Yeshayahu, "The 'Final Solution' – The Slovak Version," *East European Quarterly* 4, No 4 (1971), p. 431.

Jelinek, Yeshayahu A., "Slovaks and the Holocaust: Attempts at Reconciliation," *Soviet Jewish Affairs*. 19, No. 1 (1989), pp. 57–68

Jelinek, Yeshayahu A., "In Search of Identity: Slovakian Jewry and Nationalism (1918-1938)," in: *A Social and Economic History of Central European Jewry*. New Brunswick: Transaction Publishers, c1990, pp. 207-227.

Jelinek, Yeshayahu and Robert Rozett, "Slovakia," in: *Encyclopedia of the Holocaust*. Edited by Israel Gutman. New York: Macmillan Publishing Co., 1990, Vol. 4, pp. 1364-1370.

Klein-Pejšová, Rebekah, Among the Nationalities: Jewish Refugees, Jewish Nationality, and Czechoslovak State Building, 1914-38. Ph.D. Dissertation, Columbia University, 2006.

Klein- Pejšová, Rebekah, *Mapping Jewish Loyalties in Interwar Slovakia*. Bloomington, IN: Indiana University press, 2015. 216p.

Klein-Pejšová, Rebekah (2009), "Abandon Your Role as Exponents of the Magyars': Contested Jewish Loyalty in Interwar Czechoslovakia," *AJS Review.* 33, No. 2 (2009), pp. 341–62.

Klein-Pejšová, Rebekah, "An Overview of the History of Jews in Slovakia," in: Synagoga Slovaca. See - http://www.slovak-jewish-heritage.org/history-of-jews-in-slovakia.html

Kubátova, Hana, *The Jews in Czech and Slovak Imagination, 1938-89.* Brill, 2018. 286p.

Kulka, Erich (1989), "The Jews in Czechoslovakia between 1918 and 1968," in: *Czechoslovakia: Crossroads and Crises, 1918–88.* Edited by Norman Stone and Eduard Strouhal. London: Palgrave Macmillan, 1989, pp. 271–96.

Láníček, Jan, *Czechs, Slovaks and the Jews, 1938-48: Beyond Idealization and Condemnation.* New York: Palgrave Macmillan, 2013. 265p.

Mandel, Louis, *The Tragedy of Slovak Jewry in Slovakia.* 1950. 66p.

III. Slovak American History

A. GENERAL SURVEYS

1. United States

Alexander, June Granatir, "Slovak Americans," in: World Culture Encyclopedia - Countries and their Culture Forum. See - http://www.everyculture.com/multi/Pa-Sp/Slovak-Americans.html

Bartalska, Lubica, *Slovak America*. Fila Gabriela Advertising, 1999. 113p.

Čapek, Thomas, Jr., "The Slovaks in America, in: *The Cech (Bohemian) Community of New York*. New York: Czechoslovak Section of America's Making, 1921, pp. 77-93.

Čulen, Konštantín, *History of Slovaks in America*. Translated by Daniel C. Nečas. St. Paul, MN: Czechoslovak Genealogical Society International, 2007. 440p.

Miller, Kenneth D. *The Czecho-Slovaks in America*. New York: George H. Doran, 1922

Fernice, Gregory C., "Slovak Immigration to the United States in Light of American Czech and Slovak History," *Nebraska History* 74, No. 3 and 4 (Fall/Winter 1993), pp. 130-35.

Krajsa, Joseph C., ed., *Slovaks in America: A Bicentennial Study*. Middletown, PA: The Slovak League of America, 1978. 494p.

Panorama: A Historical Review of Czechs and Slovaks in the United States. Cicero, IL: CNCA, 1971. 328 p.

Payne-Pikus, Monique, "Slovak Americans," in: *Encyclopedia of Race, Ethnicity and Society*. Edited by Richard T. Schaefer. SAGE Publications, 2008, Vol. 1, pp. 1238-1241.

Rechcigl, Miloslav, Jr., *Czechs and Slovaks in America: Survey, Essays, Reflections and Personal Insights Relating to the History and the Contributions of Czech and Slovak Immigrants in America and their Descendants*. Boulder, IN: East European Monographs, and New York: Columbia University Press, 2005.

Roucek, Joseph S., *The Czechs and Slovaks in America*. Minneapolis Lerner Publications, 1967.

"Slovak Americans," in: *Encyclopedia of Race, Ethnicity, and Society*. Edited by Richard T. Schaefer. Los Angeles: Sage Publications, 2008, Vol. 1, pp. 1238-1241.

Kre'pi, Bill, "Slovak Americans," in: *Multicultural America*. Edited by Carlose E. Cortes. Los Angeles: Sage, 2013, Vol. 4, pp. 1966-1967.

Staško, Jozef, *Slovaks in the United States of America: Brief sketches of their history, national heritage and activities*. Cambridge, MA: Dobra kniha, 1974. 79p.

Stolarik, M. Mark, "Slovak Migration from Europe to North America 1870-1918," *Slovak Studies* 20 (1980), p. 5-137.

Stolarik, M. Mark "Slovaks," in: *Harvard Encyclopedia of American Ethnic Groups*. Cambridge, MA: Belknap Press of Harvard University Press, 1980, pp. 926-34.

Stolarik, M. Mark, *The Slovak Americans*. New York: Chelsea House, 1988. 112p.

Stolarik, M. Mark, *Where My Home? Slovak Immigration to North America (1870–2010)* (Immigration from Europe to North America). Bern: Peter Lang AG, 2012. 392p.

Tibor, M. Martina, *The Slovaks in America to the End of the Nineteenth Century*. Middletown, PA: Jednota Printery, 1979.

2. Canada

"About Slovaks and Slovak Immigration Part I – Canada," in: Slovak Cathedral of Transfiguration. See - http://cathedral.latorica.com/slovaks-part-1/

Čermák, Josef. *Fragmenty ze života Čechů a Slováků v Kanadě*. Zlín: Ateliér IM, 2000.

Čermák, Josef, *It all Started with Prince Rupert*. The Story of Czechs and Slovaks in Canada. Luhačovice: Atelier IM Publishing Co., 2003. 365p.

Čulen, Konstantin, *Slovaks in Slovakia and Canada*. Winnipeg: Canadian Slovak League, 1955.

Gellner, John and John Smerek, *The Czechs and Slovaks in Canada*. Toronto: University of Toronto Press, 1969. 184p.

Hikl, Mario. *A Short History of the Czechoslovak People in Canada*. Toronto: Across-Canada Press, 1955.

Jakešová, Elena. "Slovak Emigrants in Canada as Reflected in Diplomatic Documents (1920-1938)," *Slovakia* 35.64-65 (1991-1992): 7-35

Jakešová, Elena, and M. Mark Stolárik, "Slovaks," in: *Encyclopedia of Canada's Peoples*. Edited by Paul Robert Magocsi. Toronto: University of Toronto Press, 1999, pp. 1168-1179.

Kaye, V.J., "Canadians of Slovak Origin: A Brief Survey," *Canadian Slavonic Papers / Revue Canadienne des Slavistes*, Vol. 4 (1959), pp. 147-154.

Kirschbaum, Joseph M., *Slovaks in Canada*. Canadian Ethnic Press Association of Ontario, 1967. 468p.

Kirschbaum, Stanislav J., "Slovak Canadians," in: the Canadian Encyclopedia. See - https://www.thecanadianencyclopedia.com/en/article/slovaks/

Magocsi, Paul R. *Encyclopedia of Canada's Peoples*. Toronto: University of Toronto Press, 1999.

Mihal, Ondrej, *Slovaks in Canada through their Own Eyes*. Toronto: Slovak Canadian Culture, 2003.

Raska, Jan, Mistrusted Strangers at Home: Czechs, Slovaks, and the Canadian 'Enemy Aliens' Registration Issue, 1938-1942," *International Journal of Canadian Studies*, Issue 38 (2008), pp. 91-117.

Raska, Jan, Freedoms Voices: Czech and Slovak Immigration to Canada during the Cold War. Ph.D. Thesis, University of Waterloo, Waterloo, Ontario, Canada, 2013.

Reguly, Bob, "The Saga of Slovak Settlement in Canada," in:" Slovak Canadian Heritage Museum. See - http://www.slovakcanadianheritagemuseum.ca/articles/the-saga-of-slovak-settlement-in-canada/

"The Saga of Slovak Settlement in Canada," in: Slovak Canadian Heritage Museum. See - http://www.slovakcanadianheritagemuseum.ca/articles/the-saga-of-slovak-settlement-in-canada/

"Slovak Canadians," in: The Canadian Encyclopedia. See - https://www.thecanadianencyclopedia.ca/en/article/slovaks/

"Slovak Communities Info," in: Kanadský Slovák. See - https://www.kanadskyslovak.ca/index.php/slovak-community

"Slovak Emigrants in Canada as Reflected in Diplomatic Documents, 1920-1938," *Slovakia*, Vol. 35, o. 64/65 (January 1991), pp. 7–35.

Pavla Špačková, Immigration of Czechs and Slovaks to Canada. Bakalářská práce. Olomouc. See - https://theses.cz/id/5ua111/BP_Spackova_Pavla.pdf

Stolárik, M. Mark, *Slovaks in Canada and the United States, 1870-1990: Similarities and Differences*. Ottawa: Department of History, University of Ottawa, 1992. 32p.

3. Latin America

Kybal, Milič,"Czechs and Slovaks in Latin America," in: *The Czechoslovak Contribution to World Culture.* Edited by Miloslav Rechcigl, Jr. The Hague-London-Paris: Mouton & Co., 1964, pp. 516-522.

Kybal, Vlastimil, *Po československých stopách v Latinské Americe.* Prague: Nákladem České akademie věd a umění v Praze, 1935.

Polišenský, J., La emigración checoslovaca a América Latina 1680-1945. Problemas y fuentes," *Jahrbuch für Geschichte von Staat, Wirtschaft und Gesellschaft Lateinamerikas,* 13 (1976), pp. pp. 216-248.

LaMigrace. Portal sobre la migración checa y slovaca a América Latina. See - http://lamigrace.ff.cuni.cz/es/paraguay-2/personalidades/

Lenghardtová, Jana and Jana Paľková, Perceptions of Latin America in Slovakia and their Reflections at the University of Economics in Bratislava," *Ekonomické rozhľady / Economic Review,* 43, No. 2 (2014), pp. 121-140.

Rechcigl, Miloslav, Jr. "On the Tracks of Czechs in Latin America," in: *Behind the Sea of Beer. History of Immigration of Bohemians and Czechs to the New World and their Contribution.* Bloomington, IN: AuthorHouse, 2017, pp. 61-67.

Reynolds, Matthew, "Latin Americans still Dancing the Slovak Nights away," in: *The Slovak Spectator,* Augsut 21, 2000.

Štěrba, F. C., *Češi a Slováci v Latinské Americe.* (Přehled jejich kulturního přínosu). Washington-New York: SVU, 1962. 61p.

Vasiljev, I., Vystěhovalectví Čechů a Slováků do Latinské Ameriky před druhou světovou válkou.," *Český lid,* 73, No. 4 (1986), pp. 239-243.

B. EARLY HISTORY

1. Surveys

Berta, John, "Slovak Beginnings in America," *Jednota Annual Furdek* 25 (1986), pp. 165-172.

Čulen, Konštantín, "The Pioneers," in: Čulen, pp. 15-21.

Dobrotková, Marta, "Slovenskí priekopníci v Amerike," in: Dobrodruh.sk. See - https://www.dobrodruh.sk/historia/slovenski-priekopnici-v-amerike

Pauco, Jozef, *Slovenskí priekopníci v Amerike. Slovak pioneers in America.* Cleveland, OH: Prvá Katolícka slovenská jednota, 1972. 359p.

Puskás, Julianna, *From Hungary to the United States (1880-1914)*. Budapest: Akadémiai Kiadó, 1982.

Rechcigl, Miloslav Jr., "In the Footprints of the First Czech (and Slovak) Immigrants in America," *Czechoslovak and Central European Journal* 9 (1990), pp. 75-90.

Rechcigl, Miloslav Jr., "Early Jewish Immigrants in America from the Czech Historic Lands and Slovakia," *Rev. Soc. Hist. Czechoslovak Jews* 3 (1990-91), pp. 157-79.

Rechcigl, Miloslav, Jr., "The First American Settler from Slovakia," *Naše Rodina* 8, No. 3 (September 1996), p. 100.

Rechcigl, Miloslav, Jr., "The Immigration to America from the Czechlands and Slovakia in the 17th and 18th Centuries," in: *Selected Papers from the 2003 SVU North American Conference*, Cedar Rapids, Iowa, 26-28 June 2003, pp. 1-8.

Rechcigl, Miloslav, Jr., "The First Slovaks in America" in: *Beyond the Sea of Beer. History of Immigration of Bohemians and Czechs to the New World and their Contributions*. Bloomington, in: AuthorHouse, 2017, pp.40-46.

Rudzik, Roman, "Early Slovak Immigration to America and its Influences on the 21st Century." See - http://www.slovak-garden.com/uploads/3/4/6/2/34629022/early_slovak_immigration.pdf

Tybor, M. Martina, "The Slovak Presence in America up to 1890," in *Slovaks in America*. A. Bicentennial History, pp. 3-22.

Zatko, James J., "Beginnings of the Slovaks in America," *Slovakia* 15 (1963), pp.1-37.

2. Pioneers

Móric Benyovszky (Benovský) (1746-1786), b. Vrbové, Slovakia; Count, soldier of fortune, globetrotter.

Bio: Tybor, Martina, "The Slovak Presence in America up to 1890," in: *Slovaks in America*. A Bicentennial Study. Middletown, PA: The Slovak League of America, 1978, p.p. 7-8; *Memoirs and Travels of Mauritius Augustus Count de Benyowsky. Magnate of the Kingdom of Hungary and Poland*. London, 1789-90; "Beňovský, Móric," in: *Slovenský biografický slovník*. Martin: Matica slovenská, 1996, Vol. 1, pp. 220-221; Čulen, Konstantin, "The Beňovský. Brothers in America," in: *History of Slovaks in America*. Minneapolis, MN: CGSI, 2003, p. 17

NOTABLE AMERICANS WITH SLOVAK ROOTS

Franciscus Xaver Eder (1727-1773), b. Banská Štiavnica, Slovakia; a Bohemian Jesuit; was sent as a missionary with other Bohemian Jesuits to South America. He worked in Peru. He is remembered for writing an authoritative account of the hard and distressful life in the Majos Mission, where the missionaries resembled 'living corpses' rather than human beings. It was published in 1791, almost 20 years after his death, under the title *Description Provinciae Moxitarum in Regno Peruano*. After his return, he served as a R.C. priest in Banská Štiavnica.
Bio: "Éder Xavér Ferenc," in: Wikipedia. See - https://hu.wikipedia.org/ wiki/ Éder_Xavér_Ferenc; Encyclopedia, Vol. 1, p. 9.

Andrew Jelik (ca 1730-1783), b. Baja, Slovakia; adventurer
Bio: Tybor, Marttina, "The Slovak Presence in America up to 1890," in: *Slovaks in America. A Bicentennial Study*. Middletown, PA: The Slovak League of America, 1978, pp.4-5; Čulen, Konstantin, "The Adventurous Journey of Andrej Jelik," in: *History of Slovaks in America*. Minneapolis, MN: CGSI, 2003, pp. 16-17.

John l. Polerecky (1748-1830), b. France, of Slovak father; Major of Lauzun's Polish Lancers, veteran of the American Revolutionary War
Bio: George J. Krajsa, "Major L. Polerecky, an Officer of Slovak Heritage in the American Revolution," Jednota 18 (1979), pp. 21- 231; "The Slovaks Were There - Major John Polerecky Fought for American Independence," *Slovakia* 7, No. 3-4 (September-December 1957), p. 84;" Ján Ladislav Polerecký," in: Wikipedia. See - https://sk.wikipedia.org/wiki/ Ján_Ladislav_Polerecký

Isaac Ferdinand Šarošy (aka Izák Šároši, Isaacus Sharoshi) (bf. 1695-), b. Slovakia; Protestant preacher, with the colony of Francis Daniel Pistorius, Germantown, PA; in America since 1695; returned to Europe after two years.
Bio: Tybor, Marttina, "The Slovak Presence in America up to 1890," in: *Slovaks in America*. A Bicentennial Study. Middletown, PA: The Slovak League of America, 1978, p. 4.

Anton Schmidt (1725-1793), b. Bratislava, Slovakia; first known permanent settler from Slovakia in America; member of the renewed '*Unitas fratrum,*' Bethlehem, PA
Bio: Rechcigl, Miloslav, Jr., "The First American Settler from Slovakia," *Naše Rodina* 8, No. 3 (September 1996), p. 100.

C. REGIONAL AND LOCAL HISTORIES

1. United States

Alabama

Simon, Staci, Study of the Slovak Community at Brookside, Alabama. MA. Thesis, University of Alabama, 1997.
"Unique Heritage. Brookside, Alabama." See - http://www.brooksidealabama. com/?page_id=17

Alaska

Kopanic, Michael J., "Slovaks in Alaska? Alexander Liska's Life," *Jednota*, Sept. 23, 2015, pp. 18-19. See -https://www.fcsu.com/wp-content/uploads/ jednota-archives/2015/SEPT-23RD-ISSUE-15.pdf

Arkansas

Earl, Jack, "Little Slovakia in Arkansas," *Arkansas Democrat Sunday Magazine*, January 27, 1952, pp. 1-2.
Hanson, Aprille, "Slovak parishioners mix flour and sugar with devotion," *Arkansas Catholic*, June 16, 2015.
Metrailer, Jamie, "Slovak (Prairie County)," in: *The Encyclopedia of Arkansas History and Culture*. See - http://www.encyclopediaofarkansas.net/ encyclopedia/entry-detail.aspx?entryID=5362
"Slovak, Arkansas," in: Wikipedia. See - https://en.wikipedia.org/wiki/ Slovak,_Arkansas

California

Bazovsky, John L., "Early Slovaks in Los Angeles (1883-1945)," *Slovak Studies* 13 (1973), pp. 203-16.
"Slovaks with the Highest Percentage of Slovaks in California." See - http:// zipatlas.com/us/ca/city-comparison/percentage-slovak-population.htm
"Czechs & Slovaks in California," in: Home / Facebook Website

Colorado

Kedro, James, "Czechs and Slovaks in Colorado, 1860-1920," *The Colorado Magazine* 54, No. 2 (Spring 1977), pp. 93-125.

Connecticut

McDougal, Diana, *The American-Slovak Community in Bridgeport.* Bridgeport, 1954. 23 p.

District of Columbia

"Slovaks in Washington, D.C." See - http://www.slovakcooking.com/2010/blog/slovaks-in-washington-dc/

Florida

"Czech and Slovak Presence in Florida," in: American Czech-Slovak Cultural Club. See - See - http://acscc.org/czechpresence.html
Hudak, Andrew F., Jr., *Slovaks in Florida.* Winter Park, FL: Agency Da Vel, 1991. 112p.
Kopanic, Michael J., "The Slovako-Czech Settlement in Masaryktown, Florida," *Almanac of the National Slovak Society,* Vol. CIII (1995), pp. 87-90.
"Masaryktown, Florida," in: Wikipedia. See - https://en.wikipedia.org/wiki/Masaryktown,_Florida
Petrik, Robert, "Czechs and Slovaks in Florida." Paper delivered at the SVU conference at Coe College, Cedar Rapids, IA on June 27, 2003. See - http://acscc.org/Papers/svu_062703b.html
Slovak Garden, Winter Park, FL - Official Website: http://www.slovak-garden.com/about.html

Illinois

Brunner, Emily, "Slovaks," in: *Encyclopedia of Chicago.* See - http://www.encyclopedia.chicagohistory.org/pages/1152.html
Fasiang, Robert M. and Robert Magruder, *Slovaks if Chicagoland.* Mt Pleasant, SC: Arcadia Publishing, 2014. 128p.
Hletko, Peter, "The Slovaks of Chicago," *Slovakia* 19, No. 42 (1962), pp. 32-63.

Kopanic, Michael J., "Slovak Immigration to the Chicago Area and Illinois before World War II," in: Czechoslovak Genealogical Society International Conference. See - https://www.cgsi.org/sites/default/files/2013_chicago_syllabus_e.pdf

Kugler, John, A Study of Czechoslovak Immigration and their Contributions to Vocational Education in Chicago between 1875and 1935. A Master's Thesis, Chicago State University, 2003.

Nemecek, Paul M. "Early Slovaks in Chicago," *Naše Rodina* (December 2012), Vol. 24, No.4: pp. 156-158.

Palickar, Stephen J., "The Slovaks of Chicago," *Illinois Catholic Historical Review*, 4, No. 1 (July 1921), pp. 180-196.

Reichmann, John J., *Czechoslovaks of Chicago*, Chicago: Czechoslovak Historical Society of Chicago, 1937. 112p.

Zahrobsky, Mary L., The Slovaks in Chicago. M.S. Thesis, University of Chicago, 1924

Indiana

Lane, James B., "Calumet Region Slovaks." See - http://northwestindianahistorianjamesblane.blogspot.com/2014/07/calumet-region-slovaks.html

"Cities with the Highest Percentage of Slovaks in Indiana," in: Zip Atlas. See - http://zipatlas.com/us/in/city-comparison/percentage-slovak-population.htm

"Whiting, Indiana: Generational Memory 1991-1993. 88 interviews," in: IU CSHM collection. See - http://www.dlib.indiana.edu/reference/cshm/ohrc102.html

"Zip Codes with the Highest Percentage of Slovaks in America." in: Zip Atlas. See - http://zipatlas.com/us/in/zip-code-comparison/percentage-slovak-population.htm

Iowa

"A Czech and Slovak Community," in: Iowa Pathways. See - http://www.iptv. org/iowapathways/mypath/czech-and-slovak-community

Louisiana

"Cities with the Highest Percentage of Slovaks in Louisiana," in: Zip Atlas. See - http://zipatlas.com/us/la/city-comparison/percentage-slovak-population.htm

Hlavac, James, *A Hidden Impact: The Czechs & Slovaks of Louisiana from the 1720s to Today.* Bloomington, IN: iUniverse, 2006. 432p.

Massachusetts

Copithone, Alan C., The Role of Slovak Immigration in the Development of a Second Protestant Church in Hatfield, Mass. Hatfield, MA: The Author, 1971. See - https://archive.org/stream/roleofslovakimmi00copi/roleofslovakimmi00copi_djvu.txt

Michigan

Benesh, Anton, "Michigan Czechs and Slovaks," in: *Panorama: A Historical Review of Czechs and Slovaks in the United States.* Cicero, IL: Czechoslovak National Council of America, 1970, pp. 54-57.

"Cities with the Highest Percentage of Slovaks in Michigan," in: Zip Atlas. See - http://zipatlas.com/us/mi/city-comparison/percentage-slovak-population.htm

Minnesota

"Bohemian Flats," in: Wikipedia. See - https://en.wikipedia.org/wiki/Bohemian_Flats

Hukriede, Stephen, The Other Side of the Chasm: Slavic Life in Northeast Minneapolis, 1880-1920. Thesis, Macalester College, 1989.

Stolarik, M. Mark, "The Slovaks," in: *They Chose Minnesota.* A Survey of the State's Ethnic Groups. Ed. June Drenning Holmquist. St. Paul: Minnesota Historical Society Press, 1981, pp. 352-61.

Missouri

"Bohemians & Czechs in St. Louis," in: St. Louis Genealogical Society. See - https://stlgs.org/research-2/community/ethnic/bohemians-czechs
"Czech & Slovak Community of Las Vegas," in: Home / Facebook. See - https://www.facebook.com/czechslovakvegas/

Nebraska

"Cities with the Highest Percentage of Slovaks in Nebraska," in: Zip Atlas. See - http://zipatlas.com/us/ne/city-comparison/percentage-slovak-population.htm

New Jersey

Kopanic, Michael J., "Slovaks in New Jersey: An Overview," in academia.edu See - https://www.academia.edu/37609105/Slovaks_in_New_Jersey_An_Overview
"Slovaks," in: *Encyclopedia of New Jersey*, pp. 749-750.
"Slovakia, New Jersey, in Summertime," *Happy Hungry Journey*, August 21, 2011.

New York

Bušek, Vratislav and Ján Shintay, "The Czechs and Slovaks of New York," in: *Panorama. A Historical Review of Czechs and Slovaks in the United States of America.* Cicero, IL: Czechoslovak National Council of America, 1970, pp. 18-29.
Crosseite, Barbara, "In Search of the Czechoslovak East Side," *The New York Times*, September 10, 1976.
"Czechs and Slovaks in New York," in: Slavs of New York. See - http://nycslav.blogspot.com/2010/01/czechs-and-slovaks-in-new-york.html
Kasinec, Edward, "Slovaks," in: *The Encyclopedia of New York City*. 2nd ed. New Haven, CT: Yale University Press, 2010.
Kopanic, Michael, Jr., The Slovaks in Cleveland, 1870-1930: Neighborhoods, Politics and Nationality Relations," *Czechoslovak & Central European Journal*, Vol. 9, N. 1/2, Jan. 1990, pp. 115–33.
Mažár, Imrich, *A History of the Binghamton Slovaks: Over a period of Forty Years, 1879-1919.*

Edited by Wilhelmina Mažár Satina. Translated by Thomas Janacek. Phoenix: Via Press, 2003.

Shelley, Thomas J., "Neither Poles nor Magyars nor Bohemians: The Slovak Catholics of Yonkers, New York," *Records of the American Catholic Historical Society of Philadelphia* Vol. 105, No. 1/2 (Spring-Summer 1994), pp. 16-31.

Shelley, Thomas J., *Slovaks on the Hudson. Most Holy Trinity Church, Yonkers and the Slovak Catholic Archdiocese of New York, 1894-2000.* Washington, DC: The Catholic University of America Press, 2002. 273 p.

Šimko, Vlado, "Evolution of Our Ethnic Community in New York City," in: BBLA. See - http://www.bohemianbenevolent.org/index.php/about/pastpresent

Sutherland, Anthony X, The Slovaks of Haverstraw. Np: The Author, 986. https://hrvh.org/utils/getfile/collection/hsrc/id/2763/filename/2744.pdfpage/page/5

Tanzone, Daniel F., *Slovaks of Yonkers, New York.* Middletown, PA: Jednota Printery, 1975. 126p.

"Walking Tour: Czech and Slovak Yorkville," in: Slavs of New York. See - http://nycslav.blogspot.com/2008/07/walking-tour-czech-and-slovak-yorkville.html

North Carolina

"Czechs and Slovaks in North Carolina: How are they doing?" in: Czechmate Diary. See - http://czechmatediary.com/2008/11/13/czechs-and-slovaks-in-north-carolina-how-are-they-doing/

"North Carolina Language School becomes Meeting Point for Czech and Slovak Expats," in: Radio Praha in English. See - http://www.radio.cz/en/section/in-focus/north-carolina-language-school-becomes-meeting-point-for-czech-and-slovak-expats

Ohio

"A Century Later, Six Ethnic Clubs in Barberton still Surving," *Akron Beacon Journal,* Ohio. com, September 1, 20014. See - https://www.ohio.com/akron/news/a-century-later-six-ethnic-clubs-in-barberton-still-surviving

"Cleveland and Its Neighborhoods - Slovaks," in: google Sites. See - https://sites.google.com/site/clevelandanditsneighborhoods/home/ethnic-groups-in-cleveland/slovaks

Hornack, Joseph J., "Cleveland, Ohio and Cuyahoga County 1880 to the Present and its Slovak Identification," in: Slovak Institute. See - http://www.slovakinstitute.com/Cleveland.htm

Hruska, Steve, and Genevieve Novicky, Eds., *The History of the Slovak People of the Mahoning Valley*. Youngstown, Ohio: The Slovak Bicentennial Committee of Youngstown and Mahoning County, 1976.

Kopanic, Michael J.,"The Slovak National Home in Cleveland," *Almanac of the National Slovak Society*, 1990, pp. 46-52.

Kopanic, Michael J., "Slovak Magyar Relations in Cleveland, 1880 1930," in Western Reserve Studies Symposium (1989), pp. 1-24. See - http://www.case.edu/artsci/wrss/documents/Kopanic.pdf

Kopanic, Michael J., "Slovaks in Cleveland, 1870-1930. Neighborhoods, Politics and Nationality Relations," *Czechoslovak and Central European Journal* 9 (1990), pp. 115-33.

Kopanic, Michael J., "The Slovaks," in: *Identity, Conflict, and Cooperation: Central Europeans in Cleveland, 1850-1930. Edited by* David C. Hammack, John J. Grabowski, and Diane L. Grabowski. Cleveland: Western Reserve Historical Society, 2003, pp. 249-306.

Ledbetter, Eleanor E., *The Slovaks of Cleveland with Some General Information on the Race*. Cleveland: Mayor's Advisory War Committee, 1918. 32 p.

Megles, Susi, Mark Stolarik, and Martina Tybor, *Slovak Americans and their Communities of Cleveland*. Cleveland: Ohio State University Press, 1978.

Pankuch, Jan, *History of the Slovaks in Cleveland and Lakewood*. Minneapolis, MN: Czechoslovak Genealogical Society, 2001. 301 p.

Sabo, Gerald, "Slovaks," in: *Encyclopedia of Cleveland History*. See - https://case.edu/ech/articles/s/slovaks

Sabol, John T. and Lisa A. Alzo, *Cleveland Slovaks*. Mt Pleasant, SC: Arcadia Publishing,2009. 128p.

Sciranka, John C., "Slovak Pioneer Life in Youngstown and Mahoning Valley, Ohio," *Jednota Annual Furdek*, 9 (January 1970), pp. 119-125.

"Slovak American Culture in Ohio," in: Revolvy. See - https://www.revolvy.com/folder/Slovak-American-culture-in-Ohio/387442

"Slovak Ohioans," in: Ohio History Central. See - http://www.ohiohistorycentral.org/w/Slovak_Ohioans

Summers, Susan J. and Loretta A. Ekoniak, *Slovaks of the Greater Mahoning Valley*. Mt Pleasant, SC: Arcadia Publishing, 2011. 128p.

Wilkes, Paul, "It's not so much fun to go home again -," *The New York Times*, January 24, 1971.

Oklahoma

"Cities with the Highest Percentage of Slovaks in Oklahoma," in: Zip Atlas. See - http://zipatlas.com/us/ok/city-comparison/percentage-slovak-population.htm

Oregon

"Czechs & Slovaks in Oregon," in: Home / Facebook. See - https://www.facebook.com/CZ.SK.OR/

Pennsylvania

Alzo, Lisa A., *Slovak Pittsburgh*. Mt Pleasant, SC: Arcadia Publishing, 2006. 128p.

Alzo, Lisa A., *Pittsburgh's Immigrants*. Mt Pleasant, SC: Arcadia Publishing, 2006. 128p.

Alzo, Lisa A., "Slovaks Settled Here: Identifying Early 20th Century Immigrant Cluster Communities in Pittsburgh," in: Lisa Also. See - http://www.lisaalzo.com/articles/PITT2006.pdf

Ardan, Brian., *The Anthracite Coal Region's Slavic Community*. Arcadia Publishing, 2009. 128p.

"Slovaks," in: The Peoples of Pennsylvania. An Annotated Bibliography of Resource Materials. Compiled by David E. Washburn. Pittsburgh: University of Pittsburgh Press, 1981, pp. 189-205.

Bodnar, John, ed., *The Ethnic Experience in Pennsylvania*. Lewisburg: Bucknell University Press, 1973.

Budd, Joseph P., We Do know English: Philadelphia's Czechoslovak Presbyterian Church of Jan Hus, 1926-1967. M.A. Thesis, University of Delaware. See - http://udspace.udel.edu/bitstream/handle/19716/5471/Joseph_Budd_thesis.pdf;sequence=1

Dvorchak, Robert, "Slovaks Reconnect with their Heritage," in: Pittsburgh Post-Gazette, May 20, 2001. See - http://northwestindianahistorianjamesblane.blogspot.com/2014/07/calumet-region-slovaks.html

Kalčik, Susan. "Fortune,' Stepchildren: Slovaks in Pennsylvania," *Pennsylvania Folklife*, Vol. 44, No. 2, Winter 1994-1995, pp. 50–69. See - https://digitalcommons.ursinus.edu/pafolklifemag/143/

Kushner, Jozef A., *Slováci Katolíci v Pittsburghého Biskupstva* (Slovak Catholics in the Pittsburgh Diocese). Passaic, NJ: Slovak Catholic Sokol, 1946.

McCarthy, Charles A., "Slovak Pioneers in Pennsylvania's Anthracite Coal Region," *Jednota Annual Furdek*, 20 (January 1981), pp. 397-401.

Pauliny, Milan, *History of Bethlehem Slovaks in the United States of America*. Passaic, NJ: Slovak Catholic Sokol, 1921.

Reuscher, J.A., "Slovaks and Slovakia," in: *The Encyclopedia of Greater Philadelphia*. See - http://philadelphiaencyclopedia.org/archive/slovaks-and-slovakia/

"Slovaks," in: *The Peoples of Pennsylvania. An Annotated Bibliography of Resource Materials*. Compiled by David E. Washburn. Pittsburgh: University of Pittsburgh Press, 1981, pp. 189-205.

Stolarik, M. Mark, *Growing Up in the South Side: Three Generations of Slovaks in Bethlehem, Pennsylvania, 1880-1976*. Lewisburg: Bucknell University, 1985. 147 p.

Triebs, Samuel. "Taking Root on Rocky Soil: Slovak Settlement on Pittsburgh's South Side, 1880-1920." MA thesis, Duquesne University, 1999.

Zduleczna, Christine, "The Czechoslovaks of Philadelphia," in: *The Foreign-Born of Philadelphia*. Philadelphia: International Institute of Philadelphia, 1927.

Texas

"Around the World in Houston: Discover Slovakia & the Czech Republic." See - https://365thingsinhouston.com/2018/01/04/around-the-world-in-houston-discover-slovakia-and-the-czech-republic/

"Cities with the Highest Percentage of Slovaks in Texas," in: Zip atlas. See - http://zipatlas.com/us/tx/city-comparison/percentage-slovak-population.htm

Official Site: "Slovaks in Texas." - See - https://www.facebook.com/Slovaks-in-Texas-Slovaci-v-Texase-907624209266440/

Virginia

"Celebrating Czech and Slovak Traditions," in: Virginia Humanities. See - https://www.virginiahumanities.org/2013/09/celebrating-czech-and-slovak-traditions/

"In New Bohemia, traditions old and new," The Progress-Index, October 15, 2016

Llovio, Louis, Preserving their Past: Prince George Czechs and Slovaks Look to Honor their Immigrant Heritage Prince George looks to honor 19th-century immigrant heritage," *Richmond Times-Dispatch*, November 19, 2013.

"Virginia CzechSlovak Heritage Society," in: Home. See - http://www.virginiaczechslovak.org/index.html

Vlk, Bruce A. "New Bohemia in the New World: Czech and Slovak Immigration and Assimilation in Prince George County, Virginia." *Czechoslovak and Central European Journal*, Vol. 25, No. 2, Summer 2012, pp. 75–102.

West Virginia

"Cities with the Highest Percentage of Slovaks in West Virginia," in: Zipatlas. See - http://zipatlas.com/us/wv/city-comparison/percentage-slovak-population.htm

"Fighting bigotry from West Virginia to Slovakia," in: Not in our Town, September 25, 2014. See - https://www.niot.org/blog/fighting-bigotry-west-virginia-slovakia

"Slovak businesswoman's 3-month stay in WV a 'strong experience,'" *Charleston Gazette-Mail*, May 27, 2015.

Wisconsin

Hosmanek, John J., "Slovak Immigrants to Wisconsin," in: *Selected Papers from the 2003 SVU North American Conference*, Cedar Rapids, Iowa, 26-28 June 2003.

Reck, Bill, "Slovaks in Milwaukee," in: Encyclopedia of Milwaukee. See - https://emke.uwm.edu/entry/slovaks/

2. Canada

Alberta

"Edmonton Slovak Community," in: Kanadský Slovák. See - ttps://www.
kanadskyslovak.ca/index.php/edmonton

British Columbia

"A look at the Slovak Community," in: The Source. See - http://thelasource.
com/en/2018/09/24/a-look-at-the-slovak-community/
"Slovak Immigrants in British Columbia," in: ppt video online. See - https://
slideplayer.com/slide/1434451/
"Slovenské začiatky v Britskej Kolumbii," Časopis Slovo z Britskej Kolumbie,
April 16, 2018. See - http://slovozbritskejkolumbie.ca/node/35
"Vancouver Slovak Community," in: Kanadský Slovák. See - https://www.
kanadskyslovak.ca/index.php/vancouver/vancouver-slovak-community
"Vancouver Slovak Organizations," in: Kanadský Slovak.
See-https://www.kanadskyslovak.ca/index.php/vancouver/vancouver-slovak-
organizations/64-vancouver-slovak-organizations

Manitoba

"History of CCBA," in: CCBA Home. See - http://www.czechslovak
benevolentassoc.ca/html/history_of_ccba.html
"Winnipeg Slovak Community," in: *Kanadský Slovak*. See - https://www.
kanadskyslovak.ca/index.php/winnipeg-/winnipeg-slovak-community

Ontario

"Bradlo - an Immigrant's Memories. See - http://www.slovak.com/bradlo/
immigrants_memories.html
Kitchener-Waterloo Slovak Community. In: Kanadský Slovák. See - https://
www.kanadskyslovak.ca/index.php/kitchener
"Ottawa Slovak community," in: Kanadský Slovák. See - https://www.
kanadskyslovak.ca/index.php/ottawa/ottawa-slovak-community
"Ottawa Slovak Organizations," in: Kanadský Slovák. See - https://www.
kanadskyslovak.ca/index.php/ottawa/ottawa-slovak-organizations

"The Slovak Community," in: *Toronto's Many Places*. By Tony Ruprecht. 5th ed. Toronto: Dundurn Press, 2011, pp. 357-360.
"Toronto Slovak Community," in: Kanadský Slovák. See: https://www. kanadskyslovak.ca/index.php/toronto/toronto-slovak-community

Quebec

"Montreal Slovak Community," in: Kanadský Slovak. See - https://www.kanadskyslovak.ca/index.php/montreal/montreal-slovak-community/84-montreal-slovak-community10
"Welcome to Montreal," in: La Mason Slovaque. See - http://www.slovak. com/montreal/

Saskatchewan

Anderson, Alan, "Czech and Slovak Settlements," in: The Encyclopedia of Saskatchewan. See - http://esask.uregina.ca/entry/ czech_and_slovak_settlements.html

3. Latin America

Argentina

Baďura, B., K historii prvních spolků českých a slovenských vystěhovalců v Argentině," *Sborník k problematice dějin imperialismu*, 11 (1981), pp. 290-302.
"Bibliografía. Lista de la blibliografía sobre la migración checoslovaca a Argentina.," in: LaMigrace. See - http://lamigrace.ff.cuni.cz/es/argentina-2/ bibliografia/
Botik, Jan, *Slováci v argentínskom Chacu* (Slovaks in Argentine's Chaco. Bratislava: Lúč, 2002. 300p.
Dubovický, I, "Kolonizační pokusy v Argentině a meziválečná Československá Republika," *Češi v cizině*, 3 (1988), pp. 193-236.
Dubovicýy, Ivan, "Formování českého a slovenského etnika v Argentině," *Češi v cizině*, 4, (1989). 12p.
Jančárik, E. Stanislav. *Slovenská Argentína*, Matica slovenská, 1996.
Kapitola, Luděk, "K historii slovenské emigrace v Argentině," *Slováci v zahraničí*, 6 (1980), pp. 28-43.

Míšek, R., "Origen de la emigración checoslovaca a la Argentina," *Ibero-Americana Pragensis*, 1 (1967), pp. 123-132.

Mismo, El, Argentinskí Slováci v podvečer druhej svetovej vojny," *Slováci v zahraničí* 10 (1984), pp. 28-39.

"K historii slovenské emigrace v Argentině," in: *Slováci v zahraničí* 6, Matice Slovenská, 1980, pp. 28-41.

"Slovaks of Argentina," in: People Groups. See - http://www.peoplegroups. org/explore/groupdetails.aspx?peid=17367

Brazil

Barteček, Ivo, Československá kolonizace v Brazilii," *Češi v cizině*, 3 (1988), pp. 237-251.

Barteček, Ivo, "České a slovenské vystěhovatelství do Brasilie před druhou světovou válkou," *Latinská Amerika - Dějiny a současnost*, 2 (1989), pp. 161-180.

Kybal, Vlastimil, "Kolik je nás Čechoslováku v Brazilii?" (How many are we Czechoslovaks in Brazil?), in: *Jižní Amerika a Československo*. Praha, 1928, pp. 142-145.

"Little Pieces of Slovakia in Brazil," The Slovak Spectator, January 23, 2012. See - https://spectator.sme.sk/c/20042224/little-pieces-of-slovakia-in-brazil. html

Minarechová, Radka, "Little Pieces of Slovakia in Brazil," in: *The Slovak Spectator*, January 23, 2012. See - https://spectator.sme.sk/c/20042224/little-pieces-of-slovakia-in-brazil.html

Mismo, El, "Československá kolonizace v Brazilii," *Češi v cizině*, 3 (1988), pp. 237-251.

Chile

Jiránek, Jiří and Ivo Barteček, *Češi a Slováci v Chile ve 20. století*. Olomouc: Univerzita Palackého, 2013. 272p.

Cuba

Nálevka, Vladimír, "La Colonia chechoslovaca en Cuba durante y la secunda guerra mundial," *Ibero-Americana Pragensia*, 4 (1970), pp. 231-236.

Mexico

Barteček, Ivo, *Československý antifašistický exil německého jazyka v Mexiku: studie a dokumenty.* Olomouc: Univerzita Palackého, 1999. 102p.

Nicaragua

"Nicaragua - The First Country where for the first time...," in: MiliMundo Travel Blog. See - https://milimundo.com/ nicaragua-the-first-country-where-for-the-first-time/
"Slovaks in Nicaragua," in: CP Compatriots. See - http://www.compatriots. com/tab_page.php?type=jobs&nationality=Slovaks&country=Nicaragua

Paraguay

Dubovický, Ivan, "K otázce evropského přistěhovalectví do Paraguaye" (European immigration to Paraguay), *Acta Universitatis Carolinae—Philosophica et Historica* 3, *Studia Ethnographica,*7 (1991), pp. 77-98.

Patagonia (Argentina & Chile)

Bielik, F., "Zo života Slovákov a Čechov v Patagonii," *Slováci v zahraničí,* 11 (1985), pp. 148-152.

D. CHRONOLOGY

Fedor, Helen, *The Slovaks in America. Chronology. Selected Bibliography.* Washington, DC: Library of Congress, N.d.
Matica Rožňava, "Chronológia Slovákov v Amerike do konca 19. storočia" (Chronology of Slovaks in America till the End of the 19th Century), in: www. maticaroznava.sk. See - https://www.maticaroznava.sk/?p=9324

IV. Immigration and Settlement

A. EMIGRATION AND ITS CAUSES

Abscondo, Top Ten Reasons why Americans can be Thankful they don't Live in Slovakia," See http://www.abscondo.com/abscondo/2012/11/top-10-reasons-why-an-american-would-not-want-to-come-to-slovakia.html

Balch, Emily G., "Slovak Emigration," in: *Our Slavic Fellow Citizens*. New York: Charities Publication Committee, 1910, pp. 85-119.

Bodnar, John, *The Transplanted: A History of Immigrants in Urban America*. Bloomington: Indiana University Press, 1985, pp. 153, 166.

Čulen, Konstantin, "The Causes of Slovak Emigration," in: Čulen, pp. 25-30.

Čulen, Konstantin, "Some Statistics on Slovak Emigration," in: Čulen, pp. 31-44.

"Czech and Slovakian Immigrants," in: Immigration to United States. See - http://immigrationtounitedstates.org/455-czech-and-slovakian-immigrants.html

"Emigration," in: Miller, pp. 42-45.

Ference, Gregory C., "Slovak Immigration to the United States in the Light of American, Czech, and Slovak History, *Nebraska History*, Vol. 74, No. 3 & 4 (Fall/Winter 1993), pp. 130-135.

Glettler, Monika. "The Hungarian Government Position on Slovak Emigration, 1885-1914,"

in: *Overseas Migration from East-Central and Southeastern Europe, 1880-1940*. Edited by

Julianna Puskás, Akadémiai Kiadó, 1990, pp. 107–18.

Grygier, Nanette. East European Migration to Northwest Pennsylvania : A Case Study of

Crossingville, Pennsylvania. MA Thesis, University of Pennsylvania, 2004.

Kaščáková, Janka, and Dalibor Mikuláš, editors, *Emigration to the English-Speaking World*.

Ružomberok : Catholic University in Ružomberok, Faculty of Arts and Letters, 2006.

Kosa, John, "A Century of Hungarian Emigration 1850-1950," *The American Slavic and East European Review*, 16 (December 1957), pp. 502-503.

Krajsa, Joseph C., "Slovaks: A Part of the Great Emigration to America," *Slovakia* 21, No. 44 (1971), pp. 145-63.

Puci, J., "A Few Notes on Some Aspects of Slovak Emigration to the U. S. A.," in: Kaščáková, J. and D. Mikuláš (Eds.), *Emigration to the English-Speaking World.* Ružomberok: Faculty of Philosophy, Catholic University in Ružomberok, 2006, pp. 119-127.

Puskas, Julianna, Emigration from Hungary to the United States Before 1914," *Studia Historica ASH,* No. 11. Budapest: Akademiai Kiadó, 1975, p. 7.

Stasko, Joseph, "Distinctive Characteristics of Slovak Immigration to America," *Czechoslovak and Central European Journal,* 9, No. 1/2 (Summer/Winter 1990), pp. 91-102.

Stolarik, M. Mark, Slovak Migration from Europe to North America, 1870-1918," *Slovak Studies,* 20 (1980), pp. 5-137.

Tajtak, Ladislav, "Slovak Emigration and Migration in the Years 1900-1914," *Studia Historica Slovaca,* 10 (1978), p. 48 ff.

Tajtak, Ladislav, "Slovak Emigration: Its Causes and Consequences," in: *Overseas Migration from East-Central and Southeastern Europe, 1880-1940.* Ed. By Julianna Puskas. Budapest: Akademiai Kiado, 1990, pp. 74-88.

Tibor, Frank, "From Austria-Hungary to the United States: National Minorities and Emigration 1880–1914," *Nationalities Papers: The Journal of Nationalism and Ethnicity,* Vol. 24, No. 3, Sept. 1996, pp. 409–23.

Vasiljev, I., Vystěhovalectví Čechů a Slováků do Latinské Ameriky před druhou světovou válkou." *Český lid,* 73, No. 4 (1986), pp. 239-243.

Vida, István Kornél, *The True Cause of Freedom: The Kossuth Emigration and the Hungarians' Participation in the American Civil War.* A Dissertation, The University of Debrecen, 2008.

Wheeler, Glenn E., "Slovak Emigration to the United States," in: Genealogical and Local History of Ličartovce, Prešov, Slovakia. See - https://sites.google.com/site/licartovcegen/slovak-emigration-to-the-united-states.

"Why Emigrate," in: Slovakia Genealogy Research Strategies. See - https://www.iabsi.com/gen/public/why_emigrate.htm

B. IMMIGRATION AND SETTLEMENT

Alexander, June Granatir, "Staying Together: Chain Migration and Patterns of Slovak Settlement in Pittsburgh Prior to World War," *Journal of American Ethnic History* 1 (Fall 1981), pp. 56-83.

Alexander, June Granatir, "Slovaks and Slovak Americans, 1870-1940," in: *Immigrants in American History: Arrival, Adaptation, and Integration.* Santa Barbara, CA: ABC0-CLIO, 2013, pp. 603-612.

Alexander, June Granatir, "Slovaks and Slovak Americans, 1940 - Present," in: *Immigrants in American History: Arrival, Adaptation, and Integration.* Santa Barbara, CA: ABC0-CLIO, 2013, pp. 1265-1274.

Čulen, Konštantín, "The Founders of Slovak Settlements," in: Čulen, pp. 67-72.

Ference, Gregory C., "Slovak Immigration to the United States in Light of American, Czech and Slovak History," *Nebraska History,*74, No. 3 & 4 (Fall-Winter, (1993), pp. 130-135.

"Immigration," in: Miller, pp. 47-54

Kopanic, Michael J., "With Feet Planted in Two Lands: An Overview of Emigration to North America from Czechoslovakia," *Slovo* (Magazine of the National Czech & Slovak Museum & Library), Vol. 12, No. 1 (Summer 2011), pp. 10-13.

Raška, Jan, Freedom's Voice: Czech and Slovak Immigration to Canada during the Cold War. A Ph.D. Thesis, University of Waterloo, Waterloo, Ont., Canada, 2013.

"The Saga of Slovak Settlement in Canada," in: Slovak Canadian Heritage Museum. See - http://www.slovakcanadianheritagemuseum.ca/articles/the-saga-of-slovak-settlement-in-canada/

"Slovak Communities Info," in: Kanadský Slovák. See - https://www.kanadskyslovak.ca/index.php/slovak-community

Stasko, Joseph, Distinctive Characteristics of Slovak Immigration to America," *Czechoslovak and Central European Journal,* 9, No. 1 / 2 (Summer / Winter 1990), pp. 91-102.

Stolarik, M. Mark. "Building Slovak Communities in North America," in: The *Other Catholics*. Edited by Keith P. Dyrud, Michael Novak, and Rudolph J. Vecoli. New York: Arno Press, 1978, pp. 89-109.

Wingfield, Nancy M., "Czechoslovak Jewish Immigration to the United States, 1938-1945," Czechoslovak & Central European Journal, Vol. 11, No. 2, Jan. 1993, pp. 38–48.

Zecker, Robert M., *Streetcar Parishes: Slovak Immigrants Build Their Nonlocal Communities, 1890-1945*. Susquehanna University Press, 2010. 329p.

C. ASSIMILATION AND ACCULTURATION

Alexander, June Granatir," Slovaks and Slovak Americans, 1870-1940," in: Immigrants in American History. Arrival, Adaptation and Integration. Edited by Elliot Robert Barkan. Santa Barbara, CA: ABC-CLIO, 2013, Vol. 2., pp. 603-612.

Alexander, June Granatir," Slovaks and Slovak Americans, 1940-Present," in: Immigrants in American History. Arrival, Adaptation and Integration. Edited by Elliot Robert Barkan. Santa Barbara, CA: ABC-CLIO, 2013, Vol. 3, pp. 1265-1274.

"Assimilation," in: Miller, 104-118.

Chimbos, Peter D.,"A Comparison of the Social Adaptation of Dutch, Greek and Slovak Immigrants in a Canadian Community," *The International Migration Review*, 6, No. 3 (Autumn 1972), pp. 230-244.

Horna, Jarmila L.A., "Social Problems in Integration of Immigrants from Czechoslovakia," in: *Czechoslovak National Association of Canada Conference on Cultural and Social Integration of Immigrants from Czechoslovakia*. Edited by Victor Fic. Toronto: Czechoslovak National Association of Canada, 1983, pp. 31-48.

Roucek, Joseph S., "Problems of Assimilation: A Study of Czechoslovaks in the United States," *Sociology and Social Research* 17 (September/October 1931), pp. 62-71.

Roucek, Joseph S., "Passing of American Czechoslovaks," *American Journal of Sociology* 39 (March 1934), pp. 611-625.

Stein, Howard, F. and Robert F. Hill, "Adaptive Modalities among Slovak- and Polish-Americans: Some Issues in Cultural Continuity and Change," *Anthropology* 3, No. 1-2 (1979), pp. 95-107.

Stein, Howard F., "The Slovak- and Rusyn-American Experience: Ethnic Adaptation in the Steel Valley of Western Pennsylvania, *Mind and Human Interaction*, 4, No. 2 (April 1993), pp. 83-91.

D. MELTING POT VS. MULTICULTURALISM

Novak, Michael, *Rise of Unmeltable Ethnics*: Politics and Culture in the Seventies. New York: Macmillan, 1973. 376p.

Palmer, Howard, Mosaic versus the Melting Pot?: Immigration and Ethnicity in Canada and the United States," *International Journal* 31 (1976), pp. 488-528

Stolarik, M. Mark, Multiculturalism in Canada: A Slovak Perspective," *Canadian Ethnic Studies*, Vol. 35, No. 2 (May 2003), pp. 123–28.

E. ETHNIC IDENTITY

Alexander, June Granatir, *Ethnic Pride, American Patriotism: Slovaks and Other New Immigrants in the Interwar Era*. Philadelphia, PA: Temple University, 2004. 278 p.

Kopanic, Michael J., "Slovaks in America," in: *Hungary Through the Centuries. Studies in Honor of Steven Béla Várdy and Ágnes Huszár Várdy*. Ed. Richard P. Mulcahy. Boulder: East European Monographs, distributed by Columbia University Press, 2011, pp. 431-450.

Kopanic, Michael J., "The Slovaks in the USA," in: *Studies in Ethnic Identity: Wandering Slovak People*. Edited by Yoshimoto Kawasaki. Tokyo: Chuo University Press, 2007, pp. 209-241.

Novak. Michael, *Unmeltable Ethnics: Politics and Culture in American Life*. Piscataway, NJ: Transection Publishers, 1995. 486p.

Riecanska, Eva, "Contemporary Ethnicity, Maintenance of Ethnic Culture and Ethnic Change: The Case of the Slovak Americans in Western Pennsylvania," *Human Affairs*, 8, No. 1 (June 1998), pp. 68-84.

Stein, Howard F., An *Ethno-Historic Study of Slovak American Identity*. Salem, NH: Ayer Co. Publishers, 1981.

Stolarik, M. Mark, "The Slovak Search for Identity in the USA, 1870-1918," *Canadian Review of Studies in Nationalism* 20, No. 1-2 (1993), pp. 45-55.

Zecker, Robert M. "Where Everyone Goes to Meet Everyone Else: The Translocal Creation of a Slovak Immigrant Community," *Journal of Social History*, Vol. 38, No. 2, Winter 2004, pp. 423–53.

F. HOME-COUNTRY GOVERNMENT'S REACTION
TO EMIGRATION

Sum, Anton, Czecho-Slovak Government and Immigration," *Foreign-Born*. A Bulletin of International Service, April 1921, p. 178.

G. EFFECT OF EMIGRATION AND REIMMIGRATION
ON SLOVAK SOCIETY

Brown, Jennifer, "Sharing an American Traditions: How an Expat in Bratislava Hosts Thanksgiving (and why)," see - https://www.welcometobratislava. eu/sharing-an-american-tradition-how-an-expat-in-bratislava-hosts-thanksgiving-and-why/

Jakešová, Elena, "The Impact of Emigrants and Reimmigration on Slovak Society (1880's - 1920's)," *Društvena istraživanja*, 7 (1933-34), pp. 27-42.

V. People

A. ANTHROPOLOGY

"Who Are the Czecho-Slovaks?" in: Miller, pp. 11-17.

Piskor, Steve, *Gypsy Violins Hungarian Slovak Gypsies in America*. Saroma, 2012. 244p.

Stein, Howard, F. and Robert F. Hill, "Adaptive Modalities among Slovak- and Polish-Americans: Some Issues in Cultural Continuity and Change," *Anthropology* 3, No. 1-2 (1979), pp. 95-107.

B. DEMOGRAPHY

Čulen, Konstantin, "Some Statistics on Slovak Emigration," in: *History of Slovaks in America*. Minneapolis, MN: CGSI, 2003, pp. 30-44.

"Distribution and Location," in: Miller, pp. 47-54.

Janda, Kenneth, "More Slovaks in the U.S. than Czech? Who Says? When and Where?" See - http://janda.org/bio/Habsburgs/More%20Slovaks%20 in%20the%20U.S.pdf

"Slovak American Demographics," in: améredia. See - http://www.ameredia. com/resources/demographics/slovak.html

US Department of Labor, Report of the Department of Labor: 1919: Report of the Secretary of Labor and Reports of Bureaus.Washington, DC: GPO, 1920, pp. 486-87.

US Department of Commerce, Bureau of the Census, Fourteenth Census of the United States Taken in the Year 1920. Vol. 11. Population 1920. General Report and Analytical Tables. Washington, DC: GPO, 1922, p. 973.

C. Language

1. General

Alexander, June Granatir, "Language and Leisure: Getting the Younger Generation's Perspective," in: *Ethnic Pride, American Patriotism. Slovaks and Other New Immigrants in the Interwar Era.* Philadelphia: Temple University Press, 2004, pp. 132-159.

Budd, Joseph P., We Do Know English: Philadelphia's Czechoslovak Presbyterian Church of Jan Hus, 1926-1967. M.A. Thesis, University of Delaware, 2009.

Hammer, Louise. B., "American Slovak Speech," *Národný Kalendár-Almanac for the Year of 1990.* Pittsburgh: National Slovak Society, 1990, pp. 64-65.

Hammer, Louise B.,"Language Death: The Slovak Language in America," *Good Shepherd,* 1993, pp. 87-94.

Hammer, Louise. B. and Ivor Ripka, *Speech of American Slovaks.* Bratislava: Veda, 1994. 163p.

Henzl, Věra M., "Slavic Languages in the New Environment," in: *Language in the USA.* Edited by Charles A. Ferguson and Shirley Brice Heath. Cambridge: Cambridge University Press, 1981, pp. 293-321.

"Historical Slovak Literacy," in: Slovak Studies Program. See - https://www.pitt.edu/~votruba/qsonhist/literacyslovakiahungarykingdom.html

Kvetánová, Viktória, "Linguistic Research about Slovaks in the USA," in: Slovak Spot. See - See - https://groups.google.com/forum/#!msg/slovak-spot/7By-bRc3c0s/HknNKsiBlZ4J

"Linguist: Slovak Surviving well under pressure from English," *The Slovak Spectator,* February 3, 2003. See - https://spectator.sme.sk/c/20018335/linguist-slovak-surviving-well-under-pressure-from-english.html

Magocsi, Paul Robert. "Slavic Immigrant Cultures in North America: The Language Factor," *Slavic Languages in Migration.* Edited by Michael Moser and Maria Polinsky. Slavische Sprachgeschichte No. 6, Lit, 2013, pp. 11-21.

McCabe, Marta, Parental Experiences with Children's Heritage Language Maintenance and Loss: Cases of Eleven Czech and Slovak Transnational Immigrant Families in the Southeastern United States. Ph.D. Dissertation, University of North Carolina, Chapel Hill, 2014.

McCabe, Marta, "Czech and Slovak Mothers Struggling to Maintain Children's Heritage Language in North Carolina," in: Immigration and Education in

North Carolina. Edited by X. L. Rong and J. Hilburn. Rotterdam: Sense Publishers, 2016, pp. 241-266.

McCabe, M., "Transnationalism and Language Maintenance: Czech and Slovak as Heritage Languages in the Southeastern United States," *International Journal of the Sociology of Language,* Vol. 238 (2016), pp. 169–191.

Meyerstein, Goldie Piroch, *Selected Problems of Bilingualism among Immigrant Slovaks.* University of Michigan, 1959. 398p.

Meyerstein, Goldie Piroch, Bilingualism among American Slovaks: Analysis of Loans. *Publication of the American Dialect Society,* Vol. 46, Issue 1 (November 1966), pp. 1-19.

Potocek, Cyril J., "The Slovaks and their Language," *Sbornik Sokol* (1960), pp. 488-492.

Sabatos, Charles, "Between Two Worlds: Slovak Language and American Identity in Out of this Furnace," *Comparative American Studies,* 11, No. 1 (March 2013), pp. 74-88.

"Slovak Language Lessons," in: Slovak Treasures - and American Slovaks. See - http://www.slovakcooking.com/language/

"Slovaks Reconnect with their Heritage," *Pittsburgh Post-Gazette,* May 20, 2001. See - http://old.post-gazette.com/magazine/20010520slovaksmag2.asp

Stolarik, M. Mark, "A Historical Perspective on the Declining Use of the Slovak Language over Three Generations in the United States of America," *Národný Kalendár-Almanac for the Year of 1990.* Pittsburgh: National Slovak Society, 1990, pp. 65-67.

2. Anglicisms

Katreniakoá, Zdena, *Anglicizmy v slovenčině* (Anglicism on the Slovak Language). Banská Bystrica: Metodicke centrum, 2002.

Kráľová, Zdena, Anglicizmy v slovenčine z hľadiska didaktickej komunikácie. Banská Bystrica: Metodické centrum, 2002. 32p.

Štujberová, Elena, The Anglicisms in the Slovak Language. Bakalárska práca, Fakulta aplikovaných jazykov EU v Bratislava, 2015. 51p.

Ulašin, Bohdan, "Lexical Anglicisms in Spanish and Slovak: A Contrastive Study," *Verba Hispanica,* Vol. 23, No. 1 (2015), pp. 163-178.

3. Slovak Names

"Slovak Name," in: Wikipedia. See - https://en.wikipedia.org/wiki/Slovak_name

"Slovak Names," in: Behind the Names. See -. See - https://www.behindthename.com/names/usage/slovak

"Slovak Names - Top 100 First Names in Slovakia & Statistics," in: Students of the World. See - http://www.studentsoftheworld.info/penpals/stats.php3?Pays=SLO

D. FOOD AND CUISINE

The Anniversary Slovak-American Cook Book. By the First Catholic Slovak Ladies Union. Allegro Editions, 2015. 438p.

Bodnar, John, "Kolachi Nut Rolls - A Slovak Family Legacy," in: See - https://cnneatocracy.wordpress.com/tag/john-bodnar-cnn/

Brendel, Toni and Sidonka Wadina, *Slovak Recipes*. Penfield Books, 2009. 172p.

Brieda, Luboš, "Slovak Cooking." See - http://www.slovakcooking.com/about.

Contempierogi: Breakfast Machanka: Traditional Recipe." See - http:/contempierogi.blogspot.com/2009/12/breakfast-machanka-traditional-recipe.html

Contempierogi, "A Modern Twist of Favorite Slovak-American Recipes. See - http://contempierogi.blogspot.com/

Eleuterio, Susan, "Slovakia," in: *Ethnic American Food Today: A Cultural Encyclopedia.* Edited by Lucy M. Long. Lanham - Boulder - New York - London: Rowman & Littlefield, 2015, pp. 565-567.

Kowis, Agnes, *Serenko Cookbook:* An Ageless Mid-West Slovak/American Tradition.CreateSpace, 2013. 226p.

Golis, Otilia, *Otilia's Slovak Kitchen.* 2nd ed. The Author, 2018. 40p.

Petrzala, Peter, *My Slovak Kitchen.* CreateSpace, 2017. 174p.

"Slovak Food, Recipes, Culture, Language Lessons…," in: Slovak Treasures - and American Slovaks. See - http://www.slovakcooking.com/

E. TRADITIONS & CUSTOMS

Brendel, Toni, *Slovak American Touches*: Family Recipes, History, Folk Arts. Penfield Books, 2008. 192p.

Cincebeaux, Helene Baine., *Slovakia!:Traditions Old and New*. The Author, 2010.

Dvorchak, Robert, "Slovaks Reconnect with their Heritage," in: Pittsburgh Post-Gazette, May 20, 2001. See - http://old.post-gazette.com/magazine/20010520slovaksmag2.asp

Kováč, Edward, Jr., *Slovenské zvyky* (Slovak Customs). Scranton, PA: Obrana Press, 1953.

"Traditions," in: Slovak Treasures - and American Slovaks. See - http://www.slovakcooking.com/category/blog/traditions

F. FOLKLORE

Brendel, Toni, *Slovak American Touches: Family Recipes, History, Folk Arts*. Penfield Books, 2008. 192p.

Cincura, Andrew, Slovak and Ruthenian Easter Eggs in America: The Impact of Culture Contact on Immigrant Art and Custom," *Journal of Popular Culture*, 4 (1970), pp. 155-193.

Cincebeaux, Helen, *Treasures of Slovakia*. Martin: Neographia, 1993.

Cincebeaux, G Helen, *A Treasury of Slovak Folk Dress*. Rochester, NY: Best Printers, 2014. 136p.

Hammer, Louise B., "Slovak Folk Music and Religious Christmas Music," *Národný Kalendár-Almanac for the Year of 1991*. Pittsburgh: National Slovak Society, 1990, pp. 64-65.

Kováč, Edward, Jr. *Slovenské zvyky* (Slovak Customs), Scranton, PA: Obrana Press, 1953.

"The Lúčina Slovak Folklore Ensemble," in: smartculturesoure.org. See - http://www.smartculturesource.org/hostorganizationprofile/lúčina-slovak-folklore-ensemble

Nettl, Bruno and Ivo Moravcik, Czech and Slovak Songs Collected in Detroit," *Midwest Folklore* 5 (1953), pp. 37-49.

"Slovak Communities," in" *Encyclopedia of American Folklife*. Edited by Simon J. Bronner. London and New York: Routledge, 2006, pp. 1139-1143.

"Slovak Heritage Live," a quarterly newsletter. Summary of the Summer Issue, Vol. 13, No.2 (Summer 2005). See - http://www.slovakheritage.org/SHLnewsletter/20052summer.htm

"Slovak Folk Art - Straw Eggs and Weaved Whips," in: Slovak Treasures - and American Slovaks. See - http://www.slovakcooking.com/2011/blog/slovak-folk-art/

G. ETHNOGRAPHY

Stein, Howard F., "Structural Change in Slovak Kinship: An Ethnohistoric Inquiry," *Ethnology*, 14, No. 1 (January 1975), pp. 99-108.

Stein, Howard, F., Some Anthropological Reflections: Inaugural Meeting of Slovak Studies Association," *Jednota*, 26, December 1979.

Stein, Howard E., *An Ethno-Historic Study of Slovak American Identify*. New York: Arno Press, 1980. 526p.

Stein, Howard F., "An Ethnohistory of Slovak-American Religious and Fraternal Associations: A Study in Cultural Meaning, Group Identity and Social Institutions," *Slovakia*, 29, No. 53-54 (1980-1981), pp. 53-101.

Stein, Howard F., "Ethnographic Research on Rusyns in America," *Carpatho-Rusyn American*, 13, No. 2 (Summer 1990), pp. 7-10.

Thurova, Jana, Through One Immigrant's Eyes: Autoethnography of a Slovak Woman Living in North America. M.A. Thesis, Athabasca University, Athabasca, Alberta, Canada, 2009.

H. FESTIVALS

1. General

Pirkova-Jakobson, Svatava, "Harvest Festivals among Czechs and Slovaks in America," *The Journal of American Folklore*, Vol. 69, No. 273 (July - September 1956), pp. 266-280.

2. Individual States

Arkansas

Slovak Heritage Day, Prairie Co., AR - February 14
"Slovak Heritage Day planned for Feb. 14," *Arkansas News*, February 3, 2018

California

Czech, Moravian, and Slovak Folklore Festival- La Mesa, CA - around May 19
Website: https://czechandslovakcottage.com/events/2018/5/19/8th-annual-czech-moravian-and-slovak-folklore-festival

San Diego Czech-Moravian-Slovak Festival - San Diego, CA - about February 19
Website: http://czechfolks.com/2011/02/18/first-san-diego-czech-moravian-slovak-festival-tomorrow/

Indiana

Slovak Day - Valparaiso; Merrillville, IN
Website: https://www.nwitimes.com/news/local/porter/valparaiso/slovak-day-offers-mass-food-dance-and-music/article_50e910ca-0357-50d4-a27a-741a55aeaac6.html

Maryland

Czech and Slovak Festival, Towson, MD - around October
Website: http://cshamaryland.org/events/

Michigan

Sokol Detroit Czech and Slovak Festival, Dearborn Heights, MI -
Website: http://www.czechevents.net/events/details/8832

Minnesota

Czech and Slovak Festival - organized by Sokol Minnesota -
Website: https://www.sokolmn.org/csfestival/

Missouri

Slovakfest, St. Louis, MO - November 3
Website : http://www.slovakfest.com/

Nebraska

Omaha Czech-Slovak Festival - Omaha, NE - around April 29
Website: http://www.omahaczechclub.com/czech_slovak_folklore_
festival.html

New Jersey

Slovak Heritage Festival, East Brunswick, NJ - around September 23
Website: https://njvendors.com/events/counties-m-w/middlesex/
east-brunswick-nj-september-slovak-heritage-festival/

Slovak Heritage Museum - Holmdel, NJ - around September 28
Website: https://www.facebook.com/events/slovak-heritage-festival-
holmdel-nj/627652147349389/

Slovak Heritage Festival, Middlesex County Fair Grounds - around September
23
Website: https://www.facebook.com/slovakfestival/

New York

Czech & Slovak Festival - Bohemian Hall - Beer Garden - around May 28
Website: http://bohemianhall.com/event/czech-and-slovak-festival/

Oklahoma

Oklahoma Czech and Slovak Festival
Website: Oklahoma Czech and Slovak Festival. See - http://www.wflains.org/about-western/blog/2017/10/oklahoma-czech-and-slovak-festival/

Pennsylvania

Pitts Slovak Heritage Festival - Pittsburgh
Website: http://www.slovakcooking.com/2010/blog/pitt-festival/

Virginia

Czech & Slovak Folklife Festival - Prince George County - around October 20
Website: http://virginiaczechslovak.org/index.html

Wisconsin

Czech-Slovak Festival - Phillips, WI - around June 15-17
Website: http://www.czech-slovak-festival.com/

VI. Religion

A. GENERAL

Alexander, June Granatir, *The Immigrant Church and Community. Pittsburgh's Slovak Catholics and Lutherans, 1830-1915*. Pittsburgh: University of Pittsburgh Press, 1987. 198 p.

Alexander, June Granatir, "Religion and Ethnic Identity in a Slavic Community: Pittsburgh's Slovak Catholics and Protestants," *Studi Emigrazione*, Vol. 28, No.103 (September 1991), pp. 423–441.

Alexander, June Granatir, Slovak Churches: Religious Diversity and Ethnic Communities," *Pennsylvania Folklore*, 44, No. 2 (Winter 1994-95), pp. 70-77.

Kirschbaum, Joseph M., *Religious Life of Slovaks in Canada*. 2010

Miller, Kenneth D., "Religious Conditions," in his: The Czecho-Slovaks in America. New York: George H. Doran Company,1922, pp. 119-168.

Stolarik, M. Mark, "Slovak Religious Institutions in the United States and Canada," *Jednota Annual Furdek*, 27 (January 1988), pp. 81-87.

Stolarik, M. Mark, Slovak Immigrants Come to Terms with Religious Diversity in North America," *Catholic Historical Review*, 96, No. 1 (January 2010), pp. 56-84.

Tanzone, Daniel F., "Religious Developments among the Slovaks in America," in: *Slovaks in America: A Bicentennial Study*, pp. 57-66.

B. ROMAN-CATHOLIC CHURCH

1. General

Alexander, June Granatir, "The Laity in the Church: Slovaks and the Catholic Church in Pre-World War Pittsburgh," *Church History* 53, No. 3 (September 1984), pp. 363-78.

Cierny, Fr. Karol, S.J. Superior, "The Slovak Jesuits of Canada," *Jednota Annual Furdek*, 27 (January 1988), pp. 110-113.

Čulen, Konstantin, "The Cult of SS Cyril and Methodius among the Slovaks in USA and Canada," *Slovakia* 22, No. 45 (1972), pp. 98-113.

Gonda, Gerard, "Slovak Benedictine Monks of St. Andrew Abbey, Cleveland," *Jednota Annual Furdek*, 27 (January 1988)), pp. 88-94.

Hrobak, Philip A., *Slovak Catholic Parishes and Institutions in the United States and Canada*. Cleveland: The First Catholic Slovak Union, 1955. 183 p.

Katolícké farnosti Amerika. See - http://www.kfamerika.estranky.sk/clanky/zoznam-farnosti.html

Kremenik, Sister Anne, "History of the Conference of Slovak Religious," *Jednota Annual Furdek*, 27 (January 1988), pp. 150-153.

Portasik, Richard, *Slovak Franciscans in America*. Pittsburgh, PA: Franciscan Fathers, 1966.

Reisteter, Fr. William, O.F.M., Custos, "Slovak Franciscans in America," *Jednota Annual Furdek*, 27 (January 1988), pp. 105-109.

Shelley, Thomas J., *Slovaks on the Hudson: Most Holy Trinity Church, Yonkers, and the Slovak Catholics of the Archdiocese of New York, 1894-2000*. Catholic University of America Press, 2002

Slovak Catholic Parishes and Institutions in the United States and Canada. Cleveland: The First Catholic Union, *1955. 183p.*

"Slovak Parishes," in: *Slovaks in America*. A Bicentennial Study, pp. 297-399.

Stolarik, M. Mark, "Lay Initiative in American-Slovak Parishes, 1880-1930," *Records of the American Catholic Historical Society of Philadelphia* 83 (September-December 1972), pp. 151-156.

Stolarik, M. Mark, "Slovak Catholics in America," in: *The Encyclopedia of American Catholic History*. Edited by Michael Glazier and Thomas J. Shelley. Collegeville, MN: The Liturgical Press, 1997, pp. 1323-1327.

Tybor, M. Martina, *Slovak American Catholics*. Middletown, PA: First Catholic Slovak Union, 1976.

Zubek, Theodoric J., "The Influence of Slovak Catholics in the United States and Canada on their Social and Religious Environment," *Slovak Studies* 24 (1984), pp. 139-75.

2. Priests

Joseph Victor Adamec (1935-), b. Bannister, MI, Philadelphia, PA, of Slovak ancestry; Bishop of R.C. Diocese of Altoona-Johnstown, PA
Bio: "Joseph Victor Adamec," in: Revolvy. See - https://www.revolvy.com/topic/Joseph+Victor+Adamec; "Joseph Victor Adamec," in: Wikipedia. See - https://en.wikipedia.org/wiki/Joseph_Victor_Adamec

Joseph S. Altany (1903-1986), b. Tarentum, Pa, of Slovak descent; R.C. priest, Msgr., Papal Prelate with the title Rt. Rev., pastor of St. Michael Parish, Munhall, PA (s. 1937).
Bio: "Altany Jozef," in: Religia Slovakia. See - http://religiask.blogspot. com/2017/11/altany-jozef.html

Bonaventure Babik (?- 1986), b., R.C. priest, pastor in All Saints Parish in Canton, OH (1975-86); taught Slovak at University of Akron in Continuing Education.

Gabriel (Julian) Balazovic (1949-), b. Dolná Krupa, Slovakia; Brother, O.S.B.;
Bio: "Bro. Gabriel (Julian) Balazovic," in: St. Andrew Abbey. See - https:// standrewabbey.org/people/bro-gabriel-julian-balazovic

John Balberchak (1914-1995), b. Edwardsville, PA, of Slovak immigrant parents; R.C. priest, Msgr., Papal Prelate, pastor, St. Joseph parish, Hazleton, PA
Bio: "John A. Balberchak, died," *Hazleton Standard-Speaker,* June 6, 1995.

Jozef Ballun (1890-1936), b. Trstená, Slovakia; R.C. priest, O.F.M., Franciscan; took the name Fulgencius, Fulgenec; leader of a monastery in Bratislava. In 1926, sent as a missionary to the USA, and became very popular. Died in Gary, Indiana.
Bio: "P. Fulgenc Jozef Ballun, O.F.M." See - http://www.frantiskani.sk/ nekr/02/ballun.htm

Thomas V. Banick (1938-), b. Dunmore, PA, of Slovak descent; R.C. priest, Msgr., pastor of St. Mary's Church of the Immaculate Conception, Wilkes-Barre, PA
Bio: "Monsignor Banick, long-serving pastor, to retire," *The Citizens' Voice,* August 23, 2013.

Joseph A. Banik (-1967), b.; R.C. priest; pastor of St. John the Baptist Church, Central City, PA (s. 1924), national chaplain of Jednota (1933-44).

Joseph A. Baran (1902-1984), b. Bethlehem, PA, of Slovak descent; R.C. priest, Msgr.; pastor of Saint Michael's Catholic Church, Lansford, PA (for

22 years). He was an assistant pastor of St. Michael's 1930-36, and pastor of St. Joseph's Catholic Church, Sheppton, Schuylkill County, for 19 years. In August of 1955, he was named pastor of St. Michael's Church, where he served until retiring in 1978. He was nationally recognized for his part in bringing peace to the strife-ridden anthracite coal mines of northeastern Pennsylvania in 1937 and 1939.
Bio: "Msgr. Joseph Baran, 82, 'Miners' Priest,' *The Morning Call*, March 30, 1984.

Louis Baska (1888-1973), b. Kansas City, KS, of Slovak descent; R.C. priest, O.S.B., monk, St. Benedict Abbey, Atchison, KS, also with St. Benedict College, Atchison
Bio: "Fr Louis Martin Baska," in: Find A Grave. See - https://www.findagrave.com/memorial/53282041/louis-martin-baska

Jack Baštigal (1937-), b. Drumheller, Alberta, Canada, of Slovak descent; R.C. priest; pastor, Ascension Catholic Parish (1982-94); St. James Parish, Okotoks, Alberta (s. 1994)
Bio: "Jack Bastigal," in LinkedIn. See - https://www.linkedin.com/in/fr-jack-bastigal-53788563/; "Father Bastigal Celebrated 50th Anniversary of Priesthood," *Kanadský Slovak*, May 22, 2018.

Francis J. Beeda (ca 1930-), b. Scranton, PA, of Slovak descent; R.C. priest, STL, Msgr., pastor of St. Joseph's RC Church (1985-2009), Hazleton, PA, the oldest Slovak church in the US

George A. Benedick, b. of Slovak descent; R.C. priest, Msgr., pastor of St. John's, Luzerne, PA

John Bendik (1942-), b. Kingston, PA, of Slovak descent; R.C. priest, Msgr.; assoc. pastor, Scranton, PA; campus ministry, East Stroudsburg University (14 years), Misericordia University (until 1986); pastor of Our Lady of the Snow parish (1986-95), pastor of the parish communities of St. Casimir, St. John the Evangelist Church, Pittston, PA (s. 1996).
Bio: "Monsignor Bendik retiring after 50 years in priesthood," in: *Pittston News*, June 18, 2017.

James Benish (fl. 1970), b. of Slovak descent; R.C. priest, O.F.M.C; pastor of Sts. Cyril & Methodius Slovak Roman Catholic parish, Montreal, Canada (1939-51, 1966-70)
Bio: "Sts. Cyril & Methodius Slovak Roman Catholic Parish, Montreal, Quebec, Canada." See - https://slovakcatholic.weebly.com/history.html

Method Cyril Billy (1910-1995), b. PA, of Slovak descent; Franciscan friar, R.C. priest; chaplain in Army Air Corps (1942-46), professor of theology at Catholic University of America
Bio: "Chaplain Method Cyril Billy," in: The Arrowhead Club. See - https://thearrowheadclub.com/2017/08/23/chaplain-method-cyril-billy/

Andrew R. Biros, Slovak Canadian; R.C. priest, Msgr.; Toronto, Ont., Canada

Victor A. Blahunka (1884-1959), b. Lúčky, Slovakia; in UIS s. 1912; R.C. priest, the first Slovak to be named a monsignor in the USA, religious writer on Christian philosophy, nationality activist; pastor of Sacred Heart of Jesus Catholic in Chicago (1921-59); chaplain of the First Catholic Slovak Women's Union.
Bio: in -Paučo, Jozef, *Slovenski priekopnici v Amerike*, Cleveland: Prva Prvá Katolícka Slovenská Jednota, 1972: pp. 29-30.

Peter E. Bolerasky (1927-2009), in Moquah, WI, of Slovak immigrant parents; R.C. priest, Msgr.; pastor at St. Stephen the King in Streator (1974-2002);
Bio: "Reverend Monsignor Peter E. Bolerasky," in: Solon-Telford Funeral Home. See - https://www.solontelford.com/notices/Monsignor-Bolerasky

Matthew Bonk (1968-), b. Milan, MI, of Slovak descent; R.C. priest, C.Ss.R, pastor in St. Louis, MO, Baton Rouge, LA, Brooklyn Center, MN (s. 2015)
Bio: "Father Matthew Bonk, C.Ss.R.," in: Redemptorists Evangelization. See - https://redemptoristsevangelization.org/father-matthew-bonk-c-ss-r/

Matthew Brozovic (1931-2016), b. Briar Hill, PA, of Slovak descent; Franciscan friar, O.F.M., R. C. priest
Bio: "Fr. Matthew Brozovic," *Pittsburgh Post-Gazette*, February 4, 2016.

Michael Brunovsky (1964-), b. Cleveland, OH, of Slovak descent; R.C. priest, O.S.B., monk at St. Andrew Abbey, Cleveland; teacher, at present academic dean, at Benedictine HS, Cleveland
Bio: "Visiting Monk: Rev. Michael Brunovsky, O.S.B.," in: Behind the Pine Curtain, See - /www.behindthepinecurtain.com/wordpress/visiting-monk-rev-michael-brunovsky-osb/

John Bukovský (orig. John Fukna) (1924-2010), b. Cerova-Lieskové, Slovakia; naturalized US citizen; R.C. priest, SDW, Archbishop, a Vatican diplomat. He was consecrated titular Archbishop of Tabalta in August 1990. He was the Apostolic Nuncio in Romania from 1990 to 1994. In 1994, he became the first Apostolic Delegate to the Russian Federation.
Bio: "John Bukovsky," in: Wikipedia. See - https://en.wikipedia.org/wiki/John_Bukovsky

Timothy (Dennis) Buyansky (1942-); b. Cleveland, OH; R.C. priest, O.S.B., monk, prior, St. Andrew Abbey, Cleveland; teacher, librarian and music director of Benedictine HS, Cleveland
Bio: "Fr. Tim Tales a Bow," in: Benedictine High School - Focus on the Faculty. See - https://saintjohnofthecross.org/documents/2018/5/Father%20Tim%20article%201.pdf

Emil Černaj (1923-2000), b. Žiar nad Hronom, Czech.; R.C., priest, missionary in Philippines, USA and Australia.
Bio: "Emil Černaj," in: wikipedia. See - https://sk.wikipedia.org/wiki/Emil_Černaj

Michael J. Churak (1911-1988), b. Perth Amboy, NJ, of Slovak descent; R.C. priest, Msgr., pastor of Holy Trinity Church, Perth Amboy, NJ, supreme chaplain of the Slovak Catholic Federation of America

Stephen J. Daday (1916-1993), b. R.C. priest, Msgr.; pastor at St. Theresa's Catholic Church, Hellertown for 19 years. Before that he was principal at Allentown Central HS (1953-65).
Bio: "Monsignor Daday Dies at 77," *The Morning Call,* January 23, 1993.

Alexander Dianiska (1867-1923), b. Banská Bystrica, Slovakia; in US s. 1903; R.C. priest, author, translator, Plymouth, PA; worked closely with Rev.

Matthew Jankola in establishing the Congregation the Sisters of Saints Cyril and Methodius in Danville, PA.
Bio: in - Pauco, Jozef, "Dr. Alexander Dianiska," *Slovakia*, 42 (1969), pp. 108-116; Paučo, Jozef, *Slovenski priekopníci v Amerike,* Cleveland: Prvá Katolícka Slovenská Jednota, 1972, pp. 45-50; "Alexander Dianiska," in: Wikipedia. See - "Alexander Dianiska," in: Wikipedia. See - https://sk.wikipedia.org/wiki/Alexander_Dianiska.

Rudolf Dilong (1905-1986), b. Trstená, Slovakia; R.C. priest, O.F.M., poet, playwright, novelist
Bio: "Rudolf Dilong," in: Wikipedia. See - https://sk.wikipedia.org/wiki/Rudolf_Dilong; "Fr. Rudolph Alphones Dilong," in: Find A Grave. See - https://www.findagrave.com/memorial/113406361/rudolph-alphonse-dilong

Benedict J. Dobrencin (1912-1967); of Slovak descent; R.C. priest, O.S.B., monk, St. Andrew Abbey, principal of Benedictine High School, Cleveland, OH

Stephen J. Drab (1914-2003), b. Usovský Salgov, Slovakia; R.C. priest; in US s. 1954; Diocesan Priest of the Greensburg Diocese, and a resident of Connellsville Pennsville, PA
Bio: "Rev. Fr. Stephen J. Drab," in: Frank Kapr Funeral Home. See - https://www.kapr.com/notices/RevFrStephen-Drab

Michael A. Dravecky (1907-2001), b. of Slovak descent; R.C. priest, Papal Prelate with the title Rt. Rev., pastor of Holy Trinity Church, Duquesne, PA (1962), then in McKeesport, PA (1963-1974).
Bio: "Rev. Msgr. Michael Dravecky," in: Find A Grave. See - https://www.findagrave.com/memorial/175141060/michael-dravecky

Francis J. Dubosh (1890-1967), b. Cleveland, OH, of Slovak ancestry; R.C. priest, Msgr.; pastor of Saints Cyril and Methodius Catholic Church, Lakewood, OH, supreme chaplain of Jednota; president of the Slovak League (1943-45), president of the Slovak Catholic Federation of America (1937-38).
Bio: "Rev. Fr. Francis Joseph Dubosh," in: Find a Grave. See- https://www.findagrave.com/memorial/120789128/francis-joseph-dubosh; -Dubelko, Jim, "Balancing Slovak Identity and Patriotism. Monsignor Dubosh During

World War II," in: Cleveland Historical. See - https://clevelandhistorical.org/items/show/583?tour=41&index=7

Robert G. Duch (1938-1964), b. North Braddock, PA, of Slovak descent; R.C. priest; Ph.D.; pastor, Saint Scholastica Parish, Pittsburgh, PA (1994-2008), pastor of Saint Barnabas Parish, Swissvale, PA (1983- 1994); author of Successful Parish Leadership: Nurturing the Animated Parish (1990).
Bio: Curriculum vitae. See - https://www.futurechurch.org/sites/default/files/robert%20duch%20Curriculum%20Vitae%5B1%5D.pdf

Joseph J. Dulik (1884-1936), b. Rovné, Trenčín District, Slovakia; R.C. priest, pastor of Holy Ghost Parish in Olyphant, PA; president of the Slovak Catholic Federation after WWI and chaplain of the First Catholic Slovak Union; treasurer of the Slovak Catholic Matica Slovenská.
Bio: Pauco, Joseph, "Father Joseph J. Dulik," *Slovakia*, 47 (1974), pp. 70-80.

Joseph Aloysius Durick (1914-1994), b. Dayton, TN, of Slovak descent; R.C. priest, Bishop, first Slovak-American Bishop in the US, civil rights advocate
Bio: "Bishop Joseph Durick, 79, Civil Rights Advocate," The New York Times, June 28, 1994; "Joseph Aloysius Durick," in: Wikipedia. See - https://en.wikipedia.org/wiki/Joseph_Aloysius_Durick

Justin (David) Dyrwal (1964-), b. Pittsburgh, PA; R.C. priest, O.S.B., pastor of Assumption parish, Broadview Heights, OH, monk at St. Andrew Abbey, Cleveland
Bio: "Fr. Justin (David) Dyrwal, O.S.B.," in: St. Andrew Abbey. See - https://standrewabbey.org/people/fr-justin-david-drywal

Karol Florek (1896-d.), b. Budapest; R.C. priest, pastor of the St. Michael Slovak Catholic Parish
Bio: "Florek, Karol," in: Droba, p. 104.

James Forgáč (1919-1944), b. of Slovak descent; R.C. priest, O.S.B., monk, St. Andrew's Abbey, Cleveland; theologian; teacher at Notre Dame College, OH and at University of Ottawa, Canada
Bio: "Rev. James A. Forgac," in: Find A Grave. See - https://www.findagrave.com/memorial/162453893/james-a.-forgac

Stephen Furdek (1855-1915), b. Trstená, Slovakia; R.C. priest, in Us. S. 1882. Father Furdek was first assigned to St. Wenceslas Church, the first parish in Cleveland to serve Czech Catholics. He served there until May 1883. He then established a parish for Czechs near E. 55th and Broadway, which was placed under the patronage of Our Lady of Lourdes. Except for a short time ministering to St. Prokop's parish, he would spend the rest of his life serving the Lourdes parish. In 1888, he organized St. Ladislaus Church, the first parish to serve both Slovaks and Hungarians in Cleveland.
Bio: "Furdek, Stephan," in: *Encyclopedia of Cleveland History*. See - https://case. edu/ech/articles/f/furdek-stephanTybor, M. Martina, "Father of American Slovaks, Stephen Furdek," *Slovakia* 16 (1966), pp. 25-40; "Stephen Furdek," in: Wikipedia. See - https://en.wikipedia.org/wiki/Stephen_Furdek

Ronald William Gainer (1947-), b. Pottsville, PA, of Slovak descent; R.C. priest, Bishop of Harrisburg, PA, former second Bishop of Lexington. KY
Bio: "Ronald William Gainer," in: Wikipedia - See https://en.wikipedia.org/ wiki/Ronald_William_Gainer

Joseph A. Gajdosik (1909-1982), b. R.C. priest; pastor at Holy Name Church in Monessen
Bio: "Reverend Joseph A. Gajdosik," in: BillionGraves. See - https:// billiongraves.com/grave/Joseph-A-Gajdosik/11559514

Frederick T. Gasparovic (d. 1966), b. of Slovak descent; R.C. priest; pastor at St. Andrew parish, North Catasauqua, PA (1948-66)

Erwin Emerick Gellhof (1859-1933), b. Huncovce, Slovakia; R.C. priest, pastor of St. Stephen's Church at Streator, IL, later pastor of the Slovak congregation at Connellsville, PA.; chaplain of the First Catholic Slovak Union; one of the founders of the Matica Slovenska in America.
Bio: "Rev. Emerick Gellhof," in: *Genealogical and Personal History, of Fayette Co. Pennsylvania*. New York: Lewis Historical Publishing Company, 1912, Vol. 1, p. 215; Paučo, Jozef, *Slovenski priekopnici v Amerike*, Cleveland: Prvá Katolícka Slovenská Jednota, 1972, pp. 130-31.

Stanislaus F. Gmuca (1894-1977), b. Johnstown, PA, of Slovak descent; R.C. priest, O.S.B., first abbot of St. Andrew Svorad Abbey, Cleveland, OH (1934-1946)
Bio: "Gmuca, Rt. Rev. Stanislaus F. O.S.B.," in: *Catholic Who's Who*, 14 (1960-1961), p. 172; "Rev. Stanislaus Frank Gmuca," in: Find A Grave. See - https://www.findagrave.com/memorial/189602795/stanislaus-frank-gmuca

Gerard (Martin) Gonda (1953-), Cleveland, OH, of Slovak descent; R.C. priest, O.S.B.; monk, St. Andrew Abbey, Cleveland; English teacher, principal, at Benedictine HS, Cleveland
Bio: "Fr. Gerard (Martin) Gonda, O.S.B.," in: St. Andrew Abbey. See - https://standrewabbey.org/people/fr-gerard-martin-gonda

Anton Gracik (1878-1956), b. Slovakia; R.C. priest; writer; first Slovak pastor serving miners in Byesville, OH (1905), Holy Trinity, Ford City, PA (1907-10), Holy Trinity Church, Duquesne, PA (1910-14), SS. Cyril and Methodius, Clifton, NJ (1920-1955), St. Stephen the Martyr, Newark, NJ (1920-1955). He was Secretary and President of the Slovak Catholic Federation; editor of *Dobrý pastier* and *Ave Maria*; wrote *Katekizmus pre katolícke slovenské školy v Amerike* (1918).
Bio: in - Paučo, Jozef, *Slovenski priekopnici v Amerike*. Cleveland: Prvá Katolícka Slovenská Jednota, 1972: pp. 139-144.

Rudolf Grega, b. Slovakia; immigrated to Canada at age 5; R.C. priest; pastor in Richmond, VA (till 2012); pastor of Sts. Cyril & Methodius, Slovak Roman Catholic Parish, Montreal, Canada (2013-16).
Bio: in - Sts. Cyril 7 Methodius Slovak Roman Catholic Parish, Montreal, Canada. See - https://slovakcatholic.weebly.com/history.html

Roger William Gries (1937-), b. Cleveland, OH, of Slovak descent, R.C. priest, O.S.B., president of Benedictine HS, Cleveland, abbot, St. Andrew Abbey, Cleveland (1981-2001), Auxiliary Bishop (2001-13).
Bio: "Roger William Gries," in: Wikipedia. See - https://en.wikipedia.org/wiki/Roger_William_Gries

Andrew Gregory Grutka (1908-1993), b. Joliet, IL, of Slovak parents; R.C. priest, pastor, first Bishop of the Diocese of Gary, Indiana (1956-1984)
Bio: "Grutka, Most Rev. Andrew Gregory," in: *Catholic Who's Who* 14 (1960-1961, p. 11; "Grutka, Andrew Gregory," in" *Who's Who in America*, 41; "Andrew Gregory Grutka," in: Wikipedia. See - https://en.wikipedia.org/wiki/Andrew_Gregory_Grutka; "Grutka, Andrew Gregory," in: *Indiana's 200: The People Who Shaped the Hoosier State*. Edited by Linda C. Cugin and James E. St. Clair. Indianapolis: Indiana Historical Society Press, 2015; Kopanic, Michael J., "Rev. Andrew G. Grutka, D.D.: Slovak-American Bishop of Gary Indiana," Part 1, *Národný Kalendár, Vol.* CIX (2001), pp. 111-18; Bonta, Anthony, Andrew G. Grutka, First Bishop of the Diocese of Gary, Indiana (1957 to 1984): "Where There is Charity, There is God." Ph.D. Dissertation, Marquette University, 2012. See -https://epublications.marquette.edu/dissertations_mu/179/

Joseph Hajduch (1920-2005), b. Whiting, IN, of Slovak descent; R.C. priest, C.PP.S; parochial vicar and pastor of parishes in Nebraska, Ohio, Indiana, Wisconsin and North Dakota; chaplain at St. Francis Convent, Rice Lake, WI
Bio: "Rev. Joseph Hajduch," in: Roger Linder's Web Log. See - http://rocemabra.com/news/item=20160919-5

Thomas L. Holoman (1928-2011), b. Calumet, PA; R.C. priest, Msgr., pastor of varies Catholic churches in Nebraska, including in Curtis, Cheney, Lincoln, Bee, Brainard, Loma, Denton, later residing in Greensburg, PA.
Bio: "Monsignor Thomas L. Holoman," *Greensburg Tribune Review*, March 21, 2011; "Msgr. Holoman Dies at 83," *Southern Nebraska Register*, March 25, 2011.

Edward C. Homco (1919-2000), b. Whiting, IN, of Slovak descent; R.C. priest; C.PP.S.; pastor of St. John the Baptist Catholic Church, Whiting, IN (s. 1957)
Bio: "Rev. Edward C. Homco," in: Find A Grave. See - https://www.findagrave.com/memorial/10125223/edward-c-homco

Michael Homco (1922-1971), b. IN, of Slovak descent; R.C. priest, C.PP.S.; Whiting, IN
Bio: "Rev. Edward C. Homco," in: Find A Grave. See - https://www.findagrave.com/memorial/10125223/edward-c-homco

Michael William Hornak (1901-1986), b. Slovakia; R.C. priest
Bio: "Rev. Michael William Hornak," in: Find A Grave. See - https://www.findagrave.com/memorial/166683919/michael-william-hornak

Klemo J. Hrtánek (1889-1971), b. Velká Bytča, Slovakia; in US s. 1904; R.C. priest, monsignor; St. Martha, Leechburg, PA and St. Anne, Homestead, PA; noted builder of strong parishes; trained Pittsburgh diocese priests; headed diocese financial dept. He was president, Slovaks Catholic Students of America; assisted founding the Cleveland Benedictine monastery; president, Slovak Catholic Priests of the Pittsburgh Diocese.
Bio: in - Paučo, Jozef, *Slovenski priekopnici v Amerike*, Cleveland: Prvá Katolícka Slovenská Jednota, 1972, pp. 145-149.

Florian Hudac (1916-1969), Slovak American R.C. priest, O.S.B.; monk, St. Andrew Abbey, Cleveland; professor, Benedict High School, Cleveland (s. 1937).
Bio: Rev. Florian M. Hudac," in: Find A Grave. See - https://www.findagrave.com/memorial/162448187

John J. Humensky (1907-1984), b. Youngstown, OH, of Slovak parents; R.C. priest; theologian; STD; pastor of St. Anthony- St. Bridget Church, Cleveland; pastor of Nativity B.V.M. Slovak Parish (s. 1956); pastor, SS. Cyril & Methodius Slovak Church, Lakewood, OH (1968-77). He was named Diocesan Director of Hospitals (1949-68); a member of the Federal Hospital Council (s. 19640; president of Catholic Hospital Association.
Bio: "Fr. John J. Humensky," in: ancestry Message Boards. See - https://www.ancestry.com/boards/thread.aspx?mv=flat&m=2&p=surnames.humensky

Andrew S. Hvozdovic (1961-), b. Wilkes-Barre, PA, of Slovak descent; R.C. priest, pastor at Epiphany Parish in Sayre, PA, Diocese of Scranton; Supreme Chaplain, Slovak Catholic Sokol; National President, Slovak Catholic Federation.
Bio: *Facebook Messenger*, Sep. 13, 2018.

Matthew Jankola (1872-1916), b. Budapest, of Slovak parents from Trstená, Orava; in US s. 1893; R.C. priest, leader and educator. Founder of the Sisters

of SS. Cyril and Methodius; served parishes in northeast PA; pastor, SS. Cyril a Methodius in Bridgeport, CT, 1907-1916.
Bio: "Matúš Jankola," *Literárny týždenník*. See - https://www.literarnytyzdennik.sk/products/matus-jankola-2-7-1872-5-5-1916/; Tybor, M. Martina, "Matthew Jankola 1872-1916: Slovak-American Priest, Leader, Educator," *Slovakia* 22, No. 45 (1972), pp. 161-92; "Rev. Fr. Matthew John Jankola," in: Find A Grave. See - https://www.findagrave.com/memorial/10287992/matthew-john-jankola

Michael E. Jasko (1905-1973), b. Ohio, of Slovak descent; R.C. priest, O.S.B.; pastor of St. Benedict's Church, Cleveland, OH (s. 1940).
Bio: "Jasko, M.," in: Cleveland Clergy of 1942. See - http://usgenwebsites.org/OHCuyahoga/Religions/cleveclergy.html

Ignatius Jaskovic (d. 1990), b. Šariš, Slovakia; R.C. priest; in US s. 1882; first Slovak Catholic priest to come to America; pastor of St. John the Baptist Church, Mt. Carmel, PA; founder of St. Joseph Church, Hazleton, PA (s. 1882), later moved to Duquesne, PA, before returning to Europe.
Bio: "The History of St. Joseph Slovak Roman Catholic Church, Hazleton, Pennsylvania," in: sscmparish.com. See - http://sscmparish.com/cgi-bin/history.cgi?sid=jmrNIeOb

Joseph Job (1891-d.), b. Slanica, Slovakia; R.C. priest, founder of the St. Paul's Parish in Chicago Heights, pastor of the St. Simon's Church (s. 1931)
Bio: Droba, pp. 103-104.

Michal Judt (1876-1942), b. Špania Dolina, Slovakia; R.C. priest, poet, writer; in US s. 1913,
Bio: "Michal Judt," in: Wikipedia. See - https://sk.wikipedia.org/wiki/Michal_Judt

John E. Kalicky (1934-), b. Whiting, IN; R.C. priest, C.PP.S.; pastor of St. John the Baptist Catholic Slovak parish, Whiting, IN (s. 1991)
Bio: "Fr. John Kalicky, retiring from St. John the Baptist Church in Whiting after more than 30 years as pastor," *The Times*, June 26, 2014.

Michael Kallock, b. Oci Suchji, Slovakia; R.C. priest, in US s. 1920; pastor, St. John Baptist Church, Central City, PA (1920-1924).

Joseph Kasperek (fl. 1896), b. of Slovak ancestry; pastor of St. Mary's of the Assumption Church, McAdoo, first pastor of St. Joseph Catholic Church, Sheppton, PA (1896)

Joseph Kelchak (1926-2018), b. Gary, IN, of Slovak descent; R.C. priest; pastor of parishes in Webster, Rheinlander, Barron and Centuria, WI; served in over 53 parishes, senior priest at St. John the Evangelist Parish in St. John, IN; hospital chaplain, missions for the Chippewa Indians; author of dozen books on the liturgy, family, and marriage counseling.
Bio: "Fr. Kelchak continues to be 'instrument of Holy Spirit'" *Catholic Herald,* May 7, 2015; "Rev. Joseph Kelchak," in: Legacy.com. See - https://www. legacy.com/obituaries/nwitimes/obituary.aspx?n=joseph-kelchak&pid=190 716647&fhid=24901

Joseph J. Kloss (-1972) ; R.C. priest, Prelate, Msgr.; St. Mary's Catholic Church, Martins Ferry, OH

Štefan Kočiš (1892-1952), b. Domanovce, Slovakia ; R.C. priest, Msgr.; immigrated to US, 1905; Holy Trinity Church, Struthers, OH; first secretary of the Slovak Catholic Federation (1919-24); founded many new chapters; assisted Slovak Benedictines in Cleveland; head of St. Adalbert Society in the USA, 1922; chaplain of FCSU, 1932.
Bio: Paučo, *Jozef, Slovenski priekopnici v Amerike,* Cleveland: Prvá Katolícka Slovenská Jednota, pp. 225-228.

Theodore Kojis (1909-1984), b., R.C. priest, O.S.B., 2nd abbot (1946-66), St. Andrew Abbey, Cleveland.
Bio: "Rev. Theodore George Kojis," in: Find A Grave. See - https://www. findagrave.com/memorial/162460621/theodore-george-kojis

Stephen A. Kollar (1894-1974), b.; R.C. priest; pastor, Holy Family Church, Scranton, PA

Ondrej E. Komara (1883-1932), b. Levoča, Slovakia; RC priest, editor, writer; pastor, St. John Nepomucene, Bridgeport, CT; obtained support of

President Taft for Slovaks; helped found magazine *Ave Mária* and *Božské Srdce Ježiša* (Sacred Heart of Jesus).
Bio: Paučo, Jozef, *Slovenski priekopnici v Amerike*, Cleveland: Prvá Katolícka Slovenská Jednota, 1972 pp. 233-235

Joseph Korman (1882-1958), b. Slovakia; in US s. 1900; R.C. priest. He was ordained at St. Peter's Cathedral, Scranton, on Aug. 30, 1913, and assumed his first pastorate at St. Anthony's Church, Larksville, PA. A few months later he became pastor of Holy Rosary Church, Ashley, PA and on Aug. 1, 1914, he went to Hazleton, PA, as pastor of Holy Trinity Church. He became pastor of the Freeland church, PA on Oct. 1, 1916.
Bio: "Rev. Joseph Korman," in" in: find A Grave. See - https://www.findagrave.com/memorial/156834179/joseph-korman

Benjamin Kosnáč (1969-), b. Bratislava; R.C. priest, pastor of Ss. Cyril and Methodius Slovak Catholic Church, Sterling Heights, MI (1998-2017); he then returned to Slovakia
Bio: "Fr. Ben Kosnac," in: Vocation boom. See - https://www.vocationboom.com/fr-ben-kosnac/; "Faithful Priest Encourages Prayer, Fasting, & Voting For Upcoming Election," in: CatholicNetCast.com. See - http://catholicnetcast.com/blog/files/tag-father-ben-kosnac.html; "Rev. Benjamin Kosnac honored at farewell festivities at Sterling Heights, Mich. Parish," *Slovak Catholic Falcon*, May 3, 2017, p. 4.

John Kostik (1894-1970), b. Tovarné, Slovakia; R.C. priest, C.PP.S; pastor, St. John the Baptist, Whiting, IN (1925-45); rector, St. Charles Seminary (1945-4); missionary in South American vicariate, Chile (1947-62).
Bio: "Father John Kostik, CPPS." See - http://www.dcdiocese.org/images/necrology/KostikJohn8-9-70.pdf

Joseph L. Kostik (1890-1970), b. Tavarné, Slovakia; R.C. priest, STD, in US s. 1920, locating in Cleveland. There he was assigned to St. Elizabeth's Catholic Church as assistant pastor. He came to Youngstown in April 1922, and at that time he built St. Elizabeth's Church, school, and sisters' home in Campbell, OH. He remained pastor until 1967. He was super chaplain of Jednota.
Bio: "End of Era," *Youngstown News*, December 11, 2010.

Jerome Koval (1917-1993), Slovak American; R.C. priest, O.S.B., 3rd abbot, St. Andrew Abbey, Cleveland (1966-81)
Bio: "St. Andrew Abbey," in: Encyclopedia of Cleveland History. See - https://case.edu/ech/articles/s/st-andrew-abbey

Stephen Krasula (1887-1970), b. Namestovo, Slovakia; R.C. priest, Domestic Prelate, pastor of St. John Nepomucene Church, NYC (s. 1916)
Bio: "Msgr. S.J. Krasula, Led Slovak Group," *The New York Times*, March 15, 1970; "Krasula, Right Rev. Stephen," in: *Catholic Who's Who*, 14 (1960-1961), p. 250.

John Krispinsky (1895-1991), son. of Slovak immigrant parents, R. C. priest; 2nd pastor of Our Lady of Mercy, ministering to the parish from 1927 until 1964. In addition to his parish duties, Father Krispinsky was active in Slovak national causes.
Bio: "Rev. John W. Krispinsky," in Cleveland Historical. See - https://clevelandhistorical.org/index.php/files/show/4716

Ján Kubašek (1885 1950), b. Stará Ľubovňa, Slovakia; R.C. priest, chaplain in Yonkers, NY, pastor at Yonkers parish for 38 years; politician, publicist; signatory of the Pittsburgh Agreement
Bio: "Ján Kubašek," in: Wikipedia. See - https://sk.wikipedia.org/ wiki/ Ján_Kubašek; "Ján Kubašek," in: Stará Lubovňa. See - https://www.staralubovna.sk/jan-kubasek/

Emeric A. Kucharic (1888-1968), b. Slovakia; R.C. priest; assistant pastor at St. Agnes' Church, Philadelphia and St. Michael's Lansford; as pastor of St. Stephen, Shenandoah, St. Mary, Mahoney City, Sacred Heart, Palmaerto, Immaculate Conception, St. Clair and for 27 years at St. Andrew parish, North Catasauqua, PA (1921-1948).
Bio: "Rev. Emeric A. Kucharic dead in Allentown," *Jim Thorpe Times News*, March 8, 1963.

Dominik Kulata (1940-), b. Nova Bela, Poland, of Slovak descent; R.C. priest, pastor in Frackville, PA, Tremont, PA and Allentown, PA
Bio: "Kulata, Dominik," *Slovak Catholic Falcon*, July 15, 2015, p. 5.

Joseph A. Kushner, Slovak American; pastor of St. Dominic's, Donora, PA (s. 1930. Prior to that he was pastor of St. Cyril and Methodius at Charleroi and served the mission church at St. Edward's in Fayette City; president of the Slovak Catholic Federation (s. 1950).
Bio: "To honor retiring pastor a in Donora," *Monessen Valley Independent*, June 1, 1968.

John J. Lach (1894-1960), b. Hibernia, NJ, of Slovak descent; R.C. priest, pastor of Immaculate Conception Church, Whiting, IN;
Bio: "Lach, Rev. John Joseph," in: *Catholic Who's Who*, 14 (1960-1961), p. 252; "Lach, John Joseph," in: Droba, p.104

Edward Francis Lajack (1942-2016), b. Lakewood, OH, of Slovak descent; R.C. priest, parochial vicar, Cleveland, OH (1978); pastor, SS. Cyril and Methodius, Barberton (1979), national chaplain of the First Catholic Ladies Association 8 years)
Bio: "In Memoriam: Father Francis Lajack," *Fraternally Yours*, 103, No. 3 (December 2016), p. 18.

John M. Lefko (1912-2002), b. Lower East side of New York City, of Slovak descent; ordained R.C. priest; C.PP.S; assistant pastor at St. John the Baptist Catholic Slovak Church, Whiting, IN (s. 1938), becoming pastor in 1945. In 1953 he left for St. Joseph's College, Rensselaer, IN.
Bio: "Father John Lefko," in: Memorials (L-Z). See - https://www.nwitimes.com/uncategorized/memorials-l---z/article_f4bb9ac2-875c-52d4-b985-84bdeea8f02b.html

Francis Lendacky (1934-2016), R.C. priest; parochial vicar at Ambler, Philadelphia, and Phoenixville, PA. He served first as administrator and then pastor of St. Agnes-St. John Nepomucene, Philadelphia's only remaining Slovak parish, since 1978.
Bio: "Slovak pastor and Legion of Mary leader, Father Francis Lendacky, dies," in: CatholicPhilly.com. See - http://catholicphilly.com/2016/06/news/obituaries/slovak-pastor-and-legion-of-mary-leader-father-francis-lendacky-dies/

Felix Litva (1919-2006), b. Mikšová, Bytča, Slovakia; R.C. priest, S.J.; literary and church historian, translator; Provincial of Slovak Jesuits in Canada (1968-75); Provincial of Slovak Jesuits abroad (s. 1989).
Bio: :Felix Litva," in: Wikipedia. See - https://sk.wikipedia.org/wiki/Felix_Litva; "Felix Litva," in: Find A Grave. See - https://www.findagrave.com/memorial/165436496

Lawrence Lovasik (1913-1986), b. Tarentum, PA, of Slovak descent; R.C. missionary priest, SVD, Divine Word Seminary, Girard, PA
Bio: "Lawrence Lovasik," in: Wikipedia. See - https://en.wikipedia.org/wiki/Lawrence Lovasik; "Lovasik, Rev. Lawrence George (S.V.D.)," in: *Catholic Who's Who*, 14 (1960-1961), p. 261.

George Stephen Luba (1897-1961), b. Budapest, of Slovak descent; R.C. priest, O.S.B., pastor, prior of St. Andrew's Abbey (1935-49)
Bio: "Luba, Rev. George Stephen (O.S.B.)," in: *Catholic Who's Who*, 14 (1960-1961).

Edward J. Luca (1929-2014), b. Lorain, PA, of Slovak descent; R.C. priest, pastor of St. Teresa of Avila Parish, Sheffield Village, OH; on Board of Directors of Cannon Law Society of America
Bio: "In Remembrance - Reverend Edward J. Luca," in: Catholic Diocese of Cleveland. See - https://www.dioceseofcleveland.org/in-remembrance-rev-edward-j-luca-jcd/

Andrew F. Lukas (1923-2012), b. Ostrovany, Czech; R.C. priest; pastor in Benwood, WV, Vienna, VW, Camden VW, Fairmont, VW and Monongah, VW.
Bio: "Reverend Father Andrew F. Lukes, in: Ross Funeral home. See - https://www.rossfh.com/notices/ReverendFatherAndrew-Lukas

Hubert Macko (1899-1971), b. Jaklovce, Slovakia; R.C. priest, O.S.B., pastor of Ligonier, Wilpen, Rachelwood, Vandergrift, PA; editor of the Slovak Catholic weekly *Slovenský Svet* (s. 1926)
Bio: "Macko, Hubert," *Catholic Who's Who, 1947*, Vo. 7, p. 286; "Macko, Hubert," in: *Who's Who in the East*, 1942-43

Albert Michael Marflak (1946-2012), b. Donora, PA, of Slovak ancestry; R.C. priest; O.S.B.; monk, St. Andrew Abbey, Cleveland; teacher, chaplain and president of Benedictine High sS School, Cleveland. Father Albert had a wide range of experience in priestly ministry, having been pastor of St. Benedict Parish, administrator of Most Holy Trinity Romanian Byzantine Parish in Chester Township. He assisted in the Eparchy of St. George, Canton, Ohio, Byzantine Eparchy of Parma, St. Elias, Melkite Greek Catholic Parish, and St. Gregory the Great Parish in S. Euclid. He was chaplain of Knights of Columbus, International Order of the Aihambra, and the Slovak Catholic Federation.
Bio: "Father Albert Marflak O.S.B.," *Penn Trafford Star,* May 30, 2012.

Andrew P. Marinak (1928-), b. Steelton, PA, of Slovak descent; R.C. priest; pastor at Str. John of Arc, Hershey, PA, Holy Cross parish, Mt. Carmel, PA, Our Lady of Seven Sorrows of BVM, Middletown, PA, Corpus Christi, Chambersburg, PA. He then returned to his hometown parish of St. James in Steelton and then was assigned to Sacred Heart, Cornwall, PA, when he retired.
Bio: "The Rosary Meditation Companion. See - http://rosarycompanion. org/about.html

Ján Martvoň (1857-1948), b. Hruštín, Slovakia; R.C. priest; in US since 1889; pastor, St. Ladislaus Church, Cleveland (2 years), then at St. Andrew in Johnstown and finally a pastor at St. Stephans Slovak Catholic Church, (s. 1984). Several other parishes have sprung from the original church of St. Stephans, among them being St. Mary's Greek Catholic, St. Rochas' Croatian, St. Casimir's Polish Church, St. Emericus Magyar, SS. Peter and Paul, and St. Francis Church.
Bio: "Biography of Rev. John Martvon," in Cambria County Biographies. See - http://www.onlinebiographies.info/pa/camb/martvon-j.htm; "Rev. John Martvon (1857-1948), in: Cleveland Historical. See - https://clevelandhistorical.org/index.php/files/show/5790

Edward M. Matash (1931-2011), b. Passaic, NJ, of Slovak descent; R.C. priest, Msgr., pastor of St. Joseph Church in Bayonne, NJ; president of the Slovak Catholic Federation of U.S.A.
Bio: "Monsignor Edward M. Matash," *Star-Ledger,* Feb. 18, 2011.

Felix Mikula (1906-1979), b. Vieska, Slovakia; R.C. Priest, Port Arthur, TX
and Cleveland, OH
Bio: "Mikula, Felix," in: *SVU Directory* 4; "Mikula, Felix," in Pejskar 2, pp.
17-18.

Elemir J. Mikus (1927-2013), b. Ružomberok, Czech.; R.C. priest; in US s.
1971; pastor of SS. Cyril and Methodius Slovak parish in Detroit, MI
Bio: "Rev. Elemir J. Mikus, 86, Michigan Slovak pastoral activist, laid to rest,"
Slovak Catholic Falcon, October 2, 2013, p. 17.

Paschal Michael Mino (1911-1972), b. Mestisko, Slovakia; R.C. priest,
Franciscan Friar, TOR, associate professor of mathematics, St. Francis
College, Loretto, PA
Bio: "Mino, Paschal Michael," in: *American Science,* 10

Clement M. Mlynarovich (1887-1971), b. Hasprunka, Slovakia; R.C. priest,
author, poet, pastor, Assumption Parish, East Chicago, IN (s. 1915); voted
most popular Slovak in America (1931)
Bio: "Mlynarovich, Very Rev.," in: *Catholic Who's Who,* 7 (1946-1947), pp.
310-311; "Mlynarovich, Clement M." in: Droba, p. 105-106; "Miloš Klement
Mlynarovič," in LIC. See - http://www.litcentrum.sk/slovenski-spisovatelia/
milos-klementmlynarovic#curriculum_vitae

Thomas Nasta (fl. 2017); b. USA, of Slovak descent; R.C. priest; chaplain
and on Board of Directors, First Catholic Slovak Union of the United States of
America and Canada; *Jednota* writer. Pastor at St. Gabriel, Sorrowful Mother,
West Pottsgrove, Stowe, PA; pastor of Sacred Heart Parish, Swedesburg, PA
Bio: "Goodbye to Our Ladys of Ransom," in: *Northeast Times,* June
14, 2017. See - https://northeasttimes.com/goodbye-to-our-lady-of-
ransom-c66307a5bb10

William N. Novicky (1921-2001), b. R.C. priest, Msgr., pastor of St. Gregory
the Great Church for 25 years; head of the Cleveland Catholic schools
Bio: "Monsignor William Novicky, school chief," World News, October
16, 2001; "Rev. William N. Novicky," in: Find A Grave. See - https://www.
findagrave.com/memorial/124349256/william-n.-novicky

Joseph Novorolsky (1907-1970), b. Reading, PA, of Slovak descent; pastor of St. Peter Parish, Westfield, MA (1937-70).
Bio: "History St. Peter Parish," See - http://stp-stc.com/about-us/staff/

Clement A. Ockay (1915-1994), R.C. priest; Msgr., pastor of St. Joseph's Slovak R.C. Church, Bayonne, NJ (s. 1968)
Bio: "Rev. Clement A. Ockay," in: Find A Grave. See - https://www.findagrave.com/memorial/162576109/clement-a-ockay

Roman Ondečko (1917-1998), b. New York, NY, of Slovak descent; R.C. priest, O.F.M.C; pastor of Sts. Cyril & Methodius Slovak Roman Catholic Parish, Montreal, Canada (1973-1997).
Bio: "Rev. Roman Ondecko," in: Find A Grave. See - https://www.findagrave.com/memorial/65889907/roman-ondecko

Fabian Onderovsky (1908-1971), b. Wilkes-Barre, PA, of Slovak descent; R.C. priest, OMC; pastor of St. Joseph's Church, Endicott, NY
Bio: "Fr. Fabian Onderovsky," in: Find A grave. See - https://www.findagrave.com/memorial/21519871/fabian-onderovsky

Thomas J. Orsulak (1962-), b. Lansford, PA, of Slovak descent; pastor in Reading, PA.
Bio: "Orsulak, Thomas J.," *Slovak Catholic Falcon*, July 15, 2015, p. 5.

Joseph Michael Osip (1895-d.), b. Abaujská, Slovakia; in US s. 1902; R.C. priest; curate, St. Ambrose Church, Endicott (1930-34); St. Anthony Church, Syracuse (1934); pastor, St. Ann's Church, Binghamton, NY (s. 1934). Domestic Prelate (1952).
Bio: "Osip, Rt. Rev. Msgr. Joseph," in *Catholic Who's Who*, 14 (1960-1961), p. 364

Anthony (Norbert) Ozimek (1941-2015), b. Cleveland, OH, of Slovak descent; R.C. priest, O.S.B.
Bio: "In Remembrance - Reverend Anthony (Norbert) Ozimek, O.S.B." - See: http://www.dioceseofcleveland.org/in-remembrance-reverend-anthony-norbert-ozimek-osb/

Stephen Panik (1893-1953), b. Trstená, Slovakia; R.C. priest; pastor at SS. Cyril and Methodius in Bridgeport, CT; organized the creation of Father Panik Village, one of the largest housing projects in the USA during the New Deal.

Bio: Rierden, Andi, "The Last Farewell to Father Panik Village," *The New York Times,* October 17, 1993; "Father Panik Village," in: Wikipedia. See - https://en.wikipedia.org/wiki/Father_Panik_Village

Joachim (Joseph) Pastirik (1941-), b. Cleveland, OH, of Slovak descent; R.C. priest, O.S.B., monk, St. Andrew Abbey, Cleveland, teacher at Benedictine HS, Cleveland

Bio: "Fr Joachim (Joseph) Pastirik," in: St. Andrew Abbey. See - https://standrewabbey.org/people/fr-joachim-joseph-pastirik

John B. Pastorak (1849-1979), b. Slovakia; R.C. priest, O.S.B., pastor in Schenectady, NY, Sheffield, MA, Saunders Co., NE.

Bio: "John Pastorak Sermons," in: Archives & Special Collections, University of Nebraska–Lincoln Libraries. See - http://archivespec.unl.edu/findingaids/ms088-pastorak-unl.html

Andrew Pavčo (1863-1932), b. Slovakia; R.C. priest, writer, third pastor at St. John's, chaplain of First Catholic Slovak Union U.S.A.

Bio: Rev. Andrew Pavco," in: Find A Grave. See - https://www.findagrave.com/memorial/120183805/andrew-pavco

Paul Pekarik (1905-1994), b. Humenné, Slovakia; R.C. priest, pastor of St. Ann's Church, Emmaus, PA (1931-75); supreme chaplain of the First Catholic Slovak Union

Bio: "Rev. Paul Pekarik, 89, Ex-pastor of Catholic Church in Emmaus," *The Morning Call,* November 29, 1994.

Joseph Julius Petrovits (1886-d.), b. Štrkovec, Slovakia; R.C. priest, pastor in Shamokin, Steelton and Berwick, PA

Bio: "Petrovits, Joseph Julius," in: *Catholic Who's Who,* 1947, Vol. 7, p. 358.

Placid Pientek (1918-2018), b. Manhattan, NY, of Slovak parents; R.C. priest, O.S.B., monk at St. Andrew Abbey in Cleveland, teacher at Benedictine

HS in Cleveland; oldest monk among 700 monks of the American Cassinese Congregation of Benedictine monasteries
Bio: "Obituary for Fr. Placid Pientek, O.S.B." See - https://5060.sites. ecatholic.com/documents/2018/5/Obituary%20for%20Fr.pdf "Rev. Fr. Placid Frank Pientek," in: find A Grave. See - https://www.findagrave.com/memorial/189589364/placid-frank-pientek;

Andrew Pier (1910-2003), b. Blandburg, PA, of Slovak descent; R.C. priest, O.S.B., monk of St. Andrew Svorad Abbey in Cleveland; wrote a popular column in *Jednota*.
Bio: "Fr. Andrew Pier," in: Find A Grave. See - https://www.findagrave.com/memorial/123979568/andrew-pier

Joseph Pier (1912-2006), b. Blandburg Cambria co., PA, of Slovak ancestry; R.C. priest
Bio: "Rev Joseph Pier," in: Find A Grave. See - https://www.findagrave.com/memorial/123979329/joseph-pier

Michael Cyril Polcha (1908-d.), b. Dunmore, PA, of Slovak ancestry; R.C. priest; Rt. Rev.; curate, Rock Lake, PA (1933), Pittston (1933); pastor, Montdale (1942-48), Elmhurst (1950-58); Swoyerville (s. 1958), all in PA.
Bio: "Polcha, Rt. Rev. Msgr. Michael Cyril," in: *Catholic Who's Who*, 14 (1960-1961), p. 374.

Richard A. Portasik (1926-2012), b. Ford City, PA, of Slovak immigrant parents; R.C priest, O.F.M.; of Bellevue, a priest of the Franciscan Province of St. John the Baptist; a prolific writer and preacher; earned the admiration of the Roman Catholic Church for the spiritual renewal retreats he organized throughout the United States and Slovakia. He wrote history of Slovak Franciscans in the US.
Bio: "Priest organized retreats in U.S., Slovakia," in: TribLive. See - https://triblive.com/obituaries/newsstories/2243212-74/portasik-rev-richard-slovak-bellevue-slovakia-holy-catholic-family-organized ; "Rev. Richard A. Portasik," in: Find A Grave. See - https://www.findagrave.com/memorial/93975290/richard-a.-portasik

John Porubský (1874-1953), b. Slovakia; R.C. priest, pastor in Larksville, PA, Binghamton, NY, Jessup, PA and Miners Mills, PA
Bio: "Porubsky, John," in: *Catholic Who's Who* 7, 1946-1947.

Cyril J. Potocek (1911-2003), b. Harlem, of Slovak descent; R.C. priest, Msgr.; pastor of the Church of Holy Cross, Sleepy Hollow (1961-86).
Bio: "Monsignor Cyril J. Potocek," *The Journal News,* September 27, 2003.

Leo Rehak (1894-1961), b. Colorado, of Slovak descent; R.C. priest, O.S.B., pastor, St. Andrew Parish, Cleveland, OH.

Richard Rohr (1943-), b. Topeka, KS, of Slovak descent; priest, O.F.M., preacher, writer
Bio: "Richard Rohr," in: Wikipedia. See - https://sk.wikipedia.org/wiki/Richard_Rohr; Block, Stephanie, "What Are Fr. Richard Rohr and CAC Up to Now," in: Catholic Media Coalition. See - http://www.catholicmediacoalition.org/rohr_CAC.htm

Andrew J. Romanak (1896-1977), b. Newark, NJ, of Slovak descent; R.C. pastor emeritus of St. Mary's R. C. Slovak Church, Passaic, NJ; also served at Sacred Heart R. C. Church, where he spent 18 years; Rockaway, NJ; director of youth in the Diocese of Pat, examiner of the clergy, elected by Pope to Domestic Prelate, with the title of Right Rev. Monsignor.
Bio: "In memoriam to the Rt. Rev. Msgr. Andrew J. Romanak," in: *Congressional Record,* March 8, 1977.

John George Rusnak (-2015), b. Roebling, NJ, of Slovak descent; ordained R.C. priest in 1962; missionary in Costa Rica (7 years); left the priesthood and obtained Ph.D. and lived in Arizona. He became a full time clinician, consultant and instructor in state Community Colleges, ASU and at the University of Phoenix until his retirement in 2000.
Bio: "John George Rusnak Ph.D.," in azz central. See - https://www.legacy.com/obituaries/azcentral/obituary.aspx?page=lifestory&pid=175395732

Štefan Sevastian Sabol (1909-2003), b. Prešov, Slovakia; R.C. priest; O.S.B.; surviving victim of Soviet and Hungarian prosecutions. During the Hungarian invasion of Carpatho-Ukraine, in 1938–1939 he was a chaplain in Carpathian Sich in Khust. On December 16–18, 1948 in Prague Sabol was sentenced in absentia to life in prison for cooperation with the Ukrainian Insurgent Army. He died in Warren, Michigan.

Christopher (Robert) Schwartz (1946-), R.C. priest, O.S.B.; monk, 6th abbot, St. Andrew Abbey (2008-13)
Bio: "Right Reverend Christopher (Robert) Schwartz, O.S.B.," in: St. Andrew Abbey. See - https://standrewabbey.org/people/right-reverend-christopher-robert-schwartz

John E. Senglar, b. Mahoney City, PA, of Slovak descent; R.C. priest, S.T.L.; Msgr.; pastor of Sacred Heart Church, Phoenixville (s. 1962). He served as assistant at St. John the Evangelist Church. Philadelphia, and at SS. Cyril and Methodius. Bethlehem. From 1935 to 1944 he was a member of the faculty of Roman Catholic High School. He became pastor of St. John Nepomucene Church. Philadelphia. in September. 1944, and, in March. 1962, pastor of Sacred Heart. Phoenixville.

Richard John Sklba (1935-), b. Racine, WI, of Slovak ancestry; auxiliary bishop of the Archdiocese of Milwaukee (1979–2010). He was President of the Catholic Biblical Association of America (1982). Sklba served as chairman of the US Conference of Catholic Bishops' Committee on Ecumenical and Interreligious Affairs (2005-08); retired 2010.
Bio: "Richard J. Sklba," in: Wikipedia. See - https://en.wikipedia.org/wiki/Richard_J._Sklbahttps://en.wikipedia.org/wiki/Richard_J._Sklba

Bernard A. Slimak (1912-1999), b. Ohio, of Slovak descent; R.C. priest, O.S.B.
Bio: "Rev. Bernard A. Slimak," in: Find A Grave. See - https://www.findagrave.com/memorial/162448188/bernard-a.-slimak

Edward A. Slosarcik (1924-2005) b. Chicago, of Slovak descent; a leader in Chicago's Slovak community on the city's South Side and south suburbs. Pastor from 1977-1993 at St. John the Baptist Slovak Church. Wrote articles for *Sursum Corda*, a newsletter for retired priests, and was co-editor if the *Orava/Spiš Newsletter* quarterly (1996-2005) with Dr. Michael Kopanic, Jr.
Bio: "Rev. Edward A. Slosarcik, 81," *Chicago Tribune*, June 22, 2005; "Rev.

Edward A. Sloracik," in: Find A Grave. See - https://www.findagrave.com/memorial/11205610/edward-a.-slosarcik;"

John S. Sobota (1883-1955), b. Blacovce, Slovakia; R.C. priest, Domestic Prelate with the title Right Rev. Msgr.; pastor of Sacred Heart Slovak Church, Wilkes-Barre, PA (s. 1929).
Bio: "John S. Sobota," *Hazleton PA Standard-Sentinel,* March 24, 1955.

John J. Spitkovsky (1928-1987), b. Slovakia; R.C. priest, pastor of Assumption BVM parish, then pastor of St. Denis (s. 1984).
Bio: "Father John J. Spitkovsky," *Chicago Tribune,* December 29, 1987.

Victor Stevko (1927-2014), b. New York, NY, of Slovak ancestry; of Slovak ancestry; R.C. priest; S.V.D. He e professed vows in 1949 and was ordained to the priesthood in 1957 in the US. His first assignment was at St. Anselm, one of the oldest African-American parishes in Chicago. In 1960, he moved to Indonesia, where he served as a missionary for decades. Most recently, Father Stevko lived in the Marsfield SVD Community in New South Wales, Australia.
Bio: "Victor Stevko," *The Sydney Morning Herald,* September 9, 2014; "Father Victor Stevko - Obituary," in: www.facebook.com/Divine.Word.Missionaries.Chicago.Province/posts

Francis P. Straka (1956-2017), b. Reading, PA, of Slovak descent; R.C. priest, pastor in Bethlehem, Northampton, PA, Hellertown, PA, West Reading, Emmaus, PA
Bio: "Straka, Francis P.," *Slovak Catholic Falcon,* July 15, 2015, p. 5.; "Rev. Francis Straka," *Jednota,* January 18, 2017, p.17

Michael P. Sverchek (1910-1997), b. Lansford, PA, of Slovak descent; R.C. priest, pastor of St. Joseph Catholic Church. Shepton, PA (1955-1992)
Bio: "Rev. Michael Sverchek, Retired Schuylkill Pastor," *The Morning Call,* December 28, 1997

Robert J. Terentieff (1936-2011), Slovak American; R.C. priest, artist, teacher; St. Andrew parish and SS. Cyril and Methodius, Bridgeport, CT; religious comics; designed stained glass windows and mosaics for churches,

schools, libraries, hospitals, in New England and Mid-Atlantic states; saying 'art is like a prayer.'
Bio: Dion, Jill, "Art show spotlights work of the late Father Robert Terentieff," Milford Mirror.com., May 2, 2013. See - https://www.milfordmirror.com/6156/art-show-spotlights-work-of-the-late-father-robert-terentieff/; Simko, Michael V., "Father Robert J. Terentieff: Student, Artist, Teacher, and Priest," *Jednota Annual Furdek*, 12 (January 1973), pp. 141-144.

Gregory Vaniscak (1884-1938), b. R.C. priest, O.S.B., founder of the Slovak Benedictine Abbey of Saint Andrew Svorad, Cleveland, OH
Bio: Pauco, Joseph, "Reverend Gregory Vaniscak, O.S.B.," *Slovakia*, 47 (1974), pp. 67-71; "Rev. P. Gregory K. Vaniscak,", in: Find A Grave. See - https://www.findagrave.com/memorial/162313515/p-gregory_k-vaniscak

Joseph Viater (1930-1996), Slovak American; R.C. priest, Msgr.; served at St. Margaret Mary, in Hammond, Calumet Region, St. Monica and Luke Church, Gary, IN; author of *Slovak-English Liturgies (Slovak Catholic Federation)* (1988).
Bio: "Msgr. Joseph J Viater," in: Find A Grave. See - https://www.findagrave.com/memorial/154154956/joseph-j-viater

František Vlossák (1864-1956), b. Bobrov, Slovakia; R.C. priest; in US s. 1891. He served as chaplain and administrator in several locations, last time in South Bethlehem, then as a temporary chaplain in multiple monasteries and in the camp of Catholic Veterans.
Bio: "František Vlossák," in: Wikipedia. See - https://sk.wikipedia.org/wiki/František_Vlossák

William Wichinsky (-1937), b. Slovakia; R.C. priest; in US s. 1923; was assigned to the Immaculate Conception Church in Bitumen, PA. From Hooversville he went to Coupon, where he died on January 17, 1937.

Augustine Yurko (1911-1990), b. Youngstown, OH, of Slovak descent; R.C. priest, O.S.B.; prior of the Abbey; pastor of the Assumption parish, Royalton, OH (s. 1977)
Bio: "Rev Augustine Yurko," in: Find a Grave. See - https://www.findagrave.com/memorial/162465463/augustine-yurko

Joseph Zalibera (1882-1967), b. Slovakia; R.C. priest; pastor of Ss. Cyril and Methodius Slovak Church, Detroit, MI (1926-57); co-founder of Slovak Dominican Sisters, Oxford, MI,
Bio: "Fr. Joseph Zalibera," in: Find A. Grave. See - https://www.findagrave.com/memorial/28019751/joseph-zalibera.

Augustine Juraj Zan (1911-1999), b. Prievedza, Slovakia; R.C. priest; chaplain, professor of theology, Teachers Training College S. Hart, Danville, PA.
Bio: "Zan, Rev. Augustine Juraj," in: *American Catholic Who's Who*, 1977, Vol. 21, p. 582.

Raphael A. Zbin (1921-2001), Slovak American; R.S.; priest; pastor of St. Andrew's Parish, Cleveland (s. 1976); teacher of biology at Benedictine High school, Cleveland; Monk of the Year in 1997.
Bio: "Rev. Raphael A. Zbin," in: Find A Grave. See -- https://www.findagrave.com/memorial/168231625/raphael-a.-zbin

Clement Zeleznik (1931-), b. Cleveland, OH, of Slovak descent; R.C. priest, O.S.B., Rt. Rev.; 5th abbot of St. Andrew Abbey in Cleveland (2001-08).
Bio: "Abbot Clements Corner," in: Loyola Retreat House. See - https://loyolaretreathouse.com/wp/abbot-clements-corner-2/

David Allen Zubik (1949-), b. Sewickley, PA, of Slovak and Polish ancestry; the twelfth Bishop of Roman Catholic Diocese of Pittsburgh, PA
Bio: "David Zubik," in: Wikipedia. See - https://en.wikipedia.org/wiki/David_Zubik; Rodgers, Ann, "Zubik named Bishop of Diocese of Pittsburgh," Pittsburgh Post-Gazette, July 18, 2007.

Peter Zupan (1880-1968), b. of Slovak descent; R.C. priest, O.S.B., pastor of St. Benedict Catholic Church, Greensburg, PA (1913-16); teacher at St. Vincent College

Anselm (John) Zupka (1940-); b. Cleveland, OH, of Slovak descent; R.C. priest, O.S.B., 4th Superior, St. Andrew Abbey, Cleveland, chaplain at Walsh University, teacher at Benedictine HS
Bio: "Father Anselm Zupka, 3rd," in: LinkedIn. See - https://www.linkedin.com/in/father-anselm-zupka-1a08b93/

3. Nuns

a. Congregations

Boleslava, Sister M., "Daughters of St. Francis of Assisi Care of the Elderly, Sick, and Handicapped," *Jednota Annual Furdek*, 27 (January 1988), pp. 98-100.

Fedor, Sister Mary Ann, O.P, "Slovak Dominican Sisters of Oxford, Michigan," *Jednota Annual Furdek*, 27 (January 1988), pp. 101-104.

"History," in: Notre Dame Sisters. See: http://www.notredamesisters.org/history.html

"A History of the School Sisters of St. Francis," in: School Sisters of St. Francis. See - http://schoolsistersosf.org/pages/history.php

Machalica, Sister M. Methodia, O.S.B., "History of the Slovak Benedictine Sisters of Our Lady of Sorrows," *Jednota Annual Furdek*, 27 (January 1988), pp. 95-97.

"Our Early History," in: Sisters of Saints Cyril and Methodius. See - https://sscm.org/about-us/our-history/#toggle-id-5

Petrašek, Mary Emerentia, *A Brief History of the Congregation of the Sisters of SS. Cyril and Methodius, told in five decades, 1909-1959.* Danville, PA: The Sisters of SS. Cyril and Methodius, 1959?

Regis, Sister M. V.S.C., "Vincentian Sisters of Charity Helping to Make the World a Holy Place" *Jednota Annual Furdek*, 27 (January 1988), pp. 122-126.

"Sisters of Saints Cyril and Methodius." Official Site. See - https://sscm.org/

Urda, Teresa, SSCM, "A Reflection given to the Sisters of Saints Cyril and Methodius during their Centennial year: Mother M. Cyril Conway 1859 - 1942," *Good Shepherd (Dobry Pastier)*, The Slovak Catholic Federation, 2009. See: www.sistersofihm.org/dotAsset/227baff3-12c1-407b-a88d-8dfb7ca88f43.doc

Zajac, Thomas M., "School Sisters of St. Francis: A Mission to Educate All Men and Women," *Jednota Annual Furdek*, 27 (January 1988), pp. 118-121.

b. Individuals

Sister Rose Mary Abbick (1914-1992), b. Kansas City, KS, of Slovak descent; R.C. nun; SS.C.M. She was Principal and Superior at the Holy Trinity School in Gary. She was the first, girl's principal at Andrean High School from 1959 to 1969. Sister was also principal from 1969 to 1978 at the St. Cyril Academy.

She returned to Andrean to teach religion from 1980 to 1992. Sister taught in New Jersey, South Carolina, Pennsylvania and Indiana.
Bio: "Sr Rose Mary Abbick," in: Fin A Grave. See - https://www.findagrave.com/memorial/188804424/rose-mary-abbick

Sister Linda Marie Bolinski (1950-), b. SS.CM, general superior of the Sisters of SS Cyril and Methodius, Danville, PA. Sister Linda Marie has taught at both the elementary and secondary levels and served the congregation as director of vocations. From 1979 to 1988, she was assistant superintendent of religious education in the Harrisburg, Pa., diocesan office. She was principal of St. Columba School in Bloomsburg, Pa., and for 15 years served as principal of Blessed Sacrament School in Charleston.
Bio: "Two familiar faces to lead Sisters of Sts. Cyril and Methodius," The Catholic Miscellany, July 17, 2008. See - http://themiscellany.org/2008/07/17/two-familiar-faces-to-lead-sisters-of-sts-cyril-and-methodius/

Sister M. Catherine Laboure Bresnock, Slovak American; SS.C.M.; director of Jankola Library and Slovak Museum Danville, PA (s. 2011).
Bio: "Jankola Library and Slovak Museum." See - http://jankolalibrary.sscm.org

Mother M. Cyril Conway (1859-1942), b. Pittston, PA, of Slovak descent; General Superior, Sisters of Saints Cyril and Methodius
Bio: Urda, Teresa, "A Reflection given to the Sisters of Saints Cyril and Methodius during their Centennial year: Mother M. Cyril Conway 1859 - 1942." See - www.sistersofihm.org/dotAsset/227baff3-12c1-407b-a88d-8dfb7ca88f43.doc

Teresa Demjanovich (1901-1927), b. Bayonne, NJ, of Slovak ruthenian ancestry; American Ruthenian Catholic Sister of Charity, who has been beatified by the Catholic Church
Bio: Conklin, Margaret, *An American Teresa*. Long Island City, NY: Color Graphic Press, 1981; "Teresa Demjanovich," in: Wikipedia. See - https://en.wikipeia.org/wiki/Teresa_Demjanovich

Sister M. Tarcisia Gregorovic, SS.C.M. (-), b. Whiting, IN, of Slovak descent; translator of works in Slovak into English, including Glagolithic and Roman-Slavonic liturgy.
Bio: See - Carmen, Dr. B.V. and Slamka, Irene, *The Slovak Encyclopaedia*. New York: Slovak Academy, 1981. p. 54.

Sister M. Gabriel Hricko, SS.C.M. (1942-2017), b. of Slovak descent; editor of periodical *Fialky* (Violets), 1925-40; writer of Slovak language course books for children: *Cyril číta* (1954), *Metod myslí* (1959), *Cyril a Metod hovoria slovensky*, Cleveland: First Catholic Slovak Union, 1971.
Bio: See - Bolecek, Dr. B.V. and Slamka, Irene, *The Slovak Encyclopaedia*. New York: Slovak Academy, 1981. p. 57.

Sister Cecilia Kondrc (1911-1985), b. Bratislava; in US s. 1953; a Slovak nun. She had her story of escape from communist secret police told in a 1954 book, *The Deliverance of Sister Cecilia*. William Brinkley, a reporter for *Life* magazine, authored the article. Claudette Colbert played Sister Cecilia in a one-hour telecast on Climax Mystery Theater in May 1955.
Bio: "Spotlight on Family: Sister Cecilia Kondrc," in: Family History Tracing. See - http://familyhistorytracing.blogspot.com/2010/03/spotlight-on-family-sister-cecilia.html

Sister Theresa Novak (1940-2010), b. Canton, OH, of Slovak descent; she entered the Vincentian Sisters of Charity from Sacred Heart Parish, Canton and served for 55 years. She had a Master of Social Work from West Virginia University. Upon earning a Master of Social Work degree, Sister served for five years as Director of Community Relations for the Diocese of Steubenville. She was then appointed as Director of Catholic Charities for the Diocese of Steubenville, OH, a position she held for ten years. She was then appointed as Director of Catholic Charities for the Diocese of Steubenville, Ohio, a position she held for ten years. When she later received her Nursing Home Administrator License, she became the Administrator of the Villa de Marillac Nursing Home in Pittsburgh, Pa. serving there for ten years. When the Vincentian Collaborative System was formed, Sister Theresa was appointed the first Executive Director in which capacity she ministered for eleven years. At the time of her death, she was the Chairperson of the Pennsylvania Council on Aging.
Bio: "Theresa Novak," *Jednota*, August 4, 2010, p. 16.

Sister Bernadette Marie Ondus, SS.C.M, Slovak American; chaplain at sisters of Saints Cyril and Methodius; teacher, editor of *Dobry Pastier/Good Shepherd;* author of *Basic Composition (Student Workbook)*, 2002.
Bio: "Bernadette Marie Ondus," in: LinkedIn. See -
https://www.linkedin.com/in/bernadette-marie-ondus-b29b33144/

Mother M. Emerentia Petrasek, SS.C.M; Slovak American; Superior General of the Sisters of Saints Cyril and Methodius, Danvillle, PA; educator, promoter of Slovak culture
Bio: Pauco, Jozef, "Matka M. Emerentia Petrásková, SS.C.M.," *Kalendár Jednota* (1969), pp. 131-134.

Mother M. Valeria Romanchek (1920-2017), Slovak American, SS.CM, 8th Superior General of the Sisters of Saints of Cyril and Methodius, founder of the Conference of Slovak Religious.
Bio: "City Native Heads Religious Order," *Standard-Speaker,* August 23, 1972, p. 21.

Sister M. Rosamund (née Helen C. Dupak) (1920-2017), b. Exeter, PA, of Slovak descent; joined the Sisters of Saints Cyril and Methodius (SS.C.M.) in Denville. She was Superior and principal at St. Columba School in Bloomsburg (1971-79); assistant to the General Superior of Sister of SS. Cyril and Methodius (1980-84); in 1984, she returned to St. Columba's and taught fourth grade until 1988 n 1984, she returned to St. Columba's and taught fourth grade until 1988. Sister Rosamund served as administrator at Maria Hall, Danville (1994-98), after which she engaged in various ministries at St. Methodius Convent. She published in *Slovak Studies.*
Bio: "Sister M. Rosamund," *The Danville, News,* January 18, 2017. See:
http://www.stcyrilacademy.org/class_profile.cfm?member_id=3228835

Sister M. Martina Tybor (1908-1998), b. Bridgeport, CT, of Slovak a descent; professed in Sisters of SS Cyril and Methodius (s. 1928); teacher, translator
Bio: "Tybor, Sister M. Martina," in *Catholic Who's Who, 1977,* Vol. 21, p. 539; "Jankola Library and Slovak Museum." See - http://jankolalibrary.sscm.org

Sister Teresa Urda (1942-2017), b. Torrington, CT, of Slovak descent; SS.C.M.; teacher, writer and editor. She wrote the history of the first hundred years of the Sisters of Saints Cyril and Methodius.
Bio: "Sister Teresa Urda," in: SS.C.M. See - https://sscm.org/sister-teresa-urda-ss-c-m-74/

Sister M. Paschal Valent (1910?-2003), b. Etna, PA, of Slovak descent; SS.C.M.; teacher and writer. She wrote an MA Thesis - The influence of early church music on the development of Slovak folksongs, Catholic University of America, Washington, DC, 1968; and authored Survey of Slovak Church Music (1958).
Bio: See - Bolecek, Dr. B.V. and Slamka, Irene, *The Slovak Encyclopaedia.* New York: Slovak Academy, 1981, p. 116.

Sister M. Mercedes Voytko (1931- 2016), b. Humboldt, PA, of Slovak descent; SS.C.M.; teacher, director of Jankola Library and Slovak Museum (1992-2007). Before that, she taught school in Indiana and Pennsylvania. In 1976 she served on the General Council of the order. In 1988, she was elected General Superior.
Bio: "Sister M. Mercedes Voytko, SS.C.M., 85," in: Sisters of Saints Cyril and Methodius. See - https://sscm.org/sister-m-mercedes-voytko-ss-c-m-85/; "Jankola Library and Slovak Museum." See - http://jankolalibrary.sscm.org

Sister M. John Vianney Vranak, Slovak American; SS.C.M.; director of Jankola Library and Slovak Museum (2007-10)
Bio: "Jankola Library and Slovak Museum." See - http://jankolalibrary.sscm.org

Mother M. Pius Yakubov (1894-1966); b. of Slovak descent; SS.C.M.; General Superior. Under her leadership, ground for a new school was broken in June 1929, and the cornerstone was laid in September— just before the start of the Great Depression. Despite the world-wide economic downturn, construction of a Gothic style academy continued, thanks to the incredible generosity of supporters. The new school opened in September 1931.
Bio: "Mother M. Pius Yakubov," in: SS.C.M. See - https://sscm.org/about-us/our-history/#toggle-id-5.

C. GREEK-CATHOLIC CHURCH

1. General

"Byzantine Catholic Eparchy of Passaic, New Jersey," in: Byzantine Hierarchy and Clergy. See - http://www.tccweb.org/byzantinehierarchyclergy. htm#eparchypassaic- "Byzantine Catholic Eparchy of Parma," in: Byzantine Hierarchy and Clergy. See - http://www.tccweb.org/byzantinehierarchyclergy. htm#eparchyparma
"Byzantine Catholic Archeparchy - Pittsburgh, Pennsylvania," in: Byzantine Hierarchy and Clergy. See - http://www.tccweb.org/byzantinehierarchyclergy. htm#archeparchyPittsburgh
"Slovak Catholic Eparchy of Saints Cyril and Methodius of Toronto," in: Wikipedia. See - https://en.wikipedia.org/wiki/ Slovak_Catholic_Eparchy_of_Saints_Cyril_and_Methodius_of_Toronto
Patek, George, "Slovak Greek Catholics in America," *Slovak Studies* 5, *Historica* 3 (1965), pp. 259-68.

2. Priests

Nicholas Chopey (1876-1961), b. Hungary; priest of Greek Rite Catholic Church, pastor, St. Mary's Church, Wilkes-Barre, PA. (s. 1903)
Bio: "Chopey, Very Rev. Nicholas," in: *Catholic Who's Who*, 7 (1946-1947), p. 62; "Rev Nicholas Chopey to Have Jubilee Sunday," in: Newspapers.com. See - https://www.newspapers.com/clip/3343476/nicholas_chopey_jubilee/

Nicholas Duda (1882-d.), b. Košice, Slovakia; Greek-Catholic priest, pastor in Swotersville, PA, Old Forge, PA, Pleasant City, OH, Hazleton, PA, Cleveland, OH, Sheffield, PA, Pittsburgh, PA.
Bio: *History of Pittsburgh and Environs.* New York-Chicago: The American Historical Society, 1922, Vol. 5, p. 353.

Michael Dudick (1916-2007), b. St. Clair, PA, to Rusyn immigrant parents; Greek-Catholic priest. He served parishes in Pennsylvania and Ohio. Pope Paul VI conferred the rank of Right Reverend Monsignor in 1963. He was ordained a bishop and enthroned in 1968 as the second bishop of the Byzantine Catholic Eparchy of Passaic in Saint Michael's Cathedral, Passaic. Bishop Dudick served as a member of the Congregation for the Oriental Churches and was a member of the Committee for the Revision of Eastern Canon Law. He also served on the Board of Overseers for Harvard University and on the Board of Regents of Seton Hall University, South Orange, New Jersey.

Bio: "Michael Dudick," in: Wikipedia. See - https://en.wikipedia.org/wiki/Michael_Dudick; "Michael J. Dudick," in: Find A Grave. See - https://www.findagrave.com/memorial/19671422/michael-j.-dudick

Nicholas T. Elko (1909-1991), b. Donora, PA, of Slovak descent; Greek-Catholic priest, first Bishop of the Byzantine Catholic Metropolitan Church of Pittsburgh. In 1967, he was transferred to Rome, where he was elevated to the dignity of Archbishop and appointed the ordaining prelate for Byzantine Catholics in Rome and head of the Ecumenical Commission on the Liturgy. Archbishop Nicolas returned to the United States in 1970 and became the Auxiliary Archbishop of the (Latin) Archdiocese of Cincinnati, Ohio, a position he held for 14 years.

Bio: "Elko, Nicholas," in: Wikipedia. See - https://en.wikipedia.org/wiki/Nicholas_Elko; "Bishop Nicholas T. Elko," in: The Byzantine Catholic Archeparchy of Pittsburgh. See - http://www.archpitt.org/bishop-nicholas-t-elko/

John Fetsco (1929-2009), b. Pringle, PA, of Slovak descent; Greek Catholic priest, CSsR, Apostolic Administrator of Saints Cyril and Methodius, Toronto, Canada (1996-2001).

Bio: "Father John Fetsco, C.Ss.R." See - http://www.catholic-hierarchy.org/bishop/bfetsco.html; Obituary - John Fetsco," *Times Leader,* June 28, 2009.

Francis J. Fuga (orig. Figa) (1923-1987), b. Vinné, Slovakia; Slovak Greek-Catholic priest, Msgr., administrator of the parish in Hamilton, Canada; general vicar; editor of periodical Mária, publisher of books and almanacs; chairman of Matica Slovenská Abroad.

Bio: "František Fuga," in: Wikipedia. See - https://sk.wikipedia.org/wiki/František_Fuga; and Bolecek, Dr. B.V. and Slamka, Irene, The Slovak Encyclopaedia. New York: Slovak Academy, 1981. p. 52.

Julius N. Grigassy (1886-1959), b. Czech.; priest of Greek-Byzantine Rite; Very Rev.; pastor, Petrikovce, Slovakia (1910-14); pastor, Uniontown, PA (1924-25); SS. Peter and Paul Greek Catholic Church, Braddock, PA (s. 1925);

secretary to Bishop of Pittsburgh Greek-Byzantine Rite (1924-48). Author of works in church history.

Bio: "Grigassy, Very Rev. Julius, Sr.," in: *Catholic Who's Who*, Vol. 14, p. 179; "Rev. Julius N. Grigassy," in: Find A Grave. See - https://www.findagrave.com/memorial/151152834/julius-n.-grigassy

Joseph P. Hanulya (1873-1962), b. Nižné Repaše, Slovakia; Greek-Catholic priest, in US s. 1904. He served as pastor in Syracuse, NY, Duquesne, PA, Pittsburgh, PA, and, 1918, he was named pastor of Holy Ghost Byzantine Catholic Church in Cleveland. His Cleveland congregation was almost entirely of Rusin descent, and Hanulya soon embarked on serving not only his parishioners' spiritual needs, but also helping them preserve their cultural heritage. In the course of that commitment, Hanulya authored some twelve works, ranging from a Rusin grammar and reader to historical and catechetical works.

Bio: "Hanulya, Joseph P.," *Catholic Who's Who*, 1910, Vol. 7, 181-182; "Hanulya, Joseph P.," in: *Encyclopedia of Cleveland History*. See - https://case.edu/ech/articles/h/hanulya-joseph-p

Daniel Ivancho (1908-1972), b. Yasinia, Subcarpathian Ruthenia; Czech.; in US s. the age of eight; priest of Greek-Catholic Church. When Bishop Basil became ill, Father Daniel was named his coadjutor. On November 5, 1946, he was ordained a bishop at St. Paul (Latin) Cathedral in the Oakland section of Pittsburgh. When in May 1948, Bishop Basil lost his long and painful battle with cancer and fell asleep in the Lord, Bishop Daniel assumed the leadership of the Exarchate.

Bio: "Daniel Ivancho," in: Wikipedia. See - https://en.wikipedia.org/wiki/Daniel_Ivancho; "Bishop Daniel Ivancho," in: The Byzantine Catholic Archeparchy of Pittsburgh. See - http://www.archpitt.org/bishop-daniel-ivancho/; "Rev. Daniel Ivancho," in: Find A Grave. See - https://www.findagrave.com/memorial/123162598/daniel-ivancho

Michael Jackovics (1875-1949), b. Pušovce, Slovakia; Greek-Catholic priest; pastor of St. Michael's United Greek-Catholic Church, Passaic, NJ; spiritual leader of the Greek Catholic Union of the United States

Bio: "St. Michael's United Greek-Catholic Church," in: *History of Passaic and its Environs*. New York - Chicago: Lewis historical Publishing Company, 1922,

Vol. 1, pp. 554-557, "Father Michael Jackovics," in: Find A Grave. See - https://www.findagrave.com/memorial/105453126/michael-jackovics

Irenej Janický (1878-d.), b. Prešov, Slovakia; Greek-Catholic priest; in US. S. 1904. He served at Saint Michael's Greek Catholic Church in Passaic, New Jersey from 1905 to 1915 and again during 1917. In 1920 he was serving at St. Mary's Greek Catholic Church in Trenton, New Jersey. In 1922 he returned to Slovakia and served the Greek Catholic village churches of Nižná Pisaná (1922-30) and Sulín (1930-36)
Bio: "Irenej Janicky," in: in: Byzantine Clergy. See - http://www.tccweb.org/byzantinehierarchyclergy.htm

Stephen Janický (1852-1931), b. Tichý Potok, Slovakia; Greek-Catholic priest; in US. S. 1908. He served various Greek Catholic churches in America from 1908 to 1931. He was appointed the full time pastor of Saint Michael's Greek Catholic Church in McAdoo, Pennsylvania in 1909. He served the faithful of this parish for a full twenty-three years. During his tenure as resident priest of St. Michael's Father Stefan also served at St. Mary's Greek Catholic Church in Hazleton, Pennsylvania in 1914 and again from November 1916 to April of 1917.
Bio: "Stephen Janicky," in: Byzantine Clergy. See - http://www.tccweb.org/byzantinehierarchyclergy.htm

John Kallok (1907-1977), b. Suché, Slovakia; Greek-Catholic priest, historian, author, editor of *Byzantine Catholic World*, pastor of St. George's Greek Catholic Church, West Alquippa, PA, founder of *The Chrysostom*, a monthly
Bio: "Kallok, Rev. John," in: *Catholic Who's Who*, 1947, Vol. 7, p. 215; "Rev. John Kallok," in: Find A Grave. See - https://www.findagrave.com/memorial/184072776/john-kallok

Joseph Kapusnak (1934-2014), b. Johnstown, PA, of Slovak ancestry; Greek Catholic priest.
He served the following parishes as pastor, St. Mary Parish, Bradenville, from 1971 to 1973, St. Michael Parish, Sheffield and Lewis Run, from 1973 to 1996, St. Nicholas and St. George Parishes, Youngstown, Ohio, from 1996 to 1997, St. Nicholas Parish, Perryopolis, from 1997 to 1999 and St. Stephen Parish, Leisenring, from 1997 until his death.

Bio: "Reverend Joseph Kapusnak," in: Byzantine Catholic Archeparchy of Pittsburgh. See - http://www.archpitt.org/fallen-asleep-in-memoriam/; "Fr. Joseph Kapusnak," in: Find A Grave. See - https://www.findagrave.com/memorial/132534462/joseph-kapusnak

Stephen John Kocisko (1915-1995), b. Minneapolis, MN, of Slovak descent; Greek-Catholic priest. He was the son of Anna Zelenak a Greek Catholic of Carpatho-Rusyn decent and John Kocisko a Lutheran of Slovak descent. Both John and Anna were born in the village of Bystre, Slovakia. Not long after his birth the family returned to Slovakia. By 1910, he had returned to America. He was ordained to priesthood in Rome and then returned to the US and was assigned churches in Detroit Michigan, Lyndora and Michigan, Pennsylvania. He was named to the Exarchate's Matrimonial Tribunal and also served as a professor at the Byzantine Catholic Seminary of Saints Cyril and Methodius in Pittsburgh. In 1956, Father Stephen Kocisko was enthroned as a bishop at the Cathedral of Saint Paul of the Roman Catholic Diocese of Pittsburgh. Bishop Kocisko began his tenure at Holy Ghost Parish in Pittsburgh. For the next number of years he performed his duties as auxiliary bishop and also was appointed Rector of the Seminary and also as Vicar General. In 1963, the Pope installed Bishop Stephen Kocisko as the first Bishop of the Byzantine Catholic Eparchy of Passaic. In 1967, Bishop Kocisko was elevated as the replacement of Bishop Elko as head of the Ruthenian Byzantine Catholic Church in America. In 1969, Pope Paul VI appointed Bishop Stephen Kocisko to the status of Archbishop. Later, on June 11, 1969 Archbishop Stephen Kocisko was enthroned as the first Metropolitan in the history of the Rusyn faithful. At the time of his resignation (1990), Metropolitan Kocisko had served as a priest for fifty years and thirty-five years as a Bishop/Metropolitan.
Bio: "Stephen J. Kocisko," in: Byzantine Clergy. See - http://www.tccweb.org/byzantinehierarchyclergy.htm

Rev. Stephen Kozák (1890-1944), b. Slovakia; in US s. 1920; Greek-Catholic priest; pastor of St. John Chrysostom Byzantine Catholic Church, Pittsburgh, PA. He served from 1932-until his death in 1944. He oversaw construction of the present church, which opened in 1935, during the 25th anniversary celebration of that parish.
Bio: "Rev. Stephen Kozak," in: Find A Grave. See - https://www.findagrave.com/memorial/138460772/stephen-kozak

Emil A. Kubek (1857-1940), b. Štefurov, Slovakia; Greek-Catholic priest; in US s. 1904. He served at Saint Mary's Greek Catholic Church in Mahanoy City, PA from 1904 to 1940. ather Kubek, who was an accomplished agronomist, taught his parishioners the art of keeping and raising bees and how to grow various crops. He was an author of various novels, poems and published the only novel in his native Prešov dialect (Rusnak) *Marko Soltys* and also penned *Narodny povísti i stichi* which was a four volume set of tales and poems which was published by Okrana in Scranton, PA (1922-1923). His most important work was considered his dictionary in Slavonic-Rusnak-Hungarian.

Bio: Kupensky, Nick, "'No! We Won't Die,' in: Rediscovering Emil Kubek." See - https://www.ncsml.org/wp-content/uploads/2015/01/No-We-Wont-Die-Rediscovering-Emil-Kubek.pdf; "Rev. Father Emil A. Kubek," in: Byzantine Clergy. See - http://www.tccweb.org/byzantinehierarchyclergy.htm

Milan Lach (1973-), b. Kežmarok, Slovakia; Greek-Catholic priest. In, 2017, the Holy Father, Pope Francis, appointed Bishop Milan Lach, S.J., as Apostolic Administrator for the Byzantine Catholic Eparchy of Parma, Ohio. The 44 year old Greek Catholic Jesuit is the first European-born Bishop to serve the Byzantine Catholic Eparchy of Parma, Ohio. Prior to that he had been serving as the auxiliary Bishop of the Greek Catholic Archeparchy of Prešov, Slovakia.

Bio: "Milan Lach," in: Wikipedia. See - https://en.wikipedia.org/wiki/Milan_Lach, "Youngest bishop to head diocese in North America 'a gift' to U.S. church," Our Sunday Visitor, July 25, 2018; "Milan Lach," in: Byzantine Clergy. See - http://www.tccweb.org/byzantinehierarchyclergy.htm

Gabriel Martyak (1859-1934), b. Vyškovce, Slovakia; Greek-Catholic priest; in US s. 1894. He served at St. John the Baptist Greek Catholic Church in Lansford, Pennsylvania from 1895 until his death in 1934. From January 1898 to August 1903 he was pastor of St. Mary's Greek Catholic Church in Freeland, Pennsylvania. In 1903 he returned to Slovakia and served Greek Catholic churches in Bardejov, 1903 to 1910, Beloveza, 1905 to 1906 and Andrejova, 1905 to 1908. He returned to the United States and served Greek Catholic churches, including Saint Mary's Protection Greek Catholic Church in Homer City, Pennsylvania, from 1910 to 1934. In 1920 The Very Reverend Gabriel Martyak was instrumental in assisting Mother Macrina Melynychuk the first Ruthenian Greek Catholic Convent of the Order of Saint Basil the Great. In 1916 Right Reverend Monsignor Martyak was appointed Apostolic

Administrator of the Ruthenian Greek Catholic Church in the United States. He held this position until 1924.

Bio: "Right Reverend Monsignor Gabriel Martyak," in: Byzantine Clergy. See - http://www.tccweb.org/byzantinehierarchyclergy.htm

Nicholas Martyak (1879-1954), b. Vápeník, Slovakia; Greek-Catholic priest; in US s. 1907. Upon arrival in the U.S. Father Martyak served at St. Mary's Greek Catholic Church in McAdoo, Pennsylvania for two months. In December of 1907 he became the pastor of St. John the Baptist Greek Catholic Church in Hazleton, Pennsylvania. Father Martyak's pastorate at St. John's spanned 47 years until his death in 1954. As pastor of St. John's Father Martyak took a congregation of 200 families and built the parish to well over 500 families.

Bio: "Rev. Father Nicholas Martyak," in: in: Byzantine Clergy. See - http://www.tccweb.org/byzantinehierarchyclergy.htm

Viktor Martyak (1865-d.), b. Vel'ka Pol'ana, Slovakia; Greek-Catholic priest; in US s. 1893. He served Greek Catholic churches from 1893 to 1901. In 1893 Father Viktor was the first priest to serve St. John the Baptist Greek Catholic Church in Hazleton, Pennsylvania. He was instrumental in the organization and growth of SS Peter and Paul Greek Catholic Church in Beaver Meadows, Pennsylvania. He returned to Slovakia and served Greek Catholic village churches in Čukalovce(1901-05) and Hostovice (1905-37).

Bio: "Reverend Father Viktor Martyak," in: Byzantine Clergy. See - http://www.tccweb.org/byzantinehierarchyclergy.htm

Emil John Mihalik (1920-1984), b. Pittsburgh, PA, of Slovak descent; his father having been in born in the Carpatho-Rusyn village of Hrabské, Slovakia. Emil was ordained as a Greek-Catholic priest. His first assignment was as assistant pastor at a parish in Hazleton, Pennsylvania. After serving in Hazleton he was transferred to Saints Peter and Paul Byzantine Catholic church in Struthers, Ohio as Administrator. He served as Administrator of Saints Peter and Paul Byzantine Catholic Church in Endicott, New York and was pastor of Saint Thomas Byzantine Catholic Church in Rahway, NJ (1961-69). In 1968 he was named the Chancellor for the Byzantine Catholic Eparchy of Passaic. After the creation of the new Eparchy of Parma in 1969, Father Mihalik was appointed as Bishop. During his tenure, approximately 18 new churches were constructed, and he ordained twenty-three priests. He also assisted with the establishment of a new order of Sisters, the Byzantine Nuns of St. Clare.

Bio: "Emil john Mihalik," in: Wikipedia. See -https://en.wikipedia.org/wiki/ Emil_John_Mihalik;

"Bishop Emil John Mihalik," in: Byzantine Clergy. See - http://www.tccweb.org/byzantinehierarchyclergy.htm

Nicholas Blasius Molchany (1866-1918), b. Bajerovce, Slovakia; Greek-Catholic priest; in US s. 1894. Father Nicholas was pastor of various congregations in Braddock, Pennsylvania; Freeland, Pennsylvania; and Kingston, Pennsylvania. He was pastor of Saint Michaels Greek Catholic Church, Passaic, New Jersey from 1901 to 1906. In each of these parishes new church edifices were erected during his pastorate. His final assignment was at Assumption of the Blessed Virgin Mary Greek Catholic Church in Youngstown, Ohio.

Bio: "Reverend Father Nicholas Molchany," in: Byzantine Clergy. See - http://www.tccweb.org/byzantinehierarchyclergy.htm

Vladimir Peter Molchany (1856-1904), b. Bajerovce, Slovakia; Greek-Catholic priest; in US s. 1891. He served in various Greek Catholic churches in America. As of 1900 he was serving St. Mary's Greek Catholic Church in Kingston, Pennsylvania.

Bio: "Rev. Vladimir Peter Molchany," in: Find A Grave. See - https://www. findagrave.com/memorial/135787305/vladimir-peter-molchany

Marián Andrej Pacák (1973-), b. Levoča, Czech.; C.Ss.R.; Canadian Slovak Greek Catholic hierarch, who serves as the third Eparchial Bishop of the Slovak Catholic Eparchy of Saints Cyril and Methodius of Toronto (s. 2018). Before that he served as the chaplain of the Redemptoristine Nuns Monastery of the Most Holy Trinity of Vranov nad Topľou-Lomnica (Slovakia).

Bio: "Marián Andrej Pacák," in: Wikipedia. See - https://en.wikipedia.org/ wiki/ Marián_Andrej_Pacák; "Fr. Marián Andrej Pacák, C.Ss.R. is appointed as Eparchial Bishop of the Saints Cyril and Methodius of Toronto of the Slovaks (Canada)," Redemptorists Scala News, July 5, 2018.

John Stephen Pazak (1946-), b. Gary, IN, of Slovak descent; C.Ss.R., a member of the Congregation of the Most Holy Redeemer, commonly known as the Redemptorists. Since July 2016, the Eparch of the Ruthenian Catholic

Eparchy of the Holy Protection of Mary, Phoenix, AZ. Before that he served as Eparch of the Slovak Catholic Eparchy of Saints Cyril and Methodius of Toronto (2000-2016).

Bio: "Bishop John Pazak, C.Ss.R. Is Transferred to Phoenix, Arizona," in: archbishopterry,blogspot.com. See - http://archbishopterry.blogspot.com/2016/05/bishop-john-pazak-cssr-is-transferred.html; "John Stephen Pazák," in: Wikipedia. See - https://en.wikipedia.org/wiki/John_Stephen_Pazak

Michael Rusnak (1921-2003), b. Beaverdale, PA, of Slovak descent; R.C. priest and bishop, C.Ss.R. Family returned to Slovakia during the Depression; ordained in Slovakia, imprisoned after WWII for refusing to collaborate with the Communist regime; escaped to the USA and moved to Canada. He laid the foundation for the Slovak Byzantine Catholic Church in Canada; established new parish and started the publication, *Maria*; wrote prayer books and published religious songs. Attended Vatican II Council. In 1981, Pope John Paul II appointed him the first Bishop of the Slovak Byzantine Catholic Eparchy in North America -- the Eparchy of SS. Cyril and Methodius Auxiliary Bishop of the Ukrainian Catholic Eparchy of Toronto; served on Vatican commission for Oriental churches and Canon Law reform.

Bio: : "Michael Rusnak," in: Wikipedia. See - https://en.wikipedia.org/wiki/Michael_Rusnak; "Bishop Michael Rusnak - Eternal Memory," in: The Byzantine Forum. See -
http://www.byzcath.org/forums/ubbthreads.php/topics/752/Re:%20Bishop%20Michael%20Rusnak%20--%20E

William C. Skurla (1956-), b. Duluth, MN, of Slovak descent; ordained as Greek Catholic priest. He as ordained to the Episcopacy and enthroned as the Third Bishop of the Byzantine Catholic Eparchy of Van Nuys (now the Eparchy of Phoenix) on April 23, 2002 in Phoenix, Ariz. In December 2007 he was appointed Fourth Bishop of the Eparchy of Passaic (N.J.) and was enthroned at St. Michael Cathedral in Passaic on Jan. 29, 2008. On January 19, 2012, Bishop William was named by Pope Benedict XVI to succeed Metropolitan Basil M. Schott as the fifth Metropolitan of the Byzantine Catholic Metropolitan Church of America and eighth Archbishop of the Byzantine Catholic Archeparchy of Pittsburgh. Leader of the Metropolitan Church in the USA, Metropolitan William heads the Council of Hierarchs,

comprised of the bishops of the Byzantine Catholic eparchies of Passaic, Parma, and Phoenix.
Bio: "William C. Skurla," in: Wikipedia. See - https://en.wikipedia.org/wiki/William_C._Skurla; "Archbishop William C. Skurla, D.D.," in: The Byzantine Catholic Archeparchy of Pittsburgh. See - http://www.archpitt.org/metropolitan-archbishop/

George Thomas Thegze (1883-d.), b. Berezovo, Slovakia; pastor of Greek Catholic Churches in Charleroi, PA, Gary, IN, Binghamton, NY, Pittsburgh, PA.
Bio: "Thegze, George Thomas," in: Droba, p. 106; "Rev. George Thegze," in: *History of Pittsburgh and Environs*. New York and Chicago: The American Historical Society, 1922, p. 289.

Alexis Gabriel Vislocky (1885-d.), b. Sedliská, Slovakia; Greek-Catholic priest; in US 1920. He served as resident pastor at St. Mary's Patronage of the Mother of God Greek Catholic Church in New York, New York for 32 years. He later served at St. John the Baptist Greek Catholic Church in Rahway, New Jersey. Father Vislocky authored many publications, articles and language grammars in Rusnak and Hungarian.
Bio: "Reverend Father Alexis Vislocky," in: Byzantine Clergy. See - http://www.tccweb.org/byzantinehierarchyclergy.htm

Gabriel Vislocky (ca 1855-1918), b. Vápeník, Slovakia; Greek-Catholic priest; in US. S. 1890. He served Greek Catholic churches in Pennsylvania including Saints Cyril & Methodius Greek Catholic Church Olyphant, Holy Ghost Greek Catholic Church, Jessup and Saint Mary's Greek Catholic Church, Scranton from 1890 to 1892. He returned to Slovakia in 1892 and served the village Greek Catholic churches in Bukovce, 1892 to 1895 and Ol'ka from 1895 to 1918.
Bio: "Reverend Gabriel Vislocky," in: Byzantine Clergy. See - http://www.tccweb.org/byzantinehierarchyclergy.htm

Nestor Volenszeky (1913-), b. Slovakia; Greek-Catholic priest; in US s., pastor in Trauger, Pa, Youngstown, OH, Scranton, Pa, Sheffield, PA and Pittsburgh, PA.
Bio: *History of Pittsburgh and Environs*. New York-Chicago: The American Historical Society, 1922, Vol. 5, p. 102.

D. Eastern Orthodox Church

1. General

Wisnosky, Marc, "American Carpatho-Russian Orthodox Diocese," in: Encyclopedia of Christianity in the United States. Edited by George Thomas Kurian an and Mark A. Lamport. Lanham-Boulder-New York-London: Bowman & Littlefield, 2016, Vol. 5, pp. 66-68; American Carpatho-Russian Orthodox Diocese of the U.S.A. - Diocesan History. See - https://www.acrod.org/diocese/history/; "Russian Orthodox Church Outside Russia," in: Wikipedia. See - https://en.wikipedia.org/wiki/Russian_Orthodox_Church_Outside_Russia
"Orthodox Church in America," in: Wikipedia. See - https://en.wikipedia.org/wiki/Russian_Orthodox_Church

2. Priests

Orestes Peter Chornock (1883-1977), b. Ortuťová, Slovakia; ordained as Greek Catholic priest in Prešov. In 1910, he immigrated to the US and served Greek Catholics parishes in Chicago, IL Cleveland, OH and Duquesne, PA (St. Michael's Greek Catholic Church) and for over three decades (1911-46) served St. John the Baptist Greek Catholic Church in Bridgeport, CT. He opposed the Latinization of the Eastern rite in the Unites States of America and, in 1930s, together with some of the Transcarpathian clergy, set up an independent American Carpatho-Russian Orthodox Greek Catholic church, which came under the jurisdiction of the patriarch of Constantinople. In 1939 Chornock was consecrated bishop and in 1965 he was promoted to metropolitan.
Bio: "His Eminence, Metropolitan Orestes (Chornock)," in: American Carpatho-Russian Orthodox Diocese of the U.S.A. See - https://www.acrod.org/diocese/formerbishops/metropolitanorestes/
"Rev. Orestes Peter Chornock," in: Gian A Grave. See - https://www.findagrave.com/memorial/59233067/orestes-peter-chornock

Peter Kohanik (1880-1969), b. Becherov, Slovakia; baptized in the Greek Catholic Church; in 1892 he moved with his family to the US, where he converted to Orthodoxy. He was ordained into the priesthood and in 1903 he

and his wife left for the US. n 1903, Fr. Kohanik was appointed rector of St. John the Baptist Church in W. Charleroi, Pennsylvania, where he served until 1905 when he was transferred to Archangel Michael Church in Pittsburgh, replacing Fr. John Nedzelinsky. He served there for five years. He was dean of the Pittsburgh deanery, and then the Wilkes-Barre deanery. From 1916 to 1923 he was editor of the Mutual Aid Society newspaper *Light,* and during the years 1916, 1917, and 1921-1923 of the *Russian Orthodox Almanacs.* In 1924, Fr. Peter accepted an invitation to organize a new parish in Passaic, New Jersey thus becoming, on July 12, 1925, the first priest of the newly established Church of St. John the Baptist, a position he retained until his repose. In 1947, he was appointed Dean of New Jersey deanery. In 1951 he was awarded the right to wear the miter, later elevated to the rank of protopresbyter.
Bio: "Peter Kohanik," in: orthodoxwiki.org. See - https://orthodoxwiki.org/Peter_Kohanik

Metropolitan Nicholas (orig. Richard Smiško) (1936-2011), b. Perth Amboy, NJ, of Slovak descent; Metropolitan Bishop of Amissos and Primate of the American Carpatho-Russian Orthodox Diocese of the USA. He was elevated to the rank of Archimandrite in 1976 and was elected by the Holy Synod of the Ecumenical Patriarchate of Constantinople as Auxiliary Bishop for the Ukrainian Orthodox Church in America and was consecrated as Bishop of Amissos (modern day Samsun) on March 13, 1983. Following the death of Bishop John (Martin) in September 1984, Bishop Nicholas was chosen as the third ruling hierarch of the American Carpatho-Russian Orthodox Diocese and was enthroned in Christ the Saviour Cathedral by Archbishop Iakovos of America on April 19, 1985. He was elevated to the rank of Metropolitan, by Ecumenical Patriarch Bartholomew I on November 24, 1997. In recognition for his labors Metropolitan Nicholas received the Saints Cyril and Methodius Award given by the Orthodox Church of Czechoslovakia.
Bio: "Nicholas (Smisko)," in: Wikipedia. See - https://en.wikipedia.org/wiki/Nicholas_(Smisko);
"Media Coverage of the Repose of Metropolitan Nicholas." See - https://www.acrod.org/diocese/formerbishops/metropolitan/news-information/media-coverage/"His Eminence, Metropolitan Nicholas," in: Orthodox Church in America. See - https://oca.org/in-memoriam/metropolitan-nicholas;

Laurus Škurla (1928-2008), b. Ladomirová, Czech; in US s. 1946. Together with his brothers, he joined the Holy Trinity Monastery in Jordanville, New

York, established in 1928 by the Russian Orthodox Church Outside of Russia. Father Laurus was ordained to the priesthood in 1954 and advanced within the church. He became Bishop, Russian Orthodox Church Outside Russia. He was First Hierarch of the Russian Orthodox Church Outside Russia, the fifth cleric to hold that position.

Bio: "Laurus Škurla," in Wikipedia. See - https://en.wikipedia.org/wiki/ Laurus_Škurla; "His Eminence Metropolitan Laurus (Vassily Skurla)," in: St. John the Baptist Cathedral. See -https://www.stjohnthebaptist.org.au/ en/documents/laurus.html

Alexis Georgievich Toth (1853-1909), b. nr. Prešov, Slovakia; Greek Catholic priest, theologian, and missionary priest. Having resigned his position as a Byzantine Catholic priest in the Ruthenian Catholic Church, became responsible for the conversions of approximately 20,000 Eastern Rite Catholics to the Russian Orthodox Church, which contributed to the growth of Eastern Orthodoxy in the United States and the eventual establishment of the Orthodox Church in America. He was canonized by the Orthodox Church in 1994.

Bio: "Alexis Toth," in: Wikipedia. See - https://en.wikipedia.org/wiki/ Alexis_Toth; "Saint Alexis of Wilkes Barre." See - https://saintalexispalmcoast. org/alexis.html

Stephen Varzaly (1890-1957), b. Fulianka, Slovakia; a leading priest, journalist, and cultural activist for Rusyns in the United States. He completed his elementary, university and theological studies in Prešov (1914), where he was ordained as a Greek-Catholic priest. a year later. In 1920, he came to America on assignment to the parish of the St. Nicholas Greek Catholic Church in New Castle, PA. After 12 years, he was called to the parish of Saint Michael's Greek Catholic Church in Rankin, PA, where he served until his death in 1957. In 1937, Varzaly, by then stationed for six years at St. Michael Greek Catholic Church in Rankin, PA, joined three dozen other Byzantine rite priests to form a Carpatho-Rusyn diocese independent of Rome and the Latin rite bishops of the United States.

Bio: "Stephen Varzaly," in: Wikipedia. See - https://en.wikipedia.org/wiki/ Stephen_Varzaly; "Rev. Fr. Stephen Varzaly," in: Find A Grave. See - https:// www.findagrave.com/memorial/21803794/stephen-varzaly

E. LUTHERAN CHURCH

1. General

Dolack, George, *A History of the Slovak Evangelical Lutheran Church in the United States of America, 1902-1927.* St. Louis: Concordia Publishing House, 1955. 207p.

Gluchman, Vasil, *Slovak Lutheran Social Ethics.* Lewiston, NY: Edwin Mellen Press, 1997. 162p.

Grandquist, Mark, "Slovak Lutherans: A tough-minded people," in: Metro Lutheran. See - http://metrolutheran.org/2010/08/slovak-lutherans-a-tough-minded-people/

A History of the Slovak Zion Synod., LCA. N.p.: Lutheran Church of America, 1977.

"A History of the Slovak Zion Synod Lutheran Church in America," in: *Slovaks in America.* A Bicentennial Study, pp. 400-406.

Mazak, S. G., "A Brief History of the Slovak Lutheran Synod of the United States," *Concordia Institute Quarterly* 3 (1930), pp. 80-86; 4 (1931), pp. 105-11.

"Synod of Evangelical Lutheran Churches," in: Wikipedia. See - https://en.wikipedia.org/wiki/Synod_of_Evangelical_Lutheran_Churches

2. Ministers

John Adam (1928-2005), b. North Braddock, PA, of Slovak descent; Lutheran minister. Upon ordination, he was the pastor of Dr. Martin Luther Church in Muskegon, MI, and served there until 1969. He then received a call to become pastor of St. Paul's Lutheran Church, Danbury, CT (1969-81).In 1981, he was elected Bishop of the Slovak Lutheran Zion Synod. In addition to his service at St. Paul's, he shared his ministry in the Danbury area through monthly Sermons on WLAD. Upon retirement in 1991, Pastor Adam was requested to serve three years as an Interim Pastor at St. Mark's Lutheran Church in Butler, PA.

Bio: "John Adam, Former Bishop of ELCA Slovak Zion Synod, Dies," in: ELCA. See - http://godsworkourhands.org/News-and-Events/5596; "Obituary of Pastor Adam," in: Cornell Memorial Home. See - https://cornellmemorial.com/tribute/details/6358/Pastor-Adam/obituary.html

Daniel Jonathan Adamcik (1905-1990), b. Plymouth, PA, of Slovak descent; Lutheran minister, pastor in Lakefield, MN, Minneapolis, MN, Laramie, WY, Midwest City, OK, Globe, AZ; treasurer of Slovak Zion Synod of the United Lutheran Church of America
Bio: "Adamcik, Daniel Jonathan," in: *Who's Who in the West*, 11.

John Bajus (1901-1971), b. Raritan, NJ, of Slovak descent; Lutheran minister. He served at St. John Church, Granite City, Illinois, then at the West Frankfort-Stanton, Illinois, parish. By 1949 Bajus was at Zion Evangelical Lutheran Church, Chicago, Illinois. The congregation moved to Norridge in 1963; he remained the pastor there until 1971, the year of his death; president of the Slovak Luther League (1928-30), editor of its *Courier* (1929-46). He served as first vice-president of the SELC from 1949 to 1959 as well as serving on its board of directors. He served as the SELC's archivist from 1949 to 1969.
Bio: "John Bajus," in: Sundry Thoughts. See - https://neatnik2009.wordpress.com/tag/slovak-evangelical-lutheran-church/; Re. john Bajus," in: Fine A Grave. See - https://www.findagrave.com/memorial/144863874/john-bajus

Luther John Bajus (1927-2018), b. of Slovak descent; Lutheran minister; pastor at Zion Evangelical Lutheran Church in Norridge (1971-2018).
Bio: "Luther J. Bajus," *Chicago Tribune*, May 1, 2018

Daniel Bella (1869-d.), b. Nemecká Lupča, Slovakia; in US s. 1889; Lutheran minister; a charter member of the Holy Trinity- Slovak Lutheran Church in Chicago; served Trinity Church in Cleveland, OH (1889-1905), St. Paul's Slovak Lutheran Church, East Port Chester, CT (s. 1905). Bella was a charter member of the Slovak Evangelical Lutheran Church, and in addition to serving his own congregation and the Slovaks in Hatfield, MA, he served in many other scattered Slovak congregations.
Bio: "Daniel Bella," in: The Role of Slovak Immigration in the Development of a Second Protestant Church in Hatfield, Mass," in: Eartford Seminary Foundation. See - https://archive.org/stream/roleofslovakimmi00copi/roleofslovakimmi00copi_djvu.txt

Igor Vladimir Bella (1933-2015), Bridgeport, CT; son of the Slovak immigrant father, Lutheran minister and theologian Rev. Dr. Julius Igor Bella. He grew up in Bridgeport. He moved to Bratislava, Slovakia before moving to Geneva, Switzerland where he began his academic career while attending the Ecole Internationale and the University of Geneva. Igor went on to seminary at the Hamma Divinity School in Springfield, Ohio. After graduation, he moved to Strasbourg, France to work on his PhD at the University of Strasbourg. He was ordained Lutheran minister in Toledo, OH. He served several parishes throughout Ohio including Clinton, Martins Ferry, and Deshler.

Bio: "Igor Vladimir Bella," *Monadnock Ledger-Transcript*, December 22, 2015. See - http://www.legacy.com/obituaries/ledgertranscript/obituary.aspx?page=lifestory&pid=176981849; "Remembering Igor Bella," *The Dublin Advocate*, February 2016. See - https://dublinadvocate.com/2016/02/february-2016/

John M. Bellan (1892-1974), b. Turčok, Slovakia; Lutheran minister. He served Slovak congregations in Northampton, Philadelphia, Pottstown, Palmerton, Pa., and in Trenton and Camden, N.J. 1920-1925; Holy Emmanuel, Mahanoy City, and Sts. Peter and Paul, Freeland, 1925-1929, following which he served Slovak Church's in Torrington, Conn. St. John, Hatfield, Mass., Stafford Springs, Conn., Martin Luther, Cairnbrook, PA., 1930-1942. He was a US Army Chaplain, 1942-1952. From 1952-1961 he served Incarnation, Jamaica, N.Y. and following retirement served as vice-pastor of St. John, Mahanoy City.

Bio: Rev. John. Bellan," in: Find A Grave. See - https://www.findagrave.com/memorial/160740185/john-m-bellan

Matthew F. Benko (1891-d.), Slovakia; Lutheran minister; visiting pastor of the congregation First Slovish Evangelical Lutheran of Detroit; pastor in Lansford, PA; president of the Slovak Evangelical Lutheran Sion Synod

Bio: "Rev. M. Fred Benko," in: 1940 Census. See - https://www.ancestry.com/1940-census/usa/Ohio/Reverend-M-Fred-Benko_10hrgh

George Billy (1903-1958), Lutheran minister, pastor of Dr. Martin Luther Slovak Evangelical Lutheran Church, Gary, IN; pastor, Holy Trinity Evangelical Lutheran Church, Little Falls, NY (1934-1958).

John Body, Lutheran minister, pastor of the Peter and Paul Church, nr. Halsted (s. 1919); editor of *Slovak Lutheran*
Bio: See - *The Lutheran World Almanac and Annual Encyclopedia* for 1921, Volume 2, p.57

Ladislav Boor (1862-1918), b. Krajné, Slovakia; Lutheran Minister, pastor in Chicago, Braddock, PA, Lansford, PA
Bio: "Boor, Ladislav, Rev.," in: *Panorama*, p. 190

John Samuel Bradač (1889-1977), b. Myjava, Slovakia; Lutheran minister, pastor of the Slovak Lutheran Church (s. 1912), Whiting, IN, president of the Slovak Evangelical Lutheran Synod of U.S.A. (1922-39).
Bio: "Bradac, John Samuel," in: Droba, p. 109; "Rev. John Samuel Bradac," in: Find A Grave. See - https://www.findagrave.com/memorial/137898515/john-samuel-bradac

John Michael Brndjar (1938-2016), b. Danbury, CT, of Slovak descent; Lutheran minister, theologian, pastor of Ss. Peter and Paul Lutheran Church, Hazleton, PA, Freeland, PA and dean of the Eastern district of the Slovak Zion synod; president of Lutheran Welfare Service of Northeastern PA, founder of Hospice Saint John, the first Lutheran-sponsored US hospice, etc.
Bio: "The Rev. Dr. John Michael Brndjar," *The Morning Call*, February 3, 2016.

Juan Čobrda (1930-2010), b. Príovce, Czech.; Lutheran minister, heading a national church body in Argentina and the Slovak Zion Synod in the US; Bishop of the Lutheran Church in Argentina
Bio: "Juan Čobrda," in: Wikipedia. See - https://en.wikipedia.org/wiki/Juan_Čobrda

Andrew A. Daniel (1891-1980), b. Slovakia; Lutheran minister; pastor of the First Slovich of Detroit (1914-52); president of the Slovak Synod (SELC) (1939-49).
Bio: "Rev. Andrej A. Daniel," in: WIX. Com. See - http://ourredeemertaylor.wixsite.com/ourredeemer/history

Koloman Derek (1905-1961), b. Banská Bystrica, Slovakia; Lutheran minister, pastor, Bronx, NY
Bio: "Derek, Koloman," in: Pejskar 2, pp. 9-10.

Albert D. Dianiska (1879-1939), b. Sabinov, Slovakia; in US s. 1904; Lutheran minister. He served pastorates in Beckville, Freeland and Mahanoy City, PA. In 1915 the family moved to Cleveland, Ohio, where Rev. Dianiska served as pastor of Dr. Martin Luther Slovak Evangelical Lutheran Church. From 1930 until his untimely death from heart disease in 1939, he served as missionary pastor to congregations in Ohio, Pennsylvania, Michigan and Sarnia, Ontario, Canada.
Bio: "Rev. Albert D. Dianiska," in: Find A Grave. See - https://www.findagrave.com/memorial/56970156/albert-d-dianiska; "Ancestors of Albert Daniel Josef Dianiska." See -http://home.earthlink.net/~jeansgenealogy/ad_ancst.html

Thomas S. Drobena (1934-), b. Chicago, IL, of Slovak ancestry; Lutheran minister, pastor of Holy Trinity Lutheran Church, Stafford Springs, CT and Trumbul, CT
Bio: "Drobena, Thomas S.," in: *SVU Directory* 8; "CV: Thomas S. Drobena." See - https://cambridge.academia.edu/ThomasDrobena/CurriculumVitae

Cyril Droppa (1809-1890), b. Liptov, Slovakia; Lutheran minister, pioneer pastor in Streator, IL (1884-87), then at Freeland, PA, a member of the Evangelical Lutheran Ministerium of Pennsylvania

Andrew Dzurovcik (1947-), b. Chicago, IL, of Slovak descent; pastor of Holy Trinity Lutheran Church, Pleasant City: Zion Lutheran Church, Clark (1989-2016); SELC president
Bio: "Pastor Andrew Dzurovcik to retire from Zion Lutheran after 27 years," *Suburban News,* June 14, 2016. See - https://www.nj.com/suburbannews/index.ssf/2016/06/pastor_andrew_dzurovcik_to_ret.html

Ľudovít A. Engler (1875-1927), b. Klenovec, Gemer District, Slovakia; in US s. 1902);
Lutheran pastor, author; national activist persecuted by Hungary; founder of St. Mark's parish (1911); writer of short stories.
Bio: "Engler, Ľudovít Ondrej," in: najkrajsikraj.sk. See - http://www.najkrajsikraj.sk/engler-ludovit-ondrej/; Paučo, Jozef, *Slovenski priekopnici v Amerike.* Cleveland: Prva Katolicka Slovenska Jednota, 1972, pp. 60-61.

Daniel M. Estok (1923-2007), Slovak American; Lutheran minister; pastor of St. Lucas Evangelical Lutheran Church, St. Louis, MO; pastor of St. Paul Lutheran Church, Westport, CT
Bio: "Rev. Estok to Install Son as Pastor Sunday," *The Plain Speaker,* October 21, 1949.

Michael Estok (1898-1962), b. Houser Mills, Poconos, of Slovak descent; Lutheran minister; pastor of St. John's Evangelical Lutheran Church, Hazleton, PA (s. 1922)
Bio: *Standard-Speaker,* January 22, 1962.

George Gona, Lutheran minister, pastor of the Sion Slovak Evangelical Lutheran Church, Norridge, IL

George Michael Hanko (1937-2014), b. Westmoreland City, of Slovak descent; Lutheran minister; pastor at St. Mark Lutheran Church of Duquesne where he held both Slovak and English services.
Bio: "The Rev. George Michael Hanko," in: William Snyder & Forgie Snyder Funeral Home. See - https://www.snyderfuneralservices.com/obituaries/The-Rev-George-Hanko/#!/Obituary

Ivon Porter Harris (1940-2005), b. Irvington, NJ, of Slovak descent; Lutheran minister; Dean, Western Conference, Slovak Zion Synod; pastor in Northampton, PA, Hazleton, PA, Binghamton, NY and Chicago, IL
Bio: "Reverend Ivon Peter Harris," *Chicago Sun-Times,* July 6-7, 2005.

Karol Hauser (1853-d.), b. Moravia; Lutheran minister, minister of the Synod of Missouri, founder of a Slovak church in Minneapolis, MN. A Jewish convert to Lutheranism who had come to the U.S. in 1885; helped form the Slovak Lutheran congregation in Bohemian Flats, MN.
Bio: "Holy Emmanuel Slovak Lutheran Church, Minnesota," See - https://www.housesofworship.umn.edu/slovak-emmanuel

William P. Hinlicky (1921-2000), Lutheran minister, pastor of Zion Slovak Evangelical Lutheran Church, Newark, NJ (1960-64); pastor, Raritan, NJ (1964-84)
Bio: "William P. Hinlicky," in: Find A Grave. See - https://www.findagrave.com/memorial/27016678/marie-m-hinlicky

John Horarik (1901-1968), Lutheran minister; pastor of Zion Slovak Evangelical Lutheran Church, Newark, NJ (1932-37); pastor in Toronto, Ontario, Canada; pastor, St. Mark Lutheran Church, Steubenville, OH (s. 1959)

David P. Hudak (ca 1940-), Lutheran minister; pastor of Holy Trinity Church, Streator, IL (1980-1992); pastor of St. Peter Lutheran Church, Schaumburg, IL (1992-2012; Lutheran minister, Christ Lutheran Church, Siloam Springs, AR (s. 2012.
Bio: "David Hudak," in: LinkedIn. See - https://www.linkedin.com/in/david-hudak-26116991/

S. Cyril Hurnyak (1944-), b. PA, of Slovak descent; Lutheran minister; pastor of Zion Lutheran Church, Penn Hills, PA
Bio: "Rev. Stephen Hurnyak," *Pittsburgh Tribune Review*, February 10, 2002.

Stephen C. Hurnyak (1918-2002), b. Hauto, PA, of Slovak decent; Lutheran minister; pastor in Mahanoy City, PA, Freeland, PA, Charleroi, PA (from 1940 for 52 years)
Bio: "The Rev. Stephen C. Hurnyak," *Valley Independent*, February 11, 2002; "Rev. Stephen Hurnyak," *Pittsburgh Tribune Review*, February 10, 2002. See - http://www.legacy.com/obituaries/triblive-pittsburgh-tribune-review/obituary.aspx?n=stephen-hurnyak&pid=182336335.

Joseph Kolarik (1886-1946), b. Modrá, Slovakia; in US s. 1905; Lutheran minister, pastor in St. John's Lutheran Church, Tarentum, PA (1912-21); Cole Ridge, OH (1923-27); Raritan NJ (1927-36), Holy Immanuel, Pittsburgh, PA (1936-45).
Bio: "Brief Notes on My Life," in: The Kolarik Family Tree. See - http://kolarikr.tripod.com/extra/brief-notes.htm; "Rev. Joseph Kolarik," in: Find A Grave. See - https://www.findagrave.com/memorial/145351790/joseph-kolarik

Josef Milan Kolarik (1913-1990), b. Tarentum, PA, of Slovak ancestry; Lutheran minister; pastor, St. Paul's Lutheran Church, Braddock, PA
Bio: "J. Milan Kolarik," in: Find A Grave. See - https://www.findagrave.com/memorial/28285347/j-milan-kolarik

John Kovac (1906-), b. Brdárka, Slovakia; Lutheran minister, pastor in Emporia and Prince George, VA, Akron, OH, St. Louis, Mo, president Synod Evangelical Church (s. 196), editor of church periodical (1956-66).
Bio: "Kovac, John," in: *Who's Who in the Midwest,* 13

John Daniel Kovac (1922-2007), b. Hazleton, PA, of Slovak descent; Lutheran minister; pastor in Tarentum, PA, Central City, PA, Linn, KS, Deshler, NE, Utica, NE and Seward NE.
Bio: "Obituary: Rev. John Kovac," *York News-Times,* February 20, 2007; "Rev. John Daniel Kovac," in: Find a Grave. See - https://www.findagrave.com/memorial/28477327/john-daniel-kovac

John Kovacik (1905-2000), b. Necpaly, Slovakia; Lutheran minister; pastor at St. John the Evangelist Slovak Lutheran Church, Lansford, PA (1934-700; vice pastor at St. Matthew Lutheran Church, Mount Carmel, PA
Bio: "Rev. Dr. John Kovacik, Retired Lutheran Pastor," *The Morning Call,* Mach 11, 2000.

Ladislav Kozak (1948-), b. Slovakia; Lutheran minister; in Canada s. 1991; pastor of St. Paul's Slovak Lutheran Church, Toronto (s. 1991).
Bio: "Z kostela sv. Pavla," in: satellite 1-416. See - http://zpravy.org/1/2008/15/Narozeniny.html

Edward A. Kucera (1928-), b. St. Louis, MO, of Slovak descent; ordained Lutheran minister; served Ascension LC in Montreal Quebec, Canada until 1962. He served Sts. Peter & Paul LC (Sharon, PA) for 32 years, from 1962 until retirement, August 30, 1994, where he conducted worship in both English and Slovak. On February 14, 1971, he dedicated their new church at a cost of $340,000.00. During retirement, he served as interim pastor at various congregations in Ohio and Pennsylvania. He also accepted preaching assignments in Dallas, TX and St. Louis MO
Bio: "Meet Rev. Edward A. Kucera, EM," in: *The Lutheran Beacon,* December 17, p. 3.

Wilma Kucharek (1954-), b. Johnson City, NY, of Slovak descent; Lutheran minister, Bishop of the Slovak Zion Synod
Bio: "Wilma Kucharek," in: Wikipedia. See - https://en.wikipedia.org/wiki/Wilma_Kucharek

John Joseph Kucharik (1917-2001), b. Garfield, NJ, of Slovak descent; Lutheran minister; pastor of John Huss Lutheran Church, Kensington, PA (1941-50); associate pastor at Holy Trinity Lutheran Church, Garfield, NJ (1950-68); pastor at St. Luke Lutheran Church, Oviedo, FL (1968-82)
Bio: "Rev. John Joseph Kucharik," *Orlando Sentinel*, Nov. 6 -7, 2001; "John joseph Kucharik," in: WikiTree. See - https://www.wikitree.com/wiki/Kucharik-1

Joseph Daniel Kucharik (1920-1999), b. Akron, OH, of Slovak descent; Lutheran minister; pastor, Zion Slovak Evangelical Lutheran Church, Newark, NJ (1964-1988); secretary of of the Synod.
Bio: "Joseph Daniel Kucharik," in: WikiTree. See - https://www.wikitree.com/wiki/Kucharik-12

Joseph R. W. Kucharik (1886-1965), b. Necpaly, Slovakia; Lutheran minister; pastor, Holy Trinity Slovak Evangelical Lutheran Church, Garfield, NJ (1913-20).
Bio: "Joseph R. W. Kucharik (1886-1965). In: WikiTree. See - https://www.wikitree.com/wiki/Kucharik-2

Paul Kushner (1927-1995), Lutheran minister; pastor of Holy Cross Lutheran Church, Cambria City Johnstown, PA (for 21 years)
Bio: "Paul Kushner," in: Find A Grave. See - https://www.findagrave.com/memorial/105899194/paul-kushner

Drahotin Kvačala (1860-1918), b. Slovakia; Lutheran minister, pastor of the Slovak Lutheran Church in Braddock; St. John's Slovak Lutheran Church
Bio: "Kvacala, Drahotin Rev.," in: Cambria County, PA Genealogy. Obituary index. See - http://www.camgenpa.com/obit/scans/_prgs/obDetl.php?recd=35639; "Rev. Drahotin Kvacala," in: Find A Grave. See - https://www.findagrave.com/memorial/183154958/drahotin-kvacala

Daniel Z. Laucek (1846-1911), Lutheran minister, pastor of St. John's Slovak Lutheran Church, Nanticoke, PA, first president of the Slovak Evangelical Lutheran Synod (1902-05).

John Liptak, Lutheran minister, ordained and installed pastor in Raritan, NJ (1937-64)
Bio: "Rev Liptak," in: St. Paul Evangelical Lutheran Church." See - http://www.stpaulraritan.org/history.htm

Samuel Lichner (1878-d.), Modra, Slovakia; M.D.; ordained Lutheran minister in PA (1908), pastor, Slovak Church, Northampton, PA (1908-09), Lansford, PA (1909-10); Holy Trinity Slovak Church, Chicago, IL (s. 1910). Bio: The Philadelphia Seminary Biographical Record 1864-1923. By Luther D. Reed. Mt. Airy, Philadelphia, 1923, p. 214.

Robert Edward Matej (1937-2016), b. Jessup, PA, of Slovak descent; Lutheran minister. He served SELC District congregations in Hazleton, PA, Stamford, CT, Lakewood and Massillon, OH.
Bio: "Robert E. Matej." See - https://www.meaningfulfunerals.net/obituary/3728967?fh_id=13315

Stephen Gerald Mazak (ca 1905-), b. of Slovak descent; Lutheran minister; pastor of Zion Slovak Evangelical Lutheran Church (1929-30), pastor of St. John Church, Cudahy, WI (1932)

Stephen Gerald Mazak, Jr. (1930-2013), b. New Jersey, of Slovak descent; Lutheran minister; pastor of churches in Willow Springs, IL, Baltimore, MD, Murray KY and Conover, NC. He also served as professor and Dean of Students at Concordia Senior College, Ft. Wayne, IN and Lenoir Rhyne College, Hickory, NC.
Bio: "Pastor Stephen Gerald Mazak Jr.," in Dignity Memorial. See - https://www.dignitymemorial.com/obituaries/pelham-al/stephen-mazak-5453773

Richard Allan Mazak (1932-), b. Milwaukee, WI, of Slovak descent; Lutheran minister; physicist; pastor in San Angelo, TX (1973-79), Newton, NC (s. 1979).
Bio: "Richard Allan Mazak," in: Prabook. See - https://prabook.com/web/richard_allan.mazak/1099409na

John A. Mihok (1918-1974), Lutheran minister, pastor of St. Paul Lutheran Church, Braddock, PA

C. Molnar, Lutheran minister, assistant pastor of Holy Trinity Slovak Evangelical Lutheran Church, Chicago

Jerry Mraz (1933-), b. Partizánska Lupča, Czech.; in US s. 1939; Lutheran minister; parish pastor at Holy Trinity Lutheran Church in Akron, Ohio (1966-72); pastor of Holy Trinity Slovak Lutheran Church, Northampton (s. 1972). He is Evangelical outreach director for the Slovak Zion Synod. He had broadcast religious programs to Czechoslovakia over Radio Free Europe, had organized Slovak broadcasts in New York. Mraz reorganized the Northampton Clergy Association; was instrumental in starting Northampton Home Health Care Services, an organization that provides volunteer services for a variety of needs and was associate chaplain at St. Luke's Hospital.
Bio: "Northampton Pastor Wins the Golden Deeds Award," *The Morning Call,* May 26, 1988; "Pastor Mraz," *Hope Home News,* 38, No. 1 (February 2011). See - http://www.hopecherryville.org/publications/newsletters/2011/201102_newsletter.pdf

Ludevit Novomesky, Lutheran minister, pastor in the Raritan community (s. 1887); president of Slovak Zion

John Stefan Obeda (1929-2018), b. Chicago, IL; Lutheran minister; he served as pastor in various congregations in Texas, Michigan and Ontario, including Our Redeemer Evangelical Lutheran Church, Taylor, MI (1964-66); then took a call to Trinity, Wyandotte and later served in London, Ontario, where he is today retired. He also served as chaplain to area hospitals and nursing homes; and after retiring, still served as a guest pastor or organist.
Bio: "Obeda, John Stefan," in: Westview Funeral Chapel. See - http://www.westviewfuneralchapel.com/pages/obituaries/details.php?p=3864; "John Stefan Obeda," in: yourlifemoments.ca. See - http://yourlifemoments.ca/sitepages/obituary.asp?oid=1096675

Milan A. Ontko (ca. 1920-2002), b. Passaic, NJ, of Slovak descent; pastor of St. Paul Lutheran Church; president of SELK (1969-71)
Bio: "Milan Ontko," in: Find a Grave. See - https://www.findagrave.com/memorial/63469700/john-pelikan

John Pelikan Sr. (1870-1930), b. Slovakia; in US s. 1902; Lutheran minister; president of SELC (1905-13).
Bio: "Rev. John Pelikan," in: Find A Grave. See - https://www.findagrave. com/memorial/63469700/john-pelikan

Ján Jaroslav Pelikán (1898-after 1973) b. Záriečie, Slovakia; in US s. 1902; Lutheran minister, pastor of Lutheran churches in Jessup, PA (1919-20), Pleasant City, OH (1920-21), Veľká pod Tarou, Slovakia (1921-23), Akron, OH (1923-28), Chicago (1928-33) and Pittsburgh, PA (s. 1933). He was vice president of the Czechoslovak Group of A Century of Progress (1933) and editor of *Svedok*, an official monthly of the Slovak Lutheran Synod of U.S.A.
Bio: "Pelikan, Jaroslav Jan," in: Droba, p. 110;.

Paul A. Pruta (1887-1954), b. Ďanová, Slovakia; Lutheran minister, ordained in PA (1912); pastor of the Holy Trinity Slovak Lutheran Church in Little Falls, NY (1912-20), then in the Holy Trinity Slovak Lutheran Church, Irwin, PA (s. 1920), president of the Sion Synod
Bio: "Rev Paul A. Pruta," *The Pittsburgh Press*, April 5, 1954, p. 23.

Paul Rajcok (1893-1927), b. Slovakia; Lutheran minister, first resident pastor of St. Paul Evangelical Lutheran Church, Raritan, NJ (1913-27).
Bio: "Rev Paul John Rajcok," in: Find A Grave. See - https://www.findagrave. com/memorial/141994207/paul-john-rajcok

Paul Rafaj (1895-1962), b. Turany, Slovakia; in US s. 1910; Lutheran minister, pastor at the St. Stephen's Lutheran Church in Dickson, PA (s. 19 21); president of SELC (1949-63).
Bio: "Rafaj, Paul," in: *Who's Who in the East*, 1951; "The Rev. Paul Rafaj," *The New York Times*, March 17, 1962; Pavel Rea Rafaj," in: Find a Grave See - https://www.findagrave.com/memorial/30154668/pavel-rea-rafaj

Michael Rehak, 3rd (), b. of Slovak descent; Lutheran minister, psychologist; interim pastor, South Central Synod of WI ELCA (s. 1999); director of the Institute for Congregational Identity (s. 1998)
Bio: "Meet the Director." See- http://congregationalidentity.org/meet.html

Andrew Rolik (1896-1981), b. Brdárka, Slovakia; Lutheran minister, pastor, St. Matthew Evangelical Church, Barberton, OH; writer, Slovak national

activist. He immigrated to USA in 1909 and became one of the foremost publicists of the Slovak spirit in America; wrote poetry, translated it from English and published religious songs in Slovak journals and almanacs.
Bio: "Rev Andrew Rolik": Find A Grave. See- https://www.findagrave.com/memorial/185941496/andrew-rolik ; Rolik, Andrej," in: ECAV. http://www.ecav.sk/?p=info /INFHistória/osobnosti/rolik_andrej_ (1896_–_1981)

Karol Salva (1849-1913), b. Liptovská Sielnica, Slovakia; teacher, journalist, publicist, Protestant minister in Pleasant City and in Cleveland, OH
Bio: "Karol Salva," in: Wikipedia. See - https://sk.wikipedia.org/wiki/Karol_Salva

John Shintay (1912-1993), b. New York, NY, of Slovak descent; Lutheran minister, pastor of Holy Trinity Slovak Lutheran Church, New York, NY
Bio: "Shintay, John," in: *SVU Directory* 7; "Shintay, John Rev.," in: *Panorama*, p. 278; "Rev. John Shintay," Find A Grave. See - https://www.findagrave.com/memorial/131891081/john-shintay

Rudolph S. Shintay (1915-2010), b. New York, NY, of Slovak descent; Lutheran minister; pastor of Trinity Slovak Lutheran Church, in Chicago (1967-83); editor and chairman of Youth Ministries of the Slovak Lutheran Zion Synod
Bio: "Rev. Rudolph Shintay," in: Saul Funeral Homes, Inc. See - http://www.saulfuneralhomes.com/obituary/Rev.-Rudolph-Shintay/Chicago-IL/774517

August A. Skodacek (1913-1996), b. Indiana, of Slovak descent; Lutheran minister; Dean of the Central District, Slovak Evangelical Union of America; writer of Lutheran religious literature.

Martin Slabey, Lutheran minister; pastor, Holy Trinity Evangelical Lutheran church (1920-1925)

Thomas J. Smrcka (-1934); Lutheran minister; pastor of Holy Trinity Evangelical Church (1925-1934).

Bohuslav D. Tuhy (1914-1975), b. Wilkes-Barre, of Slovak descent; Lutheran minister, pastor of Our Savior Evangelical Lutheran Church, Chatham,

Ont., Canada; pastor, Zion Slovak Evangelical Lutheran Church, Newark, NJ (1938-1960).
Bio: "Rev. Bohuslav Daniel Tuhy," in: Find A Grave. See - www.findagrave. com/memorial/58964812/bohuslav-daniel-tuhy

Stephen Tuhy (1883-1961), b. Slovakia; Lutheran minister; pastor of St. Matthew Lutheran Church, Wilkes-Barre, PA (1910-1961); president of SELC (1913-19);
Bio: "Rev. Stephen Tuhy," in: Find a Grave. See - https://www.findagrave. com/memorial/58965071/stephen-tuhy

Stephen M. Tuhy (1909-1967), b. Pleasant City, OH, of Slovak descent; pastor of St. Luke's Lutheran Church, Oviedo, FL (1934-69); resided in Florida
Bio: "A Shepherd to Lead them," in: St. Lukes Lutheran Church. See - http://stlukes-oviedo.org/assets/images/pageDownloads/file/sample_page. pdf; "The Funeral of Rev. Stephen M. Tuhy, December 29, 1967," in: Central Florida Memory. See - https://digital.library.ucf.edu/cdm/ref/collection/ CFM/id/153428

Jaroslav Vajda (1919-2008), b. Lorain, OH, of Slovak father; ordained as Lutheran minister; pastor of parishes in Cranesville, PA (1945-49), Alexandria, IN (1949-53), Tarentum, Pa (1953-63) and St. Louis, MO (1963-76). He was noted primarily as an American hymnist.
Bio: "Jaroslav Vajda," in: Wikipedia. See - https://en.wikipedia.org/wiki/ Jaroslav_Vajda

John Vajda (fl. 1946), Lutheran minister; pastor of parishes in Emporia, VA, Racine, WI, and finally in East Chicago, IN, at Holy Trinity Slovak Lutheran Church (s. 1926)
Bio: "Rev John Vajda, pastor Holy Trinity Lutheran Church East Chicago, Il," in: *The Times*, November 7, 1947, p. 27. See - https://www.newspapers. com/clip/17571928/rev_john_vajda_pastor_holy_trinity/

Paul Visoky, Slovak American; Lutheran minister; pastor of St. Matthew Evangelical Lutheran Church (1962-95).

John Zabadal (1893-1979), a Slovak American; Lutheran minister; resided Hermitage, Mercer Co., PA
Bio: "Rev. John Zabadal," in: Find A Grave. See -
https://www.findagrave.com/memorial/15449882/john-zabadal

Nicholas Zipay, Jr. (1927-2015), of Slovak ancestry; Lutheran minister; Rev. Zipay was called to Sts. Peter and Paul Lutheran Church in Central City, PA, Our Redeemer Lutheran Church in Detroit, MI, Cross of Christ Lutheran Church in Cudahy, WI and Sts. Peter and Paul Lutheran Church in Lorain, OH before his retirement in 1989.
Bio: "Rev. Nicholas Zipay, Jr.," in: Legacy.com. See - https://www.legacy.com/obituaries/nwitimes/obituary.aspx?page=lifestory&pid=176268480; "Nicholas Zipay, Jr." in: Our Redeemer Evangelical Lutheran Church, Taylor, MI. See - http://ourredeemertaylor.wixsite.com/ourredeemer/history;

John Zornan, Jr. (1893-1979), a Slovak American; Lutheran minister; pastor of Immanuel Slovak Lutheran Church (1936-1942); president of the Slovak Zion Synod of the Lutheran Church
Bio: "Slovak Zion Synod Elects," The New York Times, May 29, 1970. .com

F. BAPTIST CHURCH

1. Surveys

Vojta, Vaclav. *Czechoslovak Baptists.* Minneapolis: Czechoslovak Baptist Convention in America and Canada, ca 1941. 276p.

2. Ministers

Paul Bednar, b. Slovakia, Baptist minister; pastor of the First Slovak Baptist Church, Cleveland
Bio: See - *The Slovaks of Cleveland* by Eleanor E. Ledbetter

Mrs. John Kana, of Yonkers, New York, was formerly a member of the First Slovak Baptist Church in Creighton, PA, and was the first Slovak woman missionary in the United States.

Andrew Slabey (1866-1928), b. Slovakia; Baptist minister, in US s. 1899; pastor, First Slovak Baptist Church, Philadelphia; pioneer missionary among the Slovaks in America, builder of churches. He taught Slovak language and literature at Columbia University (1935-36); pastor, Bethlehem Slovak Congregational Church in Duquesne, PA (1936-83).
Bio: "Rev. Andrew Slabey," in: Find A Grave. See - https://www.findagrave.com/memorial/159549951/andrew-slabey

Andrew Paul Slabey (1889-1983), b. Verba, Slovakia; Baptist minister, theologian, translator, Moravian Archives, Bethlehem, PA
Bio: "Slabey, Andrew Paul," in: *SVU Directory* 5; "Slabey, Andrey P.," in: *Panorama*, p. 17; "Interview with Dr. Andrew Paul Slabey, Jr.," The morning Call, September 22, 1968. See - https://www.newspapers.com/clip/22217258/interview with dr andrew paul slabey/

Matthias Steucek (1852-1935); b. Vavrisovo Slovakia; raised as Lutheran, missionary; in 1903, he immigrated to US, settling in Creighton PA. Founder and missionary pastor of the first Slovak Baptist Church in North America (Creighton, PA). For a while it was difficult to obtain religious literature printed in the Slovak language. This difficulty was removed when the Rev. Mr. Steucek purchased a printing press and published and distributed many thousands of tracts. He also published the first Slovak Baptist paper in America, *The Friend of Peace*.
Bio: "The Beginning of the Slovak Missionary Work," *The Standard*, February 9, 1907; "Rev Matthias Steucek," in: Find a Grave. See - https://www.findagrave.com/memorial/42830517/matthias-steucek

G. EVANGELICAL BRETHREN CHURCH

John Jerry Bravenec (1933-2006), b. Houston, TX, of Slovak descent; pastor of Caldwell Brethren Church, Snook Brethren Church and Dimebox Brethren Church
Bio: "Rev. John Jerry Bravenec," in: Find A Grave. See - https://mays.tamu.edu/news/tag/lorence-bravenec/

H. CALVIN PRESBYTERIAN UNION

Alois Husak, Pittsburgh, PA; minister at Troy Hill, PA

George Kmecik, Slavonic ordained Presbyterian minister; Lackawanna Presbytery; missionary in Scranton and Troop, PA

Ryan J. Landino (1983-), b. Bethlehem, PA, of Slovak descent; Presbyterian minister; pastor, First Presbyterian Church, Geneseo, NY (s. 2016); Lead Presbyter for Transformation (involves networking, resourcing and supporting the 95 Presbyterian Churches of Great Rivers Presbytery, a geographic region of west central Illinois.
Bio: "Former Slovak minister now leads Geneseo First Presbyterian," *Dispatch-Argus,* April 2, 2016; "Pastor lands Presby lead title," *Dispatch-Argus,* June 1, 2018

Vladimir J. Lisy, minister in charge of Braddock Slovak

John Sabol, Slovak Presbyterian ordained minister, Northumberland Presbytery; pastor of Slovak Church, Mt. Carmel, PA.

Anna Shimko, missionary in Raccoon, PA

Michael J. Tomasula (1899-1964), b. Lúčky, Slovakia; in US s. 1914; Presbyterian minister; pastor of Slovak Presbyterian Church, Mt. Carmel, PA (1937-42); pastor, John Calvin United Presbyterian Church, Raccoon, PA (for 27 years).
Bio: "Rev. Michael J. Tomasula," in: Find A Grave. See - https://www.findagrave.com/memorial/157328143/michael-j.-tomasula

I. LDS CHURCH (JESUS CHRIST OF LATTER-DAY SAINTS)

2. Apostles

David Allan Bednar (1952-), b. Oakland, CA, of Slovak ancestry; a member of the Quorum of the Twelve Apostles of LDS Church
Bio: "David A. Bodnar," in: Wikipedia. See - https://en.wikipedia.org/wiki/David_A._Bednar

J. CONGREGATIONAL CHURCH

Andrew John Moncol (1877-1974), b. Klenovec, Slovakia; pastor of St. Cyril Congregational Church (1922-39), Cleveland, OH
Bio: "Moncol, Andrew John," in: *Encyclopedia of Cleveland History.* See - https://case.edu/ech/articles/m/moncol-andrew-john

Edward Alfred Steiner (1866-1956), b. Senica, Slovakia; Congregational Church minister, educator, professor of applied Christianity, writer on immigration
Bio: Steiner, Edward Alfred, *From Alien to Citizen: The Story of my Life in America.* Boston: Pilgrim Press, 1914; Spitzer, Yanny, "Edward A. Steiner: A Writer on Immigration." See - https://yannayspitzer.net/2012/08/24/edward-a-steiner-a-writer-on-immigration/; "Edward Alfred Steiner," in: *Encyclopedia,* Vol. 2, p. 11

K. JUDAISM

1. General

Kisch, Guido, *In Search of Freedom.* A History of American Jews from Czechoslovakia 1592-1948. London: E. Goldston, 1949. 373 p.
Rechcígl, Miloslav, Jr. "Early Jewish Immigrants in America from the Czech Historic Lands and Slovakia," *Review of the Society for the History of Czechoslovak Jews,* Vol. 3, 1990-1991, pp. 157–79.

Rechcigl, Miloslav, Jr., *American Jews with Czechoslovak Roots. A Bibliography, Bio-Bibliography and Historiography.* Bloomington, IN: AuthorHouse, 2018. 388p.
Wingfield, Nancy M., "Czechoslovak Jewish Immigration to the United States, 1938-1945." *Czechoslovak & Central European Journal,* Vol. 11, No. 2, Jan. 1993, pp. 38–48.

2. Rabbis

Alexander Altmann (1906-1987), b. Košice, Slovakia; an Orthodox Jewish scholar and rabbi. He emigrated to England in 1938 and later settled in the United States, working productively for a decade and a half as a professor within the Philosophy Department at Brandeis University.
Bio: "Alexander Altmann," in: Wikipedia. See - https://en.wikipedia.org/wiki/Alexander_Altmann

Solomon Baum (1868-d.), b. Šebeš, Slovakia; rabbi, Cantor
Bio: *American Jewish Year Book.* Philadelphia: Jewish Publication Society of America, 1903, Vol.5, p. 44.

Aaron Albert Siegfried Bettelheim (1830-1890), b. Hlohovec, Slovakia; rabbi
Bio: Albert Siegfried Bettelheim," in: *The Jewish Encyclopedia.* New York - London: Funk and Wagnalls Company, 1916, Vol. 3, pp. 129-130.

Sender Deutsch (1922-1998), b. Veľké Berezné, Czech.; rabbi, leader of one of the largest Hasidic Jewish groups in the US, and editor of *Der Yid*
Bio: "Rabbi Sender Deutsch, 76, Editor, Publisher of Der Yid," *The New York Times,* September 13, 1998; "Deutsch, Sander," in: *Who's Who in the East,* 9

Sigmund Drechsler (1845-1908), b. Brezová, Slovakia; Dr.; rabbi, in US s. 1887, settling in Cleveland, OH, where he served as a rabbi.
Bio: *American Jewish Yearbook,* Vol. 5, p. 51; "Rabbi Sigmond Drechsler," in: Find A Grave. See - https://www.findagrave.com/memorial/139813612/sigmond-drechsler

Shmuel Ehrenfeld 1891-1980), b. Mattersdorf, Austria, of Slovak ancestry; rabbi, Torah leader
Bio: "Shmuel Ehrenfeld," in: Wikipedia. See - https://en.wikipedia.org/wiki/ Shmuel_Ehrenfeld

Menahem M. Eichler (1870-d.); b. Budkovce, Slovakia; rabbi
Bio: *American Jewish Year Book*, 5664 (Sept. 22 to Sept. 1904), p. 51.

Henry Englander (1877-1951), b. Prešov, Slovakia; rabbi
Bio: *American Jewish Year Book*, 5664 (Sept. 22 to Sept. 1904), p. 52; "Funeral Rites in Texas for Pioneer Rabbi," Jewish Telegraph Agency, September 27, 1934

Maurice Faber (1854-1934), b. Široké, Slovakia; rabbi
Bio: *American Jewish Year Book*. Philadelphia: Jewish Publication Society of America, 1903, Vol.5, p. 53.

Zachariah Gelley (1933-2018), b. Topoľčany, Slovakia; Holocaust survivor; rav (rabbi), K'hal Adath Jeshurun (KAJ) in the Washington Heights neighborhood of upper Manhattan in New York City. Rav Gelley was a noted talmid chochom and manhig, who guided KAJ, which is comprised of an elementary yeshiva for boys and girls, a Bais Yaakov middle school for girls, a mesivta high school for boys, a bais medrash and kollel, a mikvah, a kashrus supervisory organization, a chevra Kadisha.
Bio: "Rav Zachariah Gelley zt" l, Rov of KAJ," in: matzav.com. See - http:// matzav.com/rav-zachariah-gelley-ztl-rov/

David L. Genuth (1901-1974), b. Romania, of Slovak descent; rabbi; one of Cleveland's most influential Orthodox rabbis for more than 40 years.
Bio: "David L. Genuth," in: Wikipedia. See - https://en.wikipedia.org/wiki/ David_L._Genuth

Juda Glasner (1918-2005), b. Hanušovce, Czech.; rabbi, Cong. Mishkan Yicheskel, Tujunga, CA (s. 1964).
Bio: "Juda Glasner," in: *Encyclopedia*, Vol. 1, p. 290.

Henry R. Goldberger (1899-1946), b. Zemplín, Slovakia; rabbi, Erie, PA
Bio: *Who's Who in American Jewry.* New York: Jewish Bibliographical Bureau, 1926, Vol. 1, p. 206

Samuel Greenfield (1870-d.), b. Košice, Slovakia; rabbi
Bio: *American Jewish Year Book.* Philadelphia: Jewish Publication Society of America, 1903, Vol.5, p. 50.

Sigmund Hecht (1849-d.), b. Hliník nad Hronom, Slovakia; rabbi
Bio: *American Jewish Year Book.* Philadelphia: Jewish Publication Society of America, 1903, Vol.5, p. 62.

Adolph Huebsch (1830-1884), b. Sv. Mikuláš, Slovakia, rabbi
Bio: Rechcigl, Miloslav, Jr., "Adolph Huebsch," in: *Encyclopedia of Bohemian and Czech American Biography.* Bloomington, IN.: AuthorHouse, 2016, Vol. 1, p. 292

Alois Kaiser (1840-1908), b Sobotište, Slovakia; American chazzan and composer, founder of American cantorate
Bio: "Alois Kaiser," in Wikipedia. See - https://en.wikipedia.org/wiki/Alois_Kaiser; "Kaiser, Alois," in: JewishEncyclopedia.com. See - http://jewishencyclopedia.com/articles/9137-kaiser-alois; Foster, Mark S., "Kaiser, Alois," in: *National Biography*, Vol. 11. Pp. 344-346.

Alexander Kaufman (1886-d.), b. Bardejov, Slovakia; rabbi, editor, publisher, St. Louis, MO.
Bio: *Who's Who in American Jewry.* New York: Jewish Biographical Bureau, 1927, Vol. 1, p. 312.

David Klein (1868-d.), b. Lipany, Slovakia; rabbi
Bio: *American Jewish Year Book,* 5664 (Sept. 22 to Sept. 1904), p. 68.

Henry Klein (1859-d.), b. Lipany, Slovakia; rabbi
Bio: *American Jewish Year Book.* Philadelphia: Jewish Publication Society of America, 1903, Vol. 5, pp. 68-69.

Jacob Klein (1870-d.), b. Veľká Ida, Slovakia; rabbi
Bio: *American Jewish Year Book.* Philadelphia: Jewish Publication Society of America, 1903, Vol.5, p. 69.

Philip Klein (1849-d.), b. Bardoňovo, Slovakia; rabbi
Bio: *American Jewish Year Book.* Philadelphia: Jewish Publication Society of America, 1903, Vol.5, p. 69.

Mayer Kopfstein (1866-d.), b. Bratislava, Slovakia; rabbi
Bio: *American Jewish Year Book.* Philadelphia: Jewish Publication Society of America, 1903, Vol. 5, p. 70.

Joseph Saul Kornfeld (1876-), b. Zlaté Moravce, Slovakia; rabbi, Pine Bluff, AR
Bio: *American Jewish Year Book.* Philadelphia: Jewish Publication Society of America, 1903, Vol. 5, p. 70

David Lefkowitz, (1875-1955.), b. Prešov, Slovakia; rabbi, Cong. Bnai-Yeshurun, Dayton, OH (1900-20, Temple Emanu-El, Dulles, TX (s. 1920) Bio: "Lefkowitz, David," in: *Who's Who in America,* 18; "Lefkowitz, David," in: *Who's Who in American Jewry,* Vol. 1, p. 354; "Lefkowitz, David," in: Who's Who in the Central States, 1929; "David Lefkowitz," in: Wikipedia. See - https://en.wikipedia.org/wiki/David_Lefkowitz.

David Lefkowitz, Jr. (1911-1999), b. Dayton, OH, of Slovak ancestry; rabbi, Shreveport, LA
Bio: "Davis Lefkowitz, Jr. Papers," in: American Jewish Archives, MS collection No. 650;

Morris Mandel (1875-d.), b. Biel, Slovakia; rabbi; rabbi of Congregation Adas Israel, Washington, DC (1898-1901); Beth Israel Congregation, Atlantic City, NJ (1901-03); vice president, Federation of American Zionists (1899-1900); resided in Allentown, PA.
Bio: "Mandel, Morris," in: American Jewish Year Book, Vol. 6, p. 220.

Bernard Dov Marton (1909-1990), b. Velete; rabbi; educated in Czechoslovakia; in US s. 1933; rabbi of Congregation Sharei Zedek, the Sea Gate Sisterhood and Talmud Torah in Brooklyn, NY; rabbi of First

Congregation Anshe S'fard of Borough Park, Brooklyn, NY (s. 1941), In 1945 Marton became rabbi of Congregation Kenesseth Israel in San Francisco, CA. He founded and served as dean of the Hebrew Academy of San Francisco, an Orthodox Jewish day school. He also founded, published, and edited the *Jewish Courier*, a monthly newspaper, and was appointed West Coast Chairman of the Rabbinical Alliance. He left San Francisco in 1952 to become Executive Vice-President and Provost of the Yeshiva Torah Vodaath schools in Brooklyn, NY. In the fall of 1952 Marton became rabbi of Congregation Adas Israel and Mishnayes in Newark, NJ. In 1955, Marton left Newark for a 'lifetime position' at Congregation B'nai Reuben in Los Angeles.
Bio: "Bernard Dov Marton Papers," in: Yeshiva University: See - http://libfindaids.yu.edu:8082/xtf/view?docId=ead/bernardmarton/ bernardmarton.xml;query=;brand=default

Shmuel Mendlowitz (1926-2017), b. Williamsburg; son of the legendary Rav Shraga Feivel Mendlowitz; Rav, founder and menahel of Mesivta Bais Shraga of Monsey, NY
Bio: "HaravShmuel Mendlowitz Zt"l," in: Hamodia. See - https://hamodia.com/2017/01/05/bde-harav-shmuel-mendlowitz-ztl/; "Rav Shmuel Mendlowitz zt"l," in: matzav.com, January 5, 2017. See - http://matzav.com/rav-shmuel-mendlowitz-ztl/

Shraga Feivel Mendlowitz (1886-1948), b. Svetlice, Slovakia; rabbi; leader of American Orthodoxy and founder of key institutions such as Torah Vodaath, a Yeshiva in Brooklyn, and Torah U'Mesorah, an outreach and educational organization. In the words of rabbi Moshe Feinstein: "Were it not for him, there would be no Torah study and no Fear of Heaven at all in America."
Bio: "Mendlowitz, Shraga Feivel (1886-1948), in: *Orthodox Judaism in America: A Biographical Dictionary and Source Book*. By Moshe D. Sherma. Westport, CT: Greenwood Press, 1996, pp. 152-153; "Shraga Feivel Mendlowitz," in: Wikipedia. See - https://en.wikipedia.org/wiki/Shraga_Feivel_Mendlowitz

Baruch Meyer (1964-), b. Orange, NJ; rabbi; Chief rabbi of Bratislava
Bio: "Barcu Meyer," in: Wikipedia. See - https://en.wikipedia.org/wiki/Baruch_Myers

Ignatius Mueller (1857-d.), b. Prešov, Slovakia; rabbi
Bio: *American Jewish Year Book.* Philadelphia: Jewish Publication Society of America, 1903, Vol. 5, p. 84.

Morris Newfield (1869-d.), b. Humenné, Slovakia; rabbi
Bio: *American Jewish Year Book. American Jewish Year Book.* Philadelphia: Jewish Publication Society of America, 1903, Vol. 5, p. 85.; "Newfield, Morris," in: *Who's Who in American Jewry,* New York: Jewish Biographical Bureau, 1926, vol. 1, p. 458.

Samuel Rosenblatt (1902-1983), b. Bratislava, Slovakia; rabbi, Trenton, NJ, and since 1927 onward served Congregation Beth Tefiloh in Baltimore, MD.; head of the Baltimore Board of rabbis (1952), Mizrachi (1938-42) and the American Jewish congress (1942-47)
Bio: *Who's Who in American Jewry.* New York: Jewish Biographical Bureau, 1927, Vol. 1, p. 514; "Rosenblatt, Samuel," in *Who's Who in the East,* 1930; "Rosenblatt, Samuel," in: encyclopedia.com. See - https://www.encyclopedia.com/religion/encyclopedias-almanacs-transcripts-and-maps/rosenblatt-samuel

Emanuel Schoenbrun (1859-), b. Veľké Kapušany, Slovakia; rabbi, Cleveland, OH
Bio: "Schoenbrun, Emanuel," *American Jewish Year Book.* Philadelphia: Jewish Publication Society of America, 1903, Vol. 5, p. 96.

Morris Sessler (1880-d.), b. Hlohovec Slovakia; rabbi; held positions in Alexandria, VA, Wheeling, VA, Providence, RI, and New Orleans, CA.
Bio: "Sessler, Morris," in: *American Jewish Year Book,* Vol 6, p. 283.

Solomon H. Sonneschein (1839-1908), b. Svatý Martin, Slovakia, educated in Moravia; rabbi
Bio: "Rabbi Sonneschein Resigns; He was brilliant and popular, but had many enemies," *The New York Times,* September 10, 1891; *The American Jewish Year Book,* 1903-1904, p. 101.

Benjamin Szold (1829-1902); b. Zemianske Sady, Slovakia; American rabbi and scholar, Temple Oheb Shalom, Baltimore, MD
Bio: "Benjamin Szold," in: Wikipedia. See - https://en.wikipedia.org/wiki/Benjamin_Szold

Morris Wechsler (1849-d.), b. Michalovce, Slovakia; rabbi
Bio: *American Jewish Year Book*. Philadelphia: Jewish Publication Society of America, 1903, Vol. 5, p. 104.

Alexander Sandor Wiesel (1894-), b. Slovakia; rabbi, Montgomery AL, Shreveport, LA (s. 1926)
Bio: "Wiesel, Alexander Sandor," in: *Who's Who in American Jewry*, Vol. 1, pp. 647-648.

Mayer Winkler (1882-1944), b. Veľpolie, Slovakia; rabbi, Los Angeles
Bio: *Who's Who in American Jewry*. New York: Jewish Biographical Bureau, 1927, Vol. 1, p. 650.

David Wirtschafter (ca 1969-), b. Lexington, KY, of Slovak ancestry; rabbi at Amos Jewish Congregation in IA and then at Temple Adath Israel in Lexington
Bio: "Rabbi David Wirtschafter," in Gravatar Profile. See - http://en.gravatar.com/rabbidavidw; Miller, Jonathan, "Temple Adath Israel Welcomes rabbi David Wirtschafter Home," *Shalom. Newspaper of the Jewish Federation of the Bluegrass*, 14, No. 5 (June/July 2015), pp. 1-2.

Stephen S. Wise (1874-1949), b. Budapest, of Slovak ancestry; Reform rabbi and Zionist leader
Bio: Voss, Carl H., *Rabbi and Minister: The Friendship of Stephen S. Wise and John Haynes Holmes*. New York: Prometheus, 1980; Wise, Stephen S., *The Challenging Years*. New York: Putnam, 1949; Urofsky, Melvin I., "Wise, Stephen Samuel," in: *National Biography*, Vol. 23, pp. 690-692.

VII. The Society

A. SOCIAL ORGANIZATION

Alexander, June Granatir, "Diversity within Unity: Regionalism and Social Relations among Slovaks in Pre-War I Pittsburgh," *Western Pennsylvania Historical Magazine* 70 (October 1987). pp. 317-38.
"Social Conditions," in: Miller, pp. 65-118.
Tomaskovic-Devey, Barbara, and Donald Tomaskovic-Devey, "The Social Structural Determinants of Ethnic Group Behavior: Single Ancestry Rates among Four White American Ethnic Groups," *American Sociological Review*, Vol. 53, No. 4, 1988, pp. 650-59

B. FAMILY ORGANIZATION

Stein, Howard F., "The Slovak-American 'Swaddling Ethos': Homeostat for Family Dynamics and Cultural Continuity," *Family Process*, Vol. 17, Issue 1 (March 1978), pp. 31-45.

C. HEALTH & WELFARE

Stein, Howard F., "Cultural Specificity in Patterns of Mental Ilness and Health: A Slovak-American Case Study," *Family Process*, 12 (March 1973), pp. 69-82.
Stein, Howard F., "A Dialectical Model of Health and Illness Attitudes and Behavior among Slovak-Americans," *International Journal of Mental Health*, Vol. 5, No. 2 (Summer 1976), pp. 117-137.
Stein, Howard, F., "Aging and Death among Slovak Americans: A Study in the Thematic Unity of the Life Cycle," *The Journal of Psychological Anthropology*, Vol. 1, No. 3 (Summer 1978), pp. 297-320.

1. Pioneer Physicians

Adolph Barkan (1845-1935), b. Ľubotice, Prešov Dist., Slovakia; physician, ophthalmologist; spent almost half his 91 years in a very successful career on the West Coast.
Bio: "Barkan, Adolf," in: *American Science*, 3; "Adolph Barkan (1845-1935), European Ophthalmologist in San Francisco," *JAMA Ophthalmol.*, 132, No. 3 (2014), pp. 346-340.

Matej Benczur (1860-1928), b. Jasenová, Slovakia; physician, who practiced in Buenos Aires and on Punta Arenas, the southernmost town in Chile. He is a well-known novelist under the penname, Martin Kukučín. He went to Southern America in 1908. He became the first physician of the International Red Cross in Pantagonia. A polyclinic in Punta Arenas was named in his honor. In 1922-24 he was back in Slovakia and then he resided in Croatia.
Bio: "Martin Kukučín," in: Wikipedia. See - https://sk.wikipedia.org/wiki/Martin_ Kukučín

Benjamin Berger (1884-1968), b. Hrabovec, Slovakia; physician, dermatologist, urologist, NYC
Bio: *Who's Who in American Jewry*. New York: Jewish Biographical Bureau, 1926, Vol. 1., p. 45.

Bernard Bettelheim (1811-1869), b. Bratislava, Slovakia; physician, surgeon; in US s. 1854; served in the Civil War as a surgeon; resided in Brookfield, MO
Bio: *Lincolns Hungarian Heroes*, p. 48; Bernard Jean Bettelheim," in: Wikipedia. See - https://en.wikipedia.org/wiki/Bernard_Jean_Bettelheim

Emil Bunta (1887-1965), b. Slovakia; pioneer physician, Chicago. He received M.D. from Rush Medical College (1914). Intern, Cook County Hospital (1914-16), resident alienist, Cook County Psychopathic Hospital (1916), resident physician, Oak Forest Infirmary (1917-18), instructor in diseases of the nervous system, Loyola University Medical School (s. 1920), becoming clinical professor. For many years he was on the staff of the City of Chicago Municipal Tuberculosis Sanatorium.
Bio: "Deaths," in JAMA Network. See - https://jamanetwork.com/journals/jama/article-abstract/655349; "Dr. Emil Bunta," in: Find a Grave. See - https://www.findagrave.com/memorial/22432568/emil-bunta

Julius Carmen (orig. Alfonz Zhorský (1868-1936); b. Levoča, Slovakia; in US since around 1890; pseudo doctor, with a diploma in pharmacy; residing in Detroit, MI; author of a remarkable book - *Domáci lekár a radca* (Home physician and adviser) - of some 1200 pages, published around 1920, at a cost of $12 (some $150 in today's currency). Despite its cost, it was the second most read book, after Bible, by Slovak Americans.
Bio: Prof. Igor M. Tomo, "Július Carmen alias Alfonz Zhorský," in: Slovenské Slovo. See - https://slovenskeslovo.sk/slovenske-osobnosti/659-julius-carmen-alias-alfonz-zhorsky; Pavol, Vencel, *Zabudnutý génius Július Carmen alias Alfonz Zhorský národovec alebo špión?* Luferna, 2007.

Siegmund Dembitz (ca 1795-d.), b. Bratislava, Slovakia; physician; physician; in 1899, he immigrated to Cincinnati, OH, where he opened his medical practice.
Bio: "Siegmund Dembitz," in: Geni. See - https://www.geni.com/people/Dr-Sigmund-Dembitz/6000000009370051948

Louis Fischer (1864-1944), b. Košice, Slovakia; physician, pioneer pediatrician, specialist on diseases of children. He received his M.D. from New York University Medical College in 1884 and started the practice of general medicine at the age of 20. He was attending physician at Willard Parker, Sydenham and Riverside Hospital in NYC. He later became associated with the Heckscher Foundation for Children and was for many years a member of the medical advisory board of the NYC Department of Health.
Bio: *Who's Who in America*, 18; "Fischer, Louis," *American Jewish Year Book*, Vol. 6, p.91; "Obituaries: Louis Fischer, MD 1864-1944," *Am. J. Dis. Child*, 69, No. 5 (1945), p. 331ff,

Arnold Galambos (1884-1974), b. Komárno, Slovakia; physician, internist, New York, NY
Bio: "Galambos, Arnold, in: *Who's Important in Medicine*, 2

Joseph Alysius Gazda (1881-d.), b. Široká, Slovakia; physician and surgeon, Chicago
Bio: "Gazda, Joseph Alysius," in: Droba, p. 259.

Arpad G. C. Gerster (1848-1923), b. Košice, Slovakia; physician, surgeon
Bio: Gerster, Arpad G., *Recollections of a New York Surgeon*. New York: P. B.
Hoeber, 1917; Nelson, Clark W., "Gerster, Arpad Geyza Charles," in: *National
Biography*, Vol. 8, pp. 875-876.

Duro Guca (1876-d.), b. Petrovac, Yugoslavia; general practitioner, first
Slovak physician in Chicago (s. 1909), resided in Berwyn, IL
Bio: "Duro Guca," in: *History of Medicine and surgery and Physicians and Surgeons of
Chicago*. Chicago: Biographical Publishing Corporation, 1922, p. 551.

Sandor Horwitz (1867-d.), b. Michalovce, Slovakia; physician, practiced in
Peoria, IL (s. 1895), city physician, chief physician, Hospital for Contagious
Diseases (s. 1910)
Bio: "Sandor Horwitz," in: *Peoria and County, Illinois: A Record of Settlement*.
Chicago: S. J. Clarke Publishing Co., 1912, Vol.2, pp. 256-260; *Biographical
Encyclopedia of America*, 1940

Joseph Kornitzer (1824-1906), b. Nové Mesto and Váhom, Slovakia, of
Moravian parents, a noted physician; in US s. 1868. From 1873 to 1892 resided
in Topeka, KA and since then a practitioner of Socorro, NM. For twenty-six
years a specialist in tuberculosis.
Bio: "Joseph Kornitzer," in: *Encyclopedia*, Vol. 3, p.1896.

Joseph Darwin Nagel (1867-d.), b. Hlohovec, Slovakia; physician;
consulting physician, French Hospital, New York, NY and at St. Chrysostom's
Dispensary; visiting physician to Red Cross Hospital. Author of *Diseases of the
Mind and Nervous System*.
Bio: "Nagel, Joseph Darwin," in: *Who's Who in New York City and State*. 5th ed.
New York: W. F. Brainard, 1911., p.696.

Henry Roth (1872-d.), b. Smoľinské, Slovakia; physician, surgeon, NYC
Bio: *Who's who in American Jewry*. New York: Jewish Biographical Bureau, 1926,
Vol. 1., p. 523.

M. P. Sasko (1873-d.), b. Brezová, Slovakia; physician, Chicago
Bio: "Sasko, M. P.," in: *History of Medicine and Surgery and Physicians and Surgeons
of Chicago*. Chicago: Biographical Publishing Corporation, 1922, p. 792.

D. LAW

1. Attorneys

Sean Adams, b. Cornwall, Ont., Canada, of Slovak mother; lawyer, practicing in Cornwall, Canada, associated with the firm Adams, Sherwood, Swalny & Follow;
Bio: "Slovak-Canadian Lawyer Sean Adams Received a Diamond Jubilee Medal," *Kanadský Slovak*. See - https://www.kanadskyslovak.ca/index.php/short-news/313-slovak-canadian-lawyer-sean-adams-received-a-diamond-jubilee-medal

John A. Balko (1900-d.), b. Turčiansky Sv. Martin, Slovakia; lawyer, Chicago, treasurer of the Tatran Slovak Union
Bio: "Balko, John A.," in: Droba, p. 181.

George Ben (1925-1978), b. Czech.; lawyer, politician, Toronto, Canada
Bio: "Ben, George," in: *Naše Hlasy* p. 43; "George Ben," in: Wikipedia. See - https://en.wikipedia.org/wiki/George_Ben; "George Ben pulls Humber upset," *The Toronto Daily Star*. Toronto, October 17, 1967, p. 10.

Jeffrey R. Boffa (1960-), b. New York, NY, of Slovak descent; lawyer; associate at NY law firm of Wachtell, Lipton, Rosen & Katz
Bio: "Jeffrey R. Boffa," in: Prabook. See - https://prabook.com/web/jeffrey_r.boffa/3155239

Lewis Naphtali Dembitz (1833-1907), b. Zirke, Prussia, of Slovak father and Bohemian mother; lawyer, legal scholar, politician, Louisville, KY
Bio: Kleber, John E., "Dembitz, Lewis Naphtali," in: *The Kentucky Encyclopedia*. University Press of Kentucky; pp. 247–248; "Lewis Naphtali Dembitz," in: Wikipedia. See - https://en.wikipedia.org/wiki/Lewis_Naphtali_Dembitz

John Michael Dluhy (1903-1979), b. Chicago, IL, of Slovak descent; lawyer, attorney with Waldman & Waldman Law Firm, treasurer of the Southwest Lawyers Association, president of Club Furdek, Chicago
Bio: "Dluhy, John Michael," in: Droba, pp. 181; "John M. Dluhy, Sr.," in: Find A Grave. See -
https://www.findagrave.com/memorial/184186581/john-m.-dluhy;

John Gregory Duch (1960 -2017), b. of Slovak descent; lawyer, attorney, practicing in Elmwood Park and Rochelle Park, NJ; member of the Wyckoff Education Foundation, assistant lacrosse coach
Bio: "John Duch, Former Wyckoff Education Foundation, Lacrosse Coach, Died Sunday," in: *Wyckoff Patch*, October 11, 2017.

Duane A. Dudik (1949-2009), b. McKeesport, PA, of Slovak ancestry; attorney at Pleasant Hills; partner with the downtown firm of Scoratow and Dudik.
Bio: Vondas, Jerry, "Family came first for compassionate Pleasant Hills attorney," in: TRIB Live, September 17, 2009. See - https://triblive.com/x/pittsburghtrib/obituaries/news/s_643504.html

William T. Dzurilla (1953-), b. Carteret, NJ, a grandson of Slovak immigrants; attorney, with Boies, Schiller & Flexner law firm, Fort Lauderdale, FL
Bio: "William T. Dzurilla," in: Wikipedia. See - https://en.wikipedia.org/wiki/William_T._Dzurilla

Steven F. Fabry (1960-), b. Vienna, of Czech and Slovak parents; lawyer, general attorney, US Department of State, Washington, DC
Bio: "Fabry, Steven F." in: *SVU Directory* 8

George Edward Fedor (1909-1997), b. Slovakia; lawyer, practiced in Cleveland, OH; partner of the firm, Fedor & Fedor; law director, City of Lakewood (1956-58); director of Home Federal Savings Bank, Lakewood, OH
Bio: "Fedor, George Edward," in: *Who's Who in the Midwest*, 14; "George Edward Fedor," in; Prabook. See - https://prabook.com/web/george_edward.fedor/61159

Richard C. Folta (1935-), b. Juneau, AK, of Slovak descent; lawyer, attorney at law practicing in Haines, AK, author

Bohunka Ostrovska Goldstein, Slovak American; lawyer; admitted to NY Bar in 1997; she has own practice eunder her name, in New York, NY. She specializes in immigration law, with extensive experience in family-based petitions, including adoptions, business-based immigration matters, defense

in removal proceedings, citizenship applications, as well as non-immigrant visas and waivers.
Bio: "Attorney Profile." See - http://www.bohunkagoldstein.com/attorney-profile.html; "Bohunka Goldstein," in: LinkedIn. See - https://www.linkedin.com/in/bohunkagoldstein/; "Bohunka O. Goldstein," in: Avvo. See - https://www.avvo.com/attorneys/10279-ny-bohunka-goldstein-946222.html

John Walter Golosinec (1905-1994), b. Chicago, IL, of Slovak parents; attorney at law, Chicago, director of Security Federal Savings and Loan Association
Bio: "Golosinec, John Walter," in: Droba, p. 182; "John W. Golosinec," *Chicago Tribune*, January 25, 1994.

Blanka (Richter) Gyulai (1904-2004), b. Považská Bystrica, Slovakia; lawyer, practicing in Montreal, becoming Q.C. in 1974, member of the Order of Canada
Bio: "Gyulai, Blanka," in: *SVU Directory* 8; "Blanka (Richter) Gyulai Obituary," Montreal Gazette, December 11-13, 2004.

Vlado Hajtol (ca 1977-), b. Slovakia; in Canada s. 2001; lawyers, specializing in estate assistance, real-estate purchases or sales, or business law, with Allan Snelling LLP, Kanata North, Canada;
Bio: "Vlado Hajtol,": in: Allan Snelling LLP. See - https://compellingcounsel.com/slovak-lawyer-in-canada-slovensky-pravnik-v-kanade/

Emanuel Hertz (1870-1940), b. Rebreny, Slovakia; pioneer lawyer; historian, collector of Lincolniana
Bio: "Emanuel Hertz," in: Hertz, Emanuel Collection, 1921-1937, University of Illinois Library, Urbana-Champaigne; "Hertz, Emanuel," in: Jewish Virtual Library. See - http://jewishvirtuallibrary.org/hertz-emanuel.

Cyril Francis Hetsko (1911-1997), b. Scranton, PA, of Slovak descent; lawyer, corporation executive, practiced in NYC (s. 1938); general counsel, American Brands, Inc. (1964-77), senior vice president (1969-77).
Bio: "Hetsko, Cyril Francis," in: *Who's Who in Commerce and Industry*,13; "Cyril Francis Hetsko," in: Prabook. See - https://prabook.com/web/cyril_francis.hetsko/394666; Gilpin, Kenneth N.," Cyril F. Hetsko, 85, an Executive at American Tobacco Company," *The New York Times*, March 24, 1997.

Jeffrey F. Hetsko (1950-), b. Glen Ridge, NJ, of Slovak descent; lawyer, attorney with Sanders LLP, Atlanta, GA, specializing in commercial leasing and real estate.
Bio: "Jeffrey F. Hetsko," in: Prabook. See - https://prabook.com/web/jeffrey_f.hetsko/3063973

Emanuel Hertz (1870-1940), b. Rebrény, Slovakia; pioneer lawyer, historian, collector of Lincolniana
Bio: "Hertz, Emanuel," in: *Who's Who in America*, 18; Hertz, Emanuel. Collection, 1921-1937, University of Illinois at Urbana-Champaign, Library; "Hertz, Emanuel," in: Jewish Virtual Library. See - http://www.jewishvirtuallibrary.org/hertz-emanuel

David Hirshfield (1867-d.), b. Slovakia; attorney, jurist, magistrate of NYC
Bio: *Who's Who in American Jewry*. New York: Jewish Biographical Bureau, 1926, Vol.1, p.272.

John R. Hlavacka (1903-1990), b. Budapest, of Slovak descent; attorney-at-law, Chicago, president of the Slovak Lawyers Association, director of the Slovak Building and Loan Association
Bio: "Hlavacka, John R.," in: Droba, p.183.

Annmarie Barrie Honan (1959-2014), b. Kearny, NJ, of Slovak descent; lawyer, owned her own law practice, specializing in real estate law, Eufaula, AL; author of thirty-two books
Bio: "Annmarie Honan," *Fraternally Yours*, vol. 102, No. 2 (November 2015), p. 14.

Mark R. Hornak (1956-), b. Homestead, PA, of Slovak descent; lawyer. While in law school, he served as editor-in-chief of the *University of Pittsburgh Law Review* and was inducted into the Order of the Coif. He was an associate, then a partner at the Pittsburgh law firm Buchanan, Ingwersoll & Rooney, specializing in civil litigation, labor and employment law, media defense and governmental representation. For 15 years, he also was solicitor of the Sports & Exhibition Authority of Pittsburgh and Allegheny County. Recognized as "Best Lawyer in America," as one of the "Top 50 Lawyers" in Pittsburgh, and as Pittsburgh's 2012 Lawyer of the Year in labor law. From 1989 to 1993,

he served as an Adjunct Professor of Law at the University of Pittsburgh, teaching employment litigation.
Bio: "Mark R. Hornak," in: Wikipedia. See - https://en.wikipedia.org/wiki/ Mark_R._Hornak

Paul Frank Hrabko (1946-), b. Youngstown, OH, possibly of Slovak descent; lawyer, real estate executive
Bio: "Hrabko, Paul Frank," in: *Who's Who in Commerce and Industry,* 13.

Anna Janega (c. 1978-), of Slovak parents; lawyer. As provincial Vice-President of Canadian Manufacturers and Exporters, Ann Janega works with businesses, consumers, and non-governmental organizations to create and sustain economic prosperity for the community. Because of her commitment to helping businesses succeed, she was recognized as a Champion for Women in Business. Ann Janega is a former RCMP constable and the former Director of Public Affairs at Dalhousie University in Halifax.
Bio: "Ann Janega," in: LinkedIn. See - https://www.linkedin.com/in/ann-janega-3372661/?originalSubdomain=ca; "Citizenship Judge Ann Janega," in: Kanadský Slovak. See - https://www.kanadskyslovak.ca/index.php/ short-news/530-citizenship-judge-ann-jan

Kris J. Janovcik (ca 1966), Slovak Canadian; lawyer, attorney, partner at Tapper Cuddy LLP, focusing his practice ion child protection, civil litigation and commercial litigation.
Bio: "Kris J. Janovcik," in: Tapper Cuddy LLP. See - http://www.tappercuddy. com/lawyers/kris-j-janovcik.html

Peter P. Jurchak (Yurchak) (1900-1948), b. Anita, PA, of Slovak descent; attorney, who represented coal miners in Northeastern Pennsylvania.
Bio: "Peter P. Yurchak," in: Wikipedia. See - https://en.wikipedia.org/wiki/ Peter_P._Jurchak

Stephen Jurco (1913-1985), b. Vrbové, Slovakia; lawyer, practiced law in Chicago (1935-42, 1946-60), senior partner of the law firm, Querrey Harrow Gulanick & Kennedy Ltd., with offices in Wheaton, Arlington Heights and

Waukegan, village attorney (1955-62), one of the founders of the Bank & Trust Co. of Arlington, president of NCICA (s. 1974)
Bio: "Jurco, Stephen," in: *Who's Who in Law*, 2; "Stephen Jurco, 71, Attorney and Arlington Heights Official," *Chicago Tribune*, February 5, 1985.

Andrew Katz (1939-), b. Košice, Czech.; lawyer,

Edward L. Kerpec (1910-1973), of Slovak descent; attorney; general counsel of FCSU
Bio: Oak Park Oak Leaves Archives, June 20, 1973, p. 61

Louis Andor Komjathy (1898-d.), b. Kozelnik, Slovakia; lawyer, in private practice in Detroit MI

Andrew Kozacik (1906-1993), of Slovak parents; attorney, Whiting, IN
Bio: "Andrew M. Kozacik," in: Find A Grave. See - https://www.findagrave.com/memorial/160915767/andrew-m.-kozacik

John Louis Krajsa, Jr. (1946-2012), b. of Slovak descent; lawyer, with additional training in taxation; ; president of AFC Reverse Mortgage which he founded in 2004. Before that he and his brother owned and operated AFC First Financial Corporation. He served as an attorney for the USDA in Washington, DC, where he helped create the rural industrial loan program. He was a Captain in the US Marine Corps during the Vietnam War.
Bio: "John Krajsa,", The morning Call, November 15, 2012.

George J. Kubes (fl. 2018), Slovak Canadian; lawyer; practices in Toronto and has his own law firm, specializing in divorce and family law, Canadian immigration law; solicitor of the Supreme Court of Ontario.
Bio: "George J. Kubes. Toronto Lawyer, Barrister, Solicitor & Notary." See - https://www.torontodivorcelawyernotary.com/profile

Jacob Julius Lieberman (1887-d.), b. Slovakia; lawyer; member of firm, Goldman & Lieberman (1926-33), Benjamin. Lieberman & Elmore; (s. 1933); assistant City and County attorney, Denver (1914-21); special counsel, City and County of Denver, (1921-23).
Bio: "Lieberman, Jacob Julius," in: *Who's Who in Law*, Vol. 1, p. 555.

William Liebermann (1872-d.), b. Plešany, Slovakia; lawyer, Brooklyn, NY

Bio: "Liebermann, William," in: *Who's Who in American Jewry.* New York: Jewish Biographical Bureau, 1926, Vol. 1, p. 389.

Theodore Macejko, Jr. (1938-2011), b. Youngstown, OH, of Slovak descent; lawyer. He practiced in Struthers and Youngstown, OH, with his father, in Macejko & Macejko law firm, specializing in the field of general civil trial practice in all courts, insurance products liability, medical legal, corporate, real estate, municipal and probate law, family aw, criminal law, insurance subrogation and litigation. He served as assistant Mahoning County prosecutor (1972-76, 1984-88). He was president of the Mahoning County Bar Association and served also as a visiting Judge in the Struthers courts on various occasions.

Bio: "Atty. Theodore T. Macejko Jr.," in: The Vindicator, August 5, 2018; "Theodore Macejko," in: Prabook. See - https://prabook.com/web/theodore. macejko/1260150

Cynthia M. Maleski (1951-), b. Natrona Heights, PA, of Slovak descent; attorney, president of First Catholic Slovak Ladies Association (FCSLA); named 2013 Fraternalist of the Year by the Fraternal Societies of Greater Pittsburgh, https://triblive.com/news/allegheny/3691721-74/maleski-fraternal-insurance

Steven Olenick, b. of Slovak descent; lawyer, leading sports attorney, partner in the NY firm, Loeb & Loeb, LLP

Bio: "Steven M. Olenick," in: Loeb & Loeb LLP. See - https://www.loeb. com/attorney-stevenmolenick

Kenneth M. Olex (1935-), b. New Jersey, of Slovak descent; deputy attorney general, NJ; head of law division of NJ, Dept. of Law and Public Safety.

Samuel Papanek, Jr. (1905-d.), b. Chicago, IL, of Slovak parents; lawyer, Assistant State Attorney of the State of Illinois

Bio: "Papanek, Samuel, Jr.," in: Droba, p. 292.

John E. Pavlik (1898-1985), b. Slovakia; attorney-at-law, Chicago, specializing in chancery and municipal law; village attorney for Lansing (1928-30) and city attorney for Calumet City (1934-45).
Bio: "Pavlik, John E.," in: Droba, pp. 182-183; "Pavlik, 87, judge for 30 Years," *Chicago Tribune*, October 8, 1985.

Richard Pikna, lawyer, partner in the firm Pikna, Rayner & Bartkiw, Hamilton, Ont., Canada
Bio: "Pikna, Richard," in: Naše Hlasy, p. 45

Paull Martin Poliak (1920-2015), b. Monaca, PA, of Slovak parents; maritime lawyer, founding partner of Madden, Poliak, McDougall and Williamson, in Seattle, WA
Bio: "Paul Martin Poliak," in: The Co-op Funeral Home of People's Memorial. See - https://funerals.coop/obituaries/2015-obituaries/september-2015/paul-poliak.html

Andrew Charles Putka (1926-2015); b. Cleveland, OH, of Slovak descent; lawyer, banker, chief Executive Officer, American National Bank, Parma, OH, 1963-1969; director finance, City of Cleveland, 1971-1974; director port control, 1974-1978; director, Cleveland Hopkins International Airport, 1974-1978, Oho State legislator
Bio: "Putka, Andrew Charles," in: *Who's Who in the Midwest*, 13; "Andrew Charles Putka" in: Prabook. See - https://prabook.com/web/andrew_charles.putka/334518

Alan Rudolph Rado (1906-), b. Trenčín, Slovakia; lawyer, practicing attorney, New York, NY (1946-1950), legal adviser to US Department of Commerce (1951-1953); adj professor of law, New York University School of Law (s. 1962).

Michael S. Rehak (1867-1935), b. Czech.; lawyer, vice president of the Slovak Lawyers' Association
Bio: "Michael Rehak," in: My Heritage Family Trees. See - https://www.myheritage.com/names/michael_rehak

Edgar R. Rombauer (1868-1930), b. Belleville, IL, of Slovak descent; lawyer, practicing in St. Louis, as a partner in the firm Rombauer & Rombauer (s.1892).
Bio: "Edgar R. Rombauer," in: *Centennial History of Missouri.* St. Louis - Chicago: The S. J. Clarke Publishing Co., 1921, Vol. 3, pp. 587-588; "Edgar R. Rombauer," in: Find A Grave. See - https://www.findagrave.com/ memorial/83500298/edgar-r.-rombauer

John J. Rusinak, Slovak American; attorney, Detroit, MI; served as prosecuting attorney of Wayne County for 27 years, first Slovak attorney appointed to that public office

E. Randol Schoenberg (1966-), b. Brentwood, Los Angeles, CA, of Slovak and Czech descent; US attorney and genealogist. He specializes in legal cases related to the recovery of looted or stolen artworks, particularly those by the Nazi regime during the Holocaust. Schoenberg is widely known as one of the central figures of the 2015 film Woman in Gold, which depicted the case of Maria Altmann against the government of Austria. Schoenberg is portrayed by Ryan
Bio: "E. Randol Schoenberg," in: Wikipedia. See - https://en.wikipedia.org/ wiki/E._Randol_Schoenberg

Emanuel Schwartz (1890-d.), b. Belina, Slovakia; lawyer; attorney, practicing in New York, NY (s. 1916).
Bio: "Schwartz, Emanuel," in: *Who's Who in Law,* Vol. 1, p. 833.

Suanne M. Sirotnak (1968-), of Slovak descent; lawyer, Senior Counsel West for the Alcohol and Tobacco Tax and Trade Bureau, within the US Treasury Department, San Francisco, CA
Bio: "Law Career Takes Alumna West to Wine Country," in: Journal Summer 10 + Covers.indd. See - https://www.scranton.edu/alumni/pdf/ CALProfilePDF/Sirotnak.pdf

Paul George Skalny (1967-), b. Bratislava, Czech.; lawyer, managing director of Davis, Agnor, Rapaport & Skalny, LLC, Columbia, MD
Bio: "Skalny, Peter George," in: *SVU Directory* 8, "Paul G. Skalny," in: Davis/ Agnor/ Rapaport/ skalny Attorneys at Law. See - https://www.darslaw.com/ paul-skalny

Julius Solar (1909-1985), b. Opatová, Slovakia; lawyer, Dept. of Justice, San Mateo, CA
Bio: "Solar, Julius," in: *SVU Directory* 5, "Solar, Julius," in: Pejskar 3, p.202

Joseph Steller (1897-d.), b. Dolná Lehota, Slovakia; attorney-at-law, Chicago
Bio: "Steller, Joseph," in: Droba, p. 184; "Steller, Joseph," in: *Catholic Who's Who,* 1947, Vol. 7, 5. 417.

John W. V. Stephens, b. Czech., of Slovak descent; lawyer, member of the firm McMillan, Binch, Stuarrt, Berry, Dunn, Corrigan & Howland, Toronto, Canada
Bio: "Stephens, John W. V." in: *Naše Hlasy,* p. 7

Max David Steuer (1870-1940), b. Humenné, Slovakia; in US s. 1876; trial lawyer
Bio: "Max David Steuer," *Who Was Who in America* 4; "Max Steuer," in: Wikipedia. See - https://en.wikipedia.org/wiki/Max_Steuer

Michael S. Striker (1905-1975), b. Budapest, of Slovak father; in New York s. 1938; trained as mechanical engineer, economist and a lawyer; leading patent attorney, NYC
Bio: "Michael S. Striker, 69, Dies; International Patent Lawyer," *The New York Times,* September 6, 1975

Joseph J. Talafous (1929-2008), b. New York, NY, of Slovak parents; attorney, Talafous & Talafous, Jersey City, NJ (s. 1959); assistant prosecutor, Hudson County, NJ (1962-63); City of Jersey City (1965-72); Judge, Municipal Court, Jersey City (1974-77); commissioner, NJ Governor's Commission International Trade
Bio: "Joseph John Talafous, Sr.," in: Prabook. See - https://prabook.com/web/joseph_john_talafous_.sr./911801

Joseph G. Tomascik (1914-1970), b. Wilkes-Barre, PA, of Slovak descent, lawyer; attorney, United States Department of Agriculture and Civil Aeronautics Administration; public opinion analyst and translator, United States Library of Congress; Special Deputy Attorney General of the Commonwealth of Pennsylvania; Assistant Professor, government,

King's College (1948-1952); Assistant District Attorney, Luzerne County; PA legislator
Bio: "Joseph G. Tomascik," in: PA House of Representatives. See - https://vasj. com/news/former-euclid-mayor-bill-cervenik-72-named-president-of-vasj

Michael Jacob Tremko (1892-d.), b. Taylor, PA; attorney-at-law, Chicago
Bio: "Tremko, Michael Jacob," in: Droba, p. 185

Martin Valko (ca 1975-), b. Levoča, Czech.; immigration lawyer, managing partner, Chavez & Valko LLP, Dallas, TX; Hon. Consul of the Slovak Republic to Texas
Bio: "Martin Valko," in: Chavez & Valko, LLP. See - https://www.keyvisa. com/Attorneys/Martin-Valko.shtml

Matus Varga, b. Slovakia; lawyer; founder and managing member of the Varga Immigration Attorneys PLLC, in Bonita Springs, FL; has practiced s. 2012; adjunct professor at Florida State University College of Law, teaching immigration enforcement and procedures.
Bio: "Matus Varga, Esquire." See - https://www.vargasimmigration.com/ attorneys

Stephen Vasak (1946-), b. Čaklov, Czech.; lawyer, practicing attorney at Hackensack, NJ (s. 1973); adjunct professor of taxation at Farleigh Dickinson University; legal aide to NJ Senate minority leader (s. 1978)
Bio: "Vasak, Stephen," *Who's Who in Law*, 2; "Steve Vasak," in: northjersey. com.See - https://www.legacy.com/obituaries/northjersey/obituary.aspx?n= stevevasak& pid=165752443&fhid=17130

Ryan Peter Vlcko (1982-), b. Florida, of Slovak descent; lawyer, specializing in health law, and administrative law, and real state contract, serving Grand Blanc, MI and Swartz Creek, MI
Bio: "Vlcko, Ryan Peter," in: *SVU Directory*, 9; "Ryan Peter Vlcko," in: Lawyers.com. see - https://www.lawyers.com/grand-blanc/michigan/ ryan-peter-vlcko-168512060-a/

John A. Willo (1890-d.), b. Youngstown, OH, of Slovak descent; lawyer, Youngstown, OH, president of Fraternal Society Law Association, president, Ohio Fraternal Cong., general counsel of National Slovak Soc. of U.S.
Bio: "Willo, John A.," in: *Catholic Who's Who*, 1961, Vol. 14, p. 479.

Andrew Nathaniel Witko (1896-d.), b. Plavnica, Slovakia; attorney-at-law, Chicago
Bio: "Witko, Andrew Nathaniel," in: Droba, pp. 186-187.

Luba D. Yamoah (ca 1983-), b. Bratislava, Slovakia; lawyer; she practices in Cambridge, Ont., Canada and is associated with the firm Pavey Law LLP. Her practice focuses almost exclusively on family law and she also assists the firm's clients in the areas of wills and residential real estate. Prior to joining the firm in 2010, she practiced extensively in the area of family law at full service law firm in Kitchener.
Bio: "Luba D. Yamoah," in PAVEY Law LLP. See - https://www.paveylaw.com/our-people/luba-d-yamoah/

Donald A. Zamborsky (1947-), b. Allentown, PA, of Slovak descent; attorney, specializing in estate planning, probate and adoption
Bio: "Donald Zamborsky," in: MyLife.com. See - https://www.mylife.com/don-zamborsky/donzamborsky

Edward J. Zamborsky (1941-2017), b. Allentown, PA, of Slovak descent; lawyer, attorney practicing in Allentown, PA, specializing in matrimonial law
Bio: "Edward J. Zamborsky, Esquire," *The Morning Call*, October 21, 2017.

Edward Michael Zelenak (1953-), b. Dearborn, MI, of Slovak descent; lawyer, city attorney for municipalities of Lincoln Park and Southgate, MI; president of Wayne State University Law School's Alumni Association
Bio: "Zelenak, Edward Michael," in: *Who's Who in Politics*, 4; "Edward M. Zelenak," in: Wayne Law. See - https://law.wayne.edu/international/zelenak

Stephen C. Zidek (1901-d.), b. Chicago, IL, of Slovak parents; attorney-at-law, Chicago
Bio: "Zidek, Stephen C," in: Droba, p. 187

Ludka Zimovcak (ca 1978-), b. Slovakia; lawyer; one of the managing attorneys of the Nachman Phulwani Zimovcak Law Group, P.C., Ridgewood, NJ, specializing in business and family immigration and nationality law. Bi: "Ludka Zimovcak Esq.," See - https://visaserve.com/lawyer/Ludka-Zimovcak-Esq._cp14190.htm

Steven E. Zlatos (ca. 1951-), Slovak American; lawyer; he is an experience trial layer in both state and federal courts. He has been a member of the law firm, Woodard, Emhardt, Moriarty, McNett & Henry, LLP (s. 1981). Prior to joining the Firm in 1981, he served as Deputy Attorney General for the State of Indiana from 1977 to 1981 and was the chief attorney in the Environmental Section. Bio: "Steven E. Zlatos. See - http://www.uspatent.com/professionals/? show=9&pdf=download

E. WOMEN - FEMINISM

1. General

Alzo, Lisa A., *Three Slovak Women*, Baltimore: Gateway Press, 2001.
Alzo, Lisa A., Silent Voices: Identifying the Historical Significance of Slovak Immigrant Women," Selected Papers from the 2003 SVU North American Conference, Cedar Rapids, Iowa, 26-28 June 2003. See - https://svu2000. org/conferences/2003_Iowa/09.pdf
Bolchazy, Janine M., *The Status of Slovak American Women in Pennsylvania: 1875-1914*. Cleveland, OH: First Catholic Union, 1984. 30 p.
Dobrotková, Marta, A Slovak Woman and America. Destinies of Slovak Women in the U.S. between 1891 to 1939. Spolok Slovákov v Poľsku, 2011. 152p.
Horna, Jarmila L.A. "The Entrance Status of Czech and Slovak Immigrant Women," in: Two Nations, Many Cultures: Ethnic Groups in Canada, ed. Jean Leonard Elliott. Scarborough: Prentice-Hall Ltd., 1979, pp. 270-279.
Jason, Sonya. *Icon of Spring*. University of Pittsburgh Press, 1993.
"Slovak female pilot masters the American skies!" in: GANDER. See - https:// gander.sk/en/pribehy/slovak-female-pilot-masters-the-american-skies

Tehie, Janice. A Trans-Generational Study of Education and Employment among Slovak Women on the 'Mountain Top', 1900-1995. Ph.D. Dissertation, Pennsylvania State University, 1996.

Thurova, Jana, Through One Immigrant's Eyes: Autoethnography of a Slovak Woman Living in North America. M.A. Thesis, Athabasca University, Athabasca, Alberta, Canada, 2009.

2. Indiviaduals

Anna Hurban (1855-1828), Gbely, Slovakia; formed the First Catholic Slovak Ladies Association (FCSLA) in 1892 with 8 other women.
Bio: James M O'Toole, The Faithful, https://books.google.com/books?isbn=0674033825 ; https://case.edu/ech/articles/f/first-catholic-slovak-ladies-assn

F. KINSHIP AND COOPERATION

Alexander, June Granatir, *Ethnic Pride, American Patriotism: Slovaks and Other New Immigrants in the Interwar Era*. Philadelphia, PA: Temple University Press, 2004. 278p.

Bell, Thomas, *Out of This Furnace*. Pittsburgh: University of Pittsburgh Press, 1976 (originally published 1941), pp. 327-330.

Bodnar, John, "Ethnic Fraternal Benefit Associations: Their Historical Development, Character, and Significance," in: *Records of Ethnic Fraternal Benefit associations in the United States: Essays and Inventories*. Edited by Susan H. Shreve and Rudolph J. Vecoli. St. Paul: Immigration History Research Center, University of Minnesota, 1981, pp. 5–14.

Cude, Michael Robert. Transatlantic Perspectives of the Slovak Question, 1914-1918. Ph.D. Thesis, University of Colorado, Boulder, CO, 2012.

Custer, Richard D., "Old Countrymen, New Neighbors: Early Carpatho-Rusyn and Slovak Immigrant Relations in the United States," *Slovo*, November 25, 2016. See - https://www.ncsml.org/wp-content/uploads/2015/01/Old-Countrymen-New-Neighbors.pdf

Dvorchak, Robert, "Slovak Reconnect with their Heritage," *Pittsburgh Post-Gazette*, May 20-2001.

Ference, Gregory C., *Sixteen Months of Indecision: Slovak American Viewpoints toward Compatriots and the Homeland from 1914 to 1915 as Viewed by the Slovak Language Press.*
Selinsgrove, PA: Susquehanna University.
Gosiorovský, Miloš, "Contribution to the History of the Slovak Workers' Society in the United States of America," *Historica, Sborník Filozofickej Fakulty Univerzity Komenského*, XII-XII (1961-1962), pp. 11-12.
Pichlík, Karel, "Relationships between Czechs and Slovaks in the United States during the First World War," *Nebraska History* 74 (1993), pp. 189-194
Stein, Howard F., "Structural Change in Slovak Kinship: An Ethnohistoric Inquiry," *Ethnology*, 14, No. 1 (January 1975), pp. 99-108.
Terenzani, Michaela, "Report Assesses Slovaks 'Attitudes to Foreigners," *The Slovak Spectator,* July 16, 2022. See - https://spectator.sme.sk/c/20044024/report-assesses-slovaks-attitudes-to-foreigners.html
Zecker, Robert Michael, 'All our Own Kind here': The Creation of a Slovak -American Community in Philadelphia, 1890--1945, pp. 344-345, 370-371.
Zecker, Robert M., "Negrov Lyncovanie" and the Unbearable Whiteness of Slovaks: The Immigrant Press Covers Race," American Studies, 43:2 (Summer 2002), pp.43-72.
Zecker, Robert, "Where Everyone Goes to Meet Everyone Else: The Translocal Creation of a Slovak Immigrant Community," *Journal of Social History*, 38, No. 2 (December 2004), pp. 423-453.

G. LABOR MOVEMENT

1. General

Beik, Mildred, *The Miners of Windber: The Struggles of New Immigrants for Unionization, 1890s-1930s.* University Park, PA: Penn State University Press, 2006. 480p.
Beik, Mildred,"The Significance of the Lattimer Massacre: Who Owns Its History?" *Pennsylvania History*, Vol. 69, No. 1 (January 2002), pp. 58–70.
Gosiorovský, Miloš, "Contribution to the History of the Slovak Workers' Society in the United States of America," *Historica, Sborník Filozofickej Fakulty Univerzity Komenského*, XI-XII (1961-1962), pp. 11-12.

Stolarik, M. Mark, "Slovak Immigration to the United States and Its Relation to the American Socialist and Labor Movement," *Slovakia* 33, No. 60-61 (1987-88), pp. 47-62.
Stolarik, M. Mark, Slovak-Americans in the Great Steel Strike," *Pennsylvania History* 64, No. 3 (Summer 1997), pp. 407-418.
Stolarik, M. Mark, A Slovak Perspective on the Lattimer Massacre," *Pennsylvania History*, 69, No.1 No. 1 (January 2002), pp. pp. 31-41.

2. Individuals

John T. Kmetz (1893-1968), b. Lepuhov, Slovakia; labor union official, with United Mine Workers of America (s. 1901), president, Dist. 50, UMWA, Washington, DC; Intl. Bd. Mem. Dist 1, UMWA
Bio: "Kmetz, John T.," in: *Who's Who in Labor.* New York: The Dryden Press, 1946, p. 193.

Joseph W. Knapik (1908-d.), b. Johnsonburg, Pa, of Slovak descent; labor union official, with Textile Workers Union of America, Federation of Dyers, Finishers, Printers and Bleachers of America (CIO); president, Dyers' dept., TWUA, Peterson, NJ
Bio: "Knopik, Joseph W.," in: *Who's Who in Labor.* New York: The Dryden Press, 1946, p. 193.

Michael Joseph Kosik (1898-d.), b. Dupont, PA; labor union official, with United Mines Workers of America (AFL) (s. 1913); president, district One, Scranton, PA.
Bio: Kosik, Michael Joseph," in: *Who's Who in Labor.* New York: The Dryden Press, 1946, p.196.

Mike Petrak (1892-d.), b. Carlton, MI, of Slovak descent; labor union official, with United Steelworkers of America (CIO) (s. 1936), Local 1196; assistant director, District 19, Tarentum, PA
Bio: "Petrak, Mike," in: *Who's Who in Labor.* New York: The Dryden Press, 1946, p. 278.

Jacob M. Rosenblatt (1890-d.), b. possibly in Slovakia; labor union official, with Employees International Union (AFL) (s. 1911), Local 23076; Office Sec., Local 9 ILGWU (s. 1918), New Yok, NY
Bio: "Rosenblatt, Jacob M.," in: *Who's Who in Labor.* New York: The Dryden Press, 1946, p. 306.

Joseph Stephen Sadecky, Jr. (1907-d.), b. Tarentum, PA, of Slovak descent; labor union official; with Federation of Glass, Ceramic & Silica Sand Workers of America (CIO) (s. 1935); Local 12; Wage Committeeman and Rec. Sec., Tarentum Indl. U. Council, Tarentum, PA; member of Bd. Indl. Development Council
Bio: "Sadecky. Joseph Stephen, Jr.," in: *Who's Who in Labor.* New York: The Dryden Press, 1946, p. 310.

Frank Sitek (1912-d), b. Detroit, Mi, possibly of Slovak descent; labor union official, with United Packinghouse Workers of America (CIO) (s. 1938), Dist. Dir., UPWA-CIO, District 7, Detroit, MI.
Bio: "Sitek, Frank," in: *Who's Who in Labor.* New York: The Dryden Press, 1946, p. 329.

Richard J. Spisiak (1912-d.), b. Buffalo, NY, of Slovak descent; labor union official, with United Automobile, Aircraft and Agricultural Implement Workers of America (CIO) (s. 1937; Rec. Sec., Local 42 Buffalo, NY; vice president, NY State Indl. U. Council.
Bio: "Spisiak, Richard J.," in: *Who's Who in Labor.* New York: The Dryden Press, 1946, p. 337.

Norman Harold Weigel (1908-d.) b. Cogan House, PA, of Slovak descent; labor union official, with United Electrical, Radio and Machine Workers of America (CIO) (s. 1937), Local 506; Fin. Sec., Erie Indl. U. Council, Erie, PA; business manager, The Peoples Press
Bio: "Weigel, Norman Harold," in: *Who's Who in Labor.* New York: The Dryden Press, 1946, p. 370.

Paul Zazrivy, Jr. (1910-d), b. Slovakia; labor union official, with United Gas, Coke and Chemical Workers of America (CIO) (s. 1940), Local 148;

Intl. Rep., UGCCWA CIO, Cleveland, OH; president, Greater Cleveland District Indl. U. Council
Bio: "Zazrivy, Paul, Jr.," in: *Who's Who in Labor.* New York: The Dryden Press, 1946, p. 388.

H. URBANIZATION

Alexander, June Granatir, "Diversity within Unity: Regionalism and Social Relations among Slovaks in Pre-War I Pittsburgh," *Western Pennsylvania Historical Magazine* 70 (October 1987). pp. 317-38.
Barton, Joseph, *Peasants and Strangers: Italians, Rumanians, and Slovaks in an American City, 1890-1950* (Harvard Studies in Urban History). Cambridge, MA: Harvard University Press, 1975. 240p.
Stolarik, M. Mark. *Immigration and Urbanization: The Slovak Experience, 1870-1918.* New York: AMS Press, c1989. 290p.

I. LEADERSHIP

"Leadership," in: Miller, pp. 86-89.
McClure, Archibald, "The Slovaks," in: *Leadership of the New America Racial and Religious.* New York: George H. Doran Company, 1916, pp. 110-118.

J. CHARACTER - ATTITUDE - BEHAVIOR

Bell, Thomas, *Out of This Furnace.* Pittsburgh: University of Pittsburgh Press, 1976, (originally published 1941), pp. 327-330.
"Moral Standards," in: Miller, pp. 70-71.
Goska, Danusha V., 'No Opportunity for Song': A Slovak Immiogrant's Silencing Analyzed through her Pronoun Choice. See - https://scholarscompass.vcu.edu/cgi/viewcontent.cgi?referer=https://www.google.com/&httpsredir=1&article=1249&context=esr
Hudson, Brian. The Development of Slovak Nationalism in the United States, 1880-1914. MA Thesis, Western Washington University, 1999.
Laurence, Patricia Ondek," The Garden in the Mill: The Slovak Immigrant's View of Work," *Melus,* 10, No. 2 (Summer, 1983), pp. 57-68.

Stein, Howard F., "Envy and the Evil Eye among Slovak-Americans: An Essay in the Psychological Ontogeny of Belief and Ritual," *Ethos*, 2 (1974), pp. 15-46.

Stein, Howard F., An *Ethno-Historic Study of Slovak American Identity*. Salem, NH: Ayer Co. Publishers, 1981.

Terenzani, Michaela, "Report Assesses Slovaks 'Attitudes to Foreigners," *The Slovak Spectator*, July 16, 2022. See - https://spectator.sme.sk/c/20044024/report-assesses-slovaks-attitudes-to-foreigners.html

Zecker, Robert M., "'Negrov Lyncovanie' and the Unbearable Whiteness of Slovaks: The Immigrant Press Covers Race," *American Studies*, 43, No. 2 (Summer 2002), pp. 43-72.

Zecker, Robert M., *Race and America's Immigrant Press. How the Slovaks Were Taught to Think Like White People*. New York: Continuum, 2011.

K. IMAGE

Bicha, Karel D., "Hunkies: Stereotyping the Slavic Immigrants, 1890-1920," *Journal of American Ethnic History*, Vol. 2, No. 1 (Fall, 1982), pp. 16-38

Geiger, Taylor, Six Stereotypes about Slovaks that Simply aren't True," in: culture trip. See - https://theculturetrip.com/europe/slovakia/articles/6-stereotypes-about-slovaks-that-simply-arent-true/

Graf, Sylvie, "Accuracy of Slovak National Stereotypes: Result of Judgment or Intuition?" *Studia psychologica*, Vol. 53, No. 2 (2011), pp. 201-213.

Karas, Nicholas Stevensson, *Hunky: The Immigrant Experience*. Bloomington, IN: AuthorHouse, 2004. 580p.

Roucek, Joseph S., "The American Czechs, Slovaks, and Slavs in the Development of America's "Climate of Opinion," in: *Czechoslovakia Past and Present*. Edited by Miloslav Rechcigl, Jr. The Hague-Paris, 1968, Vol. 1, pp. 815-843.

Roucek, J. S., "The Image of the Slav in U.S. History and Immigration Policy,"*American Journal of Economics and Sociology*, Vol. 28, No. 1 (1969), pp. 29-48.

Stevo, Allan, "Honkey, Honkey, Honkie," in: Honkey - 52 Weeks in Slovakia. See - http://www.52insk.com/2016/honkey/

Wtulich, Josephine, *American Xenophobia and the Slav Immigrant: A Living Legacy of Mind and Spirit*. Boulder, IN: East European Monographs, 1994. 214p.

VIII. Economy

A. GENERAL

Andic, V.E. "Trends in Czech and Slovak Economic Enterprise in the New World," in: *The Czechoslovak Contribution to World Culture*. B Edited by Miloslav Rechcigl, Jr. The Hague: Mouton & Co., 1964, pp. 523-527.
"Economic Conditions," in: Miller, pp. 55-64.
Krause, Paul, *The Battle for Homestead, 1880-1992: Politics, Culture, and Steel*. Pittsburgh: University of Pittsburgh Press, 1992

B. LIVING CONDITIONS

Krause, Paul, "Labor Republicanism and 'Za Chlebom': Anglo-Americans and Slavic Solidarity in Homestead," in: *Struggle a Hard Battle:Essays on Working-Class Immigrants*. By Dirk Hoerder. DeKalb, IL, 1986.
Stolarik, M. Mark, Slovak Immigration to the United States and its Relation to the American Socialist and Labor Movements," *Migracijske teme*, 4, no. 1-2 (1988), pp. 145-155.
Whaples, Robert, "The Standard of Living among Polish-and Slovak-Americans: Evidence from Fraternal Insurance Records 1880–1970," *The Biological Standard of Living on Three Continents*. Edited by John Komlos, Westview Press, 1995

C. OCCUPATIONS

Bodnar, John, *Immigration and Industrialization: Ethnicity in an American Milltown*. Pittsburgh: University of Pittsburgh Press, 1977.
"Occupations," in: Miller, pp. 55-64.
Zecker, Robert M. "They Roamed All over Fixing Things: The Migratory Tinkers of Slovakia," *Journal of American Ethnic History*, Vol. 35, No. 1, Fall 2015, pp. 38-70.

D. MERCHANTS AND OTHER BUSINESSMEN

Lillian M. Baar (1916-1988); b. Chicago, of Czech and some Slovak ancestry; a pioneer woman realtor in the western suburbs of Chicago, co-owner of Baar and Baar Realtors, Berwyn, IL
Bio: "Baar, Lilian Mary," in: *Who's Who in the Midwest*, 14; "Baar, Lillian Mary," in: Who's Who in Finance and Industry, 21; "Realtor Lillian M. Baar, 72," *Chicago Tribune*, April 27, 1988.

Steven A. Bachleba (1931-), b. Slovakia; businessman, co-owner of Typographic Art, Hamden, CT
Bio: "North Haven vet, 83, pens book on his family's immigration story," *New Haven Register,* November 9, 2014.

Method M. Balco (1818-2013), b. Newark, NJ, of Slovak descent; owner and president of Balco Catholic Supply of Verona, North Caldwell, NJ
Bio: "Method M. Balco," *The Star Ledger,* February 8, 2013

Peter Baycura (1923-1996), b. Visny Cabiny, Czech.; Peter Baycura & Assoc., advt. agency, Butler, PA (s. 1948)
Bio: "Baycura, Peter," in: *Who's Who in the East*, 12; "Baycura, Peter," in: *Who's Who in Commerce and Industry*, Vol. 14, p.1480.

Ivan Bielek (1886-1942), b. Dohňany, Slovakia; in US s. 1906; vice-president and director of the Czecho-Slovak Commercial Corp. of America, an import company founded in 1918; editor, *Národné noviny;* president, Slovak League of America (1920-1923); signatory of Pittsburgh Agreement.
Bio: "Ivan Bielek" in: Wikipedia. See - https://sk.wikipedia.org/wiki/Ivan_Bielek; "Ivan Bielek," in: History of Pittsburgh and Environs. New York and Chicago: The American Historical Society, 1922, pp. 331-332.

Milan Čarnogurský (1935-2007), b. Slovakia; builder of highways and airports in northern Canada
Bio: "Carnogursky, Milan," *The Vancouver Sun,* June 26, 2007.

Joseph Chaban (1892-d.), b. Priechod, Slovakia; restaurant owner, Chicago
Bio: "Chaban, Joseph," in: Droba, p. 72.

Joseph Chilla (1881-1958), b. Pusté Pole, Slovakia; dealer in real estate and insurance, Chicago, IL. Founder and secretary of the Liberty Savings and Loan Association and a founder and secretary of the Slovak House Association.
Bio: Chilla, Joseph," in: Droba, p. 73.

Joseph Domko (1874-d.), b. Mošovce, Slovakia; wholesale grocer, Chicago
Bio: "Domko, Joseph," in: Droba, p. 74

Stefan Facuna (1881-d.), b. Rakovo, Slovakia; shoe merchant, Chicago
Bio: "Facuna, Stefan," in: Droba, p. 73.

Anna Suzana Feriencik (1881-1972), b. Mošovce, Slovakia; organizer and president of Czecho-Slovak arts studios in the principal cities of the US, residing in Chicago
Bio: "Feriencik, Anna Suzana," in: Droba, p. 76.

Miroslav Fillo (1905-1986), b. Košice, Slovakia; business executive, founder and co-owner of House Lumber Ltd. and Alpa Industries Inc., Toronto, Canada
Bio: "Fillo, Miroslav," in: Pejskar 3, p. 53

István Kálmán Foyta (1895-1978), b. Trenčín, Slovakia; business executive

Vladimír Paul Gavora (1931-2018), b. Brezová pod Bradlom; economist by training; owner of shopping centers, beverage stores and other businesses in Alaska, Canada
Bio: "V. Paul Gavora," *Daily News-Miner,* May 27, 2018.

Julius Glaser (1862-1941), b. Mýto pod Ďumbierom, Slovakia; commissions dry goods merchant, St. Louis, MO, director, Boatmen's National Bank
Bio: "Glaser, Julius," in: *Who's Who in American Jewry,* Vol. 1, p. 197; "Julius Glaser," in: *The Book of Missourians.* Ed. By M. L. Van Nada. Chicago-St. Louis: T.J. Steele & Co., 1906, p. 204.

Ján Gömöry (1909-1982), b. Dobšiná, Slovakia; businessman, Toronto, then in Montreal, Canada
Bio: "Ján Gömöry," in: Pejskar 2, p. 216.

John D. Hertz (1879-1861), b. Sklabiňa, Slovakia; founder of Yellow Cab Co., first reliable taxi service in US; founder of the famous Hertz Corporation, for renting automobiles with branches all over the world
Bio: "Hertz, John Daniel," in: *Who's Who in America*, 18; "Hertz, John D." *Who's Who in American Jewry*, Vol. 1, p. 263; "Hertz, John Daniel," in: *Who's Who in Commerce and Industry*, 4.

Joseph Hoffman (1924-2017), b. Slovakia; contractor and developer, Canada

Travis Kalanick (1976-), b. Los Angeles, CA, of Slovak ancestry; businessman; co-founder of Scour, a peer to peer file sharing application, Red Swoosh, a peer-to-peer content delivery network, and Uber, a transportation network company
Bio: "Travis Kalanick," in: Wikipedia. See - https://en.wikipedia.org/wiki/Travis_Kalanick

Henry Kallan (1947-), b. Šahy, Czech.; in US s. 1968; president and owner of the Library Hotel Collection; regarded as one of the industry's most innovative independent hoteliers.
Bio: Hirschowitz, Sharon, "Spotlight on Henry Kallan, President, Library Hotel Collection. See- https://www.luxuryhotelassociation.org/2017/05/spotlight-on-henrykallan-president-library-hotel-collection/

Andrew Konrady (1893-1977), b. Haniska, Slovakia; dealer in coal business, Konrady Coal Co., Gary, IN
Bio: "Konrady, Andrew," in: Droba, p. 78.

Edward Kováč (1873-1939), b. Brádno, Slovakia; trained as carpenter; then entrepreneur; built a modern furniture factory.
Bio: See - Bolecek, Dr. B.V. and Irene Slamka, *The Slovak Encyclopaedia.* New York: Slovak Academy, 1981, p. 68; Paučo, Jozef, *Slovenski priekopnici v Amerike*, Cleveland: Prvá Katolícka Slovenská Jednota, 1972, pp. 242-248.

Michael Kozacik (1873-1941), b. Horná Lhota, Slovakia; banker, president of the Lake Land Co., president of the Kozacik Hardware Co., Whiting, IN
Bio: "Kozacik, Michael," in: Droba, pp. 78-79; "Kozacik, Michael," in: Find a Grave. See - https://www.findagrave.com/memorial/93578867/michael-kozacik

Edward J. Luchansky (1911-2004), b. Middletown, NJ, of Slovak descent; merchant, proprietor of Eddie's Food Market, Bridgeport, CT
Bio: "Edward j. Luchansky," *Connecticut Post,* March 9, 2004.

Thomas W. Matey, Sr. (1931-2017), b. Warren, OH, of Slovak descent; business executive; executive with Inland Steel, Indianapolis; developer of the Las Olas Beach Club timeshare resorts in Satellite Beach and Cocoa Beach. An early leader in the timeshare industry, affiliated with Resort Condominiums International since 1979.
Bio: "Thomas W. Matey sr.," *Florida Today,* Sept. 16, 2017

Dusty Miklas (fl. 1999), b. Šipkové, Slovakia; town engineer, contractor and real estate developer, Canada, president and chief executive officer at Invar Building Corp.
Bio: "Dusty Miklas," in: myhomepage.ca. See - https://myhomepage.ca/whos_who/dusty-miklas/;

Paul Miklas (fl. 2007), b. Canada, of Slovak father; builder; president of Valleymade Building AMA Corp., Toronto, Canada
Bio: "Bridle Path builder knows the whims of the rich," in: The Globe and Mail. See - ttps://www.theglobeandmail.com/real-estate/bridle-path-builder-knows-the-whims-of-the-rich/article686008/

Emil Novak (1919-1978), b. Melčice, Czech.; businessman, Montevideo, Uruguay
Bio: "Novak, Emil,", in: Pejskar 2, p. 225.

Samuel Papanek (1871-d.), b. Brezová, Slovakia; wool dealer, Chicago
Bio: "Papanek, Samuel," in: Droba, p.80

Nathan Pereles (1824-1879), b. Sobotište, Slovakia; pioneer Jewish grocery merchant in Milwaukee, attorney specializing in commercial and real estate law
Bio: "Nathan Pereles," in: *The Columbian Biographical Dictionary and Portrait Gallery of the Representative Men of the US. Wisconsin Volume.* Chicago: The Lewis Publishing Co., 1895,
Part 2, pp. 437-442.

Peter Kornel Piacek (1921-1996), b. Slovakia; founder and president of Alpina Salami, Inc., Laval, QC, Canada
Bio: "Piacek, Kornel," *The Gazette,* Montreal, QC, February 25, 2007

Adam Podkrivacky (1889-d.), b. Rovné, Slovakia; realtor, insurer, Chicago, IL
Bio: "Podkrivacky, Adam," in: *Catholic Who's Who,* 1961, Vol. 14, p. p. 362.

Peter A. Rafaeli (1932-), b. Bratislava, Czech.; president, PAR Development Corp., Spring House, PA
Bio: "Rafaeli, Peter A.," in: *SVU Directory* 8

Morris Rich (orig. Mauritius Reich) (1847-1928), b. Košice, Slovakia; the founder of what would become Rich's Department Store retail chain, Atlanta, GA
Bio: Rich's. A Southern Institution. Charleston, SC: The History Press, 2012

Walter Henry Rich (1880-1947), b. Atlanta, GA, of Slovak descent; president of Atlanta's largest department store, Rich's Inc.
Bio: Harris, Leon, "The Riches of Atlanta," in: *Merchant Princes.* New York: Harper & Row, 1979, pp. 135-155; "Rich, Walter Henry," in: *Who's Who in Commerce and Industry,* 4, p. 794; "Walter H. Rich," in: Find A Grave. See - https://www.findagrave.com/memorial/78289000/walter-h.-rich

Richard H. Rich (orig. Rosenheim) (1902-1981); b. Atlanta, GA, of Slovak ancestry on his mother's side; merchant and business executive; with Rich's Inc., becoming its director and eventually president and chairman of the executive committee
Bio: "Richard H. Rich," in: Richard H. Rich Papers. See - https://findingaids. library.emory.edu/documents/rich575/#descriptive_summary

Steve Robert (1922-), b. Michalovce, Czech.; automobile dealer, Robert Motors Ltd., Toronto, Canada (s. 1952) - first Canadian Volvo dealers
Bio: "Steve Robert," in: *Naše Hlasy,* p. 32.

Pavel Rohon (1920-), b. Bystrička, Czech.; president, Samoth Realty Corp., Teaneck, NJ
Bio: "Rohon, Pavel," in: SVU *Directory* 8

Leslie Ruzsa (1901-d.), b. Hucín, Slovakia; owner of L' Europe Tavern, Toronto, Canada.
Bio: Leslie Ruzsa," in: *Naše Hlasy,* p. 32.

Jacob Schmidt (1889-1965), b. Bardejev, Slovakia; in US since 1907; clothing merchant, at Yorktown, TX (s. 1915), later also at Beeville and San Marcos, TX.
Bio: "Schmidt, Jacob," in: Handbook of Texas Online. See - https://tshaonline.org/handbook/online/articles/fscjs

Frank J. Semancik, Jr. (1949-2006), b. Poughkeepsie, NY, of Slovak descent; owner of Speedo's Paint & Body shop, Poughkeepsie
Bio: "Frank Semancik," in: Legacy.com. see - https://www.legacy.com/obituaries/name/frank-semancik-obituary?pid=178424446

Joseph Spanik (1893- d.), b. Brezany, Slovakia; meat merchant, Chicago
Bio: "Spanik, Joseph," in: Droba, p. 82.

Otto Stanek (1921-), b. Považská Bystrica, Czech.; realtor, O. Stanek Real Estate, Toronto, Canada
Bio: "Otto Stanek," in: *Naše Hlasy,* p. 35.

John Stefka (1882-d.), b. Čachtice, Slovakia; building contractor, Chicago
Bio: "Stefka, John," in: Droba, p. 83

Frank Sura, b. Slovakia; immigrated to Canada in the interwar years; contractor and developer

John Svatik, b. Slovakia; pioneer wool dealer, Chicago

Albert B. Tabola (1898-d.), b. Vlkovce, Slovakia; dealer in real estate, loans and insurance (s. 1923), Chicago
Bio: "Tabola, Albert B," in: Droba, p. 83.

James 'Jim" R. Trueman (1935-1986), b. American businessman and automobile racing team owner, founder of Red Roof Inn Motels
Bio: "Jim Trueman," in: Wikipedia. See - https://en.wikipedia.org/wiki/Jim_Trueman; "James Trueman, 51, Owner of Winning Car in Indy 500," *The New York Times,* Jun 13, 1986.

Joseph Vaschak (ca 1850-ca 1920), b. Richnava, Slovakia; was the first Slovak as director of funeral home in Mahoning and Shenango Valleys and founder of funeral home in Youngstown, OH in 1907, which operates today under the name of Vaschak-Kirila Funeral Home.
Bio: "Vaschak-Kirila," in: In the beginning. See - https://www.vaschak-kirilafh.com/in-the-beginning

Joseph 'Jožo' Weider (1908-), b. Žilina, Slovakia; founder of Blue Mountain Pottery Ltd., Blue Mountain Gateway and Blue Mountain Winter Park, Collingwood, Ont., Canada - ceramics, manufacturing and distribution. Motel and restaurant. Winter sports (skiing).
Bio: "From the Vault: Celebrating 75 Years of Blue Mountain Resort – Part 1," in: Mountain Life Live It Up. See - https://www.mountainlifemedia.ca/2017/01/vault-celebrating-75-years-blue-mountain-resort/; "1941. Jozo Weider Opens Blue mountain Ski Resort," in: Blue Mountain. See - https://www.bluemountain.ca/mountain/history

Aaron Weiss (1894-d.), b. Michalovce, Slovakia; founder of the shoe chain company, Triangle Shoe Co., Wilkes-Barre, PA
Bio: "Weiss, Aaron," in *Who's Who in the East,*1951

E. Agribusinessmen

Andrew Duda (1873-1958), b. Velčice, Slovakia; in US s. 1909; rancher, philanthropist, and entrepreneurial farmer in Florida and acquired the nickname 'the celery king;' grew from his family's small farm to an international agricultural corporation (A. Duda & Sons) at the small Slovak colony of Slavia, Florida.
Bio: Find A Grave. See - https://www.findagrave.com/memorial/26416442/andrej-duda

Paučo, Jozef, *Slovenski priekopnici v Amerike*, Cleveland: Prva Katolicka Slovenska Jednota, 1972, p. 51;

David Duda (fl. 2009), b. Florida, of Slovak descent; trained as business administrator; president and CEO of A. Duda &Sons, Inc. (s. 2009)
Bio: "David Duda," in: LinkedIn. See - https://www.linkedin.com/in/david-duda-81834ba/

Koerner Rombauer (1934-2018), b. Escondido, CA, of Slovak descent; commercial pilot, the founder of Rombauer vineyards, NapaValley, CA
Bio: "Koerner Rombauer," in: Rombauer Vineyards. See - https://www.rombauer.com/koerner-rombauer/; "Koerner Rombauer, Founder of Rombauer Vineyards, Dies at 83," in: Wine Spectator. See - https://www.winespectator.com/webfeature/show/id/Koerner-Rombauer-Dies-at-83; "Koerner Rombauer," in: Legacy.com. See - https://www.legacy.com/obituaries/sfgate/obituary.aspx?n=koerner-rombauer&pid=188994390

F. MANUFACTURERS

Peter Baran (1874-1936), b. Potok, Liptov, Slovakia; in US s. 1898; established a leather factory in Newark, NJ, Chapel Leather Co., later renamed Peter Baran & Sons; made quality leather products by improving the production procedure and used alligator leather; "Baran Alligators" became famous in America and worldwide for their quality.
Bio: Paučo, Jozef, *Slovenski priekopnici v Amerike*, Cleveland: Prva Katolicka Slovenska Jednota, 1972, pp. 21-22.

Ethan Becker (1945-), b. of Slovak descent; son of Marion and John William Becker and grandson of Irma Starkloff Rombauer, the original author of *The Joy of Cooking*. Ethan studied at Cordon Bleu in Paris in 1971 and 'was entrusted with' authorship of *Joy of Cooking* in 1976 from his mother. the 1980s he founded Becker Knife and Tool which in time partnered with BlackJack Knives. Becker Knife and Tool later partnered with Camillus Cutlery Company (until Camillus' bankruptcy in 2007) to produce Ethan's knife designs which are currently produced by Ka-Bar Knives and manufactured in

the USA. Ethan is also the creator of the 'Becker Patrol Pack,' manufactured by Eagle Industries, the CMI Figure 8 Descender and other climbing gear.
Bio: "Ethan Becker," in: Wikipedia. See - https://en.wikipedia.org/wiki/Ethan_Becker; "Ethan Becker,' in: The Joy of Cooking. See - http://www.thejoykitchen.com/all-about-joy/ethan-becker

Joseph Bellon (fl. 1878), the presumed first known Slovak immigrant to Canada, who landed in Toronto in 1878. Bellon served in the Canadian Expedition sent to quell the Riel Rebellion. He and his brother later established s wireworks factory.

Rudolph Hans Bunzl (1922-2016), b. Vienna, of Slovak ancestry; manufacturer, founder of American Filtrona Corp.
Bio: Robertson, Ellen, "Rudolph H. Bunzl, retired president of America Filtrona Corp., dies at 94," *Richmond Times-Dispatch*, October 18, 2016; "Rudolph Hans Bunzl," in: GENi. See - https://www.geni.com/people/Rudolph-Bunzl/6000000014958397072

Walter Henry Bunzl (1913-1988), b. Vienna, of Slovak father and Czech mother; ;manufacturer, Textile & Paper Supply Corp., Atlanta, GA
Bio: "Walter H. Bunzl," in: Find A Grave. See - ttps://www.findagrave.com/memorial/186875205/walter-h-bunzl

John Filko (1892-1965), b. Bánovce, Slovakia; president of the F. & B. Manufacturing Company, engineers, makers of tools, dies and automotive parts, (Chicago).
Bio: "Filko, John," in: Droba, p. 76.

Imrich Gora (1906-d.), b. Trenčianska Tepla, Slovakia; founder of Top Paper Products, manufacturers of packaging materials, Guelph, Ont., Canada
Bio: "Imrich Gora," in: *Naše Hlasy*, p. 29.

Jay Greenfield (ca. 1958-), b. the oldest son of Martin Greenfield; vice president and co-owner of Martin Greenfield Clothiers,
Bio: "The Mystery of Trump's Suits, Solved," *The New York Times*, October 6, 2016.

Martin Greenfield (1928-), b. Pavlovo, Czech.; in US s. 1947; an American master tailor, based in Brooklyn, NY, specializing in men's suits. He has been described as the best men's tailor in the United States. His list of clients includes six US Presidents, as well as other notable politicians and celebrities. His company, Martin Greenfield Clothiers, has also fashioned men's suits for clothing lines DKNY and Rag & Bone, and the television show Boardwalk Empire. Greenfield is a Holocaust survivor, having been imprisoned as a teenager at Auschwitz, where the rest of his immediate family were killed. Bio: "Martin Greenfield," in: Wikipedia. See - https://en.wikipedia.org/wiki/Martin_Greenfield; Francis, Enjoli and Eric Noll, "Martin Greenfield, Holocaust Survivor, Is Now Tailor to the Famous," in abcNEWS, February 3, 2017. See - https://abcnews.go.com/Business/martin-greenfield-holocaust-survivor-now-tailor-famous/story?id=44020819; Farmer, Ann, "A Tailor, Called Upon by Designers and Politicians," *The New York Times*, November 5, 2010; "The Mystery of Trump's Suits, Solved," *The New York Times*, October 6, 2016.

John Stanislav Jurik (1891-), b. Podhradie, Slovakia; banker and realtor, president of the Cedar Lake Realty Co., Crown Point, IN and Anna Rose Co., Chicago
Bio: "Jurik, John Stanislav," in: Droba, p. 77

Jerry Kane (1947-), b. Prague, Czech., of Slovak parents; president, CEO and chairman of Sam Kane Beef Processors Inc.
Bio: "Jerry Kane," in: *Encyclopedia*, Vol. 1, p. 143.

Sam Kane (1919-2010), b. Spišské Podhradie, Czech.; founder of meatpacking company, Corpus Christi, TX
Bio: Rechcigl, Miloslav, Jr., "Sam Kane," in: *Encyclopedia*, Vol. 1., p. 144.; "Sam Kane of Corpus Christi - Holocaust Survivor," in: TexAg, January 4, 2010. See - https://texags.com/forums/49/topics/1561812

Stephen Andrew Kubanik (1919-), b. Makov, Czech.; in. US s. 1936; display and wire products manufacturer; partner in A & J Wire Display Corp. (1952).
Bio: "Kubanik, Stephen Andrew," in: Who's Who in Commerce and Industry, 14.

Estée Lauder (1908-2004), b. Corona, Queens, NY, of Czechoslovak ancestry; founder of eponymous cosmetics company
Bio: "Estée Lauder," in: Wikipedia. See - https://en.wikipedia.org/wiki/ ; Estee Lauder, *Estee: A Success Story.* New York: Random House, 1985; Israel, Lee, *Estee Lauder: Beyond the Magic.* An Unauthorized Biography. New York: Macmillan, 1985; Alpern, Sara, "Estee Lauder," in: *Jewish Women: A Comprehensive Historical Encyclopedia.* Shalvi Publishing, Ltd., 2006; Kent, Jacqueline C., *Business Builders in Cosmetics.* Minneapolis, MN: The Oliver Press, 2003.

Jan Matejovič (1929-2014), b. Slovakia; founder of Drummond Metal Products Ltd., manufacturers of aluminum extrusions, building supplies and drapery hardware, Toronto, Canada
Bio: "Jan Matejovic," in: *Toronto Star,* June 24, 2014.

Anton Olach, b. Slovakia; pioneer furniture manufacturer, Chicago

John Ondrey, and his brother **Walter Ondrey,** b. in Piešťany, Slovakia; owners of Lido Industrial Products Ltd., manufacturers of plastic containers and plastic extrusions, Toronto, Canada
Bio: "John Ondrey, Walter Ondrey," in: *Naše Hlasy,* p. 31.

John Polachek (1873-1955), b. Slovakia; began his career by taking charge of the William H. Jackson Co. factory (for 9 years) and then had charge of the Tiffany Studio factories (for 7 years); founder of the John Polachek Bronze & Iron Co. (1910) and took over eight other largest bronze manufacturing companies in US to form the General Bronze Corp.; chair of the Bd. and president until he retired in 1934 ; president and director of other corporations; resided in New York, NY
Bio: "Polachek, John," in: *Who's Who in Commerce and Industry,* 1, p. 756.

Morris Printz (1843-1931), b. Košice, Slovakia; pioneer in establishing cloak industry, Cleveland, OH
Bio: *A History of Cleveland and its Environs.* Chicago: Lewis Publishing Co., 1918, Vol. 3, pp. 502-503

Alexander Printz (1869-d.), b. Košice, Slovakia; president of Printz-Biederman Co., NYC, extensive manufacturers of ladies' garments.
Bio: "Alexander Printz," in: *A History of Cleveland and its Environs.* Chicago: Lewis Publishing Co., 1918, Vol. 3, pp. 502-503

John Rybovich (1882-1970), b. Yugoslavia, of Slovak descent; in US s. 1902; married Anna (1881-1982), a Czechoslovak native. He was a carpenter and cabinetmaker by training; founder of Rybovich & Sons Boat Works (s. 1930s), repair and refit center, Florida
Bio: "The Rybovich History 1900-1929)," See - http://michaelrybovich andsons.com/history.html

John Rybovich, Jr. (1913-1993), b. Florida, of Slovak descent; boatbuilder; designer and builder of the first modern sportfishing boats and incorporating new technology; inducted into IGFA Fishing Hall of Fame.
Bio: "The Rybovich History 1900-1929)," See - http://michaelrybovichandsons. com/history.html; "John Rybovich, Jr.," in: IGFA. See - https://www.igfa. org/Museum/HOF-Rybovich-J.aspx;

John Saksun (1922-), b. Zalobin, Czech.; The Queensway Machine Products, Ltd., manufacturers of aircraft and machine parts, Toronto, Canada
Bio: "John Saksun," in: *Naše Hlasy*, p. 33.

Andrew Schustek (1871-1909), b. Slovenská Lupča, Slovakia; manufacturer of moving picture supplies, Andrew Schustek & Co., Chicago
Bio: "Schustek, Andrew," in: Droba, pp. 81-82.

Vlastimil Šurák (1927-), b. Brezová pod Bradlom, Czech.; founder of Surak Leather Co., Chicago (1954-99), Chicago
Bio: "Vlastimil John Surak," in: NCSML Oral Histories. See - https://www. ncsml.org/exhibits/vlastimil-john-surak

Joseph Tapajna, b. Slovakia; pioneer paper manufacturer, Whiting, IN

John Židek, b. Slovakia; wandering 'drotar,' pioneer manufacturer, Chicago

G. CORPORATE EXECUTIVES - ENTREPRENEURS

Aexander Sandor Aranyos, b. Žilina, Slovakia; corporate executive, with Freehauf Trailer Co., Detroit, MI (s. 1953), president of Freehauf International Ltd. (s. 1957)
Bio: *Who's Who in Commerce and Industry*, Vol. 14, p. 31; "Aranyos, Alexander Sandor," in: *Who's Who in America*, 33; "Aranyos, Alexander Sandor," in: *Who's Who in Commerce and Industry*, Vol. 14.

John Stephen Bugas (1908-1982), b. Rock Springs, WY, of Slovak parents; lawyer; corporate executive; second in command at Ford Motor Company during the presidency and chairmanship reign of Henry Ford II; philanthropist, politician
Bio: "John Bugas," in: Wikipedia. See - https://en.wikipedia.org/wiki/John_Bugas#cite_ref-Progressive_5-0; "John S. Bugas is Dead at 74; Was Top Executive at Ford," *The New York Times*, 1982.

Milan V. Fabry (1922-1997), b. Prešov, Czech.; vice president for operations, Sears World Trade, Washington, DC
Bio: "Fabry, Milan V., in: *SVU Directory* 7

Edward A. Garba (1922-2005), b. Newark, NJ (of Slovak descent; vice president of the Interpublic Group of Companies, Inc., Manhattan, NY; president of the Slovak-American Cultural Center, New York, NY
Bio: "Edward A. Garba," *The Journal News*, August 16, 2001.

John Hertz, Jr. (1908-1968), b. Chicago, IL, of Slovak descent; with Buchanan & Co., adv. agency (s. 1936), chairman bd. and director; director, Fifth Avenue Coach Co., NY, city Omnibus Corp., Omnibus Corp. of America; residing in NYC.
Bio: "Hertz, John, Jr.," in: *Who's Who in Commerce and Industry*, 6

Alexander Kerney (1910-1993), b. Rožňava, Slovakia, investor, and steelmaker, business executive, Toronto, Canada
Bo: Alexander Kerney and Gizelle Kerney," in: Veridicus Mercuius. See - http://veridicusmercurius.blog.cz/0605/kerney-alexander

John L. Krajsa (1911-1991), b. Allentown, PA, of Slovak descent; he operated the consumer and mortgage lending company since 1947. Before that he was manager of the Allentown office of the Standard Loan Service Co.; chairman of the Allentown Area Hospital Authority, served on the board of governors of the Allentown-Lehigh County Chamber of Commerce, 1961-63, and 1976-80. Krajsa was named to the First and Sixth Ward Old-timers Hall of Fame in 1963, and in 1987, he was the net winner of the Lehigh and Northampton Counties Golf Association Senior Championship.
Bio: "John Krajsa, 79, President of Allentown Financial Corp.," *The Morning Call*, February 12, 1991.

Aerin Lauder (1970-), b. New York, NY, of Czech. ancestry, a granddaughter of Estée Lauder; an American billionaire heiress and businesswoman, style and image director for the Estée Lauder companies.
Bio: "Lauder, Aerin," in: Wikipedia. See - https://en.wikipedia.org/wiki/Aerin_Lauder

Leonard Lauder (1933-), b. New York, NY, of Czech. descent, son of Estée Lauder; American billionaire businessman, chairman of The Estée Lauder Companies (until 1999); art collector, humanitarian
Bio: "Lauder, Leonard," in: Wikipedia. See - https://en.wikipedia.org/wiki/Leonard_Lauder

Ronald Lauder (1944-), b. New York, NY, of Czech. descent, American businessman, heir to the Estée Lauder Corporation, philanthropist.
Bio: "Ronald Lauder," in: Wikipedia. See - https://en.wikipedia.org/wiki/Ronald_Lauder

William P. Lauder (1960-), b. New York, NY, of Czech. descent, a grandson of Estée Lauder; American billionaire businessman, and executive chairman of the Estée Lauder companies
Bio: "Lauder, William P.," in: Wikipedia. See - https://en.wikipedia.org/wiki/William_P._Lauder

Jacob Max Lowy (1908-), b. Bardejov, Slovakia; industrialist, real estate executive
Bio: "Lowy, Jacob Max," in: *Who's Who in Commerce and Industry*, 14

Dušan 'Dusty' Miklas, b. Sipkové, Czech.; in Canada s. 1938; Canadian town engineer and planner, entrepreneur, president and chief executive officer of Invar Building Corp., Toronto
Bio: "Dusty Miklas," in: Bloomberg. See their website; "Dusty Miklas," in: myhomepage.ca. See - https://myhomepage.ca/whos_who/dusty-miklas/

Peter Munk (1927-2018), b. Budapest, of Slovak descent (the family came originally from the Nitra District in Slovakia) ; in Canada s. 1950; industrial tycoon, investor, philanthropist; one of the richest men in Canada; founder of Barrick Gold (the world's largest gold-mining corporation) and the multi-billion-dollar Canadian construction and development firm Trizec Properties.
Bio: "Peter Munk," in: Wikipedia. See - https://en.wikipedia.org/wiki/Peter_Munk; "Peter Munk, 90, Dies; Built World's Biggest Gold Mining Company," *The New York Times*, March 30, 2018.

Steve Obsitnik (1967-), b. Stamford, CT, of Slovak descent; US Naval Academy and the Wharton School graduate; electrical engineer by training; entrepreneur; president, COO & CFO, Calabrio Inc. (2002-05); Venture Advisor, SRI International (2005-08); chairman & CEO, Quintel Technology (2007-12); High Tech CEO, Saugatuck Advisory (s. 2012); adjunct professor of business and entrepreneurship, Sacred Heart University (s. 2010); also a politician-a politician
Bio: "Steve Obsitnik," in: Ballotpedia. See - https://ballotpedia.org/Steve_Obsitnik; "Steve Obsitnik," in: LinkedIn. See - https://www.linkedin.com/in/steveobsitnik/

Milan Francis Ondrus (1923-), b. Bratislava, Czech.; lawyer, public information specialist with Voice of America and Radio Free Europe; executive with Dow Chemical Co. (s. 1957), with Brunswick Co., with FMC Corp.; president of American Chamber of Commerce in Germany and Belgium.
Bio: "Ondrus, Milan Francis," in: *Who's who in Commerce and Industry*, Vol. 14, p. 989; "Obituary: Milan Ondrus, 91, fled Czechoslovakia,

Dow Chemical executive," in: NewCanaanAdvertiser, August 26, 2014. See - https://ncadvertiser.com/120969/obituary-milan-ondrus-91-fled-czechoslovakia-dow-chemical-executive/

Joseph J. Prischak (1931-), Pennsylvania, of Slovak parents, who came from Prešov; corporate executive and philanthropist. President and CEO of the Pastek Group, Erie, PA. The company quickly became a leader in industrial production and engineering. They have developed a number of standards and procedures that are currently being used in the mining industry. Their clients included significant firms such as. IBM, Eastman Kodak, Polaroid. more than 30 years at the head of the company, this company has increased enormously from several tens to more than 2 000 employees.
Bio: "Joseph J. Prischak," in: Bloomberg. See - https://www.bloomberg. com/research/stocks/private/person.asp?personId=1476498&privcapId= 4258867; "Erie Businessman, Philanthropist Joseph Prischak Named Honorary Alumnus," in: *Penn State News*, June 12, 2014. See - https://news. psu.edu/story/318242/2014/06/12/erie-businessman-philanthropist-joseph-prischak-named-honorary-alumnus.

Michael P. Rich (1938-), b. Atlanta, GA, of Slovak descent; with Rich's department store, Atlanta, GA (s. 1962), senior vice president (s. 1972)
Bio: "Rich. Michael P.," in: *Who's Who in America*, 42.

Richard H. Rich (1901-), b. Atlanta, GA, of Slovak father; director, M. Rich & Bros. Co., Atlanta, GA (s. 1926), treasurer (1929-44). president (s. 1948), director of Trust Co
Bio: "Rich, Richard, H." in: *Who's Who in America* 28.

Stephen Boleslav Roman (1921-1988), b. Veľký Ruskov, Czech.; prominent Canadian mining engineer, and mining executive, called the 'Uranium King of Canada.'
Bio: Loun, George, "Stephen B. Roman," in: *Builders of Fortune.* Toronto: Pitt Pub. Co., 1963, pp. 55-60; La Bourdais, Donat Marc, "Stephen B. Roman," in: *Canada and the Atomic Revolution.* Toronto: McClelland, 1959, pp. 110-117; "Stephen Boleslav Roman," in: Wikipedia. See - https://en.wikipedia. org/wiki/Stephen_Boleslav_Roman; McKay, Paul. *The Roman Empire: The Unauthorized Life and Times of Stephen Roman.* Toronto: Key Porter Books Limited, 1990; "Roman, Stephen Boleslav," in: *Who's Who in the East,* 14.

Helen E. Roman-Barber (1946-), b. Canada, of Slovak descent; director of Roman Corporation Limited (s. 1973), serving as chairman on the board and chief executive officer, Toronto, Canada
Bio: "Helen E. Roman-Barber," in: Bloomberg. See - https://www.bloomberg.com/research/stocks/private/person.asp?personId=8093047& privcapId=873910

Richard Francis Schubert (1936-), b. Trenton, NJ, of Slovak ancestry; executive of Bethlehem Steel Corp., president of American Red Cross
Bio: "Schubert, Richard Francis," in: *SVU Directory* 8; Wirth, Paul, "Former Steel Exec Quits Red Cross," *The Morning Call*, April 19, 1989

John Slezak (1896-1984), b. Stará Turá, Slovakia; mechanical engineer, Col., US Army, chairman of the board of the Kable Printing Co. (1947-72), and was on the board of directors of the Hazeletime Corp., the Clayton Mark Co. and the Roper Corp.
Bio: "Slezak, John," in: Wikipedia. See - https://en.wikipedia.org/wiki/John_Slezak; "Slezak, John," in: Droba, p.165; "Slezak, John," in: *SVU Directory* 5

Allen Alexander Staub (1905-1930), b. Košice, Slovakia; in US. s. 1913; conglomerate executive; senior vice president, Misco Industries, Inc., Wichita, KS (s. 1945).
Bio: "Staub, Allen Alexander," in: *Who's Who in Finance and Industry*, 21

Milton Staub (1904-1981), b. Košice, Slovakia; engineering and construction executive; president and general manager, Gustav Hirsch Orgn., Inc., Columbus, OH (s. 1929); president, Skyway Broadcasting Corp. (s. 1959); vice president, Elyrian Lorain Broadcasting Corp., Elyria, OH (1959-); vice president and treasurer, director, Carl Centner, Inc. (s. 1951); president director, Intercity Auto Service, Inc. (s. 1951); president director, Eastmoor Electric Co., Columbus, OH, etc.
Bio: "Staub, Milton," in: *Who's Who in Commerce and Industry*, 14.

H. BANKERS AND FINANCIERS

Čapek, Thomas and Thomas Capek, Jr., *The Czechs and Slovaks in American Banking.* New World: Fleming H. Ravell Co., 1920. 60p.

Michal Bosák (1869-1937), b. Okruhle, Slovakia; banker and shipping agent, philanthropist
Bio: Čulen, Konštantín, *Michal Bosák.* Scranton, PA: Slovenská obrana, 1958; Nissley, Erin l. "Local History: Immigrant found his fortune in Scranton," *The Times-Tribune,* January 31, 2016; "Michal Bosák," in: Wikipedia. See - https://sk.wikipedia.org/wiki/Michal_ Bosák; Bosák, Martin and Bosák, Rudolf, *Michael Bosák: An American Banker from Šariš.*Košice: IBIS Publishing, 1990.

Joseph J. Chilla (1881-1958), b. Pusté Pole, Slovakia; banker, founder and secretary of the Liberty Savings and Loan Association, founder and secretary of the Slovak House Association, dealer in real estate and insurance, Whiting, IN.
Bio: Chilla, Joseph," in: Droba, p. 73; "Joseph J. Chilla," in: Indiana Biography. See - http://debmurray.tripod.com/indiana/indbioref-145.htm

Ivan Štefan Dexner (1860-1938), b. Nagykálló, of Slovak father; banker; secretary of the Slovak League of America
Bio: Paučo, Jozef, *Slovenski priekopnici v Amerike,* Cleveland: Prva Katolicka Slovenska Jednota, 1972, pp.43-44; "Dexner Ivan," in: Národná banka Slovenska. Archive website. See - https://www.nbs.sk/sk/publikacie/archiv-nbs/osobnosti-penaznictva-na-slovensku/daxner-ivan

Rudolf Fraštacký (1912-1988), b. Mošovce, Slovakia; Czechoslovak politician; exile politician settling in Toronto, Canada; banker, founder of the Metropolitan Trust Co., Toronto
Bio: Bio: "Fraštacký, Rudolf," in: SVU Directory 6; "Fraštacký, Rudolf," in: Pejskar 3, pp. 57-68; Cvetkova, Tatiana, "Rudolf Fraštacký 1912-1988," in: Národná banka Slovenska. Gallery of Personalities, BIATEC 11, No. 3 (2003), pp. 29-30.

John Stanislav Jurik (1891-d.), b. Podhradie, Slovakia; banker and realtor, organizer of the Robey State Bank, vice president of its successor Depositors State Bank
Bio: "Jurik, John Stanislav," in: Droba, p. 77.

Michael Kozacik (1873-1941), b. Horná Lhota, Slovakia; banker, president of the American Trust and Savings Bank, Whiting, IN, president of the Lake Land Co., president of the Kozacik Hardware Co., Whiting, IN
Bio: "Kozacik, Michael," in: Droba, pp. 78-79; "Kozacik, Michael," in: Find a Grave. See - https://www.findagrave.com/memorial/93578867/michael-kozacik

Wendell Stephen Platek (1897-d.), b. Horný Hričov, Slovakia; banker, assistant bank cashier, Roseland National Bank, Chicago
Bio: "Platek, Wendell Stephen," in: Droba, pp. 80-81.

Carl Pohlad (1915-2009), b. Des Moines, IA, of Slovak ancestry; American financier, the owner of the Minnesota Twins baseball franchise
Bio: "Carl Pohlad," in: Wikipedia. See - https://en.wikipedia.org/wiki/Carl_Pohlad

Peter Víťazoslav Rovnianek (1867-1933), b. Dolný Hričov, Slovakia; businessman, banker, journalist; founder of Slovaktown, AR
Bio: "Peter Víťazoslav Rovnianek," in: Wikipedia. See - https://sk.wikipedia.org/wiki/Peter_Víťazoslav_Rovnianek

Stephen Joseph Skriba, Jr. (1918-2004), b. Chicago, IL, of Slovak descent; aeronautical engineer, banker, Clyde Savings, Greenville, NC
Bio: "Stephen Joseph Skriba, Jr.," *Chicago Tribune,* October 10, 2004; "Stephen Joseph Skriba, Jr.," *The Greenville News,* September 30, 2004.

John A. Sotak (1856-1927), b. Slovakia, banker; established in 1909 the Tatra Savings & Loan Co., together with Joseph Dovalosky, and Michael Phillips, renamed State Savings & Loan Co. in 1946. At one time, it became the 9th largest bank in Cleveland Ohio area.
Bio: "John A. Sotak," in: Find A Grave. See - https://www.findagrave.com/memorial/123306831/john-a.-sotak

Henry Spira (1862-1942), b. Veľká Lesná, Slovakia; banker, president, Spira Savings & Loan Association, Spira International Express Co., Cleveland, OH
Bio: *Who's Who in American Jewry*, Vol. 1, 589; "Spira, Henry," in: *Encyclopedia of Cleveland* History. See- https://case.edu/ech/articles/s/spira-henry

I. BROKERS

Vaclav T. Kočlík (1925-2017), b. Košice, Czech.; investment broker, Unionville, Ont., Canada
Bio: "Vaclav T. Kočlík," in: SVU Directory, 8; "Frank Koclik Obituary," in: Niagara-on-the-Lake - ObitTree.

David J. Machlica, managing partner, Manhattan Investment Partners, LLC (MIP) and managing principal of Venue Strategies, LLC, MIP's affiliate
Bio: "David J. Machlica," in: Manhattan Investment Partners, LLC. See - http://www.manhattaninvest.com/david-machlica.html

Ronald S. Papánek (1934-), b. Mostová, Czech.; president, REP, Investments Ltd., Chicago, IL
Bio: "Papánek, Ronald S.," in: *SVU Directory* 8

Ron Papanek (1963-), b. Chicago, IL, of Slovak descent; managing director, head of Symbiont's Data business, a blockchain advocate
Bio: "Ron Papanek," in: SIFMA. See - https://www.sifma.org/people/ron-papanek/

Zdenka Kurčíková Prokop (1952-), b. Nižná Boca, Czech.; broker, Ear Wadmont Realty, Brentwoods, TN
Bio: "Prokop, Zdenka Kurčíková," in: *SVU Directory*, 8

IX. Public Life

A. POLITICS - ACTIVISM

Cude, Michael Robert, Transatlantic Perspectives on the Slovak Question, 1914-1948. Ph.D. Dissertation, University of Colorado, Boulder, CO, 2012.

Cude, Michael, "The Imagined Exiles: Slovak-Americans and the Slovak Question during the First Czechoslovak Republic," *Studia Historica Gedanensia*, Vol. 5 (2014), pp.287-

Hletko, Peter P., "The Slovaks and the Pittsburgh Pact," *Slovakia* 18, 41 (1968), 5-54.

"It's only Politics," in: Slovaks in Canada in the year 2000. See - http://www. slovak.com/stephens/politics.html

Krause, Paul, *The Battle for Homestead, 1880-1992: Politics, Culture, and Steel.* Pittsburgh: University of Pittsburgh Press, 1992

Laska, Vera, "Czechs and Slovaks," in: *America's Ethnic Politics.* Eds. Joseph S. Roucek and Bernard Eisenberg. Westport: Greenwood Press, 1982, pp. 133-53.

Mamatey, Victor S., "The United States and Czechoslovak Independence," in: *Czechoslovakia: Crossroads and Crises, 1918–1988.* New York: St. Martin's Press, 1989.

Matocha, B. P., "Work of the Czechoslovaks in America," *Current History*, Vol. 10, No. 1, 2 (May 1919), pp. 309–312.

Paučo, Joseph, "American Slovaks and the Beginnings of Czecho-Slovakia," *Slovakia,* 16, No. 39 (1966), pp. 63-75.

Pergler, Charles, *America in the Struggle for Czechoslovak Independence.* Philadelphia: Dorrance, 1926.

Shain, Yossi, *Marketing the American Creed abroad: Diasporas in the U.S. and their Homelands.* Cambridge University Press, 1999. 314p.

Smith, Tony, *Foreign Attachments: The Power of Ethnic Groups in the Making of American Foreign Policy.* Cambridge, Mass.: Harvard University Press, 2000.

Stolarik, M. M., "The Role of American Slovaks in the Creation of Czecho-Slovakia, 1914-1918," *Slovak Studies*, 8, Historica 5 (1968).

Stolarik, M. Mark, "Slovak Immigration to the United States and its Relation to the American Socialist and Labor Movements," *Migracijske teme*, Vol. 4, No. 1-2 (1988), pp. 145-155.

Stolárik, M. Mark, "The Slovak League of America and the Canadian League in the Struggle for the Self-determination of the Nation, 1907–1992," *Slovakia*, 39, 72 & 73 (2007), pp. 7–35.

Tomek, Prokop "The Highs and Lows of Czech and Slovak Émigré Activism," In: *Anti-Communist Minorities in the U.S.: Political Activism of Ethnic Refugees.* Edited by Ieva Zake. New York: Palgrave Macmillan, 2009, pp. 109–126.

B. US GOVERNMENT

1. Executive Branch

a. US Cabinet

John T. Kmetz (1893-1968), b. Lepuhov, Slovakia; labor union official; Assistant Secretary of Labor, having been appointed by President Truman (1947).
Bio: "Truman Picks Kmetz, Lewis Aide, As Assistant Secretary of Labor," *The New York Times*, October 1, 1947.

John Slezák (1896-1986), b. Stará Tura, Slovakia; Colonel, mechanical engineer, businessman, Under Secretary of the Army (1954-55).
Bio: "Slezák, John," in: *SVU Directory* 5; "Slezak, John," in: *Who's who in America*, 28; "John Slezak," in: Wikipedia. See - https://en.wikipedia.org/ wiki/John_Slezak; "Slezak, John," in: Droba, p.165

b. US Agencies

David Eli Lilienthal (1899-1981), b. Morton, IL, of Slovak ancestry; American attorney, chairman of Tennessee Valley Authority (TVA) and of the Atomic Energy commission.
Bio: "Lilienthal, David Eli," in: *Biographical Dictionary of American Business Leader.*, AG, Westport, CT: Greenwood Press, 1983, pp. 796-799; Neuse, Steven M., "David E. Lilienthal: Exemplar of public purpose," *International Journal of Public Administration*, 14, No. 6 (1991), pp. 1099-1148; Neuse, Steven

M., *David E. Lilienthal: The Journey of an American Liberal.* University of
Tennessee Press, 1996; Keene, Ann t., "Lilienthal, David Eli," in: *National
Biography,* Vol. 13, pp. 651-652.

Sanford 'Sandy' J. Ungar (1945-), b. Slovak ancestry; journalist, director
of Voice of America
Bio: "Stanford J. Ungar," in: Wikipedia. See - https://en.wikipedia.org/wiki/
Sanford_J._Ungar

c. Diplomats

Norman L. Eisen (1960-), b. Los Angeles, CA, of Slovak descent; lawyer,
US Ambassador to the Czech Republic (2011-2014).
Bio: "Norman L. Eisen," in: Wikipedia. See - https://en.wikipedia.org/wiki/
Norman_L._Eisen

John Karch (1923-2010), b. Velká Domaša, Czech.; in US. s. 1934; US
Navy veteran; US diplomat; Chief of the European Division at the Voice of
America from (1960-68); professor at the National War College, Washington
(1979-82); Counselor with the US Mission to International Organizations,
Vienna (till 1996).
Bio: "Longtime FCSU Member and Jednota Contributor Dr. John Karch
Passed Away on September 7, 2010," *Jednota,* Vol. 119, No. 5831, November
10, 2010, p. 17.

Ronald Lauder (1944-), b. New York, NY, of Czech. Ancestry, American
businessman, philanthropist, US Ambassador to Austria (1986-87).
Bio: "Ronald Lauder," in: Wikipedia. See - https://en.wikipedia.org/wiki/
Ronald_Lauder

Vincent Obsitnik (1938-), b. Moravany, Czech.; Ambassador of the US of
America to the Slovak Republic (2007-09)
Bio: "Vincent Obsitnik," in: Wikipedia. See - https://en.wikipedia.org/wiki/
Vincent_Obsitnik

Michael J. Senko (1950-), b. Washington, DC, of Slovak parents; career
foreign service officer. Served as U.S. Ambassador to the Republic of the
Marshall Islands and the Republic of Kiribati (s. 2001), having been nominated

by President William Jefferson Clinton. He entered the Foreign Service in 1977 and served in a variety of consular, administrative, political and management positions in the Dominican Republic, Uruguay, El Salvador, Mongolia, Belize, Bosnia and Herzegovina, and Washington. He also served in the Marshall Islands, where he opened the U.S. Status Liaison Office in 1984. Ambassador Senko last served as Policy Planning Director in the Bureau of International Narcotics and Law Enforcement Affairs.
Bio: "Michael J. Senko," in US Department of State Archive. See - https://2001-2009.state.gov/outofdate/bios/s/2910.htm

László Újházy (1795-1870), b. Budimir, Slovakia; son of a landowner of the lesser nobility; in US s. 1849, arriving in NYC with the first group of Hungarian refugees; after the unsuccessful Hungarian revolution; lawyer by training; Kossuth's representative with the US government; founder of a Hungarian colony, New Buda in Iowa. Ujhazy and his family settled near San Antonio, TX, where he farmed and ranched. He served as Abraham Lincoln's consul at Ancona, Italy (1862-64).
Bio: "Újházy László," in: Wikipedia. See - https://hu.wikipedia.org/wiki/ Újházy_László; Vassady, Béla, New Buda: A Colony of Hungarian Forty Eighters in Iowa," *The Annals of Iowa*, 51 (1991), pp. 26-52; "Ujhazi, Laszlo," in Handbook of Texas. See - https://tshaonline.org/handbook/online/articles/ fuj01

2. Legislative Branch

a. General

Rechcigl, Miloslav Jr., *U.S. Legislators with Czechoslovak Roots from Colonial Times to Present: With Genealogical Lineages*. Washington, DC: SVU Press, 1987. 65 p.

b. US Congressmen

Victor l. Berger (1860-1929), b. Nieder Rebbach, Austria, of Slovak parents; journalist, US Congressman from Wisconsin
Bio: "Victor L. Berger," in: Wikipedia. See - https://en.wikipedia.org/wiki/ Victor_L._Berger

Mark Critz (1962-), b. Irwin, PA, of Slovak ancestry; former US Representative for Pennsylvania's 12ᵗʰ Congressional district
Bio: "Mark Critz," in: Wikipedia. See - https://en.wikipedia.org/wiki/Mark_Critz

Joseph M. Gaydos (1926-2015), b. Braddock, PA, of Slovak ancestry; Democratic member of the U.S. House of Representatives from Pennsylvania
Bio: Joseph M. Gaydos," in: Wikipedia, see: https://en.wikipedia.org/wiki/Joseph_M._Gaydos; "Gaydos, Joseph M.," in: *Who's Who in the East*, 18

John Katko (1962-), b. Syracuse, NY, of Slovak ancestry; attorney and politician, attorney and politician, Republican member of the US House of Representatives from New York's 24ᵗʰ district Bio: "John Katko," in: Wikipedia. See - https://en.wikipedia.org/wiki/John_Katko

Daniel Mica (1944-), b. Binghamton, NY, of Slovak descent; Republican US Representative from Michigan
Bio: "Dan Mica," in: Wikipedia. See - https://en.wikipedia.org/wiki/Dan_Mica

John L. Mica (1943-), b. Binghamton, NY, of Slovak ancestry; Republican US Representative from Florida's 7ᵗʰ congressional district (1993-2017)
Bio: "John Mica," in: Wikipedia. See - https://en.wikipedia.org/wiki/John_Mica

Tom Ridge (1945-), b. Munhall, PA, of Slovak ancestry; politician, former Republican US Representative from Pennsylvania's 21ˢᵗ district
Bio: "Tom ridge," in: Wikipedia. See - https://en.wikipedia.org/wiki/Tom_Ridge

Philip Ruppe (1926-), b. Laurium, MI, of Slovak ancestry; former Republican US Representative from Michigan's 11ᵗʰ district
Bio: "Philip Ruppe," in: Wikipedia. See - https://en.wikipedia.org/wiki/Philip_Ruppe

Claudine Schneider (1947-), b. Clairton, PA, of Slovak ancestry; former US Representative
Bio: "Claudine Schneider," in: Wikipedia. See - https://en.wikipedia.org/wiki/Claudine_Schneider

Joe Sestak (1951-), b. Secane, PA, of Slovak ancestry; former Democratic US Representative from Pennsylvania's 7th district
Bio: "Joe Sestak," in: Wikipedia. See - https://en.wikipedia.org/wiki/Joe_Sestak

James Traficant (1941-2014), b. Youngstown, OH, of Slovak descent; politician, member of the US House of Representatives from Ohio
Bio: "James Traficant," in: Wikipedia. See - https://en.wikipedia.org/wiki/James_Traficant

Peter John Visclosky (1949-), b. Gary, IN, of Slovak ancestry; Democratic US Representative from Indiana's 1st district. He called himself the "Slovak Kid" and gained votes with hot dog dinners.
Bio: "Pete Visclosky," in: Wikipedia. See - https://en.wikipedia.org/wiki/Pete_Visclosky

3. Judicial Branch

George W. Folta (1893-1955), b. Braddock, PA, of Slovak immigrant parents; bear hunter in Alaska, lawyer, prosecutor, solicitor, presiding judge of the first Federal Judicial District of Alaska, appointed by President Truman.
Bio: Folta, Richard C., *Of Bench and Bears: Alaska's Bear Hunting Judge.* 2nd ed. Great Northwest Publishing, 2002; Rainery, Richard, "Folta," in: City and Borough of Juneau. See - http://www.juneau.org/library/museum/GCM/readarticle.php?UID=857&newxtkey=

Felix Frankfurter (1882-1965), b. Vienna, of Czech and Slovak ancestry; attorney, professor, jurist, Associate Justice of the Supreme Court of the US
Bio: Hirsch, H. N., *The Enigma of Felix Frankfurter.* Quid Pro, LLC, 2014. 230p.; Lash, Joseph P., *From Diaries of Felix Frankfurter.* W.W. Norton & Co., 1975. 366p.; Thomas, Helen Shirley, *Felix Frankfurter: Scholar on the Bench.* Baltimore: The John Hopkins University Press, 1960. 381p.

Mark R. Hornak (1956-), b. Homestead, PA, of Slovak descent; lawyer, appointed US District Judge by President Barack Obama on October 19, 2011
Bio: "Mark R. Hornak," in: Wikipedia. See - https://en.wikipedia.org/wiki/ Mark R. Hornak; "Mark R. Hornak, District Judge," in: US District Court Western District of Pennsylvania. See - http://www.pawd.uscourts.gov/ content/mark-r-hornak-district-judge

Olga Jurco (1916-2004), b. Illinois, of Slovak descent; lawyer, Federal Magistrate judge; first woman to occupy judicial position in the Northern District of Illinois as US Magistrate (for 14 years)
Bio: "Olga Jurco," *Chicago Tribune*, January 7, 2004.

John Glover Roberts, Jr. (1955-), b. Buffalo, NY, of Slovak descent; lawyer, 17th Chief Justice of the Supreme Court of the US (s. 2005), nominated by President George W. Bush. He was previously a Judge of the United States Court of Appeals for the District of Columbia Circuit (2003-05).
Bio: "John Roberts," in: Wikipedia. See - https://en.wikipedia.org/wiki/ John_Roberts

John Smietanka (1941-), b. Chicago, IL, of Slovak descent; lawyer, prosecutor for Berrien Co., MI; US attorney in Western Michigan, appointed by President Reagan (1981-1994)
Bio: "John Smietanka," in: Wikipedia. See - https://en.wikipedia.org/wiki/ John_Smietanka

Jacob Weinberger (1882-1974), b. Slovakia; lawyer, in private practice, Denver, CO (1904) and Gila County,
AZ (1905-11), in San Diego, CA (1911-41); city attorney for San Diego (1941-43); judge of the Superior Court of San Diego County (1943-45); appointed, by President Truman, Federal Judge, to the seat on the US District Court for the Southern California, first in Los Angeles (1946-49), then San Diego (1949-74)
Bio: "Weinberger, Jacob," in: *Directory of American Judges*. Chicago: American directories, 1955; Jacob Weinberger," in: Wikipedia. See - https://en.wikipedia. org/wiki/Jacob_Weinberger

Edward Weinfeld (1901-1988), b. Manhattan, NY, of Slovak descent; lawyer, Federal Judge of the US District Court for the Southern District of New York
Bio: "Edward Weinfeld," in: Wikipedia. See - https://en.wikipedia.org/wiki/ Edward_Weinfeld

5. Military Service

a. General

White, Lewis, M., ed. *On All Fronts: Czechs and Slovaks in World War II.* Boulder: East European Monographs; distributed by Columbia University Press, New York, 1991. 296p.

b. Soldiers

Jan Ambruš (1899-1994), b. Gorna Mitropolia, Bulgaria, of Slovak descent; Slovak aerobatics and fight pilot, with French Air Force and the British Royal Air Force during World War II, after communist takeover of ČSR, he settled in the US, where he worked as design engineer
Bio: "Jan Ambrus," in: Wikipedia. See - https://en.wikipedia.org/wiki/ Jan_Ambrus

Jerry George Capka (1922-1978), b. Middletown, PA, of Slovak descent; US Army Lieutenant Colonel, recipient of Legion of Merit for action during Vietnam War (1965).
Bio: "Jerry George Capka," in: Military Times Hall of Valor. See - https:// valor.militarytimes.com/hero/98535; "Col. Jerry George Capka," in: Find a Grave. See - https://www.findagrave.com/memorial/125817730/ jerry-george-capka

Péter Pál Dobozy (1832-1919), location of his birth uncertain but could be Slovak ancestry; soldier in Hungarian revolution of 1848; in US s. 1861; Civil War veteran; adjutant of General Asboth; commander of the 4th Colored Heavy Artillery Regiment which he organized; mustered in 1866 at Pine Bluffs, AR. After the Civil War, resided in Missouri as a farmer.
Bio: "Dobozy, Peter Paul," in: *Lincoln's Hungarian Heroes*, p. 50; "LTC Peter Paul Dobozy," in: Find A Grave. See -https://www.findagrave.com/

memorial/77856851/peter-paul-dobozy; "Dobozy Péter Pál," in: Wikipedia.
See - https://hu.wikipedia.org/wiki/Dobozy_ Péter_Pál

Joseph E. Durik (1922-1942), b. Pennsylvania, of Slovak descent; apprentice
seaman, killed in action, following the accidental firing of a torpedo aboard
destroyer Meredith. For his selfless conduct in giving first aid to an injured
shipmate although wounded himself, Apprentice Seaman Durik was
posthumously commended by Admiral Chester W. Nimitz. The destroyer
escort Durick was named in his honor.
Bio: "Joseph E. Durik," in: Wikipedia. See - https://en.wikipedia.org/wiki/
Joseph_E._Durik

Michael J. Estocin (1931-1967), b. Turtle Creek, PA, of Slovak descent;
US Navy officer and a recipient of the United States military's highest
decoration—the Medal of Honor—for his actions in the Vietnam War. He
was presumably lost during action. The US Navy named the guided missile
frigate USS Estocin (FFG-15), launched in 1979, in his honor.
Bio: "Michael J. Estocin," in: Wikipedia. See - https://en.wikipedia.org/wiki/
Michael_J._Estocin

Ján Fiala (1822-1871), b. Slovakia; emigrated to America; surveyor building
railroads and mapping Missouri; a colonel in the Civil War, prepared plans to
defend St. Louis and organize German recruits; wounded.
Bio: "John T. Fiala Papers (1860-1871)," in: Missouri Historical Society Archives,
St. Louis. See - http://mohistory.org/collections/item/resource:103165.

George William Folta (1919-2003), b. Juneau. AK, of Slovak descent;
submarine sailor, Capt., US Navy, serving long career, spanning World War
II, Korea and Viet Nam
Bio: "Captain George William USN Retired," in: SubmarineSailor.com. See -
http://www.submarinesailor.com/InMemorium/FoltaGeorgeW.asp

Cornelius Fornet (1818-1894), b. Stráže pod Tatrami, Slovakia; engineer;
soldier in Hungarian war of 1848; in US s. 1849; in 1852 went back to Europe
to get married and returned to US with his wife; in Civil Ware served under
General John C. Frémont, as a Major of engineers; after recovery from a
serious accident, he was sent to New Jersey by General Hall to organize the
22nd Volunteer Infantry Regiment of NJ. He was appointed first colonel of

the Regiment but, due to injuries, he returned to Hungary, where he became government official.

Bio: "Fornet, Cornelius," in: Lincoln's Hungarian Heroes, p. 54; "Fornet Kornel," in : Wikipedia. See - https://hu.wikipedia.org/wiki/Fornet_ Kornél

Andrew Gálfy-Gállik (1818-1883), b. Brzotín, Slovakia; merchant in Košice; Hungarian army officer; came to America, settling in Cincinnati, OH; in 1862, enlisted in the 58th Ohio Infantry Regiment, in which he was appointed major. After being captured, he was exchanged and then served on the gunboat 'Mound City. After the War, he studied medicine and then practiced in Boston, then in Cincinnati and finally in Kansas City. In 1881, he returned to Košice.

Bio: "Gálfy-Gállik, Andrew, in: Lincoln's Hungarian Heroes, p. 55; "Gallik, András, Gálfy," in: Arcanum. See - https://www.arcanum.hu/en/online-kiadvanyok/Lexikonok-magyar-eletrajzi-lexikon-7428D/g-gy-757D7/gallik-andras-galfy-7585C/

Anthony (Antal) Gerster (1825-1897), b. Košice, Slovakia; uncle of Dr. Arpad G. Gerster; civil engineer, military officer in the 1848 Hungarian Revolution; in US s. 1852; served in the Civil War as a Captain of the engineer corps under General John C. Frémont with General Alexander Asboth and later served under the Generals Rosecrans and Grant; with the 5th Missouri Infantry, then the 27th Missouri Infantry. After the War, he organized Gerster's Independent Company of Pioneers, an independent company of military engineers, responsible for building, repairing, or destroying fortifications and bridges. He died in California in 1897.

Bio: "Gerster's Independent Company of Pioneers," in: Wikipedia. See - https://en.wikipedia.org/wiki/Gerster%27s_Independent_Company_of_Pioneers; "Gerster Antal," in: Wikipedia. See: https://hu.wikipedia.org/wiki/Gerster_Antal; Gerster Anthony," in: Lincoln's Hungarian Heroes, p. 55.

John Joseph Greytak (1902-1973), b. PA, of Slovak descent; Admiral, US Navy

Bio: "Adm. John Joseph Greytak," in: Find A Grave. See - https://www.findagrave.com/memorial/117616482/john-joseph-greytak

Matej Kocak (1882-1918), b. Gbely, Slovakia; US Marine Corps sergeant, posthumous recipient of the Army and Navy Medals of Honor
Bio: "Matej Kocak," in: Wikipedia. See - https://en.wikipedia.org/wiki/Matej_Kocak; Sciranka, John C., "Sergeant Matej Kocak, United States Marine Corps," *Furdek* (1974), pp. 147-149.

Gabriel de Korponay (1809-1866), b. near Košice, Slovakia; in US s. 1844; Mexican-American War and Civil War veteran; with the rank Colonel. He performed recruiting duty in 1847 and commanded a company of cavalrymen in the war. On July 5, 1848, he routed a detachment of Comanches on the Santa Fe Trail in an engagement that is remembered as 'Gabriel's Barbecue'. In the Civil War, Korponay commanded the 28th PA Volunteer Infantry Regiment. He was also known for popularizing the polka dance and taught fencing.
Bio: "Image - Gabriel de Korponay," in: Library of Congress. See - https://www.umbrasearch.org/catalog/12f4969772d9e51bb9369ee9a7eda75683998b75;"Gabriel's Barbecue on the Santa Fe Trail." See - https://www.santafetrailresearch.com/research/gabriels-barbeque.html

Eugene Arthur Kozlay (1826-1883), b. Slovakia; civil engineer; Brigadier General (USA), officer in the Union Army during the Civil War; recruited by President Lincoln to organize a volunteer regiment, designated the 54th New York Voluntary Infantry in 1861. As Colonel in command, his regiment participated in actions at Shenandoah, the Battle of Cross Keys, the Battle of Chancellorsville and the first day of the Battle of Gettysburg on July 1, 1863. In 1864, the regiment took part in various engagements at Seabrook, John's Island, James' Island and at Santee River in the South Carolina campaign. In March 1865, the 54th entered Charleston, South Carolina where it remained until it was ordered to Hart's Island, New York Harbor, and there mustered out of the service of the United States, on April 14, 1866. After the war, as a civil engineer, he helped construct the first elevated railroad in Brooklyn, NY.
Bio: "Brigadier General (USA), Eugene A. Kozlay," in: GENi; "Eugene Arthur Kozlay," in: Find A Grave. See - https://www.findagrave.com/memorial/10508959/eugene-arthur-kozlay;

John C. Kubanic (1970-), b. Greensburg, PA, of Slovak descent; trained in military history and organizational management; graduate of Air Command and Staff College, Maxwell Air Force Base, AL and of Air University, AL, and of the National War College. Washington, DC. He holds the rank of Brigadier General, US air Force and is the Commander, Warner Robins Air Logistics Complex, Robins Air Force Base, Georgia. As the commander, he serves a world-class workforce of over 7,200 military and civilian personnel. Bio: "Brigadier General John C. Kubinec," in: US Air Force. See - https:// www.af.mil/About-Us/Biographies/Display/Article/949525/brigadier-general-john-c-kubinec/; Napsha, Joe, "Hempfield Area graduate Kubinec rises to brigadier general in Air Force," in: TRIB Live. See - https://triblive. com/news/westmoreland/11111363-74/kubinec-force-academy

Theodore Majthenyi (1838-1909), b. Nitra, Slovakia; a Baron, was son of Baron Joseph Majthenyi, member of the landed gentry and prominent politician, a member of upper chamber of Hungarian parliament. Having taken part in the War of Independence, the father was forced to flee. Theodore was only 13 years old when he had to follow his father to exile. They settled in New Buda, Iowa, but soon moved to Davenport. When the Civil War came, Theodore volunteered in the 2nd Iowa Infantry regiment as a Sargent. In St. Louis, he was transferred to the Frémont Body Guard. He was promoted to a 2nd Lieutenant and adjutant within a month. When Frémont was removed, Majthenyi obtained commission as a Captain in Company K of 1st Indiana Cavalry Regiment in 1862, serving until December 1864. He was appointed 2nd Lieutenant of the 5th US Cavalry in February 1866 and elevated to 1st Lieutenant in October. He resigned from the service in December 1868. Bio: "Theodore Majthenyi," in: *The Bracken Rangers: Company K, 28th Regiment, 1st Indiana Cavalry.* By Robert Allan Stevens. 2nd ed. Miami-Los Angeles: Three Stars Press, 2011, pp. 83-85.

Richard Marcinko (1940-), b. Lansford, PA, of Slovak grandfather; US Navy SEAL commander and Vietnam War veteran; the first commanding officer of SEAL Team Six and Red Cell
Bio: "Richard Marcinko," in: Wikipedia. See - https://en.wikipedia.org/wiki/Richard_Marcinko

Edward C. Meyer (1928-), b. St. Mary's, PA, of Slovak descent; US Army General, Chief of Staff of the US Army
Bio: "Edward C. Meyer," in: Wikipedia. See - https://en.wikipedia.org/wiki/Edward_C._Meyer-

Gejza Mihalotzy-Mikulas (aka Géza Mihalótzy/ Michalovič) (1825-1864), b. Zemplín region, Slovakia; moved to Chicago. On Feb. 4, 1861, he sent Abraham Lincoln a letter requesting recognition a group of volunteers from Upper Hungary, Poland, and from Bohemia; they became the Lincoln's shooters of Slavic origin and joined the Union's 24th Volunteer Illinois Regiment. He Fought at Perryville on October 8, 1862 during Kentucky campaign, and in Jan. 1862-63, at the bloody battle of Stones Rive. In 1864, Mihaloczy died in 1864 after sustaining injuries at the Battle of Buzzard's Roost Gap in Georgia.

Bio: Dobrotková, Marta, "Slovenskí priekopníci v Amerike," in: Dobrodruh. sk. See - https://www.dobrodruh.sk/historia/slovenski-priekopnici-v-amerike; Karamanski, Theodore J., "Civilians, Soldiers, and the Sack of Athens, Alabama," in: Illinois Periodicals Online. http://www.lib.niu.edu/1997/iht429748.html

Joseph Nemeth (1816-1881), b. Lošonec, Slovakia; officer in the Hungarian revolutionary forces. After the surrender of the of the revolutionary forces, he eventually arrived in the US in November 1851, settling initially in New York. In 1853, he settled in St. Louis. He made excellent use of his experience with horses and started a practice as surgeon and horse doctor. At the start of the Civil War, he enlisted in the 5th Missouri Infantry Regiment as 1st lieutenant and adjutant and was mustered out in August 1861. He reenlisted as a Major in the battalion Benton Hussars and served as its commander until the unit was incorporated into 5th Missouri Cavalry in February 1862. He was then appointed Colonel and the commander of the entire regiment. He was discharged in November 1862. Subsequently he settled down in Chicago and continued his practice as a veterinary surgeon

Bio: Vida, pp. 277-278.

George P. Novotny (1921-2018); b. Toledo, OH, of Slovak descent; enlisted in the US Army Air Corps, soon after the bombing of Pearl Harbor; he was assigned to the 325th Fighter Group on May 14, 1943 he left the states and spent the next 13 months in North Africa and Italy flying the P-40 Warhawk, the P-47 Thunderbolt and the P-51 Mustang. He was a celebrated World War II P-47 Ace and known as "Toledo's War Ace" and participated in 57 missions. (To receive the title of "Ace", a fighter pilot must have shot down five or more

enemy aircraft in "air-to-air" combat.) He was credited with a ninth aerial victory over Budapest on April 13, 1944.
Bio: "George P. Novotny," in: Voran Funeral Home. See - https://www.voranfuneralhome.com/obituary/George-P.-Novotny/_/1774947

John L. Polerecky (1748-1830), b._France, of Slovak father; Major of Lauzun's Polish Lancers, veteran of the American Revolutionary War
Bio: George J. Krajsa, "Major L. Polerecky, an Officer of Slovak Heritage in the American Revolution," Jednota 18 (1979), pp. 21- 231; "The Slovaks Were There - Major John Polerecky Fought for American Independence," *Slovakia* 7, No. 3-4 (September-December 1957), p. 83-87; "Ján Ladislav Polerecký," in: Wikipedia. See - https://sk.wikipedia.org/wiki/ Ján_Ladislav_Polerecký

John J. Remetta (1911-1992), Slovak American; Maj. General; assistant commander of the 28th Division

Raphael Guido Rombauer (1838-1912), b. Mukačevo, of Slovak father (from Levoča); the youngest of the Rombauer brothers. He was taken to America by his family and he followed his older brothers' footsteps when he volunteered in the Civil War. Similarly, to them, he sought service at the 1st Missouri Infantry Regiment, in which he served as sergeant. After three months, he became a lieutenant and adjutant to Colonel Gustav Wagner, chief of Artillery at Cairo, IL. They belonged under the supervision of General Ulysses Grant. Because of secrecy, much of the communication was conducted in Hungarian and it was Raphael's responsibility to do the translation from Hungarian to English for Grant. Later became Captain of the 1st Illinois Light Artillery Regiment. In October 1864 he was elevated to Major and in February 1865, he became chief of artillery at Memphis. After the War, he was involved with the expanding railroad business and later established his own enterprise. Rombauer Coal Co. in Missouri
Bio: "Maj. Raphael Guido Rombauer," in: Find A Grave. See - https://www.findagrave.com/memorial/116037267/raphael-guido-rombauer; "Rombauer Rafael Guido," in: Wikipedia. See - https://hu.wikipedia.org/wiki/Rombauer_Rafael_ Guidó

Robert Julius Rombauer (1830-1925), b. Mukačevo, of Slovak father (from Levoča); 1850, he immigrated to America with his mother, settling down first in Iowa, then in St. Louis, MO. In 1861, he played a major role in rallying the

pro-Union elements in St. Louis and became Lieutenant Colonel in the 1st Regiment of US Reserve Corps in Missouri, later as Colonel in command of the 1st Missouri Infantry. Towards the end of the Civil War, he was the commander of the 5th Regiment City Guard in St. Louis, organized in 1864 to protect the city during Major General Sterling Price's invasion of Missouri. At the end of the civil War, he returned to civil life in St. Louis, and worked as an editor of the local paper, the *New World.* He was much interested in education and was one of the most devoted proponents of the founding the St. Louis Public Library. He even became president of the library for some time, as well as president of the Board of Assessors and Board of Education. He is the author of one of the best histories of the Union movement in St. Louis.
Bio: "Rombauer Gyula Robert," in: Wikipedia. See - https://hu.wikipedia. org/wiki/Rombauer_ Gyula_Róbert

Roderick E. Rombauer (1833-1924), b. Szeleszto, of Slovak father; fought in the Hungarian War of Independence with his three brothers. In 1851, he immigrated with mother and six siblings from Hamburg to New York, settling, in Iowa. He was probably the most successful of Tivadar's children. He studied law in Quincy, IL at the office of Williams and Lawrence and later attended the Harvard University Law School. He then practiced the law in St. Louis. During the Civil War, Roderick served with the 1st Regiment of the US Reserve Corps in Missouri, as a Captain. He took part in organizing a home guard unit and was involved in battles in southeast Missouri. Having overcome typhoid fever, he then joined General Frémont on his staff. After the War, he continued his legal practice. He became judge of the Circuit Court of St. louis county (1867-70) and then served on the bench of the St. Louis Court of Appeals (1884-96), nine years as presiding judge. He was still practicing law in 1913, at the age of 80.
Bio: Rombauer, Roderick E., *The History of a Life.* The Author, 1903; "Rombauer E. Roderick," in: Wikipedia. See - https://hu.wikipedia.org/ wiki/Rombauer_E._Roderick; Roderick Emil Rombauer," in: Find A Grave. See - https://www.findagrave.com/memorial/95173680;

Roland Rombauer (1837-1898), b. Mukačevo, of Slovak father. He was still a young child when the Hungarian War of liberation was raging and was taken to the US by his mother, following the head of the family, Tivadar Rombauer. He was only 14 years old. Similarly, to his brothers, he enlisted at Company A of the 1st Missouri Infantry Regiment as a Private. After 3 months, he served

as Sergeant in the Company of the 1ˢᵗ Missouri Light Artillery Regiment. He later joined the 1ˢᵗ Florida Cavalry, as Captain, first becoming assistant provost marshal of the District of West Florida, under the command of Brig. General Alexander Asboth and later provost marshal. He was mustered out on November 15, 1865. Subsequently he settled down in St. Louis and worked as a cashier in a bank. Later moved to the West and set off a mining enterprise in Montana, and later was official in the forestry service. He died suddenly of a heart attack in November 1898.
Bio: "Rombauer, Roland," in: Vida, pp. 295-296; "Capt. Roland Theodore Rombauer,", in: Find A Grave. See - https://www.findagrave.com/ memorial/124603894/roland-theodore-rombauer

Matthias Ernest Rozsafy (orig. Ruzicska) (1828-1893), b. Komárno, Slovakia, presumably of Czech origin; a pioneer journalist. As a twenty-year old, took part in the 1848 revolution, during which he almost lost his life. In 1850, he succeeded to come to America and for a time lived in New York and then did some farming in North Carolina on the Fair Oaks plantation; later he operated a farm in Peekskill, NY. In the civil War, he served under General Pope as a Captain of the 1ˢᵗ West Virginia Light Artillery Regiment; was mustered out as a Major by brevet. After the War, he lived in New York, and later moved to Washington, DC, where he had a government position and later had his own patent bureau. He died in Washington and was buried in Arlington National Cemetery.
Bio: "Rozsafy Matthias Ernest," in: Lincoln Hungarian Heroes, pp. 77-79.

Károly Semsey (1830-1911); b. Kračúnovce, Slovakia; officer in Hungarian army with the rank captain; in US s. 1859; veteran of Civil War with the rank Major of the 45ᵗʰ New York Volunteer Infantry Regiment. After the War, worked in the Customs Office and then in the immigration service.
Bio: "Semsey, Karoly," in: Wikipedia. See - https://hu.wikipedia.org/wiki/ Semsey_ Károly; "Semsey, Charles," in: *Lincoln's Hungarian Heroes*, p. 81; "Charles Semsey," in: Vesvary Collection Newspaper. See - http://vasvary. sk-szeged.hu/newsletter/04jun/beszedits.html

Thomas W. Sima (1932-), b. Hannastown, PA, of Slovak descent; Lieutenant Colonel, US Air Force; Vietnam War (1964-74), POW, recipient of Distinguished Cross w/Valor.
Bio: "Thomas W. Sima," in: Veteran Tributes. See -

http://www.veterantributes.org/TributeDetail.php?recordID=983

John Sopko (1930-), Tahanovce, Slovakia; a Rusyn-Slovak American; solider for America during the Korean War. He was highly decorated with several silver and bronze stars for his service and was nominated for the Medal of Honor.
Bio: "American War Hero and Survivor of Holocaust Returns to Slovakia 64 Years Later," in: PRWEB. See - https://www.prweb.com/releases/2005/06/prweb249269.htm

Michael Strank (1919-1945), b. Jarabina, Czech.; US Marine Corps sergeant, killed in action during the Battle of Iwo Jima in World War II; one of the six flag-raisers who helped raise the second US flag atop Mount Suribachi on February 23, 1945, 145, as shown in the iconic photograph Raising the Flag on Iwo Jima. The Marine Corps War Memorial located in Arlington, Virginia, which was modeled after the flag-raising photograph, depicts bronze statues of each of the six Marine flag-raisers.
Bio: "Michael Strank," in: Wikipedia. See - https://en.wikipedia.org/wiki/Michael_Strank

Walter Robert Tkach (1917-), b. La Belle, PA, of Slovak descent; command surgeon of Air Force Systems Command, Andrews Air Force Base, MD; White House physician, who served 3 presidents.
Bio: "Walter Tkach, 72; Served as the Doctor to Three Presidents," *The New York Times*, November 9, 1989; "Major General Walter Robert Tkach," in: http://www.af.mil/About-Us/Biographies/Display/Article/105421/major-general-walter-robert-tkach/

5. Other

Juraj Slávik (1929-), b. Prague, of Slovak parents; with US Government cultural exchange program, Washington, DC
Bio: "Slávik, Juraj Ľudevít Ján," in: *SVU Directory* 8; "Juraj Slavik," in: NCSML Oral Histories. See - https://www.ncsml.org/exhibits/juraj-slavik/

C. STATE AND MUNICIPAL GOVERNMENT

1. Governors

Tom Ridge (1945-), b. Munhall, PA, of Slovak ancestry; politician, 43rd Governor of Pennsylvania
Bio: "Tom Ridge," in: Wikipedia. See - https://en.wikipedia.org/wiki/Tom_Ridge

Jesse Ventura (orig. James George Janos) (1951-), b. Minneapolis, MN, of Slovak ancestry; former professional wrestler, 38th Governor of Minnesota
Bio: "Jesse Ventura," in: Wikipedia. See - https://en.wikipedia.org/wiki/Jesse_Ventura

2. State Legislators

Andrew Paul Bugas (originally Bugos) (1865-1948), b. Lučina, Slovakia; in US. s. 1882, initially settling in Mahanoy City, PA. Later he moved to Rock Springs, Wyoming. He was engaged in grocery, bakery and saloon business. In 1901 he was elected to the Wyoming State Legislature as a Republican and served six terms until 1907. He was apparently the first Slovak to enter American politics. In 1902 he married Helena, also from Slovakia, and from 1903 to 1929 they had a total of eight sons and two daughters.
Bio: "Andrew P. Bugas," in: *Progressive Men of the State of Wyoming.* Chicago, IL: A. W. Bowen & Co., 1901, pp. 644-645; "John Bugas," in: Wikipedia. See - https://en.wikipedia.org/wiki/John_Bugas

George Edward Fedor (1909-1997); b. Slovakia; lawyer, Member Ohio House of Representatives from Cuyahoga County District (1949-1952).
Bio: "Fedor, George Edward," in: *Who's Who in the Midwest,* 14; "George Edward Fedor," in: Prabook. See - https://prabook.com/web/george_edward.fedor/61159

Joseph Aloysius Ferko (1895-1964), b. Philadelphia, PA, of Slovak descent; a pharmacist and founder of Ferko String Band. He was popular enough to be

elected as a PA State Representative on both the Republican and Democratic ticket (1935).
Bio: "Joseph A. Ferko," in: PA House of Representatives. See - https://www. legis.state.pa.us/cfdocs/legis/BiosHistory/MemBio.cfm?ID=1811&body=H

Jules Filo (1909-1991), b. Czech.; member of the PA State House of Representatives (1948, reelected to serve 9 more terms), appointed to PA Commission on Interstate Cooperation (1967-68)
Bio: "Jules Filo," in: PA House of Representatives. See - http://www.legis. state.pa.us/cfdocs/legis/BiosHistory/MemBio.cfm?ID=1329&body=H; "Filo, Jules," in: *Who's Who in US Politics,* 2

George C. Hasay (1948-), b. Nanticoke, PA; manager, Hasay Chevrolet, Inc., Shickshinny, PA; elected as a Republican to the PA House of Representatives for 1973 term, reelected to serve 16 consecutive terms thereafter
Bio: "George C. Hasay," in: PA House of Representatives. See - http://www. legis.state.pa.us/cfdocs/legis/BiosHistory/MemBio.cfm?ID=62&body=H

Joseph Hirkala (1923-1987), b. Passaic, NJ; of Slovak descent; member of NJ Assembly (1967, 1969); member of NJ Senate (1971, 1973, 1977, 1981 and 1983)
Bio: "Joseph Hirkala Is Dead; A Jersey State Senator," *The New York Times,* January 3, 1987.

George A. Hricko (1883-1963), b. Drifton, PA; member of PA State House of Representatives (1924,1927), presumably first American legislator of Slovak descent, president of Jednota (1926)
Bio: "George A. Hricko," in: Prabook. See - https://prabook.com/ web/george_a.hricko/934357; "George A. Hricko," in: PA House of Representatives. See - http://www.legis.state.pa.us/cfdocs/legis/BiosHistory/ MemBio.cfm?ID=3338&body=H

Sid Michaels Kavulich (1956-), b. Taylor, PA, of Slovak descent; communications specialist, Democrat, serving Lackawanna County in the PA House of Representatives (s. 2011).
Bio: "Sid Michaels Kavulich," in: PA House of Representatives. See - http://www.legis.state.pa.us/cfdocs/legis/home/member_information/

house_bio.cfm?id=1213; "Sid Michaels Kavulich," in: Wikipedia. See - https://en.wikipedia.org/wiki/Sid_Michaels_Kavulich

Joseph Klein (1908-), b. Košice, Slovakia; insurance executive, politician, member of the Indiana State House of Representatives (1936, 1938, 1946, 1948)
Bio: "Klein, Joseph," in: *Who's Who in US Politics* 1952

Frank Leonard Malinczak (1925-), b. Fredericktown, PA, of Slovak descent; owner of Malinczak Gas and Oil Co. (s. 1952); Pennsylvania State Representative (1965-66), county commissioner, Fayette County, PA (196-71)
Bio: "Malinczak, Frank Leonard," in: *Who's Who in US Politics,* 2

John L. Mica (1943-), b. Binghamton, NY, of Slovak ancestry; member of the Florida House of Representatives from the 41st district (1976-1980)
Bio: "John Mica," in: Wikipedia. See - https://en.wikipedia.org/wiki/John_Mica

Frank Mrvan (1933-), b. East Chicago, IN; of Slovak descent; accountant and bank financial officer; politician; member of the Indiana Senate, Democratic Party (1979-95).
Bio: "Frank Mrvan," in: Wikipedia. See - https://en.wikipedia.org/wiki/Frank_Mrvan

Stephen R. Olenick (1910-2003), b. Youngstown, OH, of Slovak descent; city councilman, Youngstown, OH (1946-54); Ohio State senator (1955-62), auditor, Mahony County (s, 1962); supreme auditor, Slovak Catholic Sokol, Passaic, NJ; supreme treasurer (s. 1962
Bio: "Olenick, Stephen R.," in: *Who's Who in American Politics,* 2

Michael Allen O'Pake (1940-2010), b. Reading, PA, of Slovak descent; lawyer, attorney (s. 1966), elected as a Democrat to PA House of Representatives (1969-71), to Pa State Senate (1973-2010)
Bio: "Michael A. O'Pake," in: PA House of Representatives. See - http://www.legis.state.pa.us/cfdocs/legis/BiosHistory/MemBio.cfm?ID=172&body=H; "O'Pake, Michael A.," in: *Who's Who in American Politics,* 2

Raymond L. 'Ray' Pavlak (1926-1994), b. South Paul, MN; lawyer; member of the MN State House of Representatives (1965-66, 1967-72, 1973-74).
Bio: "Pavlak, Raymond L. 'Ray,'" in: MN Legislative Reference Library -Legislators Past & Present. See - https://www.leg.state.mn.us/legdb/fulldetail?ID=10511; "Raymond Pavlak, 68, district judge for 20 years," *Star Tribune* (Minneapolis, MN), April 2, 1994; "Ray Pavlak," in: Wikipedia. See - https://en.wikipedia.org/wiki/Ray_Pavlak

James Michael Petro (1948-), b. Cleveland, OH, probably of Slovak descent; lawyer, Republican politician, member of Ohio State House of Representatives (1981-91);
Ohio State auditor (1994, re-elected 1968), Ohio attorney general (2003-07).
Bio: "Petro, James Michael," in: *Who's Who in American Politics,* 8

Andrew Charles Putka (1926-2015); b. Cleveland, OH, of Slovak descent; lawyer, banker, member Ohio House of Representatives, 1953-1956, Ohio Senate, 1957-1958.
Bio: "Putka, Andrew Charles," in: *Who's Who in the Midwest,* 13; "Andrew Charles Putka," in: Prabook. See - https://prabook.com/web/andrew_charles.putka/334518

Steve Seventy (1927-1988), b. Pittsburgh, Pa, of Slovak father; accomplished accordion player, owner of Seventy's Music, Pittsburgh, teacher; elected to PA House of Representatives in 1978, served 4 more consecutive terms
Bio: "Steve Seventy," in: PA House of Representatives. See - http://www.legis.state.pa.us/cfdocs/legis/BiosHistory/MemBio.cfm?ID=420&body=H; "Steve Seventy," in: Wikipedia. See - https://en.wikipedia.org/wiki/Steve_Seventy

Mary K. Sotak (fl. 1956), b. Cleveland, of Slovak descent; member of the Ohio House of Representatives (1944-45), member of Cleveland City Council (1947); Delegate to Democratic National Convention from Ohio, 1948, 1956 (alternate).

Jerome Stano (1932-2011), b. Cleveland, OH, of Slovak descent;
Bio: "Jerome Stano," in: Wikipedia. See - https://en.wikipedia.org/wiki/Jerome_Stano; "Jerome P. Stano," *The Plain Dealer,* August 31-Sept. 1, 2011.

Joseph G. Tomascik (1914-1970), b. Wilkes-Barre, PA, of Slovak descent, lawyer, elected as Democrat to the PA House of Representatives (1961-1962) Bio: "Joseph G. Tomascik," in: PA House of Representatives. See - https://vasj. com/news/former-euclid-mayor-bill-cervenik-72-named-president-of-vasj

Judy Baar Topinka (1944-2014), b. Riverside, IL, of Czech and Slovak ancestry; journalist, member of the Illinois House of Representatives (1981-85) and in the Illinois Senate (1985-1995). She also served as the State chairwoman of the Republican Party.
Bio: "Judy Baar Topinka," in: Wikipedia. See - https://en.wikipedia.org/wiki/Judy_Baar_Topinka

3. Mayors

Andrew W. Banick (1906-1986), b. Dunmore, PA, of Slovak descent; Mayor of Carteret, NJ
Bio: "Andrew W. Banick," in: Find A Grave. See - https://www.findagrave. com/memorial/97237248/andrew-w-banick

Mary Jancosek Bercik (1914-1996), b. of Slovak descent; Mayor of Whiting, IN (1957-64). When her husband died in the office, the city council appointed Mary Jancosek Bercik to serve for two years, completing the unexpired term of Mayor William Bercik. Mary Bercik went on to seek and win the Mayoral office for the next four years.
Bio: "Mary Jancosek Bercik," in: IN.gov. See- https://www.in.gov/icw/files/2015-03-11_Mary_Jancosek_Bercik.pdf

Robert Bercik (1938-), b. Whiting, IN, of Slovak descent; Mayor of Whiting, IN (1988-2003). He was the owner-operator of Whiting Service Station and served as the Street Commissioner of Whiting from 1962 to 1974.
Bio: "Robert J. Bercik," in: Mayors - Whiting. See - https://whiting.lib.in.us/mayors/

Stephen J. Bercik (1921-2003), b. of Slovak descent; politician, Mayor of Elizabeth, NJ. (1956-64); served of the Waterfront Commission of New York Harbor (1966-71); in 1972 he was appointed a municipal judge.
Bio: "Deaths: Bercik, The Honorable Steven J.," *The New York Times,* June 16, 2003; "Stephen Bercik," in: Wikipedia. See - https://en.wikipedia.org/wiki/Stephen_Bercik

William Bercik (1876-1957), b. Whiting, IN, of Slovak descent; Mayor of Whiting, IN (1956-1957). He was extremely active in church, fraternal and civic affairs throughout the community. In 1957, William Bercik was serving his second year of a four year mayoral term when he succumbed to a heart attack.
Bio: "William Bercik," in: Mayors - Whiting. See - https://whiting.lib.in.us/mayors/

Michael J. Blastick (1905-1969), served as Mayor of Whiting, IN (1955-56). In December 1954, he resigned to become the Lake County auditor.

William R. Cervenik (1976-), of Slovak descent; certified public accountant, Mayor, City of Euclid, OH
Bio: "Former Euclid Mayor Bill Cervenik '72 named president of VASJ," in: Villa Angela-St. Joseph HS. See - https://vasj.com/news/former-euclid-mayor-bill-cervenik-72-named-president-of-vasj

Miller M. Duris (1928-2014), b. Rainier, OR, of Slovak descent'; Democratic politician, Mayor of Hillsboro, Oregon
Bio: "Miller M. Duris," in: Wikipedia. See - https://en.wikipedia.org/wiki/Miller_M._Duris

Frank R. Franko (1920-fl 1961), b. of Slovak descent; a Democrat; Mayor of Youngstown, OH (1960-1961)

William Grenchik, b. Whiting, IN, of Slovak descent; Mayor of Whiting, IN (1964-1968) and 1976-1988). He enlisted in the US air Force for two years. In 1947, he was employed by the American Trust and Savings Bank of Whiting. Since 1962, he became active in his travel agency.
Bio: "Joseph Grenchik," in: Mayors - Whiting. See - https://whiting.lib.in.us/mayors/

Andrew S. Kovacik (1916-1988), b. of Slovak immigrant parents; Mayor of Whiting, IN (1948-1954).In 1942, he joined the US Army, where he served as a member of the Counter Intelligence Corps for two years.
Bio: "Andrew S. Kovacik." In: Mayors - Whiting. See - https://whiting.lib. in.us/mayors/

Frank X. Kryzan (1914-2010), b. Youngstown, OH; lawyer, practiced law with his brother Anthony in Youngstown, OH; president of City Council; Mayor of Youngstown, OH (1954-60); one of the first politicians in Ohio to support the bid of then Senator John F. Kennedy for Presidency of the US.
Bio: "Frank X. Kryzan," *The Times,* Crown Point, IN, March 16, 2010; "Frank X. Kryzan," *The Vindicator,* July 21, 2018

Robert A. Pastrick (1930-2018), of Slovak descent; Mayor of East Chicago, IN (1973-2004). He was also on the city council for 12 years and controller for seven years.
Bio: "Former East Chicago Mayor Pastrick dead at 88," *Chicago Tribune,* August 7, 2018.

John Petruska (1920-2015), b. Cleveland, OH; 'hands on" Mayor, Parma, OH (1967-1987), president of the city council (1967); award-winning roller skater, Word War II veteran
Bio: "John Petruska, former Parma mayor: Obituary," in: Cleveland. com. See - https://www.cleveland.com/parma/index.ssf/2015/09/ john_petruska_former_parma_may.html

Joseph Stahura (1956-), b. Whiting, IN, of Slovak descent; a Democrat; Whiting City Councilman (served 20 years), Mayor of Whitney, IN (s. 2004; in 2018 in his 4th term.)
Bio: "Joseph Stahura," in: MyLife.com. See - https://www.mylife.com/ joseph-stahura/e791264115810

Nick Wasicsko (1958-1993), b. Yonkers, NY, of Slovak descent; lawyer, politician; Mayor of Yonkers, NY (s. 1987), the youngest Mayor of Yonkers. As mayor he fought for the desegregation of public housing. Once out of

office, Wasicsko practiced law, taught at John Jay College of Criminal Justice, and hosted a local radio talk show.
Bio: "Nick Wasicsko," in; Wikipedia. See - https://en.wikipedia.org/wiki/Nick_Wasicsko

Joseph John Zahorec (1920-1984), b. Lorain, OH, of Slovak descent; owner of Zahorec Realty for 24 years; Mayor of Lorain, OH (1972-79, 1983-84).
Bio: "Zahorec, Joseph John," in: *Who's Who in American Politics*, 1977-78; "Joseph Zahorec," in: Find A. Grave. See - https://www.findagrave.com/memorial/49504464/joseph-zahorec

Stephen A. Zona (1899-1969), politician, Mayor of Parma, OH (1952-1957)

4. Judges

George E. Benko (1931-), possibly of Slovak decent; Sandusky-Sanilac County probate judge, Michigan
Bio: "Benko, George E.," in: *The American Bench* 1977.

Steven J. Bercik (1921-2003), b. of Slovak descent; judge to the Juvenile and Domestics Court of Union County, NJ, serving as presiding judge from 1977-88.
Bio: "Deaths: Bercik, The Honorable Steven J.," *The New York Times*, June 16, 2003; "Stephen Bercik," in: Wikipedia. See - https://en.wikipedia.org/wiki/Stephen_Bercik

Nanette Dembitz (1913-1989), b. Washington, DC, of Slovak descent; a lawyer; General Counsel of New York Civil Liberties Union (1988-67); Judge of the Family Court of New York (1967-81).
Bio: "Nanette Dembitz," *The New York Times*, June 22, 1972; Anderson, Susan Heller, "Judge Nanette Dembitz, 76, Dies; Served in New York Family Court," The New York Times, April 5, 1989.

Frank Robert Franko (1920-), b. Youngstown, OH, of Slovak descent; lawyer, practicing attorney, Youngstown (1946-54), city prosecutor, Youngstown (1948-54) judge Municipal Court of Youngstown, (1954-59)
Bio: "Franko, Frank Robert." In: *Directory of American Judges*. Chicago: American Directories, 1955

David Gertler (1911-1995), b. Komárno, Slovakia; lawyer, in private practice, New Orleans (1939-63); judge, Civil Dist. Court, New Orleans, LA (s. 1963); co-founder, with his son Mike, of the firm Gertler Law Firm (s. 1975-), specializing in mesothelioma law
Bio: "Gertler, David," in: *Who's Who in the South*, 11; "Gertler Law Firm." See - https://www.mesotheliomalawyers.net/attorneys/gertler-law-firm/; "David Gertler," in: Prabook. See - https://prabook.com/web/david.gertler/1664369

John Herman Hausner (1932-2010), b. Detroit, MI, of Slovak descent; lawyer, assistant US attorney (1969-73), chief assistant US attorney, Eastern District Michigan (1973-76); Judge 3rd Judicial Circuit Michigan, Wayne County (1976-1994); also, a poet
Bio: "Judge John H. Hausner," in: Legacy.com. See - https://www.legacy.com/obituaries/name/john-hausner-obituary?pid=182227697; "John Herman Hausner," in: Prabook. See - https://prabook.com/web/john_herman.hausner/929500

Otto Michael Kaus (1920-1996), b. Vienna, of Slovak ancestry; lawyer, Justice of the Supreme Court of California
Bio: "Otto Kaus," in: Wikipedia. See - https://en.wikipedia.org/wiki/Otto_Kaus

John S. Kolena (1918-1989), b. Loraine, OH, of Slovak descent; lawyer, practicing attorney in Lorain, OH (s. 1951), assistant city prosecutor, Lorain (1951-56), judge, Lorain Municipal Court (1965-79).
Bio: "Kolena, John S.," in: *The American Bench* 1977.

Frank X. Kryzan (1914-2010), b. Youngstown, OH; lawyer, politician, municipal judge, Youngstown, OH (1973-1984).
Bio: "Frank X. Kryzan," *The Times*, Crown Point, IN, March 16, 2010; "Frank X. Kryzan," *The Vindicator*, July 21, 2018

John J. Leskovyansky (1925-2006), b. Senecaville, OH, of Slovak descent; lawyer, assistant prosecutor, Youngstown, OH; judge, municipal court (1961-72), judge, Ohio Court of Common Pleas, Mahoning County (1972-78)
Bio: "Leskovyansky, John J.," in: *The American Bench*, 1977; "John Joseph Leskovyansky," in: Prabook. See - https://prabook.com/web/john_joseph.

leskovyansky/390655; "Domestic relations judge for 24 years," *The Vindicator*, May 10, 2006.

Peter J. Marutiak (1923-1985), b. California, PA, of possible Slovak ancestry; lawyer, judge of Shiawassee Circuit Court, Michigan (1969-74)
Bio: "Marutiak, Peter J.," in: *The American Bench* 1977.

Mark J. Mihok (1953-), b. of Slovak descent; lawyer, municipal judge, Lorain, OH (s. 2002)
Bio: "The Honorable Judge Mark J. Mihok," in: Lorain Ohio. See - http://www.cityoflorain.org/476/Judge-Mihoks-Office

Paul J. Mikus (1910-1995), b. possibly of Slovak descent; lawyer, prosecutor, Lorain County, OH; judge, Lorain County, OH
Bio: "Mikus, Paul J.," in: *The American Bench* 1977

George J. Novicky; b. possibly of Slovak descent; judge, Parma Municipal Court, OH (-1979);
Bio: "Novicky, George J.," in: *The American Bench* 1977

Raymond L. 'Ray' Pavlak (1926-1994), b. South Paul, MN; lawyer; practicing attorney with the firm Pavlak & Lacy (1965-74); judge, 1st Judicial District Court, MN (1974-94), also MN State legislator
Bio: "Pavlak," in: *The American Bench* 1977; "Raymond Pavlak, 68, district judge for 20 years," *Star Tribune* (Minneapolis, MN), April 2, 1994; "Ray Pavlak," in: Wikipedia. See -https://en.wikipedia.org/wiki/Ray_Pavlak

John Edward Pavlik (1898-1985), b. Bratislava, Slovakia; lawyer, practicing attorney (s. 1924), city attorney, Calumet City, IL (1935-45), judge, City Court of Calumet City, IL (1945, 1951 and 1957); associate circuit judge (1964), circuit judge (1971), presiding judge of the 6th Municipal District (1971).
Bio: "Pavlik, John Edward," in: *Directory of American Judges*. Chicago: American Directories, 1995; "Pavlik, 87, judge for 30 Years," *Chicago Tribune*, October 8, 1985.

Roderick E. Rombauer (1833-1924), b. Szeleszto, of Slovak father; revolutionary in 1848 War; in US s. 1851; Civil War veteran. He studied law in Quincy, IL at the office of Williams and Lawrence and later attended the

Harvard University Law School. He then practiced the law in St. Louis. After the Civil War, he continued his legal practice. He became judge of the Circuit Court of St. louis county (1867-70) and then served on the bench of the St. Louis Court of Appeals (1884-96), nine years as presiding judge. He was still practicing law in 1913, at the age of 80.
Bio: Rombauer, Roderick E., *The History of a Life*. The Author, 1903; "Roderick Emil Rombauer," in: find A Grave. See - https://www.findagrave.com/memorial/95173680; "Rombauer, Roderick E.," in: *Encyclopedia of the History of St. Louis: A Compendium of History*. New York - Louisville, St. Louis: The Southern History Co., 1899, Vol. 4, pp. 1935-1936; Rombauer E. Roderick," in: Wikipedia. See - https://hu.wikipedia.org/wiki/Rombauer_E._Roderick

John J. Sirotnak (1901-1975), b. of Slovak descent; judge of the Common Pleas Court, Lackawanna County, PA, General Counsel of the FCSU

Louis D. Stefan (1925-1994), b. Philadelphia, PA, possibly of Slovak ancestry; lawyer, judge of PA county of Common Pleas (s. 1970); Orpheus County judge (s. 1985),
Bio: "Stefan, Louis Damon," in: *The American Bench* 1977; "Collision with Tractor-trailer Kills Montgomery County Judge in N.J.," *The Morning Call*, September 11, 1994.

Aron Steuer (1898--1985), b. New York, NY, of Slovak descent; justice of City Court New York (1929-); justice of the Supreme Court New York (1932-1961); justice of the Appellate Division New York (1961-1974).
Bio: "Steuer, Aron," in: *Who's Who in Law*, 1; "Steuer, Aron," in: *Who's Who in East*, 12; "Steuer, Aron," in: *Directory of American Judges*. Chicago: American Directories, 1955; Kolbert, Elizabeth, "Aron Steuer, Served as Appellate Justice in New York Court," *The New York Times*, May 6, 2014; "Aaron Steuer," in: nycourts.gov. See - https://www.nycourts.gov/courts/ad1/centennial/Bios/asteuer2.shtml

Robert J. Stolarik (1929-), b. Williston Park, NY; of Slovak descent; lawyer, family court judge (1969), Rockland County Court judge, NY, State Supreme Court judge in Rockland County (s. 1979)
Bio: "Stolarik, Robert J.," in: *The American Bench* 1977; "Man in the News; Judge in the Brink's Case," *The New York Times*, September 20, 1982.

George Stephen Tenesy (1887-1948), b. Slovakia; lawyer, municipal judge, Cleveland (1934-35); chief counsel, Unemployment Compensation Commission, Cleveland (s. 1937).
Bio: "Tenesy, George Stephen," in: *Who's Who in Law.* Edited by J. Schwarz. New York: 1937, Vol. 1, p. 929.

Joseph E. Wargo (ca 1911-1987), b. of Slovak descent; lawyer, municipal judge, Anoka County Probate Court, MN (1968-79)
Bio: "Anoka County feathers its nest with a bird-lover's gift," *Star Tribune.* See - http://www.startribune.com/anoka-county-feathers-its-nest-with-a-bird-lover-s-gift/14849186/

Stephen A. Zona (1899 -1969), politician, judge, Parma, OH (1964-1969)

5. Other Officials

Peter Billick (1909-2014), b. Thompson, PA, of Slovak descent; trained as architect; joined the police force in Gary, IN, retiring as captain (1951); chief of investigating staff of district attorney; assistant supt., plant protection, Gary Works of US Steel (1951); president, Gary Deanery, NCCM (1950--51); ran, unsuccessfully, on Republican ticket in primary, for Mayor of Gary (1951); organizer of Indiana State Lodge, Fraternal Order of police (1935).; director of Aldering Settlement House; Slovak Club.
Bio: "Billick, Peter," in: *Catholic Who's' Who,* Vol. 5, p. 24

John Fusek (1885-d.), b. Vrbovce, Slovakia; dealer in real estate and insurance business; alderman, East Chicago
Bio: Fusek, John," in: Droba, p. 290.

Andrew Hedmeg (1908-1988), b. Bratislava, Slovakia; physician, director of Adams County Health Department, Natchez, MS (1937-52); director of the division of preventive medicine and director of division of local health services, LA Board of Health (1952-66); president of LA State Board of Health, New Orleans, LA (s, 1966)
Bo: "Hedmeg, Andrew," in: *Who's Who in the South,* 11

Samuel Kostelny (1894-d.), b. Brezová, Slovakia; commissioner of the West Chicago Parks and treasurer of the West Chicago Park Board
Bio: "Kostelny, Samuel," in: Droba, p. 291-292.

Michael Kozacik (1873-1941), b. Horná Lhota, Slovakia; banker, Whiting, IN; first Democratic alderman elected to the city council in Whiting, Indiana
Bio: "Kozacik, Michael," in: Droba, pp. 78-79; "Kozacik, Michael," in: Find a Grave. See - https://www.findagrave.com/memorial/93578867/michael-kozacik

Stephen, J. Skriba (1892-1960), b. Šimonovany, Slovakia; real estate and insurance broker, manager, Mortgage Home Owners Loan Corp., Chicago
Bio: "Skriba, Stephen J.," in: Droba, pp. 292-293; "Stephen Joseph Skriba, Sr., in: Find A Grave. See - https://www.findagrave.com/memorial/152164348/stephen-joseph-skriba

Judy Baar Topinka (1944-2014), b. Riverside, IL, of Czech and Slovak ancestry; politician, 71[St] Treasurer of Illinois (1995-2007); and 7th Comptroller of Illinois (2011-2014).
Bio: "Judy Baar Topinka,", in: Wikipedia. See - https://en.wikipedia.org/wiki/Judy_Baar_Topinka

D. CIVIC AND COMMUNAL WORK

1. Religious Workers

Joseph Victor Adamec (1935-), b. Bannister, MI, of Slovak descent; R.C. priest; National President of Slovak Catholic Federation (s. 1973)
Bio: "Adamec, Rev. Joseph," in: *Catholic Who's Who*, 21 (1976-1977).

Joseph S. Altany (1903-1986), b. Tarentum, Pa, of Slovak descent; R.C. priest, Msgr., Papal Prelate with the title Rt. Rev., president of the Slovak Catholic Foundation; editor of the monthly *Dobrý pastier.*
Bio: "Altany Jozef," in: Religia Slovakia. See - http://religiask.blogspot.com/2017/11/altany-jozef.html

MILOSLAV RECHCIGL, JR.

Sidonia Cyd Bettelheim (1866-1959), b. Hungary, of Slovak ancestry; resident directress of Emanu El Sisterhood, NYC
Bio: "Bettelheim, Cyd," *The American Jewish Yearbook*, 7 (1905-1906), p.43.

Samuel Bettelheim (1873-1942), b. Bratislava, Slovakia; Zionist, organizer of the Agudath Israel in America
Bio: "Samuel Bettelheim Reported Dead in Hungary" in: Jewish Telegraph Agency, June 25, 1942; "Bettelheim, Samuel," in: *Who's Who in American Jewry*, Vol. 1, pp. 57-58.

Francis J. Dubosh (1890-1967), b. Cleveland, OH, of Slovak ancestry; R.C. priest, Msgr.; supreme chaplain of Jednota; president of the Slovak League (1943-45), president of the Slovak Catholic Federation of America (1937-38). Bio: "Rev. Fr. Francis Joseph Dubosh," in: Find a Grave. See- https://www. findagrave.com/memorial/120789128/francis-joseph-dubosh;

Joseph Hušek (1880-1947), b. Ružomberok, Slovakia; editor, president of Federation of Slovak Catholics, president of Slovak League of America, founder and president of Slovak Educational Institute of America, founder and president of Friends of Slovak Freedom
Bio: "Husek, Joseph," in: *Catholic Who's Who*, 7 (1946-1947), p. 286.

Matthew Jankola (1872-1916), b. Slovakia; R.C. priest, the founder of the Sisters of SS. Cyril and Methodius
Bio: Tybor, M. Martina, "Matthew Jankola 1872-1916: Slovak-American Priest, Leader, Educator," *Slovakia* 22, No. 45 (1972), pp. 161-92; Jankola Book Honoring the Centennial of the Birth of Father Matthew Jankola (1872-1916) Slovak-American Priest, Patriot, Educator, and Founder of the Sisters of SS. Cyril and Methodius.

Stefan Kistiak (1889-1970), b. Brezová, Slovakia; machinist, inspector of the Slovak Lutheran Church of St. Peter and Paul, vice president of the Slovak Evangelical Society, Chicago
Bio: "Kistiak, Stefan," in: Droba, p. 218.

Rebekah Kohut (1864-1951), b. Košice, Slovakia; in US s. 1862; social welfare activist, president of Ahawath Chesed Sisterhood
Bio: Rebekah Bettelheim Kohut,", in: Jewish Women's Archive. Encyclopedia. See - https://jwa.org/encyclopedia/article/kohut-rebecca; Kohut, Rebekah. Papers. AJA, Cincinnati, Ohio, and American Jewish Historical Society, Waltham, MA; "Rebekah Bettelheim Kohut," in: Wikipedia. See - https://en.wikipedia.org/wiki/Rebekah_Bettelheim_Kohut; "Rebekah Kohut, Noted American Jewish Women's Leader, Dies at age of 86," *The Wisconsin Jewish Chronicle*, August 17, 1951; Wald, Lillian D., "American Jewry's First Lady. Rebekah Kohut on the Golden Jubilee in Public Life," *The Wisconsin Jewish Chronicle*, November 15, 1935; "Kohut, Rebekah," *The American Jewish Yearbook*, 7 (1905), p. 76; Sorin, Gerald, "Kohut, Rebekah Bettelheim," in: *National Biography*, Vol. 12, pp. 874-875.

Stephen Krasula (1887-1970); b. Namestovo, Slovakia; R.C. priest; Rt. Rev.; pastor, St. john Nepomucene Church, NYC (s. 1916); hon. president of the Slovak Catholic Federation
Bio: "Msgr. S.J. Krasula, Led Slovak Group," *The New York Times*, March 15, 1970.

Joseph Kroslak (1890-1938), b. Streda, Slovakia; president of Nitra of the Slovak Evangelical Society, accountant of the Slovak Evangelical Lutheran Church of St. Peter and Paul.
Bio: "Kroslak," in: Droba, p. 222:

Herman Moskowitz (1921-2018), b. Pavlovce, Czech.; attended the world-famous Munkatch Yeshiva. Having been recognized for his beautiful voice, he was elevated to its High Holidays choir. Having survived the Holocaust, he came to Cincinnati, OH, in 1948. He became the long-standing shamos (sexton) of then Congregation Ohav Shalom in Avondale and then Roselawn - serving for 25 years.
Bio: "Obituary – Herman Moskowitz," in: *The American Israelite*, February 15, 2018. See - http://www.americanisraelite.com/social_news/obituaries/article_e9af9ae4-127c-11e8-ba0c-3b37609daa4b.html

Jozef Murgaš (1864-1929), b. Tajov, Slovakia; R.C. priest, founder of the Slovak Catholic-Federation
Bio: Palickar, Stephen J., *Rev. Joseph Murgas, Priest-Scientist: His Musical Wireless and the First Radio: Biography.* New York, 1950. 164 p.; Palickar, Stephen J., *A Pictorial Biography of Rev. Joseph Murgas, Pioneer Inventor in the Field of Wireless Telegraphy and Radio.* Wilkes-Barre, PA: Murgas Memorial Foundation, 1953. 83p.

Ján Kubašek (1885 1950), b. Stará Ľubovňa, Slovakia; R.C. priest, chaplain in Yonkers, NY, politician, publicist, founder of the Association of Slovak Catholics.
Bio: "Ján Kubašek," in: Wikipedia. See - https://sk.wikipedia.org/ wiki/ Ján_Kubašek; "Ján Kubašek," in: Stará Lubovňa. See - https://www. staralubovna.sk/jan-kubasek/

Lawrence Lovasik (1913-1986), b. Tarentum, PA, of Slovak descent; R.C. missionary priest, SVD, founder of the Sisters of the Divine Spirit, a missionary congregation of women and the Family Service Corps, secular institute devoted to charitable work
Bio: "Lawrence Lovasik," in: Wikipedia. See - https://en.wikipedia.org/wiki/ Lawrence_Lovasik

Samuel Papánek (1870-1956), b. Brezová pod Bradlom, Slovakia; founder of National Wood Co., one of the founders of the Holy Trinity Slovak Evangelical Church, Chicago
Bio: "Papánek, Samuel," in: *Panorama*, pp. 259-260.

Ján Podmajersky (1868-d.), b. Sobotište, Slovakia; president of the Slovak Evangelical Society (1912-1929), Chicago
Bio: "Podmajersky, Ján," in: Droba, pp. 227-228.

Martin Potucek (1888-d.), b. Slovakia; president of the Slovak Evangelical Society, Chicago
Bio: "Potucek, Martin," in: Droba, p. 228.

Ronald Lauder (1944-), b. New Tork, NY, of Czech. descent, American businessman, heir to the Estée Lauder Corporation, political activist, president of the World Jewish Congress
Bio: "Ronald Lauder," in: Wikipedia. See - https://en.wikipedia.org/wiki/Ronald_Lauder

Mary (née Mandula) Rezak (1924-2009), b. Gary, IN, of Slovak descent; a clubwoman; president of the Rosary Alter Society, first president of American Legion Auxiliary Slovak Unit # 367, president of the Gary Deanery Council of Catholic Women
Bio: "Mary Rezak," *Post-Tribune*, December 11-12, 2009.

Alexander Seelenfreund B. (1869-1920), b. Vienna; educated in Košice, Slovakia; in US s. 1883; resided in Chicago. He was leader of the International Order of B'nai B'rith, of which he had been secretary of the International Constitution Grand Lodge; first president of the B'nai B'rith Council of Chicago; founder of the Anti-Defamation League and the Covenant Club.
Bio: "Seelenfreund, Alexander B." in: *History of Jews in Chicago*, p.662; "Alexander B. Seelenfreund Funeral 10:30 This Morning from Forth's Chapel--World Leader Dies," in: Foreign Language Press See - https://flps.newberry.org/article/5423972_8_1_1010

Joseph Simonides (1881-1969), b. Slovenské Pravno, Slovakia ; president of the Slovak Evangelical Union, Chicago
Bio: "Simonides, Joseph," in: Droba, p. 230.

Henrietta Szold (1860-1945), b. Baltimore, MD, of Slovak ancestry; Jewish Zionist leader and founder of Hadassah
Bio: Kessler, B. (ed.). *Daughter of Zion: Henrietta Szold and American Jewish Woman.* 1995;
Lowenthal, Marvin, *Henrietta Szold: Life and Letters.* New York: Viking, 1942; Kessler, B. (ed.). *Daughter of Zion: Henrietta Szold and American Jewish Woman.* 1995; Lowenthal, Marvin. Henrietta Szold: Life and Letters. New York: Viking, 1942; Reinharz, S. and M. Raider (eds.), *American Jewish Women and the Zionist Enterprise* (2005); Shargel, B.R. *Lost Love: The Untold Story of Henrietta Szold* (1997); "Carey, Charles W., "Szold, Henrietta," in: *National Biography*, Vol. 21, pp. 241-23.

Samuel Woolner (1845-1911), b. Senica, Slovakia; distiller, financier, president of Union of American Hebrew Congregations
Bio: "Woolner, Samuel," *The American Jewish Yearbook*, 7 (1905-1906), p. 117; "Samuel Woolner," in: Peoria City and County, Illinois. Chicago: S. J. Clarke Publishing Co., 1912, pp. 807-809.

2. Communal Workers

Anton Štefan Ambrose (1867-1941), b. Kobyly, Bardejov District, Slovakia; in US s. 1882; pioneer journalist; co-founder of Národny slovenský spolok (National Slovak Society (1890) and its president (1901-12). It was the first Slovak Fraternal Society in America. During 1921-38, he served as press secretary of the Czechoslovak Government in Prague, responsible for information for the Czechoslovaks abroad. In 1938, he returned to the US.
Bio: "Ambrose, Anton Štefan," in: Encyclopedia Beliana. See - https://beliana.sav.sk/heslo/ambrose-anton-stefan

Mary H. Babnič (1923-2008), b. Youngstown, OH, of Slovak descent; trained as a nurse; served with US Army in various army hospitals in TX, KY, CO, CA and NY and after World War II, she served with the US Army Air Corp of Nurses (1946-53). She was also very active in the Youngstown Slovak community. She was president of the American Slovak Cultural Association in the Mahoning Valley. She was most known for her broadcasts of the WKTL Radio Slovak Hour over many years.
Bio: Kopanic, Michael J., "The Queen of Slovak Culture in Youngstown, Ohio – Mary H. Babnič (1923-2008)." Posted on academia.edu. See - https://www.academia.edu/37290303/The_Queen_of_Slovak_Culture_in_Youngstown_Ohio_Mary_H._Babnič_1923-2008

Eward J. Behuncik (1912-1994), b. Bridgeport, CT, of Slovak descent; lawyer, national president of the Slovak League (1967-1985), founder of the Slovak League of America Heritage Foundation, and the American Fund for Slovak Refugees, one of the founders of the Slovak World Congress.
Bio: "Biographical Notes," in: Edward J. Behuncik Papers. See - https://hsp.org/sites/default/files/legacy_files/migrated/findingaidmss170behuncik.pdf

Ján Beliansky (1922-2008), b. Veľký Klíž, Slovakia; in US s. 1952; Slovak national activist; editor, of the First Catholic Slovak Jednota newspaper; founder and Executive Director of the Slovak Research Institute, Cleveland. Bio: "In Memoriam: Jan (John) Beliansky," *Jednota*, February 20, 2008. See - https://www.fcsu.com/wp-content/uploads/jednota-archives/2008/ JEDNOTA-FEB-20-08.pdf

Charles (Karol) Belohlavek (1886-1942), b. Holíč, Slovakia; printer, journalist, founder and president of Slovak Garden, a Home for American Slovaks (1949)
Bio: "Biographical Note," in: Register of the Papers of Charles Belohlavek. See - http://www2.hsp.org/collections/Balch%20manuscript_guide/html/ belohlavek.html

David G. Blazek (1950-), b. Pittsburgh, PA, of Slovak descent, president of the National Slovak Society of the U.S.A. (s. 1994)
Bio: "David G. Blazek, FIC," in: NSSLife. See - http://nsslife.org/staff/ david-g-blazek-fic/

Toni Brendel (1986-), b. US, of Slovak descent; an amateur historian and author; a founding member and former President of the Phillips Wisconsin Czechoslovakian Community Festival; State Director of the Miss Czech-Slovak Wisconsin Queen Pageant held annually in Phillips for 10 years; In 2002, she was named Phillips Citizen of the Year and was the first woman to serve on the Board of Directors of the Phillips Area Chamber of Commerce. She is the proprietress of the Phillips High School Alumni Tourist House. Bio: "Mraz - Lugerville Project." See - http://www.lugervilleproject.com/ families/mraz.html

Božena Buchta, b. Stamford, CT, of Slovak parents; Financial Secretary of the Evangelical Slovak Women's Union, president of the 'Slovak Priadky' Bio: "Buchta, Božena," in: Droba, pp. 213-214.

Adolph Cierny, Jr. (1916-1983), b. Chicago, IL, of Slovak parents; president, District L. Štúr, Sokol U.S.A. (1953-196i), supreme vice president, Sokol U.S.A. (1955-58), president of the Supreme Court, Sokol U.S.A. (1969), on Board of directors, Czechoslovak National Council of America. Bio: "Cierny, Adolph, Jr.," in: *Panorama*, p. 115.

Konštantin Čulen (1904-1964), b. Brodské, Slovakia; journalist turned historian, author, second director of the Slovak Institute in Cleveland (1956-1959)
Bio: "Konštantín Čulen," in: LIC. See - http://www.litcentrum.sk/ slovenski-spisovatelia/konstantin-culen

Ján Denďúr (1898-1998), b. Petrovec, Báčka, Yugoslavia, of Slovak descent; migrated to Chicago in 1920. Teacher and editor of *Naš svet* and the monthly *Slovenka* (s. 1940); one of the founders of the Matica slovenská in America, and developer of the National Slovak School, a workingmen's educational organization, and the National Slovak School's amateur theaters in Cicero and Berwyn, Illinois.
Bio: See - Bolecek, Dr. B.V. and Irene Slamka, *The Slovak Encyclopaedia*. New York: Slovak Academy, 1981, p. 45; "Ján Denďúr (1898-1988)," in: Jan Denďúr Papers. See - https://hsp.org/sites/default/files/mss/ finding_aid_3032_dendur.pdf;

Mary Ann Doucette (née Háčková), president of the Canadian Slovak League

Anna Drienska (1865-), b. Brezová, Slovakia; president of the Supreme Court of 'Živena' (s. 1933), president of the Ladies Auxiliary of the Slovak Charitable Association
Bio: Drienska, Anna," in: Droba, p. 214.

Francis J. Dubosh (1890-1967), b. Cleveland, OH, of Slovak ancestry; Monsignor, R.C. priest, president of the Slovak League of America
Bio: Dubelko, Jim "Balancing Slovak Identity and Patriotism. Monsignor Dubosh During World War II," in: Cleveland Historical. See - https:// clevelandhistorical.org/items/show/583?tour=41&index=7

Margaret Dvorsky (1933-), b. Montreal, Que., Canada, of Slovak parents; pillar of Canadian Slovak community.
Bio: "Rest in Peace, Margie Dvorsky," in: Kanadsky Slovak. See - https://www.kanadskyslovak.ca/index.php/toronto/events-in-toronto/ 816-rest-in-peace-margie-dvorsky

Loretta Ekoniak (1953-) b. Youngstown, OH, Slovak descent; president, American Slovak Cultural Association of the Mahoning Valley, Youngstown, Ohio Area.
Bio: "Loretta Ekoniak," in: LinkedIn. See - https://www.linkedin.com/in/loretta-ekoniak-a3563726/

Morris Engelman (1872-), b. Bardejov, Slovakia; insurance agent, communal worker, secretary of Union Orthodox Jewish Congregations, organizer of Ohab Zedek Sisterhood
Bio: *Who's Who in American Jewry*. New York: Jewish Biographical Bureau, 1926, Vol. 1, pp. 141-142; "Morris Engelman," in: *Distinguished Jews of America*. New York, 1917, Vol. 1, pp. 115-116.

Michael Fabian (1886-1966), b. Lackovo, Slovakia; in soft drink retail business, Chicago, club officer, president, of the Tatran Slovak Union, treasurer of the Slovak Citizens' League, treasurer of the first Catholic Slovak Union
Bio: "Fabian, Michael," in: Droba, pp. 214-215.

Mikuláš Ferjenčík (1904-1988), b. Polomka, Slovakia; military veterinarian, General of Czechoslovak Army, resistance fighter, vice president of the Czechoslovak National Council of America, Chicago
Bio: "Ferjenčík, Mikuláš," in: Pejskar 3, pp. 45-53; "Mikuláš Ferjenčík," in: Wikipedia. See - https://en.wikipedia.org/wiki/ Mikuláš_Ferjenčík; "Ferjenčík, Mikuláš," in: Panorama, p. 113; "Mikuláš Ferjenčík," in: Wikipedia. See - https://en.wikipedia.org/wiki/Mikuláš_Ferjenčík

Stephen Furdek (1855-1915), b, Trstená, Slovakia; priest, a writer, and a co-founder of the First Catholic Slovak Union (Jednota), in 1891, the national fraternal organization, whose membership was 45,000 by 1915, and its periodical *Jednota*. In n 1892, he helped organize the FCSU's sister organization, the First Catholic Slovak Ladies Association. He was the first president of the Slovak League of America, which later played a large role in the call for an independent Czechoslovak state. He wrote profusely, writing books, pamphlets, and poetry in both Czech and Slovak on religious, political, and educational topics.

Bio: Tybor, M. Martina, "Father of American Slovaks," *Slovakia* 16, No. 39 (1966), pp. 25-40; "Stephen Furdek," in: Wikipedia. See - https://en.wikipedia. org/wiki/Stephen_Furdek

George S. Galos (1902-1985, b. Zvolen, Slovakia; accountant, club officer, recording secretary of the Association of Slovak Catholic Lodges of the First Catholic Slovak Union, Chicago
Bio: "Galos, George S.," in: Droba, p. 215.

Ignác Gessay (1874-1928), b. Tvrdošín, Slovakia; journalist, co-founder of Slovak League of America
Bio: "Ignác Gessay," in: Wikipedia. See - https://sk.wikipedia.org/wiki/ Ignác_Gessay

Mary Hamrlik (1895-1979), b. Jablonica, Slovakia, president of the Gary Branch of the Slovak Gymnastic Union Sokol of America, Gary, IN
Bio: "Hamrlik, Mary," in: Droba, p. 216.

Joseph Herbach (1873-d.), b. Slovakia; editor, publisher, communal worker, president of Hebrew Sheltering Home, president of Home for Infants, director of Federation for Jewish Charities, etc. Philadelphia
Bio: *Who's Who in American Jewry*. New York: Jewish Biographical Bureau, 1926, Vol. 1., p. 259.

Peter P. Hletko (1902-1973), b. Chicago, IL, of Slovak ancestry; physician, president of the Slovak League of America (1935-39, 1963-64)
Bio: "Peter Hletko," in: Slovenské zahraničie. Portál Slovakov vo svete. See - http://www.slovenskezahranicie.sk/sk/osobnost/93/peter-hletko; Krajsa, Joseph C., "Dr. Peter P. Hletko," *Slovakia*, 44 (1971), pp. 54-57; "Hletko, Peter Paul," in: *Catholic Who's Who*, Vol. 14, p. 208.

John A. Holy (1922-), b. Nová Baňa, Slovakia; in US s. 1949; president of the Slovak League of America (1976-2002); worked at Slovak Catholic Sokol.
Bio: See - http://www.slovakcatholicsokol.org/efalcon/20180718falcon.pdf

Nina Holy (1932-), b. New York, lived in Koseča, Slovakia when 2-15 years-old. Accountant and auditor; Slovak League of America general secretary; New Jersey Slovak Festival co-chairperson.

Bio: See - http://www.fcsla.org/fraternallyyours-0805.pdf

Joseph J. Hornack (1934-2016), b. Cleveland, OH, of Slovak and Czech descent; assoc. director of the Slovak Institute and Reference Library, Cleveland;
Bio: "Joseph J. Hornack," *The Plain Dealer*, March 17-18, 2016.

Maria Hrabina (1896-), b. Jasenia, Slovakia; clubwoman, treasurer and director of the Slovak Catholic Charitable Association, Chicago
Bio: "Hrabina, Maria," in: Droba, p. 216.

Thomas M. Hricik (1930-2010), b. Pleasant Unity, PA, of Slovak descent; national president of the First Catholic Slovak Union of the US and Canada (for 12 years); recipient of the Ellis Island Medal of honor
Bio: "Thomas M. Hricik," *Greensburg Tribune Review*, January 6, 2010.

George A. Hricko (1884-1962), b. Freeland, Luzerne Co., PA, of Slovak descent; coal miner, grocery merchant, president of the First Catholic Slovak Union (s. 1926), residing in Olyphant, PA
Bio: "Hricko, George A.," in: *Catholic Who's Who*, Vol. 7, p. 204.

Steve J. Hruska (1920-2004), b. Johnstown, PA, of Slovak descent; as a child returned to Slovakia with his parents. He returned as a young man settling in Youngstown, Oh. He served as the Supreme president of the Slovak Catholic Sokol, 1985-91.
Bio: Source: Daniel Tanzone

František Hrušovský (1903-1956), b. Dolné Lovčice, Slovakia; historian, director of the Slovak Institute, Cleveland (1952-1956)
Bio: "František Hrušovský," in: Wikipedia. See - https://sk.wikipedia.org/wiki/František_Hrušovský

Andrew F. Hudák (1928-2016), b. Kecerovské Pekľany, Czech.; president of Florida Slovak Garden and Cultural Center, director of the Slovak Institute and Library at St. Andrew's Abbey, Cleveland
Bio: "Andrew F. Hudak Jr.," *The Plain Dealer*, April 1-3, 2016.

Anna Hurban (1855-1828), b. Gbely, Slovakia; formed the First Catholic Slovak Ladies Association (FCSLA) in 1892 with 8 other women.
Bio: James M O'Toole, *The Faithful. History of Catholics in America*. Cambridge, MA: The Balknap Pres of Harvard University Press, 2008, pp. 93-95, 306. See - https://books.google.com/books?isbn=0674033825 ; https://case.edu/ech/articles/f/first-catholic-slovak-ladies-assn.

Rose Schury Hurbanek (1901-1997), b. Slovakia; co-founder and the first president of the Keystone Pride Chapter of the Zivena Beneficial Society, founded in 1930
Bio: "Rose Schury Hurbanek," in: Rose Schury Hurbanek Papers and Photographs 1925-1995.
See - http://historicpittsburgh.org/islandora/object/pitt%3AUS-QQS-mss719/viewer

Františka C. Jakabčínová (1873-1933), b. Poproč, Slovakia; president of First Catholic Slovak Ladies Assn. for 30 years; active in Slovak-American life; helped found Slovak Catholic Matica slovenská and build Slovak schools for girls in Danville, PA, and Benedictine High School, Cleveland; active with Slovak Catholic Federation.
Bio: Paučo, *Jozef, Slovenski priekopnici v Amerike*, Cleveland: Prvá Katolícka Slovenská Jednota, pp. 199-201.

Ján Janček, Jr. (1881-1933), b. Ružomberok, Slovakia; news editor, writer; organizer of the Czechoslovak Legion in Russia (1916); Secretary of the Slovak League of America (1917); signatory of the Pittsburgh Agreement (1919)
Bio: "Jan Janček, Jr., in: Pittsburgh Agreement. See - https://en.wikipedia.org/wiki/Pittsburgh_Agreement #Ján_Janček,_Jr._(1881_-_1933); see also: *Slovenský Biografický Slovník*. Martin: Matica Slovenska, 1987, Vol. 1, p. 520.

Kris J. Janovcik (ca 1966-), Slovak Canadian; lawyer; President, Slovak Canadian National Council, Manitoba Chapter (1999- 2015), Vice-President, Slovak Canadian National Council, Manitoba Chapter (1997- 1999).
Bio: "Kris J. Janovcik," in: Tapper Cuddy LLP. See - http://www.tappercuddy.com/lawyers/kris-j-janovcik.html

Veronika Kalafut, b. Passaic, NJ, of Slovak parents; clubwoman, auditor of the Slovak Catholic Sokol
Bio: "Kalafut, Veronika," in: Droba, p. 217

Gustine Kasovsky, b. Chicago, of Slovak descent; bookkeeper, auditor and president of Slovak Catholic Charitable Association, Chicago
Bio: "Gustine Kasovsky," in: Droba, p. 218.

Daniel J. Kisha (1937-2016), b. Johnstown, PA, of Slovak ancestry; chemical Engineer; Chaired the Johnstown Slavic Festival committee, and member of the Slovak Heritage Association of the Laurel Highlands. Owned and operated Slovak Import Company 2000-2016, which promoted commerce with Slovakia
Bio: "Daniel Kisha Obituary," in: *Tribune Democrat*, December 17, 2016. See - http://obituaries.tribdem.com/obituary/daniel-kisha-1937-2016-857454192

Margaret A. Kluka (1908-2001), b. Benwood, WV, of Slovak descent; organized the Barberton Slovak Chorus in 1967 and recorded an album "Songs of Slovakia". She was secretary and Junior Eldress of the Children's Branch 166 of the Slovak Catholic Sokol. She founded the Slovak Heritage Society of Northeast Ohio in 1980 and organized the annual Chirstmas Eve supper in Barberton, Ohio.
Bio: "Margaret Ann Skvarka Kluka," in: Find A. Grave. See -https://www.findagrave.com/memorial/97739109/margaret-ann-kluka.

Milan Kobulský (1947-), b. Prešov, Czech.;in US s. 1969; engineer with NASA; director of the Slovak Institute, Cleveland (s. 2016); residing in Medina, OH
Bio: "Milan Kobulský," in: Slovak Institute directors. See - http://www.slovakinstitute.com/Directors.htm

Anna Margaret Kocur (1887-d.), b. Nižná Orava, Slovakia; founder of the society of Our Lady Helper of Christians, founder and president of the Slovak Charitable Organization; founder of the Slovak Catholic Home for the Aged, Chicago
Bio: "Kocur, Anna Margaret," in: Droba, p. 219

John A. Kocur (1887-1948), b. Turzovka, Slovakia; in Us s. 1905; secretary of the Slovak League of America; was helpful to Slovak exiles.
Bio: "Kocur, John A.," in: *History of Pittsburgh and Environs.* New York - Chicago: The American Historical Society, 1922, Vol. 5, pp. 353-354; Paučo, Jozef, *Slovenski priekopnici v Amerike,* Cleveland: Prvá Katolícka Slovenská Jednota, 1972, pp. 229-231.

Frank Kohut (1897-d.), b. Dolná Lehota, Slovakia; deputy clerk of the Municipal Court; chairman of the American Slovak Democratic Club, Chicago
Bio: Kohut, Frank," in: Droba, pp. 219-220.

Božena Kosman (1880-d.), b. Prievidza, Slovakia; clubwoman, assistant director of the Ľudevít Štúr division of the Slovak Sokol, Chicago
Bio: "Kosman, Božena," in: Droba, pp. 220-221.

Andrej V. Kozák (1877-1949), b. Markušovce, Slovakia; musician; organist; treasurer, FCSU; helped build Jednota Printery in Middletown, PA and fund Sisters of SS. Cyril and Methodius, Danville, PA; participated in founding Slovak Catholic Federation.
Bio: Paučo, Jozef, *Slovenski priekopnici v Amerike,* Cleveland: Prvá Katolícka Slovenská Jednota, 1972, pp. 245-248.

Julia Krajcovic (1897-d.), b. Klin, Slovakia; one of the founders and president of the Slovak Catholic Charitable Association, president of the Union of all the Chicago Branches of the first Catholic Slovak Ladies Union
Bio: "Krajcovic, Julia," in: Droba, p. pp. 221-22.

Samuel Krc (1873-d.), b. Senica, Slovakia; club officer, treasurer of the Tatran Slovak Union, of the Slovak Evangelical Society and the Tatra Benefit Society, Chicago
Bio: "Krc, Samuel," in: Droba, p.222.

John Kubicek (1884-1970), b. Turoluka, Slovakia; owner of dry goods store (Kubicek's Bazaar), Chicago, one of founders and honorary president of the Slovak American Charitable Association, one of organizers and director

of the Halsted Exchange National Bank, secretary of the Czechoslovak Chamber of Commerce of Chicago
Bio: "Kubicek, John," in: Droba, p. 223.

John Kulhan (1923-2014); b. Vinodol, Czech.; engineer, Slovak patriot, Czechoslovak Army officer, POW; in US s. 1950; political activist. Founder and first VP of the Slovak Cultural Center of New York; president of the Slovak Catholic Sokol; secretary of the Slovak World Congress.
Bio: Marchant, Robert, "Veteran Honored for Eastern Front Battle," *The Journal News*, October 3, 2005. See - https://www.iabsi.com/gen/public/ john_kulhan.htm; "John Kulhan, Decorated Slovak World War II Hero and Author, Passed Awa," *Slovak Catholic Falcon*, October 22, 2014; Kenny, Joe, "John Kulhan," in: Slovakia Genealogy Research Strategies. See - https:// www.iabsi.com/gen/public/john_kulhan.htm

Anna Kvačala, b. Piešťany, Slovakia; auditor and vice-president of the First Catholic Slovak Ladies Union, Chicago
Bio "Kvacala, Anna," in: Droba, pp. 223-224

John J. Lach (1894-1960), b. Hibernia, NJ, of Slovak descent; R.C. priest, president of the Slovak Catholic Athletic Association, president of the Midwest Slovak Catholic Association, organizer of Father Lach's Band, director of the Calumet Park Cemetery
Bio: "Lach, Rev. John Joseph," in: *Catholic Who's Who*, 14 (1960-1961), p. 252; "Ján J. Lach," in: Wikipedia. See - https://sk.wikipedia.org/wiki/Ján_J._Lach

Elizabeth Lipovsky (1908-1996), b. Bethlehem, PA, of Slovak descent; national auditor and board member of the First Catholic Slovak Ladies Association (FCSLA) (1940), editor of the Society's monthly *Fraternal Yours* (1960-66), national president of FCSLA (1964-1976).
Bio: "Elizabeth 'Betty' Lipovsky, 88," *The Morning Call*, December 21, 1996.

Paul M. Makousky (1961?-), b. Minnesota, of Slovak and Czech ancestry; Saint Paul, MN - one of the founding members of the Czechoslovak Genealogical Society International, Executive Committee member, organizer of CGSI conferences, editor of the *Naše rodina*, Slovak and Czech ethnic origins.

Irene Matuschak (1911-2009), b. Pittsburgh, PA, of Slovak descent; gymnastics teacher, Slovak community activist, esp. in the Slovak League and Slovak Catholic Sokol; produced and narrated a bilingual radio program, "Melodia: The Musical Voice of the People" on WCVI in Connellsville during the 1950s.; judge at the 1948 London Olympics; worked to return villages annexed by Poland, wrote The Abandoned Ones: The Tragic Story of Slovakia's Spis and Orava Regions, 1918-1948 (2008).
Bio: "Irene Matuschak Obituary," *Greensburg Tribune Review*, October 3 24, 2009. See -
http://www.legacy.com/obituaries/triblive-tribune-review/obituary.aspx?page=lifestory&pid=177340238

Peter Molčan (1949-), b. Sabinov, Prešov, Czech.; cabinetmaker, secretary of the Slovak Society of Canada.

Ferdinand Mondok (1903-1995), b. Dolný Lopašov, Slovakia; R.C. priest; HS teacher; politically active in the World War II Slovak Republic; member of Slovenský snem; forced to leave Slovakia in 1945, immigrated to Canada in 1950; active in Slovak National Council and Montreal Slovak community.
Bio: "Ferdinand Mondok," in: Obec Lopašov. See - http://www.obecdlopasov.sk/obec-15/historia-obce/slavni-rodaci-z-obce-dolny-lopasov/ferdinand-mondok/

Joseph Ondrejkovic (1890-1964), b. Turčiansky Sv. Martin, Slovakia; founder and director of the Slovak National Theater, Chicago, residing in Berwyn, IL
Bio: "Ondrejkovic, Joseph," in: Droba, pp. 224-225

Stefan Osusky (1907-1997), b. Chicago, of Slovak parents; dentist, Chicago, president of the Slovak Students League of America
Bio: "Osusky, Stefan," in: Droba, pp. 223-224

Ján Pankúch (1869-1952), b. Šariš Country, Slovakia; newspaper editor and publisher, Cleveland, OH, president of the National Slovak Society
Bio: "Pankuch, John," in: *Encyclopedia of Cleveland History*. See - https://case.edu/ech/articles/p/pankuch-jan

Ján Papánek (1896-1997), b. Brezová pod Bradlom, Slovakia; lawyer, Slovak exile diplomat
Bio "Papánek, Ján," in: *SVU Directory* 7; "Papánek, Ján," in: Pejskar 4, pp. 125-131; Saxon, Wolfgang, "Jan Papanek, 95, Czechoslovak Who Stood Up to Communism," *The New York Times*, December 3, 1991; "Ján Papánek," in: Wikipedia. See - https://sk.wikipedia.org/wiki/ Ján_Papánek

Jozef Paučo (1914-1975), b. Pila, Pezinok Dist., Slovakia; in US s. 1945; writer, journalist, publicist; organizer and Secretary-General of Slovak National Council Aboad; Secretary of Slovak League in America
Bio: "Jozef Pauco," in: Databáze.knih.cz. See - https://www.databazeknih.cz/zivotopis/jozef-pauco-100732 LIC. See - http://www.litcentrum.sk/slovenski-spisovatelia/jozef-pauco#curriculum_vitae

Ľudovít Pavlo (1925-2014), b. Michalovce, Czech.; physician; specialized in family medicine; family; writer, executive president of Slovak League in America
Bio: "Zomrel Ľudovít Pavlo, čestný predseda Slovenskej ligy v Amerike," in: Úrad pre Slovákov žijúcich v zahraničí. See - http://www.uszz.sk/sk/stranka/3439/zomrel-ludovit-pavlo-cestny-predseda-slovenskej-ligy-v-amerike

Andrew Pier (1910-2003), b. Blandburg, PA, of Slovak descent; R.C. priest, O.S.B., writer, historian and preeminent activist, director of the Slovak Institute, Cleveland, OH (1959-2001)
Bio: "Fr. Andrew Pier," in: Find A Grave. See - https://www.findagrave.com/memorial/123979568/andrew-pier

Adam Podkrivacky (1889-1964), b. Rovné, Slovakia; realtor, insurer, Chicago, IL, supreme president of the First Catholic Slovak Union, vice president of Catholic Slovak Federation of America.
Bio: "Podkrivacky, Adam," in: *Catholic Who's Who*, 1961, Vol. 14, p. 362.

Edward J. Popovich (1947-2018), b. Johnstown, PA, of Slovak descent; president of the Slovak Educational Society and vice president of the Greater Johnstown Youth League
Bio: "Edward j. Popovich," in: Hindman Funeral Homes and Crematory, Inc. See - https://hindmanfuneralhomes.com/obituary/edward-j-popovich/

Andrew M. Rajec (1942-), b. Milwaukee, Wisconsin, of Slovak descent; accountant; president of the First Catholic Slovak Union (FCSU) (s. 2007); Friends of Slovakia (s. 2013); 'Slovak American of the Year.'
Bio: See - http://slovakamericancc.wixsite.com/slovakamericancc/slovak-ball-2018

Andrew Rolik (1896-1981), b. Brdárka, Slovakia; Lutheran minister, pastor, writer, Slovak national activist. He immigrated to USA in 1909 and became one of the foremost publicists of the Slovak spirit in America. He founded a children's singing group, 'Spevokol Sládkoviču;' delegate of the Slovak League visiting Czechoslovakia in 1938 in support of the Pittsburgh Agreement; wrote poetry, translated it from English and published religious songs in Slovak journals and almanacs.
Bio: "Rev Andrew Rolik": Find A Grave. See- https://www.findagrave.com/memorial/185941496/andrew-rolik; "Rolik, Andrej," in: ECAV. http://www.ecav.sk/?p=info /INFHistória/osobnosti/rolik_andrej_ (1896_-_1981)

Stephen Boleslav Roman (1921-1988), b. Veľký Ruskov, Czech.; prominent Canadian mining engineer, and mining executive; president of the Slovak World Congress.
Bio: "Stephen Boleslav Roman – the American Dream in Canada," in: AmCham Slovakia. See - http://www.amcham.sk/publications/connection-magazine/issues/2016-05/272551 stephen-boleslav-roman-the-american-dream-in-canada; "Stephen Boleslav Roman," in: Prabook. See - https://prabook.com/web/stephen_boleslav.roman/1374802; "Roman, Stephen Boleslav," in: *Who's Who in the East,* 14; McKay, Paul. *The Roman Empire: The Unauthorized Life and Times of Stephen Roman.* Toronto: Key Porter Books Limited, 1990.

Peter Víťazoslav Rovnianek (1867-1933), b. Dolný Hričov, Slovakia; businessman, journalist, founder of the first Slovak newspaper in America

(*Slovenský Denník*), founder and the first president of the National Slovak Society of the USA (1890), founder of the Slovak colony in Arkansas (Slovaktown)
Bio: Tybor, M. Martina, "Peter V. Rovnianek (1867-1933)," *Slovakia*, 40 (1967), pp. 137-143; Bolecek, Vincent, Peter V. Rovnianek. New York, 1957; "Peter Víťazoslav Rovnianek," in: Wikipedia. See - https://sk.wikipedia.org/wiki/Peter_Víťazoslav_Rovnianek

Edward Rubovitz (1840-d.), b. Seben, near Prešov, Slovakia; superintendent of the United Hebrew Charities, Zionist
Bio: "Rubovitz, Edward," *The American Jewish Yearbook*, 7 (1905-1906), p. 99.

John S. Sabol (ca 1946-), b. Cleveland, of Slovak descent; seasoned writer and editor; fraternalist, First Catholic Slovak Union
Bio: "John Sabol," in: LinkedIn. See - https://www.linkedin.com/in/john-sabol-7b881813/

Andrew Schustek (1871-1922), b. Slovenská Lupca, Slovakia; manufacturer; co-founder of two Chicago lodges of the National Slovak Society; founder of the first Slovak Sokol group in Chicago; directed the founding of a settlement in Arkansas, known as 'Slovaktown;' president of the Slovak Building and Loan Association; charter member of the Slovak Matica in America, the future Slovak League of America; treasurer of the Czechoslovak National Council of America; residing in Chicago
Bio: "Schustek, Andrew," in: Droba, pp. 81-82.

Joseph Senko (1935-), b. Pittsburgh, PA, of Slovak descent; certified public accountant. He was the founder of a non-profit Western Pennsylvania Slovak Cultural Organization (WPSCA) (1997). He was awarded the Medal of the President of the Slovak Republic for extraordinary merit in the development of friendly relations with the Slovak Republic, as well as promoting Slovakia throughout the world.
Bio: "Joseph Senko Recognized for Slovak Work," in: Honorary consulate. See - https://www.paslovakconsulate.org/consul_c.htm

Anna Šimek (1894-1977), b. Sv. Jur, Slovakia; club officer, director and secretary of the Slovak Catholic Charitable Association, president of the Slovak Catholic Sokol, Chicago
Bio: Šimek, Anna," in: Droba, p. 229.

Eva Sopocy (1890-1977), b. Horné Bzince, Slovakia; clubwoman, secretary of the First Lodge of 'Slovenské Priadky,' later general secretary of 'Slovenské Priadky,' Chicago
Bio: "Sopocy, Eva," in: Droba, p. 231.

Jan Sopoci (1925-2014), b. Slovakia; a leader in the Slovak community in the Chicago area and in New Jersey where he lived for 25 years, as Supreme Secretary of Sokol USA.
Bio: "Jan Sopoci," *Chicago Tribune*, November8-9, 2014

Joseph Spanik (1893- d.), b. Brezany, Slovakia; meat merchant, Chicago; vice president of the local chapter of the Slovak Sokol Union, treasurer of the Slovak Building and Loan Association
Bio: "Spanik, Joseph," in: Droba, p. 82.

Joseph Staško (1917-1999), b. Sedliacka Dubová, Slovakia; journalist and retired librarian; president of the Slovak Historical Association of America; resides in Canada.
Bio: "Jozef Stasko," in: https://cs.wikipedia.org/wiki/ /Jozef_Staško

Imrich Stolárik (1909-2000), b. Turzovka, Slovakia; accountant, president of the Canadian Slovak League, prolific writer; leader of Slovak community in Ottawa
Bio: "Stolarik, Imrich," The Citizen, Ottawa, ON. See - https://www.genealogiequebec.com/necro/avis-de-deces/560699-STOLARIK-Imrich

Paul Leslie Strigner (1926-), b. Slovakia; president of Sokol, Ottawa, Canada
Bio: "Paul Leslie Strigner," in: *Naše Hlasy*, p. 57.

Paul Sturman (1904-1990); bookkeeper and accountant, writer; president of Wilsonian Club, Washington, DC; resided in Arlington, VA
Bio: "Paul Sturman," *The Washington Post*, March 3, 1990.

Joseph Suchy (fl. 1992), editor of magazine *Maria*; secretary of Slovak World Congress; resided in British Columbia, Canada.

Joseph J. Talafous (1929-2008), b. New York, NY, of Slovak parents; attorney, Jersey City, NJ (s. 1959). President, Slovak League American Heritage Foundation (s. 1976); Vice president, Slovak League of America. Bio: "Joseph John Talafous, Sr.," in: Prabook. See - https://prabook.com/web/joseph_john_talafous_.sr./911801

Daniel F. Tanzone (1947-), b. Yonkers, NY, of Slovak descent; fraternalist, editor of the *Slovak Catholic Falcon* (s. 1980); active in the Slovak League of America, serving as national president (1895-93). Recipient of numerous w awards.

Victor Tibensky (1889-d.), b. Hrnčiarovce, Slovakia; director of the Ludevit Štúr Division of the Slovak Gymnastic Union Sokol, Chicago
Bio: "Tibensky, Victor," in: Droba, p. 233.

László Újházy (1795-1870), b. Budimir, Slovakia; son of a landowner of the lesser nobility; in US s. 1849, arriving in NYC with the first group of Hungarian refugees, after the unsuccessful Hungarian revolution; lawyer by training; Kossuth's representative with the US government; founder of a Hungarian colony, New Buda in Iowa, but the plan failed to attract many exiles. Ujhazy and his family settled near San Antonio, TX, where he farmed and ranched. He served as Abraham Lincoln's consul at Ancona, Italy (1862-64). Helped found the Republican Party in Bexar Co. during the Reconstruction.
Bio: "Újházy László," in: Wikipedia. See - https://hu.wikipedia.org/wiki/Újházy_László; Vassady, Béla, New Buda: A Colony of Hungarian Forty Eighters in Iowa," *The Annals of Iowa*, 51 (1991), pp. 26-52; "Ujhazi, Laszlo," in Handbook of Texas. See - https://tshaonline.org/handbook/online/articles/fuj01

Stephen F. Ungvarsky (1911-2001), b. Trauger, PA, of Slovak descent; executive secretary of the First Slovak Union of USA and Canada;
Bio: "Ungvarsky, Stephen F.," in: *Catholic Who's Who*, 21 (1976-1977); "Stephen F. Ungvarsky Obituary," *Greensburg Tribune Review*, December 4, 2001.

Andrew Joseph Valuchek (1911-1997), b. Smithfield, PA, of Slovak descent; founder of the American Fund for Czechoslovak Refugees, president of Czechoslovak National Council, director of American Council for Nationality Service, Washington, DC
Bio: "Valuchek, Andrew Joseph," in: *SVU Directory* 7; Saxon, Wolfgang, "Andrew Valuchek, Democratic Liaison and Publisher, 85," The New York Times, March 31, 1997.

Michael J. Vargovich (1897-1986), b. Slovakia; realtor, McKeesport, national president of First Catholic Slovak Union of America (s. 1940)
Bio: "Vargovich, Michael J.," *Catholic Who's Who,*1971, Vol. 14, p. 460.

Hermina M. Vlk (1884-d.), b. Kúty, Slovakia; clubwoman, president of the 46ᵗʰ Lodge of the Catholic Order of Foresters, one of the founders of the Busy Ladies Club,

Thomas Klimek Ward (1944-), b. Joliet, IL, of Slovak descent; founder and chairman of the Slovak American Cultural Society of the Midwest (1991); author; Honorary Consul of the Slovak Republic in Chicago.
Bio: "Honorary Consul Builds on His Slovakian Roots," Chicago Tribune, March 21, 1997. See - http://articles.chicagotribune.com/1997-03-21/news/9703210233_1_slovak-republic-consul-office

Mary Wargos, b. Chicago, IL, of Slovak parents; club officer, secretary of Club Furdek, secretary of the Junior Order of the First Catholic Slovak Ladies Union Chicago
Bio: "Hermina M. Vlk," in: Droba, p. 134.

Michael J. Zahorsky, of Slovak descent; labor union official, president of the first Catholic Slovak Union

3. Activists & Reformers

Michael Badnarik (1954), b. Hammond, IN, of Slovak ancestry; software engineer, political figure, radio talk show host, former Libertarian Party nominee for US President
Bio: "Michael Badnarik," in: Wikipedia. See - https://en.wikipedia.org/wiki/Michael_Badnarik

Method M. Balco (1818-2013), b. Newark, NJ, of Slovak descent; owner and president of Balco Catholic Supply of Verona, North Caldwell, NJ; vice president of the World Slovak Congress, president of the Slovak Americans of America
Bio: "Balco, Method Matthew," in: *Catholic Who's Who*, 21 (1976-1977); "Method M. Balco," *The Star Ledger*, February 8, 2013.

William Bila (1969-), b. New York, NY, of Slovak Romani descent; living in New York; studied business management and organizational behavior and has worked for auditing companies. He has long been involved in commemorating the annihilation of Romani people by the Nazis.
Bio: "Interview with Romani American William Bila about the Roma Holocaust," in: romea.cz. See - http://www.romea.cz/en/news/world/ interview-with-romani-american-wiliam-bily-about-the-roma-holocaust; "William Bila," in: LinkedIn. See - https://www.linkedin.com/in/billbila/

Lewis Naphtali Dembitz (1833-1907), b. Zirke, Prussia, of Slovak father and Bohemian mother; lawyer, a staunch unionist, frequent antislavery agitator, member of the new Republican Party, member of the Republican Convention that nominated Abraham Lincoln for the President. Louisville, KY
Bio: Kleber, John E., "Dembitz, Lewis Naphtali," in: *The Kentucky Encyclopedia*. University Press of Kentucky; pp. 247–248; "Lewis Naphtali Dembitz," in: Wikipedia. See - https://en.wikipedia.org/wiki/Lewis_Naphtali_Dembitz

John Hvasta (1927-2013), b. Miglesov, Czech.; in US s. 1938. After his military service, he returned to Czechoslovakia, where he was later jailed on false espionage charges, but he succeeded to escape to US Embassy. Eventually he got back to the US, where he became a freelance filmmaker of documentary films and after coming to Washington be became a political activist on behalf of the Slovak cause.
Bio: "John Hvasta, 85, was devoted Slovak activist," *Slovak Catholic Falcon*, Vol. 52, No. 4990, May 15, 2013, p. 14.

Julia Indichova (1949-), b. Košice, Czech.; American reproductive healthcare activist and author
Bio: "Julia Indichova," in: Wikipedia. See - https://en.wikipedia.org/wiki/ Julia_Indichova

John Kulhan (1923-2014), b. Vinodol, Czech.; engineer, Slovak patriot, Czechoslovak Army officer, POW; in US s. 1950, political activist, author, in US residing in Bronxville, NY. Involved in Republican Party. Recipient of the Presidential Legion of Honor signed by 4 Presidents.
Bio: Marchant, Robert, "Veteran Honored for Eastern Front Battle," *The Journal News*, October 3, 2005. See - https://www.iabsi.com/gen/public/john_kulhan.htm; "John Kulhan, Decorated Slovak World War II Hero and Author, Passed Away," *Slovak Catholic Falcon*, October 22, 2014; Kenny, Joe, "John Kulhan," in: Slovakia Genealogy Research Strategies. See - https://www.iabsi.com/gen/public/john_kulhan.htm

Michael Lucas (1926-), b. Slovakia; an artist, designer and political activist residing in Toronto, Ont., Canada. He is the Chair of the Executive Committee of the Canadian Friends of Soviet People, founded in 1991, and was formerly the chair of the USSR-Canada Friendship Association from 1972 until 1991. He is also the chair of the International Council of Friendship and Solidarity with Soviet People, operating out of Toronto.
Bio: "Michael Lucas," in: Wikipedia. See - https://en.wikipedia.org/wiki/Michael_Lucas_(political_activist)

Nell Newman (1959-), b. New York, NY, of Slovak descent; a former actress who performed under the name of Nell Potts; an environmentalist, biologist, and a prominent supporter of sustainable agriculture, who became an entrepreneur when she founded an organic food and pet food production company, Newman's Own Organics. In 2014, Newman received the prestigious Rachel Carson Award from The National Audubon Society for her environmental leadership. In 2017, Newman was inducted into the Specialty Food Hall of Fame, which "honor(s) individuals whose accomplishments, impact, contributions, innovations, and successes within the specialty food industry deserve praise and recognition.
Bio: "Nell Newman," in: Wikipedia. See - https://en.wikipedia.org/wiki/Nell_Newman

Daniel 'Dan' Samuel Senor (1971-), b. Utica, NY, of Slovak ancestry; columnist, writer, a Pentagon and White House adviser, foreign policy adviser to US presidential candidate Mit Romney
Bio: "Dan Senor," in: Wikipedia. See - https://en.wikipedia.org/wiki/Dan_Senor

Margit Šlachta (1884-1974), b. Košice, Slovakia; social activist. In 1920 she was the first woman to be elected to the Diet of Hungary, and in 1923 she founded the Sisters of Social Service, a Roman Catholic religious institute of women. Slachta told her sisters that the precepts of their faith demanded that they protect the Jews, even if it led to their own deaths. One of Šlachta's sisters, Sára Salkaházi was executed by the Arrow Cross, and Slachta herself was beaten and only narrowly avoided execution. The sisters rescued probably more than 2000 Hungarian Jews. In 1985, Yad Vashem recognized Margit Šlachta as Righteous among the Nations. She died in Buffalo, NY.
Bio: "Margit Slachta," in: Wikipedia. See - https://en.wikipedia.org/wiki/ Margit_Slachta

Debora Steinerman (1924-), b. Slovakia, child of a Holocaust survivor; lawyer, co-founder of Vermont Holocaust Memorial (s. 2017)
Bio: "Debora Steinerman," in: Vermont Holocaust Memorial. See - https:// www.holocaustmemorial-vt.org/steinerman/
"Debora Steinerman," in: LinkedIn. See - https://www.linkedin.com/in/ debora-steinerman-5237148/

Rose L. Gerak Tenesy (1890-1992), b. Cleveland, OH, of Slovak descent; first woman ward leader for the Cuyahoga Co. Democratic Party (1920-40)
Bio: "Tenesy, Rose L. Gerak," in: *Encyclopedia of Cleveland History.* See - https:// case.edu/ech/articles/t/tenesy-rose-l-gerak

Peter Zapletal (1914-), b. Nitra, Slovakia; compiler of *Tragedy of Slovak Jews* (1984).
Bio: "Zapletal, Peter," in: SVU Directory, 9

Zvi Weinberg (1935-2006), b. Brekov, Slovakia; politician, Zionist, advocate for peace in Middle East, educator
Bio: "Zvi Weinberg," in: Wikipedia. See - https://en.wikipedia.org/wiki/ Zvi_Weinberg

4. Paranormals

Ryan Daniel Buell (1962-), b. Corry, PA, of Slovak descent; American paranormal investigator, author and producer. Founder of the Paranormal

Research Society when he was a 19-year-old student at Pennsylvania State University.
Bio: "Ryan Buell," in: Wikipedia. See - https://en.wikipedia.org/wiki/Ryan_Buell

5. Local Politicians

Jean Ann Milko (1934-), b. Braddock Hill, PA, of Slovak descent; vice chair of Allegheny County Democratic Party, PA; delegate to the Democratic National Convention from PA (1972, 2000, and 2008) ; member of the Democratic National Committee from PA (2004).
Bio: "Milko, Jean Ann," in: *Who's Who in American Politics*, 7; "Jean Milko," in: Wikipedia. See - https://en.wikipedia.org/wiki/Jean_Milko

Steve Obsitnik (1967-), b. Stamford, CT, of Slovak descent; US Naval Academy graduate, electrical engineer by training; entrepreneur; a Republican politician; was 2018 Republican candidate for Governor of Connecticut but lost the primary.
Bio: "Steve Obsitnik," in: Ballotpedia. See - https://ballotpedia.org/Steve_Obsitnik; "Steve Obsitnik," in: LinkedIn. See - https://www.linkedin.com/in/steveobsitnik/

Dennis Spisak (1959-), b. Youngstown, OH, Slovak descent; Slovak radio announcer; teacher; a Green Party candidate for Governor of Ohio in the 2014 elections; ran on a ticket with Suzanne Patzer as lieutenant governor. He has served on the Struthers City School System Board of Education since 2005.
Bio: "Dennis Spisak," in: Ballotpedia.org. Encyclopedia of American Politics. See - https://ballotpedia.org/Dennis_Spisak

E. CANADIAN POLITICIANS

1. Legislative Branch

<u>George Ben (1925-1978</u>), b. Slovakia; lawyer, politician, a member of the Ontario legislature (1965-71).
Bio: "George Ben," in: Wikipedia. See - https://en.wikipedia.org/wiki/
George Ben; "City maverick, George Ben, dead at 53," *The Toronto Star,*
December 18, 1978.

<u>Timothy Patrick "Tim" Hudak (1967-),</u> b. Fort Erie, Ont., Canada; a
Progressive Conservative member of the Ontario legislature (1995-2016)
Bio: "Tim Hudak," in: Wikipedia. See - https://en.wikipedia.org/wiki/
Tim_Hudak; "Tim Hudak," in: Legislative Assembly of Ontario. See -
https://www.ola.org/en/members/all/tim-hudak

<u>Peter Kormos (1952-2013),</u> b. Welland, Canada, of Slovak descent; criminal
lawyer, politician, a member of the Ontario legislature (1988-2011)
Bio: "Peter Kormos, former NDP MPP has died," *The Star,* March 30, 2013;
"Former NDP politician Peter Kormos dead at 60," CBC News, March 30,
2013; Dimatteo, Enzo, RIP Peter Kormos, 1952-2013," *NOW* Magazine,
March 21, 2013.

<u>William A. Kovach (1909-1966),</u> b. Passburg, Alberta, Canada, of Slovak
descent; politician, a member of the Alberta legislature (1948-66)
Bio: "William Kovach," in: Wikipedia. See - https://en.wikipedia.org/wiki/
William_Kovach

<u>Natalia Kusendova (fl. 2014),</u> b. of Slovak and Polish descent; a Canadian
politician, who was elected to the Legislative Assembly of Ontario in the
2018 provincial election. She represents the riding of Mississauga Centre as
a member of the Progressive Conservative Party of Ontario. Before being
elected, she worked as a nurse.
Bio: "Natalia Kusendova," in: Wikipedia. See - https://en.wikipedia.org/
wiki/Natalia_Kusendova

Michelle Rempel (1980-), b. Winnipeg, Manitoba, Canada, of Slovak descent; politician, a Conservative member of the Canadian House of Commons (2011-)
Bio: "Michelle Rempel," in; Wikipedia. See - https://en.wikipedia.org/wiki/Michelle_Rempel

Anthony Roman (1936-1992), b. Veľký Ruskov, Czech.; politician, a member of the Canadian House of Commons (1984-88)
Bio: "Tony Roman," in: Wikipedia. See - https://en.wikipedia.org/wiki/Tony_Roman

Paul Sazabo (1948-), b. Toronto, Ont., Canada, of Slovak descent; a member of the Canadian House of Commons (1993-2011)
Bio: "Paul Szabo," in: Wikipedia. See - https://en.wikipedia.org/wiki/Paul_Szabo

2. Executive Branch

Timothy Patrick "Tim" Hudak (1967-), b. Fort Erie, Ont., Canada; politician, Minister of Northern Development and Mines, then Minister of Culture, Tourism and Recreation, and Minister of consumer and business services
Bio: "Tim Hudak," in: Wikipedia. See - https://en.wikipedia.org/wiki/Tim_Hudak; Paikin, Steve, "Untangling the complicated legacy of Tim Hudak," in: TVO.org. See - https://tvo.org/blog/current-affairs/untangling-the-complicated-legacy-of-tim-hudak; "OREA welcomes Tim Hudak as new CEO," in: OREO Website.

Peter Kormos (1952-2013), b. Welland, Canada, of Slovak descent; criminal lawyer, politician, Minister of Consumer and Commercial Relations, then Minister of Financial Institutions
Bio: Luxen, Micah, "Peter Kormos, former NDP MPP has died," *The Star,* March 30, 2013; "Former NDP politician Peter Kormos dead at 60," CBC News, March 30, 2013; Dimatteo, Enzo, RIP Peter Kormos, 1952-2013," *NOW* Magazine, March 21, 2013.

Michelle Rempel (1980-), b. Winnipeg, Manitoba, Canada, of Slovak descent; politician, Minister of State for Western Economic Diversification Bio: "Michelle Rempel," in; Wikipedia. See - https://en.wikipedia.org/wiki/ Michelle_Rempel

3. Mayors

Anthony Roman (1936-1992), b. Veľký Ruskov, Czech.; politician, Township Councilor (1966-68), Mayor of the Town of Markham, Ont., Canada (1970-84) Bio: "Tony Roman," in: Wikipedia. See - https://en.wikipedia.org/wiki/ Tony_Roman

4. Judges and Justices of Peace

Vladimir Bubrin (fl. 2005), b. of Slovak descent; Justice of Peace, Ontario Court of Justice. Since 1994, justice of the peace Vladimir Bubrin has been a member of the Immigration and Refugee Board where he adjudicated refugee claims. He has also worked in the Community Development Branch of the Ministry of Citizenship (Ontario) and been an investigator in the Office of the Ontario Ombudsman. He has published various articles and reviews in academic journals and community newspapers.
Bio: "Attorney General Announces Justice of the Peace Appointments," in: Newsroom. See - https://news.ontario.ca/mag/en/2005/09/attorney-general-announces-justice-of-the-peace-appointments-1.html

Anna Janega (c. 1978-), of Slovak parents; lawyer; Citizenship Judge at Citizenship & Immigration Canada, Halifax area (s. 2014). She is responsible for making decisions on citizenship applications, presiding over citizenship ceremonies and administering the oath of citizenship to new citizens.
Bio: "Ann Janega," in: LinkedIn. See - https://www.linkedin.com/in/ann-janega-3372661/?originalSubdomain=ca; "Citizenship Judge Ann Janega," in: Kanadsky Slovak. See - https://www.kanadskyslovak.ca/index.php/ short-news/530-citizenship-judge-ann-janega.

G. SLOVAK DIPLOMATS ASSIGNED TO AMERICA

1. United States

Peter Burian (1959), b. Hlohovec, Slovakia; a diplomat. Following the breakup of Czechoslovakia on 1 January 1993, he was appointed chargé d'affaires at the newly independent Slovakia's Embassy in Washington, D.C. and, shortly after, deputy chief of mission. In December 2008. he became the Slovak Ambassador to the US.
Bio: "Peter Burian," in: Wikipedia. See - https://en.wikipedia.org/wiki/Peter_Burian

Martin Bútora (1944-), b. Slovakia; a Slovak sociologist; university professor, diplomat; Slovak Ambassador to the US (1999-2003)
Bio: "Martin Bútora," in: Wikipedia. See - https://en.wikipedia.org/wiki/Martin_ Bútora

Vladimír Hurban (1883-1949), b. Turčiansky Svatý Martin, Slovakia; Minister to the USA and Cuba (1936-1946); member of the Czechoslovak National Council (1939-1946"
Bio: Weldon, Shawn, "Vladimir Hurban," in: Register of the Papers of Vladimir Hurban." See -
http://www2.hsp.org/collections/Balch%20manuscript_guide/html/hurban.html; Rechcigl, Miloslav, Jr., "Vladimir Hurban," in: *Encyclopedia, Vol.* 1 pp. 390-391.

Ladislav Krno (1909-1972), b. Brezno pod Hronom, Slovakia; Consul General of Czechoslovakia in Chicago (1945-1948)
Bio: "Krno, Ladislav Gejza," in: *SVU Directory* 2; "Krno Ladislav Gejza," in: *Who's Who in the Midwest,* 18 "Krno, Ladislav," in: Pejskar 1, p. 135; "Krno Ladislav Gejza," in: MZV Website.

Ivan Korčok (1964-), b. Banská Bystrica, Czech.; the 7th Slovak Ambassador to USA (s. 2018). Previous positions: State Secretary of the Ministry of Foreign and European Affairs of the Slovak Republic; State Secretary of the Ministry of Foreign and European Affairs of the Slovak Republic; Plenipotentiary of the Government for the Slovak Presidency in the Council of the EU (2015- 17); Head of the Delegation of the Slovak Republic on the

Accession Talks to NATO (2003); State Secretary, Slovak Ministry of Foreign Affairs (2001-005).
Bio: "Ivan Korčok," in: Embassy of the Slovak Republic in Washington. See -https://www.mzv.sk/web/washington-en/about_us/ambassador

Rostislav Káčer (1965-), b. Nova Banna, Slovakia; Slovak Ambassador to the US (2003-08)
Bio: "Rastislav Kacer," in: The Aspen Institute. See - https://www. aspeninstitutece.org/people-profile/rastislav-kacer/; "Káčer,_Rostislav," in: SVU Directory 9

Peter Kmec (1966-), b. Nitra, Slovakia; lawyer, diplomat; Ambassador of the Slovak Republic to the US (2012-18)' Foreign Advisor to Prime Minister of the Slovak Republic (20180)
Bio: "Peter Kmec," in: LinkedIn. See - https://www.linkedin.com/ in/peter-kmec-34868864/; "Ambassador from Slovakia: Who is Peter Kmec," in: AllGov. See - http://www.allgov.com/news/appointments-and-resignations/ambassador-from-slovakia-who-is-peter-kmec-130413? news=849725

Branislav Lichardus (1930-), b. Liptovský Mikuláš, Slovakia; physician; scientist; the first Ambassador of the Slovak Republic to the US (1994-98).
Bio: "Prof. MUDr. Branislav Lichardus DrSc.," in: osobnosgti.sok. See - https://www.osobnosti.sk/osobnost/branislav-lichardus-180

Ivan Rohal-Ilikov (1917-2002), b. Lukov u Bardejeva, Czech (1928-36); Czechoslovak Ambassador to Canada (1968-69); Czechoslovak Ambassador to the US (1969-71).
Bio: "Ivan Rohal-Ilikov," in: *Encyclopedia*, p. 394.

Juraj Slávik (1890-1969), b. Dobrá Niva, Slovakia; lawyer, author, translator, diplomat, Czechoslovak Ambassador to the United States
Bio: "Slávik, Juraj," in: *SVU Directory* 2; "Slávik, Juraj," in: Pejskar 1, pp. 42-45; "Juraj Slávik," in: Wikipedia. See - https://sk.wikipedia.org/wiki/Juraj_ Slávik; Rechcigl, Miloslav, Jr., Juraj Slávik," in: *Encyclopedia*, Vol. 1 pp. 394-395; "Slávik, Juraj Michal Daniel," in *Panorama*, pp. 281-282.

Stanislav Suja (1940-), b. Vigláš u Zvolena, Czech.; Czechoslovak Ambassador to the US
Bio: "Stanislav Suja," in: *Encyclopedia,* Vol. 1, p. 395.

2. Canada

Vincent Bužek (1931-), b. Skalité, Czech.; Czechoslovak Ambassador to Canada (1982-86).
Bio: "Vincent Bužek," in: *Encyclopedia,* Vol. 1, p. 391.:

Andrej Droba (1975-), b. Slovakia; economist, a diplomat; Ambassador of the Slovak Republic to Canada (2014-18).
Bio: "Andrej Droba," in" Wikipedia. See - https://sk.wikipedia.org/wiki/Andrej_Droba

Anton Hykisch (1932-), b. Banská Štiavnica, Slovakia; a Slovak writer, politician and diplomat. Hykisch was a member of the Slovak National Assembly (Slovak Parliament) from 1990 to 1992 and the first Slovak Ambassador of the Slovak Republic to Canada from 1993 to 1997.
Bio: "Anton Hykisch," in: Wikipedia. See - https://en.wikipedia.org/wiki/Anton_Hykisch

Ján Janovic (1925-), b. Dolný Kubín, Czech.; Czechoslovak Ambassador to Canada (1986-90)
Bio: "Ján Janovic," in: *Encyclopedia,* Vol. 1, p. 398

Milan Kollar, b. Zvolen, Slovakia; lawyer, diplomat; Slovak Ambassador to Canada (ca 2010-2014)
Bio: "Milan Kollar ends Term as Slovak Ambassador," in: *Kanadský Slovak.* See - https://www.kanadskyslovak.ca/index.php/ottawa/events-in-ottawa/569-milan-kollar-ends-term-as-slovak-ambassador

Zdenka Kremplová (1957-), b. Slovakia; Foreign Minister of Slovakia (1997-98); Slovak Ambassador to Canada (1998);
Bio: "Zdenka Kramplová," in: Wikipedia. See - https://en.wikipedia.org/wiki/Zdenka_ Kramplová

Miroslav Mikolášík (1952-), b. Dolný Kubín, Slovakia; a Slovak politician; Ambassador Extraordinary and Plenipotentiary of the Slovak Republic to Canada (1999-2002).
Bio: "Miroslav Mikolášík," in: Wikipedia. See - https://en.wikipedia.org/wiki/Miroslav_ Mikolášik

Štefan Murín (1934-2007), b. Stariná, Czech.; Czechoslovak Ambassador to Canada (1976-82).
Bio: "Stefan Murin," in: *Encyclopedia*, Vol. 1, p. 398.

Stanislav Opiela (1952-) b. Levoča, Slovakia; economist, diplomat; CDA to Canada (1997-98, 1999); Slovak Ambassador to Canada (2005-10).
Bio: "Diplomat: his Excellency Stanislav Opiela, Ambassador of the Slovak Republic," in: BigChili. See - http://www.thebigchilli.com/feature-stories/diplomat-his-excellency-stanislav-opiela-ambassador-of-the-slovak-republic

Ivan Rohal-Ilikov (1917-2002), b. Lukov u Bardejeva, Czech (1928-36); Czechoslovak Ambassador to Canada (1968-69); Czechoslovak Ambassador to the US (1969-71).
Bio: "Ivan Rohal-Ilikov," in: *Encyclopedia*, Vol. 1, p. 394.

Štefan Rozkopal (1965-), b. Slovakia; diplomat; CDA to Canada (2002-05); head of the Office of the Slovak President (s. 2015)
Bio: "Head of the Office of the President." See - https://www.prezident.sk/en/page/about-office/

Rudolf Schuster (1934-), b. Košice, Czech.; Czechoslovak Federal Ambassador to Canada (1990-92); President of Slovakia (1999-2004).
Bio: "Rudolf Schuster," in; Wikipedia. See - https://en.wikipedia.org/wiki/Rudolf_Schuster; "Rudolf Schuster," in: *Encyclopedia*, Vol. 1, p. 399.

Peter Zeleňák, b. Slovakia; diplomat; CDA to Canada (1998-99); deputy head of mission, Washington, DC
Bio: "Peter Zeleňák," in Linked.In. See - https://www.linkedin.com/in/peter-zelenak-8b10b623/

Miroslav Žemla (1925-), b. Krškany, of Czech father; Czechoslovak Ambassador to Canada (1964-68)
"Bio: "Miroslav Žemla," in: *Encyclopedia*, Vol. 1, p. 400.

3. Latin America

Jozef Adamec, b. Slovakia; Slovak Ambassador to Mexico (2005-10)

Jan Bratko, b. Slovakia; foreign trade specialist; diplomat; Slovak Ambassador to Mexico (1993-98)
Bio: "Jan Bratko," in: In LinkedIn. See - https://www.linkedin.com/in/jan-bratko-96214558/

Milan Cigáň (1962-), b. Slovakia; diplomat; Slovak ambassador to Brazil (2002, s. 2012)
Bio: "Milan Cigáň." See - https://www.mzv.sk/web/brazilia-en/about_us/ambassador

Vladimír Gulla (1953-), b. Košice, Czech.; Czechoslovak charge d'affaires in Brazi (1980), Czechoslovak Ambassador to Brazil (1988-90).
Bio: "Vladimir Gulla," in: *Encyclopedia*, p. 401.

Branislav Hitka, b. Slovakia; lawyer; diplomat; Slovak Ambassador to Chile (1996-2000); Mexico (2001-05); Argentina (s. 2009)
Bio: "Branislav Hitka." See - https://www.mzv.sk/web/buenosaires-en/about_us/ambassador

Miroslav Jenča (1965-), b. Krompachy, Slovakia; an Ambassador of the Slovak Republic to Mexico (1998-2001).
Bio: "Miroslav Jenča," in: Wikipedia. See - https://en.wikipedia.org/wiki/Miroslav_Jenča

Ján Jurišta (1944-), b. Svrčinovec, Czech.; Czechoslovak Ambassador to Argentina (1982-89).
Bio: "Ján Jurišta," in: *Encyclopedia*, p. 402

Ladislav Kocman (1923-1988), b. Holíč, Czech.; Czechoslovak Ambassador to Cuba (1963); named but never sent there
Bio: "Ladislav Kocman," in: *Encyclopedia*, p. 402

Alexander Kunoši (1908-1962), b. Terešve, Slovakia; Czechoslovak Ambassador to Argentina (1947-1951)
Bio: "Alexander Kunosi," in: *Encyclopedia*, p. 403.

Roman Roubal (1929-), b. Bratislava, of Czech parents; Czechoslovak Ambassador to Chile (1900-92).
Bio: "Roman Roubal," in: *Encyclopedia*, p. 405.

Tibor Zlocha (1929-1995), b. Břeclav, of Slovak father; Czechoslovak Ambassador to Argentina (1991-92), also representing Paraguay

4. United Nations, New York

Peter Burian (1959-), b. Hlohovec, Slovakia; a career diplomat; a Slovakia's permanent representative to the UN (2004-08).
Bio: "Peter Burian," in: Wikipedia. See - https://en.wikipedia.org/wiki/Peter_Burian

Vladimír Houdek (1912-), b, Ružomberok, Slovakia; Czechoslovak Ambassador to UN (1948-50)
Bio: "Vladimír Houdek," in: *Encyclopedia*, p. 406.

Miloš Koterec (1962-), b. Partizánske, Slovakia; a career diplomat from Slovakia. He was sent to the Permanent Mission of Slovakia to the U.N. from '95-'99. He then went on to work at the Permanent Mission to NATO for Slovakia in 2001. In 2009 he was appointed as the Permanent Representative to the U.N. for Slovakia.
Bio: "Miloš Koterec," in: Wikipedia. See - https://en.wikipedia.org/wiki/Miloš_Koterec

Eduard Kukan (1939-), b. Trnava nad Váhom, Czech.; Czechoslovak Ambassador to UN
(1991); a permanent Representative of Slovakia to the UN (1993), Special Envoy for the Balkans (1991–2001).

Bio: "Eduard Kukan," in: *Encyclopedia*, p. 408; "Eduard Kukan," in: Wikipedia. See - https://en.wikipedia.org/wiki/Eduard_Kukan

Karel Kurka (1922-2000), b. Trnava, Czech.; politician, diplomat; Czechoslovak Ambassador to UN, New York, NY
Bio: "Kurka, Karel," in: *Encyclopedia*, Vol. 1, p. 408; "Karel Kurka," in: Wikipedia. See - https://cs.wikipedia.org/wiki/Karel_Kurka

Michal Mlynár, b. Slovakia; trained as a teacher; diplomat; Slovak Ambassador to UN (s. 2017)
Bio: "New Permanent Representative of Slovakia Presents Credentials," in: UN. See https://www.un.org/press/en/2017/bio5001.doc.htm; "Michal Mlynar," in: LinkedIn. See - https://www.linkedin.com/in/michal-mlyn%C3%A1r-b351312/;

Ján Papánek (1896-1991), b. Brezová pod Bradlom, Slovakia; Czechoslovak Ambassador to UN (1946-48).
Bio: "Ján Papánek," in: *Encyclopedia*, p. 409; "Ján Papánek," in: Wikipedia. See - https://sk.wikipedia.org/wiki/ Ján_Papánek

František Ružička (1966-), b. Lučenec, Slovakia; international relations specialist, diplomat; Slovak Ambassador to UN (s. 2012).
Bio: "New Permanent Representative of Slovakia Presents Credentials," in UN. See - https://www.un.org/press/en/2012/bio4396.doc.htm

Peter Tomka (1956-), b. Banská Bystrica, Slovakia; a diplomat. Following the division of Czechoslovakia, he served as Slovakia's Deputy Permanent Representative to UN from 1993 to 1994. From 1994 to 1997, he served as Slovakia's Ambassador to the United Nations.
Bio: "Peter Tomka," in: Wikipedia. See - https://en.wikipedia.org/wiki/ Peter_Tomka

G. SLOVAK EXILE POLITICIANS AND DIPLOMATS

Pavol Blaho (1903-1987), b. Skalica, Slovakia; agricultural engineer, resistance fighter, politician, member of the Council of Free Czechoslovakia
Bio: "Blaho, Pavol," in: *SVU Directory* 5; "Blaho, Pavol," in Pejskar 3, pp. 13-14.

Emanuel Theodore Böhm (1909-1990), b. Vrútky, Slovakia; chemist, politician; elected member of the Czechoslovak Parliament representing Slovak Democratic Party; in 1947 resigned and went to exile; in US s. 1954.
Bio: "Böhm, Emanuel Theodore," in: *Who's Who in the East*, 18; "Emanuel Böhm," in: Wikipedia. See - https://sk.wikipedia.org/wiki/ Emanuel_Böhm

Leopold Danihels (1923-2003); b. Záhorská Ves, Czech.; business executive. He was a co-owner of a casino in Las Vegas, dedicated to renting and renting real estate. He was elected president of the Slovak World Congress
Bio: "Leopold Danihels," in: Wikipedia. See - https://sk.wikipedia.org/wiki/ Leopold_Danihels

Jozef Dieska (1913-1995), b. Dolná Lehota, Slovakia; philosopher, member of the Council of Free Czechoslovakia
Bio: "Jozef Dieska," in: Masaryk University. See - https://www.phil.muni.cz/ fil/scf/komplet/dieska.html

Albert Dutka (1905-1982), b. lawyer, Slovak exile diplomat; resided in St. Petersburg, FL
Bio: "Dutka, Albert," in: Pejskar 2, p. 295.

Mikuláš Ferjenčík (1904-1988), b. Polomka, Slovakia; military veterinarian, General of Czechoslovak Army, resistance fighter, vice president of the Czechoslovak National Council of America, Chicago
Bio: "Ferjenčík, Mikuláš," in: Pejskar 3, pp. 45-53; "Mikuláš Ferjenčík," in: Wikipedia. See - https://en.wikipedia.org/wiki/ Mikuláš_Ferjenčík; "Ferjenčík, Mikuláš," in: Panorama, p. 113; "Mikuláš Ferjenčík," in: Wikipedia. See - https://en.wikipedia.org/wiki/ Mikuláš_Ferjenčík

Mikuláš Franek (1903-1968), b. Príbovce, Slovakia; politician,
Bio: "Mikuláš Franek," in: Wikipedia. See - https://cs.wikipedia.org/wiki/
Mikuláš_Franek

Viera Fraštacká (1919-1994); b. Bratislava, Czech., member of Council of
Free Czechoslovakia, residing in Toronto, Canada
Bio: "Fraštacká, Viera," in: Pejskar 4, p. 205.

Rudolf Fraštacký (1912-1988), b. Mošovce, Slovakia; business executive,
politician, member of the Council of Fee Czechoslovakia, residing in Toronto,
Canada
Bio: "Fraštacký, Rudolf," in: *SVU Directory* 6; "Fraštacký, Rudolf," in: Pejskar
3, pp. 57-68; Cvetkova, Tatiana, "Rudolf Fraštacký 1912-1988," in: Národná
banka Slovenska. Gallery of Personalities, *BIATEC* 11, No. 3 (2003), pp. 29-
30; "Rudolf Fraštacký," in: Wikipedia. See - https://cs.wikipedia.org/wiki/
Rudolf_ Fraštacký

Fedor Hodža (1878-1968), Budapest, of Slovak descent; lawyer, Slovak exile
politician, member of the Council of Free Czechoslovakia
Bio: "Hodža, Fedor," in: Pejskar 1, pp. 86-88; "Fedor Hodža," in: Wikipedia.
See - https://en.wikipedia.org/wiki/Fedor_ Hodža

Ľadislav Hudák (1911-1989), b. Lesné, Slovakia; Slovak exile diplomat,
member of the Council of Free Czechoslovakia
Bio: "Hudák, Ľadislav," in: Pejskar 3, p. 98.

Matej Josko (1907-1969), b. Liptovský Sv. Mikuláš, Slovakia; Slovak exile
politician, secretary of the Council of Free Czechoslovakia and editor of its
Zpravodaj
Bio: "Josko, Matej," in: Pejskar 1, p. 65; "Matej Josko," in: Wikipedia. See -
https://cs.wikipedia.org/wiki/Matej_Josko

Joseph Marian Kirschbaum (1913-2001), ; b. Dolné Vestenice, Slovakia;
politician, diplomat; in Montreal, Canada (s. 1949); in Toronto, Canada (s.
1957); co-founder and chairman of the Assembly of the Slovak Liberation
Council and executive vice-chairman of the Slovak World Congress.
Bio: Joseph Marian Kirschbaum," in: Wikipedia. See - https://sk.wikipedia.
org/wiki/Jozef_M._Kirschbaum

Ivan S. Kerno (1891-1961), b. Myjava, Slovakia;_a Czechoslovak lawyer and diplomat. Upon the establishment of the United Nations following the Second World War, Kerno became Assistant to Secretary-General Trygve Lie and was in charge of the Legal Department. Between 1946 and 1952 he held the post of the first legal councilor of the United Nations and the deputy of the UN Secretary General for legal matters. After February 1948 and the communist coup d'etat in Czechoslovakia, he remained in the United States.
Bio: "Ivan S. Kerno," in: Wikipedia. See - https://en.wikipedia.org/wiki/Ivan_S._Kerno

Štefan Kočvara (1896-1973), b. Myjava, Slovakia; lawyer, Slovak exile politician, member of the Council of Free Czechoslovakia
Bio: "Kočvara, Štefan" in: *SVU Directory* 3' "Kočvara, Štefan," in: Pejskar 1; pp. 65-66; "Stefan Kočvara," in: Wikipedia. See - https://cs.wikipedia.org/wiki/ Štefan_Kočvara

Ladislav Krno (1909-1972), b. Brezno pod Hronom, Slovakia; Slovak exile diplomat, residing in Berwyn, IL
Bio: "Krno, Ladislav," in: Pejskar 1, p. 135; "Krno, Ladislav Gejza," in: *SVU Directory* 2

Martin Kvetko (1912-1995), b. Muránska Dlhá Lúka, Slovakia; veterinarian, exile politician, cofounder the Council of Free Czechoslovakia, founder and head of Stála konferencia slovenských demokratických exulantov
Bio: "Kvetko, Marttin," in: SVU *Directory* 7; "Martin Kvetko," in: Wikipedia. See - https://sk.wikipedia.org/wiki/Martin_Kvetko

Jozef Lettrich (1905-1969), b. Turčianské Teplice, Slovakia; lawyer, Slovak exile politician, member of the Council of Free Czechoslovakia
Bio: "Lettrich, Jozef," in: *SVU Directory* 2; "Lettrich, Jozef," in: Pejskar 1, pp. 19-21; "Jozef Lettrich," in: Wikipedia. See - https://sk.wikipedia.org/wiki/Jozef_Lettrich; "Jozef Lettrich, 64, Slovak Foe of Nazis and Communists, Dies," *The New York Times*, December 2, 1969; "Lettrich, Jozef," in *Panorama*, pp. 235-236.

Eugen Lőbl (1907-1987), b. Halíč, Slovakia; economist, politician; after the Soviet invasion of Czechoslovakia in 1968, he immigrated to the US. He served a vice president of the Slovak World Congress.
Bio: "Eugen Lőbl," in: Wikipedia. See - https://cs.wikipedia.org/wiki/ Eugen_Löbl; "Eugen Loebl, 80, Dies; Former Czech Official," *The New York Times,* August 9, 1987.

Albert Pavol Mamatey (1870-1923), b. Kláštor pod Znievom, Slovakia; Slovak exile politician, signatory of Pittsburgh Agreement
Bio: "Albert Mamatey," in: *History of Pittsburgh and Environs.* New York - Chicago: The American Historical Society, 1922, vol. 5, pp. 128-129; "Albert Pavol Mamatey," in Wikipedia. See - https://sk.wikipedia.org/wiki/ Albert_Pavol_Mamatej

Ferdinand Mondok (1903-1995), b. Dolný Lopašov, Slovakia; R.C. priest; HS teacher; politically active in the World War II Slovak Republic; member of Slovenský snem; forced to leave Slovakia in 1945, immigrated to Canada in 1950; active in Slovak National Council and Montreal Slovak community.
Bio: "Ferdinand Mondok," in: Obec Lopašov. See - http://www. obecdlopasov.sk/obec-15/historia-obce/slavni-rodaci-z-obce-dolny-lopasov/ ferdinand-mondok/

Jozef August Mikuš (1909-2005), b. Krivá, Slovakia; lawyer, diplomat, exile politician, university teacher; co-founder of the Slovak World Congress
Bio: "Jozef August Mikuš," in: Wikipedia. See - https://sk.wikipedia.org/ wiki/Jozef_August_Mikuš

Anton Moravčík (1903-1965), b. Veresvar, Slovakia; member of World War II Slovak parliament; emigrated after WWII; editor of the Slovak Catholic Sokol newspaper.
Bio: See: Bolecek, Dr. B.V. and Irene Slamka, *The Slovak Encyclopaedia.* New York: Slovak Academy, 1981, p. 80.

Jozef Mrázek (1910-1979), b. Lamač, Slovakia; journalist, with RFE, NYC, exile politician, member of Council of Free Czechoslovakia
Bio: "Mrázek, Jozef," in: ČSDS Website. See - http://www.csds.cz/cs/ g6/934-DS.html; "Mrázek, Jozef," in: Pejskar 2, p. 170.

Michal Múdry-Šebík (1909-1978), b. Drietomá, Slovakia; lawyer, journalist, chief of Czechoslovak Desk, Radio Free Europe, New York, NY, exile politician, member of Council of Free Czechoslovakia
Bio: "Múdry-Šebík, Michael," in: *SVU Directory* 4; "Múdry-Šebík, Michael," in: Pejskar 2, p. 170; Múdry-Šebík, Michael," in: *Czechoslovakia Past and Present*, Vol. 2, p. 1821.

Štefan Osuský (1889-1973), b. Brezová pod Bradlom, Slovakia; Slovak exile politician and diplomat, member of the Council of Free Czechoslovakia
Bio: "Osuský, Štefan," in: Pejskar 1, pp. 142-144; "Stefan Osusky," in: Wikipedia. See - https://en.wikipedia.org/wiki/ Štefan_Osuský; "Osuský, Stefan," in: *Panorama*, p. 256.

Betka Papanek (19900-1995), b. Chicago, of Slovak parents; founder and president of the National Council of Women of Free Czechoslovakia, founder and president of the Council of European Women in Exile
Bio: "Papanek, Betka," in: *SVU Directory* 7; "Papanek, Betka," in: *Panorama*, pp. 256-257

Ján Papánek (1896-1997), b. Brezová pod Bradlom, Slovakia; lawyer, Slovak exile diplomat
Bio "Papánek, Ján," in: *SVU Directory* 7; "Papánek, Ján," in: Pejskar 4, pp. 125-131; Saxon, Wolfgang, "Jan Papanek, 95, Czechoslovak Who Stood Up to Communism," *The New York Times*, December 3, 1991; "Ján Papánek," in: Wikipedia. See - https://sk.wikipedia.org/wiki/ Ján_Papánek; Jan Papanek, Anti-Stalinist Czechoslovak," *Chicago Tribune*, December 8, 1991; "Papanek, Ján," in: *Panorama*, pp. 257-258; "Papanek, Ján," in: *Czechoslovakia Past and Present*, Vol. 2, pp. 1824-1825.

Pavol Pláňovský (1912-1984), b. Prešov, Slovakia; journalist, politician politician, member of Council of Free Czechoslovakia; cofounder of Stála konferencia slovenských demokratických exulantov, residing in Montreal, Canada
Bio: "Pavol Pláňovský," in: Wikipedia. See - https://cs.wikipedia.org/wiki/ Pavol_ Pláňovský

Emil Ransdorf (1920-1974), b. Nové Zámky, Czech.; exile student leader, founder of Czech Students Abroad, member of the Council of Free Czechoslovakia
Bio: "Ransdorf, Emil," in" *SVU Directory* 3

Imrich Vitzak Rosenberg (1913-1986), b. Nové Mesto and Váhom, Slovakia; lawyer, activist, Zionist, realtor, in exile he resided in Ottawa, Canada
Bio: "Rosenberg, Imrich Vitzak," in *SVU Directory* 5, "Rosenberg, Imrich Vitzak," in Pejskar 3, p. 186; Rosenberg, Truda, "Curriculum vitae of Dr. Imrich Itzhak Rosenberg," in: Rosenberg, Dr. Imrich MG 31, H 158. See-http://data2.archives.ca/pdf/pdf001/p000000214.pdf

Pavol Rusnak, b. Liptovský Mikuláš, Slovakia; business executive, president of the Slovak World Congress
Bio: "Slovak World Congress gets new president," in: *The Slovak Spectator,* October 9, 1996.

Karol Sidor (1901-1953), b. Ružomberok, Slovakia; Slovak nationalist politician, commander of the Hlinka guard, immigrated to Montreal, Canada
Bio: "Karol Sidor," in: Wikipedia. See - https://en.wikipedia.org/wiki/Karol_Sidor

Ján Šikura (1902-1978), b. Mošovce, Slovakia; lawyer, Slovak exile politician, member of Council of Free Czechoslovakia, resided in Canada
Bio: "Šikura, Ján," in: Pejskar 2, p. 64

Juraj Slávik (1890-1969), b. Dobrá Niva, Slovakia; Slovak exile politician and diplomat, member of the Council of Free Czechoslovakia, resided in Washington, DC, writer, translator
Bio: "Slávik, Juraj," in: *SVU Directory* 2; "Slávik, Juraj," in: Pejskar 1, pp. 42-45; "Juraj Slávik," in: Wikipedia. See - https://sk.wikipedia.org/wiki/Juraj_Slávik; "Slávik, Juraj Michal Daniel," in: Panorama, p. 281; "Slávik, Juraj," *Czechoslovak Contribution*, p. 648.

Julius Solar (1909-1985), b. Opatova, Slovakia; lawyer, Slovak exile diplomat
Bio: "Solar, Julius," in: *SVU Directory* 5, "Solar, Julius," in: Pejskar 3, p.202

Jozef Staško (1917-1999), b. Sedliacka Dubová, Slovakia; Czechoslovak politician; jailed by Communists; in Us s. 1961; became librarian in NYC. Bio: "Jozef Staško," in: Wikipedia. See - https://cs.wikipedia.org/wiki/Jozef_ Staško

Pavol Viboch (1896-1981), b. Zvolen, Slovakia; Slovak exile politician, member of the Council of Free Czechoslovakia
Bio: "Viboch, Pavol," in: Pejskar 1, p. 92; "Pavol Viboch," in: Wikipedia
See - https://cs.wikipedia.org/wiki/Pavol_Viboch

Ján Žák () member of the Council of Free Czechoslovakia

X. Cultural Life

A. GENERAL

Pier, Andrew V., "Our Slovak Heritage in America," in: *Slovaks in America. A bicentennial Study*, pp. 79-88.

Rechcigl, Miloslav Jr., "Cultural Contributions of Americans with Roots in Slovakia", *Kosmas* 14, No. 1 (Fall 2000), pp. 112-95-106.

Tanzone, Daniel F., "Slovak Contributions to the American Cultural Mosaic," *Slovakia* 25, No. 48 (1975), pp. 119-27.

B. EDUCATION

1. General

"Future of Czech-Slovak Studies in America," 20th SVU World Congress, Washington, DC, August 9-13, 2000.

Gregorovic, M. Consuela, "Contributions of Rev. Matthew Jankola to Slovak Catholic Education in the United States," *Slovak Studies* 16 (1976), pp. 7-54.

Palickar, Stephen, "The First Slovak Girls Academy, Danville, Pennsylvania," *Student Life* (December 1928), pp. 53-55.

Kugler, John, A Study of Czechoslovak Immigration and their Contributions to Vocational Education in Chicago between 1875and 1935. A Master's Thesis, Chicago State University,2003.

Rechcigl, Miloslav Jr., *Educators with Czechoslovak Roots*. U.S. and Canadian Roster. Washington, DC: SVU Press, 1980. 122 p.

Stolarik, M. Mark. "Immigration, Education and the Social Mobility of Slovaks, 1870-1930." *Slovakia* 27, No. 50 (1977): 80- 90.

Votruba, Martin, "Slovak Studies Program, University of Pittsburgh," in: University of Pittsburgh. See - https://www.pitt.edu/~votruba/skprogram/skprogram.html

2. Teachers

Bonaventure Babik (?-1986), R.C. priest, O.F.M.; assistant pastor of St. Mary's parish, Clifton (1975-86); teacher of Slovak University of Akron, in the department of Continuing Education.
Bio:

John Bača (1934-), b. Vehec, Slovakia; in US s.1947; with Chrysler, vocational teacher in engineering and design.
Bio: Baca, John, *A Humble Beginning: My Life*, Saline, MI: Allegra Print Imaging, 2011;m "Author's Background," *Jednota*, October 12, 2011.

Arthur Aaron Dembitz (1870 -d.) b. Louisville, KY, of Slovak descent; on editorial staff of *The American Hebrew*, New York (1892-97); private teacher of Hebrew, NYC (1892-97); instructor in Jewish history, Gratz College, Philadelphia (s. 1897).
Bio: "Dembitz, Artur Aaron," in: *American Jewish Year Book*, Vol. 6, p. 81.

Božena Hilková Fox, b. Michalovce, Slovakia; teacher of Slovak at Pittsburgh's Kolar Club, Carlow University and Allegheny County Community College
Bio: Little information about her can be found in "Slovaks Reconnect with their Heritage." See - http://old.post-gazette.com/magazine/20010520slovaksmag2.asp

Michael Gerdelan (1914-), b. Sečovská Polianka, Slovakia; teacher, poet; published in Slovak periodicals.
Bio: See - Bolecek, Dr. B.V. and Irene Slamka, *The Slovak Encyclopaedia*. New York: Slovak Academy, 1981, p. 53.

Anna Puchy Matko (1916-2012), b. Newark, NJ, of Slovak descent; teacher. Began teaching in Mountainside, NJ, in 1966, where she became a beloved teacher in all three schools in the district, Echobrook, Beechwood, and Deerfield, teaching third grade, until 1980.
Bio: "Anna Puchy Matko," in: Union Funeral Home Lytwyn & Lytwyn. See - http://www.unionfuneralhome.com/obituary/Anna-Puchy-Matko/Mountainside-NJ/1103736

Dennis Ragan (1952-), b. Pittsburgh, PA, of Slovak father; studied Slovak in Bratislava and at University of Pittsburgh; after working in marketing for some 16 years (1999-2015), he switched to teaching of Slovak language; part-time instructor of Slovak at Westmoreland County Community College (s. 2002); Online instructor of Slovak language and culture, Czechoslovak Genealogical Society Intl. (s. 2018).
Bio: "Dennis Ragan," in; LinkedIn. See - https://www.linkedin.com/in/dennisragan/

Ethel Shintay (1899--2017), b. Johnstown, PA; teacher in NY Public schools, as well as an English as a second language instructor
Bio: "Shintay, Ethel," in: *SVU Directory* 8; "Ethel Shintay," in: *Asbury Park Press*, December 30, 2017.

Michael J. Vaschak (1954-2018), b. Youngstown, OH, of Slovak descent; trained as educational administrator; school teacher in Campbell City schools (for 35 years)
Bio: "Michael J. Vaschak," in: The Vindicator, September 3, 2018. See -http://www.vindy.com/news/tributes/2017/jan/18/michael-j-vascha/

C. Journalism & Publishing

1. Surveys

Bakay-Záhorská, Michaela and Zdena Kráľová, *Slovak Cultural Heritage in the USA - Periodicals*. Nitra: Pedagogická fakulta UKF, 2015. 117p.
Čulen, Konštantín, "The Beginnings of the Slovak Press in America," in: Čulen, pp. 161-163.
Duben, Vojtěch N., "Czech and Slovak Press Outside Czechoslovakia," in: *The Czechoslovak Contribution to World Culture*. The Hague / London /Paris: Mouton & Co., pp. 528-545.
Fodiak, William P., "Slovak Newspapers in the United States," *Jednota Annual Furdek* 23 (1984), pp. 27-46.
Kona, William, "The Oldest Slovak Newspaper in the U.S.A." *Slovakia* 15, No. 38 (1965), pp. 38-50.

Olekšák, Peter and Albert Kulla, "The Slovak Periodical Press Historical Development, Current Content, New forms of Access," *Slavic and East European Information Resources*, 8, No. 2 / 3 (December 2007), pp. 21-29.
Paučo, Draga, "Slovak American Journalism," in: *Slovaks in America. A Bicentennial Study*, pp. 67-78.
Paučo, Joseph, "Slovak Journals in the United States," *Furdek* (1974), pp. 99- 104.
Stolarik, M. Mark, "Slovak American Newspapers, 1885-1975: A Preliminary Listing," *Slovakia* 32, No. 58 and 59 (1985-86), pp. 34-70.
Pier, Andrew, "The Oldest Slovak Newspaper in America," *Slovakia*, 42 (1969), pp. 96-99.
Stolarik, M. Mark, "The Slovak-American Press," in: *The Ethnic Press in the United States. A Historical Analysis and Handbook*. Ed. by Sally M. Miller. Westport, CT: Greenwood Press, 1987, pp. 355-368.
Stolarik, M. Mark, "The Slovak Press in the Late 19th and Early 20th Centuries, with Particular Emphasis on the Slovak-American Press, 1885-1918," in: *Dve domovini - Two Homelands*, 2- 3 (1992), pp. 141-164.
Wynar, Lubomyr R., "Slovak Press," in his *Guide to the American Ethnic Press*. Kent, OH: Kent State University School of Library Science, 1986. Pp. 44-57.
Zahorska, Michaela B., Zdena Kralova and Helen Baine Cincebeaux, "The Historic Background of the Slovak Press in the USA," *Communications*, Vol. 3 (2014, pp. 36-40.

2. Journalists

a. Surveys

Tybor, M. Martina, "First Slovak Newspapermen in America," *Slovakia* 18, No. 41 (1968), pp. 121-31

b. Individuals

John Adam (1928-2005), b. North Braddock, PA, of Slovak descent; Lutheran minister;
co-editor, *Sion* (Zion), monthly, Pittsburgh, PA (s. 1929)
Bio: "Obituary of Pastor Adam," in: Cornell Memorial Home. See - https://cornellmemorial.com/tribute/details/6358/Pastor-Adam/obituary.html

Margot Adler (1946-2014), b. Little Rock, AR, of Czech and Slovak descent; an American_journalist, author, lecturer, Wiccan priestess, and New York correspondent for National Public Radio (NPR)
Bio: "Margot Adler," in: Wikipedia. See - https://en.wikipedia.org/wiki/Margot_Adler

Anton Štefan Ambrose (Ambrosi) (1867-1941), b. Kobyly, Bardejov District, Slovakia; in US s. 1882; pioneer journalist, founder of *Slovak v Amerike*, the oldest newspaper and still in print in the US.
Bio: "Ambrose, Anton Štefan," in: Encyclopedia Beliana. See - https://beliana.sav.sk/heslo/ambrose-anton-stefan

Julius Behul (fl. 2012), a Slovak Canadian; editor-in-chief, *Kanadsky Slovák*

Charles (Karol) Belohlavek (1886-1942), b. Holíč, Slovakia; printer, journalist, editor of *Slovensky Hlasnik*, newspaper of the Slovak Evangelical Union, publisher and editor of *Floridsky Slovak*
Bio: "Biographical Note," in: Register of the Papers of Charles Belohlavek. See - http://www2.hsp.org/collections/Balch%20manuscript_guide/html/belohlavek.html

Meyer Berger (1898-1959), b. New York City, of Czechoslovak ancestry; journalist, reporter
Bio: Meyer M Berger," in: Wikipedia. See - https://en.wikipedia.org/wiki/Meyer_Berger; "Meyer Berger, 60, of times is Dead, Reporter Got Pulitzer Prize in '50," *The New York Times*, February 9, 1959.

Shanik Berman (1959-), b. Mexico City, Mexico, of Slovak ancestry; Showbiz journalist, Mexico
Bio: "Shanik Berman," in: Wikipedia. See - https://en.wikipedia.org/wiki/Shanik_Bermantolaryngologist

Ivan Bielek (1886-1943), b. Slovakia; journalist, editor, *The National News*, Pittsburgh, PA, president of Slovak League of America, signatory of the Pittsburgh Agreement
Bio: "Ivan Bielek," in: *History of Pittsburgh and Environs*, New York and Chicago: The American Historical Society, 1922, pp. 331-332.

Ján E. Bor (pseudonym of Dr. Ernest Žatko) (1907-1991), b. Žabokreky, Slovakia; trained as a linguist and held the post of professor of Roman literature at University of Bratislava; became a columnist and traveled abroad; in 1948 he immigrated to Argentina, where he remained, working as a journalist.
Bio: "Jan E. Bor." See - http://jebiography.blogspot.com/2006/09/who-was-jan-e_27.html?m=0

John Cieker (1912-1993), Slovak American; resided in Parma and then in Cleveland, OH; editor, *Živena*, monthly, Pittsburgh, PA
Bio: "John C. Cieker," in: Find A Grave. See - https://www.findagrave.com/memorial/115829288/john-c-cieker

Helene Cincebeaux (1938-), b. Johnson City, NY, of Slovak descent; editor of *Slovakia: A Slovak Heritage Magazine*, Rochester
Bio: "Helene Baine Cincebeaux," in: Homestead. See - http://helenezx.homestead.com/

John Denďúr (1898-), b. Petrovec, Yugoslavia; printer, teacher, journalist, publisher, editor of *Náš Svet*, a Slovak weekly, dramatic director of the Slovak Worker's Society
Bio: "Dendur, John," in Droba, p. 45.

Sender Deutsch (1922-1998), b. Veľké Berezné, Czech., rabbi, leader of one of the largest Hasidic Jewish groups in the US, and the longtime chief editor of *Der Yid*, a Yiddish-language weekly newspaper
Bio: "Rabbi Sender Deutsch, 76, Editor, Publisher of Der Yid," *The New York Times*, September 13, 1998; "Deutsch, Sander," in: *Who's Who in the East*, 9

Rudolf Dilong (1905-1986), b. Trstená, Slovakia; R.C. priest, O.F.M., author, editor, *Listy svatého Františka* (Leaflets of Saint Francis), monthly, Pittsburgh, PA
Bio: "Rudolf Dilong," in: Wikipedia. See - https://sk.wikipedia.org/wiki/Rudolf_Dilong; "Fr. Rudolph Alphones Dilong," in: Find A Grave. See - https://www.findagrave.com/memorial/113406361/rudolph-alphonse-dilong

Ján Eliáš (1910-), b. Jaklovce, Slovakia; teacher, editor of *Slovenska Ocine* (1961-64); contributor to Slovak periodicals in Canada.
Bio -See - Bolecek, Dr. B.V. and Irene Slamka, *The Slovak Encyclopaedia*. New York: Slovak Academy, 1981, p. 49.

Joseph J. Falatko (1925-20011), Slovak American; reporter for *Freeland News*, Freeland, PA
Bio: "Joseph J. Falatko," *Standard-Speaker*, April 12, 2011

John Adolf Feriencik (1865-1925), b. Zvolen, Slovakia; in US s. 1894; journalist, writer; editor of *Slovenský Hlásnik* (Slovak Herald), the weekly publication of the Slavonic Evangelical Union of America; founder of the *Osveta* magazine in Cleveland.
Bio: "John Adolph Feriencik," in: *Cleveland and Environs*. Chicago-New York: Lewis Publishing Company, 1918, vol. 2, pp. 328-330; "Ján Adolf Ferienčík," in: Wikipedia. See - https://sk.wikipedia.org/wiki/Ján_Adolf_Ferienčík.

Jozef Filek (1867-1905), b. Slovakia; journalist, editor, *Slovenské katolícke noviny* (Hazelton, PA).
Bio: See, Konštantín Čulen, *Slovenské časopisy v Amerike*. Cleveland, 1970, pp. 20, 55-56.

Ignac Gessay (1874-1928), b. Tvrdošín, Slovakia; journalist with Ján Pankúch
Bio: "Ignác Gessay," in: Wikipedia. See - https://sk.wikipedia.org/wiki/Ignác_Gessay

Milan Alexander Getting (1878-1951), b. Bytča, Slovakia; publisher of *Slovenský Sokol*, signatory of Pittsburg Agreement
Bio: "Getting, Ivan Alexander," in: *Who's Who in America*, 41; "Getting, Milan Alexander," in: Wikipedia. See - https://sk.wikipedia.org/wiki/Milan_Alexander_Getting

George Gross (1923-2008), b. Bratislava, Czech.; Canadian sport journalist worked for several newspapers, mostly for *Toronto Sun*
Bio: "George Gross," in: Wikipedia. See - https://en.wikipedia.org/wiki/George_Gross_(journalist)

Thomas B. Harnyak (1894-1987), b. South Side, PA, of Slovak descent; R.C. priest, pastor of churches in Fairchance and Shoaf and Whitaker, before moving to St. Joachim at Greenfield, PA; editor of *Svornost* (Harmony), bi-monthly, Pittsburgh, PA
Bio: "Rev. T. B. Harnyak," The Pittsburgh Press, August 13, 1987.

Stefan Hreha (1918-2015), b. Čemerné, Slovakia; in Canada since 1936; founder of the weekly *Kanadský Slovak* (The Canadian Slovak) and its first editor (1942-53).This was the official organ of the Canadian Slovak League, which has the distinction of has the distinction of being the only surviving Slovak weekly in North America that has been published, without interruption, for over 70 years. In 1952 he was hired by Crane Canada where he rose to the position of Advertising Production Manager.
Bio: "Obituary: Stefan Hreha," in: Montreal, QC - dignity Memorial. See - https://www.dignitymemorial.com/en-ca/obituaries/montreal-qc/ stefan-hreha-6556395

Philip Anthony Hrobak (1904-1964), b. Cleveland, OH, of Slovak descent; editor of *Jednota*, manager of Jednota printery, author, Middletown, PA
Bio: "Hrobak, Philip A.," in: *Catholic Who's Who*, 1961, Vol. 14, p. 215.

Joseph Hušek (1880-1947), b. Ružomberok, Slovakia; editor and manager of *Jednota* (s. 1904)
Bio: "Husek, Joseph," in: *Catholic Who's Who*, 7 (1946-1947); "Jozef Hušek," in: Wikipedia. See - https://sk.wikipedia.org/wiki/Jozef_ Hušek

Stephen Huska (1888-d.), b. Brezová, Slovakia; teacher, journalist, editor of the *Slovenský Sokol* periodical, with *Slovenský Národný Denník*, Chicago, with *Tatran* monthly, co-founder and editor the *Nové Časy*, a Slovak national weekly, residing in Chicago
Bio: Huska, Stephen," in: Droba, pp. 45-46

Teresa 'Terri' Ivanec (1954-), b. Cleveland, OH, of Slovak descent; her grandmother was born in Orava, Slovakia; a holder of a Master's degree in English from the University of Kansas. She spent a decade in Atlanta, Georgia, where she honed her skills as an in-house magazine editor and senior writer for Dun & Bradstreet Software. Returning to Cleveland in 1990s, she worked as an article writer, newsletter editor, and magazine contributor for some of the Midwest's premier manufacturers, healthcare organizations, advertising and public relations agencies, and community leaders. Since January 2000, she has held the position of editor of Slovak newspaper *Jednota*. Bio: "A Warm Welcome," *Jednota*, January 6, 2000, p. 3.

Wanda Jablonski (1920-1992), b. Czech.; American journalist; founder, owner, editor of *Petroleum Intelligence Weekly*, NYC (s. 1961) Bio: "Jablonski. Wanda Mary," in: *Who's Who in America*, 41; "Jablonski, Wanda," in: Wikipedia. See - https://en.wikipedia.org/wiki/Wanda_Jablonski; Rubino, Anna, *Queen of the Oil Club: The Intrepid Wanda Jablonski and the Power of Information*. Boston, MA: Beacon Press, 2009.

Ján Janček, Jr. (1881-1933), b. Ružomberok, Slovakia; news editor, writer; founder and editor Slovenský Sokol (1905) Bio: "Janček, Ján, Jr." *Slovenský Biografický Slovník*. Martin: Matica Slovenska, 1987, Vol. 1, p. 520.

Matúš Jankola (1872-1916), b. Budapest, of Slovak parents; in US s. 1893; R.C. priest; writer, playwright, editor, publisher Slovak patriot. Bio: "Matúš Jankola (* 2. 7. 1872 Budapešť – † 5. 5. 1916 Bridgeport, Connecticut, USA)," *Literárny Týždenník*. See -https://www.literarny-tyzdennik.sk/products/matus-jankola-2-7-1872-5-5-1916/; Pauco, Jozef, *Matúš Jankola, kňaz a národovec*. Danville, PA, 1959.

J. Jesenský, b. Slovakia; journalist, editor, *Rovnost' l'udu* (Equality of People), Chicago, IL (s. 1906); supported the radical Social Democratic Party in America. Bio: "Non-English Press of the Communist Party USA - Slovak - Rovnost' Ludu," in Wikipedia. See - https://en.wikipedia.org/wiki/ Non-English_press_of_the_Communist_Party_USA#Slovak; Konštantín Čulen, *Slovenské časopisy v Amerike*. Cleveland, 1970, p. 106

Ondrej E. Komara (1883-1932), b. Levoča, Slovakia; RC priest, editor, writer; helped found magazine *Ave Mária* and *Božské Srdce Ježiša* (Sacred Heart of Jesus). Bio: Paučo, Jozef, *Slovenski priekopnici v Amerike*, Cleveland: Prvá Katolícka Slovenská Jednota, 1972 pp. 233-235

Martin Kopunek (1889-1959), b. Bukova, Slovakia; Fraternal leader, editor of *Dobrý Pastier* (Good Shepherd), the periodical of the Slovak Catholic Federation.
Bio: See: Bolecek, Dr. B.V. and Slamka, Irene, *The Slovak Encyclopaedia.* New York: Slovak Academy, 1981, p. 65.

Edward Kováč (1873-1939), b. Brádno, Slovakia; trained as carpenter; editor, *Národné Noviny* (National News), semi-monthly, Pittsburgh (s. 1910); editor *Slovenská Obrana.*
Bio: See - Bolecek, Dr. B.V. and Irene Slamka, *The Slovak Encyclopaedia.* New York: Slovak Academy, 1981, p. 68; Paučo, Jozef, *Slovenski priekopnici v Amerike,* Cleveland: Prvá Katolícka Slovenská Jednota, 1972, pp. 242-248.

John Kovacik (1905-2000), b. Necpaly, Slovakia; Lutheran minister, co-editor of *Sion* (Zion), monthly, Pittsburgh, PA
Bio: "Rev. Dr. John Kovacik, Retired Lutheran Pastor," The Morning Call, Mach 11, 2000.

Joseph Charles Krajsa (1917- 1998), b. Allentown, PA, of Slovak ancestry; Slovak fraternalist, editor of *Jednota* (Union), Catholic Slovak weekly, Middletown, PA (s. 1964); also, editor of *Kalendar* and Annual *Furdek* (s. 1964).
Bio: "Krajsa, Joseph Charles," in: *Catholic Who's Who* 21 (1976-1977), p. 294; "Joseph C. Krajsa, Jednota Editor, Former Athletic Director," *The Morning Call,* June 12, 1998.

Jozef Borivoj Krčméry (1865-1925), b. Badín, Slovakia; publicist, journalist, banker, Pittsburgh, PA
Bio: "Jozef Borivoj Krčméry," in: Wikipedia. See - https://sk.wikipedia.org/wiki/Jozef_Borivoj_ Krčméry

Michael Laucik (1878-1965), b. Vrbica, Slovakia; journalist, grocer, teacher, editor of *Kruh Mládeže,* organ of the young Folk's Circle of the National Slovak Society of America, residing in Chicago
Bio: "Laucik, Michal," in: Droba, pp. 46-47.

George Stephen Luba (1897-1961), b. Budapest, of Slovak descent; R.C. priest, O.S.B., teacher, St. Procopius Academy (1917-27); founder and principal of Benedictine HS, Cleveland (s. 1927); pastor, St. Andrew's, Cleveland

(1929-30); prior, St. Andrew's Abbey (1935-48); editor of *Ave Maria* (Slovak monthly) (s. 1936), *Ženská Jednota* bi-monthly (s. 1937)
Bio: "Luba, Rev. George Stephen (O.S.B.)," in: *Catholic Who's Who*, 14 (1960-1961).

Hubert Macko (1899-1971), b. Jaklovce, Slovakia; R.C. priest, O.S.B., pastor, teacher, editor of the Slovak Catholic weekly *Slovenský Svet* (s. 1926)
Bio: "Macko, Hubert," in: *Catholic Who's Who*, 1947, Vo. 7, p. 286

John Matlocha (1879-1944), b. Zvolen, Slovakia; editor and publisher, editor of *Tatran*, a monthly journal, owner of the Mally Press, Printers and Binders Co., residing in Chicago
Bio: "Matlocha, John," in: Droba, p. 47; "John Matlocha," in: Find A Grave. See - https://www.findagrave.com/memorial/179872074/john-matlocha

George Mihalcik (1945-2973), b. of Slovak descent; reporter, New Castle, PA
Bio: "George Mihalcik," *New Castle News*, February 8, 1973

Dennis Mikolay (1989-d.), b. Middletown, NJ, of Slovak ancestry; political columnist, blogger, author, activist;
Bio: "Dennis Mikolay," in: Wikipedia. See - https://en.wikipedia.org/wiki/Dennis_Mikolay

Peter Minarik (), b. editor, TV JOJ; resides in Chicago
Bio: "Peter Minarik" in: Krajanske Centrum Tatran. See - http://www.krajanskecentrum.com/ludia/

Ján Okáľ (1915-1990), b. Hubová, Slovakia; teacher, writer, editor; Matica Slovenska employee; emigrated to Italy, then to USA in 1950. Was editor, *Slovák v Amerike* (1951–58), *Literary Almanac of Slovak in America*, the *Bulletin of the World Congress of the Slovaks* (1979-90). He wrote prose, poetry, and books for children.
Bio: "Ján Okáľ," in: LIC. See - http://www.litcentrum.sk/slovenski-spisovatelia/jan-okal

Stephen J. Palickar (1885-1955), b. Olyphant, PA, of Slovak immigrant parents; they came from Stropkov, Slovakia. Descen. He was professional journalist, writer.
Bio: See - Bolecek, Dr. B.V. and Irene Slamka, *The Slovak Encyclopaedia*. New York: Slovak Academy, 1981, p. 86.

Ján Pankúch (1869-1952), b. Prešov, Slovakia; newspaper editor and publisher, long-time editor and publisher of *Hlas* (The Voice), Cleveland's only Slovak newspaper
Bio: "Pankuch, John," in: *Encyclopedia of Cleveland History*. See - https://case. edu/ech/articles/p/pankuch-jan; Dubelko, Jim, "Slovak Journalist Jan Pankuch," in: Cleveland Historical. See - https://clevelandhistorical.org/ items/show/598; "Pankuch, Jan," in: *Encyclopedia of Cleveland History*. See - https://case.edu/ech/articles/p/pankuch-jan

Draga Paučo (1922-2003), b. Slovakia; editor, *Slovak v Amerike*, weekly, Middletown, PA (s. 1889)
Bio: "Draga Divinska," in: *Czechoslovakia Past and Present*, Vol. 1, p. 876.

Joseph Paučo (1914-1974), b. Slovakia; journalist, publicist, publisher of *Slovak in America*, Middletown, PA
Bio: Kirschbaum, Joseph M, "Dr. Pauco's Writing and the History of American Slovaks," *Furdek* (1974), pp. 75-80; Kirschbaum, Josef M., comp., *Jozef Pauco, 1914-1974*. Cleveland, OH: Slovak Institute, 1974.

Jaroslav John Pelikan, Sr. (1898-1974), b. Slovakia; Lutheran minister; pastor, Trinity Slovak Lutheran Church, Chicago, IL; president of the Slovak Alliance; editor, Svedok (The Witness), monthly, Pittsburgh, PA
Bio: See - United States Census, 1940; United States Social Security Death Index, https://www.familysearch.org/search/record/results?count =20&query=%2Bgivenname%3AJaroslav~%20%2Bsurname%3A Pelikan~.

John Porubský (1874-1953), b. Zniev, Slovakia; R.C. priest, prolific writer and journalist
Bio: "Porubsky, John," in: *Catholic Who's Who* 7, 1946-1947), pp. 363-364.

František Pucher-Čiernovodský (1861-1905), b. Svätý Jur, Slovakia; journalist, editor of *Slovak v Amerike*
Bio: "František Pucher-Čiernovodský," Slovak v Amerike, September 2018. See - http://www.slovakvamerike.com/

Eric Reguly (ca 1952 -), b. Vancouver, BC, Canada, of Slovak descent; son of Robert Reguly; a Canadian newspaper columnist. He is a feature columnist for *The Globe and Mail*, where he contributes to the paper's financial section, Report on Business. He also contributes to Report on Business Magazine and Globe Auto and is an occasional commentator on Report on Business Television.
Bio: "Eric Reguly," in: Wikipedia. See - https://en.wikipedia.org/wiki/Eric_Reguly

Robert Reguly (1931-2011), b. Fort William, Ont., Canada; of Slovak parents; three-time National Newspaper Award-winning journalist. He was one of Canada's top news reporters in the 1950s and 1960s. He was at the forefront of the mid-20th century news war between the *Toronto Telegram* and the *Toronto Star*. In 1981, he became a spokesperson for the Ontario Ministry of the Environment. After his retirement, he became a successful freelance writer, writing mainly for outdoors magazines.
Bio: "Robert Reguly," in: Wikipedia. See - https://en.wikipedia.org/wiki/Robert_Reguly; "Journalist Robert (Bob) Reguly has died," *Kanadský Slovak*. See - http://kanadskyslovak.ca/index.php/home/64-community-short-news?start=33

Peter Víťazoslav Rovnianek (1867-1933), b. Dolný Hričov, Slovakia; businessman, banker, journalist; founder of Slovaktown, AR. He was the founder of the first Slovak newspaper in America; editor of several Slovak papers, especially the first Slovak daily in Pittsburgh.
Bio: "Peter Pavol Rovnianek," in: Geni. See - https://www.geni.com/people/Peter-V%C3%AD%C5%A5azoslav-Rovnianek/6000000021154797645; "Peter Víťazoslav Rovnianek," in: Wikipedia. See - https://sk.wikipedia.org/wiki/Peter_Víťazoslav_Rovnianek

Rosalie Ruman (1925-), b. Slovakia; writer, Montreal, P.Q., Canada
Bio: Ruman, Rosalie," in: *SVU Directory*, 9

Stephen Reistetter (1914-2006), b. Lipany, Slovakia;. Emigrated after war; edited Kanadsky Slovak; in 1955, helped found the Nitra Folk Dancing group; charged with kidnapping 3,000 Slovakian Jews in 1942 in Bardejov, Slovakia, but acquitted for lack of evidence. See: https://billiongraves.com/grave/Stefan-Reistetter/1327815 and https://webcache.googleusercontent.com/search?q=cache:FiC9eCEo4r8J:https://www.jta.org/1990/05/29/archive/canadas-first-war-crimes-trial-ends-in-acquittal-to-jews-dismay+&cd=8&hl=sk&ct=clnk&gl=us

Fedor Ivan Salva (1901-1988), b. Ružomberok, Slovakia, son of Karol Salva. Journalist and national activist. Editor of *Slovenská Obrana* (Scranton) and *Národné Noviny*; member of the Slovak delegation which visited President Roosevelt in 1937.
Bio: See - Bolecek, B.V., and Irene Slamka, *The Slovak Encyclopaedia*. New York: Slovak Academy, 1981, p. 94.

Karol Salva (1849-1913), b. Liptovská Sielnica, Slovakia; teacher, journalist, publicist, editor of *Amerikánsko-Slovenské Noviny, Rarášek* and *Slovenský Denník*, published in Pittsburgh, publisher
Bio: "Karol Salva," in: Wikipedia. See - https://sk.wikipedia.org/wiki/Karol_Salva

Edward Schwartz-Markovič (1850-1933), b. Tepla, Slovakia; pioneer journalist in Streator, IL, publisher of *Nova Vlast* (New Home).
Slovenský Biografický Slovník. Martin: Matica Slovenská,1994, Vol. 6, pp. 248-49.

John C. Sciranka (1902-1980), b. Allegheny City, PA, of Slovak descent; journalist, editor of *Katolicky Sokol*, residing in Passaic, NJ
Bio: Tanzone, Daniel, "John C. Sciranka: outstanding Slovak American fraternalist," *Jednota Annual Furdek*, 17, (January 1978), pp. 51-160.

Ján Slovenský (1856-1900), b. Krompachy, Slovakia; journalist, founder of mimeographed weekly *Bulletin,* Pittsburgh, PA, together with Julius Wolf published *Amerikanszko-Szlovenszke Noviny* (American-Slovak News).
Bio: "Janko Slovenský,": in: Wikipedia. See - https://sk.wikipedia.org/wiki/Janko_Slovenský

Mikuláš Šprinc (1914-1986), b. Krompachy, Slovakia; R.C. priest; poet, prose writer, essayist, editor, translator and teacher; editor of the journal of most for 30 years.
Bio: "Mikuláš Šprinc," in: Wikipedia. See - https://sk.wikipedia.org/wiki/ Mikuláš Šprinc; "Mikuláš Šprinc," in: LIC. See -http://www.litcentrum.sk/ slovenskispisovatelia/mikulas-sprinc

Joseph Staško (1917-), b. Sedliacka Dubová, Slovakia; journalist and retired librarian; editor and writer for the *SKS Bulletin* and for the periodical *Horizont* Bio: "Jozef Stasko," in: https://cs.wikipedia.org/wiki/ /Jozef_Staško

Anthony X. Sutherland (1944 -), b. Stony Point, NY, of Slovak descent; historian, editor of Slovak-American newspaper *Jednota* (1995-2009).
Bio: "A Fond Farewell," *Jednota*, January 6, 2010, p. 3. See - https://www.fcsu. com/wp-content/uploads/jednota-archives/2010/JEDNOTA-JAN-6TH-10. pdf

Daniel F. Tanzone (1947-), b. Yonkers, NY, of Slovak descent; fraternalist, editor of the *Slovak Catholic Falcon* (s. 1980); active in the Slovak League of America, serving as national president (1895-93). Recipient of numerous awards.
Bio: "Daniel F. Tanzone," in: Find A Grave. See - https://www.findagrave. com/memorial/118560254/daniel-f.-tanzone

Adalbert Tholt-Veľkoštiavnický (1852-1940), b. **Ružomberok**, Slovakia; in US s. the eighties in the 19ᵗʰ century; journalist; editor, including *Slovenská svornosť*, Connelsville, PA (1896),
Slovák v Amerike, Slovenský denník and, in 1905–1909, editor of *Amerikánsko-ruský viestnik*.
Bio: *Slovenský Biografický Slovník*. Martin: Matica Slovenská,1994, Vol 6, p. 56.

Stephen J. Tkach (1894-1981), editor, *Bratrstvo* (Brotherhood), monthly, Wilkes-Barre, PA (s. 1899)
Bio: "Stephen J. Tkach, Sr.," in: Find A Grave. See - https://www.findagrave. com/memorial/132651597/stephen-j.-tkach

Wendel Tylka (1889-1977), b. Námestovo, Slovakia; journalist, editor; emigrated 1913; studied printing at St. Procopius, Lisle, IL; founded Tylka

Brosthers Press, Chicago; edited a Catholic weekly with Peter Hletko, Osadné hlasy (Community Voice).
Bio: See - *Slovenský Biografický Slovník*. (Martin: Matica Slovenská,1994, Vol. 6, p. 160.

Stanford J. Ungar (1945-), b. of Slovak ancestry; journalist, Dean at American University, President of Goucher College
Bio: "Stanford J. Ungar," in: Wikipedia. See - https://en.wikipedia.org/wiki/Sanford_J._Ungar; "Sanford. J. Ungar, Goucher's 10th President," in Goucher College. See: http://www.goucher.edu/explore/who-we-are/history/gouchers-presidents/sanford-ungar

Stephen Varzaly (1890-1957), b. Fulianka, Slovakia; a leading priest, journalist, and cultural activist for Rusyns in the United States. From 1930 to 1937 Varzaly served as editor-in-chief of *Amerikansky Russky Viestnik* (1892-1952), the longest-running Rusyn-American newspaper in America and the official publication of the Greek Catholic Union of Rusyn Brotherhoods, a fraternal benefit society based in Pennsylvania. Many Carpatho-Rusyns, including Varzaly, believed clerical celibacy to be so inherently unnatural as to lead inevitably to promiscuity and sexual abuse. During the celibacy conflict Varzaly used the newspaper to argue against *Cum Data Fuerit* and for continuation of a traditional married clergy within the Church. He joined, eventually, with the other clergy and laity to formally fight the Pope's decree.
Bio: "Stephen Varzaly," in: Wikipedia. See - https://en.wikipedia.org/wiki/Stephen_Varzaly

George Virchick, Jr. (1914-d.), minister of Presbyterian Church; pastor in Mount Carmel, PA; editor, *Calvin*, Pittsburgh, PA, monthly
Bio: See -The Peoples of Pennsylvania: An Annotated Bibliography of Resource Materials by David E. Washburn, p. 205.

Július Wolf (1860-1930), b. Krompachy, Slovakia; journalist, together with Ján Slovenský was publisher of *Amerikanszko-Szlovenszke Noviny* (American-Slovak News). Written in eastern dialect with Magyar orthography with pro-Hungarian political leaning.
Bio: *Slovenský Biografický Slovník*. Martin: Matica Slovenská,1994, Vol. 6, p. 378.

Andrew Yurkovsky (1962-), b. New Haven, CT, reporter, *Manchester Herald*, CT, *Stars and Stripes*
Bi: "Yurkovsky, Andrew," in: *SVU Directory* 8; "Articles by Andrew Yurkovsky, Stars and Stripes Journalist," in: Muck Rack. See - https://muckrack.com/andrew-yurkovsky/articles

Jozef Žák-Marušiak (1885-1979), b. Laksárska Nová Ves, Slovakia; editor of *Národné Noviny*, Pittsburgh and *Rovnost Ľudu*, Chicago
Bio: "Žak-Marušiak, Jozef," in: Pejskar 3, p. 262; "Žák-Marušiak, Joseph," in: Panorama, p. 310.

Ernest Žatko (1907-1991), columnist. See - **Ján Elen Bor**

Julius Žorna-Horský (1865-1902), b. Slovakia;_editor, *Americko-Slovenské Noviny*, Cleveland (s. 1886); *Bulletin*, Pittsburgh 1885-86); *Americký Slovak*, Cleveland (s. 1892); *Bratrstvo* (s. 1899).
Bio: "Žorna-Horský Julius," in: Slovo z Britskej Kolumbie. See - http://slovozbritskejkolumbie.ca/taxonomy/term/1686

Daniel M. Zornan (1925-1986), b. of Slovak descent; president of the United Lutheran Society; editor, *United Lutheran*, monthly, Ligonier, PA
Bio: "Daniel Mildred Zorna," in: mylife. See - https://www.mylife.com/daniel-mildredzornan/E963172237680

3. Radio and TV Correspondents and Hosts

Damon Amendolara (1979-), b. Warwick, NY, of Italian and Slovak descent; host on the CBS Sports Radio Network
Bio: "Damon Amendolara," in: Wikipedia. See - https://en.wikipedia.org/wiki/Damon_Amendolara

Mary H. Babnič (1923-2008), b. Youngstown, OH, of Slovak parents; program director and announcer for the Struthers WKTL Radio Slovak, 1983-2007.
Bio: Kopanic, Michael Jr., Jr., "The Queen of Slovak Culture in Youngstown, Ohio –Mary H. Babnič (1923-2008)," Jednota, October 1, 20008, p. 14.

John J. Biroš (1905-1982), voice of the Cleveland Slovak Radio Club's 'Slovak Hour' program
Bio: "John J. biro," in: Find A Grave. See - https://www.findagrave.com/memorial/25607675/john-j-biro

Milan Chvostek (1932-), Slovak Canadian; producer / director of the Canadian Broadcasting Corporation
Bio: "Milan Chvostek," in: Wikipedia. See - https://en.wikipedia.org/wiki/Milan_Chvostek

Miroslav Dobrovodský (1939-2009), b. Žilina, Czech.; journalist, broadcaster, chief of Slovak Service, VOA, USIA, Washington, DC
Bio: "Dobrovodský, Miroslav," in: *SVU Directory* 8; "Miroslav S. Dobrovodský: Za hlasom Ameriky," *SME Kultúra,* June 13, 2018.

Jan Juraj Frajkor (1934-), b. Montreal, P.Q., Canada; journalist, professor of TV News and current affairs production, and Online journalism, Carleton University, Ottawa, Canada; executive director, Frajkor Enterprises
Bio: "Frajkor, Jan Juraj," in: *SVU Directory* 8; "Jan Juraj," in: LinkedIn. See - https://www.linkedin.com/in/jan-juraj-george-frajkor-b8715a12/

Alois Havrilla (1891-1952), b. Prešov, Slovakia; radio announcer, also singer, composer and conductor
Bio: "Havrilla, Alois," in: *Who's Who Today in Musical World,* 1938; *Biographical Dictionary of Music,* 1973.

Michael Hlinka (ca 1958-), b. Etobicoke, Canada, of Slovak descent; one of the most popular CBC Metro morning columnists
Bio: "Michael Hlinka," in: Annick Press. See - http://www.annickpress.com/author/Michael_Hlinka

Johny Hryzny (1931-2009), b. Chicago, IL, of Slovak descent; drum player; popular polka disk jockey; owner of the Personality Lounge, Polka Radio DJ for 43 years; president of U.P.A. (United Polka Association) International
Bio: "Johny Hryzny - Living Category - Inducted 1983," in: International Polka Association. See - http://www.ipapolkas.com/blog/otw-portfolio/johnny-hyzny-living-category-inducted-1983/; "Death Notice: John C. Hryzny," *Chicago Tribune,* April 17, 2009

Chris Jansing (orig. Kapostasy) (1957-), b. Fairport Harbor, OH, of Hungarian and Slovak descent; American television news correspondent
Bio: "Chris Jansing," in: Wikipedia. See - https://en.wikipedia.org/wiki/Chris_Jansing

Vincent V. Kalnik (1895-1957), b. Horny Hričov, Slovakia; founder and director of the first Slovak Radio hour, Chicago
Bio: "Kalnik, Vincent V.," in: Droba, pp. 217-218

Milan Kobulsky (1947-), b. Prešov, Slovakia; in US s. 1969; director of the Slovak Institute (s. 2016-); Slovak radio announcer.
Bio: Kobulsky, Milan, "Cleveland Slovak Radio čítam aj správy z Prešovského večerníka" *Prešovský Večerník*, August 11, 2017. See - http://www.povecernik.sk/rozhovory/207824/milan-kobulsky-v-cleveland-slovak-radio-citam-aj-spravy-z-presovskeho-vecernika

Braňo Lajda (1917-2000), b. Myjava, Czech; lawyer, economist, writer-editor, Voice of America, USIA
Biol: "Lajda, Braňo," in: *SVU Directory 7*

Jozef Mrázek (1910-1979), b. Lamač, Slovakia; journalist, with Radio Free Europe, New York
Bio: "Mrazek, Jozef," in: ČSDS Website. See - http://www.csds.cz/cs/g6/934-DS.html; "Mrázek, Jozef," in: Pejskar 2, p. 170.

Anne Mroczkowski (1953-), b. Hamilton, Ont., Canada, to a Polish and Slovak immigrant family; Canadian TV reporter and news anchor. She is the former co-anchor of Global News Hour, along with Leslie Roberts, a job she started on June 1, 2010. Roberts announced Mroczkowski's departure on-air in August 2013. Since leaving the news business, Mroczkowski is now a media consultant and occasional actor.
Bio: "Anne Mroczkowski," in: Wikipedia. See - https://en.wikipedia.org/wiki/Anne_Mroczkowski

Michael Múdry-Šebík (1909-1978), b. Drietomá, Slovakia; lawyer, journalist, chief of Czechoslovak Desk, Radio Free Europe, New York, NY, politician, member of Council of Free Czechoslovakia
Bio: "Múdry-Šebík, Michael," in: *SVU Directory* 4; "Múdry-Šebík, Michael," in: Pejskar 2, p. 170.

Anna Tomcik Olson (1968-), b. Atlanta, GA, of Slovak descent; a professionally trained pastry chef. She resides in Welland in the Niagara region of Ontario, Canada. She is the host of Bake with Anna Olson on Food Network Canada. She was previously the host of Food Network Canada's Fresh with Anna Olson, Sugar and Kitchen Equipped.
Bio: "Anna Olson," in: Wikipedia. See - https://en.wikipedia.org/wiki/Anna_Olson skating

John T. Sabol (ca 1945-), b. Cleveland, OH, of Slovak father; editor, writer; president, JTS Consulting LLC, Cleveland; host of the New Czech Voice of Cleveland Radio Program (s. 2016).
Bio: "John Sabol," in: LinkedIn. See - https://www.linkedin.com/in/john-sabol-7b881813/

Ľudovít Šebesta (1922-1983), b. Ružomberok, Czech.; journalist, reporter, editor with Radio Free Europe, New York, NY
Bio: "Šebesta, Ľudovít," in: Pejskar 2, pp. 179-180.

Joe Schlesinger (1928-), b. Vienna, of Slovak parents; Canadian TV journalist and author, member of the Order of Canada
Bio: "Joe Schlesinger," in: Wikipedia. See - https://en.wikipedia.org/wiki/Joe_Schlesinger

Dennis Spisak (1959 -), b. Youngstown, OH, Slovak descent; certified teacher; radio program director; radio announcer, WTCL, Warren, OH (1977-79); radio announcer, production, WCLT-AM-FM, Newark, OH (1981-82); music director, sports announcer, WOSE-FM, Port Clinton, OH (1982-84); radio announcer, WCPZ-FM, Sandusky, OH; teacher instructor, program director, WCWT-FM, Centerville, OH (s. 1985)
Bio: "Dennis Stephen Spisak," in: Prabook. See - https://prabook.com/web/dennis_stephen.spisak/238101

Ivan Trebichovsky (1910-1973), b. 1910-1973), b. Trenčín, Slovakia; lawyer, journalist, reporter, with Radio Free Europe, New York, NY
Bio: "Trebichovsky, Ivan," in: Pejskar 2, p. 65; "Trebichovsky, Ivan," in: *SVU Directory* 2.

Lara Trump (née Yunaska) (1982-), b. Wilmington, NC, of Slovak descent; TV host, TV producer. She is married To Eric Trump; the second son od President Trump. She is the producer/host of Real News Update and the former producer of Inside Edition.
Bio: "Lara Trump," in: Wikipedia. See - https://en.wikipedia.org/wiki/Lara_Trump

Joseph Valenčik (1929-2015), b. Slovakia, in US s. 1953; WERE Cleveland Slovak Radio Club announcer; fraternalist.
Bio: Source: Michael Kopanic, Jr., and "Jozef Valencik Obituary," *The Plain Dealer*, December 15-16, 2015. See - https://obits.cleveland.com/obituaries/cleveland/obituary.aspx?n=jozef-valencik&pid=176903675&fhid=5819

Teofil Bohumír Vozárik (1912-1973), b. Podtúreň, Slovakia; lawyer, editor, Voice of America, USIA, Washington, DC.
Bio: "Vozárik, Teofil," in: Pejskar 2, p. 189; "Teofil Bohumír Vozarik," in: Wikipedia. See - https://sk.wikipedia.org/wiki/Teofil_Bohumír_Vozárik

4. Bloggers

iJustine (orig. Justine Ezarik) (1984-), b. Pittsburgh, PA, of Slovak ancestry; YouTube personality, host, actress and model
Bio: "iJustine," in: Wikipedia. See - https://en.wikipedia.org/wiki/IJustine

5. Publishers, Printers

Ladislaus Joseph Bolchazy (1937-), b. Michalovce, Czech.; publisher, president, Bolchazy-Carducci Publishers, Mundelein, IL - a company devoted to the ancient world, classics and textbooks.
Bio: "Bolchazy-Carducci," in: *SVU Directory* 8; "In Memoriam: Ladislaus J. Bolchazy, Ph.D.," in: CAAS-CW. See - http://caas-cw.org/wp/2013/02/15/in-memoriam-ladislaus-j-bolchazy-ph-d/; "Ladislaus "Lou" Bolchazy, Ph.D.," in: Bolchazy--Carducci Publishers, Inc. See - http://www.bolchazy.

com/cw_contributorinfo.aspx?ContribID=2967&Name=Ladislaus+ "Lou"+Bolchazy%2C+PhD

Eugene Fodor (1905-1991), Levice, Slovakia; writer and publisher of travel literature; founder of the eponymous travel-guide series. He created *Fodor Modern Guides*, operating mainly from Paris but moved to Litchfield, Connecticut in 1964, and lived there until his death. Fodor was elected to the American Society of Travel Agents (ASTA) World Travel Congress Hall of Fame, the only travel editor to be so honored.
Bio: "Eugene Fodor," in: Wikipedia. See - https://en.wikipedia.org/wiki/ Eugene_Fodor_(writer); Smallwood, James M., "Fodor, Eugene," in: *National Biography*, Vol. 8, p. 159.

Stephen Furdek (1855-1915), b. Trstená, Slovakia; R.C. priest; pastor of Our Lady of Lourdes, Cleveland; the founder and publisher of Jednota, the journal of the First Catholic Slovak Union.
Bio: "Furdek, Stephan," in: *Encyclopedia of Cleveland History*. See - https://case. edu/ech/articles/f/furdek-stephan

Nina Hečková (1958-), b. Dunajska Streda, Slovakia; management information specialist; composition specialist, RR Donnelley, Financial Printing (2000-08); Senior proofreader, Franklin Templeton Investments (2010-14); composition specialist, RR Donnelley, Palo Alto, CA (2014-14); publishing, San Francisco area.
Bio: "Hečková, Nina," in: SVU Directory, 9; "Nina Heckova," in: LinkedIn. See - https://www.linkedin.com/in/nina-heckova-6b75524/

Benjamin W. Huebsch (1875-1964), b. New York, NY, of Slovak ancestry; publisher, NYC
Bio: "B. W. Huebsch," in: Wikipedia. See - https://en.wikipedia.org/wiki/ B._W._Huebsch; Rechcigl, Miloslav, Jr., "Benjamin W. Huebsch," in: *Beyond the Sea of Beer.* p. 776; *Dictionary of American Biography*, Suppl. 7, (1981), pp. 373-375.

Mirko Janecek (1927-2017), b. Bratislava, Czech.; publisher of *Nový Domov* (New Homeland), *Hlas Nových* (Newcomers' Voices), *Kanadské Listy* (Canadian Papers), from the basement of his Mississauga home, Canada for 42 years.
Bio: "Janecek, Mirko," in: *Encyclopedia,* Vol. 2, p. 993, "Mirko Janecek Obituary," *Toronto Star,* January 14, 2017.

Joseph J. Krajsa (1947-2007), b. Allentown, Pa, of Slovak descent; manager of Jednota Press and manager of Jednota Estates. He was also sales and marketing manager of at Triangle Press, Harrisburg.
Bio: "Joseph J Krajsa," *The Morning Call,* August 26, 2007.

John J. Lach (1894-1960), b. Hibernia, NJ, of Slovak descent; R.C. priest, pastor of Immaculate Conception Church, Whiting, IN, owner of *Slovak v Amerike,* the oldest Slovak newspaper in US (s. 1951);
Bio: "Lach, Rev. John Joseph," in: *Catholic Who's Who,* 14 (1960-1961), p.252.

Charles Mally (1887-), b. Previdza, Slovakia; printer, Chicago
Bio: "Mally," in: Droba, p. 79.

John Spevak (1866-1905), b. Slovakia; editor and publisher, *Slovák v Amerike,* NYC

D. LIBRARIANSHIP

1. General
Ference, Gregory C., "Slavic Diaspora Library: The Slovak American Example," *Indiana Slavic Studies,* 16 (2006), pp. 73-86.

2. Librarians - Archivists

Katarina Avnet (1946-), b. Sečovce, Czech., librarian, National Library of Medicine, Bethesda, MD
Bio: "Avnet, Katarina," in: *SVU Directory* 8

Sister M. Catherine Laboure Bresnock, Slovak American; SS.C.M.; director of Jankola Library and Slovak Museum Danville, PA (s. 2011).
Bio: "Jankola Library and Slovak Museum." See - http://jankolalibrary.sscm. org

Marta Chrappa (1940-), b. Košice, Czech; music librarian. CBC, Toronto, Ont., Canada;
Bio: "Chrappa, Marta," in: *SVU Directory*, 9

Bohuslav Dérer (1924-), b. Topolčany, Czech.; lawyer, chief librarian, East York Public Library, Toronto, Ont., Canada
Bio: "Dérer, Bohuslav," in: *SVU Directory 8*

Ernestine Hudak Fagan (1920-), b. Philadelphia, PA; librarian, Colorado School for the Deaf and the Blind, Colorado Spring, CO
Bio: "Fagan, Ernestine Hudak," in: *SVU Directory 8*

Stella Solar Gabuzda (1937-), b. Žilina, Czech.; Head Librarian, Penn Wynne Library, Philadelphia, PA
Bio: "Gabuzda, Stella Solar," in: *SVU Directory 8.*

Eva Gavora (1937-), b. Užhorod; librarian, Plant Research Library, Agriculture Canada, Ottawa, Ont., Canada
Bio: "Gavora, Eva," in: *SVU Directory 8*

Sister Loretta Marie Hrubec, SS.C.M., Slovak American, SS.C.M.; librarian, Jankola Library and Slovak Museum, Danville, PA.
Bio: "Jankola Library and Slovak Museum." See - http://jankolalibrary.sscm. org/jankolacontact.html

Vladimír Kajlik (1946-), b. Perecin, Czech.; theologian, librarian, Wayne State University, Detroit, MI; now residing in the Czech Republic, applied linguist and translator, with University of South Bohemia, České Budějovice
Bio: "Kajlik, Vladimír," in: *SVU Directory 8*

Edward Kasinec (1945-), b. New York, NY, of Rusyn descent; reference librarian, curator of Slavic-Baltic Division, New York Public Library

(1984-2009), visiting fellow of Hoover Institution, research scholar with Harriman Institute, Columbia University
Bio: NYC Literacy Showcase Participants. See - http://readrussia.org/participants/bio/edward-kasinec; "Edward Kasinec Visiting Fellow," in: Hoover Institution. See - https://www.hoover.org/profiles/edward-kasinec; "Edward Kasinec," in: Institute Staff, Columbia University. See - https://nehsummerinst.columbia.edu/bios/institute-staff/; "Edward Joseph Kasinec," in: Prabook. See - https://prabook.com/web/edward_joseph.kasinec/530573

Štefan Kočvara (1896-1973), b. Myjava, Slovakia; lawyer, legal specialist, US Library of Congress, Washington, DC
Bio: "Kočara, Štefan," in: *SVU Directory* 3; "Kočvara, Štefan," in: *Czechoslovakia Past and Present*, Vol. 2, pp. 1815-1816.

Martha Kona (1930-2024), b. Bánovce nad Bebravou, Czech.; medical librarian at Rush University Medical Center; cataloguer-librarian, University of Illinois Library of Medicine and Science (1958-63).
Bio: "Martha M. Kona," *Chicago Tribune*, April 24-3-, 2014; "Martina Mistina Kona," in: Find A Grave. See - https://www.findagrave.com/memorial/128121952/martha-m-kona

William Kona (1920-1989), archivist at Rush-Presbyterian-St. Luke's Medical Center
Bio: "Rush-Presbyterian-St. Luke`s Archivist William Kona, 69," *Chicago Tribune*, December 9, 1989:

Magda Križanová (1920-), b. Prešov, Czech; BAPST Library, Boston College, Chestnut Hill, MA
Bio: "Križanová, Magda," in: *SVU Directory* 3' "Krizanova, Magda," in: Educators, p. 22

James P. Kusik, Slovak American; associate librarian, Saint Xavier University
Bio: "James P. Kusik," in: ResearchGate. See - https://www.researchgate.net/profile/James_Kusik

Irene Lettrich (1912-2011), b. Slovakia; librarian, Georgetown University, Washington, DC
Bio: "Lettrich, Irene," in: *SVU Directory* 8; "Irene Lettrich Obituary," in: *The Repository*, February 18, 2011 - Legacy.com.

Susan Katherine Martin (née Orowan) (1942-), b. Cambridge, England, of Slovak grandfather; holder of doctorate from University of California, Berkeley; in US s. 1950; American librarian. Held important positions at Harvard University, Johns Hopkins University, Princeton University, and Tufts University.
Bio: "Susan Katherine Martin," in: Prabook. See - https://prabook.com/web/ susan_katherine.martin/10544

Angela Tomko Mendiville (1948-), b. Levice, Czech.; Cataloguer, US Library of Congress, Washington, DC, resides now at Boca Raton, FL
Bio: "Mendiville, Angela Tomko," in: *SVU Directory* 8.

Joan Rafaj Olson (1933-2015), b. Dickson City, PA, of Slovak descent; first archivist, St. Olaf College, Northfield, MN (1969-98)
Bio: "Obituary for Joan Olson," in: Benson & Langehough Funeral Home & Cremation. See - See - http://www.northfieldfuneral.com/obituary/ joan-olson/#expe1

Vladimír Palic (1906-1989), b. Kochanovce, Slovakia; lawyer, bibliographer, US Library of Congress, Washington, DC
Bio: "Palic, Vladimir" in: *SVU Directory* 6; "Palic, Vladimír," in: Pejskar 3, p. 172

Elizabeth Rajec (1931-), b. Bratislava, Czech.; librarian, City University of New York, City College
Bio: "Rajec, Elizabeth," in: Educators, p. 32; "Elizabeth Rajec (née Molnar)," in: NCSML Oral Histories. See - https://www.ncsml.org/exhibits/ elizabeth-rajec/

Svato Schutzner (1923-), b. Bratislava, Czech.; rare book cataloguer, US Library of Congress, Washington, DC
Bio: "Schutzner, Svato" in: *SVU Directory* 8;

Joseph Staško (1917-), b. Sedliacka Dubová, Slovakia; librarian, chief of the periodicals dept., New York Library, also journalist
Bio: "Jozef Stasko," in: Wikipedia. See - https://cs.wikipedia.org/wiki/ / Jozef_Staško

George Jiří Svoboda (1933-2004), b. Bratislava, Czech.; historian, head, Slavic Library, University of California, Berkeley (1980-93)
"Svoboda, George Jiří," in; *Encyclopedia*, Vol. 2, p.1263; "George Jiri Svoboda," in: Prabook. See - https://prabook.com/web/george_jiri.svoboda/432631; "Svoboda, George Jiri," in: *American Scholars*, 8, Vol. 1

Sister M. Martina Tybor (1908-1998), b. Bridgeport, CT, of Slovak descent; professed in Sisters of SS Cyril and Methodius (s. 1928); teacher, translator; founder and the first director of Jankola Library and Slovak Museum, Danville, Pa (s. 1968).
Bio: "Tybor, Sister M. Martina," in *Catholic Who's Who, 1977*, Vol. 21, p. 539; https://sscm.org/sister-m-mercedes-voytko-ss-c-m-85/; "Jankola Library and Slovak Museum." See - http://jankolalibrary.sscm.org.

Sister M. Mercedes Voytko (1931- 2016), b. Humboldt, PA, of Slovak descent; SS.C.M.; teacher, director of Jankola Library and Slovak Museum (1992-2007), succeeding Sister M. Martina Tybor.
Bio: "Sister M. Mercedes Voytko, SS.C.M., 85," in: Sisters of Saints Cyril and Methodius. See - https://sscm.org/sister-m-mercedes-voytko-ss-c-m-85/; "Jankola Library and Slovak Museum." See - http://jankolalibrary.sscm.org

Sister M. John Vianney Vranak, Slovak American; SS.C.M.; director of Jankola Library and Slovak Museum (2007-10)
Bio: "Jankola Library and Slovak Museum." See - http://jankolalibrary.sscm. org

Matt Wrbican (1991-), b. New York, NY, of Slovak descent; American archivist and authority on the life of the artist Andy Warhol. Beginning in 1991 in New York City, Wrbican, as the archivist of The Andy Warhol Museum in Pittsburgh, Pennsylvania, United States, has been unpacking,

processing, preserving, and documenting an estimated 500,000 objects in Warhol's Time Capsules.
Bio: "Matt Wrbican," in: Wikipedia. See - https://en.wikipedia.org/wiki/Matt_Wrbican

Galina Dronova Zarechnak (1916-2007), b. Novocherkask, Russia; librarian, National Library of Medicine, NIH, Bethesda, Md
Bio: "Zarechnak, Galina Dronova," in: *SVU Directory* 4; "Zarechnak, Galina," *The Washington Post,* December 14, 2007.

E. CREATIVE AND NONFICTION WRITING

1. Surveys

Hribal, C. J., Ed., *The Boundaries of Twilight: Czecho-Slovak Writing from the New World.* Minneapolis: New Rivers Press, 1991.
Kovtun, George J., *Czech and Slovak Literature in English. A Bibliography,* 2nd ed. Washington, DC: Library of Congress, 1988.
Sabatos, Charles, "Slovak American Literature," in: *The Greenwood Encyclopedia of Multiethnic American Literature.* Edited by Emmanuel Nelson. Westport, CT: Greenwood Press, 2005, Vol. 4, N-S, pp. 2048-51.
Vnuk, F., "Slovak Literature in Exile," *Arena,* No. 16 (1963), pp. 4-10.
Vnuk, František, "Slovak Exile Literature," in: *Czechoslovakia Past and Present.* Edited by Miloslav Rechcigl, Jr. The Hague- Paris: Mouton, 1968, Vol. 1, pp.869-878.
Židová, Diana. "Ethnic Literature and Slovak American Research," *Ars Aeterna,* Vol. 6, No. 1, 2014, pp. 1–7.

2. Writers

Marion Rombauer Becker (1903-)1976), b. St. Louis, MO, of Slovak descent; author and illustrator. She was the co-author with her mother, Irma von Starkloff Rombauer, of the *Joy of Cooking,* first published in 1931. Elected by the New York Public Library as one of the 150 most important and influential books of the 20th century. Published by her mother, Marion is best known for the cookbook's illustrations. The friendly, chatty style cookbook is considered as the best-selling cookbook of all time. A prominent Cincinnatian, Becker

also worked as an art teacher and for Women's Wear Daily. She was one of the founders of Cincinnati's Modern Art Society and became the Society's first professional director. Also, a gardener and an environmentalist, she was a pioneer in natural gardening and wrote *Wild Wealth* which chronicled her woodland garden at the family's estate. Becker received the Oak Leaf Award from the Nature Conservancy and the prestigious Medal of Merit from the Garden Club of America. Before her death in 1976, she was a recipient of the Greatest Living Cincinnatian Award
Bio: "Marion Rombauer Becker," in: Find a Grave. See - https://www.findagrave.com/memorial/25845324/marion-rombauer-becker

Ľudo Bešeňovský (orig. Ľudovít Baran) (1910-1994), b. Liptovský Michal, Slovakia; in Canada s. 1948, residing in Winnipeg; poet, writer, teacher
Bio: "Ľudo Bešeňovský," in: Slovenskí spisovatelia. See - https://www.obecbesenova.sk/obec-1/osobnosti/ludo-besenovsky-3sk.html

Thomas Bell (orig. Adalbert Thomas Belejcak) (1903-1961), b. Braddock, PA, of immigrant Lemko Rusyn parents from Slovakia; novelist
Bio: Berko, John F., *Thomas Bell (1903-1961), Slovak American Novelist.* Cleveland, OH: Slovak Institute, 1975, 1975. 158p.; Alexander, June G., "Bell, Thomas (née Belčák)," in: *Making It in America. A Sourcebook of Eminent Ethnic Americans.* Edited by Elliot Robert Barkan. Santa Barbara, CA: ABC-CLIO, 2001, pp. 34-35.

Jaroslava Blažková (1933-2017), b. Velké Meziříčí, Moravia, but was educated and resided in Bratislava. She was a Slovak novelist, short story writer, children's writer and a journalist.
Bio: "Jaroslava Blažková," in: Wikipedia. See - https://en.wikipedia.org/wiki/Jaroslava_ Blažková

Alexander Boldizar (1971-), b. Košice, Czech.; trained as a lawyer; writer and art critic. Boldizar worked briefly as an attorney at the San Francisco and Prague offices of Baker & McKenzie, before leaving law in order to write. He has been Canadian citizen s. 1983. Boldizar has been described as 'a boisterous Borges' and writes in the existentialist satire and dark humor tradition of writers like Heller, Kafka, Musil, Hrabal, Borges, and Laurence Sterne.
Kanadský Slovak newspaper named him one of the most notable Slovaks "in Canada and probably in North America."

Bio: "Alexander Boldizar," in: Wikipedia. See - https://en.wikipedia.org/wiki/Alexander_Boldizar

Jan E. Bor (pseud. of Dr. Ernest Žatko) 1907-1911), b. Žabokreky, Slovakia; Slovak literary critic, journalist, columnist; s. 1948 he resided in Argentina
Bio: "Jan E. Bor." See - http://jebiography.blogspot.com/

Andrej Brázda-Jankovský (1915-2008), b. Slovakia; in Canada s. 1968, where he lived and worked as a novelist and journalist. A Canadian-based writer who wrote in the Slovak language.
Bio: "Andrej Brázda-Jankovský," in: Wikipedia. See - https://en.wikipedia.org/wiki/Andrej_ Brázda-Jankovský

Joseph Bruchac (1942-), b. Saratoga Springs, NY, of Slovak father; author, editor, teacher, storyteller, musician; writer of books relating to the indigenous peoples of the Americas. He wrote over 120 books and won many awards.
Bio: "Joseph Bruchac," in: Wikipedia. See - https://en.wikipedia.org/wiki/Joseph_Bruchac; Hinton-Johnson, Kaa Vonia, "Bruchac, Joseph," in: *The Greenwood Encyclopedia of Multiethnic American Literature*. Westport, CT: Greenwood Press, 2005, Vol. 1, A-C, pp. 338-339; Andres, Linda R., "Joseph Bruchac," *Children's Literature Review*, 46 (1998), pp. 1-24.

Jozef Cíger-Hronský (1896-1960), b. Zvolen, Slovakia; writer, teacher, painter, editor, publisher, publicist, residing in Luján, Argentina; president of the Slovak National Council Abroad
Bio: "Jozef Cíger-Hronský," in: Wikipedia. See - https://sk.wikipedia.org/wiki/Jozef_ Cíger-Hronský; "Jozef Ciger-Hronský," in: *Czechoslovakia Past and Present*, Vol. 1, p.875.

Ján Marian Dafčík (1923-1981), b. Žabokreky nad Nitrou, Slovakia; professor of drama and film, playwright, theater director, editor, literary critic; s. 1948 lived in Argentina.
Bio: "Ján Marián Dafčík," in: LIC. See - http://www.litcentrum.sk/slovenski-spisovatelia/jan-marian-dafcik

MILOSLAV RECHCIGL, JR.

Rudolf Dilong (1905-1986), b. Trstená, Slovakia; R.C. priest, O.F.M., poet, playwright, novelist, author of some 100 books
Bio: "Rudolf Dilong," in: Wikipedia. See - https://sk.wikipedia.org/wiki/Rudolf_Dilong; "Rudolf Dilong," in: *Czechoslovakia Past and Present*, Vol. 1, p. 873; "Fr. Rudolph Alphones Dilong," in: Find A Grave. See - https://www.findagrave.com/memorial/113406361/rudolph-alphonse-dilong

Draga Divinská (pseudonym of Draga Paučo) (1922-2005), b. Slovakia; writer, prosaist, storyteller; editor, *Slovak v Amerike*, weekly, Middletown, PA (s. 1889)
Bio: "Draga Divinska," in: *Czechoslovakia Past and Present*, Vol. 1, p. 876.

Ján Doránsky 1911-1973), b. Trstená, Orava, Slovakia; poet, playwright, novelist, residing in Montreal, Canada
Bio: "Ján L. Doránsky," in: LIC. See - http://www.litcentrum.sk/slovenski-spisovatelia/jan-l-doransky; "Ján Doránsky," in: *Czechoslovakia Past and Present*, Vol. 1, p. 877.

Natasa Durovičová (1954-), b. Bratislava, Czech; editor, International Writing Program, editor of 91st Meridian - an electronic publication, cinema historian, University of Iowa, Iowa City
Bio: "Durovičová, Nataša," in: *SVU Directory* 8; "Natasa Durovicova," in: Profiles, University of Iowa, Linkedin. See - https://www.linkedin.com/in/natasa-durovicova-6121734b/

Max Eisen (1929-), b. Moldava, Slovakia; an author, public speaker and Holocaust educator. He travels throughout Canada giving talks about his experiences as a concentration camp survivor, to students, teachers, universities, law enforcement personnel, and the community at large.
Bio: Max Eisen," in: Wikipedia. See - https://en.wikipedia.org/wiki/Max_Eisen

Carolyn Forché (1950-), b. Detroit, MI, of Slovak ancestry; poet, editor, translator
Bio: "Carolyn Forché," in: Wikipedia. See - https://en.wikipedia.org/wiki/Carolyn_ Forché

Jessica Gavora (1963-), b. Fairbanks, AK, of Slovak descent; political scientist and journalist by training; American conservative writer on politics and culture; speechwriter and formed advisor at the US Department of Justice
Bio: "Jessica Gavora," in: Wikipedia. See - https://en.wikipedia.org/wiki/Jessica_Gavora

Koloman Kolomi Geraldini (1908-1994), b. Terchová, Slovakia; poet, literary critic, translator, living in Argentina
Bio: "Koloman Kolomi Geraldini," in: Wikipedia. See - https://sk.wikipedia.org/wiki/Koloman_Kolomi_Geraldini

Lisa Jakub (1978-), b. Toronto, Ont., Canada, of Slovak descent; a Canadian writer, speaker and yoga teacher; a former actress
Bio: "Lisa Jakub," in: Wikipedia. See - https://en.wikipedia.org/wiki/Lisa_Jakub

Jozef Janek (1946-), b. Veľký Šariš, Slovakia; in US s. 1969; resides in Detroit, MI; author of books about American Slovaks, amateur historian, excellent speaker. languages Bio: See - https://www.facebook.com/AmericansofSlovakorigin17/photos/a.1680175988942192/1918622118430910/?type=3&theater

Larry Janowski (ca 1945-), b. Chicago, IL, of Slovak descent; R.C. priest, O.F.M.; Franciscan friar, writer, author of several books of poetry, fiction writer; teaches poetry at Loyola University, Chicago
Bio: "Larry Janowski," in: e-poets. See - http://voices.e-poets.net/JanowskiL/

Sonya Jason (1927-), b. Rusyn American; writer of novels and stories and freelance journalist.
Bio: Sabo, Gerald J., "Jason, Sonya," in: *The Greenwood Encyclopedia of Multiethnic American Literature*. Westport, CT: Greenwood Press, 2005, Vol. 3, I-M. pp. 1130-1131.

Kathy Kacer (1954-), b. Toronto, Ont., Canada, of Slovak parents; trained as a psychologist, a Canadian author of fiction and non-fiction for children about The Holocaust. A winner of the Silver Birch, Red Maple, Hackmatack

and Jewish Book Awards, and a finalist for the Geoffrey Bilson and Norma Fleck Awards.
Bio: "Kathy Kacer," in: kathykacer.com. See - http://www.kathykacer.com/aboutme.html; "Kathy Kacer," in: Wikipedia. See - https://en.wikipedia.org/wiki/Kathy_Kacer

Rudolf Kalenčík (1894-), b. Nové Mesto nad Váhom, Slovakia; writer of short satirical novels; wrote a satirical novel, *Doktor Šaša* (Middletown, Pa.: Jednota, 1965), *The Devil and the Soldier* (1972).
Bio: See - Bolecek, Dr. B.V. and Irene Slamka, *The Slovak Encyclopaedia*. New York: Slovak Academy, 1981, p. 63.

Ľudovít Kandra (pseud: Peter Klas) (1904-1993), b. Banská Štiavnica, Slovakia; poet, essayist, novelist, free-lance writer, lobbyist, political activist
Bio: "Kandra, Ľudovít," in: atom. See - https://biblio.uottawa.ca/atom/index.php/sandra-ludovit

Regina 'Gina' Kaus (née Wiener) (1893-1985), b. Vienna, of Slovak ancestry; novelist, screenwriter
Bio: "Gina Kaus," in: Wikipedia. See - https://en.wikipedia.org/wiki/Gina_Kaus

Esther Oravec Kemeny (1912-2008), b. Michalovce, Slovakia; pioneer woman lawyer, Holocaust survivor, author of *On the Shores of Darkness*
Bio: "Esther Oravec Kemeny," in: *SVU Directory*, 6; "Esther Kemeny," *San Francisco Chronicle* on Feb. 29, 2008' "Esther Oravec Kemeny," in: Find A Grave. See - https://www.findagrave.com/memorial/125246981/esther-kemeny

Iby Knill (1923-), b. Slovakia; survivor of the Holocaust, writer of powerful autobiographies
Bio: "A Holocaust Survivor Iby Knill," *Women's History Review*, 25, No. 6 (2016), pp. 999-1005; Harding, Louette, "They could try to dehumanize me, but inside I was still me': An Auschwitz survivor breaks her silence," in: MailOnline. See - http://www.dailymail.co.uk/home/you/article-1334982/Iby-Knill-Auschwitz-survivor-breaks-silence-They-try-dehumanise-inside-I-me.html

Heda Kovály (née Bloch) (1919-2010), b. Prague, Czech.; Holocaust survivor, writer and translator
Bio: "Heda Kovaly, Czech Who Wrote of Totalitarianism, Is Dead at 91," *The New York Times*, December 9, 2010; "Heda Margolius Kovály obituary," *The Guardian*, December 13, 2010; Heda Kovaly," in: Find A Grave. See -https://www.findagrave.com/memorial/62724236/heda-kovaly; "Hed Kovaly," *The Telegraph*. See-https://www.telegraph.co.uk/news/obituaries/culture-obituaries/books-obituaries/8192521/Heda-Kovaly.html; "Heda Margolius Kovály," in: Wikipedia. https://en.wikipedia.org/wiki/Heda_Margolius_Kovály

Fraňo Kráľ (1903-1955), b. Barton, OH, of Slovak father; poet, prosaist of Social realism and politician
Bio: "Fraňo Kráľ in: Wikipedia. See - https://sk.wikipedia.org/wiki/Fraňo_Kráľ

Andrew Krivak (1963-), b. Wilkes-Barre, PA, of Slovak descent; an American novelist. His debut novel, *The Sojourn* (2011) was nominated for the National Book Award for Fiction, won the Dayton Literary Peace Prize, and was well received critically. He also wrote a memoir about his time in the Jesuit order, *A Long Retreat: In Search of a Religious Life* (2008). He grew up in Pennsylvania, has lived in London, and has taught at Harvard, Boston College, and the College of the Holy Cross.
Bio: "Andrew Krivak," in: Wikipedia. See - https://en.wikipedia.org/wiki/Andrew_Krivak

Martin Kukučín (pseud. of Matej Benczur (1860-1928), b. Jasenová, Slovakia; physician, who practiced in Buenos Aires and on Punta Arenas, the southernmost town in Chile. He went to Southern America in 1908. In 1922-24 he was back in Slovakia and then he resided in Croatia.
He is best-known as prosaist, novelist, playwright and publicist. He was a representative of Slovak literary realism, a founder of modern Slovak prose. He was a member of the Czech Academy of sciences and Arts.
Bio: "Martin Kukucin - bibliografia," in: LIC. See - http://www.litcentrum.sk/50769 ; "Martin Kukučín," in: Wikipedia. See - https://sk.wikipedia.org/wiki/Martin_ Kukučín

Patricia Ondek Laurence (1942-), Slovak American; author, literary historian and critic; professor of English at the City University of New York. Bio: "Patricia Laurence, Writer, Professor, Critic." See - http://patricialaurence. com/; "Jane Elliot Laurence, Patricia Ondek," in: *The Greenwood Encyclopedia of Multiethnic American Literature.* Westport, CT: Greenwood Press, 2005, Vol. 3, I-M.

Matthew John Lesko, Jr. (1943-), b. Wilkes Barre, PA, of Slovak descent; author, known for his publications and infomercials on Federal grant funding. Bio: "Lesko, Matthew john, Jr.," in: *Who's Who in the East,* 18; "Matthew Lesko," in: Wikipedia. See - https://en.wikipedia.org/wiki/Matthew_Lesko

Anna Lesznai (pseud) (real name: Amália J. Moskowitz) (1885-1966), b. Budapest; she grew up in Nižný Hrušov, Slovakia, on the country estate belonging to her father Geyza Moskowitz, a physician; American writer, painter, designer, and key figure in the avant-garde. Bio: "Anna Lesznai," in: Wikipedia. See - https://en.wikipedia.org/wiki/Anna_Lesznai

Rita M. Malie (1940-2017), b. Youngstown, OH, of Slovak descent; nurse, prolific writer Bio: "Rita M. Malie," *Florida Times-Union,* April 6, 2017.

Sándor Márai (1900-1989), b. Košice, Slovakia; writer and journalist; author of 46 books Bio: "Sándor Márai," in: Wikipedia. See - https://en.wikipedia.org/wiki/Sándor_Márai

Gustáv Maršall-Petrovský (1862-1916), b. Báčsky Petrovec, Serbia; studied law in Prešov and medicine in Vienna. He was a Slovak prose writer, journalist and activist. He was sentenced for sedition against the Magyar nation and immigrated to the USA in 1880. He wrote a German textbook of the Slovak language. Most of realistic literary works take place in his native Vojvodina; also wrote the historical novel *Jánošík* (1894) and a book of short stories, *Under the American Snowdrifts* (1906). He died in Chicago during WWI. Bio: "Gustav Maršal Petrovský, in: Wikipedia. See - https://sk.wikipedia. org/wiki/Gustav_Maršal_Petrovský; "Gustáv Maršall Petrovský," in: Ústav pre kultúru vojvodinskych Slovakov. See - http://www.slovackizavod.org. rs/licnosti/5659

Stanislav Mečiar (1910-1971), b. Previdza, Slovakia; worked for Matica slovenská in Martin (s. 1934); s. 1949 resided in Argentina; editor, poet, essayist, literary critic and historian, translator.
Bio: "Stanislav Mečiar," in: LIC. See - http://www.litcentrum.sk/ slovenski-spisovatelia/stanislav-meciar

Clement K. Mlynarovich (1887-1971), b. Hasprunka, Slovakia; R.C. priest; in US s. 1914; pastor in Indiana; author, novelist, poet; co-founder of Slovak Writers and Artists abroad
Bio: "Miloš Klement Mlynarovič," in LIC. See - http://www.litcentrum.sk/ slovenski-spisovatelia/milos-klement-mlynarovic#curriculum_vitae; "Miloš K. Mlynarovič," in: *Czechoslovakia Past and Present,* Vol. 1, p. 872.

Sharona Muir (1957-), b. MA, of Slovak ancestry; writer, professor of creative writing at Bowling Green Univ.
Bio: Rechcigl, Miloslav, Jr., "Sharona Muir," in: *Encyclopedia of Bohemian and Czech-American Biography.* Bloomington, IN: AuthorHouse, 2016, Vol. 2, pp. 974-975; "Sharona Bentov Muir," in: Wikipedia. See - https://en.wikipedia. org/wiki/Sharona_Ben-Tov_Muir

Ján Okál (1915-1990), b. Hubova, Slovakia; in US s. 1950; publicist, writer, translator.
Bio: "Ján Okáľ," in: Literárne Informačné centrum. See - http://www. litcentrum.sk/slovenski-spisovatelia/jan-okal; "Ján Okál," in: "Gorazd Zvonický," in: *Czechoslovakia Past and Present,* Vol. 1, p.874

Štefan Pagáč (1920-1983), b. Trenčín, Czech; flier, jailed by Communists, writer
Bio: "Pagáč, Štefan," in: *SVU Directory* 5; "Pagáč, Štefan," in: Pejskar 2, p. 287.

Jozef Paučo (1914-1975), b. Pila, Pezinok Dist., Slovakia; in US s. 1945; writer, journalist, publicist
Bio: LIC. See- http://www.litcentrum.sk/slovenski-spisovatelia/ jozef-pauco#curriculum_vitae

Kornel Otto Piacek (1921-1996), b. Slovakia; writer and journalist; author of Karol Strmeň représentant typique de la poésie moderne slovaque, University of Montreal, 1954;
Bio: "Kornel Piacek," The Gazette, Montréal, QC, February 25, 2006.

Alejandra (Flora) Pizarnik (1936-1972), b. Avellaneda, Argentina, of Slovak ancestry; Argentine poet
Bio; "Alejandra Pizarnik," in: Wikipedia. See - https://en.wikipedia.org/wiki/Alejandra_Pizarnik

Štefan Polakovič (1912-1999), b. Chtelnica, Slovakia; philosopher, author, essayist, publicist; s. 1949 resided in Argentina.
Bio: "Štefan Polakovič," in: LIC. See - http://www.litcentrum.sk/slovenski-spisovatelia/stefan-polakovic

Nicolette Polek, Slovak American, born in Cleveland, OH; writer and pianist. Her stories have been published in the *Chicago Quarterly Review*, *New York Tyrant*, *Hobart*, *Fanzine*, *Shabby Doll House*, and elsewhere. She is currently getting her MFA in fiction at the University of Maryland.
Bio: "Nicolette Polek," in: Monster house Press. See - https://monsterhousepress.com/authors/nicolette-polek/

Darryl Ponicsan (1938-), b. Shenandoah, PA, of Slovak descent; American writer. He is best known as the author of the 1970 novel *The Last Detail*, which was adapted into a 1973 film starring Jack Nicholson. A sequel, 'Last Flag Flying,' based on his 2005 novel of the same name, was released in 2017 and he also co-wrote the screenplay with Richard Linklater. He also wrote the 1973 novel and screenplay 'Cinderella Liberty', starring James Caan. Ponicsan writes mystery novels under the pen name Anne Argula.
Bio: "Darryl Ponicsan," in: Wikipedia. See - https://en.wikipedia.org/wiki/Darryl_Ponicsa

Andrej Potocký (1893-1996), b. Sedliacka Dubová, Orava, Slovakia; Supreme National Secretary of the Canadian Slovak League

James Ragan (1944-), b. Duquesne, PA, of Slovak parents; poet, playwright and essayist. Author of 8 books and translated into 15 languages, he has read at the UN, Carnegie Hall, and for 7 heads of state including Czech President

Vaclav Havel, So. Korean Prime Minister Young-Hoon Kang and for Mikhail Gorbachev at Moscow's Int. Poetry Festival. Has appeared on CNN, C-SPAN, NPR, PBS and in 30 Anthologies. He has a Ph.D. and served for 25 years as Director of USC's Professional Writing Program and for 23 summers as Distinguished Professor at Charles University in Prague.
Bio: "James Ragan," in: Poets & Writers. See - https://www.pw.org/content/james_ragan_1

John Rekem (1917-1983), b. Trenčianska Teplá, Slovakia; R.C. priest, Msgr.; in 1949, immigrated to Winnipeg, Manitoba; published widely in literary and historical journals and Slovak newspapers in Canada and US.
Bio: "Jan Rekem," in: LIC. See - http://www.litcentrum.sk/slovenski-spisovatelia/jan-rekem

Mary Ann Malinchak Rishel (ca 1940-), Slovak American; fiction writer, professor, Department of Writing, Ithaca College
Bio: "Mary Ann Rishel," in: Ithaca College. See - https://faculty.ithaca.edu/rishel/; "Mary Ann Malinchak Rishel," in: *The Greenwood Encyclopedia of Multiethnic American Literature*. Westport, CT: Greenwood Press, 2005, Vol. 4, N-S; "Mary Ann Malinchak Rishel," in: Poets & Writers. See - https://www.pw.org/content/mary ann malinchak rishel 1

Richard Rohr (1943-), b. Topeka, KS, of Slovak descent; priest, O.F.M., preacher, writer
Bio: "Richard Rohr," in: Wikipedia. See - https://sk.wikipedia.org/wiki/Richard_Rohr; Block, Stephanie, "What Are Fr. Richard Rohr and CAC Up to Now?" in: Catholic Media Coalition. See - http://www.catholicmediacoalition.org/rohr_CAC.htm

Gregory A. Rucka (1969-), b. San Francisco, CA, of Slovak descent; American comic book writer and novelist. He is known or his work on such comics as Action Comics, Batwoman, Detective Comics, and the miniseries Superman: World of New Krypton for DC Comics, and for novels such as his Atticus Kodiak series.
Bio: "Greg Rucka," in: Wikipedia. See - https://en.wikipedia.org/wiki/Greg_Rucka

Rosalie Ruman (née Wuhl) (1925-2006), b. Czech.; writer, journalist, Montreal, Canada
Bio: "Ruman, Rosalie," in: *SVU Directory* 8; "Rosalie (Wohl) Ruman Obituary," *Montreal Gazette*, October 11, 2006.

Anne Lucas Ryba (1940 -), b. Grassflat, PA, of Slovak descent; author of family history and their immigration to the USA: Humble Beginnings. Kearnery, NE: Morris Publishing, 2000.
Bio: "Anne Lucas Ryba's book 'Humble Beginnings' still available," in: cleveland.com. See - http://blog.cleveland.com/slovakia/2010/04/anne_lucas_rybas_book_humble_b.html

Štefan Senčík (1920-2001), Starý Tekov, Slovakia; R.C. priest, S.J.; writer, translator, and novelist; editor of newsletter *Echo;* ordained in Maastricht, Netherlands.; emigrated to Australia, 1952; organized theater and served as a missionary among Slovak Bush farmers; worked at Vatican Radio, 1957-1963, 1984-1990; missionary to Canada, 1963-1984; appointed Provincial of the Mission House of the Slovak Jesuits in Cambridge, Ontario, 1969-1975; last years spent helping Catholic publishing in Trnava.
Bio: "Redaktor: Petmes - Dr. Stefan Sensik, SJ," in: Wikipedia. See - https://sk.wikipedia.org/wiki/Redaktor:Petmes

Michael V. Simko (1893-1989), Bridgeport, CT, of Slovak parents; podiatrist by education, but known as a prolific writer
Bio: "Michael V. Simko (1893-1989)," in: Tellers of Weird Tales. See - http://tellersofweirdtales.blogspot.com/2016/01/michael-v-simko-1893-1989.html

Maria K. Sinak, b. Slovakia; fiction writer, with Slovak themes; *Jej Americká Svokra*, Pittsburgh, PA: International Printing Co., 1942, and *Katka*: a novel, Detroit, MI: S.J. Bloch Pub.Co., 1946.
See - https://www.worldcat.org/search?q=au%3AMaria+K.+Sinak&qt=results_page

Juraj Slávik (1890-1969), b. Dobrá Niva, Slovakia; lawyer, author, translator, diplomat. He wrote under the pseudonym Neresnický.
Bio: "Slávik, Juraj," in: *SVU Directory* 2; "Slávik, Juraj," in: Pejskar 1, pp. 42-45; "Juraj Slávik," in: Wikipedia. See - https://sk.wikipedia.org/wiki/Juraj_Slávik; Rechcigl, Miloslav, Jr., Juraj Slávik," in: *Encyclopedia*, Vol. 1 pp. 394-395;

"Slávik, Juraj Michal Daniel," in *Panorama*, pp. 281-282; "Juraj Slavik," in: *Czechoslovakia Past and Present*, Vol. 1, pp. 875-876.

Mikuláš Šprinc (1914-1986), b. Krompachy, Slovakia; R.C. priest; poet, prosaist, essayist, translator
Bio: "Mikuláš Šprinc," in: Wikipedia. See - https://sk.wikipedia.org/wiki/Mikuláš_Šprinc; "Mikuláš Šprinc," in: *Czechoslovakia Past and Present*, Vol. 1, pp. 873-874.

Karol Strmeň (1921-1994), b. Palárikovo, Czech.; poet, translator, Cleveland, OH
Bio: "Karol Strmeň," in: Wikipedia. See - https://sk.wikipedia.org/wiki/Karol_Strmeň ; "Karol Strmeň," in: LIC. See - http://www.litcentrum.sk/slovenski-spisovatelia/karol-strmen#curriculum_vitae; "Karol Strmeň" in: *Czechoslovakia Past and Present*, Vol. 1, p. 872.

Daniel Šustek (1846-1923), b. Slovenská Ľupča, Slovakia; cabinetmaker, traveler, busionessman, writer; co-founder of Matica slovenská in the US
Bio: "Daniel Šustek," in: Wikipedia. See - https://sk.wikipedia.org/wiki/Daniel_Šustek

Agnes Tomasov (née Grossman) (1930-), b. Bardejov, Slovakia; she immigrated to Canada, following the Soviet invasion of Czechoslovakia; author of successful autobiographical Holocaust memoirs.
Bio: "Agnes Tomasov," in: Azrieli. See - http://memoirs.azrielifoundation.org/survivor/agnes-tomasov; her autobiography in *Broken by Borders*. See - https://medium.com/study-of-history/bound-by-borders-how-the-nazi-annexation-of-czechoslovakia-changed-the-life-of-agnes-tomasov-3f74349cf737

Ernst Vajda (1886-1954), b. Komárno, Slovakia; actor, playwright, novelist, but is more famous today for his screenplays.
Bio: "Ernst Vajda," in: Wikipedia. See - https://en.wikipedia.org/wiki/Ernest_Vajda

Paul Wilkes (1938-), b. Cleveland, OH, of Slovak descent; writer, journalist, who has written extensively about individual spirituality as well as the role of religion in public and personal lives.
Bio: "Paul Wilkes," in: Wikipedia. See - https://en.wikipedia.org/wiki/Paul_Wilkes

Andrej Žarnov (1903-1982), b. Kuklov, Slovakia; trained as physician; after 1952 he moved to Austria, Italy and finally to America. He was a poet, a Slovak Catholic modernist (Catholic Moderna). An author of socio-political, patriotic and reflective poems. He was also a popularizer and translator of Polish poetry works. He was president of the Association of Slovak Writers and Artists Abroad.
Bio: "Andrej Žarnov," in: Wikipedia. See - https://en.wikipedia.org/wiki/Andrej_ Žarnov; "Andrej Žarnov," in: *Czechoslovakia Past and Present*, Vol. 1, p. 876

Miloslav Zlámal (1922-1997), b. Skalica, Czech.; poet, novelist, radio and TV producer and director
Bio: "Zlámal, Miloslav," in: *SVU Directory, 7;* "Miloslav Zlámal," in: *Czechoslovakia Past and Present*, Vol. 1, p. 875.

Gorazd Zvonický (orig. Andrej Šándor) (1913-1995), b. Mikulovce, Slovakia; Salesian priest, missionary; poet, translator, pedagogue. He escaped from a concentration camp for clergy in Podolínec; moved to Italy, then Argentina. He was active with Matica Slovenska Abroad. He returned to Europe and worked at the Slovak Institute of SS. Cyril and Methodius in Rome. He influenced literary developments in Slovakia; especially known for his Marian poetry.
Bio: "Gorazd Zvonický," in: Wikipedia. See - https://sk.wikipedia.org/wiki/Gorazd Zvonický; "Gorazd Zvonický - Básnik, pedagóg, kňaz, misionár," in: oslavma.hu. See - http://www.oslovma.hu/index.php/sk/archiv/185-archivnazory/966-gorazd-zvonick-basnik-pedagog-kaz-misionar; "Gorazd Zvonický," in: *Czechoslovakia Past and Present*, Vol. 1, p.874.

F. MUSIC

1. Surveys

Lowenbach, Jan, "Czechoslovak Composers and Musicians in America," *The Musical Quarterly*, Vol. 29, No. 3 (July 1943), pp. 313-328.

2. Composers

Béla Bartók (1881-1945), b. Romania, of Slovak mother; composer, pianist, ethnomusicologist
Bio: "Béla Bartók," in: Wikipedia. See - https://en.wikipedia.org/wiki/ Béla_Bartók; "Bartok, Bela," *ASCAP Biographical Dictionary;* Knight, Ellen, "Bartók, Bela," in: *National Biography,* Vol. 2, pp. 285-287.

Ernst von Dohnányi (1877-1960), b. Bratislava, Slovakia; composer, pianist and conductor
Bio: "Ernst von Dohnányi," in: Wikipedia. See - https://en.wikipedia. org/wiki/Ernst_von_ Dohnányi; "Dohnanyi, Ernst von," in: *Biographical Dictionary of American Music,* 1973.

Miloslav Francisci (1854-1926), b. Debrecen, Hungary, of Slovak father; physician, composer of the first Slovak operettas, piano compositions, arranger of Slovak folksongs
Bio: "Miloslav Francisci," in: Wikipedia. See - https://sk.wikipedia.org/wiki/ Miloslav_Francisci

Francis Gromon (1890-1971), b. Trenčín, Slovakia; in US s, 1923; composer, conductor, teacher; conductor of light opera, NY and on tours; general music director, Hollywood film studios (1930), then Paramount Studios; composer for 9 films and musical director for 19 films.
Bio: "Gromon, Francis," in: *The ASCAP Biographical Dictionary of Composers, Authors and Publishers,* 1966; "Dr. Francis Gromon," in: Find A Grave. See - https://www.findagrave.com/memorial/6477479/francis-gromon

Andrew Hudak, Jr. (1918-), b. Cleveland, OH, of Slovak descent; accordionist, composer, arranger, conductor
Bio: "Hudak, Andrew, Jr." in: *ASCAP Biographical Dictionary,* 4.

Leslie Kondorossy (1915-1989), b. Bratislava, Slovakia; composer, conductor
Bio: "Kirk, Eelsie, "Kondorossy, Leslie," in: Grove Music Online. See - http://
oxfordindex.oup.com/view/10.1093/gmo/9781561592630.article.O006350;
Kondorossy, Leslie," in: *International Who's Who in Music,* 9 (1980); Kondorossy,
Leslie," *ASCAP Biographical Dictionary,* 4 (1980).

Georg Kreisler (1922-2011), b. Vienna, of Slovak ancestry; cabarettist,
satirist, composer, songwriter
Bio: "George Kreisler," in: Wikipedia. See - https://en.wikipedia.org/wiki/
Georg_Kreisler

Franz Lehár (1870-1948), b. Komárno, Slovakia; composer, mainly known
for his operettas, the best being The Merry Widow
Bio: "Franz Lehar," in" Wikipedia. See - https://en.wikipedia.org/wiki/
Franz_Lehár; "Lehar, Frank," in: *Who's Who in Music,* 1941

Terezka Lihani (1929-2015), b. Vrbice, Czech.; composer, singer, teacher,
writer, Parma, OH
Bio: "Lihani, Teresa," in: *SVU Directory* 8; "Terezka Svejkovsky Lihani," in:
Find A Grave. See - https://www.findagrave.com/memorial/166725091/
terezka-lihani

Thomas Pavlechko (1962-), b. Ohio into Slovak-Ukrainian family of
musicians; organist, choirmaster and composer-in-residence, at St. Martin's
Lutheran church in Austin, TX. Named the Emerging Hymn Tune Composer
by the Hymn Society in 2002, Pavlechko's hymn tunes and liturgical music are
in print in denominational hymnals and hymn collections on four continents.
He is the co-author of the principal worship planning reference books of
the Episcopal Church U.S.A, Liturgical Music for the Revised Common
Lectionary, released in three volumes by Church Publishing, New York. St.
Martin's Psalter, his collection of over 600 Psalm settings, is published in
two editions by St. James Music Press and Augsburg Fortress. Pavlechko's
commissioned compositions for orchestra, concert band, organ, chamber
and choral ensembles have received premiere performances throughout the
United States.
Bio: Thomas Pavlechko Bio," in: Mississippi conference on church Music
and Liturgy. See - http://mississippiconference.org/?page_id=128; "Thomas

Pavlechko," in: Selah Publishing Co. People. See - https://www.selahpub. com/SelahPeople/Pavlechko.html

Charles J. Roberts (1888-d.), b. Košice, Slovakia; composer, arranger, flutist; in US s. 1890; flutist, NY Philharmonic and Mozart Symphony Club (1892-93); director of music, Hoffman House, NY (1895-)
Bio: "Roberts, Charles J.," in: *The ASCAP Biographical Dictionary of Composers, Authors and Publishers,* 1980.

Arnold Schoenberg (1874-1951), b. Vienna, of Slovak father and Bohemian mother (Nachod); composer, music theorist, teacher, writer and painter. He was associated with expressionist movement in poetry and art and leader of the Second Viennese School. He immigrated to the US in 1934. He gained fame as a musical innovator and pioneer of modernism in 20th-century Western music. He created new methods of musical composition involving atonality, namely serialism and the 12-tone row. He was also one of the most-influential teachers of the 20th century; among his most-significant pupils were Alban Berg and Anton Webern.
Bio: Fiesst, Sabine, "Arnold Schoenberg," in: Oxford Bibliographies. See - http://www.oxfordbibliographies.com/view/document/obo-9780199757824/obo-9780199757824-0196.xml; "Arnold Schoenberg," in: Wikipedia. See - https://en.wikipedia.org/wiki/Arnold_Schoenberg

Lajos Serly (1855-1939), b. Bratislava, Slovakia; composer, arranger, conductor, in US si. 1935
Bio: "Lajos Serly, 84, Former Musician, Composer Conductor Dies," *The New York Times,* February 2, 1939

Tibor Serly (1900-1978), b. Lošonec, Bratislava; violist, violinist and composer.
Bio: "Serly, Tibor," *Biographical Dictionary of American Music,* 1973; "Tibor Serly," in: Wikipedia. See - https://en.wikipedia.org/wiki/Tibor_Serly

Jaroslav Vajda (1919-2008), b. East Chicago, IN, of Slovak descent; son of Lutheran pastor Rev. John Vajda; ordained as Lutheran minister, was noted as an American hymnist. Vajda did not write his first hymn until age 49. From that time until his death in 2008 at age 89, he wrote over 200 original and translated hymns that appear worldwide in more than 65 hymnals. He also

published two collections of hymn texts, numerous books, translations, and articles. Vajda served on hymnal commissions for *Hymnal Supplement* (1969) and *Lutheran Book of Worship* (1978). He was named a Fellow of The Hymn Society in the United States and Canada.
Bio: "Jaroslav Vajda," in: Wikipedia. See - https://en.wikipedia.org/wiki/ Jaroslav_Vajda; "Hymn Writer Jaroslav Vajda Dies," in: LCMS News. See - https://blogs.lcms.org/2008/hymn-writer-jaroslav-vajda-dies/

3. Conductors & Bandleaders

Kurt Herbert Adler (1905-1988), b. Vienna, of Slovak ancestry; conductor and opera house director
Bio: Randel, Don Michael, ed. "Adler, Kurt Herbert," in: *The Harvard Biographical Dictionary of Music*. Cambridge, MA: Belknap Press of Harvard University Press, 1996; "Kurt Herbert Adler," in: Wikipedia. See - https:// en.wikipedia.org/wiki/Kurt_Herbert_Adler

Joseph Aloysius Ferko (1895-1964), b. Philadelophi, PA, of Slovak descent; a pharmacist; ran drug store in North Philadelphia. Founder of the famous Ferko String Band 1922) with rosters. He was a perennial performer in Philadelphia's Mummers Parade. They gained national popularity through their hit recordings in the 1940s and 1950s. They played for Franklin D. Roosevelt's 1933 Presidential inauguration.
Bio: "Ferko String Band," in: Wikipedia. See - https://en.wikipedia.org/ wiki/Ferko_String_Band; "Memories of Joe Ferko, Mummers innovator and leader of most-honored string band ever," *Bucks County Courier Times*, January 1, 2017. See - http://www.buckscountycouriertimes.com/d029d03a-cd4a-11e6-85c5-6b331d3a44f2.html

Sammy Kaye (1910-1987), b. Lakewood, OH, of Slovak parents; bandleader and songwriter
Bio: "Kaye, Sammy," in: Wikipedia. See - https://en.wikipedia.org/wiki/ Sammy_Kaye; "Kaye, Sammy," in: *Biographical Dictionary of Music*, 1973.

Martin Majkut (1975-), b. Bratislava, Czech.; conductor, in US s. 2003; named a 2016 Emerging Artist by the League of American Orchestras; music conductor of the Rogue Valley Symphony in Ashland, OR (s. 2010). Starting

with the 2017/18 season, he assumes the music directorship of the Queens Symphony Orchestra in New York.
Bio: "Martin Majkut," in: Hudobne centrum. See - https://hc.sk/en/hudba/osobnost-detail/784-martin-majkut; "Martin Majkut," in: Diane Saldick - Building Successful Collaborations. See - http://dianesaldick.com/martin-majkut/; "Martin Majkut Conductor." See - https://martinmajkut.com/wp-content/uploads/2018/05/Majkut-Biography-April-2018.pdf

Fritz Reiner (1888-1963), b. Budapest, of Slovak descent; prominent conductor of opera and symphonic music, he reached prominence while music director of the Chicago Symphony Orchestra
Bio: "Fritz Reiner," in: Wikipedia. See - https://en.wikipedia.org/wiki/Fritz_Reiner

George Szell (1897-1970), b. Budapest, of Czechoslovak ancestry; conductor and composer
Bio: Michael Charry and Stanley Sadie, "George Szell," in: *The New Grove Dictionary of Music and Musicians*, 2nd ed. London: MacMillan, 2001, vol. 24, pp. 880–881; Rechcigl, Miloslav, Jr., "George Szell," in: *Encyclopedia of Bohemian and Czech-American Biography*. Bloomington, IN: AuthorHouse, 2016, Vol. 1, p. 575; "Szell, George," in: *Who's Who in America*, 33; Hanson, Acistslice M., "Szell, George," in: *National Biography*, Vol. 21, pp. 235-236.

Jerry (Jaroslav) Toth (1928-1999), b. Windsor, Ont., Canada, of Slovak father; saxophonist, clarinetist, flutist, arranger, composer, producer. oth played alto saxophone 1945-53 in the dance bands of Stan Patton, Bobby Gimby, Trump Davidson, and others and was co-leader 1952-7 with the trombonist Ross Culley and the saxophonist Roy Smith of a 17-piece jazz band. He was a member of Phil Nimmons' jazz bands 1956-74 and also studied orchestration with Nimmons.

Toth began playing in CBC orchestras in 1954 under Jack Kane and in later years was a leading Toronto studio musician. He was chief arranger or music director for the CBC's 'Parade' ca 1957-60 and in the mid-1960s began writing and producing jingles with his brother Rudy and others.
Bio: "Toth, Jerry," in: *The Canadian Encyclopedia*. See - https://www.thecanadianencyclopedia.ca/article/jerry-toth-emc

Rudy Toth (1925-2009), b. Krásno and Kysucou, Czech.; composer, arranger, conductor, pianist and cimbalom player. Rudy Toth began his CBC career in the late 1940s as pianist for Howard Cable, had his own radio show in 1951, and worked until ca 1965 as music director for CBC TV shows starring Joan Fairfax, Wally Koster, Denny Vaughan, and others. In the mid-1960s Toth turned increasingly to the writing of jingles, 1965-70 in partnership with his brother Jerry Toth, Dolores Claman, and Richard Morris as Quartet Productions, and 1970-80 with Jerry as Seven-O Productions. Toth's later assignments in TV included the orchestration (with Jerry) and conducting of the CBS production of Once Upon the Brothers Grimm (an Emmy Award nominee), and of several CBC specials. Toth played piano with Nimmons 'N' Nine in the late 1950s and performed on the cimbalom in works by Bartók, Kodály, and Stravinsky, with the Toronto Symphony Orchestra, the Ottawa Philharmonic, the Buffalo Symphony Orchestra, and the Ivan Romanoff Orchestra.
Bio: "Rudy Toth," in: Wikipedia, see - https://en.wikipedia.org/wiki/Rudy_Toth; "Rudy Toth," in: The Canadian Encyclopedia. See - https://www.thecanadianencyclopedia.ca/en/article/rudy-toth-emc/

Tony Toth (ca 1928-2003), b. Windsor, Ontario, Canada, of Slovak father; oboist, English hornist, saxophonist, clarinetist, copyist; in radio, TV, theater and recording orchestras. In the 1970s he was the baritone saxophonist and copyist for Nimmons 'N' Nine Plus Six and during the 1980s played in Peter Appleyard's All Star Swing Band.
Bio: "Tony Toth," in: The Canadian encyclopedia. See - https://www.thecanadianencyclopedia.ca/article/tony-toth-emc

Alexander von Zemlinsky (1871-1942), b. Vienna, of Slovak grandfather; composer, conductor and teacher
Bio: "Alexander von Zemlinsky," in: Wikipedia. See - https://en.wikipedia.org/wiki/Alexander_von_Zemlinsky

4. Classical Musicians

a. Pianists

Peter Breiner (1957-), b. Humenné, Czech.; pianist, conductor, composer, lived in Toronto, Canada (1992-2007), since 2007 in New York
Bio: "Peter Breiner," in: Wikipedia. See - https://en.wikipedia.org/wiki/Peter_Breiner

Eva Fabian-Reihs (1947-), b. Bratislava, Czech.; pianist, music teacher
Bio: "Fabian-Reihs, Eva," in: *SVU Directory*

Otto Herz (1894-1976), b. Prešov, Slovakia; pianist, soloist, professor, Manhattan School of Music (s. 1972), NYC
Bio: "Otto Herz, Professor of Music and Concert Pianist, Dies at 81," *The New York Times,* January 6, 1976.

Pierre Jasmin (1949-), b. Montreal, Canada, of Slovak descent; pianist, teacher
Bio: "Pierre Jasmin," in: The Canadian Encyclopedia. See - https://www.thecanadianencyclopedia.ca/en/article/pierre-jasmin-emc/

Rafael Joseffy (1852-1915), b. Huncovce, Slovakia; pianist, composer, teacher
Bio: "Rafael Joseffy,", in: Wikipedia. See - https://en.wikipedia.org/wiki/Rafael_Joseffy

Thaddeus J. Kozuch (1913-1991), b. Chicago, probably of Slovak descent; pianist, teacher, conductor, composer, accompanist
Bio: "Kozuch, Thaddeus J.," in: *Who's Who Today in the Musical World,* 1937.

Lili Kraus (1903-1986), b. Budapest, of Czech and Slovak ancestry; pianist
Bio: "Lily Kraus," in: Wikipedia. See - https://en.wikipedia.org/wiki/Lili_Kraus

Elena Letňanová (1942-), b. Bratislava; Czech.; pianist, associate professor with University of Dayton, OH (1987-1992).
Bio: "Letňanová, Elena," in: *SVU Directory* 8; "Personality Profile: Elena Letňanová," in: Music Centre Slovakia.

Antonia Mazán (fl. 1968), Slovak Canadian; pianist, instructor, Faculty of Music, University of Western Ontario, London, Canada.

Marienka Michna (1922-1993), b. Torrington, CT, of Slovak descent; concert pianist and opera coach.
Bio: "Marienka Michna: in: Krajsa, pp. 431-432.

Ditta Pásztory-Bartók (1903-1982), b. Rimavská Sobota, Slovakia; pianist and the second wife of the composer Béla Bartók; in US s. 1940; returned to Budapest in 1946.
Bio: "Ditta Pásztory-Bartók," in: Wikipedia. See - https://en.wikipedia.org/wiki/Ditta_Pásztory-Bartók

Vladimir G. Sasko (1875-1975), b. Slovakia; concert pianist, composer, professor of music, director of the Sasko Music School, Chicago
Bio: "Sasko, Vladimir G.," in Droba, p. 29.

Elyakim Taussig (1944-), b. Bratislava, Czech.; pianist, teacher, composer, video producer
Bio: "Taussig, Elyakim," in: The Canadian Encyclopedia. See - https://www.thecanadianencyclopedia.ca/en/article/elyakim-taussig-emc/

b. Organists

Mario Leona Fabry, b. Chicago, of Slovak parents; organist and choir director, Chicago
Bio: "Fabry, Marion Leon," in: Droba, p. 215.

Andrej V. Kozák (1877-1949), b. Markušovce, Slovakia; musician; organist at St. John the Baptist, Taylor, PA, then Sacred Heart of Jesus, Wilkes Barre, PA.
Bio: Paučo, Jozef, *Slovenski priekopnici v Amerike*, Cleveland: Prvá Katolícka Slovenská Jednota, 1972, pp. 245-248.

Martin Pavella (1888-d.), b. Padina, Yugoslavia, organist, St. Peter and Paul Slovak Evangelical Lutheran Church, Chicago,
Bio: "Pavella, Martin," in: Droba, pp. 226-227.

Thomas Pavlechko (1962-), b. Ohio into Slovak-Ukrainian family of musicians; organist, choirmaster and composer-in-residence, at St. Martin's Lutheran church in Austin, TX. As organist, he has performed at St. Patrick's Cathedral, New York, Washington National Cathedral, the Spoleto Festival, and for conferences of the American Guild of Organists, the Association of Anglican Musicians, the Association of Lutheran Church Musicians and The Hymn Society. In addition to his work with churches in Ohio, Tennessee, Texas and Virginia, Pavlechko has also served as Chapel Musician and Adjunct Faculty for the Lutheran Seminary Program in the Southwest in Austin, Texas and Adjunct Professor of Music at William and Mary's Richard Bland College in Prince William, Virginia.
Bio: Thomas Pavlechko Bio," in: Mississippi conference on church Music and Liturgy. See - http://mississippiconference.org/?page_id=128; "Thomas Pavlechko," in: Selah Publishing Co. People. See - https://www.selahpub.com/SelahPeople/Pavlechko.html

Adalbert B. Suhany (1888-1950), b. Nitranska, Slovakia; teacher, choir master, organist, organizer and director of the United Slovak Catholic choirs, Chicago
Bio: "Suhany, Adalbert B.," in: Droba, p. 232.

c. Violinists

Charles Dobias (1923-), b. Klàtova Novà Ves, Czech.; violinist, with Toronto Symphony
Bio: "Charles Dobias," in: *Naše Hlasy,* p. 39, "Dobias, Charles," in: *Who's Who in Music,* 9.

Frederick R. Dvonch (1912-1976), b. Chicago, IL, of Slovak descent; violinist and music director, conductor for Broadway shows
Bio: "Dvonch, Frederick R.," in: Droba, pp. 27-28; "Frederick Dvonch, 64, a Broadway Conductor," *The New York Times,* November 22, 19

Patinka Kopec (fl. 2017), b. Slovakia; immigrated to Israel and later to New York; American violinist, violist; teacher in the Pre-College and Upper School Divisions of the Manhattan School of Music where she serves as Co-Director and Co-Teacher of the Pinchas Zukerman Performance Program. She is also the Director of the Young Artist Program at the National Arts Centre in Ottawa, Canada.
Bio: "Patinka Kopec," in: Karwendel Music Festival. See - http://www.karwendelmusicfestival.com/patinka-kopec/; "Patinka Kopec," in: Manhattan School of Music. See - https://www.msmnyc.edu/faculty/patinka-kopec/; "Patinka Kopec," in: Heifetz International Music Institute. See - https://www.heifetzinstitute.org/program-2/faculty/2017-violin-faculty/patinka-kopec/

Herbert Thomas Mandl (1926-2007), b. Bratislava, Czech.; concert violinist, philosopher, inventor; he and his wife twice emigrated to the USA, where he studied psychology at the University of Washington in Seattle.
Bio: "Herbert Thomas Mandl," in: Wikipedia. See - https://en.wikipedia.org/wiki/Herbert_Thomas_Mandl

Theodore Pashkus (1905-1970), b. Bratislava, Slovakia; violinist, teacher
Bio: "Pashkus, Theodore," in: *Wo's Who in Music,* 1941

Lucia Popp (1939-1993), b. Záhorská Ves, Czech.; opera singer, soprano,
Bio: "Lucia Popp," in: Wikipedia. See - https://en.wikipedia.org/wiki/Lucia_Popp

Feri Roth (1899-1969), b. Zvolen, Slovakia; violinist, founder of the Roth Quartet, composer, conductor, professor at UCLA
Bio: "Roth, Feri," in: *Educators,* p. 5; "Roth, Feri," in: *Baker's Biographical Dictionary of Musicians*; "Dr. Feri Roth, Head of String Quartet," *The New York Times,* May 9, 1969; "Roth, Feri," in: *American Scholars,* 3; "Roth, Feri," in: *Who's Who Today in the Musical World,* 1937, p.349.

Tibor Serly (1901-1978), b. Lučenec, Slovakia; violist, violinist, composer; teacher of composition at Manhattan School of Music, NYC
Bio: "Tibor Serly," in: Wikipedia. See - https://en.wikipedia.org/wiki/Tibor_Serly

Ede Zathureczky (1903-1959), b. Spišská Nová Ves, Slovakia; violin virtuoso and pedagogue. He taught at Indiana University toward the end of his life.
Bio: "Ede Zathureczky," in: Wikipedia. See - https://en.wikipedia.org/wiki/Ede_Zathureczky; "Ede Zathurecky," in: Find A Grave. See - ttps://www.findagrave.com/memorial/60221300/ede-zathureczky

d. Guitarists

Tony Harmon (fl. 2008), b. Riverside, CA, Slovak American; classical guitarist. He performed on numerous television shows and special events. He composed and performed the musical soundtrack for ABC television's The William Randolf Hearst Story, and was asked to play at the Western White House for Ronald Reagan.
Bio: "Tony Harmon," in: Wikipedia. See - https://en.wikipedia.org/wiki/Tony_Harmon

4. Popular, Jazz and Pop Music Performers

Austin Adamec (1988-), b. Jacksonville, FL, of Czech and Slovak descent; guitarist
Bio: "Austin Adamec," in: Wikipedia. See - https://en.wikipedia.org/wiki/Austin_Adamec

Daniel J. Balberchak (1932-2012), b. Edwardsville, PA, of Slovak descent; carpenter by trade; a well-known musician and accordion player; played with many orchestras for about 30 years, resided in Exeter, PA.
Bio: "Daniel J. Balberchak," in: Legacy.com. See - http://www.legacy.com/obituaries/timesleader/obituary.aspx?page=lifestory&pid=165213551

Branislav Brinarski (fl. 2018), b. Senovce, Slovakia; in Slovakia performed with the folk ensembles, playing bass, gajdice, dvojačka and singing; in US s. 1998; founder of the Slovak Folk Band Pajtaši; also performed with the

Bensen-Scott and Jump Start big bands in the New York City area; provides music for Slovak Folk Ensemble Limbora; now plays with Harmonia.

Laco Déczi (1938-), b. Bernolákovo, Czech.; jazz trumpeter and composer Bio: "Laco Déczi," in: Wikipedia. See - https://en.wikipedia.org/wiki/ Laco_Décb. Denver, CO, of Slovak paternal grandfather; American rock cellist, vocalist and pianist

Jan Hammer (1948-), b. Prague, Czech., of Slovak mother; musician, composer and record producer;
Bio: "Jan Hammer, in: Wikipedia. See - https://en.wikipedia.org/wiki/ Jan_Hammer

Jozef Janis (fl. 2011), b. Slovakia; violinist; in Us s. 2002; member of the Duquesne University Tamburitzans; founder of his own Slovak folk band; now plays with Harmonia.
Bio: "Jozef Janis, Violin," in: Harmonia. See - http://www.harmoniaband. com/musicians.html

Ken Javor (fl. 2011), b. Cleveland, OH, of Czech and Slovak descent; string bass player; since the 1960s, playing initially in Cleveland in the famous Buckeye Road Hungarian neighborhood. A mainstay of Slovak music in Cleveland with a wide repertoire of Slovak folk music reflecting his over 40 years of experience, Ken has performed at concerts and community events in Europe and across the United States; now he performs with Harmonia.
Bio: "Ken Javor, Bass," in: Harmonia. See - http://www.harmoniaband.com/ musicians.html

Roger L. Latzgo (1949-), b. Pennsylvania, of Slovak descent; guitarist, pianist, composer
Bio: "Roger Latzgo," in: Latzgo.com. See - http://www.rogerlatzgo.com/; "Roger Latzgo," in: LinkedIn: See - https://www.linkedin.com/in/roger-latzgo-5400b04a/; "Latzgo, Roger L." in: SVU *Directory*, 9.

Katrina Leskanich (1960-), b. Topeka, KS, of Slovak descent. American musician, author and former lead singer of British pop rock band Katrina and the Waves whose song "Walking on Sunshine" was an international hit

in 1985 and who in 1997 won the Eurovision Song Contest for the United Kingdom with the song 'Love Shine a Light.'
Bio: "Katrina Leskanich," in: Wikipedia. See - https://en.wikipedia.org/wiki/Katrina_Leskanich

David Martinka (fl. 2018), b. Slovakia; flute musician, award winning recording artist
Bio: "David Martinka." See - https://www.redbellymusic.com/bio.cfm

Pete Parada (1974-), b. Arkport, NY, of Slovak paternal grandfather; American drummer and songwriter
Bio: "Pete Parada," in: Wikipedia. See - https://en.wikipedia.org/wiki/Pete_Parada

Joe Pat Paterek (1919-), b. Chicago, of Slovak descent; accordionist, Slovak band leader, Chicago
Bio: "Joe Pat" Paterek," in: IPA. See - http://www.ipapolkas.com/blog/otw-portfolio/joe-pat-paterek-living-category-inducted-1978/

Neyla Pekarek (1986-), b. Denver, CO, of Slovak descent; a cellist, vocalist, and pianist for the American folk-rock band, The Lumineers.
Bio: "Neyla Pekarek," in: Wikipedia. See - https://en.wikipedia.org/wiki/Neyla_Pekarek

Jim Peterik (1950-), b. Berwyn, IL, of Slovak descent; musician and songwriter, rock singer, guitarist founder of the band Survivor
Bio: "Jim Peterik," in: Wikipedia. See - https://en.wikipedia.org/wiki/Jim_Peterik

John M. Robel ('Jolly Jack') (1903-1968), b. Austria, of Slovak parents; musician, band leader
Bio: "Robel, John M.," in: *Making It in America.* A Sourcebook on Eminent Ethnic Americans. Edited by Elliot Robert Barkan. Santa Barbara, CA: ABC-CLIO, 2001, pp. 312-313.

Anne Dolores Zvara Sarosy (1923-2015), b. Campbell, OH, of Slovak descent; accomplished accordionist, had her own orchestra on WKBN Radio in the late 30s and 40s.
Bio: "Obituary for Anne Sarosy (Zvara)," in: Shrine of Remembrance. See -http://www.shrineofremembrance.com/book-of-memories/2214976/sarosy-anne/obituary.php

Isaac Slade (1981-), b. Denver, CO, of Slovak descent; American musician and the lead vocalist, main songwriter, pianist and co-founder of Colorado-based rock band The Fray.
Bio: "Isaac Slade," in: Wikipedia. See - https://en.wikipedia.org/wiki/Isaac_Slade

Dennis Thompson (orig. Tomich) (1948-), b. Michigan, of Slovak descent; drummer with proto-punk/hard rock group MC5
Bio: "Dennis Thompson," in: Wikipedia. See - https://en.wikipedia.org/wiki/Dennis_Thompson_(drummer)

Brian Tichý (1968-), b. Denville, NJ, of Slovak descent, his ancestors came from Žilina; American drummer, guitarist, songwriter and singer. He is best known as having been the drummer for Whitesnake, Billy Idol, Foreigner, and OzzyO.S.B.ourne.
Bio: "Brian Tichy," in: Wikipedia. See - https://en.wikipedia.org/wiki/Brian_Tichy

Timbuktu (orig. Jason Michael Bosak Diakité) (1975-), b. Lund, Sweden, of US-born Swedish human rights lawyer and Slovak mother; a rapper and reggae artist
Bio: "Timbaktu," in: Wikipedia. See - https://en.wikipedia.org/wiki/Timbuktu_(musician)

Jerry Toth (1928-1999), b. Windsor, Ontario, Canada, of Slovak father; Canadian saxophonist, clarinetist, flutist, arranger, composer, and record producer
Bio: "Jerry Toth," in: Wikipedia. See - https://en.wikipedia.org/wiki/Jerry_Toth

6. Classical Singers

Trude Check-Tuhy (1935-2006), b. Wilkes-Barre, PA, of Slovak descent; musician and vocalist, soloist in local churches and musicals in Wilkes-Barre.
Bio: "Trude Check-Tuhy," *Times Leader,* December 12, 2006.

Joseph Diskay (1886-d.), b. Topoľčany, Slovakia; opera singer, tenor, voice coach
Bio: "Diskay, Joseph," in: *Who's Who in Music,* 1941; "Joseph Diskay," in: Looking for Mabel Normand- Webs. See - https://www.freewebs.com/ looking-for-mabel/josephdiskay.htm

Jacqueline Marie Evancho (2000-), b. Pittsburgh, PA, of Slovak descent; an American crossover singer. She gained wide recognition at an early age and, since 2009, has issued an EP and five albums, including a platinum and gold album, and three Billboard 200 top 10 debuts.
Bio: "Jackie Evancho," in: Wikipedia. See - https://en.wikipedia.org/wiki/ Jackie_Evancho

Maria Mattei Georgevich (1918-2009), b. Bratislava, Czech.; opera singer, Montclair, NJ
Bio: "Georgevich, Maria Mattei," in: *SVU Directory* 6; "Maria Mattei Georgevich," in: Find a Grave. See - https://www.findagrave.com/ memorial/136076876/maria-mattei-georgevich

Etelka Gerster (1855-1920), b. Košice, Slovakia; opera singer, soprano. Her first American tour in 1873 was with the cast of Her Majesty's Opera Company under the direction of James Henry Mapleson. She also appeared in San Francisco, where it was reported she became ill. In 1884, she again appeared in New York working with Mapleson at the Academy of Music. Adelina Patti and Christine Nilsson, and Gerster were considered the leading singers of their time. Gerster opened a voice school in Berlin where she trained many famous singers from 1896 until 1917. Among her students were Ilona Durigo, Matja von Niessen-Stone, and Lotte Lehma. She died in Italy.
Bio: "Etelka Gerster," in: Luminous-Lint. See - http://www.luminous-lint. com/app/image/2195678312120199141554417660/; "Etelka Gerster," in: Wikipedia. See - https://en.wikipedia.org/wiki/Etelka_Gerster

Marinka Gurevich (née Revész) (1902-1990), b. Bratislava, Slovakia, of Jewish Czech descent; voice teacher, mezzo-soprano
Bio: "Marinka Gurevich," in *Encyclopedia*, Vol. 1, p. 669.

Helen Hájnik Janecek (1925-1993), b. Vranov nad Topľou, Czech.; Canadian singer, soprano, residing in Saskatchewan
Bio: "Helen Hajnik," in: Rechcigl, Miloslav, Jr., Encyclopedia of Bohemian and Czech-American Biography. Bloomington, IN: AuthorHouse, 2017, Vol., p. 670.

Maria Halama, b. Turčiansky Sv. Martin, Slovakia; concert singer
Bio: "Halama, Maria," in: Droba, p. 28

Štefan Kocán (1972-), b. Trnava, Czech.; opera singer, Bass. His American debut was at the Metropolitan Opera as Il Re in Aida, under the baton of Daniele Gatti in the 2009-10 season. The following season, he made his debut at the Lyric Opera of Chicago as Banco in a new production of Macbeth and returned to sing the role of Ramfis there the following season in Aida. Engagements with the Los Angeles Philharmonic followed in 2013, with Stefan Kocan singing the role of Il Commendatore in a new staged production of Don Giovanni and then as Ramfis in a concert version of Aida at the Hollywood Bowl, both under the baton of Gustavo Dudamel.
Bio: "Stefan Kocan," in: Official Bio. See - http://www.stefankocan.net/biography/official/ ; "Stefan Kocan," in: My Story. See - http://www.stefankocan.net/biography/my-story/

Rose Pauly (orig. Pollak) (1894-1975), b. Prešov, Slovakia; dramatic soprano, member of Metropolitan Opera (1938).
Bio: "Pauly, Rose," in: *Who's Who Today in the Musical World,* 1937, p. 325; "Rose Pauly," in: Wikipedia. See - https://en.wikipedia.org/wiki/Rose_Pauly_(singer)

Rudolf Petrak (1918-1972), b. Sučany, Czech.; leading tenor with the city Opera company (1948-1956)
Bio: "Petrak, Rudolf," in: *Biographical Dictionary of American Music,* 1973; "Rudolf Petrak, Tenor, dies at 54," *The New York Times,* March 6, 1972

Rudolph Rezso Szekely (1889-1981), b. Vrútky, Slovakia; singer, voice teacher, with Detroit Philharmonic Orchestra, MI
Bio: "Szekely, Rudolph Rezso," in: *Who's Who in Music*, 1941.

7. Popular Singers and Songwriters

Beata Begeniová (ca 1975-), b. Medzilaborce, Slovakia; has musical degree from J. P. Safarik University; folk singer, soloist on many recordings and radio broadcasts; she performs with Harmonia.
Bio: "Beata Begeniova, Vocals," in: Harmonia. See - http://www.harmoniaband.com/musicians.html

Jon Bon Jovi (orig. John Francis Bongiovi, Jr.) (1962-), b. Perth Amboy, NJ, of Italian and Slovak ancestry on his father's side; American singer, songwriter, record producer and actor
and, philanthropist
Bio: "Jon Bon Jovi," in: Wikipedia. See - https://en.wikipedia.org/wiki/Jon_Bon_Jovi

Carmel Buckingham (1998-), b. Anchorage, AK, of Slovak descent; Slovak-American singer and the lead singer of pop-punk group The House United based in Nashville.
Bio: "Carmel Buckingham," in : Wikipedia. See - https://en.wikipedia.org/wiki/Carmel_Buckingham

Celeste Buckingham (1995-), b. Zurich, Switzerland, of Slovak descent; Carmel Buckingham's older sister; grew up in Slovakia; Slovak singer and songwriter
Bio: "Celeste Buckingham," in; Wikipedia. See - https://en.wikipedia.org/wiki/Celeste_Buckingham

Annabelle Chvostek (1973-), b. Toronto, Ont., Canada, of Slovak descent; a Canadian singer-songwriter based in Montreal.
Bio: "Annabelle Chvostek," in: Wikipedia. See - https://en.wikipedia.org/wiki/Annabelle_Chvostek

Jackie Evancho (2000-), b. Pittsburgh, PA, of Slovak descent; American classical crossover singer, who gained wide recognition at an early age and,

since 2009, has issued a platinum-selling EP and seven albums, including three Billboard 200 top 10 debuts.
Bio: "Jackie Evancho," in: Wikipedia. See - https://en.wikipedia.org/wiki/Jackie_Evancho

Jack Gilinsky (1996-), b. Omaha, NE, of Slovak ancestry; singer
Bio: "Jack Gilinsky," in: FANDOM. See - http://madisonbeer.wikia.com/wiki/Jack_Gilinsky; "Jack & Jack," in: Wikipedia. See - https://en.wikipedia.org/wiki/Jack_%26_Jack

Hanka Gregušová (aka Hanka G) (1980-), b. Mongolia, of Slovak parents; in Us s. 2016; a jazz, gospel & world-music, singer and lyricist
Bio: "Hanka G," in: Wikipedia. See - https://en.wikipedia.org/wiki/Hanka_G; "Hanka G," in Jazz Folk Singer from Bratislava. See - http://www.hankag.com/

David Eric Grohl (1969-), b. Warren, OH, of Slovak descent; American musician, singer, songwriter, record producer, and film director
Bio: "David Eric Grohl," in: Wikipedia. See - https://en.wikipedia.org/wiki/Dave_Grohl

Tyler James Hilton (1983-), b. Palm Springs, Riverside, CA, of Slovak descent; an American singer-songwriter and actor.
Bio: "Tyler Hilton," in: Wikipedia. See - https://en.wikipedia.org/wiki/Tyler_Hilton

Katarina Korcek, (fl. 2017) b. Bloomfield Fields, MI, of Slovak descent; American singer; went to Slovakia in the early 90s, teaching English, and did not return
Bio: Rehák, Oliver, "Mala 24, keď prišla z Ameriky na Slovensko. Už sa nevrátila," in: Dennik N. See - https://dennikn.sk/688284/mala-24-ked-prisla-z-ameriky-na-slovensko-uz-sa-nevratila/

Josh Krajcik (1981-), b. Wooster, OH; singer and songwriter, bandleader
Bio: "Josh Krajcik," in: Wikipedia. See - https://en.wikipedia.org/wiki/Josh_Krajcik

Terezka Lihani (1929-2015), b. Vrbice, Czech.; singer, composer, writer, producer, director Cleveland, OH
Bio: "Lihani, Terezka," in: *SVU Directory*, 9; "Teresa Lihani," *The Plain Dealer*, June 9-10, 2015; "Terezka Svejkovsky Lihani," in: Find A Grave. See - https://www.findagrave.com/memorial/166725091/terezka-lihani

Austin Mahone (1996-), b. San Antonio, TX, of Slovak descent in his mother's side; American singer and songwriter.
Bio: "Austin Mahone," in: Wikipedia. See - https://en.wikipedia.org/wiki/Austin_Mahone

Waldemar Matuška (1932-2009), b. Košice, Czech.; Czechoslovak singer who became popular in his homeland in the 1960s and 1970s. In 1986, he immigrated to the US.
Bio: "Waldemar Matuska," in: Wikipedia. See - https://en.wikipedia.org/wiki/ Waldemar_Matuška

Bret Michaels (orig. Bret Michael Sychak) (1963-), b. Buttler, PA, of Slovak descent; an American singer-songwriter and musician. He gained fame as the lead singer of the glam metal band Poison who have sold over 40 million records worldwide and 15 million records in the United States alone. The band has also charted 10 singles to the Top 40 of the Billboard Hot 100, including six Top 10 singles and a number-one single, 'Every Rose Has Its Thorn.'
Bio: "Bret Michaels," in: Wikipedia. See - https://en.wikipedia.org/wiki/Bret_Michaels

Jason Mraz (1977-), b. Mechanicsville, VA, of Czech and Slovak ancestry; American singer and songwriter
Bio: "Jason Mraz," in: Wikipedia. See - https://en.wikipedia.org/wiki/Jason_Mraz

Melissa Newman (1961-), b. Hollywood, CA, of Slovak descent; an American pop singer, artist and actress
Bio: "Melissa Newman," in: Wikipedia. See - https://en.wikipedia.org/wiki/Melissa_Newman

Vladimir John Ondrasik (1965-), b. Los Angeles, CA, of Slovak paternal grandfather; an American singer, songwriter and record producer. He is best known for his piano-based rock, 'such as the top 40 hits, 'Superman (It's Not Easy)' (2001), '100 Years' (2003) and 'The Riddle" (2006).
Bio: "Five for Fighting (aka Vladimir John Ondrasik)," in: Wikipedia. See - https://en.wikipedia.org/wiki/Five_for_Fighting

Annie Parisse (1975-), b. Anchorage, AK, of Slovak descent; an American TV, film and theater actress.
Bio: "Annie Parisse," in: Wikipedia. See - https://en.wikipedia.org/wiki/Annie_Parisse

Neyla M. Pekarek (1986-), b. Denver, CO, of Slovak paternal grandfather; musician, singer and songwriter. She is the cellist and co-vocalist of the folk-rock band The Lumineers.
Bio: "Neyla Pekarek," in: Wikipedia. See - https://en.wikipedia.org/wiki/Neyla_Pekarek

Vlasta Průchová (1926-2006), b. Ružomberok, Czech.; Czech. jazz singer, mother of the renowned American pianist and composer Jan Hammer; in 1968, she and her family moved to the US;
Bio: "Vlasta Průchová," in: Wikipedia. See - https://en.wikipedia.org/wiki/Vlasta_Průchová

Chip Taylor (orig. James Wesley Voight) (1940-), b. Yonkers, NY, of Slovak descent, brother of actor Jon Voight; American songwriter, noted for writing Angel of the Morning" and "Wild Thing."
Bio: "Chip Taylor," in: Wikipedia. See - https://en.wikipedia.org/wiki/Chip_Taylor

8. Music Record Producers

Joe Bihari (1925-2013), b. Memphis, TN, of Slovak mother; co-founder of Modern Records, the Los Angeles-based record company that discovered such rhythm-and-blues performers as B.B. King, Etta James and Ike Turner.
Bio: "Joe Bihari, pioneering blues record producer who discovered B.B. King, dies at 88," *The Washington Post,* December 11, 2013; "Bihari brothers," in: Wikipedia. See - https://en.wikipedia.org/wiki/Bihari_brothers

John-Paul Kaplan (1982-), b. of Slovak parents; American record producer, composer, pianist
Bio: "John-Paul Kaplan," in: Wikipedia. See - https://en.wikipedia.org/wiki/John-Paul_Kaplan

9. Music Instrument Manufactures

John Dopyera (orig. Dopjera) (1893-1988), b. Šaštín-Stráže, Slovakia; inventor of a new Dobro resonator guitar
Bio: "John Dopyera," in: Wikipedia. See - https://en.wikipedia.org/wiki/John_Dopyera; "John Dopyera's guitar legend lives on," The Slovak Spectator, October 9, 2001.

John Rudolph Janac (1913-1981), b. Slovakia; music instrument manufacturer; partner of White Eagle Rawhide Mfg. Co. (WERCO), Chicago (1944-67), president and owner (s. 1967)
Bio: "Janac, John Rudolph," in: *Who's Who in the Midwest*,14

Martin Klema (1976-), b.Ilava, Slovakia; acoustic guitar maker
Bio: "Martin Klema," in: Klema Guitars. See - http://www.klemaguitars.com/en/martin-klema

Carl Toth (1905-1958), b. Krásno pod Kysucou, Slovakia; in Canada s. 1925, settling in Toronto; gypsy fiddler and master cabinet maker; made 10 cimbaloms (dulcimers), modifying traditional design and also a few violins; founder of Carl Toth Gypsy orchestra, Toronto.
Bio: "Carl Toth," in: The Canadian Encyclopedia. See - https://www.thecanadianencyclopedia.ca/en/article/carl-toth

10. Music Promoters and Producers

Jim Koplik (fl. 2007), b. New Rochelle, NY, of Slovak descent; American concert promoter. He has produced shows by The Rolling Stones, Paul McCartney, Bruce Springsteen, REO Speedwagon, Madonna, Billy Joel and Elton John, among others.
Bio: "Jim Koplik," in: Wikipedia. See - https://en.wikipedia.org/wiki/Jim_Koplik

G. DRAMATIC ARTS

1. Surveys

Czech and Slovak Theatre Abroad: in the USA, Canada, Australia and England Boulder, CO: East European Monographs and New York: East European Monographs, 2006
Tybor, M. Martina, "Slovak-American Theater," in: *Ethnic Theater in the United States*. Ed. Maxine Schwartz Seller. Westport, CT: Greenwood Press, 1983, pp. 447-90.

2. Actors

Camren Bicondova (1999-), b. San Diego, CA, of Slovak descent; an American actress and dancer. Bicondova is a series regular on the Fox television show Gotham, where she portrays a young Selina Kyle / Catwoman.
Bio: "Camren Bicondova," in; Wikipedia. See - https://en.wikipedia.org/wiki/Camren_Bicondova

Jessica Biel (1982-), b. American actress, model, producer, singer
Bio: "Jessica Biel," in: Wikipedia. See - https://en.wikipedia.org/wiki/Jessica_Biel

Marc Blucas (1972-), b. Butler, PA, of Slovak descent; an American actor, known for playing Riley Finn in Buffy the Vampire Slayer, Matthew Donnelly in Necessary Roughness and recently, abolitionist John Hawkes in Underground.
Bio: "Marc Blucas," in: Wikipedia. See - https://en.wikipedia.org/wiki/Marc_Blucas

David Boreanaz (1969-), b. Buffalo, NY, of Slovak descent; American actor, producer and director, known for playing the roles of vampire-turned-private investigator Angel on Buffy the Vampire Slayer (1997–2003) and its spinoff Angel (1999–2004).
Bio: "David Boreanaz," in: Wikipedia. See - https://en.wikipedia.org/wiki/David_Boreanaz

Jim Caviezel (1968-), b. Mount Vernon, WA, his paternal grandmother was of Slovak descent; film actor
Bio: "Jim Caviezel," in: Wikipedia. See - https://en.wikipedia.org/wiki/Jim_Caviezel

Akexandra Chando (1986-), b. Bethlehem, PA, of Slovak descent;_an American actress. She is known for her role as Maddie Coleman in the CBS soap opera, As the World Turns and for her dual role as identical twins, Emma Becker and Sutton Mercer in the ABC Family drama series, The Lying Game.
Bio: "Alexandra Chando," in: Wikipedia. See - https://en.wikipedia.org/wiki/Alexandra_Chando

Scarlett Chorvat (1972-), b. Bratislava, Czech.; American actress. She started playing tennis semi-professionally at the age of 15, but moved on to become a model, and finally an actress. She is best known as a model, counting numerous covers of magazines, advertising and TV commercials.
Bio: "Scarlett Chorvat," in: Wikipedia. See - https://en.wikipedia.org/wiki/Scarlett_Chorvat

Carrie Coon (1981-), b. Copley, OH, of Slovak descent; American actress. Coon is best known for starring as Nora Durst in the HBO drama series The Leftovers (2014–2017), for which she received widespread critical acclaim, winning a Critics' Choice Television Award for Best Actress in a Drama Series.
Bio: "Carrie Coon," in: Wikipedia. See - https://en.wikipedia.org/wiki/Carrie_Coon

Jamie Lee Curtis (1958-), b. Santa Monica, CA, of Slovak descent, a daughter of Tony Curtis; an American actress and author.
Bio: "Jamie Lee Curtis," in: Wikipedia. See - https://en.wikipedia.org/wiki/Jamie_Lee_Curtis

Tony Curtis (orig. Bernard Schwartz) (1925-2010), b. Bronx, NYC, of Slovak ancestry; film actor. His career spanned six decades but who achieved the height of his popularity in the 1950s and early 1960s. He acted in more than 100 films in roles covering a wide range of genres, from light comedy

to serious drama. In his later years, Curtis also made numerous television appearances.
Bio: "Tony Curtis," in: Wikipedia. See - https://en.wikipedia.org/wiki/Tony_Curtis; "Tony Curtis," in" find A Grave. See - https://www.findagrave.com/memorial/59410614/tony-curtis

Alexandra Anna Daddario (1986-), b. New York, NY, of Slovak ancestry; film actrees
Bio: Rechcigl, Miloslav, Jr., "Alexandra Anna Daddario," in: *Encyclopedia of Bohemian and Czech-American Biography*, Bloomington, IN: AuthorHouse, 2016, Vol. 2, p. 734; "Alexandra Daddario," in: Wikipedia. See - https://en.wikipedia.org/wiki/Alexandra_Daddario; Woodhall, Alex, "Woman of the Week: Alexandra Daddario," *The Gentleman's Journal*, United Kingdom, February 21, 2016.

Matthew Daddario (1987-), b. New York, NY, of Slovak ancestry; actor
Bio; "Matthew Daddario," in: Wikipedia. See - https://en.wikipedia.org/wiki/Matthew_Daddario

Paul Dano (1984-), b. Manhattan, NYC, NY, of Slovak and Czech ancestry; American actor and producer, director, screenwriter, musician
Bio: "Paul Dano," in: Wikipedia. See - https://en.wikipedia.org/wiki/Paul_Dano

Brant Daugherty (1985-), b. Mason, OH, of Slovak descent; an American actor, known for his recurring role as Noel Kahn on the teen drama television series, Pretty Little Liars.
Bio: "Brant Daugherty," in: Wikipedia. See - https://en.wikipedia.org/wiki/Brant_Daugherty

Nikita Denise (1976-), b. Czech.; a Slovak pornographic actress; in Canada s. 1998. Denise has appeared in over 400 movies, and has won several adult industry awards, including the AVN Female Performer of the Year Award in 2002.
Bio: "Nikita Denise," in: Wikipedia. See - https://en.wikipedia.org/wiki/Nikita_Denise

Lya De Putti (1897-1931), b. Vojčice, Slovakia; film actress of the silent era, noted for her portrayal of vamp characters; in US s. 1926.
Bio: "Lya De Putti," in: Wikipedia. See - https://en.wikipedia.org/wiki/Lya_De_Putti

Charles Esten (1965-), b. Pittsburgh, Pa, of Slovak descent; known professionally as Chip Esten and Charles Esten, is an American actor, singer and comedian.
Bio: "Charles Esten," in: Wikipedia. See - https://en.wikipedia.org/wiki/Charles_Esten

Patrick Joseph Fabian (1964-), b. Pittsburgh, PA, of Slovak paternal grandfather; American film, stage and TV actor. He is best known for his role on Better Call Saul as Howard Hamlin. His film roles include End Game (2006), The Last Exorcism (2010), Pig (2011) and Jimmy (2013).
Bio: "Patrick Fabian," in: Wikipedia. See - https://en.wikipedia.org/wiki/Patrick_Fabian

Oakes Fegley (2004-), b. Pennsylvania, of Slovak descent; American child actor. He is known for his supporting role as Paul Swann in the film Fort Bliss, for playing Samaritan's human avatar Gabriel in the series Person of Interest, and for starring as Pete in the 2016 Disney film Pete's Dragon.
Bio: "Oakes Fegley," in: Wikipedia. See - https://en.wikipedia.org/wiki/Oakes_Fegley

Hans Feher (1922-1958), b. Vienna, of Slovak ancestry; actor
Bio: Rechcigl, Miloslav, Jr., "Hans Feher," in: *Encyclopedia of Bohemian and Czech-American Biography*, Bloomington, IN: AuthorHouse, 2016, Vol. 2, p. 736.

Tibor Feldman (1947-), b. Slovakia, of Czech-Jewish descent, is an American actor, having played roles in movies, television shows, television commercials, and stage plays
Bio: "Tibor Feldman," in *Encyclopedia*, Vo. 2, p. 766

Willie Garson (orig. William Garson Paszaman) (1964-), b. Highland Park, NJ, of Slovak descent; an American actor. He has appeared in over 75 films, and more than 300 TV episodes. He is known for playing Stanford Blatch on the HBO series Sex and the City and in the related films Sex and

the City and Sex and the City 2, and for his role as Mozzie, in the USA Network series White Collar from 2009 to 2014. He appears on Hawaii Five-0 as Gerard Hirsch.
Bio: "Willie Garson," in: Wikipedia. See - https://en.wikipedia.org/wiki/ Willie_Garson

Michael Gladis (1977-), b. Houston, TX, of Slovak descent, an American actor. He played Paul Kinsey in the television series Mad Men; he appeared in the series' first three seasons, and as a guest star in the show's fifth season.
Bio: "Michael Gladis," in: Wikipedia. See - https://en.wikipedia.org/wiki/ Michael_Gladis

Sean Grandillo (1992-), b. Cleveland, OH, of Slovak descent; an American actor, singer and musician, known for his roles as the Voice of Otto in the 2015 Broadway revival of Spring Awakening, Eli Hudson in MTV's horror series Scream, and Brett Young in ABC's comedy series The Real O'Neals.
Bio: "Sean Grandillo," in: Wikipedia. See - https://en.wikipedia.org/wiki/ Sean_Grandillo

Anna Gunn (1968-), b. Santa Fe, NM, of Slovak descent; an American actress. She is best known for her role as Skyler White on the AMC drama series Breaking Bad, for which she won the Primetime Emmy Award for Outstanding Supporting Actress in a Drama Series in 2013 and 2014.
Bio: "Anna Gunn," in: Wikipedia. See - https://en.wikipedia.org/wiki/ Anna_Gunn

James Haven (orig. James Haven Voight) (1973-), b. Los Angeles, CA, of Slovak ancestry; American actor and producer
Bio: "James Haven," in: Wikipedia. See - https://en.wikipedia.org/wiki/ James_Haven

Glenne Headly (1955-2017), b. New London, CT, of Slovak descent; an American actress. She was widely known for her roles in Dirty Rotten Scoundrels, Dick Tracy, and Mr. Holland's Opus. Headly received a Theatre World Award and four Joseph Jefferson Awards and was nominated for two Primetime Emmy Awards.
Bio: "Glenne Headly," in: Wikipedia. See - https://en.wikipedia.org/wiki/ Glenne_Headly

Audrey Hepburn (1929-1993), b. Ixelles, Belgium, of Czech and Slovak descent; actress, model, dancer
Bio: "Audrey Hepburn," in: Wikipedia. See - https://en.wikipedia.org/wiki/Audrey_Hepburn

Steve Ihnat (1934--1972), b. Jastrabie pri Michalovciach, Czech.; American actor and director. He immigrated to Canada when he was five years old, and later became a United States citizen.
Bio: "Steve Ihnat," in: Wikipedia. See - https://en.wikipedia.org/wiki/Steve_Ihnat

Milan Jablonsky (1935-), b. Oravské Veselé, Czech.; trained as a physical educator and a coach; he defected with his wife in 1969 to Canada, after the Soviet troops invaded Czechoslovakia; became an actor, resides in Ottawa.
Bio: "Milan Jablonsky," in: LinkedIn. See - https://www.linkedin.com/in/milan-jablonsky-548b5667/

Lisa Jakub (1978-), b. Toronto, Ont., Canada, of Slovak descent; Canadian actress and writer, speaker, yoga teacher
Bio: "Lisa Jakub," in: Wikipedia. See - https://en.wikipedia.org/wiki/Lisa_Jakub

Cameron Jebo (1990-), b. Santa Clara, CA, of Slovak descent, his mom's grandfather (Robert Andrew Dopyera) was born in Krupá, Slovakia; American actor
Bio: "Cameron Jebo," in: ethnicelebs. See - http://ethnicelebs.com/cameron-jebo; "Cameron Jebo," in: LinkedIn. See - https://www.linkedin.com/in/cameron-jebo-b6674b14/

Jenteal (1976-), b. Oklahoma, of Czech and Slovak descent; former American pornographic actress
Bio: "Jenteal," in: Wikipedia. See - https://en.wikipedia.org/wiki/Jenteal

Angelina Jolie (orig. Angelina Jolie Voight) (1975-), b. Los Angeles, CA, of Slovak and Czech ancestry; actress, filmmaker, humanitarian
Bio: "Angelina Jolie," in: Wikipedia. See -https://en.wikipedia.org/wiki/Angelina_Jolie

iJustine (née Justine Ezarik) (1984-), b. Pittsburgh, PA, of Slovak descent; American comedian, internet personality, actress, model and TV host
Bio: "iJustine," in: Wikipedia. See - https://en.wikipedia.org/wiki/IJustine

Bianca Kajlich (1977-), b. Seattle, WA, of Slovak father and Italian mother; TV and film actress
Bio: "Bianca Kajlich," in: Wikipedia. See - https://en.wikipedia.org/wiki/Bianca_Kajlich

Adriana (Sklenaříková) Karembeu (1971-), b. Brezno, Czech.; fashion model and actress
Bio: "Adriana Karembeu," in: Wikipedia. See - https://en.wikipedia.org/wiki/Adriana_Karembeu

Charles Korvin (1907-1998), b. Piešťany, Slovakia; film, television and stage actor, in US s. 1940
Bio: "Charles Korvin," in: Wikipedia. See - https://en.wikipedia.org/wiki/Charles_Korvin

Ernie Kovacs (1919-1962), b. Trenton, NJ, of Slovak descent; an American comedian, actor, and writer.
Bio: "Ernie Kovacs," in: Wikipedia. See - https://en.wikipedia.org/wiki/Ernie_Kovacs

Harley Jane Kozak (1957-), b. Wilkes-Barre, PA, of Slovak descent; American actress and author
Bio: "Harley Jane Kozak," in: Wikipedia. See - https://en.wikipedia.org/wiki/Harley_Jane_Kozak

Candace Kroslak (1978-), b. Chicago, IL, of Slovak descent; American actress
Bio: "Candace Kroslak," in: Wikipedia. See - https://en.wikipedia.org/wiki/Candace_Kroslak

Peter Lorre (orig. Löwenstein) (1904-1964), b. Ružomberok, Slovakia; actor
Bio: "Peter Lorre," in: Wikipedia. See - https://en.wikipedia.org/wiki/Peter_Lorre; French, Philip, "Peter Lorre: a great screen actor remembered,"

The Observer, August 31, 2014; Youngkin, Stephen D., *The Lost One: A Life of Peter Lorre*. University Press of Kentucky, 2005; 'Boles, William C., "Lorre, Peter," in: *National Biography*, Vl. 13, pp. 929-930.

Paul Lukas (1894-1971), b. Budapest; resided in Košice; actor, specializing in comedy; winner of the Academy award for best actor (1943)
Bio: "Paul Lukas," in: Wikipedia. See - https://en.wikipedia.org/wiki/Paul_Lukas

Jes Macallan (née Jessica Lee Liszewski) (1982-), b. Sarasota, FL, of Slovak descent; an American actress. She is best known for her role as Josslyn Carver in ABC drama series Mistresses and Ava Sharpe in The CW superhero comedy-drama Legends of Tomorrow.
Bio: "Jes Macallan," in: Wikipedia. See - https://en.wikipedia.org/wiki/Jes_Macallan

Luba Mason (fl. 2018), b. Astoria, Queens, NY., of Slovak parents; American actress, jazz vocalist, songwriter and dancer. She has starred on Broadway, Off-Broadway, regional theaters in plays and musicals and television and film. As a singer, she has performed in International Jazz and Music Festivals as well as major jazz and music clubs around the country. Mason has trademarked her own musical format called Mixtura, "a blend of different musical currents.
Bio: "Luba Mason," in: Wikipedia. See - https://en.wikipedia.org/wiki/Luba_Mason; Orlando, Nick, "BWW Interviews: CAPEMAN's Luba Mason," in: Broadway World, August 3, 2010. See - https://www.broadwayworld.com/article/BWW-Interviews-CAPEMANs-Luba-Mason-20100803.

Allison McAtee (1980-), b. Erie, PA, of Slovak maternal grandmother; an American actress, best known for her role as Maggie Day in the Oprah Winfrey Network primetime soap opera, The Haves and the Have Nots and was promoted to the main cast in the fourth season.
Bio: "Allison McAtee," in: Wikipedia. See - https://en.wikipedia.org/wiki/Allison_McAtee

Ryan McCartan (1993-), b. Excelsior, MN, of Slovak descent; an American actor and singer. as an actor, he is known for his recurring role as Diggie on

the Disney Channel sitcom Liv and Maddie, and for his role as Brad Majors in the 2016 Fox musical television film The Rocky Horror Picture Show: Let's Do the Time Warp Again.
Bio: "Ryan McCartan," in: Wikipedia. See - https://en.wikipedia.org/wiki/Ryan_McCartan

Dash Mihok (1974-), b. New York, NY, of Slovak father; American actor
Bio: "Dash Mihok," in: Wikipedia. See - https://en.wikipedia.org/wiki/Dash_Mihok

Isabela Moner (2001-), b. Cleveland, OH, of Slovak descent; an American actress and singer
Bio: "Isabela Moner," in: https://en.wikipedia.org/wiki/Isabela_Moner

Brittany Anne Murphy (1977-), b. Atlanta, GA, of Italian, Irish and Slovak ancestry; American actress and singer
Bio: "Brittany Murphy," in: Wikipedia. See - https://en.wikipedia.org/wiki/Brittany_Murphy

Pola Negri (1897-1987), b. Lipno, Poland, of Slovak immigrant father (Juraj Chalupec); Polish and American stage and film actress during the silent and golden eras of Hollywood and European film
Bio: "Pola Negri," in: Wikipedia. See - https://en.wikipedia.org/wiki/Pola_Negri

Elinor 'Nell' Teresa Newman (1959-), b. New York, NY, of Slovak ancestry; child actress, environmentalist, biologist
Bio: "Nell Newman," in: Wikipedia. See - https://en.wikipedia.org/wiki/Nell_Newman

Melissa Newman (1961-), b. Hollywood, CA, of Slovak ancestry; screen actress, artist, singer
Bio: "Melissa Newman," in: Wikipedia. See - https://en.wikipedia.org/wiki/Melissa_Newman

Paul Newman (1925-2008), b. Shaker Heights, OH, of Slovak ancestry; actor, film director, producer, activist, race car driver
Bio: "Paul Newman," in: Wikipedia. See - https://en.wikipedia.org/wiki/Paul_Newman; Godfrey, Lionel, *Paul Newman Superstar: A Critical Biography.* New York, NY: St. Martin's Press, 1979; O'Brien, Daniel, *Paul Newman.* London, UK: Faber, 2004; Landry, J. C., *Paul Newman.* New York, NY: McGraw-Hill, 1983; Lax, Eric, 6). *Paul Newman: A Biography.* Atlanta, GA: Turner Pub., 1996.

Scott Newman (1950-1978), b. Cleveland, OH, of Slovak ancestry; film and TV actor, stuntman
Bio: "Scott Newman," in: Wikipedia. See - https://en.wikipedia.org/wiki/Scott_Newman_(actor)

Timothy Omundson (1969-), b. St. Joseph, Missouri, of Slovak descent; American actor. He is notable for his supporting roles as Sean Potter on the CBS television series Judging Amy, Eli on the syndicated series Xena: Warrior Princess, Carlton Lassiter in Psych, as King Richard on the musical series Galavant, and as Cain in Supernatural.
Bio: "Timothy Omundson," in: Wikipedia. See - https://en.wikipedia.org/wiki/Timothy_Omundson

Cameron Palatas (1994-), b. Los Angeles, CA, of Slovak paternal grandfather; American actor
Bio: "Cameron Palatas," in: Wikipedia. See - https://en.wikipedia.org/wiki/Nick_Palatas

Nick Palatas (1988-), b. Bethesda, MD, of Slovak descent; American actor.
Bio: "Nick Palatas," in: Wikipedia. See - https://en.wikipedia.org/wiki/Nick_Palatas

Annie Parisse (nee Cancelmi) (1975-), b. Anchorage, AS, of Italian, Slovak and Syrian ancestry; American television, film, and theater actress
Bio: "Annie Parisse," in: Wikipedia. See - https://en.wikipedia.org/wiki/Annie_Parisse

Robert Petkoff (1963-), b. Sacramento, CA, of Slovak descent; an American stage actor known for his work in Shakespearean productions and more recently on the New York City musical theater stage.
Bio: "Robert Petkoff," in: Wikipedia. See - https://en.wikipedia.org/wiki/ Robert_Petkoff

Joaquin Phoenix (orig. Joaquin Rafael Bottom)(1974-), b. San Juan, Puerto Rico, of Slovak descent; an American actor, producer and activist. For his work as an actor, Phoenix has received a Grammy Award, a Golden Globe Award and three Academy Award nominations.
Bio: "Joaquin Phoenix," in: Wikipedia. See - https://en.wikipedia.org/wiki/ Joaquin_Phoenix

Rain Joan of Arc Phoenix (née Bottom) (1972-), b. Crockett, TX, of Slovak descent; an American actress, musician and singer.
Bio: "Rain Phoenix," in: Wikipedia. See - https://en.wikipedia.org/wiki/ Rain_Phoenix

River Phoenix (orig. River Jude Bottom) (1970-), b. Madras, OR, of Slovak descent; American actor, musician, activist. Phoenix's work encompassed 24 films and television appearances, and his rise to fame led to his status as a "teen idol".
Bio: "River Phoenix," in: Wikipedia. See - https://en.wikipedia.org/wiki/ River_Phoenix

Danny Pintauro (1976-), b. Milltown, NJ, of Slovak decent; an American actor, best known for his role as Jonathan Bower on the popular American sitcom Who's the Boss? as well as his role in the 1983 film Cujo.
Bio: "Danny Pintauro," in: Wikipedia. See - https://en.wikipedia.org/wiki/ Danny_Pintauro

Pete Ploszek (1987-), b. Hinsdale, IL, of Slovak descent; an American actor. He is best known for his roles a Leonardo in the Teenage Mutant Ninja Turtles films.
Bio: "Pete Ploszek," in: Wikipedia. See - https://en.wikipedia.org/wiki/ Pete_Ploszek

Michael Rady (1981-), b. Philadelphia, PA, of Slovak descent; an American actor
Bio: "Michael Rady," in: Wikipedia. See - https://en.wikipedia.org/wiki/Michael_Rady

Vanessa Ray (née Liptak) (1981-), b. Livermore, Alameda, CA, of Slovak descent; an American actress and singer. She is best known for her role on Pretty Little Liars as CeCe Drake (Charlotte DiLaurentis), Jenny on the legal drama series Suits, Teri Ciccone on As the World Turns, and Officer Edit 'Eddie' Janko on Blue Bloods.
Bio: "Vanessa Ray," in: Wikipedia. See - https://en.wikipedia.org/wiki/Vanessa_Ray

Catherine Reitman (1981-), b. Los Angeles, CA, of Slovak ancestry; actress, film critic
Bio: "Catherine Reitman," in: Wikipedia. See - https://en.wikipedia.org/wiki/Catherine_Reitman

Stephanie Romanov (1969-), b. Las Vegas, NV, of Slovak descent; American actress and model
Bio: "Stephanie Romanov," in: Wikipedia. See - https://en.wikipedia.org/wiki/Stephanie_Romanov

Nick Roux (1990-), b. Los Angeles, CA, of Slovak descent; an American actor.
Bio: "Nick Roux," in: Wikipedia. See - https://de.wikipedia.org/wiki/Nick_Roux

Joseph Schildkraut (1896-1964), b. Vienna, of Slovak ancestry; stage and film actor
Bio: "Joseph Schildkraut," in: Wikipedia. See - https://en.wikipedia.org/wiki/Joseph_Schildkrauthttps://en.wikipedia.org/wiki/Joseph_Schildkraut

Lizabeth Scott (1922-2015), b. Scranton, PA, of Slovak descent; an American actress, known for her 'smoky voice' and being "the most beautiful face of film noir during the 1940s and 1950s.
Bio: "Lizabeth Scott," in: Wikipedia. See - https://en.wikipedia.org/wiki/Lizabeth_Scott

Thomas William Selleck (1945-), b. Detroit, MI, of Slovak descent; an American actor and film producer. He is known for starring as private investigator Thomas Magnum in the television series Magnum, P.I. (1980–1988) and as Peter Mitchell in Three Men and a Baby.
Bio: "Tom Selleck," in: Wikipedia. See - https://en.wikipedia.org/wiki/Tom_Selleck

Emil Sitka (1914-1998), b. Johnstown, PA, of Slovak descent; veteran American actor
Bio: "Emil Sitka," in: Wikipedia. See - https://en.wikipedia.org/wiki/Emil_Sitka; "Emil Sitka, Favorite Foil of 3 Stooges, Dies at 83," *The New York Times,* January 25, 1998.

Karl Slover (orig. Karl Kosiczky) (1918-2011), b. Prakovce, Slovakia; American actor best known as one of the Munchkins in The Wizard of Oz (1939). Diagnosed at an early age with pituitary dwarfism, Slover was barely two feet tall by his eighth birthday. When Slover was just nine years old, his father sent him to work for a traveling show based out of Berlin, Germany. After working with the show for several years, Slover moved to the United States where he joined another traveling show. It wasn't long before Slover began appearing in films like The Terror of Tiny Town, Block-Heads, Bringing Up Baby, and They Gave Him a Gun.
Bio: Karl Slover," in: Wikipedia. See - https://en.wikipedia.org/wiki/Karl_Slover

Magda Sonja (1886-1974), b. Hradisko, Slovakia, silent movie actress
Bio: "Magda Sonja," in: Wikipedia. See - https://en.wikipedia.org/wiki/Magda_Sonja

Martin Starr (orig. Martin James Pflieger Schienle) (1982-), b. Santa Monica, CA; an American actor and comedian. He is known for the television roles of Bill Haverchuck on the short-lived comedy-drama Freaks and Geeks (1999–2000), Roman DeBeers on the comedy series Party Down (2009–2010), and Bertram Gilfoyle in the HBO series Silicon Valley (2014–present), as well as for his film roles in Knocked Up (2007), Adventureland (2009) and Spider-Man: Homecoming (2017).
Bio: "Martin Starr," in: Wikipedia. See - https://en.wikipedia.org/wiki/Martin_Starr

Silvia Šuvadová (1975-), b. Ružomberok, Czech,; actress. She worked as a presenter and played in TV ads and TV movies. In 2002 she moved to Los Angeles.
Bio: "Silvia Šuvadová," in: Wikipedia. See - https://en.wikipedia.org/wiki/Silvia_Šuvadová

Angela Trimbur (1981-), b. Bucks County, PA, of Slovak descent; an American actress, comedian and dancer. She is best known for her role as Isabel in Trash Fire starring opposite Adrian Grenier, Tina the wild '80s party camp counselor in the horror comedy film The Final Girls (2015), and Penny Whitewall on FXX's animated series Major Lazer.
Bio: "Angela Trimbur," in: Wikipedia. See - https://en.wikipedia.org/wiki/Angela_Trimbur

Robert Urich (1946-2002), b. Toronto, OH, of Rusyn and Slovak ancestry; film, TV and stage actor, TV producer
Bio: "Robert Urich," in: Wikipedia. See - https://en.wikipedia.org/wiki/Robert_Urich

Apollonia Váňová (fl. 2018), b. Slovakia; raised nr Vancouver, BC, Canada; actress and opera singer, known for her roles as Silhouette in the film version of Watchmen and as the leading Wraith Queen and leader of a Wraith Alliance in the Stargate: Atlantis episode "The Queen". She played a role in ABC Family's Samurai Girl. She also played as Nadira, one of General Zod's Kryptonian soldiers in Man of Steel.
Bio: "Apollonia Vanova," in: Wikipedia. See - https://en.wikipedia.org/wiki/Apollonia_Vanova

Ingrid Veninger (1968-), b. Bratislava; Canadian actress, writer, director, producer, and film professor at York University. n 2011, she won the Toronto Film Critics Association's Jay Scott Prize for an emerging artist. In 2013, she won an EDA Award from the Alliance of Women Film Journalists at the Whistler Film Festival. The Globe and Mail dubbed Veninger 'The DIY Queen of Canadian Filmmaking.'
Bio: "Ingrid Veninger," in: Wikipedia. See -https://en.wikipedia.org/wiki/Ingrid_Veninger

Jon Voight (1938-), b. Yonkers, NY, of Slovak father; American actor, winner of one Academy Award, having been nominated for four, winner of four Golden Globe Awards, having been nominated for eleven
Bio: "Jon Voight," in: Wikipedia. See - https://en.wikipedia.org/wiki/Jon_Voight

Liz Tayler (1990-), b. Phoenix, AZ, of Slovak descent; American pornographic actress.
Bio: "Liz Tayler," in: Wikipedia. See - https://en.wikipedia.org/wiki/Lizz_Tayler

Apollonia Vanova, Slovakia; raised, nr Vancouver, BC, Canada; actress and opera singer.
Bio: "Apollonia Vanova," in: *Wikipedia*. See - https://en.wikipedia.org/wiki/Apollonia_Vanova

František Velecký (1934-2003), b. Zvolen, Czech.; Slovak actor; a particular figure of Slovak acting, being antipode to venerated mainstream showbiz celebrities. Although he had never received any formal training (in acting) he managed to earn a great respect of both filmmakers and audience members. He performed in some 50 Slovak, Czech, German, Hungarian and UK/US movies.
Bio: "František Velecký," in: Wikipedia. See - https://en.wikipedia.org/wiki/František_Velecký

Ingrid Veninger (1968-), b. Bratislava, Czech.; a Canadian actress, writer, director, producer, and film professor at York University
Bio: "Ingrid Veninger," in: Wikipedia. See - https://en.wikipedia.org/wiki/Ingrid_Veninger

Matt Wayne (1986-), b. York, PA, of Slovak ancestry; illusionist, producer and TV personality
Bio: "Matt Wayne," in: Wikipedia. See - https://en.wikipedia.org/wiki/Matt_Wayne_(magician)Helene

Gisela Werbezirk (1875-1956), b. Bratislava, Slovakia; actress, in US s. 1938; known for Jobbra én, balra te (1918), A Scandal in Paris (1946) and Frau Braier aus Gaya (1926).
Bio: "Gisela Werbezirk," in: Wikipedia. See - https://de.wikipedia.org/wiki/Gisela_Werbezirk

Devon Werkheiser (1991-), b. Atlanta, GA, of Slovak descent; American actor, voice actor, singer-songwriter and musician.
Bio: "Devon Werkheiser," in: Wikipedia. See - https://en.wikipedia.org/wiki/Devon_Werkheiser

Cornel Wilde (1912-1989), b. Prievidza, Slovakia; actor and film director
Bio: "Cornell Wilde," in: Wikipedia. See - https://en.wikipedia.org/wiki/Cornel_Wilde

Rebecca Wisocky (1971-), b. York, PA, of Slovak descent; American film, television and stage actress. She is best known for her role as Evelyn Powell in the Lifetime comedy-drama series Devious Maids.
Bio: "Rebecca Wisocky," in: Wikipedia. See - https://en.wikipedia.org/wiki/Rebecca_Wisocky

Devon Werkheiser (1991-), b. Atlanta, GA, of Slovak descent; an American actor, voice actor, singer, songwriter and musician.
Bio: "DevomWerkheiser," in: Wikipedia. See -

Winter Ave Zoli (1980-), b. New Hope, PA, of Slovak descent; an American actress and model, best known for her role as Lyla Winston in FX's TV series Sons of Anarchy.
Bio: "Winter Ave Zoli," in: Wikipedia. See - https://en.wikipedia.org/wiki/Winter_Ave_Zoli

Chris Zylka (orig. Christopher Michael Settlemire) (1985-), b. Warren, OH, of Slovak descent; an American actor and model
Bio: "Chis Zylka," in: Wikipedia. See - https://en.wikipedia.org/wiki/Chris_Zylka

3. Dancers - Choreographers

a. Groups

Czechoslovak Moravan Club of Binghamton, NY, founded 1935.
See - http://czechoslovakmoravianclub.com/wp/

Limbora Slovak Folk Ensemble of New York established in 1966.
See: http://www.limbora.szm.com/en.htm and https://www.facebook
.   c   o   m   /
fslimboranyc/?hc_ref=ARQFQXQHcWQKZh5rlk-x4sQOtKOsd_6LXQ
thg-M09nwekA_8GEXs1o4JovhI1-QHQdY&fref=nf&__xts__[0]=68.
ARDMjp-YYqvlsSvKtXBXUrzUzjJ5NOhVlmRypzFSoboNQDDqZ662H
oqVbMQYpTU97EWp6cELVTjYBF3kqiBHrsqVEyD2V793MlSaxneXW
P0OlE4JnPq34OxD1JcTBcHwT_gTl-k&__tn__=kC-R

Lučina Slovak Folklore Ensemble of Cleveland. Lučinka Children's Ensemble.
See: http://www.lucina.org

Pittsburgh Area Slovak Folk Ensemble (PÁS), Malý PÁS children's
Monroeville, PA.
See: http://www.pasfolkensemble.com/

Sarisan Slovak Folk Ensemble, Junior Sarisan Slovak Folk Ensemble, Detroit,
MI, director Milan Straka
See - https://www.sarisanusa.com

Slavjane Folk Ensemble, director Dean Poloka. A children's performing
ensemble that preserves the ethnic heritage of all Slavic heritages, esp.,
Carpatho-Rusyn music, song and dance.
See: https://www.facebook.com/Slavjane-177074242305419/

Toronto Slovak Dancers, Milan Popik, director.
See - http://www.slovak.com/toronto_slovak_dancers/

Veselica Slovak Folklore Ensemble, Chicago, IL; *Veselicka Children's Ensemble*.
See: http://veselica.com/

Vychodna Slovak Dancers, Toronto, Ontario.
See - http://www.vychodna.com/history/

b. Individuals

Thomas Ivanec (1949-), b. Cleveland, of Slovak ancestry; founder and director of Lučenec Folk Ensemble, and the children's Lučínka Golk Ensemble.
See - http://www.lucina.org/about.html

Jozef Jantoška (fl. 1990), b. Slovakia; actor, director, choreographer, Toronto Slovak Dancers.
See - http://www.slovak.com/toronto_slovak_dancers/

Gabriel de Korponay (1809-1866), b. near Košice, Slovakia; in US s. 1844; Colonel of a PA Regiment during the Civil War. Celebrated as a teacher of dancing; he was the first to introduce the Polka in the US, which then gained immense popularity.
Bio: "Gabriel de Korponay," in: The Philadelphia Dance History. See - https://philadancehistoryjournal.wordpress.com/tag/gabriel-de-korponay/

Angie Lipchick (1954 -), b. Pittsburgh, PA, of Slovak ancestry; director and choreographer of Pittsburgh Area Slovak Folk Ensemble; librarian at St. Maurice Catholic School
Bio: See - www.pasfolkensemble.com/about-paacutes.html

Florentina Lojeková (fl. 1973), b. Bratislava; primabalerina, choreographer; in 1968 came to Canada, joining the Canadian National Ballet. For 25 years she served as professor at Ryerson University in Toronto.
Bio: Gajdošová, Eva, "Florentina Lojekova - Life of a Ballerina Started in Bratislava," in: SND Balet. See - https://2001-2009.state.gov/outofdate/bios/s/2910.htm military

Nadia Oros (fl. 1992), b. Prešov, Slovakia; instructor/choreographer, Lučenec Folk Ensemble and the children's Lučínka Folk Ensemble; formerly with Slovak Folk Ensemble, 'ŠARIŠAN.'
Bio: See - http://www.lucina.org/about.html

Dean Poloka (1971-), b. Pittsburgh, of Slovak descent; choreographer of the Slavjane Folk Ensemble, a children's Slavic Dance Ensemble; researches Carpatho-Rusyn history, language, music, song and dance; host Rusyn Radio program on WPIT-AM.
Bio: See: https://www.riversofsteel.com/folklife-directory/results/dean-poloka/

Jack Poloka (1938-2010), b. Pittsburgh, PA, of Slovak descent; in 1959 founded Slavjane Folk Ensemble, a children's Slavic Dance Ensemble; hosted Rusyn Radio program on WPIT-AM; administrative manager at Equitable Gas Co.
Bio: See - https://triblive.com/x/pittsburghtrib/obituaries/news/s_672386. html; and http://www.legacy.com/obituaries/postgazette/obituary. aspx?n=john-poloka-jack&pid=140794986

Irena Prochotsky (1941-2003), b. Klagenfurt, Austria, of Slovak descent; ballet dancer, owner of Ballet School Bethesda, MD
Bio: "Prochotsky, Irena," in: *SVU Directory* 3; "Irena Prochotsky," in: Prabook. See - https://prabook.com/web/irena.prochotsky/180673

Thomas Schramek (1945-), b. Bratislava, Czech.; of Slovak descent; Canadian ballet artist, principal dancer with the National Ballet of Canada (s. 1973), principal character artist (s. 1990), assistant mallet master (2005-2010)
Bio: "Tomas Schramek Principal Character Artist," in: The National Ballet of Canada. See - https://national.ballet.ca/Meet/Dancers/Principal-Character-Artists/Tomas-Schramek

Pavel Smok (1927-), b. Levoča, Czech.; classical ballet dancer and choreographer trained at Prague State Conservatory
Bio: "Pavel Smok," in: *Encyclopedia*, Vol. 2, p. 770.

Matt Steffanina (1986-), b. Virginia, of Slovak descent; American choreographer, actor, entrepreneur
Bio: "Matt Steffanina," in: IDA Hollywood. See - https://www.idahollywood. com/mattsteffanina

4. Models

Justin Jedlica (1980-), b. Poughkeepsie, New York, to Slovak parents; model, known as the 'Human Ken Doll'; noted for multiple cosmetic surgeries
Bio: "Jedlica and the Art of Transformation, in: Sexuality - SBS. See - https://www.sbs.com.au/topics/sexuality/article/2016/05/31/justin-jedlica-and-art-transformation; "Justin Jedlica," in: Wikipedia. See - https://en.wikipedia.org/wiki/Justin_Jedlica;

Adriana Karembeu (née Sklenaříková) (1971-), b. Brezno, Czech.; fashion model and actress
Bio: "Adriana Karembeu," in: Wikipedia. See - https://en.wikipedia.org/wiki/Adriana_Karembeu

Michaela Kocianová (1988-), b. Trenčín, Czech.; a Slovak model. She won second place in the 2004 Elite Model Look Slovak fashion contest. She has since been featured in advertisements for Monique Lhuillier and Vivienne Westwood. She has appeared in magazines such as Italian Vogue, Velvet, Spanish Vogue, Elle, British Elle, Amica, and L'Officiel. In 2009, she became the face for Piazza Sempione, an Italian designer. She resides in New York, NY.
Bio: "Michaela Kocianova," in: Wikipedia. See - https://en.wikipedia.org/wiki/Michaela_Kocianova

Karolína Kurková (1984-), b. Děčín, Czech., of Czech father and Slovak mother; a Czech model and actress. She is best known as a former Victoria's Secret Angel and Vogue cover star. Vogue editor Anna Wintour called her the 'next supermodel.'
Bio: "Karolína Kurková," in: Wikipedia. See - https://en.wikipedia.org/wiki/Karolína_Kurková

Annalaina Marks (1983-), b. Erie, PA, of Slovak descent; American model, actress, and television personality. She is known for being a contestant on the third season of America's Next Top Model.
Bio: Annalaina Marks," in: IMDb. See - https://www.imdb.com/name/nm1856236/bio? ref_=nm_ov_bio_sm

Lucia Oskerova (fl. 2017), b. Bratislava; Slovak-Canadian model and actress. She became a Fashion Week star, walking for Dolce & Gabbana, Prada, Dior, Chanel, Fashion Rocks, Leone, Boboli and Vetrina. he was cast in several outstanding network TV series including Smallville, Battlestar Galactica, The Guard, Painkiller Jane, Very Bad Men as well as in the feature film National Lampoon. She now lives between Istanbul and Los Angeles where she continues her work as a model and actress.
Bio: "Lucia Oskerova," in: About. See - http://www.luciaoskerova.biz/about

Viera Schottertova (1982-), b. Topoľčany, Slovakia; a Slovak mode. Schottertova moved to Vienna after participating in the Elite Model Look Contest. From there her international career quickly took off and she featured on covers and editorials for magazines such as Elle, Marie Claire, DS, Vogue and major advertising drummer campaigns for Armani, Bernd Berger, Bolero, Chanel cosmetics, Custo Barcelona, Gant, Horizons, Lou lingerie, Mango, Marc Cain, Olivier Strelli, Red Point, Rimmel, Tag woman, TaiFun, Trixi Schober, Walter Leder, Women's Secret, Yera. She has also appeared in Victoria's Secret catalogs.
Bio: "Viera Schottertova," in: Wikipedia. See - https://en.wikipedia.org/wiki/Viera_Schottertova

Katarina Van Derham (1975-), b. Ľubochňa, Slovakia; American model, actress and publisher
Bio: "Katarina Van Derham," in: Wikipedia. See - https://en.wikipedia.org/wiki/Katarina_Van_Derham

5. Internet Personalities - YouTube Stars

David Dobrík (1996-), b. Košice, Czech.; YouTuber. He is known for his work on An Interrogation (2015), FML (2016) and Airplane Mode (2016). He has a successful channel on YouTube with over 6 million subscribers, where he posts vlogs about skits and his daily life.
Bio: "David Dobrik," in: IMDb. See - https://www.imdb.com/name/nm7228036/

Breanne Ezarik (1987-), b. Pittsburgh, PA, of Slovak descent; an American internet personality.
Bio: "Breanne Ezarik," in: ethnicelebs. See - http://ethnicelebs.com/breanne-ezarik

Jenna Ezarik (1989-), b. Pittsburgh, PA, of Slovak descent; an American internet personality
Bio: "Jenna Ezarik," in: ethnicelebs. See - http://ethnicelebs.com/jenna-ezarik

Gabrielle Jeannette Hanna (1991-), b. New Castle, PA, of Slovak descent; an American YouTuber, Viner, author, comedian, actress, singer, and songwriter. She has risen to fame through YouTube, gaining over 6,000,000 subscribers. She is known for her Youtube channel 'The Gabbie Show.'
Bio: "Gabbie Hanna," in: Wikipedia. See - https://en.wikipedia.org/wiki/Gabbie_Hanna

6. Directors. Producers

Martin Beck (1867-1940), b. Liptovský Mikuláš, Slovakia; vaudeville theater manager, owner, and impresario
Bio: Downer, Alan S., "Beck, Martin," in: *Dictionary of American Biography*, Suppl. 2, pp. 32-33; "Martin Beck Dies, Theatre Veteran," *The New York Times*, November 17, 1940; "Martin Beck (vaudeville)," in: Wikipedia. See - https://en.wikipedia.org/wiki/Martin_Beck_(vaudeville)

František Deák (1940-), b. Bratislava, Czech.; professor of department of theatre and dance (1974-94), dept. chair (1991-94), Dean, Division of Arts and Humanities (1994--2004), University of California, San Diego
Bio: "Deak, František," in: *Educators*, p. 6; "Frantisek Deak," UC San Diego Theatre & Dance People. See - http://www-theatre.ucsd.edu/people/faculty/emeritus/FrantisekDeak/index.htm

Ján Kadár (1918-1079), b. Budapest, of Slovak descent; film writer and director
Bio: "Kadar, Jan, in: *Who's Who in America*, 41; "Kadár, Ján," in: Wikipedia. See - https://en.wikipedia.org/wiki/Ján_Kadár; Hurd, Mary, "Kadar, Jan," in: *National Biography*, Vol. 11, pp. 326-327.

Milo Kubik (1929-2013), b. Čadca, Czech.; producer, founder of independent firm Animete Canada, later in charge of the Czech and Slovak program in Toronto
Bio: "Milo Kubik," in: *Encyclopedia*, Vol.2, p. 772.

Joseph Ondrejkovic (1890-1964), b. Turčiansky Sv. Martin, Slovakia; founder and director of the Slovak National Theater, Chicago, residing in Berwyn, IL
Bio: "Ondrejkovic, Joseph," in: Droba, pp. 224-225

Noam Pitlik (1932-1999), b. Philadelphia, PA, of Slovak ancestry; an American television director and actor. In 1979, Pitlik won an Emmy for Outstanding Directing for a Comedy Series for his work on the ABC sitcom Barney Miller.
Bio: "Noam Pitlik," in: Wikipedia. See - https://en.wikipedia.org/wiki/Noam_Pitlik

Bill Pohlad (1955-), b. Hennepin, MN, of Slovak ancestry; American film producer and director
Bio: "Bill Pohlad," in: Wikipedia. See - https://en.wikipedia.org/wiki/Bill_Pohlad

Gottfried Reinhardt (1913-1994), b. Berlin, Ger., of Bohemian and Slovak ancestry; film director and producer
Bio: Grimes, William, "Gottfried Reinhardt, 81, Film Director and Producer," *The New York Times*, July 21, 1994; "Gottfried Reinhardt," in: Wikipedia. See - https://en.wikipedia.org/wiki/Gottfried_Reinhardt

Max Reinhardt (1873-1943), b. Baden, near Vienna, of Bohemian and Slovak ancestry; theatre and film director, intendant and theatrical producer
Bio: "Max Reinhardt," in: Wikipedia. See - https://en.wikipedia.org/wiki/Max_Reinhardt

Ivan Reitman (1946-), b. Komárno, Slovakia; Canadian film producer and director
Bio: "Ivan Reitman," in: Wikipedia. See - https://en.wikipedia.org/wiki/Ivan_Reitman

Jason Reitman (1977-), b. Montreal, Canada, of Slovak ancestry; Canadian-American film director, screenwriter and producer
Bio: "Jason Reitman," in: Wikipedia. See - https://en.wikipedia.org/wiki/Jason_Reitman

Rick Sebak (1953-), b. Bethel Park, PA, of Slovak descent; American film director and producer; lives and works in Pittsburgh. Sebak is the creator of the "scrapbook documentary" genre, many of which he has created for WQED and PBS.
Bio: "Rick Sebak," in: Wikipedia. See - https://en.wikipedia.org/wiki/Rick_Sebak

Jaroslav Siakeľ (1896-1997), b. Blatnica, Czech.; resided in US s. 1912; film director and cameraman
Bio: "Jaroslav Siakeľ, in: Wikipedia. See - https://sk.wikipedia.org/wiki/Jaroslav_Siakeľ

Michael Sucsy (1973-), b. New York, NY, of Slovak descent; Golden Globe and Emmy Award-winning film director, screenwriter, and producer. He is best known for creating the HBO film Grey Gardens.
Bio: "Michael Sucsy," in: Wikipedia. See - https://en.wikipedia.org/wiki/Michael_Sucsy

Lee Unkrich (1967-), b. Cleveland, OH, of Slovak descent on his mother's side; an American director, film editor, screenwriter, and animator. He is a longtime member of the creative team at Pixar, where he started in 1994 as a film editor. He later began directing, first as co-director of 'Toy Story 2'.
Bio: "Lee Unkrich," in: Wikipedia. See - https://en.wikipedia.org/wiki/Lee_Unkrich

Ingrid N. Veninger (1968-), b. Bratislava, Czech.; multitalented filmmaker, producer, director, actor, writer
Bio: "Ingrid Veninger," in: The Canadian Encyclopedia. See - https://www.thecanadianencyclopedia.ca/en/article/ingrid-veninger/

Peter Zinner (1919-2007), b. Vienna, of Slovak ancestry; American filmmaker and producer
Bio: "Peter Zinner," in: Wikipedia. See - https://en.wikipedia.org/wiki/Peter_Zinner; "Zinner, Paul," in: Who's Who in America, 41

7. Video Makers

Michael Krivička (ca 1978-), b. Cifer, Slovakia; videographer; co-founder of Thinkmodo (s. 2011); founder and director of whoisthebaldguy (s. 2018)
Bio: "Michael Krivicka," in: LinkedIn. See - https://wd ww.linkedin.com/in/michaelkrivicka/; "His company earns $400K – $1Million for producing viral videos," in: The Viral Planet. See - https://theviralplanet.com/2017/12/03/his-company-earns-400k-1million-for-producing-viral-videos/amp/; "Michael Krivička," in: Digital RULEZZ.SK 2017. See -https://digital.rulezz.sk/2017/spikri/michael-krivicka

8. Screenwriters

Kent Osborne (1969-), b. New Jersey, of Slovak descent; an American screenwriter, actor, and producer for film and television. As a writer and storyboard artist for such animated television shows as SpongeBob SquarePants, Camp Lazlo, Phineas and Ferb, The Marvelous Misadventures of Flapjack, Adventure Time and Regular Show, he has received multiple Emmy Award nominations and has won twice for Adventure Time (in 2015 and 2017). He is currently the head writer for Cartoon Network's animated series Summer Camp Island, which premiered in 2018
Bio: "Kent Osborne," in: Wikipedia. See - https://en.wikipedia.org/wiki/Kent_Osborne

Beau Willimon (1977-), b. Alexandria, VA, of Slovak descent; an American playwright and screen writer. He is the creator of the Netflix original series House of Cards and served as showrunner for the first four seasons.
Bio: "Beau Willimon," in: Wikipedia. See - https://en.wikipedia.org/wiki/Beau_Willimon

9. Performing Arts Historians

Marinka Gurewich (1902-1990), b. Bratislava, Slovakia, of Bohemian ancestry; voice teacher and mezzo-soprano
Bio: "Marinka Gurewich, A Voice Teacher, 88," *The New York Times,* December 25, 1990;
"Marinka Gurewich," in: Wikipedia. See - https://en.wikipedia.org/wiki/Marinka_Gurewich;

H. Visual Arts

1. Architects

David Peter Baycura (1953-), b. Pittsburgh, Pa, of Slovak descent; landscape architect, real estate developer
Bio: "David Peter Baycura," in: Prabook. See - https://www.prabook.com/web/david_peter.baycura/141402

Titus de Bobula (1878-1961), b. Budapest, of Slovak descent; American architect; in US s. 1897, living and working at times in New York City and Marietta, Ohio. In 1903, he arrived in Pittsburgh, Pennsylvania, where he designed buildings for the next eight years. One of his major commissions was St. John the Baptist Greek Catholic Church in Munhall, Pennsylvania, patterned after the Rusyn Greek Catholic Cathedral of the Exaltation of the Holy Cross in Uzhhorod. The church's twin towers, which rise 125 feet, are composed of white brick in a Greek cruciform pattern set into sandstone. His last building in Pittsburgh was St. Peter and Paul Ukrainian Orthodox Greek Catholic Church in Carnegie, Pennsylvania.
Bio: "Titus de Bobula," in: Wikipedia. See - https://en.wikipedia.org/wiki/Titus_de_Bobula

Richard Bondy-Charvát (1893-1978), b. Trnava, Slovakia; agricultural engineer, politician, landscape architect, residing in Orange City, FL
Bio: "Bondy-Charvat, Richard O.," in: *SVU Directory* 3; "Bondy-Charvat, Richard O.," in: *Panorama,* p. 190.

Dana Čupková (fl. 2012), b. Slovakia; architect. She holds assistant professorship at the Carnegie Mellon School of Architecture and is a co-founder and design director of EPIPHYTE Lab, an architectural design and research collaborative. Cupkova was a founder and design director of DCm-STUDIO, an architectural design practice in New York City, and has extensive international professional experience in Europe, the United States, and Southeast Asia. She was previously in practice with Smith-Miller+Hawkinson Architects, RUR Architecture in New York City, and TR Hamzah & Yeang in Malaysia.
Bio: "Dana Cupkova," in: CMU School of Architecture. See - https://soa. cmu.edu/dana-cupkova/

John Gustav Gabriny (1923-2000), b. Rajec, Czech.; architect, Washington, DC
Bio: "Gabriny, Ivan," in: *SVU Directory* 7

Tomáš Gulíšek (ca 1970-), b. Slovakia; architect, registered in New York (s. 2000). He is a Design Principal with AE7. He is an internationally recognized designer who has worked in the US, Europe and MENA for over 17 years. Previous to AE7, Tomas was one of the founding Principals of the Burt Hill Dubai office and has been living in the MENA region for over 5 years.

Ladislav Hudec (1893-1958), b. Banská Bystrica, Slovakia; architect active in Shanghai from 1918 to 1945 and responsible for some of that city's most notable structures. After leaving Shanghai in 1947 Hudec moved to Lugano and later to Rome. In 1950 he moved to Berkeley where he taught at the University of California.
Bio: "László Hudec," in: Wikipedia. See - https://en.wikipedia.org/wiki/ László_Hudec; "Hudec: The Architect Who Made Shanghai, *"The Wall Street Journal,* September 7, 2010.

Peter Lizoň (1938-), b. Lučenec, Czech.; architect, professor of architecture, University of Tennessee, Knoxville;
Bio: "Lizoň, Peter," in: *SVU Directory* 8; "Peter Lizon," in: BIV. See -http:// web.utk.edu/~biv/biv_2003/lizon.html

Frank J. Machlica (1945-2015), b. Endicott, NY, of Slovak ancestry; architect, with Veterans Administration, Cincinnati, OH; US Air force in Dayton, OH and Camp Spring, MD; and US Navy, Washington, DC
Bio: "Machlica, Frank J.," in: *SVU Directory* 8; "In Memoriam: Francis J. Machlica, III," In: Archdiocese Denver. See - http://www.archdenmort.org/memsol.cgi?user id=1523012

Ricardo de Jaxa Malachowski (1887-d.), b. Prochorowa, nr Odessa, Ukraine, of Polish father and Slovak mother; a Peruvian architect; known as the main architect of Government Palace of Peru in Lima (1938).
Bio: "Ricardo de Jaxa Malachowski," in: Wikipedia. See - https://en.wikipedia.org/wiki/Ricardo_de_Jaxa_Malachowski

Ladislav Rado (1909-1993), Čadca, Slovakia; architect, partner of the firm Raymond Rado, New York City and Tokyo, Japan (1946-82)
Bio: 'Ladislav L. Rado; Architect, 84," *The New York Times*, October 29, 1993; "Ladislav Leland Rado," in: Prabook. See - https://prabook.com/web/ladislav_leland.rado/606091; "Rado, Ladislav Leland," in: *Who's Who in America*, 42

Emery Roth (1871-1948), b. Sečovce, Slovakia; architect; the founder of the New York architectural firm Emery Roth & Sons. Without formal training, he became one of New York's best-known architects. His buildings, characterized by rich Renaissance details, included the Belleclaire, San Remo, Normandy, Ritz Tower, St. Moritz, Drake, Dorset and Oliver Cromwell.
Bio: "Emery Roth," in: Wikipedia. See - https://en.wikipedia.org/wiki/Emery Roth; Ruttenbaum, Steven, *Mansions in the Cloud: The Skyscraper Palazzi of Emery Roth*. Balsam Press, 1986.

Julian Roth (1902-1992), b. Manhattan, NY, of Slovak descent; American architect. Following the death of his father, founder Emery Roth, he and his brother Richard took over at Emery Roth & Sons, one of the oldest and most prolific firms in New York City. National Real Estate Investor dubbed the brothers "New York's name-brand architects, designing much of Sixth

Avenue in the 1960s and 1970s." They were also a key contractor in building the World Trade Center.
Bio: "Julian Roth, "in: Wikipedia, See - https://en.wikipedia.org/wiki/Julian_Roth; "Julian Roth, 91, Dies; Architectural Designer," *The New York Times*, December 17, 1992.

Richard Roth (1905 -1987), b. Manhattan, NY, of Slovak descent, architect; chairman of the board of the firm Emery Roth & Sons. He guided the firm to a position of leadership in the design of more than 150 high-rise buildings and luxury hotels around the country. Most of them are in Manhattan, including the General Motors headquarters building on Fifth Avenue at 59th Street, the Park Lane Hotel on Central Park South and the Palace Hotel, a multi-use structure that incorporates a luxury hotel, apartments, stores, office space and the landmark Villard Houses on Madison Avenue, behind St. Patrick's Cathedral. Curtain Walls.
Bio: "Richard Roth Sr., 82, is dead," *The New York Times*, January11, 1987.

Emil Royco (1908-1996), b. St. Louis, MO, of Slovak descent; architect, Washington, DC
Bio: "Royco, Emil," in: *SVU Directory* 7

Andrew Steiner (1908-2009), b. Dunajská Streda, Slovakia; architect. During World War II, Steiner was a member of the Working Group, an illegal organization working to prevent deportations of Slovak Jews to extermination camps in Poland. After the Communist takeover in 1948, he emigrated with his family to Cuba, where he was offered the position of chief architect in an American design studio. In 1950 he settled in Atlanta in the USA. In the 1960s he became the manager of the area and town planning division at Robert and Company Associates, an architecture company based in Atlanta. He also taught at the university in Atlanta.
Bio: "Andrew Steiner," in: Wikipedia. See - https://en.wikipedia.org/wiki/Andrew_Steiner; "Endre Steiner," in: Brno Architecture Manual. See - https://www.bam.brno.cz/en/architect/37-endre-steiner

Eugene Sternberg (1915-2005), b. Bratislava, Slovakia; architect, Colorado
Bio: "Eugene Sternberg," in: Wikipedia. See - https://en.wikipedia.org/wiki/Eugene_Sternberg; "Sternberg, Eugene," in: Encyclopedia, Vol. 2, p. 918.

Stefan Andrew Yarabek (1952-), b. Dobbs Ferry, NY, of Czech and Slovak descent; landscape architect, president / owner, Hudson & Pacific Designs, Saugerties, NY
Bio "Czech Landscape Architecture - Reflections," in: Bohemian Benevolent Org. See - http://www.bohemianbenevolent.org/index.php/activities/view/czech-landscape-architecture; : "Yarabek, Stefan Andrew," in: *SVU Directory* 8

2. Painters

Adolf Benca (1959-), b. Bratislava, Czech.; painter, in US s. 1969
Bio: "Adolf Benca," in: Wikipedia. See - https://sk.wikipedia.org/wiki/Adolf_Benca

Jolan Gross Bettelheim (1900-), b. Nitra, Slovakia; artist, painter, active in New York, NY, resided in US from 1925-1956, working in the graphics art division of the works Progress Administration.
Bio: "Jolan Gross-Bettelheim,", in: Wikipedia. See - https://en.wikipedia.org/wiki/Jolan_Gross-Bettelheim; "Jolan Gross Bettelheim," in: SAAM. See - https://americanart.si.edu/artist/jolan-gross-bettelheim-390

Joseph Bodner (1925-1982), b. Florence Township, NJ, of Slovak descent; an American painter, illustrator. He often chose the vanishing West and white stallions as favorite subjects but his painting "The Resurrection of Jonathan," which was exhibited at the motion picture premiere of Jonathan Livingston Seagull, is probably his best-known work.
Bio: "Joseph Bodner," in: Wikipedia. See - https://en.wikipedia.org/wiki/Joseph_Bodner

Darina Boldizar (fl. 2015), Slovak Canadian, b. Košice, Slovakia; immigrated to Canada in 1980; after retiring from a successful real estate business, she became painter; oil painter
Bio: "Boldizar Darina," in: LinkedIn. See - https://www.linkedin.com/in/boldizar-darina-72a33ab9/; "Paintings of Darina Boldizar," in Kanadský Slovak. See - https://www.kanadskyslovak.ca/index.php/ottawa/events-in-ottawa/723-paintings-of-darina-boldizar

Maurice Braun (1877-1941), b. Bytča, Slovakia; artist, landscape impressionist; one of the most popular California impressionist painters and one of the most popular artists in San Diego.
Bio: "Maurice Braun," in: Wikipedia. See - https://en.wikipedia.org/wiki/Maurice_Braun

Marta Brestovansky (1937-), b. Czech.; Pinter, residing in Orillia, Ont., Canada
Bio: Brestovansky, Marta," in: Artists in Canada - Canada.ca

Lydia Darvaš (1935-), b. Lošonec, Czech; artist, abstract and surrealistic painter, North Miami Beach, FL
Bio: "Darvaš, Lydia," in: *SVU Directory* 8; "Lydia Darvas," in: Darvas Art Studio / LinkedIn - See - https://www.linkedin.com/in/lydia-darvas-43524538/

Oskar Ember-Spitz (1892-1952), b. Spišská Nová Ves, Slovakia; painter, portraitist

Pavol Fallat (1908-), b. Bardejov, Slovakia; a portrait painter; administrator at Slovak Catholic Sokol, Passaic, NJ.
Bio: See - Bolecek, Dr. B.V. and Irene Slamka, *The Slovak Encyclopaedia*. New York: Slovak Academy, 1981, p. 49.

Joseph Gabanek (1923-2011), b. Budapest, grew up in Slovakia; painter, portraits and landscapes, Vancouver, Canada
Bio: "Gabanek, Joseph," in: *Encyclopedia*, Vol. 2, p. 818; "Joseph Gabanek Obituary," *Vancouver Sun,* November 26, 2011.

Ladislav Guderna (1921-1999), b. Nitra, Czech.; surrealist, painter, art teacher
Bio: "Ladislav Guderna," in: Wikipedia. See - https://sk.wikipedia.org/wiki/Ladislav Guderna, "Guderna, Ladislav," in: *SVU Directory* 4; Biography. See - http://www.ladislavguderna.com/biography/exhibitions.html

Charles H. Kellner (1890-1979), b. Košice, Slovakia; painter, Chicago
Bio: "Charles Kellner," in: askArt. See - http://www.askart.com/artist/Charles_H_Kellner/70727/Charles_H_Kellner.aspx; Kellner, Charles H." in: *Who's Who in American Jewry*. Vol. 1, p.315

Joe Klamar (1965-), b. Jasná, Slovakia; immigrated in 1987 to Canada; photographer. He is the chief photographer of the French agency Agence France-Presse for the Central Europe. His specialties include political events, memorial celebrations, and celebrities. In 2009 he won the first prize in the Czech Press Photo competition for Barack Obama picture in Prague.
Bio: "Joe Klamar," in: Wikipedia. See - https://cs.wikipedia.org/wiki/Joe_Klamar

Peter Kovalik (1956-), Czech., son of Tibor Kovalik; Canadian artist, painter, residing in Toronto
Bio: Keith Norman and Rebecca Robinson, *Say Nothing: Art of Tibor and Peter Kovalik*. Oakville, Ont., Canada: Mosaic Press, 1981; Hookey, Robert, *Tibor Kovalik, Peter Kovalik: Their Canadian Decade, 1968-1978*. Cambridge, Ont.: Friends of Good Books, 1978.

Tibor Kovalik (1935-), b. Poprad, Czech; Canadian surrealistic painter, designer and illustrator of children's books, recipient of awards, residing in Lac-Beaport, Quebec
Bio: "Tibor Kovalik," in: his website. See - http://www.tiborkovalik.com/personal.en.php; Keith Norman and Rebecca Robinson, *Say Nothing: Art of Tibor and Peter Kovalik*. Oakville, Ont., Canada: Mosaic Press, 1981; Hookey, Robert, *Tibor Kovalik, Peter Kovalik: Their Canadian Decade, 1968-1978*. Cambridge, Ont.: Friends of Good Books, 1978.

Mikuláš Kravjanský (1928-), b. Czech.; painter, designer, poet, residing in Ontario, Canada
Bio: "Mikulas Kravjansky," in" Park West Gallery. See - https://www.parkwestgallery.com/artist/mikulas-kravjansky

Andrew Leonard Lukachko (1927-), b. Czech.; watercolor painter, residing in Toronto, Canada (s. 1936).
Bio: "Lukachko, Andrew Leonard," in: Artists in Canada - Canada.ca

Frank Mikuska (1930-), b. Canada, of Slovak father; painter, residing in Manitoba, Canada
Bio: His interview, in: The Frank Mikuska Donation. See - https://www.umanitoba.ca/schools/art/content/galleryoneoneone/fm02.html

Vincent Mikuska (1956-), b. Manitoba, Canada; painter, abstract painter. residing, Manitoba, Canada
Bio: "Vincent Mikuska," in: his website, Vincemikuska. See - http:// vincemikuska.com/about/

Paul Moschcowitz (1873-1942), b. Giraltovce, Slovakia; artist
Bio: *American Jewish Year Book*, Vol. 6, p. 158.

John Ignatius Perl (1806-1972), b. Galanta, Slovakia; physician, surgeon, in US s. 1924, practicing in Chicago. At the age of 46, Dr. Perl took up painting as a serious avocation and on his first attempt at a major exhibition, his work was accepted into an Art Institute of Chicago watercolor show in 1942. He exhibited at the Art Institute in 1942, 1943, 1946 and 1948 and was best known for his scenes of Chicago. He had local gallery representation at a prominent Chicago gallery at that time called The Little Gallery on Delaware Pl. Dr. Perl was an important
Bio: "John I. Perl," in: Richard Norton Gallery. See - http:// richardnortongallery.com/artists/john-perl

Joseph Plavcan (1908-1981), b. Braddock, PA, of Slovak parents; an American painter and teacher.
Bio: "Joseph Plavcan," in: Wikipedia." See - https://en.wikipedia.org/wiki/ Joseph_Plavcan

Emil Purgina (1937-), b. Bratislava, Czech.; painter, graphic artist
Bio: "Purgina, Email," in: *SVU Directory* 8; Palko, Stefan, "Emil Purgina," in: his Website. See - http://www.emilpurgina.com/biography.html

Frank Reichenthal (1895-1971), b. Lehnice, Slovakia; artist, abstract expressionist.
Bio: "Reichenthal, Frank," in: *Who's Who in the East* 7; "Frank Reichenthal, an abstract artist," *The New York Times*, April 5, 1971.

Alvena Vajda Seckar (1915-), b. McMechen, WV, of Slovak immigrant parents; painter; activist
Bio: "Alvena V. Seckar," in: *Making It in America*. A Sourcebook on Eminent Ethnic Americans. By Elliot Robert Barkan. Santa Barbara, CA: ABC-CLIO, 2001, pp. 340-341.

By Elliot Robert Barkan. Santa Barbara, CA: ABC-CLIO, 2001, pp. 340-341; Gaboury, Fred, "Alvena Seckar, Walking the Path of Artistic Activism," *People's World*, March 7, 2003.

Zoltan Leslie Sepeshy (1898-1974), b. Košice, Slovakia painter, Bloomfield Hills, MI
Bio: "Sepeshy, Zoltan Leslie," in: *Catholic Who's Who*, 7 (1946-1947), p. 401; "Sepeshy, Zoltan," in: Who's Who in America; Houghton, James, "Zoltan Sepeshy Remembered," in: Traditional Fine Arts Online. See - http://www.tfaoi.com/aa/3aa/3aa226.htm

Koloman Sokol (1902-2003), b. Liptovský Sv. Mikuláš, Slovakia; painter, graphic artist, illustrator, Bryn Mawr, PA, later resided in Tucson, AZ
Bio: "Sokol, Koloman," in *SVU Directory* 7; "Koloman Sokol," in: Wikipedia. See - https://en.wikipedia.org/wiki/Koloman_Sokol; "Kolomon Sokol," in: Osobnosti.sk. See - https://www.osobnosti.sk/osobnost/koloman-sokol-1021; Simko, Vlado, "The Life of an Artist Exile." See - http://www.tfsimon.com/koloman-sokol.htm

Helena M. Stockar (1933-), b. Bratislava, Czech.; painter, illustrator,
Bio: "Stockar, Helena M., in: *SVU Directory* 8; "Helena M. Stockar. Life Story," in: WIX. See - http://helenamstockar.wixsite.com/artist/life-story; "Helena Marie Magdalena Stockar," in: Prabook. See - https://prabook.com/web/helena_marie_magdalena.stockar/773796;
Freeman, Matt, "Helena Stockar's art on exhibit in Kennett Square," Daily Local News. See - http://www.dailylocal.com/article/DL/20130727/NEWS01/130729725

3. Illustrators

Olivia Darvaš (1960-), b. Bratislava, Czech.; book illustrator, International Voyager Pub. Inc., Miami, FL
Bio: "Darvaš, Olivia," in: *SVU Directory* 8

Edward 'Ed' Ignatius Valigursky (1926-2009), b. Arnold, PA, of Slovak descent; American illustrator; freelance artist; an art director for Ziff-Davis Publications, NYC. He illustrated books for such publishers as Bantam Books, Ballantine Books, Lippincott, Macfadden Publications, and Time-Life Books.

In 1970s he was invited to NASA to illustrate the spectacular space program for *Popular Mechanics*, where he continued to work until the 1980s. After retiring from commercial illustration in the 1990s he began to produce fine art paintings that celebrated the history of aviation.
Bio: "Ed Valigursky (1926-200)," in: Pulp Artists. See - https://www. pulpartists.com/Valigursky.html

James Warhola (1955-), b. Smock, PA, of Slovak ancestry; illustrator of more than two-dozen children's picture books. Warhola has worked for several major publishing houses, among them Warner Books and Prentice Hall. He serves as a consultant to the Andy Warhol Museum of Modern Art in Medzilaborce, Slovakia, near the Warhola ancestral village of Miková.
Bio: "James Warhola," in: Wikipedia. See - https://en.wikipedia.org/wiki/ James_Warhola

4. Cartoonists - Comics Artists

Oscar Berger (1901-1997), Prešov, Slovakia; cartoonist in Prague, later in the US
Bio: "Berger, Oscar," in: *Who's Who in America*, 41; See Berger, Oscar, *Famous Faces; Caricaturist's Scrapbook*. London, Hutchinson. 1950;
Berger, Oscar, *My Victims. How to Caricature*. Harper & Bros. NY. 195
2; "Berger, Oscar," in: *Who's Who in the East* 12; "Oscar Berger (Cartoonist), in: Wikipedia. See - https://en.wikipedia.org/wiki/Oscar_Berger_(cartoonist)

Stephen J. Ditko (1927-), b. Johnstown, PA, of Ukrainian and Slovak ancestry; comic book artist and writer, co-creator of the Marvel Comics heroes Spider-Man and Doctor Strange
Bio: "Stephen J. Ditko," in: Wikipedia. See - https://en.wikipedia.org/wiki/ Steve_Ditko

John Sikela (1907-1996), b. Veľké Kozmálovce, Slovakia; cartoonist. Along with Wayne Boring, he was one of the most important and long-lasting ghost artists on Joe Shuster's *Superman* comic. He joined the studios in 1940, where he worked close with Joe Shuster, doing pencilling and inking work. His solo work featured dynamic panels with big aerial views. Later on, he was one of the main artists on the spin-off 'Superboy' series. After the introduction of

Superboy #1 in 1949, Sikela enjoyed a long run on the title through the latter half of the 1950s and also illustrated several stories for *Adventure Comics.*
Bio: "John J. Sikela," in: Superman Super site. See - http://www.supermansupersite.com/sikela.html

5. Graphic Designers

Zuzana Ličko (1961-), Bratislava, Czech.; type-designer, graphic designer, co-founder of the graphic design magazine *Emigre* and for creating numerous typefaces, including Mrs Eaves.
Bio: "Licko, Zuzana," in: Wikipedia. See - https://en.wikipedia.org/wiki/Zuzana_Licko

Pavel Liháni)1922-2008), b. Hňúšťa, Czech.; commercial and fine artist, graphic artist, poet, journalist, co-owner of Creative Aarts Studio and Terry Art Productions, Parma, OH
Bio "Liháni, Pavel," in: *SVU Directory* 8

Louis Madarasz (1860-1910), b. San Antonio, TX, of Slovak descent on his mother' side (Ujhazy); calligrapher; regarded as one of the most highly skilled ornamental penmen of all time.
Bio: Henning, William E., An Elegant Hand. *The Golden Age of American Penmanship and Calligraphy.* New Cattle, DE: Oak Knoll Press, 2002; "Louis T. Madarasz," in: Find A Grave. See - https://www.findagrave.com/memorial/135354941/louis-t.-madarasz; "Louis Madarasz," in: Wikipedia. See - https://en.wikipedia.org/wiki/Louis_Madarasz; Joseph M. Vitolo, *Louis Madarasz. His Life and Work.* See - http://www.zanerian.com/MadaraszHisLifeAndWorks.pdf

Julia Warhola (née Julia Justina Zavacká) (1891-1972), b. Miková, Slovakia; the mother of the American artist, Andy Warhol; in US s. 1921; amateur artist, illustrator, known for her decorative penmanship
Bio: Gabelmann, Grashina, "Julia Warhola the Mother," *Tissue,* No. 3, March 12, 2013. See - http://tissuemagazine.com/story/the-mother/; "Julia Warhola," in: Wikipedia. See - https://en.wikipedia.org/wiki/Julia_Warhola

6. Printmakers

Louis Novak (1903-1983), b. Žilina, Slovakia; printmaker, printer, teacher at Wentworth Institute in Boston
Bio: "Novak, Louis," in: *Who's Who in the East*, 9; "Louis Novak," in: BHNY Fine Art. See -http://www.bhnyfineart.com/artists/novak-2?letter=n ; "Biography of Louis Novak (1903-1983)," in: artprice. See - https://www. artprice.com/artist/44860/louis-novak/biography

7. Sculptors

Christina Kenton (fl. 2017), b. Vancouver, BC, Canada; of Slovak descent; a self-taught lighter/ mixed media artist, inspired heavily from her late surrealist grandfather Ladislav Guderna; surrealistic sculptor.
Bio: See - https://ompomhappy.com/home-tours/8250-2/

Gyula Košice (orig. Ferdiand Fallik) (1924-2016), b. Košice, Czech.; Argentine sculptor
Bio: "Gyula Kosice," in: Wikipedia. See - https://en.wikipedia.org/wiki/ Gyula_Kosice

Dalya Lutwak (fl. 2018), b. Northern Galilee, Israel, of Slovak immigrant parents; an Israeli-American sculptor, living in Chevy Chase, MD
Bio: Katzman, Laura, "A Meditation of Roots: The Sculpture of Dalya Lutwak." See: https://dalya-luttwak.squarespace.com/s/DalyaLuttwakLauraESSAY1. pdf

Zdeno Mayercak (1953-), b. Žilina, Czech.; came to US as a political refugee in 1985; sculptor; professor of art, Montgomery College, Rockville, MD
Bio: "Zdeno Mayercak," in: Saatchi art. See - https://www.saatchiart.com/ zdeno.mayercak; "Zdeno Mayercak," in: Prabook. See - https://prabook. com/web/zdeno.mayercak/777090

Lyuba Durdakova Prusak (1922-2010), b. Košice, Czech.; freelance artist, sculptor, teacher, Pacific Design Center, Melrose, CA
Bio: "Prusak, Lyuba Durdaková," in *SVU Directory* 8; "Lyuba Durdakova Prusak," in: Prabook. See - https://prabook.com/web/lyuba_durdakova. prusak/772441; "Lyuba Prusak," *Daily Herald*, February 18, 2010

Klára Katherina Sever (1935-), b. Trebišov, Czech.; sculptor, Falls Church, VA
Bio: "Sever, Klára Katherine," in: *SVU Directory* 8; "Klara Sever (née Klein)," in: NCSML Histories. See - https://www.ncsml.org/exhibits/klara-sever/

8. Decorative Artists - Craftsmen

Dale Chihuly (1941-), b. Tacoma, WA, of Slovak descent; American glass sculptor and entrepreneur
Bio: "Dale Chihuly," in: Wikipedia. See - https://en.wikipedia.org/wiki/Dale_Chihuly; Kuspit, Donald B., *Chihuly* (2nd ed.). Seattle: Harry N. Abrams, Inc.,1998

Moritz Fuerst (1782-1840), b. Pezinok, Slovakia; US Mint engraver, medalist. Prior to immigrating, he was enlisted by the American consul at Livorno, Italy, in 1807, and came to the United States to work as an engraver. In 1808 he settled in Philadelphia, where he set up business as a seal and steel engraver and die-sinker. He was subsequently employed by the United States Mint in Philadelphia and soon received recognition as an early American medalist. Thirty-three of his patriotic commemoratives and portraits, including his best-known work which honored heroes of the War of 1812, are still issued by the U.S. Mint. He struck the official portraits of Presidents James Monroe, John Quincy Adams, Andrew Jackson and Martin Van Buren.
Bio: "Moritz Fuerst," in: Wikipedia. See - https://en.wikipedia.org/wiki/Moritz_Fuerst

Tatiana Krizova Lizoň (1942-), b. Ústie nad Oravou, Czech.; freelance artist, artist craftsman, fiber and quilt artist, Knoxville, TN
Bio: "Lizoň, Tatiana Krizova," in: *SVU Directory,* 9

Greta Loebl (1917-2005), b. Vienna, of Slovak descent; Jewish jewelry designer and painter
Bio: "Loebl, Great," in: Wikipedia. See - https://en.wikipedia.org/wiki/Greta_Loebl

William 'Bill' Schiffer (1882-d.), b. New York, NY, of Slovak descent, artist, jewelry designer, NYC

Bio: "Bill Schiffer, New York City, NY" in: EBTH. See - http://billschifferjewelry.com/history.html

Sidonka Widona (ca 1985-), b. Milwaukee, WI, of Slovak descent; Slovak Master folk artist, graphic designer, egg decorator, straw weaver, and folk painter.
Bio: "Sidonka Widona," in: LinkedIn. See - https://www.linkedin.com/in/sidonka-wadina-2173643a/; "Sidonka Widona," in: United States artists. See - http://usartists.squarespace.com/fellows/2015/sidonka-wadina

Eva Striker Zeisel (1906-2011), b. Budapest, Hungary, of Slovak ancestry; in US s. 1938; industrial designer, ceramist, 'maker of useful things,' as she called herself
Bio: "Eva Zeisel," in: Wikipedia. See - https://en.wikipedia.org/wiki/Eva_Zeisel

9. Photographers

Talisman Brolin (ca 1982-), b. New York, NY, of Bohemian and Slovak descent; trained as a cultural anthropologist; commercial and documentary photographer with background in photojournalism. She has been owner, photographer, Talisman PHOTO LLC, NYC (s. 2004); co-founder / owner, Top Floor White Door, NYC (s. 2016).
"Talisman Brolin," in: LinkedIn. See - https://www.linkedin.com/in/talismanbrolin/

Yuri Dojc (1946-), b. Humenné, Czech., is a Slovak-Canadian fine arts photographer known for his portraits of Slovak World War II veterans from his Last Folio project. Dojc currently resides in Toronto, Canada but photographs internationally in countries such as Brazil, Slovakia, Rwanda as well as across Canada.
Bio: "Yuri Dojc," in: Wikipedia. See - https://en.wikipedia.org/wiki/Yuri_Dojc

Tibor Gasparik (1922-1993), b. Slovak descent; photographer, Cleveland, OH
Bio: "Tibor Gasparik," in: Find a Grave. See - https://www.findagrave.com/memorial/166112970/tibor-gasparik

Patrik Jandak (1977-), b. Malacky, Czech.;_a Slovak photographer; in Canada s. 2005. Since December 2001 till June 2004 he worked as official photographer to President of Slovakia Rudolf Schuster and since June 2004 till April 2005 as photographer of Slovak President Ivan Gasparovic. In Canada, he transformed form documentary photographer to studio portrait and Fine Art nude photographer. In October 2010 started publishing monthly photography magazine *PH Magazine*.
Bio: "Patrik Jandak," in: Wikipedia. See - https://en.wikipedia.org/wiki/Patrik_Jandak

Joe (Jozef) Klamár (1965-), b. Jasná, Slovakia. Emigrated in 1987 to Canada. Photographer for the Canadian Press Agency, the Slovak Press Agency TASR and Reuters. He returned to Slovakia in 1998 and since 2012 lives in Los Angeles and works for the French company Agence France Presse. His specialties include political events, memorial celebrations, and celebrities.
Bio: "Joe Klamar," in: Wikipedia. *See* https://cs.wikipedia.org/wiki/Joe_Klamar" ; "*Expat returns home," in: The Slovak Spectator. See - https://spectator.sme.sk/c/20045868/*expat-returns-home.html and https://www.facebook.com/

Béla J. Komorowicz (1913-1990), b. Košice, Slovakia; art and commercial photographer

Vivian Maier (1926-2009), b. Bronx, NY, of Slovak descent; an American street photographer. he took more than 150,000 photographs during her lifetime, primarily of the people and architecture of Chicago, New York City, and Los Angeles, although she also traveled and photographed worldwide. Her life and work have been the subject of books and documentary films, including the film Finding Vivian Maier (2013), which premiered at the Toronto International Film Festival, and was nominated for the Academy Award for Best Documentary Feature at the 87th Academy Awards.
Bio: "Vivian Maier," in: Wikipedia. See - https://en.wikipedia.org/wiki/Vivian_Maier

Duane Michals (1932-), b. Mc. Keesport, PA, of Slovak ancestry; American photographer. Michals's work makes innovative use of photo-sequences, often incorporating text to examine emotion and philosophy.
Bio: "Duane Michals," in: Wikipedia. See - https://en.wikipedia.org/wiki/Duane_Michals; "Duane Michals," in: artnet. See - http://www.artnet.com/artists/duane-michals/

Emiline Royco Ott, b. St. Louis, MO, of Slovak parents; photographer, residing in Chevy Chase, MD
Bio: "Otto, Emiline Royco," in: *SVU Directory* 8

Robert Vano (1948-), b. Nové Zámky, Czech.; photographer, in 1967 immigrated to US, since 1995 lives in Prague
Bio: "Robert Vano," in: Wikipedia. See - https://en.wikipedia.org/wiki/Robert_Vano

10. Mixed and Multi-Genre Visual Artists

Jozef Bajus (1958-), b. Kežmark, Czech.; award winning fiber and mixed media artist; associate professor of design and director of fiber program, Buffalo State College, NY.
Bio: "Jozef Bajus," in: Buffalo State Art and Design Department. See - http://artdesign.buffalostate.edu/faculty/jozef-bajus

Jozef G. Cincík (1909-1992), b. Clopodia, Rumania, of Slovak descent; painter, sculptor, graphic artist, scenographer, art historian
Bio: "Jozef Cincík," in: Wikipedia. See - https://sk.wikipedia.org/wiki/Jozef_Cincík_(maliar)

Vera Frenkel (1938-), b. Bratislava; Czech.; multidisciplinary artist, independent video artist, writer, first recognized as a printmaker and sculptor
Bio: The Canadian Encyclopedia. See - https://www.thecanadianencyclopedia.ca/en/article/vera-frenkel/

Ian Hornak (1944-2002), b. Philadelphia, PA, of Slovak descent; American draughtsman, painter and printmaker and one of the founding artists of the Hyperrealist and Photorealism art movements

Bio: "Ian Hornak," in: Wikipedia. See - https://en.wikipedia.org/wiki/Ian_Hornak

Ali Hossaini (1962-), b. West Virginia, of Slovak descent on his mother's side; video artist; an American artist, philosopher and businessperson, described as a 'biochemist turned philosopher turned television producer turned visual poet.' He has served as an executive in a number of media and technology-oriented businesses.
Bio: "Ali Hossaini," in: Wikipedia. See - https://en.wikipedia.org/wiki/Ali_Hossaini

Beata Pies (1956-), b. Bratislava, Czech.; freelance artist, painter drawing artist, graphic artist, tapestry artist, science artist
Bio: Pies, Beata," in: *SVU Directory* 8; Beata Science Art - Gallery. See - http://www.beatascienceart.com/gallery

Zuzana Rudavská (1962-), b. Bratislava, Czech.; textile designer, jewelry designer, graphic artist, painter
Bio: "Rudavská, Zuzana," in: *SVU Directory* 8; "Zuzana Rudavska," in: Prabook. See - https://prabook.com/web/zuzana.rudavska/783665

Ondrej Rudavský (1966-), b. Bratislava, Czech.; painter, graphic artist, sculptor, art photographer, animated film maker
Bio: "Rudavský, Ondrej,": in: *SVU Directory* 8; Ondrej Rudavsky's Website. See - http://www.ondrejrudavsky.com/' "Ondrej Rudavský," in: Wikipedia. See - https://sk.wikipedia.org/wiki/Ondrej_Rudavský

Tibor Spitz (1929-), b. Dolný Kubín, Czech., is a Jewish artist of Slovak origin and a Holocaust survivor. After escaping from communist Czechoslovakia to the West he lived and worked in Canada and the United States. Currently he lives in Kingston, New York. Besides painting he has been also sculpting, making ceramics, woodcarvings and wood burnings. When he discovered that impressionists have not fully exhausted all their artistic possibilities, his painting techniques gradually gravitated toward pointillism and neo-impressionism. Besides initial hounding faces and figurative scenes associated

with Holocaust, Judaism and Jewish mystical teachings Kabbalah, he also added fishing scenes, musicians, horses, still-life and landscapes.
Bio: "Tibor Spitz," in: Wikipedia. See - https://en.wikipedia.org/wiki/Tibor_Spitz

John Regis Tuska (1931-1998), b. Yukon, PA, of Slovak descent; ceramist, painter, sculptor, papier-macheist, and art historian, Tuska cast himself as a teacher who created art along the way.
Bio: "A True Renaissance Man," in: Tuska Biography. See - http://www.tuska.com/tuska.html

Andy Warhol (orig. Andrew Warhola) (1928-1987), b. Pittsburgh, PA, of Lemko Rusyn parents of Slovakia; artist in variety of media, including painting, silk-screening, photography, film and sculpture
Bio: "Andy Warhol," in: Wikipedia. See - https://en.wikipedia.org/wiki/Andy_Warhol; Bockris, C. Victor, *Warhol: The Biography*. New York: De Capo Press, 1997; Danto, Arthur C., *Andy Warhol*. New Haven: Yale University Press, 2009.

Thomas R. Yanosky (1918-2014), b. Colver, PA, of Slovak parents; cartographer by trade, a noted artist whose media included etchings, oils, acrylics, constructions, watercolors and collages, Herndon, VA
Bio: "Yanosky, Thomas R.," in: *SVU Directory* 8; "Artist biography". See - http://www.severnart.com/tombio.html; "Thomas Yanosky Obituary," *The Washington Post*, September 7, 2014

11. Pop Artists

Bozidor Brazda (1972-), b. Cambridge, Canada, of Slovak descent; the grandson of the award-winning journalist Andrej Brázda-Jankovský. He is an artist living in New York City. Brazda's work consists of silk screens, wall texts, and audio recordings. In recent years the artist has moved away from his earlier "narrative-driven" installations to a minimalist Pop Art that reflects his continued interest in the 'edges of popular culture.' His work has appeared in purple.com, Artforum, Flash Art, artnet.com, The New York Times, Architectural Digest (France), Art in America, Interview Magazine

and Maximum Rock N Roll. Brazda plays in the post-punk band TXTR with model and singer Ruby Aldridge.
Bio: "Bozidar Brazda," in: Wikipedia. See - https://en.wikipedia.org/wiki/Bozidar_Brazda

Andy Warhol (orig. Andrew Warhola) (1928-1987), b. Pittsburgh, PA, of Slovak descent; artist, a leading figure in the visual art movement known as pop art
Bio: "Andy Warhol," in: Wikipedia. See - https://en.wikipedia.org/wiki/Andy_Warhol

12. Art Directors

Želmíra "Myra" Hatala (1942-2013), b. Michalovce, Czech.; graphic artist, fashion designer, in art advertising and printing, art director, *The Washington Post*
Bio: "Hatala, Želmíra Anna," in: *SVU Directory* 8; "Obituary: Zelmira A. Hatala," in: Dignity Memorial. See - https://www.dignitymemorial.com/en-ca/obituaries/arlington-va/zelmira-hatala-5478802; Obituaries: Zelmira 'Myra' Hatala, ad executive," The Washington Post, May 8, 2013.

Pavel Lihani (1922-2008); b. Hnúšťa, Czech.; artist and writer, co-owner of Creative Arts Studio and Terry art Production, Cleveland, OH
Bio: "Lihani, Pavel" in: *SVU Directory*, 9; "Pavel Lihani," in: Find A. Grave. See - https://www.findagrave.com/memorial/166725092/pavel-lihani

Zlata W. Pačes (1925-2013), b. Čierna Lehota, Czech.; vice president of design and production, Macmillan Educational Publishing, New York, NY
Bio: "Pačes, Zlata W." in: *SVU Directory* 8; "Zlata Paces," in: Find A Grave. See - https://www.findagrave.com/memorial/165049874/zlata-paces

13. Art Historians

Joseph C. Cincik (1909-1992)-, b. Clopodia, Romania, of Slovak descent; painter, sculptor, graphic artist, historian of fine arts, archeologist.
Bio: "Cincik, Joseph," in: *American Scholars,* 4, Vol. 1; "Jozef Cincik," in: Wikipedia. See - https://sk.wikipedia.org/wiki/Jozef_ Cincík_(maliar)

Mildred Constantine (orig. Mildred Constantine Bettelheim) (1913-2008), b. Brooklyn, NY, of Slovak descent; an American curator, who helped bring attention to the posters and other graphic design in the collection of the Museum of Modern Art in the 1950s and 1960s.
Bio: "Mildred Constantine," in: Wikipedia. See - https://en.wikipedia.org/wiki/Mildred_Constantine

Anna Gonosová (ca 1945-), b. Slovakia; art historian, specialist on Byzantine and Medieval art and architecture, University of California, Irvine, CA
Bio: "Gonosová, Anna," in: *SVU Directory* 8; "Anna Gonosova," in: UCI Faculty Profile System. See - https://www.faculty.uci.edu/profile.cfm?faculty_id=2672

Adeline Lee Karpiscak (ca 1948-), b. of Slovak descent; art historian; curator, associate director of the University of Arizona Museum; author of books
Bio: "Retirement UA Museum of Art Associate Director to Retire," in: UA News. See - https://uanews.arizona.edu/story/retirement-ua-museum-art-associate-director-retire

Thomas M. Messer (1920-2013), b. Bratislava, Czech.; art historian, director of Guggenheim Museum
Bio: "Messer, Thomas M," in: SVU Directory; "Messer, Thomas M," in: *Who's Who in America*, 33; "Thomas M. Messer," in: Wikipedia. See - https://en.wikipedia.org/wiki/Thomas_M._Messer; Weber, Bruce, "Thomas M. Messer, Museum Director Who Gave Guggenheim Cachet, dies at 93," *The New York Times*, May 15, 2013; "Messer, Thomas," in: *Panorama*, p. 246.

Zuzana Trepková Paternostrová (1944-), b. Budapest, of Slovak descent; art historian, living in Brazil
Bio: "Zuzana Trepková Paternostrová," in: Wikipedia. See - https://sk.wikipedia.org/wiki/ Zuzana_Trepková_Paternostrová

Kristina Potuckova (ca 1984-), b. Slovakia; art historian; graduate student in art and architecture of medieval Europe, at Yale university
Bio: "Kristina Potuckova." See - https://arthistory.yale.edu/people/kristina-potuckova

I. ALLIED HEALTH & SOCIAL SERVICES

1. Nurses

Mary H. Babnič (1923-2008), b. Youngstown, OH, of Slovak descent; trained as a nurse; served with US Army in various army hospitals in TX, KY, CO, CA and NY. After World War II, she served with the US Army Air Corp of Nurses (1946-53). For 38 year she also served as nurse anesthetist with Youngstown Hospital Association. She was also involved in the Slovak community.
Bio: Kopanic, Michael J., "The Queen of Slovak Culture in Youngstown, Ohio – Mary H. Babnič (1923-2008)." Posted on academia.edu. See - https://www.academia.edu/37290303/The_Queen_of_Slovak_Culture_in_Youngstown_Ohio_Mary_H._ Babnič_1923-2008; "Mary H. Babnic," in: Find A Grave. See - https://www.findagrave.com/memorial/164620757/mary-h.-babnic

Anna Kuba (1923-2016), b. Lansford, PA, of Slovak descent; registered nurse; teacher of nursing students at Jefferson Medical College and assistant professor of nursing, University of Pennsylvania School of Medicine and School of Nursing (until 1965)
Bio: "Anna Kuba," *The Morning Call*, April 30, 2017; "Anna Kuba, Nursing," in: University of Pennsylvania Almanac, May 23, 2017. See - https://almanac.upenn.edu/articles/anna-kuba-nursing https://almanac.upenn.edu/articles/anna-kuba-nursing

Virginia Marie Parobek (1961-), b. Lancaster, OH, of Slovak descent; registered nurse, Fairfield Medical Center, Lancaster, OH
Bio: "Parobek, Virginia Marie," in: *SVU Directory*, 9

Jeanette Rigelsky (née Yurko) (1931-2016), b. Youngstown, OH, of Slovak descent; nurse. She worked many years at St. Elizabeth Hospital as a registered nurse and assistant head nurse and charge nurse.
Bio: "Jeanette Rigelsky," The Vindicator, July 16, 2016.

Emilia Sabo (née Ontko) (1927-2013), b. Passaic, NJ, of Slovak descent; trained nurse; member of US Student Nurse Cadet Corps (1944-47), serving at US Merchant Marines Hospital at Staten Island; registered Nurse at

Hasbrouck Heights Hospital (1947-52), then at Beth Israel Hospital in Passaic, NJ (until 1984).
Bio: "Emilia Sabo," *The Record/Herald News,* Aug. 1-2, 2013; "Emilia 'Millie' Olga Ontko Sabo," in: Find a Grave. See - https://www.findagrave.com/memorial/114778402/emilia-olga-sabo

2. Physical Therapists

Renata Greenberg (ca 1984-), b. Bratislava, Slovakia; registered massage therapist and yoga instructor, with Transcend Wellness Connection, Aurora, Ont., Canada.
Bio: "Renata Greenberg," in: LinkedIn. See - https://www.linkedin.com/in/renata-greenberg-rmt-b4604543/?originalSubdomain=ca; "Meet our Teams," in: Transcend Wellness Connection. See - https://transcendwellnessconnection.com/team.html

3. Pharmacists

Ernest B. Buczek (1929-2008), b. Gary IN, of Slovak descent; pharmacist; opened Rexall Drugs in the Glen Park / Gary area and served the NW Indiana area community for over 45 years
Bio: "Obituary for Ernest B. Buczek," in: Burns Funeral home & Crematory. See -http://www.burnsfuneral.com/obituaries/Ernest-B-Buczek-2631/#!/Obituary

Joseph Aloysius Ferko (1895-1964), b. Philadelphia, PA, of Slovak descent; a pharmacist; ran drug store in North Philadelphia. He started, in 1905, as a stock boy in Dr. John Fralinger's pharmacy. In 1921, Ferko opened his own pharmacy. The Ferko drugstore occupied the first floor of a strange-looking, three-story triangular-shaped building on Fifth Street in the Kensington section of the city. The structure (which is still there) resembled a thin slice of layer cake, with the front door at the thin end of the building and the sales counter at the wider end. However his popularity and fame came when he founded Ferko String Band.
Bio: "Founder of the famous Ferko String Band 1922) with rosters. He was a perennial performer in Philadelphia's Mummers Parade. They gained national popularity through their hit recordings in the 1940s and 1950s. They played for Franklin D. Roosevelt's 1933 Presidential inauguration.

Bio: "Ferko String Band," in: Wikipedia. See - https://en.wikipedia.org/wiki/Ferko_String_Band

Vladimir Kopec (fl. 1974), Slovak American; pharmacist, with Wykoff Heights Hospital, Brooklyn, NY; professor at the Brooklyn College of Pharmacy of Long Island University

Jana Krehel (ca 1978-), b. Slovakia; pharmacist; senior pharmacist specialist, at EmblemHealth, New York, NY.
Bio: "Jana Krehel," in: LinkedIn. See - https://www.linkedin.com/in/janakrehel79/

Adolph Weinberger (1891-1977), b. Slovakia; pharmacist; founder and president of nation-wide chain of drug stores -Weinberger Drug Stores, Inc.; residing in Cleveland, OH
Bio: "Weinberger, Adolph," in: *Who's Who in Commerce and Industry*, 4, p. 1056; "Weinberger, Adolph," in: Encyclopedia of Cleveland History. See - https://case.edu/ech/articles/w/weinberger-adolph

Arthur George Zupko (1916-2010), b. Yonkers, NY; pharmacist, professor, St. Louis College of Pharmacy (1949-55), associate dean (1955), dean (1956-60); Provost, Brooklyn College of Pharmacy, Long Island University (1960-73), president (1973-76); president, Arnold and Marie Schwartz College of Pharmacy and Health Sciences (1976-79).
Bio: "Zupko, Arthur George," in: *Who's Who in America*, 42' "Arthur George Zupko," in: Prabook. See - https://prabook.com/web/arthur_george.zupko/404181; "Dr. Arthur George Zupko," The News-Press, February 3, 2010

4. Public Health Specialists

Jo Ann Krukar (1948-), b. Ford City, Pa, of Slovak descent; healthcare lobbyist
Bio: "Jo Ann Krukar," in: Wikipedia. See - https://en.wikipedia.org/wiki/Jo_Ann_Krukar

Lindsey Nicole Rechcigl (1994-), b. Bradenton, FL, of Czech and Slovak descent; nutritionist and public health specialist

5. Health Service Administrators

Gregory Rechcigl (1988-), b. Bradenton, FL, of Czech and Slovak ancestry; health science administrator at East Arkansas Regional Unit, Correct Care Solutions
Bio: "Greg Rechcigl," in: LinkedIn. See - https://www.linkedin.com/in/greg-rechcigl-00672836/

6. Physical Educators

Rudolph S. Bachna (1928-2012), b. Cleveland, OH, of Slovak descent; associate professor of physical education, Kent State University, Kent, OH
Bio: "Bachna, Rudolph S.," in: *Educators*, p. 43; "Rudolph M. 'Rudy' Bachna," *The Plain Dealer*, July 22, 2012; "Rudolph Bachna, in: TGFC. See - https://kentstatesports.com/sports/2016/10/12/tgfc-hall-of-fame-members-class-of-1993.aspx?id=242

Michael Duda (1909-1968), b. Donora, PA, of Slovak descent; held doctorate in education, he chose coaching as his career; he won his first teaching and coaching jobs in 1935, when he joined the Donora School District. There he learned under legendary coach James K. Russell and coached football, basketball and baseball, while also officiating at WPIAL football and basketball games. During his early teaching and coaching days, Dr. Duda became a mentor and lifelong confidant to many fine scholar-athletes, including eventual Major League Baseball Hall of Fame member Stan Musial. A tireless worker, Dr. Duda served as a teacher, guidance counselor, director of playgrounds and scoutmaster before becoming a principal in the Donora school district from 1942-1951. He then was named superintendent of the Monessen School District, a position he held until becoming president at California. Coincidentally, Dr. Duda was inducted into the Mid-Mon Valley All Sports Hall of Fame in 1956, the same year he began his California presidency. In the *Hall of Fame's Biographical Journal*, he was labeled "the quintessential scholar-athlete of the Mon Valley."
Bio: "Dr. Michael Duda - Class of - Hall of Fame - California University of Pennsylvania." See - https://calvulcans.com/hof.aspx?hof=148

Ron Petro, b. Yonkers, NY, of Slovak descent; athletic director; head men's basketball coach (1966-84) and director of athletics (1977-84); athletic director, University of Alaska, anchorage, Alaska (1984-92); director of athletics and recreation at the University of Rhode Island (1992-2004);
Bio: "Ron Petro, athletic director, 1984-92," in: The Official Home of Seawolf Athletics. See -http://www.goseawolves.com/ViewArticle. dbml?DB_OEM_ID=13400&ATCLID=205128259;
"Athletic Director Ron Petro Will Not Seek Contract Extension," in: Go. Rhody. com. See - http://www.gorhody.com/genrel/releases/010804aaa.html.

Ray J. Plutko (ca 1937-), b. McKeesport, PA, of Slovak descent; teacher and coach; Notre Dame HS, Riverside (s. 1970); administrative assistant with CIF-SS (1975); fifth commissioner of the CF-SS (1980); commissioner of HS Activities in the State of Colorado (s. 1986); principal. Charter Oak HS, CA (1992); principal at Temple City HS (1993); principal at Martin Luther King HS (1998), returning as principal to Temple City HS (2004-07).
Bio: "Ray J. Plutko," in: CIF-SS History. See - https://www.cifss.org/wp-content/uploads/2015/06/CIFSS-History-78-Ray-Plutko.pdf

7. Social Workers

Donald Pafko (1939-2017), b. Minneapolis, MN, of Slovak descent; social welfare worker, superior of department of probation and parole
Bio: "Pafko, Donald," in: *SVU Directory,* 9

Juraj Piljan (1912-1988), b. Mokrá Luka, Slovakia; director of social services, Nursing Homes, Dept, of Social Services, State of Michigan
Bio: "Piljan, Ju4

J. SPORTS

1. Baseball Players

George Alusik (1935-2018), b. Ashley, PA, of Slovak descent; American Major League Baseball (MLB) player who played five seasons with the Detroit Tigers (1958, 1961–1962) and Kansas City Athletics (1962–1964). Until Frank Thomas broke the record for home runs in consecutive games by an Athletics player,

Alusik was one of three Athletics players who held the record of hitting home runs in five consecutive games. On August 26, 1962, Alusik broke up a perfect game in the 9th inning against Twins pitcher Jack Kralick. Alusik also beat Kralick with a two-run home run on August 8, 1962.
Bio: "George Alusik," in: Wikipedia. See - https://en.wikipedia.org/wiki/George_Alusik

Ralph Branca (1926-2016), b. Mount Vernon, NY, of Slovak mother; an American professional baseball pitcher who played 12 seasons in Major League Baseball (MLB), from 1944 through 1956. Branca played for the Brooklyn Dodgers (1944–1953, 1956), Detroit Tigers (1953–1954), and New York Yankees (1954). He was a three-time All-Star. In a 1951 playoff, Branca allowed a walk-off home run to Bobby Thomson, known as the "Shot Heard 'Round the World."
Bio: "Ralph Branca," in: Wikipedia. See - https://en.wikipedia.org/wiki/Ralph_Branca

Johny Bucha (1925-1996), b. Allentown, PA, of Slovak descent; baseball player, catcher in American League Baseball (MLB)
Bio: "Johny Bucha," in: Wikipedia. See - https://en.wikipedia.org/wiki/Johnny Bucha

Dave Dravecky (1956-), b. Youngstown, OH, of Czech and Slovak ancestry; professional baseball player in MLB for San Diego Padres (1982-87) and San Francisco Giants (1987-89)
Bio: "Dave Dravecky," in: Wikipedia. See - https://en.wikipedia.org/wiki/Dave_Dravecky; "Dave Dravecky," in: *Encyclopedia*, Vol. 3, p. 2235.

Jim Honochick (1917-1994), b. Oneida, PA, of Slovak descent; American League umpire; he worked the World Series 6 times and the All-Star game 4 times; Temple University Hall of Fame inductee
Bio: "Jim Honochick," in: Wikipedia. See - https://en.wikipedia.org/wiki/Jim_Honochick; "Jim Honochick," in: Hall of Fame. See - https://owlsports.com/hof.aspx?hof=256Temple Jim Honochick," in: Find A Grave. See - https://www.findagrave.com/memorial/8040540

Scott Kazmir (1984-), b. Houston, TX, of Slovak descent; American professional baseball pitcher
Bio: "Scott Kazmir," in: Wikipedia. See - https://en.wikipedia.org/wiki/ Scott_Kazmir

Andy Kosco (1941-), b. Youngstown, OH, of Slovak ancestry; baseball outfielder in Major League
Bio: "Andy Kosco," in: Wikipedia. See - https://en.wikipedia.org/wiki/ Andy_Kosco

Jack Kralick (1935-2012), b. Youngstown, OH, of Slovak ancestry; baseball pitcher with Washington Senators and Cleveland Indians
Bio: "Jack Kralick," in: Wikipedia. See - https://en.wikipedia.org/wiki/ Jack_Kralick

Rick Krivda (1970-), b. McKeesport, PA, of Slovak ancestry; professional baseball player, Olympic gold medalist
Bio: "Rick Krivda," in: Wikipedia. See - https://en.wikipedia.org/wiki/ Rick_Krivda

John 'Johnny' Albert Kucab (1919-1977), b. Olyphant, PA, of Slovak\. ancestry; baseball pitcher with Philadelphia Athletics
Bio: "Johnny Kucab," in: Wikipedia. See - https://en.wikipedia.org/wiki/ Johnny_Kucab

Curt Leskanic (1968-), b. Homestead, PA, of Slovak descent; former American Major League Baseball relief pitcher
Bio: "Curt Leskanic," in: Wikipedia. See - https://en.wikipedia.org/wiki/ Curt_Leskanic

Evan Longoria (1985-), b. Downey, CA, of Slovak descent; nicknamed Longo, is an American professional baseball third baseman for the San Francisco Giants of Major League Baseball (MLB). He previously played in MLB for the Tampa Bay Rays from 2008 through 2017.
Bio: "Evan Longoria," in: Wikipedia. See - https://en.wikipedia.org/wiki/ Evan_Longoria

Rudy Manarcin (1930-2013), b. North Vandergrift, PA, of Slovak descent; a pitcher in Major League Baseball who played from 1955 through 1957 for the Cincinnati Redlegs (1955) and Boston Red Sox (1956–57). Listed at 6 ft 0 in (1.83 m), 195 lb (88 kg), he batted and threw right-handed.
Bio: "Rudy Manarcin," in: Wikipedia. See - https://en.wikipedia.org/wiki/Rudy_Minarcin Kadar

Andy Pafko (1921-2013), b. Boyceville, WI, of Slovak ancestry; an American professional baseball player. He played in Major League Baseball (MLB) for the Chicago Cubs (1943–51), Brooklyn Dodgers (1951–52), and Milwaukee Braves (1953–59). He batted and threw right-handed and played center field.
Bio: "Andy Pafko," in: Wikipedia. See - https://en.wikipedia.org/wiki/Andy_Pafko

Mike Piazza (1968-), b. Norristown, PA, of Italian and Slovak ancestry; baseball catcher in Major League Baseball (MLB)
Bio: "Mike Piazza," in: Wikipedia. See - https://en.wikipedia.org/wiki/Mike_Piazza

Jack Quinn (orig. Joannes Pajkos) (1883-1946), b. Štefurov, Slovakia; baseball player. He was as a pitcher in Major League Baseball. Quinn pitched for eight teams in three major leagues (the American, Federal, and National) and made his final appearance at the age of 5.
Bio: "Jack Quinn," in: Wikipedia. See - https://en.wikipedia.org/wiki/Jack_Quinn_(baseball)

George Thomas 'Shotgun' Shuba (1924-2014), b. Youngstown, OH, of Slovak ancestry; outfielder for the Brooklyn Dodgers. He played in three World Series during the 1950s but who was best remembered for his welcoming gesture to Jackie Robinson at home plate on the day Robinson, as a minor leaguer, broke baseball's color barrier.
Bio: "George Shuba," in: Wikipedia. See - https://en.wikipedia.org/wiki/George_Shuba; "George Shuba, 89, Dies; Handshake Heralded Racial Tolerance in Baseball," *The New York Times,* September 30, 2014; "George 'Shotgun' Shuba," in: Find A Grave. See - https://www.findagrave.com/memorial/136606409/george-shuba

Brian Sikorski (1974-), b. Detroit, MI; of Polish and Slovak descent; former baseball relief pitcher
Bio: "Brian Sikorski," in: Wikipedia. See - https://en.wikipedia.org/wiki/ Brian_Sikorski

Al Sima (1921-1993), b. Mahwah, NJ, of Slovak ancestry; American professional baseball pitcher
Bio "Al Sima," in: Wikipedia. See - https://en.wikipedia.org/wiki/Al_Sima

Brett Tomko (1973-), b. Euclid, OH, of Slovak ancestry; former professional baseball pitcher in Major League Baseball (MLB)
Bio: "Brett Tomko," in: Wikipedia. See - https://en.wikipedia.org/wiki/ Brett_Tomko

Elmer Valo (1921-1998), b. Rybnik, Slovakia; baseball right fielder, coach and scout in Major League Baseball
Bio: "Elmer Valo," in: Wikipedia. See - https://en.wikipedia.org/wiki/ Elmer_Valo

Jason Varitek (1972-), b. Rochester, MI, of Slovak ancestry; baseball catcher with Boston Red Sox
Bio: "Jason Varitek," in: Wikipedia. See - https://en.wikipedia.org/wiki/ Jason_Varitek

2. Football Players

Chuck Bednarik (1925-2015), b. Bethlehem, PA, of Slovak ancestry; American football player with Philadelphia Eagles of the NFL
Bio: "Chuck Bednarik," in: Wikipedia. See - https://en.wikipedia.org/wiki/ Chuck_Bednarik; Alexander, June G., "Bednarik, Charles 'Chuck,'" in: *Making it in America: A Sourcebook on Eminent Ethnic Americans.* Edited by Elliot Robert Barkan. Santa Barbara, CA: ABC-CLIO, 2001, p. 32.

Pete Billick (1933-2014), b. Gary, IN, of Slovak descent; trained in architecture; teacher of industrial arts, and track and football coach; head football coach, Andrean HS (1972-81), before that he was an assistant coach.
Bio: "Peter Lawrence 'Coach' Billick, *Post-Tribune,* January 29, 2014.

George Blanda (1927-2010), b. Youngwood, PA, of Slovak ancestry; football quarterback and kicker for the Oakland Raiders and Houston Oilers
Bio: "George Blanda," in: Wikipedia. See - https://en.wikipedia.org/wiki/George_Blanda; Litsky, Frank and Bruce Weber, "George Blanda, Hall of Fame Football Player, Dies at 83," *The New York Times*, September 27, 2010.

Joe Devlin (1954-), b. Phoenixville, PA, of Slovak descent; an American football offensive tackle in the National Football League for the Buffalo Bills in the 1970s and 1980s.
Bio: "Joe Devlin," in: Wikipedia. See - https://en.wikipedia.org/wiki/Joe_Devlin_(American_football)

Nick Drahos (1918–2018), b. Ford City, PA, of Slovak ancestry; American college football player at Cornell University, member of the Sphinx Head Society; elected to the College Football Hall of Fame in 1981.
Bio: "Nick Drahos," in: Wikipedia. See https://en.wikipedia.org/wiki/Nick_Drahos

George Gulyanics (1921-1990), b. Mishawaka, IN, of Slovak descent; professional American football player, running back and punter for the Chicago Bears
Bio: "George Gulyanics," in: Wikipedia. See - https://en.wikipedia.org/wiki/George_Gulyanics

Jim Juriga (1964-), b. Fort Wayne, IN, of Slovak descent; a former guard who played 3 seasons in the National Football League. He started in Super Bowl XXIV for the Denver Broncos.
After he finished his football career, he obtained his Doctor of Veterinary Medicine degree from Colorado State University. He currently lives with his wife Denise in Geneva, Illinois.
Bio: "Jim Juriga," in: Wikipedia. See - https://en.wikipedia.org/wiki/Jim_Juriga

Dan Marino (1961-), b. Pittsburgh, PA, of Polish, Italian and Slovak ancestry; former American football player, a quarterback for the Miami Dolphins in the NFL
Bio: "Dan Marino,", in: Wikipedia. See - https://en.wikipedia.org/wiki/Dan_Marino

Mark Markovich (1952-), b. Latrobe, P_A, of Slovak descent; professional American football player who spent four seasons in the National Football League, where he played for the San Diego Chargers and Detroit Lions. Prior to his professional career, Markovich played at the collegiate level, while attending Penn State, where he provided blocking for Heisman Trophy winner, John Cappelletti.
Bio: "Mark Markovich," in: Wikipedia. See - https://en.wikipedia.org/wiki/Mark_Markovich

Joe Pisarcik (1952-), b. Kingston, PA, of Slovak descent; an American football quarterback who played in the National Football League for eight seasons, from 1977 through 1984, after playing high school football at West Side Central Catholic H. S. (later Bishop O'Reilly, now closed), and college football at New Mexico State University. His first professional team was the Calgary Stampeders of the Canadian Football League, where he played from 1974 to 1976.
Bio: "Joe Pisarcik," in: Wikipedia. See - https://en.wikipedia.org/wiki/Joe_Pisarcik

Joe Skladany (1911-1972), b. Larksville, PA, of Slovak ancestry; American football player with Pittsburgh Pirates of the NFL
Bio: "Joe Skladany," in: Wikipedia. See - https://en.wikipedia.org/wiki/Joe_Skladany

Leo Skladany (1927-2003), b. Larksville, PA, of Slovak descent; American football defensive end in NFL for the Philadelphia Eagles and the New York Giants.
Bio: "Leo Skladany," in: Wikipedia. See - https://en.wikipedia.org/wiki/Leo_Skladany

Mike Vrabel (1975-), b. Akron, OH, of Slovak descent; an American football coach and former linebacker. He is the current head coach of the Tennessee Titans of the National Football League (NFL). He played college football at Ohio State University, where he earned consensus All-American honors. After retiring as a player following the 2010 season, he was the linebackers and defensive line coach at Ohio State for three seasons. His NFL coaching career

began in 2014 with the Houston Texans as linebackers' coach and then defensive coordinator, before being hired in 2018 as head coach of the T
Bio: "Mike Vrabel," in: Wikipedia. See - https://en.wikipedia.org/wiki/Mike_Vrabel.

Joe Zelenka (1976-), b._Cleveland, OH, of Slovak descent; football long snapper the National Football League (NFL). He was signed by the San Francisco 49ers as an undrafted free agent in 1999. He played college football at Wake Forest. Zelenka also played for the Washington Redskins, Jacksonville Jaguars and Atlanta Falcons
Bio: "Joe Zelenka," in: Wikipedia. See - https://en.wikipedia.org/wiki/Joe_Zelenka

3. Basketball Players

Jeff Bzdelik (1952-), b. Mount Prospect, IL, of Slovak ancestry; basketball coach in NBA
Bio: "Jeff Bzdelik," in: Wikipedia. See - https://en.wikipedia.org/wiki/Jeff_Bzdelik

Michal Čekovský (1994-), b. Košice, Czech.; basketball player, played basketball for university of Maryland
Bio: Michal Čekovský," in: Wikipedia. See - https://en.wikipedia.org/wiki/Michal_ Čekovský

Andrea Kuklová (1971-), b. Poprad, Czech.; former basketball player in the WNBA
Bio: "Andrea Kuklová," in: Wikipedia. See - https://en.wikipedia.org/wiki/Andrea_Kuklova

John Kundla (1916-2017), b. Star Junction, PA, of Slovak ancestry; professional basketball coach
Bio: "John Kundla," in: Wikipedia. See - https://en.wikipedia.org/wiki/John_Kundla

Charles Jerome Kupec (1953-), b. Oak Lawes, IL, of Slovak descent; American basketball player, formerly in the National Basketball Association (NBA). Kupec played college basketball at the University of Michigan. A He.

played for the Los Angeles Lakers and Houston Rockets during the 1970s, as well as in Italy during the 1980s. He won the 1982 Euroleague title with Cantu.
Bio: "C. J. Kupec," in: Wikipedia. See - https://en.wikipedia.org/wiki/C._J._Kupec

Kyle Kuric (1989-), b. Evansville, IN, of Slovak ancestry; professional basketball player with Zenit Saint Petersburg of the VTB United League
Bio: "Kyle Kuric," in: Wikipedia. See - https://en.wikipedia.org/wiki/Kyle_Kuric

Joseph Lapchick (1900-1970); b. Yonkers, NY, of Slovak descent; professional basketball player, with the Original Celtics (1920s and 1930s); head coach at St. John's University (1937-47), with New York Knicks in the NBA (until 1957), returning to St. John's (until 1965).
Bio: "Joe Lapchick," in: Wikipedia. See - https://en.wikipedia.org/wiki/Joe_Lapchick

Erin Lawless (1985-), b. Chicago, IL, is an American born-Slovak women's basketball player.
She played for Slovakia at EuroBasket Women 2011, where she was her nation's top scorer. She played club basketball in Italy, Slovakia, Russia, Turkey and Belgium between 2007 and 2015, before returning to the United States.
Bio: "Erin Lawless," in: Wikipedia. See - https://en.wikipedia.org/wiki/Erin_Lawless

Bill Mlkvy (1931-), b. Palmerton, PA, of Slovak descent; retired professional basketball player
Bio: "Bill Mlkvy," in: Wikipedia. See - https://en.wikipedia.org/wiki/Bill_Mlkvy

Bill Mokray (1907-1974), b. Passaic, NJ, of Slovak descent; American basketball statistician and historian. He was enshrined into the Basketball Hall of Fame in 1965.
Bio: "Bill Mokray," in: Wikipedia. See - https://en.wikipedia.org/wiki/Bill_Mokray

Richard Petruška (1969-), b. Levice, Czech.; retired professional basketball player and coach
Bio: "Richard Petruška," in: Wikipedia. See - https://en.wikipedia.org/wiki/ Richard_Petruška

Herb Sendek (1963-), b. Pittsburgh, PA, of Slovak ancestry; American college basketball coach
Bio: "Herb Sendek," in: Wikipedia. See - https://en.wikipedia.org/wiki/ Herb_Sendek

Mike Smrek (1962-), b. Welland, Ont., Canada, of Slovak descent; a retired Canadian professional basketball player. He was the top pick in the 2nd round of the Portland Trail Blazers in the 1985 NBA draft, and played seven seasons as a backup big man in the league.
Bio: "Mike Smerk," in: Wikipedia. See - https://en.wikipedia.org/wiki/ Mike_Smrek

Joe Sotak (1914-2007), b. Whiting, IN, of Slovak descent; professional basketball player. He played in the National Basketball League for Whiting/ Hammond Ciesar All-Americans and averaged 4.1 points per game.
Bio: "Joe Sotak," in: Wikipedia. See - https://en.wikipedia.org/wiki/ Joe_Sotak

Zuzana Žirková (1980-), b. Bojnice, Czech.; former professional basketball player with Washington Mystics in WNBA
Bio: "Zuzana Žirková," in: Wikipedia. See - https://en.wikipedia.org/wiki/ Zuzana_Žirková

4. Soccer Players

Adrian Cann (1980-), b. Thornhill, Ont., Canada, of Slovak descent; a Canadian international soccer defender
Bio: "Adrian Cann," in: Wikipedia. See - https://en.wikipedia.org/wiki/ Adrian_Cann

Ferdinand Daučík (1910-1986), b. Šahy, Slovakia; Slovak soccer player and manager. In 1967, Daučík moved to Canada to coach the Toronto Falcons of the National Professional Soccer League. This proved to be something of

a family reunion as he was joined at the club by his son Yanko, son-in-law Ladislao Kubala and grandson Branko Kubala. After returning to Spain, he had spells at Elche, Espanyol and Colonia Moscardó, among others.
Bio: "Ferdinand Daučík," in: Wikipedia. See - https://en.wikipedia.org/wiki/Ferdinand_ Daučík

Yanko Daučík (1941-2017), b. Prague, Czech., a son of Ferdinand Daučík; a professional soccer player. Yanko played for Real Betis, Real Madrid, the Toronto Falcons and RCD Español. He became one of the first Spanish footballers to play in North America when he played for Toronto Falcons of the National Professional Soccer League. This proved to something of a family reunion as Yanko was joined at the club by his father Ferdinand, brother-in-law Ladislao Kubala and nephew Branko Kubala. During the 1967 season Yanko played 17 games, scored 20 goals and made 8 assists for the Falcons and finished as the top scorer in the league.
Bio: Yanko Daucik," in: Wikipedia. See - https://en.wikipedia.org/wiki/Yanko_Daucik

David Depetris (1988-), b. San Jorge, Argentina, of Slovak descent; an Argentine-born Slovak footballer who plays as a forward for Club Olimpo on loan from Huracán.
Bio: "David Depetris," in: Wikipedia. See - https://en.wikipedia.org/wiki/David_Depetris

Dominik Jakubek (1979-), b. Santa Clara, CA, of Slovak descent; American professional footballer
Bio: "Dominik Jakubek," in: Wikipedia. See - https://en.wikipedia.org/wiki/Dominik_Jakubek

Branko Kubala (1949-2018), b. Šahy, Czech.; a professional soccer player who played as a striker. The family moved to Barcelona, Spain soon after his birth. He later moved to North America with his family, where he played for the Toronto Falcons, the St. Louis Stars, and the Dallas Tornado.
Bio: "Branko Kubala," in: Wikipedia. See - https://en.wikipedia.org/wiki/Branko_Kubala

Ladislav Kubala (1927-2002), b. Budapest; had Czechoslovak citizenship; a professional soccer-player, regarded as one of te n best players in history.

In 1967, Kubala went to Canada, where at Toronto Falcons he enjoyed something of family reunion with his father-in-law, Ferdinand Daučík, his brother-in-law, Yanko Daucik and his son Branko. He also appeared in 19 matches for Toronto, scoring 5 times.
Bio: "László Kubala," in: Wikipedia. See - https://en.wikipedia.org/wiki/László_Kubala

Josef Miso (1973-), b. Trnava, Slovakia; a Slovak football player who last played for Municipal Grecia in the Costa Rican Second Division.
Bio: "Josef Miso," in: Wikipedia. See - https://en.wikipedia.org/wiki/Josef_Miso

Adam Nemec (1985-), b. Banská Bystrica, Czech; professional footballer who plays as a forward for Slovakia national team. In his career, he has played in 6 different countries, including the US.
Bio: "Adam Nemec," in; Wikipedia. See - https://en.wikipedia.org/wiki/Adam_Nemec

Arturo Rodenak (1931-2012), b. La Plata, Argentina, of Slovak descent; an Argentine–born Chilean footballer, regarded as one of the greatest players in Rangers' history.
Bio: "Arturo Rodenak," in: Wikipedia. See - https://en.wikipedia.org/wiki/Arturo_Rodenak

Albert Rusnák (1994-), b. Výškov, Czech.; professional footballer, who plays for Major League Soccer Club Real Salt Lake as an attacking midfielder.
Bio: "Albert Rusnák," in: Wikipedia. See - https://en.wikipedia.org/wiki/Albert_ Rusnák

Leopold Šťastný (1911-1996), b. Rohoznik, Slovakia; soccer player and coach. Almost his entire career he played with the football club Šk Slovan Bratislava. For four years, he worked for the Austrian Football Union, at the end of his life, he moved to his to Canada, where he finally died nine days before his 85th birthday.
Bio: "Leopold Šťastný," in: Wikipedia. See - https://en.wikipedia.org/wiki/Leopold_Šťastný

Dionatan Teixeira (1992-2017), b. Londrina, Brazil, of Slovak descent; professional soccer, centre-back
Bio: "Dionatan Teixeira,", in: Wikipedia. See - https://en.wikipedia.org/wiki/ Dionatan_Teixeira

José Varacka (1932-), b. Buenos Aires, Argentina, of Slovak descent; an Argentine former soccer player and coach.
Bio: "José Varacka," in: Wikipedia. See - https://en.wikipedia.org/wiki / José_Varacka

Igor Vrablic (1965-), b. Bratislava, Czech.; Canadian soccer player, at both professional and international levels, as a striker.
Bio: "Igor Vrablic.," in; Wikipedia. See - https://en.wikipedia.org/wiki/ Igor_Vrablic

5. Softball Players

Joseph T. Barber (orig. Balberchak) (1931-2004), b. Edwardsville, PA, of Slovak descent; affectionately dubbed Mr. Softball; manager the Brakettes Softball, Stratford, CT (for nearly 40 years); president of the Amateur Softball Association;
Bio: "Joseph Balberchak" in: Legacy.com. See - http://www.legacy.com/ obituaries/timesleader/obituary.aspx?page=lifestory&pid=2854209

John Doslak (1918-1998), b. Lorain, OH, of Slovak descent; an outstanding softball pitcher for two decades
Bio: "John J. Doslak," in: Find a Grave. See - https://www.findagrave.com/ memorial/147176633/john-j-doslak

6. Volleyball Players

Scott Touzinsky (1982-), b. St. Louis, MO, of Czech and Slovak descent; American volleyball player
Bio: "Scott Touzinsky," in: Wikipedia. See - https://en.wikipedia.org/wiki/ Scott_Touzinsky

7. Lacrosse Players

Tomáš Hájek (1978-), b. Bratislava, Czech.; a Slovak-Canadian lacrosse player from St. Catharines, Ontario, who plays for the Philadelphia Wings in the National Lacrosse League. He played Junior lacrosse for the St. Catharines Athletics and Junior hockey for the St. Catharines Falcons.
Bio: "Thomas Hajek," in: Wikipedia. See - https://en.wikipedia.org/wiki/Thomas_Hajek

8. Hockey Players

Natalie Babonyová (1983-), b. Oshawa, Ont., Canada; a Slovak-Canadian female ice hockey forward. Babonyova participated in the 2010 Vancouver Winter Games for Slovakia.
Bio: "Natalie Babonyová," in: Wikipedia. See - https://en.wikipedia.org/wiki/Natalie_ Babonyová

Pete Backor (1919-1988), b. Fort William, Ont., Canada, of Slovak descent; a Canadian professional ice hockey defenceman of Slovak origin who played briefly for the Toronto Maple Leafs in the NHL.
Bio: "Pete Backor," in: Wikipedia. See - https://en.wikipedia.org/wiki/Pete_Backor

Ľuboš Bartečko (1976-), b. Kežmarok, Czech.; professional ice hockey forward; he most notably played in the National Hockey League (NHL) for the St. Louis Blues and Atlanta Thrashers.
Bio: "Ľuboš Bartečko," in: Wikipedia. See - https://en.wikipedia.org/wiki/ki/Ľuboš_Bartečko

Stephen Beda (1909-1985), b. Forth William, CA, of Slovak parents; Canadian hockey player, coach and referee
Bio: "Stephen Beda," Dlhá and Oravou. See - http://www.dlhanadoravou.sk/stephen-beda.html

Jiří Bicek (1978-), b. Košice, Czech.; ice hockey forward, with New Jersey Devils in NHL (1997), with the Albany River Rats in AHL; won Stanley cup 2003 with New Jersey Devils
Bio: "Jiří Bicek," in: Wikipedia. See - https://en.wikipedia.org/wiki/Jiří_Bicek

Mike Buckna (1908-1996), b. Trail, BC, Canada, of Slovak descent; Canadian amateur ice hockey player and coach.
Bio: "Mike Buckna," in: Wikipedia. See - https://en.wikipedia.org/wiki/Mike_Buckna

Peter Budaj (1982-), b. Banská Bystrica, Czech.; professional ice hockey goaltender for the Los Angeles Kings in the National Hockey League (NHL). He has previously played for the Colorado Avalanche, by whom he was drafted, the Montreal Canadiens and the Tampa Bay Lightning.
Bio: "Peter Budaj," in: Wikipedia. See - https://en.wikipedia.org/wiki/Peter_Budaj

Zdeno Chára (1977-), b. Trenčín, Czech.; Slovak professional ice hockey defenseman, currently serving as captain of the Boston Bruins of the National Hockey League (NHL). He won the James Norris Memorial Trophy while playing for the Bruins in the 2008–09 season.
Bio: "Zdeno Chára," in: Wikipedia. See - https://en.wikipedia.org/wiki/Zdeno_ Chára

Andy Clovechok (1923-2016), b. Klokočov, Czech.; Canadian professional hockey player; who played for the Vancouver Canucks in the Pacific Coast Hockey Association, for which he played 114 games, scoring 175 points. He also played for the Edmonton Flyers and Kamloops Elks. He is a member of the Alberta Sports Hall of Fame and Museum as well as the B.C. Sports Hall of Fame. Clovechok grew up in Rosedale, Alberta.
Bio: "Andy Clovechok," in: Wikipedia. See - https://en.wikipedia.org/wiki/Andy_Clovechok.

Alex Delvecchio (1931-), Fort William, Ontario, Canada, of Slovak descent on his mother's 's side; legendary Canadian professional hockey player, coach and general manager who spent his entire NHL with the Detroit Red Wings. In a playing career that lasted 24 seasons, Delvecchio played in 1,549 games, recording 1,281 points. At the time of his retirement, he was second in NHL history in games played, assists and points. He won the Lady Byng Memorial Trophy for sportsmanship and gentlemanly conduct three times, and helped the Red Wings win the Stanley Cup three times. Delvecchio was inducted

into the Hockey Hall of Fame in 1977, and in 2017 was named one of the '100 Greatest NHL Players' in history.
Bio: "Alex Delvecchio," in; Wikipedia. See - https://en.wikipedia.org/wiki/Alex_Delvecchio

Pavol Demitra (1974-2011), b. Dubnica nad Váhom, Czech; professional hockey player with NHL
Bio: "Pavol Demitra," in: Wikipedia. See - https://en.wikipedia.org/wiki/Pavol_Demitra

Martin Fehérváry (1999-), b. Bratislava, Czech.; ice hockey defenceman, with the Washington Capitals of thy National Hockey League (NHL).
Bio: "Martin Fehérváry," in: Wikipedia. See - https://en.wikipedia.org/wiki/Martin_ Fehérváry

Andrew Ference (1979-), b. Edmonton, Alberta, Canada, of Slovak descent; a former Canadian professional ice hockey defenceman. Ference started in the NHL during the 1999–2000 season and has played for the Pittsburgh Penguins, Calgary Flames, Boston Bruins, and Edmonton Oilers. In 2011, Ference helped the Bruins to their 6th Stanley Cup Championship. Ference last played for and captained the Edmonton Oilers.
Bio: "Andrew Ference," in: Wikipedia. See - https://en.wikipedia.org/wiki/Andrew_Ference

Robbie Ftorek (1952-), b. Needham, MA, of Slovak descent; former ice hockey player and coach
Bio: "Robbie Ftorek," in: Wikipedia. See - https://en.wikipedia.org/wiki/Robbie_Ftorek

Marián Gáborík (1982-), b. Trenčín, Czech.; professional ice-hockey right winger with the Ottawa Senators of the NHL
Bio: "Marián Gáborík," in: Wikipedia. See - https://en.wikipedia.org/wiki/Marián_Gáborík

Jaroslav Halák (1985-), b. Bratislava, Czech.; professional ice hockey player with New York Islanders in NHL.
Bio: "Jaroslav Halák," in: Wikipedia. See - https://en.wikipedia.org/wiki/Jaroslav_Halák

Taylor Hall (1991-), b. Calgary, Canada, of Slovak descent; professional ice hockey left winger;
Bio: "Taylor Hall,", in: Wikipedia. See - https://en.wikipedia.org/wiki/Taylor_Hall

Michal Handzuš (1977-), b. Banská Bystrica; professional ice hockey center; since joining the National Hockey League (NHL) in 1998, Handzuš has played for the St. Louis Blues, Phoenix Coyotes, Philadelphia Flyers, Los Angeles Kings, San Jose Sharks and, most recently, the Chicago Blackhawks, with whom he won the Stanley Cup with in 2013.
Bio: "Michal Handzuš," in: Wikipedia. See - https://en.wikipedia.org/wiki/Michal_Handzuš

Marián Hossa (1979-), b. Stará Ľubovňa, Czech.; professional ice hockey right winger with Chicago Blackhawks of the NHL
Bio: Marián Hossa," in: Wikipedia. See - https://en.wikipedia.org/wiki/Marián_Hossa

Marcel Hossa (1981), b. Ilava, Czech.; ice hockey player, left winger; he played in the National Hockey League (NHL) with the Montreal Canadiens, New York Rangers and Phoenix Coyotes, having been drafted by the Canadiens in the first round, 16th overall, in the 2000 NHL Entry Draft.
Bio: "Marcel Hossa," See - https://en.wikipedia.org/wiki/Marcel_Hossa

Brian Ihnacak (1985-), b. Toronto, Ont., Canada, of Slovak father; professional ice hockey forward who currently plays for HC Sparta Praha of the Czech Extraliga.
Bio: "Brian Ihnacak," in: Wikipedia. See - https://en.wikipedia.org/wiki/Brian_Ihnacak.

Peter Ihnačák (1957-), b. Poprad, Czech.; former Slovak ice hockey center; he was prohibited from playing outside of the Communist bloc because members of his family had already fled Slovakia. He went on to play eight seasons with the Toronto Maple Leafs of the National Hockey League from 1982 until 1990.
Bio: "Peter Ihnačák," in: Wikipedia. See - https://en.wikipedia.org/wiki/Peter_Ihnačák

Tomáš Jurčo (1992-), b. Košice, Czech.; ice hockey right winger currently playing for the Chicago Blackhawks of NHL
Bio: "Tomáš Jurčo," in: Wikipedia. See - https://en.wikipedia.org/wiki/Tomáš_Jurčo

Chad Kolarik (1986-), b. Abington, PA, of Slovak descent; an American professional ice hockey right wing. He is currently playing with Adler Mannheim of the Deutsche Eishockey Liga (DEL) in Germany.
Bio: "Chad Kolarik," in: Wikipedia. See - https://en.wikipedia.org/wiki/Chad_Kolarik

Tomas Kopecký (1992-), b. Ilava, Czech.; professional ice hockey right winger, in the NHL with the Detroit Red Wings, Chicago Blackhawks and Florida Panthers.
Bio: "Tomas Kopecky," in: *Encyclopedia*, Vol. 3, p. 2277; "Tomáš Kopecký," in: Wikipedia. See - https://en.wikipedia.org/wiki/ Tomáš_Kopecký

John Kubinec (1928-1995), b. Fort William, Ontario, Canada, of Slovak parents; Canadian hockey player who played defense and was active between 1949 and 1956.
Bio: "John Kubinec," in: Dlhá nad Oravou. See - http://www.dlhanadoravou.sk/john-kubinec.html

Kristián Kudroč (1981-), b. Michalovce, Czech.; former ice hockey defenceman with New York Islanders
Bio: "Kristián Kudroč", in: Wikipedia. See - https://en.wikipedia.org/wiki/ Kristián_Kudroč

Kevin Labanc (1995-), b. Staten Island, NY, of Slovak father; an American professional ice hockey right wing. He is currently playing for the San Jose Sharks of the National Hockey League (NHL). He was drafted by the Sharks in the sixth round, 171st overall, in the 2014 NHL Entry Draft.
Bio: "Kevin Labanc," in: Wikipedia. See - https://en.wikipedia.org/wiki/ Kevin_Labanc

Igor Liba (1960-), b. Prešov, Czech/; professional ice hockey player; in 1983 he was drafted by the Calgary Flames. Played with the New York Rangers (10 games, 2 goals + 5 assists) and Los Angeles Kings (37 games, 7 goals + 18

assists) in the season of 1988–1989. In the Los Angeles Kings he was playing with Wayne Gretzky in one formation.
Bio: "Igor Liba," in: Wikipedia. See - https://en.wikipedia.org/wiki/Igor_Liba

Ivan Majeský (1976-), b. Banská Bystrica, Czech.; ice hockey defenceman. He was drafted by the Florida Panthers 267th overall in the 2001 NHL Entry Draft and played a full season with the Panthers scoring 4 goals and 8 assists for 12 points. On June 21, 2003, Majeský was traded to the Atlanta Thrashers, where he scored 3 goals and 7 assists for 10 points in 63 regular season games for Atlanta. During the 2004–05 NHL lockout, which resulted in the cancellation of the 2004–05 NHL season, Majeský played in the Czech Republic for HC Sparta Praha before joining the Washington Capitals. It's with the Capitals where Majeský is famous with North American fans for his only goal for the team, a 170–foot shot from his own end that somehow managed to bounce past Pittsburgh Penguins goalie Sébastien Caron.
Bio: "Ivan Majeský," in: Wikipedia. See - https://en.wikipedia.org/wiki/Ivan_Majeský

Martin Marinčin (1992-), b. Košice, Czech.; professional hockey player, with the Toronto Marlies in AHL
Bio: "Martin Marinčin," in: Wikipedia - See -https://en.wikipedia.org/wiki/Martin_ Marinčin

Andrej Meszároš (1985-), b. Považská Bystrica, Czech.; professional ice hockey player; played in NHL with the Buffalo Sabres, Boston Bruins, Philadelphia Flyers, Tampa Bay Lightning and Ottawa Senators
Bio: "Andrej Meszároš," in: Wikipedia. See - https://en.wikipedia.org/wiki/Andrej_ Meszároš

Rudy Migay (1928-2016), b. Fort William, Ont., Canada, of Slovak descent; a Canadian ice hockey forward. Migay turned professional in 1948. He spent three years with Pittsburgh's American Hockey League (AHL) club before joining the National Hockey League (NHL)'s Toronto Maple Leafs for a seven-year tenure. This was followed by a couple of years in Rochester and later two seasons in Denver. He then moved into coaching.
Bio: "Rudy Migay," in: Wikipedia. See - https://en.wikipedia.org/wiki/Rudy_Migay

Vladimír Mihálik (1987-), b. Prešov, Czech.; professional ice hockey defenceman; he came to North America to play junior hockey in 2005, with the Red Deer Rebels of the Western Hockey League. For the 2006–07 season, he moved to the Prince George Cougars producing 26 points in 51 games before signing a three-year entry level contract with the Lightning on 6 April 2007. He started his pro career in the 2007–08 season with the Norfolk Admirals of the American Hockey League posting 16 points as a rookie. Mihálik was promoted to the Tampa Bay Lightning for the start of the 2008–09.
Bio: "Vladimír Mihálik," in: Wikipedia. See - https://en.wikipedia.org/wiki/Vladimír_Mihálik

Stan Mikita (orig. Stanislav Guoth) (1940-2018), b. Sokolče, Slovakia; professional ice hockey player with Chicago Black Hawks in NHL
Bio: "Stan Mikita," in: Wikipedia. See - https://en.wikipedia.org/wiki/Stan_Mikita' "Mikita, Stanley," in: *Who's Who in America*, 41

Ladislav Nagy (1979-), b. Šaca, Czech.; professional ice hockey forward, played 8 seasons in the National Hockey League (NHL) with the St. Louis Blues, Phoenix Coyotes, Dallas Stars and Los Angeles Kings.
Bio: "Ladislav Nagy," in: Wikipedia. See - https://en.wikipedia.org/wiki/Ladislav_Nagy

Vladimír Országh (1977-), b. Banská Bystrica, Czech.; professional ice hockey player. He was drafted into the National Hockey League (NHL) in 1995 by the New York Islanders in the fifth round (106th overall) and he has been playing in the NHL since 1997. From 1997 through to 2000, Vladimír Országh was attempting to crack the New York Islanders line-up, as he had a stint of 34 games in the NHL over those three years, tallying a total of five points. In 2001 he signed up with the Nashville Predators, where he tallied 105 points (47 goals and 58 assists) and he has also helped them earn their first play-off spot in the team's six-year history. On December 30, 2005, Országh joined the St. Louis Blues after he was claimed off waivers.
Bio: "Vladimír Országh," in: Wikipedia. See - https://en.wikipedia.org/wiki/Vladimír_Országh

Žigmund Pálffy (1972-), b. Skalica, Czech.; professional ice hockey player; he played right wing for the New York Islanders, Los Angeles Kings and Pittsburgh Penguins between 1993–2006.
Bio: "Žigmund Pálffy," in; Wikipedia. See - https://en.wikipedia.org/wiki/Žigmund_Pálffy

Richard Pánik (1991-), b. Martin, Czech.; professional ice hockey right winger with the Arizona Coyotes of the National Hockey League (NHL)
Bio:" Richard Pánik," in: Wikipedia. See - https://en.wikipedia.org/wiki/Richard_Pánik

Dušan Pašek (1960-), b. Bratislava, Czech.; a professional ice hockey forward who played 48 games in the National Hockey League. He played for the Minnesota North Stars. He won a silver medal at the 1984 Winter Olympics and represented Czechoslovakia at three Canada Cups. He also won a gold medal at the 1985 World Ice Hockey Championships.
Bio: "Dušan Pašek," in: Wikipedia. See - https://en.wikipedia.org/wiki/Dušan_Pašek

Róbert Petrovický (1973-), b. Košice, Czech.; professional ice hockey player right winger; he played in the NHL for the Hartford Whalers, Dallas Stars, St. Louis Blues, Tampa Bay Lightning and the New York Islanders.
Bio: "Róbert Petrovický," in: Wikipedia. See - https://en.wikipedia.org/wiki/Róbert_Petrovický

Peter Podhradský (1979-), b. Bratislava, Czech.; professional ice hockey player, defenceman; in 2000 NHL Entry Draft and spent three seasons with their American Hockey League affiliate the Cincinnati Mighty Ducks.
Bio: "Peter Podhradský," in: Wikipedia. See - https://en.wikipedia.org/wiki/Peter_Podhradský

Branko Radivojevič (1980-), b. Piešťany, Czech.; professional hockey player; played with Colorado Avalanche, the Phoenix Coyote, the Philadelphia Flyers, the Minnesota Wild; after a couple seasons with the Wild, he opted to go to the KHL.
Bio: "Branko Radivojevič," in: Wikipedia. See - https://en.wikipedia.org/wiki/Branko_Radivojevič

Ladislav Ščurko (1986-), b. Gelnica, Czech.; professional ice hockey center. He was drafted by the Philadelphia Flyers in the sixth round, 170th overall, in the 2004 NHL Entry Draft. Shortly after, he was drafted seventh overall in the CHL Import Draft by the Seattle Thunderbirds. In his first year in the Western Hockey League (WHL), he scored 42 points, which put him in fifth in the league for points scored by a rookie. He also set a Thunderbird record with a nine-game point streak from December 11, 2004 through January 12, 2005, during which he scored 12 points. He enjoyed similar success in fewer games the following season.
Bio: "Ladislav Ščurko," in: Wikipedia. See - https://en.wikipedia.org/wiki/Ladislav_Ščurko

Andrej Sekera (1986-), b. Bojnice, Czech.; professional ice hockey player, currently playing for the Edmonton Oilers of the National Hockey League (NHL)
Bio: "Andrej Sekera," in: Wikipedia. See - https://en.wikipedia.org/wiki/Andrej_Sekera

Juraj Šimek (1987-), b. Prešov, Czech.; professional ice hockey player. Selected by the Brandon Wheat Kings with their first choice in the 2006 Canadian Hockey League (CHL) Import Draft, Šimek made his North American debut in 2006–07 with the Wheat Kings. He scored at a near point-per-game pace, with 57 points in 58 games and received his first NHL contract in the off-season, on July 23, 2007, with the Canucks. Signed with the Canucks, he made his AHL debut with Vancouver's minor league affiliate, the Manitoba Moose, in 2007–08 and scored 17 points in 66 games. On October 6, 2008, he was traded along with Lukáš Krajíček to the Tampa Bay Lightning. On December 9, 2010, Tampa Bay traded Šimek to the Boston Bruins.
Bio: "Juraj Šimek," in: Wikipedia. See - https://en.wikipedia.org/wiki/Juraj_Šimek

Peter Smrek (1979-), b. Martin, Czech.; ice hockey defenceman. Smrek played for the Des Moines Buccaneers of the USHL during the 1998-99 season and helped them win the 1999 Clark Cup Championship. Smrek was drafted 85th overall by the St. Louis Blues in the 1999 NHL Entry Draft and made his NHL debut on February 10th, 2001 vs. the Colorado Avalanche [2] but only managed to play 6 games with the Blues, spending most of his time with the Blues' American Hockey League affiliate the Worcester IceCats. He was later traded to the New York Rangers and played 22 further games in the NHL, but again spent most of his spell in the AHL, this time with the Hartford Wolf Pack. He was then traded to the Nashville Predators and then to the Ottawa Senators, but never played another NHL game. In total, Smrek played 28 NHL games, scoring two goals and four assists for 6 points and collected 18 penalty minutes.

Bio: "Peter Smrek," in: Wikipedia. See - https://en.wikipedia.org/wiki/Peter_Smrek

Anton Šťastný (1959-), b. Bratislava, Czech.; professional ice hockey left winger; he played nine seasons with the Quebec Nordiques of the National Hockey League from 1980 until 1989.

Bio: "Anton Šťastný," in: Wikipedia. See - https://en.wikipedia.org/wiki/Anton_ Šťastný

Paul Stastny (1985-), b. Quebec City, Quebec, Canada, of Slovak ancestry; professional ice hockey center

Bio: "Paul Stastny," in: Wikipedia. See - https://en.wikipedia.org/wiki/Paul_Stastny

Peter Šťastný (1956-), b. Bratislava, Czech.; professional ice-hockey player in the National Hockey League (NHL)

Bio: "Peter Šťastný," in: Wikipedia. See - https://en.wikipedia.org/wiki/Peter_ Šťastný

Yan Stastny (1982-), b. Quebec City, Quebec, Canada, of Slovak ancestry; professional ice-hockey player

Bio: Yan Stastny," in: Wikipedia. See - https://en.wikipedia.org/wiki/Yan_Stastny

Mike Stevens (1965-), b. Kitchener, Ont., Canada; professional ice hockey player who played 23 games in the National Hockey League.

Bio: "Mike Stevens," in: Wikipedia. See - https://en.wikipedia.org/wiki/Mike_Stevens_(ice_hockey,_born_1965)

Scott Stevens (1964-), b. Kitchener, Ont., Canada, of Slovak descent; a Canadian professional ice hockey player and coach. As a defenceman, Stevens played 22 seasons in the National Hockey League (NHL) for the Washington

Capitals, St. Louis Blues and New Jersey Devils, serving as captain of the Devils from 1992 to 2004. Stevens was later inducted into the Hockey Hall of Fame in 2007, his first year of eligibility.
Bio: "Scott Stevens," in: Wikipedia. See - https://en.wikipedia.org/wiki/Scott_Stevens

Tomáš Surový (1981-), b. Banská Bystrica, Czech.; professional ice hockey left winger. Surový was drafted in the 4th round by the Pittsburgh Penguins in the 2001 NHL Entry Draft. Was called up from Wilkes-Barre Penguins in December 2005 where he earned the nickname "Killer" after jumping to Sidney Crosby's defence in a game against the Ottawa Senators. The Penguins decided against re-signing him following the 2005–06 season and he signed with Luleå HF of the Swedish Elitserien. But on July 9, 2007, Surový signed with the Phoenix Coyotes. However, his contract with Phoenix was cancelled and he returned to Linköpings HC on September 26, 2007.
Bio: "Tomáš Surový," in: Wikipedia. See - https://en.wikipedia.org/wiki/Tomáš_Surový

Marek Svatoš (1982-2016), b. Košice, Czech.; professional ice hockey winger; played in the National Hockey League (NHL) for several seasons, mostly with the Colorado Avalanche; his last stint in the NHL was in the 2010–11 season, during which he played with the Nashville Predators and Ottawa Senators after beginning the season in the Kontinental Hockey League (KHL) with Avangard Omsk.
Bio: "Marek Svatoš," in: Wikipedia. See - https://en.wikipedia.org/wiki/Marek_ Svatoš

Tomáš Tatar (1990-), b. Ilava, Czech.; professional ice hockey left winger with the Vegas Golden Knights of the National Hockey League (NHL)
Bio: "Tomáš Tatar," in: Wikipedia. See - https://en.wikipedia.org/wiki/Tomáš_Tatar

Zuzana Tomčíková (1988-), b. Zvolen, Czech.; ice hockey player, goaltender, Canadian immigrant, member of Bemidji State Beavers women's ice hockey team, Minnesota
Bio: "Zuzana Tomčíková," in: Wikipedia. See - https://en.wikipedia.org/wiki/Zuzana_ Tomčíková

Boris Valábik (1986-), b. Nitra, Czech.; professional hockey player; he played for Atlanta Thrashers, Kitchener Rangers, Chicago Wolves, Boston Bruins, Providence Bruins, Pittsburgh Penguins.
Bio: "Boris Valábik," in: Wikipedia. See - https://sk.wikipedia.org/wiki/Boris_Valábik

Thomas Vanek (1984-), b. Baden bei Wien, of Czech father and Slovak mother; an Austrian professional ice hockey left winger who currently plays for the Detroit Red Wings of the National Hockey League (NHL). He has previously played for the Buffalo Sabres, New York Islanders, Montreal Canadiens, Minnesota Wild, Florida Panthers, Vancouver Canucks and Columbus Blue Jackets. Vanek was drafted by the Sabres fifth overall in the 2003 NHL Entry Draft, making him the highest drafted Austrian in NHL history.
Bio: "Thomas Vanek," in: Wikipedia. See - https://en.wikipedia.org/wiki/Thomas_Vanek

Elmer Vasko (1935-1998), b. Duparquet, Quebec, Canada, of Slovak descent; a Canadian professional ice hockey defenceman who played 13 seasons in the National Hockey League for the Chicago Black Hawks and Minnesota North Stars and won the Stanley Cup in 1961.
Bio: "Elmer Vasko," in: Wikipedia. See - https://en.wikipedia.org/wiki/Elmer_Vasko

Mickey Volcan (1962-), b. Edmonton, Alberta, Canada, of Slovak descent; ice hockey defenceman who played 162 NHL games for the Hartford Whalers and Calgary Flames (1980-84). He was the youngest player in the NHL in the 1980–81 season.
Bio: "Mickey Volcan," in: Wikipedia. See - https://en.wikipedia.org/wiki/Mickey_Volcan

Igor Vrablic (1965-), b. Bratislava, Czech.; a Canadian former soccer player who played at both professional and international levels, as a striker.
Bio: "Igor Vrablic," in: Wikipedia. See - https://en.wikipedia.org/wiki/Igor_Vrablic

Benny Woit (1928-2016), b. Fort William, Ontario, Canada, of Slovak descent; hockey player; a National Hockey League defenceman of the 1950s.

Tomáš Záborský (1987-), b. Trenčín, Czech.; former professional ice hockey left winger with the New York Rangers of the NHL
Bio: "Tomáš Záborský," in: Wikipedia. See - https://en.wikipedia.org/wiki/ Tomáš_Záborský

Marek Zagrapan (1986-), b. Prešov, Czech.; professional ice hockey center currently playing for EHC Winterthur of the Swiss League (SL). He was drafted by the National Hockey League (NHL)'s Buffalo Sabres in the first round, 13th overall, at the 2005 NHL Entry Draft.
Bio: Marek Zagrapan," in: Wikipedia. See - https://en.wikipedia.org/wiki/ Marek_Zagrapan

Richard Zedník (1976-), b. Banská Bystrica, Czech.; professional ice hockey winger. He had a 15-year career in the National Hockey League (NHL), playing for the Washington Capitals, Montreal Canadiens, New York Islanders and Florida Panthers.
Bio: "Richard Zedník," in: Wikipedia. See - https://en.wikipedia.org/wiki/ Richard_Zedník

9. Boxers

Joe Baksi (1922-1977), b. Kulpmont, PA, of Slovak ancestry; professional boxer, heavy weight
Bio: "Joe Baksi," in: Wikipedia. See - https://en.wikipedia.org/wiki/ Joe_Baksi

Emil Brtko (1929-1985), b. USA, of Slovak descent; boxer, heavyweight
Bio: "Emil Brtko." See - http://www.sportenote.com/vedi_dettagli. asp?id=59064

Pete Latzo (1902-1968), b. Coloraine, PA, of Slovak ancestry; boxer, World Welterweight Champion
Bio: "Pete Latzo," in: Wikipedia. See - https://en.wikipedia.org/wiki/ Pete_Latzo

Kelly Pavlik (1982-), b. Youngstown, OH, of Slovak ancestry; undefeated middleweight boxing champion
Bio: "Kelly Pavlik," in: Wikipedia. See - https://en.wikipedia.org/wiki/Kelly_Pavlik

John Risko (1902-1953), b. Bohunice, Slovakia; heavyweight boxer, residing in Cleveland, OH
Bio: Kopanic, Michael J., Jr., "Risko, Johnny," in: *Encyclopedia of Ethnicity and Sports in the United States*. Edited by George B. Kirsch, Othelo Harris, and Claire E. Nolte. Westport, CT: Greenwood Press, 2000, p. 382; "Risko, John," in: Encyclopedia of Cleveland History. See- https://case.edu/ech/articles/r/risko-john

Rudy J. Sader (1902-1971), b. of Slovak descent; professional boxer; resided in Natrona Heights, PA

10. Swimmers

Florence Chadwick (1918-1995), b. San Diego, Ca, of Slovak descent; long distance swimmer, first woman to swim the English Channel in both directions, setting a time records each time.
Bio: "Florence Chadwick," in: Wikipedia. See - https://en.wikipedia.org/wiki/Florence_Chadwick

Marcel Gery (1965-), b. Smolenice, Czech.; butterfly swimmer, Canadian Olympic bronze medalist, Commonwealth Games bronze medalist for Canada
Bio: "Marcel Gery," in: Wikipedia. See - https://en.wikipedia.org/wiki/Marcel_Gery

Martina Moravcová (1976-), b. Piešťany, Czech.; a medley, butterfly and freestyle swimmer; she is a two-time Olympic silver medalist, both achieved at the 2000 Summer Olympics in Sydney, Australia. She is one of Slovakia's greatest female athletes, although she has lived in Dallas, TX, USA since she started attending Southern Methodist University in the mid-1990s.
Bio: "Martina Moravcová," in: Wikipedia. See - https://en.wikipedia.org/wiki/Martina_Moravcová

11. Tennis and Table Tennis Players

Ladislav Hecht (1909-2004), b. Žilina, Slovakia; a Jewish professional tennis player, well known for representing Czechoslovakia in the Davis Cup during the 1930s where he compiled an 18 victories-19 losses record; fled to US in 1938. After the war he continued his tennis career, becoming a no. 1 ranked player in the eastern United States.
Bio: "Ladislav Hecht," in: Wikipedia. See - https://en.wikipedia.org/wiki/Ladislav_Hecht

Helen Kelesi (1969-), b. Victoria, B.C., Canada, of Slovak ancestry; professional tennis player, member of BC Sports Hall of Fame
Bio: "Helen Kelesi," in: BC Sports of Fame. See - http://www.bcsportshalloffame.com/inductees/inductees/bio?id=324&type=person
"Helen Kelesi," in: Wikipedia. See -https://en.wikipedia.org/wiki/Helen_Kelesi;

Max Marinko (1916-1975), b. Ljubljana; international table tennis player, played for Czechoslovakia, residing in Canada
Bio: "Max Marinko," in: Wikipedia. See - https://en.wikipedia.org/wiki/Max_Marinko

Bethanie Mattek-Sands (1985-), b. Rochester, MN, of Slovak ancestry; professional tennis player, Olympic Gold medalist in mixed doubles, winner of five grand Slam titles in women's doubles and two in mixed doubles
Bio: "Bethanie Mattek-Sands," in: Wikipedia. See - https://en.wikipedia.org/wiki/Bethanie_Mattek-Sands

Jarmila Wolfe (1987-), b. Bratislava, Czech.; a Slovak-Australian tennis player. Wolfe has won two singles titles and one doubles title on the WTA tour in her career, as well as fourteen singles and nine doubles titles on the ITF Circuit in her career. She lived in Dallas, TX.
Bio: "Jarmila Wolfe," in: Wikipedia. See - https://en.wikipedia.org/wiki/Jarmila_Wolfe

12.1. Figure Skaters

Silvia Hugec (2000-), b. Paterson, NJ, of Slovak parents. She is a Slovak-American figure skater. She is the 2018 Slovak national champion and represented Slovakia at the 2018 European Championships, where she qualified to the final segment. She resides in the suburbs of Minneapolis and studies at Mounds Park Academy in Saint Paul, Minnesota.
Bio: "Silvia Hugec," in: Wikipedia. See - https://en.wikipedia.org/wiki/Silvia_Hugec

Andrew Poje (1987-), b. Kitchener, Ont., Canada, of Slovak descent; a Canadian ice dancer. With partner Kaitlyn Weaver, he is a three-time World medalist (2014 silver, 2015 and 2018 bronze), a two-time Four Continents champion (2010, 2015), a two-time Grand Prix Final champion (2014–15, 2015–16), and a two-time Canadian national champion (2015, 2016).
Bio: "Andrew Poje," in: Wikipedia. See - https://en.wikipedia.org/wiki/Andrew_Poje

Nicole Rajičová (1995-), b. Garden City, NY, of Slovak parents; figure skater
Bio: "Nicole Rajičová," in: Wikipedia. See - https://en.wikipedia.org/wiki/Nicole_Rajičová

Jozef Sabovčík (1963-), b. Bratislava, Czech., of Czech mother and Slovak father; figure skater, Olympic bronze medalist; he lives in Bountiful, UT
Bio: "Jozef Sabovčík," in: Wikipedia. See - https://en.wikipedia.org/wiki/Jozef_Sabovčík

13. Skiers

Leslie Krichko (1959-), b. Portland, OR, of Slovak ancestry; Olympic cross-country skier
Bio: "Leslie Krichko," in: Wikipedia. See - https://en.wikipedia.org/wiki/Leslie_Krichko

Anna Weider (1942-2007), b. of Slovak descent; pianist and music teacher; skier, top-ranked Canadian junior ski racer, winner of Canadian Junior Alpine Championship
Bio: "Anna (Weider) Marik Obituary," *National Post,* October 19-20, 2007.

Katherine Weider, of Slovak descent
Bio: "Katherine Weider Canning," in: Collingwood Sports Hall of Fame.
See - http://collingwoodsportshalloffame.ca/?cat=22

14. Gymnasts

Janet Bachna (fl. 1991), Slovak American; gymnast; she helped to start the
Kent State gymnastics program in 1959 and was involved as the coach of the
women's team until her retirement in 1991; during this time the Lady Flashes
participated in the AIAW National Championships 11 consecutive years.
She became the first female judge from the United States to serve as a judge
in international finals competition when she judged the World Gymnastics
Championships held in Prague, Czechoslovakia in 1962. A member of the
U.S. Olympic Committee for Women's Gymnastics for 12 years (1960-72);
Chair of the U.S. Women's Gymnastics (1964-69). She was inducted into
the U.S. Gymnastics Federation Judges' Hall of Fame in 1979, the Greater
Cleveland Sports Hall of Fame in 1984 and the Mid-American Conference
Hall of Fame in 1992.
Bio: "Janet Bachna," in: TGFC - Hall of Fame Members. See - https://
kentstatesports.com/sports/2016/10/12/tgfc-hall-of-fame-members-
class-of-1993.aspx?id=242

15. Track and Field Athletes

Istvan Barta (Berger), (1895-1948), b. Hungary, of Slovak ancestry; water
polo player
Bio: "Istvan Barta," in: Wikipedia. See - https://en.wikipedia.org/wiki/
István_Barta

Milan Jamrich (1950-), b. Nové Zámky, Slovakia; resided in Houston, TX,
biologist; American high jump record holder
Bio: "Q&A with Milan Jamrich: American HJ record-holder," in: masterstrack.
com. See - http://masterstrack.com/qa-with-milan-j/.

Ladislav Pataki (1946-2007), b. Nové Zámky, Czech.; American coach,
sports scientist, and masters track and field thrower
Bio: "Ladislav Pataki," in: Wikipedia. See - https://en.wikipedia.org/wiki/
Ladislav_Patakihockey

László Tábori (1931-2018), b. Košice, Czech.; middle- and long-distance runner, best known for equalling the 1500 metres world record and placing 4th in that event at the 1956 Summer Olympics. At the close of the Melbourne Games, Tábori decided to defect to the West with his coach, Mihály Iglói. He soon left for the United States and settled in California, where he remained for the rest of his life. Tábori returned to distance running as a coach in 1967, his training methods based directly on Iglói's. He coached the now defunct program at Los Angeles Valley College to three state championships and coached the San Fernando Valley Track Club since 1973. He was a vocal advocate of interval training. He continued coaching at the University of Southern California, coaching among others, Duane Solomon.
Bio: "László Tábori," in: Wikipedia. See - https://en.wikipedia.org/wiki/László_Tábori

16. Water polo

Jana Salat (1979-), b. Košice, Czech.; Canadian water polo player, member of the bronze medal winning Canada women's national water polo team at the 2001 World Championships in Fukuoka, Japan
Bio: "Jana Salat," in: Wikipedia. See - https://en.wikipedia.org/wiki/Jana_Salat

17. Wrestlers

The Miz (orig. Michael Gregory Mizanin) (1980-), b. Parma, OH, of Slovak descent; an American professional wrestler, actor and media personality currently signed to WWE, where he performs on the SmackDown brand under the ring name The Miz.
Bio: "The Miz," in: Wikipedia. See - https://en.wikipedia.org/wiki/The_Miz

18. Jiujitsu

Alexander Boldizar (1971-), b. Košice, Czech.; lawyer, writer. Boldizar currently lives in Vancouver, BC, Canada. He won first place in his division at the British Columbia Brazilian jiu-jitsu Championships in both 2010 and

2011, a gold medal at the 2011 Pan American Championships and a bronze at the 2013 World Masters Championships.
Bio: "Alexander Boldizar," in: Wikipedia. See - https://en.wikipedia.org/wiki/Alexander_Boldizar

19. Bodybuilders - Weightlifters

<u>John Grimek (1910-1998),</u> b. Perth Amboy, NJ, of Slovak immigrant parents; bodybuilder and weightlifter
Bio: "John Grimek," in: Wikipedia. See - https://en.wikipedia.org/wiki/John_Grimek

20. Golfers

<u>Thomas W. Matey, Sr. (1931-2017),</u> b. Warren, OH, of Slovak descent; business executive, an avid golfer; NCAA All American and captain of the ND golf team, winning many golf tournaments and championships; member of the Warren Sports Hall of Fame, Notre Dame Hall of Fame and of the prestigious Society of Seniors, home of the top senior amateur golfers in the country
Bio: "Thomas W. Matey sr.," *Florida Today*, Sept. 16, 2017

21. Horse Racing - Jockeys

<u>Bill or 'Willie' Hartack (William John Hartack Jr.) (1932-2007);</u> b. Colver, Pa, of Slovak descent; k a Hall of Fame jockey; By his third season of racing, Hartack was the US' leading jockey, going on to win that honor on three more occasions.
Bio: Kopanic, Michael J., Jr., "Hartack, William J., Jr.," in: *Encyclopedia of Ethnicity and Sports in the United States.* Edited by George B. Kirsch, Othello Harris and Claire E. Nolte. Westport, CT: Greenwood Press, 2000, pp. 207-208;Hersh, Marcus, "Five-Derby winner Bill Hartack dies," in: espn. See - http://www.espn.com/sports/horse/news/story?id=3129958; "Bill Hartack," in: Wikipedia. See - https://en.wikipedia.org/wiki/Bill_Hartack

22. Car and Motorcycle Racers

Johny von Neumann (1922 -2004), b. in US s. 1938; sports car racer. He fled the Nazi Anschluss in 1938 and landed in California. After serving in the US Army in an intelligence unit, he built a fortune importing Ferraris, Porsches and VWs. A co-founder of Cal Club, von Neumann is best remembered for providing top-quality equipment to talents like Phil Hill, Richie Ginther and Ken Miles. Bio: "John von Neumann passes away," in: Autoweek. See - https://autoweek. com/article/car-news/john-von-neumann-passes-away; "Johny von Neumann," in: Hemmings. See - https://www.hemmings.com/magazine/ hsx/2010/03/Johnny-von-Neumann/2937241.html

Marty Tripes (1956-), b. San Diego, CA, of Slovak ancestry; former American professional motocross racer
Bio: "Marty Tripes," in: Wikipedia. See - https://en.wikipedia.org/wiki/ Marty_Tripes

William 'Bill' Vukovich (1918-1955); b. Freson, CA, of Slovak descent; an American automobile racing driver. He won the 1953 and 1954 Indianapolis 500 plus two more American Automobile Association National Championship races. Several drivers of his generation have referred to Vukovich as the greatest ever encountered in American motorsport.
Bio: "Bill Vukovich," in: Wikipedia. See - https://en.wikipedia.org/wiki/ Bill_Vukovich

23. Hydro Racers

Mira Slovak (1929-2014), b. Cifer, Slovakia; airline pilot who fled Communist Czechoslovakia by hijacking his own commercial flight to West Germany, who went on to become a hydroplane racing champion, a stunt flyer and an airline pilot. Bio: "Mira Slovak Obituary," in: Hydroplane and Raceboat Museum. See - https://thunderboats.ning.com/profiles/blogs/mira-slovak-obituary; Yardley, William, Mira Slovak, a Daring Pilot Who Won freedom, then Races, dies at 84,", the New York Times, June 28, 2014; "The Incredible Story of Mira Slovak, the Flying Czech," in: Return of kings. See - http://www.returnofkings. com/46600/the-incredible-story-of-mira-slovak-the-flying-czech; Farley, Fred, "Mira Slovak - 'The Flying Czech,' in: Hydroplane History. See - http:// www.lesliefield.com/personalities/mira_slovak_the_flying_czech.htm

24. Skydiving - Parachuting

Radoslav Mulík (1944-2016), b. Nalepkovo, Slovakia; motocross, gliding and skydiving enthusiast. Emigrated in 1968; employed as a technician for Siemens Company; lived in South Africa, former Rhodesia, and SW Africa. Moved to Coppell, Texas in 1976; founded a construction business. Passionate about his sport and teaching students; founded Slovak Air Skydiving Center in Ennis, Texas. Founded the Stefan Banic Parachute Foundation.
Bio: "Slavo Mulik (1944-2016), in: International Skydiving Museum & Hall of Fame. See - http://skydivingmuseum.org/news/slavo-mulik-1944-2016 ; "Radoslav 'Slavo' Mulik," in: Dignity Memorial. See - https://www. dignitymemorial.com/obituaries/coppell-tx/radoslav-slavo-mulik-6867240

25. Sports Team Owners and Executives

Joseph T. Barber (orig. Balberchak) (1931-2004), b. Edwardsville, PA, of Slovak descent; orig. an announcer and sportscaster for WNAB radio; later became community relations administrator and then CT ASA commissioner. He became involved for 50 years with the Amateur Softball Association, becoming its president. He was elected to the National Softball Hall of Fame and the ISF Hall of Fame. Barber had played a major role in the development of Softball in not only Connecticut but throughout the United States and the world.
Bio: "Joseph Balberchak" in: Legacy.com. See - http://www.legacy.com/ obituaries/timesleader/obituary.aspx?page=lifestory&pid=2854209

John Doslak (1918-1998), b. Lorain, OH, of Slovak descent; an outstanding softball pitcher for two decades, his favorite sport was bowling, and after 35 years of service to the Lorain Bowling Association he was known as 'Lorain's Mr. Bowling." He had served three terms as president of the Lorain Bowling Association, plus 16 terms as secretary-treasurer. He has also been elected as a delegate to the American bowling congress national convention a total of 15 times.
Bio: "John Doslak inducted April 21, 1981," in: Lorain Sports Hall of Fame. See - http://www.lorainsportshalloffame.com/doslak-john/

George Gross (1923-2008), b. Bratislava, Czech.; Canadian sports journalist and soccer executive, co-founder of Eastern Canada Professional Soccer League
Bio: "George Gross," in: Wikipedia. See - https://en.wikipedia.org/wiki/ George_Gross_(journalist)

Carl R. Pohlad (1915-2009), b. Des Moines, IA, of Slovak ancestry; American financier, the owner of the Minnesota Twins baseball franchise
Bio: "Carl Pohlad," in: Wikipedia. See - https://en.wikipedia.org/wiki/Carl_Pohlad; Lavietes, Stuart, "Carl R. Pohlad, Owner of Minnesota Twins, Dies at 93," *The New York Times,* January 5, 2009

Jim Pohlad (1953-), b. of Slovak descent; owner of the Minnesota Twins of the American League
Bio: "Jim Pohlad," in: Wikipedia. See - https://en.wikipedia.org/wiki/Jim_Pohlad

K. RECREATION

1. Chess Players

Francisco Benkö (1910-2010), b. Berlin, of Czech and Slovak ancestry; an Argentine chess master and problemist.
Bio: "Francisco Benkö," in: Wikipedia. See - https://en.wikipedia.org/wiki/Francisco_ Benkö

Herman Steiner (1905-1955), b. Dunajská Streda, Slovakia; in Us s. 1921; US chess player, organizer, columnist
Bio: "Herman Steiner," in: Wikipedia. See -https://en.wikipedia.org/wiki/Herman_Steiner

2. Magicians

Matt Wayne (orig. Matthew Wayne Tomasko) (1986-), b. York, PA, of Slovak ancestry; illusionist, producer and TV personality
Bio: "Matt Wayne," in: Wikipedia. See - https://en.wikipedia.org/wiki/Matt_Wayne_(magician)

3. Stamp Collectors

XI. Learning - Scholarship - Research

A. GENERAL

Rechclgl, Miloslav Jr. and Jiri Nehnevajsa, "American Scholars and Scientists with Czechoslovak Roots - Some Key Characteristics," *Journal of Washington Academy of Sciences* 58 (1968), pp. 213-22.

B. HUMANITIES

1. Archeologists

Miriam Ruth Pelikan Pittenger (1967), b. New Haven, CT, of Slovak ancestry; daughter of eminent church historian Jaroslav Pelikan, Jr.; classist, trained at Yale and University of California-Berkeley. She became assistant professor of classics at University of Illinois, Campaign-Urbana in 1998 and associate professor of classics at Hanover College in 2005. Currently, she holds the position of full Professor of Classical Studies at Hanover College and, recently, has also been appointed Vice President of the College. She is noted for her book, *Contested Triumphs: Politics, Pageantry, and Performance in Livy's Republican Rome*, published by the University of California Press in 2008

Francis Zeman (1918-d.), b. Viničné, Slovakia; theologian, archeologist; professor of Holy Scriptures and Oriental Languages, Major Seminary, Nicolet, P.Q., Canada (s. 1952); professor of Near East, Université du Québec à Trois-Riviéres (s. 1969)
Bio: "Zeman, Francis," in: *American Scholars*, 8, Vol. 1, "Zeman, Francis," in: *Who's Who in the East*, 10; "Zeman, Francis," in: *Educators*, p.70.

2. Historians

Stolarik, M. Mark, Slovak Historians in Exile in North America, 1945-1992," *Human Affairs* (Bratislava) 6, No. 1 (1996), pp. 34-44.

John Berta (1949-), b. Brooklyn, NY, of Slovak descent; historian, speculating in Russian an East European studies; adjunct professor of history, Methodist College/ university, Fayetteville, NC (1986-2010); research analyst, US government (s. 1985); adjunct professor of history, Fayetteville State University (s. 1990).
Bio: "John Berta," in: Linked.In. See - https://www.linkedin.com/in/john-berta-21101643/

June Granatir Alexander (1948-), b. Steubenville, OH; historian, University of Cincinnati, OH
Bio: "Alexander June Granatir," in: *SVU Directory*, 8

John Andrew Berta (1949-), b. Brooklyn, NY; adjunct professor of history, Fayetteville State University, and Methodist College, Fayetteville, NC
Bio: "Berta, John Andrew," in: *SVU Directory* 8

Livia Elvira Bitton-Jackson (née Elli L. Friedmann) (1931-), b. Šamorín, Czech.; Holocaust survivor, Jewish historian, professor of history at City University of New York (for 37 years)., she then moved to Israel
Bio: "Bitton-Jackson, Livia Elvira," in: *American Scholars*, 7, Vol. 1; "Livia Bitton-Jackson," in: Wikipedia. See - https://en.wikipedia.org/wiki/Livia_Bitton-Jackson

John Bodnar (1944 -), b. Victoria, Texas, of eastern Slovak descent; grew up in Forest City, PA. He is a Distinguished Professor of History at Indiana University, described as 'the doyen of American immigration history.' He is a co-director of the Center for the Study of History and Memory. He was nominated for a Pulitzer Prize.
Bio: "John Bodnar," in: *Indiana University Honors and Awards.* See: https://honorsandawards.iu.edu/search-awards/honoree.shtml?honoreeID=1565.

Stephen Borsody (1911-2000), b. Prešov, Slovakia; lawyer, historian, diplomat, professor of history at Chatham College (s. 1947).
Bio: "Stephen Borsody," in: *Encyclopedia,* Vol. 2, pp. 1190-1191; "Borsody, Stephen," in: *American Scholars*, 8, Vol. 1; "Stephen Borsody, 89, Scholar of Hungary," *The New York Times*, November 18, 2000; "Obituary: Stephen Borsody, former Hungarian diplomat who became a professor and author," *Pittsburgh Post Gazette*, November 11, 2000.

Edita Bosak (1950-), b. Stockholm, Sweden, of Slovak descent; historian, Memorial University of Newfoundland, St. John's, Newfoundland, Canada
Bio: "Bosak, Edita," in *SVU Directory* 9

Michael Cude (1983-), b. US, a genuine Honorary Slovak who has done lots of work pertaining to Slovak Americans, although he is not of Slovak descent. ; historian, specializing in Central and Eastern Europe, and immigration and diplomatic history; assistant professor of history and program coordinator of Texas Studies, Schreiner University, Kerrville, TX
Bio: "Dr. Michael Cude," in: Schreiner University. See - https://www. schreiner.edu/academics/faculty_directory/faculty-bios/cude.aspx

Konštantin Čulen (1904-1964), b. Brodské, Slovakia; journalist turned historian, author, second director of the Slovak Institute in Cleveland (1956-1959)
Bio: "Konštantín Čulen," in: LIC. See - http://www.litcentrum.sk/ slovenski-spisovatelia/konstantin-culen

Gabriela Dudeková (1968-), b. Hurbanovo, Czech.; historian, living and working in Bratislava, Nitra and Houston, TX.
Bio: "Gabriela Dudeková," in: Wikipedia. See - https://en.wikipedia.org/ wiki/ Gabriela_Dudeková

Louis Heilprin (1851-1912), b. Miškovec, Slovakia; an American author, historian, and encyclopedia editor.
Bio: "Louis Heilprin," in: Wikipedia. See - https://en.wikipedia.org/wiki/ Louis_Heilprin

Dagmar Horna (1925-1978), b. Bratislava, Czech.; historian, political scientist, social activist, associate professor of history, Georgetown university, Washington, DC
Bio: McCarthy, "Colman, Dagmar Perman Dies, GU Teacher," *The Washington Post*, May 31, 1978.

František Hrušovský (1903-1956), b. Dolné Lovčice, Slovakia; historian, teacher, director of Slovak Institute in Cleveland (1952-1956)
Bio: "František Hrušovský," in: Wikipedia. See - https://sk.wikipedia.org/ wiki/ František_Hrušovský

Stephanie O. Husek (1909-1994), b. Cleveland, OH; historian, professor of modern European and Russian history, Bridgewater State College (s. 1974). Before that she taught at Georgia Court College, where she held the position of associate professor (s. 1949).
Bio: "Husek, Stephanie O.," in: *American Scholars*, 7, Vol. 1

Oskar Jászi (orig. Jakubovits) (1875-1957), b. Nagykaroly, of Slovak descent; social scientist, historian, politician; in US s. 1925. He joined the faculty of Oberlin College, where he settled down to a career as a history professor and wrote a series of books, the best known of which is *The Dissolution of the Habsburg Monarchy*, first published by the University of Chicago Press in 1929.
Bio: "Oszkár Jászi," in: Wikipedia. See - https://en.wikipedia.org/wiki/Oszkár_Jászi

Yeshayahu A. Jelinek 1933-2016), b. Prievidza, Czech.; Israeli historian, visiting professor at University of Colorado, University of Minnesota, Columbia University.
Bio: "Jelinek, Yeshayahu A.," in: Educators, p. 42; "Yeshayahu A. Jelinek," in: Wikipedia. See - https://de.wikipedia.org/wiki/Yeshayahu_A._Jelinek

Marcel Jesensky (ca 1983-), b. Slovakia; historian, with specialization in in international relations and diplomacy; part-time professor, Department of History, University of Ottawa. A former diplomat, he has worked at the UN in New York.
Bio: "Marcel Jesensky," in: University of Ottawa. See - https://arts.uottawa.ca/history/people/jesensky-marcel

Joseph Marian Kirschbaum (1913-2001), b. Dolné Vestenice, Slovakia; Slovak politician; in Canada s. 1949; historian, specializing in Slavonic civilizations, associate professor at University of Montreal (s. 1951).
Bio: "Kirschbaum, Joseph Marian," in: *American Scholars*, 4, Vol. 1; "Joseph Marion Kirschbaum," in: Wikipedia. See - https://sk.wikipedia.org/wiki/Jozef_M._Kirschbaum

Rebekah Klein-Pejšová (ca 1972-), Slovak-American; historian, specializing in East-European history. She is associate professor of history at Purdue

University. She has also taught at Columbia, Rutgers, and the City University of New York.
Bio: "Rebekah Klein-Pejšová." See: http://www.slovak-jewish-heritage. org/history-of-jews-in-slovakia.html; "Rebekah A. Klein- Pejsova," in: Purdue University. See - https://www.cla.purdue.edu/history/directory/ ?p=Rebekah_Klein-Pejšová

Michael J. Kopanic, Jr. (1954-), b. Youngstown, OH, of Slovak parents; historian; first with St. Francis University of Pennsylvania; with University of Maryland University College, Adelphi (s. 2007), as adjunct professor (s. 2012). He specializes in interwar trade unions, Slovak history and Slovak-American history and customs.
Bio: "Kopanic, Michael J., Jr.," in: *SVU Directory*, 9; Curriculum Vitae. See - https://umuc.academia.edu/MichaelKopanic/CurriculumVitae

Štefan Kucík (1979-), b. Trebišov, Slovakia; historian, specializing in Slovak history, ; Ph.D. degree from Prešov University; did research at University of Ottawa, Slovak institute and Reference library, Cleveland, Jankola Library, IHRC, University of Minnesota; he returned to Slovakia and is a freelancer now.
Bio: "Štefan Kucík," in: Google Sites. See - https://sites.google.com/site/ stefankucik1/curriculum-vitae

Věra Láska (1928-2006), b. Košice, Czech.; historian, professor of history and head of dept. of social sciences at Regis College, Weston, MA.
Bio: "Věra Láska," in *Encyclopedia*, Vol. 2, p. 1204; "Láska, Věra," in: *SVU Directory* 8; "Laska, Vera," in: *American Scholars*, 8, vol. 1.

Herman Lebovics (1935-), b. Czech.; historian, professor, SUNY at Stony Brook, NY (s. 1966)
Bio: "Lebovics, Herman," in: *American Scholars*, 8, Vol. 1; "Herman Lebovics," in:
Stony Brook University - Department of History. See - https://www. stonybrook.edu/commcms/history/people/faculty/lebovics

Miroslav J. Ličko (1938-), b. Banská Bystrica, Czech.; historian, teacher, Dundas,
Bio: "Ličko, Miroslav," in: *SVU Directory* 8; "Ličko, Miroslav Ján," in: WorldCat Identities. See - http://www.worldcat.org/identities/lccn-n79-17580/

Victor S. Mamatey (1917-2007), b. North Braddock, PA, of Slovak descent; professor of history, University of Georgia (s. 1967)
Bio: "Victor S. Mamatey," in: *SVU Directory* 8; "Victor S. Mamatey," in: Wikipedia. See - https://en.wikipedia.org/wiki/Victor_S._Mamatey; "Mamatey, Victor S.," in: *Panorama*, p. 243; "Mamatey, Vojtech," in: *American Scholars*, 8, Vol. 1; "Mamatey, Victor Samuel," in: *Who's Who in America*, 41; "Mamatey, Victor S.," in: *Czechoslovakia Past and Present*, Vol. 2, pp. 1819-1820.

Thomas D. Marzik (1941-2007), b. Bridgeport, CT; historian, associate professor, Saint Joseph's University, Philadelphia
Bio: "Marzik, Thomas D.," in: *SVU Directory*, 9; Miller, Randall M., "In Memoriam:
Thomas D. Marzik (1941–2007), in: AHA Perspectives on History, May 2008; Kulczycki, John J., "Thomas D. Marzik, 1941-2007), *Slavic Review*, 67, No. 2, pp. 544-545; "Marzik, Thomas David," in: *American Scholars*, 8, Vol. 1.

Todd Michael Michney (1971-), b. Cleveland, OH, of Slovak descent; historian, Georgia Institute of Technology, Atlanta, painter GA
Bio: "Michney, Todd Michael," in: *SVU Directory*, 9; "Todd Michney," in: Georgia Tech School of history and Sociology. See - https://hsoc.gatech.edu/people/person/todd-michney

Susan Mikula (1943-), b. Bratislava, Czech; historian specializing in East Europe; professor of Benedictine University
Bio: "Susan Mikula," in: NCSML Oral histories. See - https://www.ncsml.org/exhibits/susan-mikula/

Maxim William Mikulak (1913-), b. New York, NY, of Slovak descent; historian, associate professor of history, New York Institute of Technology, Old Westbury, NY (s. 1980).
Bio: "Mkulak, Maxim William," in: *American Scholars*, 7, Vol. 1.

Joseph A. Mikuš (1910-2005), b. Krivá, Slovakia; professor of history and international relations at St. John's University, Jamaica, NY and Georgian Court College 1968-77), Lakewodd, NJ
Bio: "Mikus, Joseph A." in: *Educators*, p. 29; "Joseph A. Mikus," *The Washington Post*, June 10, 2005; "Mikus, Joseph August," in: *American Scholars*, 8, Vol. 1.

Andre S. Neuschloss (1920-1994), b. Bratislava, Czech.; Jewish historian, assistant professor of history, Touro College, NY (s. 1974), visiting professor of Jewish history, Yeshiva University (s. 1971).
Bio: "Neuschloss, Andre S.," in: *American Scholars*, 8, Vol.1

Dagmar Horna Perman (1925-1978), b. Bratislava, Czech.; social activist, historian, Georgetown University, Washington, DC.
Bio: "Perman, Dagmar Horna," in: *Encyclopedia*, Vol. 2, p. 1208; "Horna, Dagmar," in: *Social Sciences*, 9; McCarthy, Colman, "Dagmar Perman Dies, GU Teacher," *The Washington Post*, May 31, 1976.

Laura Matild Polanyi (1882-1959); b. Vienna, of Slovak father; married to Slovak-born businessman Sándor Striker; in US s. 1938; trained as a historian and economist. She was the first woman to get a Ph.D. from the University of Budapest. She was active as feminist and prolific non-fiction writer; author of a biography about the American hero Captain John Smith (of Pocahontas fame), the founder of Virginia in the 17th century.
Bio: Szapor, Judith, "Laura Polanyi 1882-1957: Narrative of a Life." See - https://www.kfki.hu/~cheminfo/polanyi/9702/szapor.html

Thomas Spira (1923-2005), b. Bratislava, Czech.; modern European historian, professor of history, University of Prince Edward Island, Charlottetown, Canada (s. 1971), editor
Bio: "Spira, Thomas," in: *American Scholars*, 8, Vol. 1; "Thomas Spira," in: Wikipedia. See - https://en.wikipedia.org/wiki/Thomas_Spira

M. Mark Stolarik (1943-), b. St. Martin, Czech.; historian, president of Balch Institute for Ethnic Studies, Philadelphia (1979-91); professor of history ad department chair, University of Ottawa (s. 1992)
Bio: "Stolarik, M. Mark," in: *American Scholars*, 7, Vol. 1, "M. Mark Stolarik," in: Prabook. See - https://prabook.com/web/m.mark.stolarik/800777

Anthony X. Sutherland (1944 -), b. Stony Point, NY, of Slovak descent; historian, editor of Slovak-American newspaper *Jednota* (1995-2009), author of *The Canadian Slovak League: A history, 1932-1982* (Toronto, 1982).
Bio: "A Fond Farewell," Jednota, January 6, 2010, p. 3. See - https://www.fcsu.com/wp-content/uploads/jednota-archives/2010/JEDNOTA-JAN-6TH-10.pdf

Edward Andrew Tuleya (1919-2008), b. Bridgeport, CT, of Slovak descent; historian, professor of history, Millersville University (1968-81), curator and archivist, Slovak Museum & Archives, Middletown, PA (1983-95)
Bio: "Tuleya, Edward Andrew," in: *American Scholars,* 8, Vol. 1; "Dr Edward A. Tuleya," *York Daily Record & York Dispatch,* November 13, 2008.

Francis Stephen Wagner (1911-1999), b. Krupina, Slovakia; modern historian, subject cataloguer, Library of Congress (1965-81)
Bio: "Wagner, Francis Stephen," in: *American Scholars,* 8, Vol. 1

George Waskovich (1896-1971), b. Greenwich, CT, of Slovak descent; historian. He taught history at the College of St. Teresa, Winona, MN, St. John's University, Brooklyn, NY and Hunter College, New York, NY.
Bio: "Waskovich, George," in: *Czechoslovak Contribution,* p. 651.

Charles Wojatsek (1916-2008), b. Dvory and Žitavou, Slovakia; historian, professor of history, Bishop's University, Sherbrooke, Quebec, Canada (s. 1976)
Bio: "Wojatsek, Charles," in: *American Scholars,* 8, Vol. 1

Ronald Edward Zupko (1938-), b. Youngstown, OH; professor of modern history, authority on historical metrology, Marquette University, WI (1966-2002)
Bio: "Zupko, Ronald Edward," in: *American Scholars,* 8, Vol. 1; "Ronald Edward Zupko," in: Wikipedia. See - https://en.wikipedia.org/wiki/Ronald_Edward_Zupko

3. Genealogists

Lisa A. Alzo (ca 1965-), b. Duquesne, PA, of Slovak descent; genealogist, freelance author, lecturer, vice president of the Federation of Eastern European Family History Societies
Bio: "Lisa Alzo," in: her website. See - https://www.lisaalzo.com/about/; "Lisa A. Alzo," in: FEEFHS. See - http://feefhs.org/presenter-2017-laa

Duncan Gardiner (1940-), b. Detroit, MI, of German-Slovak ancestry, a professional genealogist, specializing in Czech, Slovak, German and Russian research, and author.
Bio: "Biography," in: his article on Karel Kundera. See - https://www.cgsi. org/sites/default/files/1995_chicago_il_conference_2.pdf

Karen A. Melis, b. PA, of Slovak ancestry; genealogist, researching Slovak roots from both sides of the ocean, specializing in the former Spiš District, Slovakia; does also DNA testing. 2011-12 Fulbright Scholarship Winner for research in Slovakia on Slovak migration.
Bio: "Karen A. Melis," in: CGSI Professional Researchers. See - https://www. cgsi.org/research/professionals

Ray Plutko (ca. 1937-), b. McKeesport, PA, of Slovak ancestry; teacher and coach at Notre Dame High School in Riverside, CA; director, Slovak Genealogical Research Center; wrote *Jednota* column;
See: "Slovak Genealogical Resource," in: FEEFHS. See - http://feefhs.org/ resource/slovakia-genealogical-research-center

Randol Schoenberg (1966-), b. Brentwood, Los Angeles, CA, of Slovak and Czech descent; a grandson of the composer Arnold Schoenberg; trained as a lawyer. Apart from his lucrative law practiced, he was known primarily as a genealogist. He is a volunteer curator on Geni, and one of Geni's most active users, managing about 160,000 profiles. He is a board member of JewishGen and the co-founder of JewishGen's Austria-Czech Special Interest Group. He founded and moderates the Jewish Genealogy Portal group on Facebook, with over 25,000 members, the largest Jewish genealogy group in existence.
Bio: "Randy Schoenberg," in: GENi. See - https://www.geni.com/ people/Randy-Schoenberg/6000000002764082210; "E. Randol

Schoenberg," in: Wikipedia. See - Reynolds.https://en.wikipedia.org/wiki/E._Randol_Schoenberg

4. Legal Scholars

Thomas Buergenthal (1934-), b. Lubochňa, Slovakia; lawyer, jurist, legal scholar; professor of law, with SUNY Buffalo (1962-77); Fulbright and Jaworski Professor of Law, University of Texas, Austin, TX (s. 1978)
Bio: "Buergenthal, Thomas," in: *American Scholars*, 8, Vol.4; "Buergenthal, Thomas," in: *Who's Who in Law*, 2; "Thomas Buerghenthal," in: Wikipedia. See - https://en.wikipedia.org/wiki/Thomas_Buergenthal; "Buergenthal, Thomas," in: *Who's Who in America*, 41

John Francis Drac (1920-), b. Zborov, Czech.; chief law librarian (s. 1957), associate professor of law (s. 1969), Chicago-Kent College of Law, Chicago, IL
Bio: "Drac, John Francis," in: *American Scholars*, 5, Vol. 4

Robert Emil Hudec (1934--2003), b. Cleveland, OH, of Slovak ancestry; lawyer, professor of law at the University of Minnesota, authority on trade law and the GATT
Bio: "Robert Emil Hudec," in: *Who Was Who* in America; Altman, Daniel, "Robert E. Hudec, 68, Expert on Global Trade Law, Dies," *The New York Times*, March 31, 2003; "Hudec, Robert Emil," in: *American Scholars*, 8, Vol. 4; "In Memory of Robert Emil Hudec (1935-2003)," in: RIETI. See - https://www.rieti.go.jp/en/miyakodayori/064.html

5. Language and Literary Scholars

John F. Abbick (1911-1974), b. of Slovak descent; R.C. priest, S.J. He was an English professor at Marquette University in Milwaukee for 20 years before joining the English department at Rockhurst College in 1969.
Bio: "Rev. John Francis Abbick." In: Find A Grave. See - https://www.findagrave.com/memorial/188807606/john-francis-abbick

Luba Barna-Gulanich (1924-), b. Bratislava, Czech.; Slavic linguist, associate professor Youngstown State University, Youngstown, OH
Bio: "Barna-Gulanich, Luba," in: *SVU Directory* 8

Ingeborg Baumgartner (1936-), b. Stubňa, Czech.; foreign language specialist, Albion College, MI
Bio: "Baumgartner, Ingeborg," in: *SVU Directory*, 9; "Ingeborg Baumgartner," in: Prabook. See - https://prabook.com/web/ingeborg.baumgartner/639756

Lucy Bednar (ca. 1954-), Slovak American; associate professor of English, James Madison University (s. 2004)
Bio: "Lucy Bednar," in: LinkedIn. See - https://www.linkedin.com/in/lucy-bednar-30244a92/

Zora Bravenec (ca. 1957-), b. Bratislava, Czech; teacher of English as a second language, Texas A&M University, College Station, TX
Bio: "Bravenec, Zora," in: *SVU Directory* 9

Bonaventure S. Buc (1910-1966), b. Slovakia; R.C. priest, O.F.M., in US s. 1950. He was professor of German and French at the Franciscan High School in Malacky (Slovakia) and at Notre Dame Catholic High School in Easton, Pennsylvania. He died prematurely on April 22, 1966, in Buffalo, NY. He was the author of Slovak Language Laboratory Course (1968).
Bio: See Foreword in his book - https://www.amazon.com/language-laboratory-Bonaventure-Catholic-America/dp/B0042UK9WS

Verona Chorvathova-Conant (1942-), b. Bratislava, Czech.; Slavic languages and literature, University of Pittsburgh
Bio: "Chorvathova-Conant, Verona," in: *SVU Directory* 8

Andrew Činčura (1917-2000), b. Slovakia; taught at University of California, Riverside, specializing in comparative literature and Slavic languages; translator; editor of *An Anthology of Slovak Literature*

Michael Dirda (1948-), b. Lorain, OH, of Slovak descent, on his mother's side. Dirda took an M.A. in 1974 and Ph.D. in 1977 from Cornell University in comparative literature. In 1978 Dirda started writing for the *Washington Post*; in 1993 he won the Pulitzer Prize for his criticism. Currently, he is a book columnist for the *Washington Post*.
Bio: "Michael Dirda," in; Wikipedia. See - https://en.wikipedia.org/wiki/Michael_Dirda

Nataša Durovičová (1954-), b. Bratislava, Czech.; Editor, International Writing Program, University of Iowa, Iowa City
Bio: "Nataša Durovičová," in *SVU Directory*; The International Writing Program. See: https://iwp.uiowa.edu/people/natasa-durovicova

Eugene Hannes Falk (1913-2000), b. Liptovský Sv. Mikuláš, professor of French and comparative literature, University of North Carolina, Chapel Hill
Bio: "Falk, Eugene H.," in: *SVU Directory*, 7; "Dr. Eugene Hannes Falk," in: Find a Grave. See - https://www.findagrave.com/memorial/181217016/eugene-hannes-falk; "Falk, Eugene Hannes," in: *American Scholars*, 8, Vol. 3; Falk, Eugene Hannes," in: *Who's Who in America*, 41

Frantisek Gallan (1946-1991), b. Slovakia; emigrated to Canada in 1968; trained in comparative literature at University of Montreal; assistant professor at the University of Pittsburgh in the department of Slavic and Comparative Literature (s. 1977); associate professor of English and film at Georgia Institute of Technology (1985-88); professor of comparative and Slavic literature, Vanderbilt University (s. 1988).
Bio: Hooquist, Michael, "Frantisek Galan (1946-1991): In Memoriam," in: SCRIBD. See - https://www.scribd.com/document/119622565/MICHAEL-HOLQUIST-FRANTISEK-GALAN-1946-1991-IN-MEMORIAM

Jozef J. Konuš (1904-95), b. USA, of Slovak descent; anglicist; author of *Slovak-English Phraseological Dictionary/Slovensko-Anglicky Frazeologicky Slovnik*. Passaic, NJ: Slovak Catholic Sokol, 1969, and *Practical Slovak Grammar*. The Author, 1939.
Bio: Böhmerová, Ada, "Some Notes on the History of Slovak Anglicist Lexicography," *Brno Studies in English* 19 (1991). See - https://digilib.phil.muni.cz/bitstream/handle/11222.digilib/104415/1_BrnoStudies English_19-1991-1_6.pdf

Tom Tibor Kovary (1920-1988), b. Bratislava, Czech.; assistant professor of modern languages, SUNY College Cortland (s. 1959). He taught at Ithaca College before (s. 1956).
Bio: "Kovary, Tom Tibor," in *American Scholars*, 8, Vol. 3

Charles Kraitsir (1804-1860), b. Smolnik, Slovakia; in US s. 1833; trained as physician but in the US did not practice. In 1837/8 he established an academy

at Ellicott's Mills, MD. Subsequently he resided in Washington, D.C., and in 1841/2 was principal of the state academy of Maryland, Charlotte's Hall. From 1842 until 1844, he delivered lectures in Boston on philology, and established a school there. In 1848 he went to Europe, but afterward returned to Boston, and in 1851 came to New York State and passed his last years in Morrisania, engaged in literary pursuits.
Bio: "Charles Kraitsir," in : Wikipedia. See - https://en.wikipedia.org/wiki/Charles_Kraitsir

Joseph R. Kupcek (1914-d.), b. Chicago, IL, of Slovak descent; professor of Russian language and literature, Southern Illinois University, Carbondale, IL (s. 1970). He taught at Creighton University before (s. 1954).
Bio: "Kupcek, Joseph R.," in: *American Scholars*, 8, Vol. 3

Richard Liba (1923-), b. Detroit, MI; literary scholar, professor of humanities, Michigan Technological University, Houghton, MI;
Bio: "Liba, Richard," in: *SVU Directory* 8

John Lihani (1927-), b. Hnúšťa, Czech.; professor of Spanish literature and linguistics, University of Kentucky, Lexington (1969-92)
Bio: "Lihani, John," in: Educators, p. 20; "John Lihani," in: Prabook. See - https://prabook.com/web/john.lihani/313492, "Lihani, John," in: American Scholars, 7, Vol.3

Milan Loupal (1937-), b. Žilina, Czech.; Slavic languages and literature specialist, University of Kansas
Bio: "Loupal, Milan," in: *SVU Directory* 3

Edward E. Mehok (1932-), b. Akron, OH, of Slovak descent; R.C. priest, English literature specialist, professor of English, Borromeo College, Oho (1961-73), vice president and Dean of men (s. 1967)
Bio: "Mehok, Edward Eugene," in" American Scholars, 7, Vol. 1.

Mária Modrovich (1977-), b. Bratislava; Czech.; novelist, short-story teller, journalist; writes in Slovak and in English; contributor to the periodical *Sme;* resides in NYC.
Bio: "Maria Modrovich," in: Lic. See - http://www.litcentrum.sk/slovenski-spisovatelia/maria-modrovich

Elmer Joseph Nagy (1916-), b. Oros, Slovakia; professor of classics, California State University, Fresno (s. 1969)
Bio: Educators, p. 2; "Nagy, Elmer J.," in: *American Scholars*, 7, vol. 3

Janet Paterson (née Kirschbaum), literature specialist at the University of Toronto
Bio: "Janet Peterson," in: University of Toronto French Department. See - http://french.utoronto.ca/profiles/23

Peter Petro (1946-), b. Bratislava, Czech.; Russian language specialist; associate professor of Russian Studies, University of British Columbia, as professor (s. 1977); coordinator of Russian program a chair of program in modern European studies.
Bio: "Petro, Peter," in: Encyclopedia.com. See - https://www.encyclopedia. com/arts/educational-magazines/petro-peter-1946

Elizabeth M. Rajec (1931-), b. Bratislava, Czech; professor of Germanic languages, literatures and linguistics, at City College of City University of New York (1964-96)
Bio: "Rajec, Elizabeth M.," in: *SVU Directory* 8; "Elizabeth Rajec," in" LinkedIn. See - https://www.linkedin.com/in/elizabeth-rajec-2a218946/

Walter Albert Reichart (1903-1999), b. Bratislava, Slovakia; professor of German, University of Michigan (s. 1940)
Bio: "Reichart, Walter Albert," in: *Who's Who in America*,

Joseph Remenyi (1892-1956), b. Bratislava, Slovakia; professor of comparative literature, Western Reserve University
Bio: "Remenyi, Joseph," *Who's Who in America*, 28; "Remenyi, Joseph," in: *Encyclopedia of Cleveland History*. See - https://case.edu/ech/articles/r/ remenyi-joseph

Samuel Rosenblatt (1902-1983), b. Bratislava, Slovakia; rabbi and scholar; professor of Jewish literature (1930-46) and thereafter Oriental languages, at Johns Hopkins University, Baltimore.
Bio: "Rosenblatt, Samuel," in: *American Scholars*, 8, Vol. 4; "Rosenblatt, Samuel," in: encyclopedia.com. See - https://www.encyclopedia.com/

religion/encyclopedias-almanacs-transcripts-and-maps/rosenblatt-samuel; "Rosenblatt, S," in" *Who's Who in American Jewry*, Vol. 1, p. 514.

Charles Daniel Sabatos (1971-), b. Pittsburgh, PA, of Slovak descent; associate professor of English and comparative literature, Yeditepe University, Istanbul, Turkey, translator
Bio: "Sabatos, Charles Daniel," in: *SVU Directory* 8; "Charles Daniel Sabatos," in: academia.edu See - https://yeditepe.academia.edu/CharlesSabatos

Gerald J. Sabo (1945-), b. Bridgeport, CT, of Slovak descent; R.C. priest, S.J., associate professor of Slavic Languages and Literatures, John Carroll University. Cleveland, OH
Bio: "Sabo, Gerald," in: *SVU Directory*, 9; "Fr. Gerald J. Sabo, S.J.," in: John Carroll University Classical and Modern Languages and Cultures. See - http://sites.jcu.edu/language/professor/fr-gerald-j-sabo/; "Fr. Gerald J. Sabo, S.J.," in: Jesuit Community. See - http://sites.jcu.edu/jesuit/pages/people/fr-gerald-j-sabo-s-j/

Ján Šimko (1920-2011), b. Zlaté Moravce, Czech; professor of English, linguist, translator, Georgetown University, feature writer at the Voice of America
Bio: "Šimko, Ján," in: *SVU Directory*, 9; "Obituary," *The Washington Post*, October 24, 2011.

Klement Šimončič (1912-2010), b. Dolna Krupá, Slovakia; Editor, Free Europe, Inc., New York, NY (1948-73); lecturer with Columbia University
Bio: "Šimončič, Klement," in: *SVU Directory*, 9; "Klement Simoncic Obituary," *Albany Times Union*, January 24, 2010; "Simončič, Klement," in: Panorama, p. 279; "Klement Šimončič," in: Wikipedia. See - https://sk.wikipedia.org/wiki/Klement_ Šimončič; "Šimončič, Klement," in: *Czechoslovakia Past and Present*, Vol. 2, 1829.

Mikuláš Šprinc (1914-1986), b. Krompachy, Slovakia; R.C. priest; poet, prose writer, essayist, editor, translator and teacher. He worked for the Vatican mission for refugees after WWI; immigrated to the USA in 1946; secretary of the Slovak Writers 'and Artists' Association. He was a teacher at Benedictine High School, professor of languages and philosophy of art at Borromeo Seminary of Ohio. He edited the journal *Most* for 30 years. He

was renowned for his sonnets, Christian meditations, and the role of man in the world.
Bio: "Mikuláš Šprinc," in: Wikipedia. See - https://sk.wikipedia.org/wiki/Mikuláš Šprinc; "Mikuláš Šprinc," in: LIC. See - http://www.litcentrum.sk/slovenskispisovatelia/mikulas-sprinc

Karol Strmeň (1921-1994), b. Palárikovo, Czech.; poet, translator, professor of modern languages, Cleveland State University, Cleveland, OH
Bio: "Karol Strmeň," in: LIC. See - http://www.litcentrum.sk/slovenskispisovatelia/karol-strmen#curriculum_vitae; "Karol Strmeň," in: Wikipedia. See - https://sk.wikipedia.org/wiki/Karol_Strmeň

Nathan Sűsskind (1906-1994), b. Stropkov, Slovakia; professor of German, City College of New York (1932-74), director of the institute for Yiddish Lexicology
Bio: "Sűsskind, Nathan," in: *American Scholars*, 7, Vol. 3; Pace, Eric, "Nathan Susskind, College Teacher, 87; Was Yiddish Expert," *The New York Times*, July 20, 1995.

Margaret Mary Vojtko (1930-2013), b. Homestead, PA, of Slovak ancestry; adjunct professor of French at Duquesne University
Bio: "Margaret Mary Vojtko," in: Wikipedia. See - https://en.wikipedia.org/wiki/Margaret_Mary_Vojtko

Martin Votruba (1948-2018), b. Štrba, Czech., senior lecturer of Slavic languages and literatures, and head of Slovak studies program, University of Pittsburgh
Bio: "Martin Votruba," in: University of Pittsburgh, Slovak Studies Program. See -http://www.pitt.edu/~votruba/skprogram/Martin_Votruba.html; Kopanic, Michael, Jr., "Professor Martin Votruba Obituary, 1948-2018," in: academia.edu. See - https://www.academia.edu/37904762/Professor_Martin_Votruba_obituary_1948-2018

Igor Michael Webb (1941-), b. Malacky, Czech.; associate professor of English, University of Massachusetts, Boston (s, 1971)
Bio: "Webb, Igor Michael," in: *American Scholars*, 7, Vol. 2

John F. Winter (1913-d.), b. Piešťany, Slovakia; professor of French literature, University of Cincinnati (s. 1967).
Bio: "Winter, John F.," in: American Scholars, 7, Vol. 3

6. Linguists

Eugene Gottlieb (1894-d.), b. Spiš, Slovakia; linguist, assistant professor of Germanics and Slavonic languages, City College, New York, NY
Bio: "Gottieb, Eugene," in: *American Scholars*, 3

Vladimír Kajlik (1946-), b. Perecin, Czech.; theologian, librarian, Wayne State University, Detroit, MI; now residing in the Czech Republic, applied linguist and translator, with University of South Bohemia, České Budějovice
Bio: "Kajlik, Vladimír," in: *SVU Directory* 8; "Dr. Vladimir Kajlik, Ph.D." in: ProZ.com

Mark Richard Lauersdorf (fl. 2018), linguist, associate professor, Linguistic Institute, University of Kentucky, Lexington;
Bio: Lauersdorf, Mark Richard," in: *SVU Directory* 8; "Mark Richard Lauersdorf," in: UK College of Arts & Sciences Linguistics. See - https://linguistics.as.uky.edu/users/mrlaue2

Goldie Piroch Meyerstein (1928-2017), b. Liptovský Mikuláš, Czech.; in US s. 1939; linguist; professor at UCLA and later as a longtime teacher in the LA public school system.
Bio: "Goldie Meyerstein," in: Sheridan Media.com. See - https://www.sheridanmedia.com/obituary/goldie-meyerstein

Nathan Susskind (1907-1994), b. Slovakia; professor of German and Jewish studies at City College, authority on Yiddish
Bio: Pace, Eric, "Nathan Suskind, College Teacher, 87; Was Yiddish Expert," *The New York Times*, July 20, 1994.

Michael Zarechnak (1920-2016), b. Vydraň, Czech.; linguist, computational linguist, Georgetown University, Washington, DC
Bio: "Zarechnak, Michael," in: Educators, p. 10; "Michael Zarechnak," *Washington Post*, April 12, 2016' "Zarechnak, Michael," in: *SVU Directory* 4

7. Philosophers

Alexander Altmann (1906-1987), b. Košice, Slovakia; rabbi; philosopher, professor of Jewish philosophy, Brandeis University, Waltham, MA (s. 1959). Bio: "Altmann, Alexander," in: *American Scholars,* 8, Vol. 4 ;"Altmann Alexander," in: *Who's Who in America,* 41

Martin F. Andic (1940-2005), b. New York, NY, of Slovak descent, philosopher, professor, University of Massachusetts, Boston
Bio: Rechcigl, Miloslav, Jr., "In Memoriam: Martin F. Andic," in academia.edu - See -https://www.academia.edu/12454388/ In_Memoriam_Martin_F._Andic_1940-2005_
"Andic, Martin," in: *SVU Directory*; "Andic, Martin," in: *American Scholars,* 8, Vol. 4.

Jozef Dieska (1913-1995), b. Dolná Lehota, Slovakia; philosopher, professor of philosophy, University of Dayton, OH (s. 1978)
Bio: "Dieska, Joseph," in: *American Scholars,* 8, Vol. 4; "Jozef Dieska," in: *Masaryk University.* See - https://www.phil.muni.cz/fil/scf/komplet/dieska. html

Lubomír Gleiman (1923-2006), b. Trnava, Slovakia; political philosopher, professor at Newton College, Franklin, MA (1957-75)
Bio: "Gleiman, Ľubomir" in: *SVU Directory* 8; Gleiman, Lubomir, *From the Maelstrom. A Pilgrim's Story of Dissent and Survival in the Twentieth Century.* Bloomington, IN: AuthorHouse, 2011; "Gleiman, Lubomir," in: *Social Sciences,* 13; "Gleiman, Lubomir," in: *American Scholars,* 8, Vol. 1

Pavel Kovály (1928-2006), b. Prague, Czech., of Slovak father; Holocaust survivor; professor of philosophy, Northeastern University, Boston
Bio: "Kovály, Pavel," in: Educators, p. 23; "Kovály, Pavel," in: Czech Literary Translators' Guild. See - http://databaze.obecprekladatelu.cz/databaze/K/ KovalyPavel.htm

Martin Beck Matuštík (1957-), b. Bratislava, Czech; philosopher, professor of philosophy and religious studies, Arizona State University
Bio: "Matustik, Martin," in: *SVU Directory* 8; "Martin Matustik," in: Arizona State University iSearch. See - https://isearch.asu.edu/profile/1268756'
"Matustik, Martin Beck," in: *Encyclopedia*, Vol. 2, p. 1179.

Charles Murin (1913-1998), b. Žabokreky, Slovakia; philosopher, associate professor of philosophy at University of Montreal (s. 1959)
Bio: "Murin, Charles," in: *American Scholars*, 8; "Charles Murin, 1913-1998," in: Forum.umontreal.ca. See - http://www.forum.umontreal.ca/numeros/1998-1999/Forum98-11-23/divers.html

Ernest Nagel (1901-1985), b. Nové Mesto nad Váhom, Slovakia; philosopher of science, professor of philosophy at Columba University (s. 1970)
Bio: Suppes, Patrick, "Nagel, Ernest," in: American National Biography Online, February 2000. Retrieved 10 April 2014; Suppes, Patrick (1994), "Ernest Nagel," in: *Biographical Memoirs of the National Academy of Sciences. National Academy of Sciences*. Retrieved 10 April 2014; "Ernest Nagel," in: Wikipedia. See: https://en.wikipedia.org/wiki/Ernest_Nagel; "Nagel, Ernest," in: *American Science, 14*; "Nagel, Ernest," in: *American Scholars*, 8, Vol. 4; "Nagel, Ernest," in: *Who's Who in America*, 33; Suppes, Patrick, "Nagel, Ernest," in: *National Biography*, Vol. 16, pp. 216-218.

Michael Novak (1933-2017), b. Johnstown, Pa, of Slovak ancestry; Catholic philosopher, author, publicist
Bio: "Michael Novak," in: Wikipedia. See - https://en.wikipedia.org/wiki/Michael_Novak; Alexander, June G., "Novak, Michael John," in: *Making It in America*. A Sourcebook on Eminent Ethnic Americans. Edited by Elliot Robert Barkan. Santa Barbara, CA: ABC-CLIO, 2001, p. 260; In Memoriam-Michael Novak. See - https://www.michaelnovak.net/in-memoriam/.

Štefan Polakovič (1912-1990), b. Chtelnica, Slovakia; theologican and philospher; professor at the Slovak University; published the first Slovak philosophical journal, *Filozofický sborník*. Emigrated to Germany in 1945, then Italy and in 1947 to Argentina. Worked as a bank officer, and later built

a thriving electronics business. After 1990, he distanced himself from the more radical nationalist interpretations prior to 1945.
Bio: "Štefan Polakovič," in: Wikipedia. See - https://sk.wikipedia.org/wiki/Štefan_Polakovič

Augustin C. Riška (1935-), b. Brodské, Czech.; philosopher, logician, philosopher of science, historian of philosophy, associate professor of philosophy, St. John's University, New York, NY.
Bio: "Riška, Augustin C.," in: *SVU Directory* 8, "Riska, Augustin," in: *American Scholars*, 8, Vol. 4; "Augustin Riška," in: Masaryk University (CZ). See - https://www.phil.muni.cz/fil/scf/komplet/riska.html

Michael John Sablica (1920-1997), b. Czech.; philosopher, theologian; assistant professor of philosophy and theology, Divine Word Seminary College (1977-)
Bio: "Sablica, Michael John," in *American Scholars*, 7.

8. Theologians

Alexander Altmann (1906-1987), b. Košice, Slovakia; an Orthodox Jewish scholar and rabbi. He emigrated to England in 1938 and later settled in the United States, working productively for a decade and a half as a professor within the Philosophy Department at Brandeis University.
Bio: "Alexander Altmann," in: Wikipedia. See - https://en.wikipedia.org/wiki/Alexander_Altmann

Julius Igor Bella (1901-d.), b. Slovakia; Lutheran minister; Dr.; professor of religion, Wittenberg University, Springfield, Ohio; father of Rev. Igor Vladimir Bella
Bio: "Bella Julius Igor," in: Educators, p. 44.

Bernard J. Bettelheim (1811-1870), b. Bratislava, Slovakia; physician, Protestant missionary to Okinawa, Army physician during Civil War
Bio: "Bernard Jean Bettelheim," in: Wikipedia. See - https://en.wikipedia.org/wiki/Bernard_Jean_Bettelheim

Daniel Černý (1983-), b. Košice, Czech.; Pontifical Oriental Institute, Rome; doctoral thesis on "The History of the Slovak Greek Catholics in Canada". See: Jednota, Aug. 22, 2018, p. 8.

Michael J. Chaback (1944-), b. Fountain Hill, PA, of Slovak descent; R.C. priest, S.T.D., Msgr., theologian, professor of theology, St. Charles Borromeo Seminary, Philadelphia (1973-92).
Bio: "Monsignor Michael J. Chaback, S.T.D., Group 10 chaplain, set to retire," *Slovak Catholic Falcon*, CIV, No. 5047 (July 15, 2015), p.2.

Ján Dolný (1981-), b. Bratislava, Czech.; RC. priest, theologian, monk
Bio: "Priest earns doctorate with scholarship through Eastern Europe collection," CNS News, May 22, 2017.

Joseph John Gavenda (1902-d.), b. Jessup, PA, of Slovak parents; R.C. priest, theologian; professor of Latin and psychology, St. Thomas Coll. and Marywood Coll., Scranton, PA, residing in Hazelton, PA
Bio: "Gavenda, Rev. Joseph John," in: *Catholic Who's Who*, Vol. 7, p. 158

John Hardon (1914-2000), b. Midland, PA, of Slovak ancestry; Jesuit priest, theologian. He has taught at the Jesuit School of Theology at Loyola University in Chicago and the Institute for Advanced Studies in Catholic Doctrine at St. John's University in New York. A prolific writer, he authored over forty books. In addition, he was actively involved with a number of organizations, such as the Institute on Religious Life, Marian Catechists, Eternal Life and Inter Mirifica, which publishes his catechetical courses.
Bio: "John Hardon," in: Wikipedia. See - https://en.wikipedia.org/wiki/John_Hardon; Cain, Michael, "Father Hardon will indeed be a hard act to follow," *Catholic Viewpoint*, January 5, 2001; "Rev. Fr. John Anthony Hardon," in: Find A Grave, see - https://www.findagrave.com/memorial/45587071/john-anthony-hardon

Paul Hinlicky (1952-), b. Portchester, NY, of Slovak descent; Lutheran minister, pastor in Blacksburg, VA, and Roanoke, VA; internationally-known theologian, professor of Lutheran Studies, Roanoke College, Salem, VA, editor of the *Lutheran forum* and *Pro Ecclesia*, author of books.
Bio: "Paul Hinlicky," in: InsideRoanoke. See - https://www.roanoke.edu/inside/a-z_index/religion_and_philosophy/faculty/dr_hinlicky;

"Curriculum vitae," in: InsideRoanoke. https://www.roanoke.edu/inside/a-z index/religion and philosophy/faculty/dr hinlicky/curriculum vitae

Joseph Andrew Komonchak (1939-), b. Nyack, NY, of Slovak descent; R.C. priest, theologian, church historian, professor of Catholic University of America, Washington, DC
Bio: "Komonchak, Joseph Andrew," in: *American Scholars*, 8, Vol. 4; Curriculum vitae, in: academia.edu. See - https://cua.academia.edu/JosephKomonchak/CurriculumVitae

John D. Kovac (1922--2007), b. Hazleton, PA, of Slovak ancestry; a Lutheran minister; pastor at St. John Evangelical Lutheran Church at Tarentum, Penn.; St. Peter and St. Paul Lutheran Church in Central City, Penn.; Immanuel Lutheran Church in Linn, Kan.; St. Peter Lutheran Church in Deshler; St. Paul Lutheran Church in Utica; and he was retired from St. John Lutheran Church in Seward. He was a member of the Lutheran Layman's League, Seward Kiwanis Club and the Kitones. He served as the circuit counselor for four different zones and was Central District (Slovak) secretary.
Bio: "Obituary: Rev. John Kovac, *York News-Times*, February 20, 2007; "Rev. John Daniel Kovac," in: Find A Grave. See - https://www.findagrave.com/memorial/28477327/john-daniel-kovac

Radoslav Lojan (1976-), b. Kamenice nad Cirochou, Slovakia; R.C. priest; Catholic theologian, with bioethics orientation; pastor, Ottawa Slovak community (2006-11); assistant and associate pastor, archdiocese of Kosice, Slovakia (s. 2002); with Catholic University of Ružomberok (s. 2014);
Bio: "Radoslav Lojan," in: LinkedIn. See - https://www.linkedin.com/in/radolojan/

Christian Robert Oravec (1937-), b. Johnstown, PA; R.C. priest, professor of systematic theology, St. Francis Sem. (1969-76), executive vice president, St. Francis College, Loretto, PA, (196-77), president (s. 1977)
Bio: "Oravec, Christian Robert," in: *Who's Who in America*, 42

Joseph Papin (1914 -1989), b. Parchovany, Slovakia; professor of religious studies, Villanova University, Villanova, PA (s. 1963), founder and director of the Villanova Theology Institute (s. 1967).
Bio: "Papin, Joseph," in: *American Scholars*, 7, Vol. 4; "J. Papin, Theology Institute Founder," The Willanovan, January 5, 2005. See - http://www. villanovan.com/news/j-papin-theology-institute-founder/article_a031fa94-3620-5c08-9c7d-14bad41387aa.html

Jaroslav Pelikan (1923-2006), b. Akron, OH, of Slovak ancestry; theologian, one of the world's foremost scholars of the history of Christianity; Sterling Professor of Religious Studies, Yale University (s. 1971).
Bio: "Pelikan, Jaroslav Jan," in: *Who's Who in America*, 33; "Obituary: Jaroslav Pelikan," *The Telegraph*, May 17, 2006; "Pelikan, Jaroslav," in: *American Scholars*, 8, Vol. 4; "Jaroslav Pelikan," in: Wikipedia. See - https://en.wikipedia.org/wiki/Jaroslav_Pelikan

Arnold John Tkacik (1919-2003), b. Parchovany, Czech.; theologian, Biblical scholar; associate professor, Kansas School of Religion, University of Kansas (1967-71); associate professor of Biblical literature, Illinois Benedictine College, Chicago, IL (1954-72, 1972-73).
Bio: "Tkacik, Arnold," in: *American Scholars*, 8, Vol. 4.

Stephen Samuel Wise (orig. Weisz) (1874-1949), b. Budapest, of Slovak and Moravian ancestry; American Reform rabbi, Zionist leader, theologian
Bio: "Stephen Samuel Wise," in: Wikipedia. See - https://en.wikipedia.org/wiki/Stephen_Samuel_Wise

Cassian Yuhaus (1923-2013), b. Hazleton, PA, of Slovak descent; R.C. priest, CP (member of the Passionists), church historian, and noted pioneer of religious renewal; professor of church history of various Passionate Monasteries in the Eastern US; president of CARA (1980--84)
Bio: "Rev. Cassian Yuhaus Obituary," *Scranton Times*, Feb. 16, 2013

Francis Zeman (1918-d.), b. Viničné, Slovakia; theologian, archeologist; professor of Holy Scriptures and Oriental Languages, Major Seminary,

Nicolet, P.Q., Canada (s. 1952); professor of Near East, Université du Québec à Trois-Riviéres (s. 1969)
Bio: "Zeman, Francis," in: *American Scholars*, 8, Vol. 1, "Zeman, Francis," in: *Who's Who in the East*, 10

Theodore Joseph Zúbek (1914-1988), b. Malacky, Slovakia; R.C. priest, O.F.M.; theologian, writer; church and literary historian, translator, publicist. He wrote a dissertation "Interventions by Joseph II into the life of Slovak Franciscans." Dean of Franciscans studying at the Faculty of Theology in Bratislava, taught in a Žilina monastery after WWII to 1950; put in a concentration camp after the communist closure of monasteries; escaped to Austria in 1951; to USA in 1952. He worked in parishes; professor of theology at Seton Hall University; editor of *Listy sv. Františeka*. From 1964-1970), he was the Superior of the Slovak Franciscans in America. Published in Slovak and English in Slovak and American journals. His most important book: *The Church of Silence in Slovakia*, Whiting, IN: J.J. Lach, 1956.
Bio: "P. Theodorik Jozef Zúbek, O.F.M.," in: Františkáni. See - http://www.frantiskani.sk/nekr/06/zubek.htm

C. SOCIAL SCIENCES

1. Anthropologists

Melville J. Herskovits (1895-1963), b. Bellefontaine, OH, of Slovak ancestry"; anthropologist
Bio: Gershenhorn, Jerry, *Melville J. Herskovits and the Racial Politics of Knowledge. Lincoln, NE: University of Nebraska Press*, 2004; Merriam, Alan P., "Melville Jean Herskovits, 1895-1963," *American Anthropologist*, Vol. 66, No. 1 (1964), pp. 83-109; "Melville J. Herskovits," in: Wikipedia. See - https://en.wikipedia.org/wiki/Melville J. Herskovits

Ivan Kalmar (1948-), b. Prague, Czech.; soon after he was born, the family moved to Komárno and later to Bratislava. When he was seventeen, he left the country and eventually arrived in the US, settling in Philadelphia. During the Vietnam War, he took up the study at the University of Toronto, where he received his master's degree and Ph.D. in anthropology. Kalmar is currently a Professor of Anthropology at The University of Toronto. He

is also involved with first-year undergraduate education at Victoria College, including the Vic One Program, where he holds the title of Hon. Newton W. Rowell Professor. In his recent research, the focus has been on western Christian views of Jews and Muslims. Currently, Kalmar is working on attitudes and policies towards Islam and Muslims in the eastern, formerly communist-ruled areas of the European Union.
Bio: "Ivan Kalmar," in: Wikipedia. See -

Lars Krutak (1971-), b. Lincoln, NE, of Slovak descent; an American anthropologist, photographer, and writer known for his research about tattoo and its cultural background. Btween 1999-2002 and 2010-2014, Krutak worked as an Archaeologist and Repatriation Case Officer at the National Museum of the American Indian and National Museum of Natural History, facilitating the return of human remains, funerary objects, sacred and ceremonial objects. Today, he is a Research Associate at the Museum of International Folk Art.
Bio: "Lars Krutak," in: Wikipedia. See - https://en.wikipedia.org/wiki/Lars_Krutak; "Lars Krutak, Tatoo Anthropologist," in Homepage of Lars Kutak. See - ice hockeyhttp://www.larskrutak.com/

Louis J. Lužbeták (1918-2005), b. Joliet, IL, of Slovak parents; missiological anthropologist and theologian. He was professor of anthropology, linguistics and sociology at the Seminary in Techny, IL. Missionary work and studied natives in New Guinea, 1952-55. Chairman of the Catholic Anthropological Association in 1962 and co-publisher of the quarterly *Anthropological Quarterly*. His acclaimed book: *The Church and Culture.* An Applied Anthropology for the Religious Worker (1963).
Bio: "Internationally esteemed anthropologist and missionary honored in memoriam Father Louis Luzbetak, 1918-2005," in: Society of the Divine Word, Chicago Province Obituaries. See - http://www.divineword.org/obituaries/louisluzbetak/

Edward Snajdr (ca 1967-), b. US., of Slovak descent; cultural anthropologist; with John Jay College of Criminal Justice, CUNY, NY (s. 2003), as associate professor (s. 2009)
Bio: "CV - Edward Snajdr." See - https://www.jjay.cuny.edu/sites/default/files/faculty/cv/snajdr%20cv%202017%20new.pdf

Oswald Werner (1928-), b. Rimovská Sobota, Czech.; originally trained as historical musicologist; anthropologist, linguist, professor at Northwestern University, Evanston, IL (s. 1971).
Bio: "Werner, Oswald," in: *Social Sciences*, 12; "Oswald Werner," in: Wikipedia. See - https://en.wikipedia.org/wiki/Oswald_Werner

2. Economists

Vojtech E. Andic (1910-1976), b. Dobronivá, Slovakia; economist, Union University, Albany, NY
Bio: "Andic, Vojtech Ervin," in *SVU Directory* 3; "Andic, Vojtech E.," in: Pejskar 1, pp. 81-85; "Andic, Vojtech Ervin," in: *Panorama*, p. 92; "Andic, Vojtech Ervin," in: *Czechoslovakia Past and Present*, Vol. 2, p. 1802; "Andic, Vojtech Ervin," in: *Czechoslovak Contribution*, p. 635.

Louis M. Baska (1888-1973), b. Kansas City, of Slovak descent; R.C. priest, O.S.B., professor of economics, Sr. Benedictine's College, Atchison, KS
Bio: "Baska, Louis M.," in *American Scholars*, 1; "Fr. Louis M. Baska," in: Find A Grave. See - https://www.findagrave.com/memorial/53282041/louis-martin-baska

Patrick Chovanec (1970-), b. LaGrange, IL, of Slovak descent; economist, chief strategist of Silvercrest Management and Adjunct Professor, School of International and Public Affairs, Columbia University
Bio: "Patrick Chovanec," in: Wikipedia. See - https://en.wikipedia.org/wiki/Patrick_Chovanec

Maurice Czikann-Zichy (1907-1986), b. Bratislava, Slovakia; economist, diplomat, professor of economics, Immaculata College, PA (1956-67), and then at St. Joseph's College, Philadelphia (1967-73).
Bio: "Czikann-Zichy, Maurice," in: *Educators*, p. 46; "Czikann-Zichy, Maurice," in: *Social Sciences*, 13, "Zichy, Maurice Czikann," in: *Who's Who in the East*, 12.

Michael Dudra (1912-1982), b. Jersey City, NJ, of Slovak descent; economist, professor at St. Francis College, Loretto, PA
Bio: "Dudra, Michael," in: *Educators*, p. 47, "Dudra, Michael," in: *Social Sciences*, 12.

L. Laszlo Ecker-Racz (1906-), b. Czech.; government economist, with US Treasury Department, dealing with fiscal economics and taxation.
Bio: "Ecker-Racz, L. Laszlo," in: *Social Sciences*, 12; Pearson, Richard, "L. Laszlo Ecker-Racz dies," *The Washington Post*, August 6, 1987.

Andrew Eliáš (1921-2017), b. Prešov, Czech.; economist, specializing in international trade and East-West trade, US Department of Commerce, Washington, DC
Bio: "Eliáš, Andrew," in: *SVU Directory* 8; Eliáš, Andrew, *I Chose America*. Bratislava: Vydavateľstvo, 2001; "Eliáš, Andrew," in: *Czechoslovakia Past and Present*, Vol. 2. 1808.

Michael Ferik (fl. 1967), b. Slovakia; trained as economist at University of Toronto; economist, Province of Ontario, Dept. of Economics
Bio: "Ferik, Michael," in: *Naše Hlasy*, p. 43.

Michael Ferik (ca 1972-), b. Toronto, of Slovak Canadian; trained in actuarial science; engagement manager, McKinsey & Co., NYC (1999-2002); senior VP, AXA Equitable, NYC (2002-09); senior VP, Guardian Life Insurance Co. of America, NYC (s. 2009); executive VP, Guardian life Insurance, NYC (s. 2014)
Bio: "Michael Ferik," in: LinkedIn. See - https://www.linkedin.com/in/michael-ferik-90650715/

Ervin Paul Hexner (1893-1968), b. Liptovsky Sv. Mikuláš, Czech.; political scientist, economist, with the International Monetary Fund and the World Bank, Washington, DC (1946-58)
Bio: "Hexner Ervin Paul: in: *Who Was Who in America* 5; "Ervin Paul Hexner," in: Wikipedia. See - https://de.wikipedia.org/wiki/Ervin_Paul_Hexner; "Hexner, Ervin Paul," in: *Social Sciences*, 9.

John V. Krutilla (1922-2003), b. Tacoma, WA, of Slovak ancestry; environmental economist
Bio: "John V. Krutilla," in: Wikipedia. See - https://en.wikipedia.org/wiki/John_V._Krutilla

Gregor Lazarčík (1923-), b. Horná Streda, Czech.; economist, professor of economics, State University of New York, Geneseo, NY (s. 1968)
Bio: "Lazarcik, Gregor," in *SVU Directory;* "Gregor Lazarcik," in Prabook. See - https://prabook.com/web/gregor.lazarcik/198779; "Lazarcik, Gregor," in: *Social Sciences,* 13; "Lazarcik, Gregor," in: *Who's Who in Commerce and Industry,* Vol. 14, p. 759; "Lazarcik, Gregor," in: *Who's Who in the East,*17.

Kari Polanyi Levitt (1923-), b. Vienna, of Slovak ancestry; Canadian economist, professor, McGill University
Bio: "Biography," in Kari Polanyi Levitt websihttp://www.karipolanyilevitt. com/biography/
"Kari Polanyi Levitt," in: Wikipedia. See - https://en.wikipedia.org/wiki/ Kari_Polanyi_Levitt

Patrick Lichner (1921-2004), b. Brezová, Czech.; economist, Inter-American Development Bank, Washington, DC
Bio: "Lichner, Patrick," in: *SVU Directory* 8; Obituary, *Washington Post,* January 13, 2004.

Eugen Lőbl (1907-1987), b. Halíč, Slovakia; economist, politician; jailed by Communists (1952-60); after the Soviet occupation of Czechoslovakia in 1968, he immigrated to the US. During 1969 till 1976 he taught economics in several universities.
Bio: "Eugen Lőbl," in: Wikipedia. See - https://cs.wikipedia.org/wiki/ Eugen_Löbl; "Eugen Loebl, 80, Dies; Former Czech Official," *The New York Times,* August 9, 1987.

Peter Minarik (ca 1968-), Slovak American; economist; senior economist, US Government Accountability Office, Washington, DC (2002-04); regional director, US Commission on Civil Rights (2004-16); Seanior Leader, Economist, Policy Research and Strategy, Phoenix, Arizona area; adjunct professor at Glendale Community College
Bio: "Peter Minarik," in: LinkedIn. See - https://www.linkedin.com/in/ peter-minarik-42b27a119/

Alexander M. Pavlik (1921-1974), b. Prievaly, Czech.; economist, president of International Hotel Corp., United International Development Enterprises, Elmont, NY
Bio: "Pavlik, Alexander M.," in: *SVU Directory* 3

George Polak (1923-1997), b. Porúbka, Czech.; economist, specializing in technological change, associate professor of economics and department chairman, West Liberty College, West Liberty, WV (s. 1963)
Bio: "Polak, George," in: *Social Sciences*

Karl Paul Polanyi (1886-1964), b. Vienna, of Slovak ancestry; economic historian, anthropologist and sociologist, political economist, social philosopher
Bio: "Karl Polanyi," in: Wikipedia. See - https://en.wikipedia.org/wiki/Karl_Polanyi

Jerry Karl Roháček (1945-), b. Poprad-Spišská Sobota, Czech.; economist, Anchorage Community College, University of Alaska
Bio: "Roháček, Jerry Karl," in: *SVU Directory* 8; "Jerry Rohacek," in: Encyclopedia, Vol. 2, p. 1318.

Ernest Šturc (1915-1980), b. Békéscsaba; lawyer, economist, director of the exchange and trade relations dept., International Monetary Fund, Washington, DC (s. 1965)
Bio: "Šturc, Ernest," in: *SVU Directory* 4; "Šturc, Ernest," in: Pejskar 2, p. 231; "Ernest Sturc Dies at 65," *The Washington Post*, October 30, 1980; "Ernest Sturc," in: Prabook. See - https://prabook.com/web/ernest.sturc/1047105; "Sturc, Ernest," in: *Panorama*, p. 290; "Sturc, Ernest," in: *Social Sciences*, 13.

Michael Šumichrast 1921-2007), b. Trenčín, Czech.; economist, VP and chief economist, National Association of Home Builders, Washington, DC
Bio: "Sumichrast, Michael," in: *SVU Directory*; Sullivan, Patricia, "World-Renowned Housing Economist Michael Sumichrast," *Washington Post*, September 5, 2009; "Sumichrast, Michael M.," in: *Social Sciences*, 12; "Šumichrast, Michael," in: *Czechoslovakia Past and Present*, Vol. 2, p. 1831.

Lucia Vojtassak (ca 1981-), b. Slovakia; economist; with University of Calgary (2001-07); assistant professor, Department of Economics, Trent

University (2007-12); instructor, Department of Economics, University of Calgary (s. 2016).
Bio: "CV: Lucia Vojtassak," See - https://econ.ucalgary.ca/manageprofile/ profiles/162-33562/lucia-vojtassak-cv.pdf

John Joseph Žák (1919-), b. Spišská Nová Ves, Czech.; lawyer, economist. J. Pomerantz, Inc., Newark, NJ
Bio: "Žák, John Joseph," in: *SVU Directory* 3; "Žák, John J.," in: *Czechoslovakia Past and Present*, Vol. 2, p. 1837.

3. Education Specialists

Emil Stephen Gavlak (1915-1993), b. Whiskey Springs, PA, of Slovak descent; teacher and principal in VA, TX, TN and FL; professor of education, University of Arizona, Tucson (1957-80)
Bio: "Emil Gavlak, former US professor, dies at age 77," in: *Arizona Daily Star*, November 28, 1993; "Emil Stephen Gavlak," in: *Educators*, p. 2

Louis Grossman (1863-1926), b. Vienna, of Slovak father; rabbi, pioneer of modern methodology of Jewish education in the US
Bio: "Rabbi Louis Grossman of Cincinnati Dies," *Jewish Daily Bulletin*, September 26, 1926

Emil Jacoby (orig. Jakubovics) (1923-), b. Čop, Slovakia; activist with Bnei Akiva, illegal Zionist organization in Europe; eventually immigrated to US where he got his training in education; appointed director of education at Valley Jewish Community Center (later becoming Adat Ari El) (1953-76), executive director of the Bureau of Jewish Education of Greater Los Angeles (1976-1993)
Bio: "Jacoby, Emil," in: *Educators*, p. 6; Ulman, Jane, "Survivor: Emil Jacoby," *Jewish Journal*, February12, 2014.

Alexander Mittelmann (1916-1975), b. Žbince, Slovakia; instructor, West Coast Teachers College, Los Angeles, CA
Bio: "Mittelmann, Alexander," in: *SVU Directory*, 1972, 3rd ed.

John Urban (1909-1998), b. Tisovec, Slovakia; science education specialist, professor and department chairman, State University of New York College of Education, Buffalo (s. 1946)
Bio: "Urban, Joseph," in" *American Science*, 11

4. Geographers and Area Specialists

Joseph Anthony Fekete (1928-), b. Bačka, Czech.; geographer, assistant professor and department chairman, State University College, Buffalo, NY
Bio: "Fekete, Joseph Anthony," in: *Social Sciences*, 1werner

Erwin Raisz (1893-1968), b. Levoča, Slovakia; cartographer, with Institute of Geographical Exploration at Harvard University, where he taught and was curator
Bio: "Erwin Raisz," in: Wikipedia. See - https://en.wikipedia.org/wiki/Erwin_Raisz; "Raisz, Erwin," in Who's Who in the East, 1951; "Cartographers: Erwin Raisz," in: Designerati. See - http://designorati.com/articles/t1/cartography/232/cartographers-erwin-raisz.php

Virginia Ann Yatsko (1966-), b. Wilkes-Barre, PA; specialist in photogrammetry with Farth Satellite Corp., Rockville, MD
Bio: "Yatsko, Virginia Ann," in: *SVU Directory* 8

5. Management and Business Administration Specialists

Vladimír Antoš (1979-), b. Stropkov, Czech.; business administrator; with Alexander J. Wayne & Associates, inv c. (s. 2002), as vice president (s. 2015).
Bio: "Vladimir Antos," in: LinkedIn. See - https://www.linkedin.com/in/vladimirantos/

Lorence Bravenec (1935-), b. Houston, TX, of Slovak descent; professor of accounting, Texas A&M University, College Station, TX
Bio: "Bravence, Lorence," in: *SVU Directory*, 9 "Life of Leisure? Not quite," in: Chrystal Houston, October 1, 2010. See - https://mays.tamu.edu/news/tag/lorence-bravenec/

Milan Jaques Dluhy (1942-2015), b. Chicago, IL, of Slovak ancestry; professor of political science and public administration, University of North Carolina, Wilmington, NC
Bio: "Milan Dluhy, former FIU professor of public administration, dies at 73," *Miami Herald*, Nvember 12, 2015; Curriculum Vitae: Milan J. Dluhy." See - http://docplayer.net/21166062-Curriculcum-vitae-milan-j-dluhy. html; "Dr. Milan Jacques Dluhy, 73, UNCW political science professor who authored 10 books," portcitydaily.com, November 11, 2015.

Tibor P. Gregor (1919-2008), b. Levoča, Czech.; corporate accountant, business management administrator, president of T. P. Gregor Associates, Toronto, Canada
Bio: "Gregor Tibor P." in: *SVU Directory* 8; "Tibor Gregr," *The Globe and Mail*, April 1, 2008

Fred Massarik (1926-2009), b. Vienna, of Czech and Slovak descent; professor of management, University of California, Los Angeles
Bio: "Massarik, Fred," in: *Educators* p. 5; "Dr. Fred Massarik," in: GENi. See - https://www.geni.com/people/Dr-Fred-Massarik/6000000021503761000

Joseph Senko (1935-), b. Pittsburgh, PA, of Slovak descent; certified public accountant. He was been a tax law specialist for the Internal Revenue Service and Adjunct Professor of income taxes at Duquesne, and a board member of various nonprofit and civic associations. He also worked for an international accounting firm, before starting his own accounting firm of McKeever Varka & Senko. He was elected treasurer of Mt.Lebanon
Bio: "Joseph Senko," in: Mt. Lebanon Democrats. See - http://www. mtlebanondemocrats.com/candidates/joseph-senko/

6. Political Scientists

Charles Sokol Bednar (1928-), b. New York, NY; political scientist, professor, Muhlenberg College, Allentown, PA
Bio: "Bednar, Charles Sokol Bednar," in: *SVU Directory* 8; "Charles Sokol Bednar," in: Prabook. See - https://prabook.com/web/charles_sokol. bednar/1707666

Alfred Diamant (1917-2012), b. Vienna, of Slovak Jewish parents; in US s. 1940; political scientist; with University of Florida (1950-60), Haverford College (1960-66), Indiana University (1967-88)
Bio: "Alfred Diamant," in: Wikipedia. See - https://en.wikipedia.org/wiki/ Alfred_Diamant; "Alfred Diamant," in: Dignity Memorial. See - http:// www.tributes.com/show/Alfred-Diamant-93814961

Andrew Eliáš (1921-2017), b. Prešov, Czech.; political scientist and economist, director of market research, US Dept. of Commerce, Washington, DC
Bio: "Eliáš, Andrew," in: *SVU Directory*

Gabriel Edward Janosik (1918-d.), b. Youngstown, OH; political scientist, professor of political science, State University of New York at Geneseo, NY
Bio: "Janosik, Gabriel Edward," in: *Social Sciences*, 9; "Edward Gabriel Janosik," in: Prabook. See - https://prabook.com/web/edward_gabriel.janosik/1696886; "Janosik, Edward Gabriel," in: Who's Who in America, 41.

Stanislav J. Kirschbaum (1942-), b. Bratislava, Czech.; in Canada s. 1949; political scientist; professor of international studies at York University, Glendon College (s. 1970). He he teaches courses on Central and Eastern Europe, nationalism, security, diplomacy, and Canadian defence and foreign policy in both English and French, primarily in the latter. In 2002 he was elected a Fellow of the Royal Society of Canada.
Bio: "Jubilee of Prof. Stanislav Kirschbaum," in: Kanadský Slovák. See - https://www.kanadskyslovak.ca/index.php/short-news/294-jubilee-of-prof-stanislav-kirschbaum

Jozef August Mikuš (1909-2005), b. Krivá, Slovakia; lawyer, diplomat, teacher of history and political science at Saint John's University, Queens, NY and then at Georgian Court College, Lakewood, NJ
Bio: "Jozef August Mikuš," in: Wikipedia. See - https://sk.wikipedia.org/ wiki/Jozef_August_Mikuš

Peter Alexander Toma (1925-2018), b. Dobšiná, Czech.; political scientist, professor of political science, University of Arizona, Tucson (s. 1966)
Bio: "Toma, Peter A.," in: *SVU Directory* 8; "Toma, Peter Alexander," in: *Educators,* p. 2; "Toma, Peter A.," in: *Panorama,* p. 296; "Peter A. Toma

Obituary," in: Tucson, AZ/ Obit Tree; "Toma, Peter Alexander," in. *Social Sciences*, 13; Toma, Peter A.," in: *Czechoslovakia Past and Present*, Vol. 2, p. 1832.

Philip Radmir Tuhy (1930-2016), b. Wilkes-Barre, PA, of Slovak descent; professor of political science, Wilkes University, Wilkes-Barre (s. 1993)
Bio: "Professor Philip Radmir Tuhy," *Citizens' Voice*, Apr. 22, 2016.

Paul Zinner (1923-2012), b. Košice, Czech.; political scientist, professor of political science, University of California, Davis, CA (s. 1965)
Bio: "International Student Profile: Paul Zinner," *Tufts Weekly*, November15, 1940; "Paul Zinner Obituary," *San Francisco Chronicle*, April 8, 2012; "Zinner, Paul Ernest," in: *Social Sciences*,13.

7. Psychologists (Social)

Elaine J. Belansky (1938-), b. Vígláš, Czech.; social psychologist and public health practitioner, Colorado School of Public Health, Aurora, CO
Bio: "Belansky, Elena J.," in: *SVU Directory* 8

Bernard Bettelheim (1811-1869), b. Bratislava, Slovakia; physician, surgeon; in US s. 1854; served in the Civil War as a surgeon; resided in Brookfield, MO
Bio: *Lincolns Hungarian Heroes*, p. 48; "Bernard Jean Bettelheim," in: Wikipedia. See - https://en.wikipedia.org/wiki/Bernard_Jean_Bettelheim

Bruno Betttelheim (1903-1990), b. Vienna, of Slovak and Bohemian ancestry; child psychologist
Bio: "Bruno Bettelheim," in: Wikipedia. See - https://en.wikipedia.org/wiki/Bruno_Bettelheim

Ladislav Čulen (1946-), b. Skalica, Czech.; clinical social worker, educational psychologist, Royal Ottawa Regional Rehabilitation Centre, Ottawa, Ont., Canada
Bio: "Čulen, Ladislav," in: *SVU Directory* 8

Daniel Droba Day (1898-1998), b. Žaškov, Slovakia; psychologist; professor of sociology, Gustavus Adolphus College (1934-35); counseling psychologist, VA Central Office (1946-56), VA Regnal Office
(s. 1956)

Bio: "Day, Daniel Droba," in: *Social Sciences*, 9; "Day, Daniel Droba," in: *Who's Who in the South*, 11

Ernest Furchtgott (1922-), b. Zlaté Moravce, Czech; psychologist, professor of psychology and department chairman, University of South Carolina, Columbia, SC (1969-92)
Bio: "Furchtgott, Ernest," in: *Social Sciences*, 13; "Ernest Furchtgott," in: Prabook. See - https://prabook.com/web/ernest.furchtgott/1704331; "Furchtgott, Ernest," in: *"Who's Who in America*, 41

Anna K. Hudec (1939-), b. Bytča, Czech.; transpersonal psychologist, therapist, founder and coordinator of WIN, bringing holistic practitioners and alternate modalities into one's awareness, Canada
Bio: "Hudec, Anne K.," in: *SVU Directory* 8; "Hudec," in: Windsor InspirationalNetwork. See - http://hudec.ca/winwin/

William Charles Kosinar (1911-1997), b. Czech.; psychologist, professor of social sciences with Kennedy-King College, Evanston, IL
Bio: "Kosinar, William Charles," in: *Social Sciences*, 12

Agnes Graig Rezler (1950-), b. Šahy, Czech.; educational psychologist, professor of health professions education, university of Illinois College of Medicine and college of Nursing, Glen Ellyn, IL (s. 1967).
Bio: "Rezler, Agnes Graig," in: *Social Sciences*, 13

Anita Miriam Riska (1938-), b. Bratislava, Czech.; child psychologist, specializing in mental retardation and geriatrics, applied behavioral specialist with Catholic Guardian Society, Group Home, Staten Island, NY
Bio: Riška, Anita Miriam," in: *SVU Directory* 8

Edgar Schein (1928-), b. Zurich, Switzerland, of Slovak ancestry; social psychologist, professor, MIT
Bio: "Edgar Schein," in: Wikipedia. See - https://en.wikipedia.org/wiki/Edgar_Schein

Melitta Schmideberg (née Klein) (1904-1983), b. Ružomberok, Slovakia; psychiatrist, psychoanalyst and author.
Bio: "Melitta (Klein) Schmideberg," in: *Encyclopedia*, Vol. 3, pp. 2114-2115.

Emanuel Windholz (1903-1986), b. Hronec, Slovakia; psychologist.
Bio: Rechcigl, Miloslav, Jr., "Emanuel Windholz," in: *Beyond the Sea of Beer,* pp. 567-568.

John Peter Zubek (1925-1974), b. Trnovec, Czech.; psychologist, professor and head, department of psychology, University of Manitoba, Winnipeg, Canada
Bio: "Biography of John Zubek," in: John Zubek Papers. See - http://www. umanitoba.ca/libraries/units/archives/collections/complete_holdings/ead/ html/zubek.shtml; Zubek, John Peter," in: *American Science,* 10, "Zubek, John Peter," in: *Social Sciences,* 12

8. Sociologists

Julius Drachsler (1889-1927), b. Bella, Slovakia; sociologist, social service expert, author
Bio: "Drachsler, Julius," in: *Who's Who in the East,* 1930; Prof. Drachsler, Noted Educator and Jewish Social Service Expert, Dies," Jewish Telegraphic Agency, July 25, 1927. See - https://www.jta.org/1927/07/25/archive/ prof-drachsler-noted-educator-and-jewish-social-service-expert-dies

Leslie Kish (1910-2000), b. Poprad, Slovakia; sociologist, statistician, professor of sociology, University of Michigan, Ann Arbor, MI (s. 1963)
Bio: "Kish, Leslie," in: *Social Sciences,* 13; "Kish, Leslie," in: *Who's Who in America,* 41; "Leslie Kish," in: Wikipedia. See - https://en.wikipedia.org/wiki/ Leslie_Kish; Pace, Eric, "Leslie Kish, 90; Improved Science of Surveys," *The New York Times,* October 14, 2000.

Ferdinand Kolegar (1927-2007), b. Bratislava, Czech.; sociologist, professor with Roosevelt University, Chicago, IL (s. 1967)
Bio: "Kolegar, Ferdinand," in: *Encyclopedia,* Vol. 2, p. 1438; "Kolegar, Ferdinand," in: *Social Sciences,* 13

John Kosa (1914-1973), b. Šafárikovo, Slovakia; sociologist, with La Moyne College, Syracuse (s. 1955)
Bio: "Kosa, John," in: *Who's Who in the East,* 12; "John Kosa: in Memoriam," *Soc. Sci. Med.* (April 1973), pp. 231-232.

Ernest Michael Kuhinka (1922-), b. Rimavská Sobota, Czech. sociologist, anthropologist, Dickinson College, Carlisle, PA; professor of medical sociology, Hahnemann Medical College and Hospital, Villanova, PA (s. 1967)
Bio: "Kuhinka, Ernest Michael," in: *Social Sciences,* 13

Egon Mayer (1944-2004), b. Caux, Switzerland, of Slovak father; sociologist, professor at Brooklyn College
Bio: "Egon Mayer," in: Wikipedia. See - https://en.wikipedia.org/wiki/Egon_Mayer_(sociologist)

Edward Alfred Steiner (1866-1956), b. Senica, Slovakia; Congregational Church minister, educator, professor of applied Christianity, writer on immigration
Bio: "Steiner, Edward Alfred," in: *Who's Who in America,* 18; Steiner, Edward Alfred, *From Alien to Citizen: The Story of my Life in America.* Boston: Pilgrim Press, 1914; Luker, Ralph E., "Steiner, Edward Alfred," in: *National Biography,* Vol. 20, pp. 633-634; Spitzer, Yanny, "Edward A. Steiner: A Writer on Immigration." See - https://yannayspitzer.net/2012/08/24/edward-a-steiner-a-writer-on-immigration/; "Edward Alfred Steiner," in: *Encyclopedia,* Vol. 2, p. 1167.

John Zeisel (1944-), b. of Bohemian and Slovak descent; sociologist and architectural designer by training. Dr. John Zeisel is founder and president of Hearthstone Alzheimer Care, a company that programs, constructs, and manages assisted living facilities for persons with Alzheimer's disease. For more than 20 years, John carried out strategic planning efforts, facility programming, design review, public approvals, post-occupancy evaluations, and development management. After receiving his doctorate from Columbia University and a fellowship degree Harvard University's Graduate School of Design. He taught at Yale University and at Montreal's McGill University, then spent eight years on the Harvard Architecture School faculty. From 1980 to 1990, he served as president of the applied research and development firm Building Diagnostics Inc. In 1994, he was the Cass Gilbert Visiting Professor in the Department of Architecture at the University of Minnesota.
Bio: "John Zeisel, Ph.D." in: Huffpost. See - https://www.huffingtonpost.com/author/john-zeisel-phd; "John Zeisel," in: LinkedIn." See - https://www.linkedin.com/in/john-zeisel-4b83a7a/; "John Zeisel, Ph.D.," in: The Caritas Project. See - http://www.thecaritasproject.info/council/zeisel.html

9. Communication Specialists

Jan Juraj (George) Frajkor (1934-), b. Montreal, Quebec, Canada, of Slovak descent; professor of journalism, Carleton University, reporter, editor, publisher, and director of *Kanadský Slovak* weekly newspaper.
Bio: "Jan Juraj (George) Frajkor," in: LinkedIn. See - https://www.linkedin.com/in/jan-juraj-george-frajkor-b8715a12/

Tilly Janowitz-Gecsei, assistant professor of communications studies, Concordia University, Montreal, Canada

10. Information Specialists

Marguerite Densky (1942-1974), b. Bratislava, Czech.; librarian; professor of library studies, University of Montreal, Montreal, Canada
Bio: "Densky Marguerite Huebsch," in: Educators, p. 69; "Densky, Marguerite 1909-1995," in: in: Université de Montréal. See - http://www.archiv.umontreal.ca/P0000/P0155.html

Edward Kasinec (1945-), b. New York, NY, of Rusyn descent; reference librarian, curator of Slavic-Baltic Division, New York Public Library (1984-2009), visiting fellow of Hoover Institution, research scholar with Harriman Institute, Columbia University
Bio: NYC Literacy Showcase Participants. See - http://readrussia.org/participants/bio/edward-kasinec; "Edward Kasinec Visiting Fellow," in: Hoover Institution. See - https://www.hoover.org/profiles/edward-kasinec; "Edward Kasinec," in: Institute Staff, Columbia University. See - https://nehsummerinst.columbia.edu/bios/institute-staff/; "Edward Joseph Kasinec," in: Prabook. See - https://prabook.com/web/edward_joseph.kasinec/530573

Benjamin Weintraub (1917-2011), b. Prešov, Slovakia; librarian; professor of library/ information science, Rutgers University 1965-86); before that he worked at the Detroit Public Library (1953-62) and at the Penn State Library (1962-65).
Bio: Weintraub, Benjamin," in: Educators, p. 30; "Benjamin Weintraub Obituary," in: app. See - https://www.legacy.com/obituaries/app/obituary.aspx?n=benjamin-weintraub&pid=150650161-

11. University Administrators

Samuel Abraham (1960-), b. Bratislava, Czech.;_received university education at University of Toronto and Carleton University, Ottawa, Canada. He is a rector of BISLA (Bratislava International School of Liberal Arts), a small liberal arts college in Bratislava, Slovakia.Fr om 1996 to 2004 he was representative of the Project on Ethnic Relations, a Princeton-based foundation focusing on resolving ethnic tensions in Central and Eastern Europe. He is also member of the advisory board of Eurozine - an internet journal of a network of European cultural journals.
Bio: "Samuel Abraham," in: Wikipedia. See - https://en.wikipedia.org/wiki/Samuel_Abraham

Michael Duda (1909-1968), b. Donora, PA, of Slovak descent; formerly a coach, became third president of California University of Pennsylvania (1956-1968); he helped the California State College transition from a teacher training institution into a four-year liberal arts university
Bio: "Dr. Michael Duda - Class of - Hall of Fame - California University of Pennsylvania," in: cal. University of Pennsylvania Athletics. See - https://www.calvulcans.com/hof.aspx?hof=148

Gary Judd (1942-), b. Humenné, Czech.; metallurgical engineer, professor, Rensselaer Polytechnic Institute (s. 1976), Dean of the faculty (1994-1997), Provost, Troy, NY
Bio: "Judd, Gary," in: *American Science, 14*

Samuel Paul Kvasnica (1931-2014), b. Flint, MI, of Slovak descent; vice president for business affairs for Malone College, OH; Mackinac College, MI; Sterling College, KS; Sioux Falls College, SD; and for Manhattan Christian College, KS, retiring in May of 1993.
Bio: "Samuel Kvasnica," *The Repository*, December 4, 2014.

Joseph J. Labaj (1921-1985), b. of Slovak descent, R.C. priest, S.J., president of Creighton University (1970-1978)
Bio: "Joseph J. Labaj, S.J.," in: Creighton University. See - https://www.creighton.edu/office-of-the-president/presidential-history/1970-1978

John Lefko (1912-2002), b. Lower East side of New York City, of Slovak descent; R.C. priest; C.PP.S. (SJB) was the first president of St. Joseph's College, East Chicago, IN in 1954, retiring in 1975.
Bio: "Father John Lefko," in: Memorials (L-Z). See - https://www.nwitimes.com/uncategorized/memorials-l---z/article_f4bb9ac2-875c-52d4-b985-84bdeea8f02b.html

Christian Robert Oravec (1937-), b. Johnstown, PA; R.C. priest, professor of systematic theology, St. Francis Sem. (1969-76), executive vice president, St. Francis College, Loretto, PA, (196-77), president (s. 1977)
Bio: "Oravec, Christian Robert," in: *Who's Who in America*, 42

Stanford J. Ungar (1945-), b. of Slovak ancestry; journalist, Dean at American University, President of Goucher College
Bio: "Stanford J. Ungar," in: Wikipedia. See - https://en.wikipedia.org/wiki/Sanford_J._Ungar; "Sanford. J. Ungar, Goucher's 10th President," in Goucher College. See: http://www.goucher.edu/explore/who-we-are/history/gouchers-presidents/sanford-ungar

Arthur George Zupko (1916-2010), b. Yonkers, NY; pharmacist, professor, St. Louis College of Pharmacy (1949-55), associate dean (1955), dean (1956-60); Provost, Brooklyn College of Pharmacy, Long Island University (1960-73), president (1973-76); president, Arnold and Marie Schwartz College of Pharmacy and Health Sciences (1976-79).
Bio: "Zupko, Arthur George," in: *Who's Who in America*, 42' "Arthur George Zupko," in: Prabook. See - https://prabook.com/web/arthur_george.zupko/404181; "Dr. Arthur George Zupko," The News-Press, February 3, 2010

D. BIOLOGICAL SCIENCES

1. Agronomists - Soil Scientists

Štefan Kliman (1904-1995), b. Hlinik and Hronom, Slovakia; soil chemist, Milwaukee, Wi
Bio: "Kliman, Srefan," in: *SVU Directory* 11

2. Animal Scientists

Daniel Vrabelová Ackley (ca 1979-), b. Bratislava, Czech.; veterinarian; practicing in Waltham, MA, associated with MSPCA-Angell
Bio: "Daniela Vrabelova Ackley, DVM, MS, DACVIM," in: MSPCA-Angell - See - https://www.mspca.org/waltham_services/meet-the-internal-medicine-team/

Sagi Danenberg (fl. 2003), b. Slovakia; veterinarian. He relocated from Israel to Canada in 2003 and passed the North American veterinary licensing examination. He is associated with North Toronto Veterinary Behavior Specialty Clinic, Thornhill, Ont. Canada. Sagi provides behavior consults for owners with their pets including dogs, cats, horses, parrots and other exotic mammals.
Bio: "Dr. Sagi Denenberg." See - http://www.northtorontovets.com/our-doctors.pml

Paul Sanley Fišer (1938-), b. Rožňava, Czech.; animal scientist, specializing in reproductive physiology and genetics; dept. of animal and poultry science, University of Guelph, Ottawa, Canada (s. 1976)
Bio: "Fiser, Paul Stanley," in; *American Science, 14*

Ján S. Gavora (1933-), b. Brezová pod Bradlom, Czech; animal and poultry geneticist and breeder, research scient with Animal Research Inst., agriculture Canada, Ottawa
Bio: "Gavora, Ján," in *SVU Directory* 8; "Gavora, Jan," in: *American Science, 14*

Eva Hadzima (fl. 2008), b. Slovakia; veterinarian; she emigrated from Slovakia in 2000; in 2006 she and her husband worked as locum veterinarians for more than 60 clinics in Calgary; in 2008, she and her husband opened their own practice in De Winton, Alberta, Canada
Bio: "Inspiring Others Will Be Her Legacy," in: Immigrant access fund. See - http://www.iafcanada.org/success-stories/inspiring-others-will-be-her-legacy/

Maros Hadzima (fl. 2008), b. Slovakia; veterinarian; in 2006 he and his wife worked as locum veterinarians for more than 60 clinics in Calgary; in

2008, he and his wife opened their own practice in De Winton, Alberta, Canada.

František Hrudka (1920-2010), b. Horká and Váhom, Czech; veterinarian, professor of microscopic anatomy, Western College of Veterinary Medicne, Universityof Saskatchewan
Bio: "Hrudka, Frantisek," in: *SVU Directory* 8; "František Hrudka," in: Rechcigl, Miloslav Rechcigl, Jr., *Encyclopedia*, Vol. 3, p. 2164.

Michael Ivan (1938-), b. Falkušovce, Czech.; animal nutritionist, research scientist, Animal Research Institute, Agriculture Canada, Ottawa, Ont., Canada
Bio: "Ivan, Michael," in: *American Science, 14*

Jim Juriga (1964-), b. Fort Wayne, IN, of Slovak descent; a former football player; veterinarian; owner of Valley Animal Hospital (2000-2015); senior consultant, Six Rings Consulting, Greater Chiacgo Area, consulting practice specializing in organizations in transition.
Bio: "Dr. Jim Juriga," in: LinkedIn. See - https://www.linkedin.com/in/ dr-jim-juriga-dvm-63082587/

Pavol Liska (c. 1970-), b. Slovakia; veterinarian; in Canada s. 2002; co-owner of Elizabeth Street Pet Hospital and Southern Alberta Veterinary Emergency (SAVE), Calgary, Alberta
Bio: "Dr. Pavol Liska, DVM" in: Elizabeth Street Pet hospital. See - http:// elizabethstreetpethospital.blogspot.com/p/blog-page.html

Moshe Oz (ca 1981-), b. Slovakia; veterinarian; in Canada s. 2006; co-owner with his wife of Rose Valley Veterinary Hospital, West Kelowna, BC, Canada
Bio: "Meet the Staff." See - http://kelownavet.ca/meet-your-staff/

Noa Oz (ca 1979-), b. Slovakia; veterinarian; in Canada s. 2006; co-owner, with her husband, of Rose Valley Veterinary Hospital, West Kelowna, BC, Canada
Bio: "Meet the Staff." See - http://kelownavet.ca/meet-your-staff/

Elizabeth Ruelle (ca 1980-), b. Slovakia; veterinarian. In addition to owning Wild Rose Cat Clinic of Calgary in Alberta, Dr. Ruelle has served

on the Calgary Academy of Veterinary Medicine as a Director-at-large and is currently on the city's Responsible Pet Ownership committee as a veterinary voice for Calgary's cat population.
Bio: "Elizabeth Ruelle, DVM, DABVP," in: Cat Healthy. See - http://www.cathealthy.ca/our-specialists/; "Wild Rose Cat Clinic of Calgary." See - http://www.catmd.ca/

3. Anatomists

Aexander A. Fedinec (1926-1998), b Prešov, Slovakia; physician, anatomist; professor of anatomy, University of Tennessee, Memphis, TN; Associate Dean
Bio: Fedinec, Alexander, in: Educators, p. 50; White, Jeanice, "Alex Fedinec, Retiring after 35 years of service at UTHSC," in: UTHSC. See - https://news.uthsc.edu/announcements/alex-fedinec-retiring-35-years-service-uthsc/

Mario S. Nemirovsky, physician, anatomist; associate professor of anatomy, Faculté de médecine, Universite de Sherbrooke, Sherbrooke, Quebec, Canada (1971-95)
Bio: "Nrmirovsky, M. S.," in: Educators, p.71.

4. Biochemists

Alica Barta (1923-), b. Levice, Czech.; asoc. professor of biochemistry, dept. of psychiatry, McGill University, Montreal, Canada
Bio: "Bartova, Alica," in: *Science*, 15

Jana Marie Bednarek (1966-), b. Bratislava, Czech; biochemist, research chemist at Walter Reed Army Medical Center, Washington, DC (s. 1981)
Bio: "Bednarek, Jana Marie," in: Encyclopedia, Vol. 2, p. 1450; "Jana Maria Bednarek," in: Prabook. See - https://prabook.com/web/jana_maria.bednarek/243323

Ladislav Dory (1951-), b. Košice, Czech.; biochemist; researching cholesterol metabolism, cardiovascular disease, oxidative stress, inflammatory response and anti-oxidant defense mechanisms. With Louisiana State University, New Orleans (1982-85), University of Tennessee Health Science Center, Memphis

(1985-93); University North Texas Health Science Center, Ft. Worth (s. 1993; as professor s. 1998).
Bio: "Ladislav Dory," in: Prabook. See - https://prabook.com/web/ladislav. dory/319943

Dezider Grunberger (1922-1999), b. Košice, Czech.; biochemist, professor of biochemistry and molecular biophysics at Columbia University, New York, NY
Bio: "Dezider Grunberger, 77, Cancer Researcher and Columbia Professor," *The New York Times*, August 15, 1999; "Dezider Grunberger, 77, Cancer Researcher and Columbia Professor," *The New York Times*, August 15, 1999; "Dezider Gruenberger," in: *Holocaust Encyclopedia*. See - https://www.ushmm. org/wlc/en/idcard.php?ModuleId=10006715; "Dezider Grunberger," in: *Encyclopedia*, Vol. 2, p. 1454; Saxon, Wolfgang, "Dezider Grunberger," in: Prabook. See - https://prabook.com/web/dezider.grunberger/646820

Martin Kuna (1909-), b. Veľké Leváre, Slovakia; biochemist, principal research scientist with Bristol-Meyers Products, Hillside, NJ (s. 1965-)
Bio: "Kuna, Martin," in: *American Science*, 11

Oksana Maslivec Lockridge (1941-), b. Czech.; biochemist, biochemical pharmacologist, biochemical geneticist, research scientist at University of Michigan (1982-1990), professor at University of Nebraska Medical Center (1990-2003)
Bio: "Lockridge, Oksana Maslivec," in: *Science*, 4; "Oksana Lockridge," in: Prabook. See - https://prabook.com/web/oksana.lockridge/318661

John H. Pazur (1922-2005), b. Zubné, Czech.; biochemist, professor of biochemistry, Penn State University (s. 1966)
Bio: "Pazur, John H." in: *Who's Who in America*, 41

Manfred Eliezer Reichmann (1925-2012), b. Trenčín, Czech., biochemist, microbiologist, professor of botany, University of Illinois, Urbana, IL
Bio: Herbert A. Strauss and Werner Roder, eds., *International Biographical Dictionary of Central European Emigrés 1933-1945*. München-New York – London – Paris: K. G. Saur, 1983, Part 12: L-Z, p. 952; "Reichmann, Manfred Eliezer," in: *American Science*,11

Dominika Truban (1983-), b. Žiar and Hronom, Czech.; physician, biochemist; postdoctoral researcher at Mayo Clinic (s. 2016).
Bio: "Dominika Truban," in: LinkedIn. See - https://www.linkedin.com/in/dominika-truban-b715a7106/

Ivan Alois Veliky (1929-), b. Žilina, Czech.; biological chemist, associate research officer, Division of Biological Sciences, National Research Council of Canada, Ottawa, Ont., Canada
Bio: "Veliky, Ivan Alois," in: *American Science*, 11

Rudolf Vrba (orig. Walter Rosenberg) (1924-2006), b. Topoľčany, Slovakia; Canadian biochemist, pharmacologist; as a teenager in 1942, was deported to the Auschwitz concentration camp in German-occupied Poland. He became known for having escaped from the camp in April 1944, at the height of the Holocaust, and for having co-written a detailed report about the mass murder that was taking place there.
Bio: "Rudolf Vrba," in: Wikipedia. See - https://en.wikipedia.org/wiki/Rudolf_Vrba

Leopold Weil (1906-), b. Košice, Slovakia; biochemist, Eastern Utilization Research Branch, US Department of Agriculture, Philadelphia, PA
Bio: "Weil, Leopold," in: *American Science*, 10

Ambrose Žitňák (1922-2000), b. Bratislava, Czech.; plant biochemist, food technologist, department of horticulture, University of Guelph, Ont., Canada
Bio: "Zitnak, Ambrose," in: *American Science*,11

5. Molecular Biologists

Milan Jamrich (1950-), b. Nové Zámky, Czech.; molecular and cellular biologist; with Baylor College of Medicine, Houston, TX (s. 1997), as professor of developmental biology (s. 2005)
Bio: "Milan Jamrich," in: Prabook. See - https://prabook.com/web/milan.jamrich/818377; "Milan Jamrich, Ph.D., a biologist and elite high jumper," in: TMC News. See - http://www.tmc.edu/news/2018/02/side-milan-jamrich-ph-d/; "Milan Jamrich, Ph.D.," in: Baylor College of Medicine. See - ://www.bcm.edu/people/view/milan-jamrich-ph-d/genetics-research-faculty-e-j-primary-appointments-molecular-and-human-genetics/b18757dd; Pierce,

Shanley, "Milan Jamrich, Ph.D.," in: TMC News. See - http://www.tmc.edu/news/2018/02/side-milan-jamrich-ph-d/; "Milan Jamrich, Ph.D.," in: Retina Research foundation. See - https://retinaresearchfnd.org/pilot-study-grants/grant-recipients/jamrich/

6. Biophysicists

Norbert Kucerka (1976-), b. Slovakia; biophysicist; with department of physics, Carnegie Mellon University, Pittsburgh University (2003-06); Canadian Neutron Beam Center, NRC, Chalk River, Ont., Canada (2006-14).
Bio: Curriculum vitae. See - http://www.norbbi.com/curriculum/curriculum.html

7. Botanists

Louis A. Hanic (1921-), b. Sečovce, Czech; phycologist, associate professor of biology, University of Prince Edward Island (s. 1971)
Bio: "Hanic, Louis A." in: *American Science, 14*

Hilary Stanislaus Jurica (1892-), b. Slovakia; R.C. priest, O.S.B., monk; professor of botany and head of dept. of biology at St. Procopius College, professor of botany and head dept. of biology at De Paul University
Bio: "Hilary Stanislaus Jurica," in: *Encyclopedia*, Vol. 2, p. 1476; "The Jurica Brothers," in: Benedictine University; "Jurica, Hilary Stanislaus," in: *American Science, 5.*

8. Ecologists

Jan M. Barica (1933-), b. Varin, Czech.; aquatic ecologist, limnologist, research manager of aquatic ecology, National Water Research Institute, Burlington, Ont., Canada
Bio: "Barica, Jan M.," in: *Science*, 15

John P. Smol (1955-), b. Montreal, Quebec, Canada, of Slovak descent; Canadian ecologist, limnologist, paleolimnologist, Queens University, Kingston, Canada
Bio: "John P. Smol," in: Wikipedia. See - https://en.wikipedia.org/wiki/John_P._Smol

9. Epidemiologists

Joseph Goldberger (1874-1929), b. Giraltovce, Slovakia; physician, epidemiologist
Bio: Parsons, Robert P., *Trail to Light: A Biography of Joseph Goldberger*. New York: The Bobbs-Merrill Corp., 1943; Erthridge, Elizabeth W., "Goldberger, Joseph," in: *National Biography*, Vol. 9, pp. 180-181; "Joseph Goldberger," in: Wikipedia. See - https://en.wikipedia.org/wiki/Joseph_Goldberger; "Goldberger, Joseph," in: *Who's Who in American Jewry*, Vol. 1, p.206.

10. Entomologists

Július A. Rudinský (1917-1980), b. Pukanec, Slovakia; forest entomologist, with Oregon State University, Corvallis, OR (s. 1966))
Bio: "Julius A. Rudinsky," *Bulletin of the Entomological Society of America*, 27, No. 4, 15 (December 1981), pp. 292–293, "Rudinsky, Julius Alexander," in: *American Science, 14.*

Pavel Svihra (1939-), b. Banská Bystrica, Czech.; forest entomologist, with Cooperative Extension, University of California, Berkeley and later also at Davis
Bio: "Svihra, Pavel," in: *American Science, 14.*

Milan Trpiš (1930-), b. Mojšova Lučka, Czech.; medical entomologist, professor at Johns Hopkins University, Baltimore
Bio: "Trpiš, Milan," in: *SVU Directory*, 9; "Milan Trpis," in: Prabook. See - https://prabook.com/web/milan.trpis/69139; "Trpis, Milan," in: *Who's Who in America*, 42; "Trpis, Milan," in: Who's Who in the East, 17

Frank Zalom (1952-), b. Chicago, IL, of Slovak descent; professor of entomology and extension entomologist, University of California, Davis, CA
Bio: "Zalom. Frank," in: *SVU Directory,*
9, "Frank Zalom, Past President," in: Entomological Society of America. See - https://www.entsoc.org/about_esa/gb/frank-zalom-vice-president-elect

11. Foresters

Miroslav Grandtner (1928-2013), b. Liptovská Teplička, Czech.; forest and plant ecologist, professor of forest and wood science, Laval Université Laval, Quebec, Canada
Bio: "Grandtner, Miroslav," in: *SVU Directory* 8; "Grandtner, Miroslav," in: Généalogie Québec. See - https://www.genealogiequebec.com/necro/avis-de-deces/1255680-GRANDTNER-Miroslav; "Grandtner, Professor Dr. Miroslav Marian," in: World Who is Who and Does What in Environment and Conservation. Edited by Nicholas Polunin. London- Sterling, VA: earthscan, 2009; "Grandtner, Miroslav Marian," in: *American Science*, 14.

Eugene Joseph Kubinsky (1922-), b. Spišská Nová Ves, Czech.; wood production scientists and technologist, ITT, Rayonier, Inc., Shelton, WA (s. 1972)
Bio: "Kubinsky, Eugene Joseph," in: *American Science, 14*

Koloman Lehotský (1906-1975), b. Spišská Ves, Slovakia; forester, head of forestry department, Clemson University, SC
Bio: "Lehotský, Koloman," in: SVU Directory; "Koloman Lehotsky," in: Prabook. See - https://prabook.com/web/koloman.lehotsky/1048598; "Lehotsky, Koloman," in: Pejskar 1, p. 299; "Lehotsky, Koloman," in: *American Science*, 11.

Joseph Eric Marian (1901-),.b. Bratislava, Slovakia; wood technologist, Forest Products Lab, University of California, Richmond, CA
Bio: "Marian, Joseph Eric." In: *American Science*, 11

Michael M. Micko (1935-), b. Ttrebišov, Czech.; wood scientist, asst. professor of wood science, University of Alberta, Edmonton (s. 1977)
Bio: "Micko, Michael," in *American Science, 14*

12. Geneticists

Mihaly Bartalos (1935-), b. Bratislava, Czech.; physician, internist, medical geneticist, Columbia University
Bio: "Bartalos, Mihaly," in: *American Science, 14*

Pavol Ivanyi (1930-2005), b. Košice, Czech.; physician, geneticist, with dept. of genetics at Columbia University, then immigrated to Holland, where he was offered a position as head of immunogenetics in Amsterdam.
Bio: "Pavol Ivanyi," in: *Encyclopedia*, Vol. 2, p. 1496; "Pavol Ivanyi (May 26, 1930-July 19, 2005)," *Immunogenetics* 57, No. 11 (December 2005), pp. 801-804.

Eva Sujansky (1936-), b. Bratislava; pediatrician, clinical geneticist in Aurora, CO, affiliated with UC Health Memorial Hospital Central
Bio: "Dr. Eva Sujansky," in: US News. See - https://health.usnews.com/doctors/eva-sujansky-38757

13. Immunologists

Jan Ivan Schulz (1946-), b. Bratislava, Czech.; physician, immunologist, internist, with Mc Gill University, Montreal, Canada
Bio: "Schulz, Jan Ivan," in: *American Science, 14*

Ján Tomáš Vilček (1933-), b. Bratislava, Czech.; biomedical scientist, microbiologist, immunologist, virologist, authority on interferon, inventor, professor of microbiology, New York University School of Medicine (s. 1973)
Bio: "Vilcek, Jan V.," in: SVU Directory 8; "Jan Vilček," in: Wikipedia. See - https://en.wikipedia.org/wiki/Jan_Vilček; "Vilcek, Jan Tomas," in: *American Science*, 11; "Vilcek, Jan Tomas," in: *Who's Who in the East*, 16

14. Microbiologists

Paul Albrecht (1917-2007), b. Prešov, Czech.; virologist, pathologist, FDA, Rockville, MD
Bio: "Albrecht, Pavel," in: *SVU Directory;* "Paul Albrecht; FDA Expert on Infectious Diseases," Washington Post, May 2, 2007' "Paul Albrecht," in: *Encyclopedia*, Vol. 2, p. 1508, "Albrecht, Paul," in: *Science*, 14.

Daniel Carleton Gajdusek (1923-2008), b. Yonkers, NY, of Slovak father; physician, pediatrician, virologist and medical researcher; recipient of the Nobel Prize in physiology and medicine for his work on kuru
Bio: McNeil, Donald G., Jr., "Gajdusek, Daniel Carleton," in: *SVU Directory* 8; "D. Carleton Gajdusek, Who Won Nobel for Work on Brain Disease, Is Dead at 85," *The New York Times*, December 15, 2008; "Gajdusek, Daniel

Carleton," in: *American Science, 14*; "Daniel Carleton Gajdusek," in: Wikipedia. See - https://en.wikipedia.org/wiki/Daniel_Carleton_Gajdusek; "Gajdusek, Daniel Carleton" in: *Who's Who in America*, 41.

Erika Ana Green (1928-), b. Lučenec, Czech.; medical microbiologist, Hoffmann-La Roche, Inc. (s. 1973)
Bio: "Green, Erika Ana," in: *American Science, 14*.

Ján Ilavský (1910-1982), b. Turčianská Blatnica, Slovakia; medical and industrial microbiologist, Schering Corp., Union, NJ
Bio: "Ilavský, Ján" in: *SVU Directory* 4, "Ilavsky, Jan," in: *American Science*, 10

George Keleti (1925-2000), b. Michalovce, Czech.; environmental and clinical microbiologist, Graduate School of Public Health, Pittsburgh, PA
Bio: "Keleti, George," in: *SVU Directory*, 7, "Keleti, George," in: *Educators*, p. 48

Jacob Gabriel Michael (1931-), b. Rimavská Sobota, Czech.; microbiologist, research associate, Harvard Medical School, Boston, MA (s. 1961)
Bio: "Michael, Jacob Gabriel," in: *American Science, 11*

Alexander Robert Neurath (1933-), b. Bratislava, Czech.; virologist, investigator with L. Kimball Research Institute, New York Blood Center (s. 1972)
Bio: "Neurath, Alexander Robert," in: *American Science, 14*

Jana Nigrin (1942-), b. Piešťany, Czech; physician, microbiologist, assistant clinical professor of medical microbiology, and immunology, University of Alberta, Edmonton, Alberta, Canada
Bio: "Jana Nigrin," in: *Encyclopedia*, Vol. 2, pp. 1513-14.

Mikuláš Popovič (1941-), b. Mukačevo, Czech.; raised and educated in Slovakia; physician, virologist; with NIH; and professor, University of Maryland. He made pivotal contributions to the field of human retrovirology: transmission of T-cell Leukemia Virus and the development of a cell system for continuous propagation of human Immunodeficiency Virus.
Bio: "Mikuláš Popovič," in: Encyclopedia, Vol. 2, p. 1515; "Mikulas Popovic Celebrates Over 40 Years of Professional Excellence in Virology," in: Marquis

Who's Who's Press Release, November 17, 2017. See - https://www.24-7pressrelease.com/press-release/446817/mikulas-popovic-celebrates-over-40-years-of-professional-excellence-in-virology

Manfred Eliezer Reichmann (1925-), b. Trenčín, Slovakia, of Bohemian mother; microbiologist and virologist
Bio: "Manfred Eliezer Reichmann," in: *Encyclopedia*, Vol. 2., p. 1561.

William Reiner-Deutsch (1898-d.), b. Senica, Slovakia; microbiologist, consulting bacteriologist, Ophthalmol. Foundation, Bayside, LI, NY (s. 1953)
Bio: "Reiner-Deutsch, William," in: *American Science*, 14; "Reiner-Deutsch, William," in: Who's Who in the East, 7.

15. Nutritionists

Eva Politzer Shrons (1955-), b. Štúrovo, Czech; nutritionist, director of nutrition support service, University of Minnesota Hospital and Clinic, Minneapolis, MN
Bio: "Shrons, Eva Politzer," in: *SVU Directory* 8

16. Pathologists

Vladimír B. Altman (1929-2010), b. Levoča, Czech.; physician, pathologist, clinical asst. professor of pathology, SUNY Downsview Medical Center, Brooklyn, NY
Bio: "Vladimír B. Altman," in: *Encyclopedia*, Vol. 2, p. 1532.

Ernest Cutz (1942-), b. Nové Zamky, Czech.; physician, pathologist, professor of pathology, University of Toronto, Canada
Bio: Ernest Cutz," in: *Encyclopedia*, Vol. 2, p. 1534.

Simon Robert Klein (1868-d.), b. Teplica, Slovakia; physician, pathologist
Bio: "Klein, Simon Robert," in: *Who's Who in the East*, 1930; "Simon Robert Klein," in: Prabook. See - https://prabook.com/web/simon_robert.klein/1111714

Stanislav Kovarik (1929-), b. Teplica, Slovakia; physician, anatomic and clinical pathologist, practicing in Oak Park, IL; associate pathologist with Chicago Medical School (1969-70);
Bio: "Kovarik, Stanislav," in: Who's Important in Medicine, 2; "Dr. Stanislav Kovarik MD," in: healthgrades. See - https://www.healthgrades.com/physician/dr-stanislav-kovarik-wchh3sky

Emil E. Palik (1909-2006), b. Iowa City, IA, of Slovak descent; physician, pathologist; pathologist and Director of Laboratories at St. John Hospital in Tulsa, OK, where he was founder and member of the Board of the St. John Tumor Clinic. He was president of the Oklahoma State Association of Pathologists. Dr. Palik was also past President of the Tulsa County Cancer Society, the Tulsa Internists Society, the Tulsa Surgical Society.
Bio: "Palik - Emil E., MD," in: Tulsa World, June 1, 2006.

Alena Roubíček (1950-), b. Radošiná, Topoľčany, Czech.; physician, clinical pathologist, Sandy Spring, MD
Bio: "Roubiček, Alena," in: *SVU Directory*, 9

Kornel Terplan (1894-1987), b. Zlaté Moravce, Slovakia; pathologist, professor of pathology, State University of New York School of Medicine, Buffalo, NY
Bio: "Terplan, Kornel," in: *American Science*, 11; "Terplan Kornel Ludwig," in: *Who's Who in America*, 33; "Dr Kornel L.Terplan," in: Find A Grave. See - https://www.findagrave.com/memorial/57069715/kornel-l-terplan

17. Pharmacologists

Joseph Jan Barboriak (1923-2009), b. Slovakia; biochemical pharmacologist, professor of pharmacology, Medical College of Wisconsin, Milwaukee, WI
Bio: "Barboriak, Joseph Jan," in: American Science, 14; "Barboriak, Joseph Jan," in: *Who's Who in America*, 41; "Barboriak, Joseph Jan," in: Who's Who in the Midwest, 9.

Desider Fleischhacker (1889-1962), b. Bratislava, Slovakia; pharmaceutical chemist, biochemist, with Rare Chems. Inc. and Endo Products, Inc. (s. 1939)
Bio: "Fleischhacker, Desider," in: *American Science*, 10.

Samuel Kuna (1912-2013), b. Veľké Leváre, Slovakia; pharmacologist, head of division of toxicology and biological sciences, at Merck & Co. Inc. and Bristol-Myers, professor of toxicology at Rutgers University Graduate School
Bio: "Kuna, Samuel," in: *American Science, 14;* "Samuel Kuna Obituary," *Star-Ledger,* July 3, 2013; "Kuna Samuel," in: *Who's Who in the East,* 14.

Milan Slavik (1930-), b. Košice, Czech.; internist, clinical pharmacologist, oncologist, with University of Kansas, Lawrence, KS (s. 1983)
Bio: "Slavík, Milan," in: *SVU Directory* 8; Rechcigl, Miloslav, Jr., "Milan Slavík," in: *Encyclopedia,* Vol. 2, p. 1555.

Julius Adalbert Vida (1928-2018), b. Lošonec, Czech.; in US s. 1956; chemist, pharmaceutical expert, with Worcester Foundation for Experimental Biology (1962-67); section head, Kendall Co., Lexington, MA (1967-75); director of chemistry, international division, Bristol-Meyers Co., NYC (s. 1975). He identified and negotiated agreements for medical advances that led to treatments for cancer, heart disease and HIV/AIDS.
Bio: "Veda, Julius Adalbert," in: *Who's Who in the East,* 17; "Julius A. Vida Ph.D.," in: PressReader. See - https://www.pressreader.com/usa/greenwich-time/20180612/281741270124014

Vladimir Zbinovsky (1913-2013), b. Warsaw, of Slovak parents; pharmacologist and biochemist; taught first at Clark University, MA; after settling at Nanuet, NY, he worked for American Cyanamid, also known as Lederle Labs. His years at American Cyanamid yielded several patents and the discovery of new antibiotics, among them minocycline.
Bio: "Vladimir Zbinovsky," *The Journal News,* November 22-23, 2013

18. Physical Anthropologists

Howard F. Stein (1946-), b. Pittsburgh, PA, genuine Honorary Slovak, with no Slovak ancestry; American; organizational, applied, psychoanalytic and medical anthropologist and poet; professor, dept. of family and preventive medicine, University of Oklahoma Health Sciences Center, Oklahoma City (1978-2012).
Bio: "Howard F. Stein," in: Ghost Ranch. See - https://www.ghostranch.org/instructors/howard-f-stein/

19. Physiologists

Arnošt Fronĕk (1923-), b. Topoľčany; physiologist, professor of surgery and professor of bioengineering, University of California School of Medicine, San Diego
Bio: "Fronĕk, Arnošt," in: *Encyclopedia*, Vol. 2, pp. 1561-52; "Fronek, Arnost," in: *American Science, 14.*

Michael F. Holick (1946-), Slovak American; trained as biochemist and physician; endocrinologist specializing in the field of vitamin D; professor of medicine, physiology and biophysics at Boston University Medical Center.
Bio: "Michael F. Holick; in: Wikipedia. See - https://en.wikipedia.org/wiki/Michael_F._Holick

Stanislav Reiniš (1931-2012), b. Nitra, Czech.; physiologist, professor of physiology, University of Waterloo, Canada
Bio: "Stanislav Reiniš," in: Encyclopedia, Vol. 2, p. 1528, 1572; "Reiniš, Stanislav," in: *SVU Directory* 8; "Stanislav Reiniš," in: Wikipedia. See - https://cs.wikipedia.org/wiki/Stanislav_Reiniš; "Reinis, Stanislav," in: *Who's Who in America*, 42.

John Allen Resko (1932-), b. Patton, PA, professor of physiology, Oregon Health and Science University in Portland (s. 1981).
Bio: Resko, John Allen, *The Gates of Saint Charles. Testing the Waters of a Religious Vocation: A Memoir.* Bloomington, IB: iUniverse, Inc., 2009.

Hans Selye (1907-1982), b. Vienna, of Slovak descent; raised in Komárno and educated in Prague; physician, pioneering Canadian physiologist and endocrinologist. He is acknowledged as the 'Father' of the field of stress research, having gained world-wide recognition for introducing the concept of stress in a medical context.
Bio: "Hans Selye," in: Wikipedia. See - https://en.wikipedia.org/wiki/Hans_Selye

Anna Širek (1921-2009), b. Veľké Šenkvice, Czech.; professor of physiology, University of Toronto, Canada
Bio: "Širek, Anna," in: *SVU Directory,* 9; "Anna Sirek," in: *Naše Hlasy*, p. 47, "Sirek, Anna," in: *American Science,* 11

Otakar Viktor Širek (1921-2006), b. Bratislava, Czech.; professor of physiology, University of Toronto, Canada
Bio: "Sirek, Otakar Viktor," in: *SVU Directory,* 9; "Otakar V. Sirek," in: *Naše Hlasy,* p. 47; "Sirek, Otakar Victor," in: *American Science,*11

Soma Weiss (1898-1942), b. Považská Bystrica, Slovakia; physician, clinical physiologist; professor of medicine at Harvard University; chief physician at Peter Bent Brigham Hospital, Boston
Bio: "Soma Weiss," in: *Beyond the Sea of Beer,* p. 769.

20. Plant Scientists

Anton Novacky (1933-2014), b. Bratislava, Czech; plant pathologist, professor, University of Missouri, Columbia
Bio: Novacky, Anton," in: *SVU Directory*; "Anton Novacky, 1933-2014," *The Columbia Daily Tribune,* July 27, 2014.

Tibor Rajhathy (1920-), b. Bratislava, Czech.; plant geneticist, cytologist, director, Ottawa Research Station and Exp. Farm, Canada Dept, of Agriculture, Ottawa physicians1976).
Bio: "Rajhathy, Tibor," in: *American Science, 14*

Nancy Rechcigl (née Palko) (1961-), b. Morristown, NJ, of Slovak descent; noted specialist on ornamental plant protection and phytopathology.
Bio: "Nancy Rechcigl," in: WikiDoc. See - http://www.wikidoc.org/index.php/Nancy_Rechcigl; "Nancy Rechcigl," in: LinkedIn. See - https://www.linkedin.com/in/nancy-rechcigl-9286872b/

Joseph Stephen Semancik (1948-), b. Barton, OH, of Slovak descent; plant pathologist and virologist, professor of plant pathology, University of California, Riverside (s. 1974).
Bio: "Semancik, Joseph Stephen," in: *American Science, 14*

21. Psychologists (Clinical)

Bruno Bettelheim (1903-1990), b. Vienna, of Slovak ancestry; clinical psychologist, psychoanalyst
Bio: "Bruno Bettelheim," in: Wikipedia. See - https://en.wikipedia.org/wiki/Bruno_Bettelheim; Pollak, Richard, *The Creation of Doctor B: A Biography of Bruno Bettelheim.* New York: Simon & Schuster, 1997.

Michelle Elizabeth Boffa (née Striker) (1936-2011); b. Vienna, of Slovak descent; in US s. 1938; clinical psychologist, psychotherapist; on faculty of Hunter College (1970-72); in private practice in Los Angeles (1972-92).
Bio: "Michelle E. Boffa," *The New York Times,* March 18, 2011.

Fred Brown (1905-2005), b. Bratislava, Slovakia; clinical psychologist, chief psychoanalyst, Mt. Sinai Hospital, New York, NY, professor of psychiatry at Mt. Sinai School of Medicine (s. 1960)
Bio: "Brown, Fred," in *Social Sciences,* 13; "Death: Brown Fred, Ph.D.," *The New York Times,* July 22, 2005; "Fred Brown," in: *Encyclopedia,* Vol. 3, p. 2099; "Brown, Fred," in: *Who's Who in the East,* 12.

Edith Eva Eger (1927-), b. Košice, Slovakia; a Holocaust survivor; clinical psychologist, running a practice out of her home in La Jolla, CA. Her specialty involved treating patients suffering from post-traumatic stress disorder. Throughout her career in psychology, Eger has done extensive consulting work with the US military, treating American veterans of wars in Vietnam, Iraq and Afghanistan. She has also helped set up shelters for female victims of domestic abuse.
Bio: Gottlieb, Lori, "What a Survivor of Auschwitz Learned from the Trauma of Others," *The New York Times,* October 6, 2017; "Dancing for the doctor who ordered her parents' death," in: CN. See - https://www.cnn.com/2015/01/25/world/auschwitz-dancing-mengele/index.html

František Engelsmann (1922-), b. Nové Mesto and Váhom, Czech.; clinical psychologist, professor, McGill University
Bio: "František Engelsmann," in: *Encyclopedia,* Vol. 3, p. 2099

Paul Anthony Mestancik (1942-), b. Bratislava, Czech.; clinical psychoanalyst, Philadelphia, PA
Bio: "Mestancik, Paul," in: *SVU Directory* 8

Alexander Newman (1947-), b. Michalovce, Czech.; psychologist, assistant professor, Hunter College; CUNY (s. 1973); private practice in clinical psychology, in NY and NJ
Bio: "Newman, Alexander," in: Who's Who in the East, 17

William Robert Reevy (1922-2017), b. Dobšiná, Czech.; clinical psychologist, psychotherapist, Troy, NY
Bio: "Reevy, William Robert," in *SVU Directory* 8; "Reevy, William Robert," in: *Social Sciences*, 12; "William R. Reevy," *The News & Observer*, March 9, 2017

Stanislav Reiniš (1931-2012), b. Nitra, Czech.; clinical physiologist, neurophysiologist, University of Waterloo, Canada, writer
Bio: "Reiniš, Stanislav," in: *SVU Directory* 8; "Stanislav Reiniš," in: Wikipedia. See - https://cs.wikipedia.org/wiki/Stanislav_ Reiniš

Melitta Schmideberg (née Klein) (1904-1983), b. Ružomberok, Slovakia; psychiatrist, psychoanalyst and author
Bio: Rechcigl, Miloslav, Jr., "Melitta (Klein) Schmideberg," in: *Encyclopedia of Bohemian and Czech-American Biography*. Bloomington, IN: AuthorHouse, 2016, Vol. 3, p. 2114-2115.

Lynn E. Sullivan, now Fiellin (née Boffa), (ca 1984-), b. of Slovak descent; physician; associate professor of medicine at Yale university school of medicine and practicing HIV physician and addiction medicine provider.
Bio: "Lynn Sullivan," in: Robert Wood Johnson Foundation - Physician Faculty Scholars. See - http://www.physicianfacultyscholars.org/meet/2009/sullivan.htmly

Emanuel Windholz (1903-1986), b. Hronec, Slovakia; psychologist
Bio: Rechcigl, Miloslav, Jr., "Emanuel Windholz," in: *Beyond the Sea of Beer*, pp. 567-568.

22. Zoologists

Edmund Jurica (1900-1972), b. Cloverdale, IL, of Slovak descent; R.C., priest, O.S.B., monk; professor of biology at St. Procopius College, Lisle, IL
Bio: "Edmund Jurica," in: Encyclopedia, vol. 2, p. 1578; "The Jurica Brothers," in: Benedictine University. See - https://benuarchives.omeka.net/exhibits/show/the-buildings-of-science-at-be/the-jurica-brothers.

John Palka (orig. Pálka) (1939-), b. Paris, of Slovak parents; trained as zoologist, with specialty in neuroscience. Was with University of Washington, Seattle (s. 1969), where he rose from assistant professor to full professor of biology, retiring as professor emeritus. In 2002.
Bio: "About the Author" - Nature's Depths. See - https://naturesdepths.com/about/

E. Medical Sciences

1. General

2. Allergists

Martin Dubravec (ca. 1964-), b. Herscher, IL, of Slovak descent; physician, allergist-immunologist, practicing in Cadillac, MI and is affiliated with Munson Healthcare Cadillac Hospital.
Bio: "Dr. Martin Dubravec," in: Sharecare. See - https://www.sharecare.com/doctor/dr-martin-s-dubravec

Vincent Dubravec (ca 1962-), b. Herscher, IL, of Slovak descent; physician, allergist-immunologist, practicing in Grand Rapids, MI; is affiliated with multiple hospitals in the area, including Mercy Health St. Mary's Campus and St. Mary's of Michigan Hospital.
Bio: "Dr. Vincent Dubravec MD," in: U.S. News. See - https://health.usnews.com/doctors/vincent-dubravec-276672

Jan Ivan Schulz (1946-), b. Bratislava, Czech.; physician; allergist, immunologist, rheumotologist, Montreal, Que., Canada; affiliated with Montreal General Hospital
Bio: "Schulz, Jan MD," in: McGill University. See - https://muhc.ca/doctor/schulz-jan-md; *Who's Important in Medicine*, 2

Anthony M. Yurchak (1936-2017), b. Wilkes-Barre, PA, of Slovak descent; physician, allergist and immunologist, with Buffalo Amherst Allergy Associates
Bio: "Dr. Anthony Yurchak Obituary," in: Amigone Funeral Home Inc. See - https://www.amigone.com/obituary/Dr.-Anthony-M.-Yurchak/Orchard-Park-NY/1726738

3. Anesthesiologists

Dusan Hanidziar (ca 1981-), b. Slovakia; Board certified anesthesiologist, practicing in Boston, MA. He is affiliated with Massachusetts General Hospital and Beth Israel Deaconess Medical Center.
Bio: "Dusan Hanidziar," in: doximity. See - https://www.doximity.com/pub/dusan-hanidziar-md

Viera Jana Kirilcuk (1932-), b. Bratislava, Czech.; anesthesiologist, New York, NY
Bio: "Kirilcuk, Viera Jana," in: *SVU Directory 8*

Jan Oravetz (1931-), b. Czech.; physician, anesthesiologist, Lakewood WA
Bio: "Oravetz, Jan," in: *SVU Directory,* 9

Stephen Joseph Prevoznik (1929-), b. McAdoo, PA; physician, anesthesiologist, Philadelphia (1962-94)
Bio: "Prevoznik, Stephen Joseph," in: *Who's Who in the East,* 17; "Stephen Joseph Prevoznik," in: Prabook. See - https://prabook.com/web/stephen_joseph.prevoznik/3497192

George Silvay (1935-), b. Košice, Czech.; physician; anesthesiologist; practicing in New York, NY and is affiliated with Mount Sinai Hospital;

professor of anesthesiology, perioperative medicine and pain medicine (s. 1982).
Bio: "Dr. George Silvay, MD, PhD." See - https://ww3.aievolution.com/ars1801/index.cfm?do=att.viewAtt&attendeeID=13255; "Silvay, George," in: Who's Important in Medicine, 2

Stephen R. Strelec (1951-), b. of Slovak descent; physician, anesthesiologist; practiced in Asheville, NC, Monroeville, PA, Pittsburgh, PA; anesthesiologist, UPMC, Pittsburgh (2001-2913); chief of anesthesia, Mission Hospital, Asheville, NC (2013-2016); clinical associate professor, University of Pittsburgh School of Medicine (s. 2016)
Bio: "Stephen R. Strelec, MD, FASE," in: LinkedIn. See - https://www.linkedin.com/in/stephen-r-strelec-md-fase-5009b279/

4. Cardiologists

Peter Ganz, b. US, of Slovak father; cardiologist, professor of medicine, University of California, San Francisco, pioneer and leader in translational and clinical cardiovascular research
Bio: "Peter Ganz," in: UCSF Profiles. See - https://profiles.ucsf.edu/peter.ganz

William Ganz (1919-2009), b. Košice, Czech.; cardiologist, co-inventor of the pulmonary artery catheter, with Cedars-Sinai Medical Center, Los Angeles, CA
Bio: "William Ganz," in: Wikipedia. See - https://en.wikipedia.org/wiki/William_Ganz; "Dr. William Ganz dies at 90; cardiologist co-invented flexible balloon catheter," *Los Angeles Times*, November 13, 2009; "William Ganz." In: *Encyclopedia*, Vol. 2, p. 1139 and Vol. 3, p. 1969; "Ganz, William," in: *American Science, 14*

Stephen H. Kliman (1949-2010), b. Milwaukee, WI, of Slovak descent; physician cardiologist, Indianapolis, IN;
Bio: "Stephen H. Kliman - Obituary," *The Indianapolis Star,* October 30, 2010.

Zoltán Meško (1928-), b. Košice, Czech; physician, cardiologist; in US s. 1969. In 1974, he moved to New York, where he served first at Brooklyn

Children's Hospital and then as an eadjunct professor at the cardiac center of St. Francis Hospital, until retirement in 1996.

Joseph Gregory Piroch (19236-2012), b. Pittsburgh, PA, of Slovak ancestry; clinical cardiologist; Lieutenant Commander, US Navy, Pensacola, FL Naval Hospital; in private practice of cardiology and internal medicine for nearly 40 years.
Bio: "Joseph G. Piroch," in: Find A Grave. See - https://www.findagrave.com/memorial/91972469/joseph-gregory-piroch

Peter Pitonak (ca 1967-), b. Slovakia: physician, cardiologist; practicing in Tyler, TX, affiliated with Trinity Clinic Cardiology, specializing in cardiovascular disease.
Bio: "Peter Pitonak, M.D." See - https://www.tmfhc.org/find-a-physician/profile/peter-pitonak/

Branislav Schifferdecker (1971-), b. Trstena, Czech.; physician, cardiologist, practicing in Oklahoma City, OK
Bio: "Branislav Schifferdecker, M.D.," in PreferUS. See - http://www.preferushc.com/detail/466

Paul Schweizer (1929-), b. Modrý Kámen, Czech.; physician, internist, cardiologist, practicing in New York, NY. He is affiliated with Mount Sinai Beth Israel, Mount Sinai Beth Israel Brooklyn and Mount Sinai St Luke's Hospital; professor at Mount Sinai Health System;
Bio: "Schweitzer, Paul," in: *SVU Directory*, 9; "Dr. Paul Schweitzer," in: sharecare. See - https://www.sharecare.com/doctor/dr-paul-schweitzer

Tibor K. Zemplenyi (1916-2010), b. Partizánska Lupča, Slovakia; cardiologist, professor, University of Southern California (1975-92)
Bio: "Zemplenyi, Tibor K.," in: *Educators*, p. 7; "Tibor Karol Zemplenyi,", in: Prabook. See - https://prabook.com/web/tibor_karol.zemplenyi/788097; "Zemplenyi, Tibor K.," in: *Who's Who in America*, 42

5. Chiropractors

Alfred Fred Kabana (1893-d.), b. Jablonica, Slovakia; chiropractor, Chicago, president of the Chicago Chiropractic Society, vice president of the Illinois Chiropractic Society
Bio: "Kabana, Alfred Fred," in: Droba, p. 297.

Samuel S. Lefkowitz (1885-), b. Veľopoljie, Slovakia; chiropractor, residing in Ridgefield Park, NJ
Bio: "Lefkowitz, Samuel S.," in: *Who's Who in American Jewry*, Vol. 1, p.354.

Elena Pedersen (ca 1966-), b. Revuca, Slovakia; chiropractor; in Canada s. 1969; chiropractor. In 1991, she moved to Vernon, B.C. and started her own practice. She sold her practice in 1994 and moved to U.S.A. She opened a practice in Mossyrock, WA in 1995 and built her new office building in 2006 where she is currently still practicing. She specializes in applied kinesiology (AK), the use of muscle testing the body to help delineate the areas of need be it chemical, structure, or electromagnetic.
Bio: Meat Our Team. See - http://mossyrockchiropractic.com/about-us/meet-our-team.html

6. Dentists

William S. Begalla (c. 1959-), b. Youngstown, OH, of Slovak descent; dentist, practicing in Youngstown, OH
Bio: "William Begalla, DDS," in: Northside Regional Medical Center. See - https://www.northsideregional.org/basic-page/501166/meet-general-dentistry-residency-faculty

William Joseph Doslak (1932-2014), b. Lorain, OH, of Slovak descent; dentist; practiced in Sheffield, Elyria and Amherst, OH.
Bio: "William Joseph Doslak," *The Morning Journal*, May 20, 2014.

Henry John Droba (1899-1986), b. Banská Bystrica, Slovakia; dentist, Chicago, associate in oral surgery, Illinois College of Dentistry
Bio: "Droba, Henry John," in: *Droba*, pp. 124-125; "Droba, Henry John," in: *American Science* 10.

Dominik Dubravec (ca 1962-), b. Herscher, IL, of Slovak descent; dentist and trained periodontologist. After first teaching and practicing at the University of Chicago's Department of Surgery, he began practicing in Kankakee, IL, in 1990. He opened his second practice in Chicago Heights (1997), later moving this practice to Frankfort (2008). In 2015 he merged his offices with Dr. Francis' Oak Brook office, to serve more effectively his patients. He e served as president of Illinois Society of Periodontists, Kankakee District Dental Society and South Suburban Chicago Dental Society.
Bio: "Dominik Dubravec, DDS, MSc." See - https://www.periodontalspecialty.com/meet-us/meet-dr-dominik-dubravec/

Leopold Greenbaum (1858-d.), b. Arva, Slovakia; dentist; assistant professor of Materia Medica and chemistry, Philadelphia Dental College (s. 1881), professor of Materia Medica, synesthesia and odontotechny (s. 1896); editor and manager of *The Stomatologist;* resided in Philadelphia
Bio: "Greenbaum, Leopold," in: *American Jewish Year Boo*k, Vol.6, p.105.

George Jancosek (1932-), b. Whiting, IN, of Slovak descent; dentist and orthodontist, Whiting IN
Bio: "Jancosek, George," in: Whiting, Indiana: Generational Memory. See - http://www.dlib.indiana.edu/reference/cshm/ohrc102.html#26n

Michael J. Kelchak (ca 1926-), b. Gary, IN, of Slovak descent; dentist, practicing in Chandler, AZ

John G. Lazur (1947-), b. Shenandoah, PA, of Slovak descent; dentist, practiced in Sunbury, PA (s.1972). In 2002, he relocated the practice w miles away, across the Susquehanna River in the borough of Shamokin Dam. In 2014, he transitioned his practice with Midwest Dental.
Bio: "John G. Lazur, DDS. A Dentist Story," in: Midwest Dental. See - https://midwest-dental.com/casestudies/dentist-story-lazur/

George Matula (1903-d.), b. Necpaly, Slovakia; dentist, Chicago
Bio, "Matula, George," in: *Droba*, p. 125; "Matula, George," in: *Panorama*, pp. 245246.

Stefan Osusky (1907-), b. Chicago, of Slovak parents; dentist, Chicago
Bio: "Osusky, Stefan," in: Droba, pp. 223-224

Adrian Palencar (fl. 2016), b. Slovakia; a graduate from Komensky University with the degree Doctor of Universal Medicine with specialty in stomatology (dentistry). He immigrated to Canada in 1968 and became a licensed Dental Surgeon in Canada in 1970. In 1975, he founded Brock Dental at Thorold, Ont., Canada. He practices in all aspects of dentistry from Implant Prosthetics, Crowns and Bridges, to his passion Orthodontics. In 2003 he received a Pinkster Award from the International Association of Orthodontics (IAO). He is a past president of the IAO Ontario section. In 2016 he joined the Pines Dental Office, Welland, Ont.
Bio: "Dr. Adrian Palencar," in: Brock Dental. See - http://www.brockdentalcare.com/dr--adrian-palencar/

Frank Popovich, dentist; professor of orthodontology, Faculty of Dentistry, University of Toronto, Canada; director of Burlington Growth Center (1961-89).
Bio: "Frank Popovich," in: *Encyclopedia*, Vol. 3, p.1922.

Richard Rehak (1937-), b. Czech.; dentist, orthodontist, Bethesda, MD
Bio: "Rehak, Richard," in: *SVU Directory*, 9

Radovan Rudik (fl. 2017), b. Trebisov, Slovakia; he grew up in Mississauga, Ont., Canada since he was 5 years old; dentist. He first practiced at Cary, Erwin, Pittsboro, Durham, and Roseboro, NC. Now he practices in Canada. He is affiliated with Moose Lake Dental, Guelph, Ont., Canada.
Bio: "Dr. Radovan Rudik," in: LinkedIn. See - https://www.linkedin.com/in/dr-radovan-rudik-aa034661/

Robert Schermer (1920-1974), b. Humenné, Czech.; dentist, private practice of prosthodontics, Cleveland, OH (s. 1946).
Bio: "Schermer, Robert." In: *Who's Who in the Midwest*, 6

Michael Šimko (1929-2008), b. Kolbas, Czech.; dentist, North Versailles, PA; reconstructive dental surgeon, associate clinical professor at Univ. of Pittsburgh Dental School
Bio: "Dr. Michael Simko Obituary," *Greensburg Tribune Rev.*, January 3, 2009.

Gustav Joseph Tilley (1888-d.), b. Passaic, NJ, of Slovak parents; dentist, Chicago, president of the Northwestern Branch of the Chicago Dental Society
Bio: "Tilley, Gustav Joseph," in: Droba, p. 126.

7. Dermatologists

Eugen Jeneux Arday (1902-1987), b. Žiar, Slovakia; physician, dermatologist, dept. of dermatology, State of California, Patton, CA
Bio: Arday, Eugene Jeneux," in: *SVU Directory* 4; "Arday, Eugene Jeneux," in: *Who's Who in the Midwest*, 6; "Dr. Eugene Jeneux Arday," in: Find A Grave. See - https://www.findagrave.com/memorial/7522953/eugene-jeneux-arday

Laszlo Biro (1929-), b. Czech.; physician, dermatologist, practiced in Brooklyn, NY (s. 1960), clinical associate professor of dermatology, SUNY, Downstate Medical Center, Brooklyn, NY (s. 1971).
Bio: "Biro. Laszlo," in: *Who's Who in the East*, 18; "Laszlo Biro," in: *Who's Important in Medicine*, 2.

Lester Hollander (1890-), b. Plavnica, Slovakia; physician, dermatologist, Montefiore Hospital, director of Pittsburgh College of Physicians
Bio: "Hollander, Lester," in: *Who's Who in American Jewry*, Vol. 1, pp. 277-278.

Jan Izakovic (ca 1964-), Slovak American; physician; dermatologist; practicing in Miami, FL; associate professor, Department of Dermatology and Cutaneous Surgery, University of Miami Hospital and Clinic
Bio: "JN Izakovic, in: esearchGate. See- https://www.researchgate.net/profile/Jan_Izakovic

Anna Ragaz (1943-2007), b. Czech.; dermatologist, pioneer in cosmetic dermatology, practicing in Seattle, WA, head of the Anna Ragaz Institute
Bio: "Ragaz, Anna," in: *Educators*, p.37; "Anna Ragaz," *The Seattle Times*, August 4, 2007.

8. Environmental Medicine Specialists

Juraj Ferin (1925-1995), b. Topolčany, Czech.; physician, professor of environmental medicine, School of Medicine and Dentistry, Rochester, NY
Bio: "Juraj Ferin," in: *Encyclopedia*, Vol. 3, p. 2072.

Milan Hazucha (1939-), b. Slovakia; professor of medicine and senior research scientist in the center for Environmental Medicine, Asthma and Lung Biology, University of North Carolina, Chapel Hill
Bio: "Milan Hazucha," in: UNC School of Medicine. See - https://www. med.unc.edu/cemalb/about-the-center/faculty-and-staff/faculty-2/ milan-hazucha/

9. Family Physicians - General Practitioners

Ladislav Ferdiand Clumecky (1922-), b. Podbrezova, Czech.; physician, practice in general medicine, Farmington, IL (1958--68), partner, Norridge Medical Centre, IL (s. 1968)
Bio: "Chlumecky, Ladislav Ferdinand," in: *Who's Who in the Midwest*, 14

Igor Dubravec (1926-2006), b. Košice, Slovakia; physician, neuroscientist; chief resident of the Kankakee State Hospital (for 5 years); settling in Herscher, where he was in private practice as a family doctor for nearly 30 years. He also served as Medical Director of the Illinois Veterans Home in Manteno for 8 years and served as chairman of the local branch of the American Academy of Family Physicians.
Bio: "Life Story / Obituary: Igor Dubravec," in: Schreffler Funeral Homes. See - https://www.lifestorynet.com/obituaries/igor-dubravec.70063

Eugene Foltin (1911-1997), b Bratislava, Slovakia; physician, specializing in family medicine, Massapequa, NY
Bio: "Foltin, Eugene," in: *Who's Who in the East*, 18

Vlado Andrew Getting (1910-), b. Philadelphia, PA; physician, professor of department of family medicine, University of South Florida (s. 1976)
Bio: "Getting, Vlado Andrew," in: *Who's Who in America*, 41

Peter Paul Hletko (1902-1973), b. Chicago, IL, of Slovak parents; physician and surgeon, Chicago, clinical instructor of neurology at the Loyola University School of Medicine
S Bio: "Hletko, Peter Paul," in: Droba, p. 260.

George Oravec Kemeny (1913-1986), b. Slovakia; Holocaust survivor, physician, associate professor of family practice, University of Illinois Medical Center, Chicago (s. 1975)
Bio: "Kemeny, George Oravec," in *SVU Directory*, 6; "Kemeny, George Oravec," in: *Educators*, p. 11; "Kemeny, George Oravec," in: *Who's Important in Medicine*, 2

Richard Lee Krajec (1944-2017), b. Ohio, of Slovak descent; physician, practiced family medicine at Ashtabula Clinic and Ashtabula County Medical Center, Ohio; medical director of Ashtabula County Hospice.
Bio: "Dr. Richard Lee Krajec," *The Star Beacon*, February 8, 2017.

Rudolph E. Medlen (1908-1991), b., of Slovak descent; physician, practicing in Uniontown; medical examiner of Jednota.
"Medlen Family Collection, 1905-1991)," PennState University Libraries. See - https://www.libraries.psu.edu/findingaids/CCHC7.htm

Ľudovít Pavlo (1925-2014), b. Michalovce, Czech.; physician; specialized in family medicine; family; writer, executive president of Slovak League in America
Bio: "Zomrel Ľudovít Pavlo, čestný predseda Slovenskej ligy v Amerike," in: Úrad pre Slovákov žijúcích v zahraničí. See - http://www.uszz.sk/sk/stranka/3439/zomrel-ludovit-pavlo-cestny-predseda-slovenskej-ligy-v-amerike

Alexander Pollak (1899-1966), b. Michalovce, Slovakia; Holocaust survivor, physician in general practice, Cleveland, OH
Bio: "Alexander Pollak," in: *Encyclopedia*, Vol. 3, p. 1944.

Anna Rezek (née Bunzl) (1895-1974), b. Vienna, of both Czech and Slovak ancestry; physician, Miami, Florida
Bio: "Anna Rezek," in: *Encyclopedia*, Vol. 3, p. 1945.

William George Rurik (1905-d.),), b. Chicago, IL, of Slovak father; physician and surgeon, Chicago, clinical instructor in medicine at the Rush Medical college
Bio: "Rurik, William George," in: Droba, pp. 260-261.

Frank Ruzicka (1931-2009), b. Bratislava, Czech.; physician, in US a. 1968, practiced in Taylor, TX (till 1990)
Bio: "Frank Ruzicka MD," *Austin American-Statesman,* Feb. 6, 2009

Emil G. Vrtiak (1890-), b. Janova, Slovakia; physician, Chicago, clinical professor of medicine, Rush Medical College, University of Chicago
Bio: "Vrtiak, Emil G.," in: Droba, p. 261; "Vrtiak," in: *History of Medicine and surgery and Physicians and Surgeons of Chicago.* Chicago: Biographical Publishing corporation, 1922, p. 873.

Edward J. Zamborsky (1902-1976), b. Freeland, PA, of Slovak descent; physician, surgeon, Allentown, PA
Bio: "Edward J Zamborsky," *The Gettysburg Times,* October 11, 1976.

10. Gastroenterologists

Vlado Šimko (1931-), b. Bratislava, Czech.; gastroenterologist, Brooklyn, NY
Bio: "Simko, Vlado," in: *SVU Directory* 8; "Vlado Šimko," in: NCSML Oral Histories: See - https://www.ncsml.org/exhibits/vlado-simko/

11. Geriatrists

Mildred Ruth Sabo (ca 1963-), b. NJ, of Slovak descent; internist, geriatrist, practicing in Brick, NJ; affiliated with Meridian Hospitals Corp.
Bio: "Dr. Mildred Sabo MD- Geriatric Medicine," in: USA Physicians Wiki. See - http://www.physicianwiki.com/dr-mildred-sabo-md-geriatric-medicine/

12. Gynecologists - Obstetricians

Brano (Branislav) Cizmar (ca 1967-), b. Slovakia; Board certified obstetrician and gynecologist. He relocated to North County from Brawley, California where he had been in private practice. He lives in San Marcos and is affiliated with Palomar Medical Center.
Bio: "Dr. Brano Cizmar, MD, FACS," in: Zocdoc. See - https://www.zocdoc.com/doctor/brano-branislav-cizmar-md-facs-24740

Milan Rastislav Henzl (1928-2005), b. Bratislava, Czech.; professor of obstetrics and gynecology, Stanford University, early leader in the field of hormonal contraception
Bio: "Milan R. Henzl," in: *Encyclopedia,* Vol. 3, pp. 1953-1954; "Milan Henzl, developer of medicine for women's health, dies at 77," Stanford Report, October 12, 2005. See - https://news.stanford.edu/news/2005/october12/med-obit-101205.html; "Henzl, Milan Rastislav," in: *American Science,* 14

Carl Jarolim (1929-), b. Košice, Czech.; physician, obstetrician, gynecologist, practicing in Chicago; clinical assistant professor of obstetrics and gynecology, Northwestern University Medical School, Evanston
Bio: "Jarolim, Carl," in: Educators, p. 15; "Jarolim, Carl," *Who's Important in Medicine,* 2; "Dr. Carl Jarolim, M.D.," in: healthgrades. See - https://www.healthgrades.com/physician/dr-carl-jarolim-wf7h9

Juraj Letko (ca 1975-), b. Slovakia; obstetrician and gynecologist with training in female pelvic medicine and reconstructive surgery, assistant professor of obstetrics and gynecology, University of Chicago
Bio: "Juraj Letko," in: University of Chicago Medicine. See - http://www.uchospitals.edu/physicians/juraj-letko.html

Edward Luchansky, Jr. (1941-2018), b. Bridgeport, CT., of Slovak descent; physician, obstetrician and gynecologist Bridgeport, CT
Bio: "Edward Luchansky," *Connecticut Post,* September 6-7, 2018. See - https://www.legacy.com/obituaries/ctpost/obituary.aspx?page=lifestory&pid=190141387

John N. Schwartz (1922-), b. Bratislava; immigrated to US from Israel in 1950; physician, obstetrician, gynecologist, practicing in Harvey IL; affiliated with Ingalls Memorial Hospital
Bio: "Schwartz, John N.," in: *Who's Important in Medicine,* 2; "Imrich A. Weiss," *Chicago Tribune,* Sept. 19, 2004

Imrich A. Weiss (1916-), b. Bratislava, Slovakia; Holocaust survivor; obstetrician, gynecologist, practicing in Chicago, IL
Bio: "Weiss, Imrich A." in: *Who's Important in Medicine,* 2; "Imrich A. Weiss," *Chicago Tribune,* September 19, 2004.

13. Internists

Josef Adriany (1908-d.), b. Dobšina, Slovakia; physician, internist, MO State Sanatorium, Mt Vernon, MO (1949-60; San Fernando Veteran's Administration Hospital, Sylmar, CA (s. 1960); clinical instructor of internal medicine, California College of Medicine, Los Angeles (s. 1965)
"Adriany, Josef," in: *Who's Who in the West*, 11.

Peter Bosak (ca 1966-), b. Slovakia; physician, internist; practicing at Auburn, WA, affiliated with MultiCare Auburn Medical Center
Bio: "Peter Bosak, MD," in: MultiCare. See - https://www.multicare.org/doctors/peter-bosak/

Paul Marian Cisarik (ca 1980-), Slovak American; physician, internist, with a focus on nutritional therapy; practicing in Cleveland, OH, with another office in Oxnard, CA; affiliated with Metro Health Medical Center, Cleveland; assistant professor at Case Western Reserve University School of Medicine.
Bio: "Paul Marian Cisarik, MD," in: doximity. See - https://www.doximity.com/pub/paul-cisarik-md

Peter Duros (ca 1962-), b. Slovakia; physician, internist, practicing in Orem, UT. He is affiliated with Timpanogos Regional Hospital
Bio: "Dr. Peter Duros," in: Sharecare. See - https://www.sharecare.com/doctor/dr-peter-duros

Thomas L. Gral (1925-), b. Nitra, Czech.; Holocaust survivor, physician, internist, also nephrologist and gerontologist, Canoga Park, CA; now residing in Sunny Isles Beach, Florida
Bio: "Gral, Thomas L.," in: *SVU Directory* 8; "Thomas Gral," in: NCSML Oral histories. See - https://www.ncsml.org/exhibits/thomas-gral/

Cyril Michael Hetsko (1942-), b. New Jersey, of Slovak descent; physician, Board-certified internist, Madison, WI; clinical professor of medicine at the University of Wisconsin School of Medicine and Public Health;
Bio: "Dr. Cyril Hetsko," in: US News. See - https://health.usnews.com/doctors/cyril-hetsko-790120; "Cyril 'Kim' Hetsko, M.D., receives Medical Society's Presidential Citation," in: Wisconsin Medical Society.

See - https://www.wisconsinmedicalsociety.org/news/cyril-kim-hetsko-md-receives-medical-societys-presidential-citation/

Martin Izakovic (ca. 1970-), b. Slovakia; physician, internist, hospitalist; Iowa City, IA; affiliated with Mercy Iowa City Hospital
Bio: Dr. Martin Izakovic," in: USNews. See - https://health.usnews.com/doctors/martin-izakovic-371844; "Martin Izakovic, 2nd," in: LinkedIn. See - https://www.linkedin.com/in/martin-izakovic-00858b130/

Ferdinand George Kojis (1901-1991), b. Podhradie, Slovakia; physician, internist, NYC
Bio: "Kojis, Ferdinand George," in: *Who's Who in the East*, 9

Lewis Benjamin Lefkowitz (1930-), b. Dallas, TX, of Slovak ancestry; internist, professor of preventive medicine at Vanderbilt University
Bio: Humphrey, Nancy, "Clinic Dedicated in Honor of Lefkowitz," *Reporter*, Vanderbilt University Medical' Center's weekly newspaper, March 9, 2001.

Joseph Miller (1906-) b. Tekovské Lužany, Slovakia; physician, internist, in private practice (s. 1941)
Bio: *Who's Important in Medicine*, 2

Fred W. Modern (1897-d.), b. Bratislava, Slovakia; physician, internist; practicing in Long Beach, CA; associate professor of medicine, Loma Linda University.
Bio: "Modern, Fred W." in: *Who's Important in Medicine*, 2; "Modern, Frederick W.S.," in: *Educators*, p.3.

John Anthony Ondrejicka (1956-2015), b. Bratislava, Czech.; physician, internist, Jacksonville, FL
Bio: "Ondrejicka, John Anthony," *Florida Times-Union*, May 3, 2015.

John Ondrejicka, Jr., (ca 1957-), b. Florida, of Slovak descent; internist, Neptune Beach, FL and Jacksonville, FL
Bio: "Dr. John Ondrejicka, MD," in: U.S. News - See - https://health.usnews.com/doctors/john-ondrejicka-425380

David Prokop (ca. 1971-), b. Slovakia; physician, internist, Bangor, Maine, affiliated with St. Joseph Hospital
Bio: "Dr. David Prokop MD," in: Physicians Profile WIKI. See - http://www. physicianwiki.org/dr-david-prokop-md-internal-medicine/

Kevin Thomas Rechcigl (1991-), b. Bradenton, FL, of Czech and Slovak descent; physician, internist, Jacksonville, FL
Bio: "Kevin Rechcigl," in: LinkedIn. See - https://www.linkedin.com/in/ kevinrechcigl/

Bartholomew Hernad Ring (1896-1975), b. Žilina, Slovakia; physician, specializing in internal medicine, Lake Placid, NY (s. 1951)
Bio: "Ring, Bartholomew Hernad," in: *Who's Who in the East* 9; Flynn, Andy, "Memories of Home," *Adirondack Daily Enterprise*, October 14, 2006.

Aurelia Rozov (1904-1993), b. Slovakia; clinical assistant professor of medicine, New York University Post Graduate Medical School, New York, NY
Bio: "Rozov, Aurelia," in: *Educators*, p. 37.

Jan Sporina (1958-), b. Slovakia; physician, internist; practicing in Calgary, Alberta, Canada; assistant professor, Cumming School of Medicine, University of Calgary
Bio: "Jan Sporina." See - http://contacts.ucalgary.ca/info/med/ profiles/1-4856228

Iveta Strananova Swaim (1968-), b. Slovakia; physician, internist; works in Charlotte, NC and is affiliated with Novant Health Presbyterian Medical Center
Bio: "Dr Iveta Swaim," in: healthgrades. See - https://www.healthgrades. com/physician/dr-iveta-swaim-xdhk2

Robert J. Vaschak (ca 1961-), b. Youngstown, OH, of Slovak descent; physician, Board certified internist; practices in Sandusky, OH
Bio: "Robert J. Vaschak," in: doximity. See - https://www.doximity.com/ pub/robert-vaschak-do

Austin Stanley Weisberger (1913-1970), b. Cleveland, OH, of Slovak ancestry; internist, hematologist; professor, Cleveland
Bio: "Austin S. Weisberger," *Blood*, 37, No. 1 (January 1971), pp. 113-114; "Austin Weisberger," 56, Cleveland Medical Leader," *The New York Times*, June 22, 1970.

Zoltan Tilson Wirtschafter (1899-1967), b. Košice, Slovakia; internist
Bio: "Dr. Zoltan T. Wirtschafter," in: Find A Grave. See - https://www. findagrave.com/memorial/107790700/zolton-t.-wirtschafter

Milan Wister (1952-), b. Piehany, Czech.; internist, Pikesville, MD
Bio: "Wister, Milan," in: *SVU Directory* 8; "Dr. Milan Wister," in: US News Doctors. See - https://health.usnews.com/doctors/milan-wister-317727

14. Nephrologists

Otto George Kuchel (1924-2012), b. Spišská Stará Ves, Czech.; physician, nephrologist, professor of nephrology, Clinical Research institute, University of Montreal
Bio: "Kuchel, Otto George," in: *American Science, 14,* "Otto George Kuchel," in: *Encyclopedia,* vol 2, pp. 1566-1567.

Peter Trnka (fl. 2014), b. Slovakia; physician, nephrologist. He worked as a pediatric nephrologist at the British Columbia Children's Hospital in Vancouver, Canada. He moved to Brisbane, Australia in 2010 and worked as a staff nephrologist at both Royal Children's Hospital and Mater Children's Hospital. He became the Director of Nephrology at Lady Cilento Children's Hospital in November 2014.

Daniel Valach (1958-), b. Slovakia; physician, nephrologist; a nephrologist in Mountain Home, AR and is affiliated with Fulton County Hospital.
Bio: "Daniel Valach," in: USNews. See - https://health.usnews.com/doctors/daniel-valach-154754

15. Neurologists - Neurosurgeons

Louis Bakay (1917-1998), b. Bratislava; Slovakia; physician, surgeon; in US s. 1948; professor and chairman, department of neurosurgery, State university of New York, Buffalo
Bio: "Louis Bakay," in: Prabook. See - https://prabook.com/web/louis. bakay/787572; "Bakay, Louis," in: *Science,* 15; "Louis Bakay," in: The Society of Neurological Surgeons. See - http://www.societyns.org/society/bio. aspx?MemberID=16527

Bibiana Bieleková (1969-), b. Bratislava, Czech.; neurologist, neuroimmunologist, National Institute of Neurological Disorders and Stroke, NIH, Bethesda, MD
Bio: "Bieleková, Bibiana," in: SVU Directory 8; "Bibiana Bielekova, M.D.," in: Principal Investigators, NIH Intramural. See - https://irp. nih.gov/pi/bibiana-bielekova; "Bibiana Bielekova," in: Euro Brain Injury 2017. See - https://braininjury.conferenceseries.com/ocm/2017/ bibiana-bielekova-national-institutes-of-health-usa

Ladislav Hinterbuchner (1922-2009), b. Slovakia; neurologist, professor of neurology at State University of New York, Brooklyn, NY.
Bio: "Ladislav Hinterbuchner," *The New York Times,* May 4, 2009: "Hinterbuchner, Ladislav," in: *American Science,* 14, "Hinterbuchner, Ladislav Paul," in: *Who's Who in the East,* 15.

Sylvia Klineová (ca 1978-), b. Slovakia; physician, neurologist in New York, NY. She is affiliated with multiple hospitals in the area, including Mount Sinai Hospital and Mount Sinai St. Luke's-Roosevelt.
Bio: "Sylvia Klineova," in: Mount Sinai - New York. See - https://www. mountsinai.org/profiles/sylvia-klineova

Natalia Murinova (ca 1966-), Slovakia; physician, neurologist. She is board certified in both neurology and headache medicine. She is affiliated with Harborview Medical Center and University of Washington Medical Center, Seattle. She is director of the UW Medicine Headache Center and a UW

associate professor of neurology. She also sees patients at the Headache Clinic at UWMC-Roosevelt and the Neurology Clinic at Eastside Specialty Center.
Bio: "Natalia Murinova," See - https://www.uwmedicine.org/Pages/bio.aspx?bioid=32475&redirect

Drahomira Sencakova (ca 1970-), b. Slovakia; physician, neurologist and psychiatrist, practicing in Minneapolis, MN, Rochester, MN and St. Louis Park, MN. She is affiliated with Park Nicollet Methodist Hospital.
Bio: "Drahomira Sencakova," in: vitals. See - https://www.vitals.com/doctors/Dr_Drahomira_Sencakova.html

Ivan Stanko (1939-), b. Topoľčany, Czech.; physician, neurologist, but also psychiatrist, practicing in Wausau, WI. He is affiliated with Marshfield Clinic and with Ascension St Clare's Hospital.
Bio: "Dr. Ivan Stanko MD," in US News. See - https://health.usnews.com/doctors/ivan-stanko-569780; "Stanko, Ivan," in: *Who's Important in Medicine*

16. Oncologists

Beata Holkova (1966-), b. Slovakia; hematologist and medical oncologist, practicing in Richmond, VA; assistant professor Department of Internal Medicine, Virginia Commonwealth University, Richmond.
Bio: "Beata Holkova, MD," in: VCU. See - https://medschool.vcu.edu/expertise/detail.html?ID=1413

Daniel Laszlo (1902-1958), b. Kosice, Slovakia; physician, internist, oncologist, div. of neoplastic diseases, Montefiore Hospital, New York, NY
Bi: "Laszlo, Daniel," in: *American Science, 9*

Katarina Leckova (ca 1972-), b. Slovakia; physician; Board certified in hematology, oncology and internal medicine; works in Lihue, HI; affiliated with Wilcox Memorial Hospital
Bio: "Katarina Leckova," in: Hawaii Pacific Health. See - https://www.hawaiipacifichealth.org/find-a-physician/search-results/Katarina-Leckova/1196

Victoria L. Seewaldt (ca. 1958-), b. Chappaqua, NY, of Slovak mother; physician, oncologist. With Division of Hematology and Oncology, Dept. of Medicine, Duke University, Durham, NC (s. 2000), as professor (2009-15);

assoc. director for Population Sciences Research, Comprehensive Cancer Center, City of Hope, Duarte, CA (s. 2015); Ruth Ziegler Professor and Chair, Department of Population Sciences, City of Hope, Duarte, CA (s. 20150.
Bio: "Victoria L. Seewaldt, MD," in: City of Hope. See - https://www.cityofhope.org/people/seewaldt-victoria

Eva Szabo (ca 1960-), b. Slovakia; physician, oncologist. After completing her medical oncology fellowship at the National Cancer Institute, Dr. Szabo led a laboratory effort studying lung cancer biology. She now holds the position of Chief of the Lung and Upper Aerodigestive Cancer Research Group at the NCI Division of Cancer Prevention.
Bio: "Eva Szabo, MD," in: NIH-NCI. See - https://prevention.cancer.gov/about-dcp/staff-search/eva-szabo-md

Zuzana Tothová, b. Slovakia; physician, medical oncologist; with Dana Farber Cancer Institute and the brad Institute at Harvard and MIT.
Bio: "Zuzana Tothova," in: '68 Center for Career Exploration. See - https://careers.williams.edu/alumni-profile/zuzana-tothova-01/

Peter Ujhazy (1957-), b. Bratislava, Czech; physician, oncologist, deputy associate director of the Translational Research Program, National Cancer Institute, NIH, Bethesda, MD
Bio: "Petr Ujhazy," in: *Encyclopedia*, Vol. 3, p. 1995; "Dr. Peter Ujhazy: Research for the Greater Good," in: NCBI- NIH. See - https://www.ncbi.nlm.nih.gov/pmc/articles/PMC5750156/; "Peter Ujhazy, M.D., Ph.D.," in: TRP Translational Research Program. See - https://trp.cancer.gov/about_trp/bios/ujhazy_peter.htm

Carmel Vernier (ca 1973-); b. of Slovak descent; physician, Board certified medical oncologist, hematologist; West Cancer Center, University of Tennessee
Bio: "Carmel Vernier," in: West Cancer Center. See - https://www.westcancercenter.org/about/team/1376/

17. Ophthalmologists

Adolph Barkan (1845-1935), b. Ľubotice, Prešov Dist., Slovakia; physician, ophthalmologist; spent almost half his 91 years in a very successful career on the West Coast.
Bio: "Barkan, Adolf," in: *American Science*, 3; "Adolph Barkan (1845-1935), European Ophthalmologist in San Francisco," *JAMA Ophthalmol.*, 132, No. 3 (2014), pp. 346-340.

Peter Fodor (ca. 1963-), b. Slovakia; physician, ophthalmologist, practicing in Gross Pointe, MI. He is certified in the subspecialty of corneal and external diseases, and has expertise in modern cataract, refractive, and anterior segment surgeries. He resides in Traverse City, MI.
Bio:" Dr. Peter Fedor," in: Great Lakes Eye Consultants. See - http://www.greatlakeseye.com/aboutPeter.html

Joseph Herman Goldberger (1910-2007), b. Washington, DC, of Slovak father; public health officer; in 1946 moved to El Reno, OK, where he set up a practice, specializing in ophthalmology.
Bio: "Joseph Herman Goldberger," in: Find a Grave. See - https://www.findagrave.com/memorial/18375058/joseph-herman-goldberger

Arthur Linksz (1900-1988), b. Hlohovec, Slovakia; ophthalmologist, NYC; clinical professor ophthalmology, New York University
Bio: "Arthur Linksz," in: *Encyclopedia*, Vol. 3, p. 1999; Flynn, John T., "Necrology Arthur Linksz," *Trans. Am. Ophthalmol. Soc.*, 86 (1988), pp. 10–11; "Linksz, Arthur," in: *American Science*, 14; "Linksz, Arthur," in: *Who's Who in the East*, 9' "Linksz, Arthur," in: *Who's Important in Medicine*, 2.rt.

Thomas Macejko (ca. 1942-), b. Youngstown, OH, of Slovak descent; physician, ophthalmologist, Board certified, practicing in Fairfield, OH.
Bio: "Dr. Thomas Macejko, MD" in: US News. See - https://health.usnews.com/doctors/thomas-macejko-295254

Ernst Waldstein (1879-1954), Slovak American; physician, ophthalmologist, practiced in NYC for 30 years.
Bio: "Dr. Ernst Waldstein, Ophthalmologist, 75," *The New York Times*, May 16, 1954

18. Optometrists

Barbora Bell (ca 1978-), b. Slovakia; in Us s. 1993; child psychologist, optometrist; with Gatos Eye Care,
Bio: "Barbora Bell, OD," in: Los Gatos EyeCare. See - http://www.lgeyecare. com/barbora-bell-od.html

Ivo Horak (ca. 1969-), b. Slovakia; optometrist, orthokeratologist; optometrist. He has been practicing optometry in Atlanta since graduating from New England College of Optometry in Boston in 1996. He recently opened his own Family Optical Practice, Eyes R Us, on Windy Hill Road in Smyrna, Georgia.
Bio: "Ivo Horak," in: LinkedIn. See - https://www.linkedin.com/in/ ivo-horak-91a51821/

Jana Kadlec (ca 1971-), a Slovak American; optometrist, practicing in Livonia, MI; she is affiliated with Levine Eyecare Center (s, 2011).
Bio: "Jana Kadlec Drennan," in: LinkedIn. See - https://www.linkedin.com/ in/jana-kadlec-drennan-057b885a/

Duane G. Krupar (ca 1944-), b. of Slovak descent; optometrist, practicing in Greensburg, PA; founder and owner of Willowbrook Eye Care Associates and VIP at Willowbrook.
Bio: "Dr. Duane Krupar, OD," in: healthgrades. See - https://www. healthgrades.com/providers/duane-krupar-2f8q4

John Lovasik, b. of Slovak descent; physician, optometrist; with University of Waterloo (1979-89), rising from assistant professor to full professor within eight years; professor of optometry, ocular physiology; director of School of Optometry, Université de Montréal, Canada
Bio: "John Lovasik," in: LinkedIn. See - https://www.linkedin.com/in/john-lovasik-63ab6610/; "John Lovasik," in: ResearchGate. See - https://www. researchgate.net/profile/John_Lovasik.

19. Orthopedists

Ronald V. Gregush (ca. 1976-), Slovak American; physician, Board certified orthopedic surgeon, specializing in orthopedic sports medicine. He has a

special interest in arthroscopic hip preservation surgery. He practices in Kirkland, WA and is affiliated with EvergreenHealth Kirkland.
Bio: "Ronald V. Gregush, MD." In: EvergreenHealth. See - https://www.evergreenhealth.com/dr-ronald-v-gregush-md-orthopedics

Michal Kozanek (ca 1980-), b. Bratislava, Slovakia; physician, orthopedic surgeon. He specializes in foot and ankle problems ranging from toe deformities to those requiring complex reconstructive surgery. He is affiliated with Lahey Hospital & Medical Center.
Bio: "Michael Kozanek, MD, Ph.D.," in: Excel. See - http://www.excelortho.com/portfolio/details/michal-kozanek-md-phd/

Irvin Neufeld (1903-1969), b. Vráble, Slovakia; orthopedic surgeon, New York Medical College, NYC
Bio: "Neufeld, Irvin," in: Educators. S, p. 36; "Neufeld, Irvin," in *SVU Directory* 1, "Neufeld, Irvin," in: *Who's Who in the East,* 7.

Tomáš Pevný (ca. 1965-), b. Mikuláš, Slovakia; biochemist, physician, with residency orthopedic surgery. His professional interests include sports medicine, especially disorders of the shoulder and knee. Dr. Pevny also specializes in total joint replacement surgery of the knee and shoulder. He practices in Aspen and is affiliated with Aspen Valley Hospital. He was president of Aspen Foundation for Sports Medicine Education and Research (2003-09).
Bio: "Tomas Pekny," in: OrthoAspen. See - https://orthoaspen.org/providers/tomas-pevny-md/

Jack Gerard Skendzel (ca. 1982-), Slovak American; physician; orthopedic surgeon, specializing in sports medicine. He practices in Woodbury, MN and is affiliated with Healtheast Woodwinds Hospital.
Bio: "Jack Gerard Skendzel," in: Orthopedic Surgeons. See - http://orthopedic.io/surgeon/jack-gerard-skendzel-md-woodbury/

20. Otolaryngologists

Milan Beres (1936-), b. Trebišov, Czech.; physician, otolaryngologist, plastic surgeon, in Trumbull, CT,
Bio: "Beres, Milan,' in: *Who's Who in the East*, 18; "Dr. Milan Beres, M.D.," in: USNews. See - https://health.usnews.com/doctors/milan-beres-742089; "Beres, Milan," in: *Who's Important in Medicine* 2

Emil Krmery (1959-), b. Nemecká Lupča, Czech.; physician, certified otolaryngologist, Los Angeles, CA.
Bio: "Krmery, Emil," in: *Who's Important in Medicine*, 2

Heinrich Neumann von Héthárs (1873-1939), b. Lipany, Slovakia; physician, otolaryngologist; the foremost ear-nose-and-throat doctor in Vienna before World War II. In 1938 he transmitted to the Evian Conference the infamous offer by the German government to sell the Austrian Jews at a price of $250 per capita to any foreign country that would accept them and pay. This offer - and the Conference delegates' refusal to accept it - is the focal point of Hans Habe's novel *The Mission* (1965).
Some years prior to the Anschluss he was contacted by Nazi Party doctors about a larynx problem that Adolf Hitler was suffering from. Prof. Dr. von Neumann, as he was by then known, refused to consider Hitler's case, and after the Anschluss was imprisoned as a Jew. Neumann devised a new and life-saving operation for opening the labyrinth, a technique that has later been general practice.
Bio: "Heinrich Neumann von Héthárs," in: Wikipedia. See - https://en.wikipedia.org/wiki/Heinrich_Neumann_von_Héthárs

Richard John Sekerak (1909-1985), b. Bridgeport, CT, of Slovak parents; physician, otolaryngologist, practiced in Bridgeport, CT (s. 1950); assistant clinical professor, Yale School of Medicine (1951-59)
Bio: "Sekerak, Richard John," in: *Who's Who in the East*, 17.

John Joseph Sirotnak (ca. 1963-), b. of Slovak descent; physician, otolaryngologist, practicing in Throop, PA, affiliated with Moses Taylor Hospital and Geisinger Community Medical Center.
Bio: "Dr. John Sirotnak," in" USNews. See - https://health.usnews.com/doctors/john-sirotnak-263279

21. Pediatricians

Renáta Albrecht (1929-d.), b. Nové Zámky, Czech.; pediatrician, Medical Officer, FDA, Rockville, MD
Bio: "Albrecht, Ranáta," in *SVU Directory,* 8

Vladimir G. Altmann (1913-2006), physician, pathologist; assistant professor of pathology, SUNY Med. Brooklyn (1973-)
Bio: "Altmann, Vladimir G.," in: *Who's Important in Medicine,* 2; "Altmann, Vladimir, G.," in: *Educators,* p.9.

Sonya Boor (ca 1967-), b. Slovakia; physician, pediatrician, practicing in Hamilton Square, and Trenton, NJ, affiliated with multiple hospitals; Fellow of the American Academy of Pediatrics and board certified by the American Board of Pediatrics

Alice R. Breder, Slovak American; born and trained in Slovakia; physician, pediatrician; practicing in Daly City, CA; affiliated with Palo Alto Medical Foundation.
Bio: "Alice R. Breder, M.D.," in: Sutter Health. See - https://www.sutterhealth. org/find-doctor/dr-alice-r-breder

Judita M. Hruza (1924-), b. Čerhov, Czech.; physician, pediatrician, Wards Island, NY
Bio: *Directory of Medical Specialists,* 19 (1979-80).

Katarina Prokopova (ca 1977-), b. Slovakia; physician, pediatrician, with practice in Skowhegan, ME. She is affiliated with Eastern Maine Medical Center.
Bio: "Katarina Prokopova," in: PCHC Pediatrics. See - https://pediatrics. pchc.com/staff/katarina-prokopova/

Vera Pozdisková Stanincová (1926-), b. Trenčín, Czech.; physician, pediatrician; associate clinical professor of pediatrics, University of California, Los Angles (s. 1978)
Bio: "Stanincova, V.P.," in: *Educators,* p.5; "Stanincova, Vera Pozdiskova," in: Who's Important in Medicine, 2.

Eva Sujansky (1936-), b. Bratislava, Czech.; pediatrician, clinical geneticist, Aurora, CO, clinical professor of pediatrics, University of Colorado Medical School
Bio: "Sujansky, Eva," in: *Educators,* p. 7; "Eva Borska Sujansky," in: Prabook.
See - https://prabook.com/web/eva_borska.sujansky/69626

John Zahorsky (1871-1963), b. Nálepkovo, Slovakia; physician, pediatrician; clinical professor, Washington University (1905-11); professor of pediatrics St. Louis University (1912-48), department chair (1928-33).
Bio: "Zahorsky, John," in: *Who's Who in America,* 28.

22. Physiatrists

Frederick William Modern (1897-d.), b. Bratislava, Slovakia; physician, physical and rehabilitation medicine specialist, associate professor at Loma Linda University (s. 1958), chief, Chronic Disease Service, VA Hospital, Long Beach, CA
Bio: "Modern, Frederick William." In: *American Science,* 11, "Modern, Frederick William," in: *Who's Who in the West,* 9; "Modern, Frederick W. S., Educators, p. 3.

Andor A. Weiss (1906-1986), b. Čop, Slovakia; professor of rehabilitation medicine
Bio: Rechcigl, Miloslav, Jr., "Andor A. Weiss," in: *Encyclopedia of Bohemian and Czech-American Biography.* Bloomington, IN: AuthorHouse, 2016, Vol. 3, p. 2025-2026.

23. Podiatrists

Ladislav Kuchár (ca 1976-), b. Slovakia; physician, podiatrist; practicing in Douglas, AZ and is affiliated with Canyon Vista Medical Center
Bio: "Ladislav Kuchar," in: Health Carefor People.
See - https://www.healthcare4ppl.com/physician/arizona/sierra-vista/ladislav-kuchar-1699973560.html

Darline M. Kulhan (ca 1950-), Saginaw Bay, MI, of Slovak descent; physician, podiatrist, practicing in Scarsdale, NY
Bio: "Dr. Darline Kulhan DPM," in" TopNPI.com See - https://www.topnpi.com/ny1881661502/dr-darline-kulhan

Michael V. Šimko (1893-1989), b. Bridgeport, CT, of Slovak descent; chiropodist, writer
Bio: "Simko, Michael," in: *Catholic Who's Who,* 7 (1946-1947); "Michael V. Simko (1893-1989), Tellers of Weird Tales, January 7, 2016; Masters, Ann V., "Dr. M. V. Simko Authors Novel of Slovak Life in Bridgeport, *Bridgeport Sunday Post,* June 23, 1968.

24. Preventive Medicine Specialists

Avlado Andrew Getting (1910-), b. Pittsburgh, PA, of Slovak descent; physician; preventive medicine specialist; professor of public health administration and chair of the department, University of Orlando; commissioner, Massachusetts Department of Public Health; clinical Professor of Public Health Practice, Harvard School of Public Health.
Bio: "Getting. Vlado Andrew," in: *Who's is Important in Medicine,* 2

25. Psychiatrists

Franz Gabriel Alexander (1891-1964), b. Budapest, of Slovak-born grandfather; physician, psychoanalyst; considered father of psychosomatic medicine. Founder and director of the Chicago Institute of Psychoanalysis (1932-56); professor in the department of psychiatry, University of Illinois Medical School in Chicago (1938-56).
Bio: "Franz Alexander," in: Wikipedia. See - https://en.wikipedia.org/wiki/Franz Alexander; Eckardt, M.H., "Franz Alexander: A unique outstanding pioneer," Journal of Am. Academy *Psychoanalysis,* 29, No. 1 (2001), pp. 105-11; "Franz Alexander," in: *Encyclopedia Britannica.* See - https://www.britannica.com/biography/Franz-Alexander;

Iveta Boyanchek (ca 1971-), b. physician; psychiatrist, practicing in Columbus, GA. She is affiliated with SFH Electrophysiologist Group in Columbus, as well as St. Francis Hospital in Columbus.
Bio: "Iveta Boyanchek," in: St. Francis Hospital. See - https://www.mystfrancis.com/find-a-doctor/iveta-boyanchek

John Michael Dluhy, Jr. (1937-), b. Chicago, IL, of Slovak ancestry; psychiatrist, Washington, DC (s. 1968)
Bio: "Dluhy, John Michael," in: *Who's Who in the East,* 18

Jan Ehrenwald (1900-1988), b. Bratislava, Slovakia; psychiatrist and psychotherapist, most known for his work in parapsychology
Bio: "Jan Ehrenwald," in: Wikipedia. See - https://en.wikipedia.org/wiki/Jan_Ehrenwald; "John Ehrenwald," in: *Encyclopedia*, Vol. 3, p. 2028.

Ladislaus Fessler (1897-1965), b. Topoľčany, Slovakia; physician, psychiatrist, New York, NY.
Bio: *Who's Important in Medicine*, 2; Hetman, Marcel, "Laci Fessler," *The Psychoanalytic Quarterly*, 34, Issue 4 (1965), pp. 629-638.

John R. 'Kip' Fisher, 3ʳᵈ (1938-2016); b. of Slovak descent; physician, with University Hospitals in Cleveland, specializing in psychiatry; president of the Slovak Sokol Camp
Bio: "John R. "Kip" Fisher MD III," *The Plain Dealer,* December 3, 2016-January 1, 2017.

Ian Frank (1902-d.), b. Tisovec, Slovakia; physician, psychiatrist, professor, School Psychiatry, The Menninger Foundation (1946-51; director, Topeka (KS) Institute of Psychoanalysis (1951-56); associate professor, SUNY, Brooklyn (s. 1961)
Bio: "Frank, Ian," in: *American Science*, 10; "Frank, Ian," in: *Who's Who in the East*, 12,

Irene Hitschmann (née Link) (1908-1986), b. Hohenems, Aust., of Slovak ancestry; psychiatrist
Bio: Rechcigl, Miloslav, Jr., "Irene Hitschmann," in: *Encyclopedia*, 2016, Vol. 3, p. 2031.

Ivan E. Homola (1933-2007), b. Kamenany, Czech.; psychiatrist, psychoanalyst, Jewish Medical Center and The Zucker Hillside Hospital, Glen Oaks, NY.
Bio: "Homola, Ivan E.," in: *SVU Directory* 8; "Ivan Homola Obituary," in: *The New York Times*, June 25, 2018.

Viliam Jonec (1928-2009), b. Košice, Czech.; psychiatrist, psychoneuroendocrinologist, State of California, Tarzana, CA
Bio: "Jonec, Viliam," in: *SVU Directory* 8; "Viliam S. Jonec M.D., Ph.D.," *Los Angeles Times*, November 22, 2009.

William Kitsko (1922-2015), b. Johnstown, PA, of Slovak descent; physician, psychiatrist, Indian Lake, PA
Bio: "William Kitsko M.D.," Pittsburgh Post-Gazette, Aug. 15-16, 2015; "Dr. William Kitsko, 93, was well-known Sokol golfer," *Slovak Catholic Falcon*, September 9, 2015, p. 18.

Jana Lincoln (ca 1970-), b. Slovakia; physician, psychiatrist, practicing in Wichita, KS. She works at University of Kansas Psychiatry Clinic and is affiliated with Via Christi Hospital and Via Christi-Saint Joseph Campus.
Bio: "Jana Lincoln," in: WebMD. See - https://doctor.webmd.com/doctor/jana-lincoln-89526ccb-2116-4e0f-9351-d038e570b73a-overview

Tomas Roth (1942-), b. Czech.; director the Sleep Disorders and Research Center at Henry Ford Hospital in Detroit (s. 1978), professor in the Department of Psychiatry at Wayne State University, School of Medicine in Detroit, MI
Bio: "About me," See - https://www.henryford.com/physician-directory/r/roth-thomas

Benyam G. Tegene (ca 1963-), b. Slovakia; physician, psychiatrist. He works in Camp Hill, PA and is affiliated with Geisinger Holy Spirit Hospital.
Bio: "Benyam G. Tegene," in: WebMD. See - https://doctor.webmd.com/doctor/benyam-tegene-10abbee9-2223-4d2c-93f7-5adf1cea52f1-overview

26. Pulmonologists

Tomas Ganz (ca 1951-), b. US, of Slovak father; physician, pulmonologist, and internist, with UCLA, professor of medicine in the David Geffen School of Medicine, UCLA
Bio: "Ganz, Tomas," in: Wikipedia. See - https://en.wikipedia.org/wiki/Tomas_Ganz

Viera Lakticová (ca 1975-), b. Slovakia; physician, internist, pulmonologist, critical care medicine specialist, practicing in New Hyde Park, Manhasset, and Long Island City, NY; assistant professor, Donald and Barbara Zucker School of Medicine at Hofstra/Northwell
Bio: "Viera Lakticova," in: Norhwell Health. See - https://www.northwell.edu/find-care/find-a-doctor/sleep-medicine/dr-viera-lakticova-md-11361692

Samira Shojaee (ca 1978-), b. Slovakia; physician, pulmonologist; assistant professor, fellowship director of Interventional Pulmonology Program, Virginia Commonwealth University School of Medicine, Richmond, VA
Bio: "Samira Shojaee, MD, MPH, FCCP," in: VCU. See - https://medschool. vcu.edu/expertise/detail.html?ID=2283

27. Radiologists

William V. Dzurek (1945-), b. Slovakia; physician, radiologist, Pottsville, PA, president of the Pennsylvania Radiological Society
Bio: *Directory of Medical Specialists*, 19 (1979-800.

Jozef Fabian (1912-1988), b. Radonica; physician, roentgenologist, Rego Park, NY
Bio: "Fabian, Jozef," in: *SVU Directory*

George S. Feher (1914-), b. Topoľčany, Slovakia; practicing in Modesto, CA; affiliated with University of California Hospital, San Francisco
Bio: "Feher, George S.," in: *Directory of Medical Specialists*

Augustine Gustave Formanek (1921-), b. Nitra, Czech.; physician, radiologist; practicing in Minnesota; professor of roentgenology, University of Minnesota, Minneapolis (s. 1972).
Bio: *Who's Who Important in Medicine*, 2

Bertram V. A. Low-Beer (1900-1955), b. Topoľčany, Slovakia; radiologist, professor at University of California, San Francisco
Bio: Rechcigl, Miloslav, Jr., "Bertram V. A. Low-Beer," in: *Encyclopedia of Bohemian and Czech-American Biography*. Bloomington, IN: AuthorHouse, 2016, Vol. 3, pp. 2047-2048.

Václav Igor Pokorný (1931-), b. Bratislava, Czech; diagnostic radiologist, Louisville, KY
Bio: "Pokorny, Vaclav Igor," in: *Directory of Medical Specialists*, 19, 1979-80; "Dr. Vaclav Pokorny," in: healthgrades. See - https://www.healthgrades.com/ physician/dr-vaclav-pokorny-xbgh3

George Rurik (ca 1928-), Slovak American; radiologist, Chicago
Bio: "Dr. George Rurik," in: USNews. See - https://health.usnews.com/doctors/george-rurik-1018103

Vladimir Savcenko (ca 1967-), b. Slovakia; physician; radiologist in Saint Paul, MN, affiliated with multiple hospitals in the area, including Northwestern Hospital and Altru Health System-Grand Forks
Bio: "Vladimir Sevcenko, MD," in: doximity. See - https://www.doximity.com/pub/vladimir-savcenko-md

Stefan Michael Skalina (1953-), b. Bratislava, Czech.; physician, pediatrician, diagnostic radiologist, practicing in Chester, PA,
Bio: "Skalina, Stefan Michael," in: *SVU Directory* 8; "Stefan M. Skalina, MD," in: Sharecare. See - https://www.sharecare.com/doctor/dr-stefan-m-skalina

28. Rheumatologists

Zuzana Foster (ca 1970-), b Slovak American; physician, rheumatologist and internist. She currently practices at Northern California Arthritis Center and is affiliated with John Muir Medical Center Walnut Creek Campus. She also practices at Northern California Arthritis Center in San Ramon, CA.
Bio: "Dr. Zuzana Foster," in: share.care. See - https://www.sharecare.com/doctor/dr-zuzana-foster

Simona Horak Nativ (ca 1979-), Slovak American; physician, pediatric rheumatologist, practicing in Morristown, NJ and Brunswick, NJ.
Bio: Simona Horak Nativ, MD," in: doximity. See - https://www.doximity.com/pub/simona-nativ-md

Ingrid Soltys (ca 1966-), b. Slovakia; physician, pediatric rheumatologist.
Bio: "Ingrid Soltys," in: LinkedIn. See - https://www.linkedin.com/in/ingrid-soltys-a059a6a8/

Peter Weiser (ca 1975-), b. Slovakia; physician, pediatrician with specialty on rheumatology. He practices in Birmingham, AL and is affiliated with Children's of Alabama. He is also associate professor of pediatrics in the

Division of Pediatric Rheumatology, at the University of Alabama School of Medicine.
Bio: "Peter Weiser, MD," in: Children's of Alabama. See - https://www. childrensal.org/dr-peter-weiser-md-rheumatology

29. Surgeons

Leslie Gabriel Farkaš (1915-2008), b. Ružomberok, Slovakia; physician, plastic surgeon, associate professor of plastic surgery, University of Toronto, Canada
Bio: "Farkas, Leslie Gabriel," in: *American Science, 14*; "Leslie G. Farkas: pioneer of modern craniofacial anthropometry," *Arch Facial Plast. Surg.*, 12, No. 3 (May-June 2010), pp. 141-2; Forrest, Christopher, "Leslie Gabriel Farkas, M.D., Ph.D., D.Sc., 1915 to 2008," *Plastic and Reconstructive Surgery*, 123, No. 6 (June 2009), pp. 1899-1900.

Arpad G. Gerster (1848-1923), b. Košice, Slovakia; surgeon
Bio: "Gerster, Arpad G.," in: Science 2, "Gerster Árpád," in: Wikipedia. See - https://hu.wikipedia.org/wiki/Gerster_ Árpád; Langer, Robert M., Arpad Gerster and Max Thorek Contributions to American Surgery," *Journal of Investigative Surgery*, Vol. 22, Issue 3 (2009), pp. 162-166.

Peter Paul Hletko (1902-d.), b. Chicago, IL, of Slovak descent; surgeon, Chicago
Bio: "Hletko, Peter Paul, M.D.," in: *Catholic Who's Who*, 7 (1946-1947), p. 198; "Hletko, Peter Paul," in: *Who's Who in the Midwest*, 19; "Dr. Peter P. Hletko," in: *Slovaks in America*. Bicentennial Study, p. 426.

August Julius Jurishica (1910-2007), b. Cudahy, WI, of Slovak descent; surgeon, assistant clinical professor, Medical College of Wisconsin, Milwaukee
Bio: "Jurishica, August Julius," in: "August J. Jurishica," *Milwaukee Journal Sentinel,* June 19-20, 2007

Oscar Karpati (1900-1990.), b. Kotešová, Slovakia; physician, specializing in surgery, practiced in Brookline, MA (s. 1949)
Bio: "Karpati, Oscar," in: *Who's Who in the East*, 9

Eugen M. Molnar (1942-), b. Bratislava, Czech.; plastic surgeon, Santa Anna, CA
Bio: "Molnar, Eugen M.," in: *Bio: SVU Directory* 8;

Alexis Victor Moschcowitz (1865-1933), b. Giraltovce, Slovakia; surgeon
Bio: Lilienthal, Howard, "Alexis Victor Moschcowitz," *Annals of Surgery*, 99, No. 3 (1934), pp. 557-558; "Moschcowitz, Alexis Victor," in: *Who's Who in American Jewry*, Vol. 1., p. 445; "Alexis Moschcowitz," in: Wikipedia. See - https://en.wikipedia.org/wiki/Alexis_Moschcowitz

John Ignatius Perl (1806-1972), b. Galanta, Slovakia; physician, surgeon, in US s. 1924. He practiced in Chicago and was connected with Augustana Hospital. He was also a painter.
Bio: *Who's Important in Medicine*, 2; "John Ignatius Perl," in: Richard Norton Gallery. See - http://richardnortongallery.com/artists/john-perl

Alan Politzer (1910-2002), b. Stráni, Czech.; physician, general surgeon, medical director, NY State Worker's Compensation Board, New York, NY
Bio: "Politzer, Alan," in: *SVU Directory* 8; "Deaths: Politzer, Dr. Alan A.," *The New York Times*, November 10, 2002.

Marián Porubský (ca 1970-), b. Slovakia; physician; Board-certified general surgeon and transplant surgeon. He also specializes in the surgical treatment of diseases of the liver, biliary tract and pancreas. He practices in Tampa, FL and is affiliated with TGMG Bayshore in Tampa, as well as Banner - University Medical Center Tucson Campus LLC in Tucson.
Bio: "Marian Porubsky, MD," in: TGMG. See - https://www.tgmg.org/find-doctor/marian-porubsky-md

Stefan Pribil (1954-), b. Bratislava, Czech., neurosurgeon, Hudson, FL
Bio: "Dr. Stefan Pribil MD," *US News*. See - https://health.usnews.com/doctors/stefan-pribil-584801; "About Dr. Pribil," in: Inspine. See - https://www.ispine.com/about-dr-pribil/

Theobald Reich (1927-), b. Svidnik, Czech.; general surgeon, with New York University School of Medicine (s. 1967), as professor of surgical research (s. 1973)
Bio: "Reich, Theobald," in: *Who's Who in America*, 41; "Theobald Reich," in: *Encyclopedia*, Vol. 3, p. 2063; "Reich, Theobald," in: *Who's Who in the East*, 17.

Boris Sepesi (ca 1979-), b. Slovakia; physician, thoracic and cardiac surgeon in Houston, TX; assistant professor, Department of Thoracic and Cardiovascular Surgery, University of Texas MD Anderson Cancer Center, Houston, TX
Bio: "Boris Sepesi, M.D., F.A.C.S.," See - https://faculty.mdanderson.org/profiles/boris_sepesi.html

Stanley C. Škoryna (1920-2003), b. Warsaw, Poland; surgeon, McGill University
Bio: "Stanley Constantine Skoryna," In: In Memoriam McGill. See - https://www.mcgill.ca/medicine/staff-resources/inmemoriam/2003

Eduard Sujansky 1936-1979), b. Slovakia; cardiac surgeon, Colorado
Bio: "Sujansky, Eduard," in: Educators, p. 7. "Dr Eduard Sujansky," in: Find A Grave. See - https://www.findagrave.com/memorial/93521073/eduard-sujansky

Max Thorek (1880-1960), b. Slovakia; surgeon; obstetrician, reconstructive surgeon. He founded the International College of Surgeons in 1935 and the International Museum of Surgical Science in a Chicago Gold Coast mansion in 1954. Dr. Thorek was also the founder of Thorek Memorial Hospital, still in operation in Chicago's Uptown neighborhood.
Bio: "Thorek, Max," in: National Biography, pp. 603-604; "Max Thorek," in: Wikipedia. See - https://en.wikipedia.org/wiki/Max_Thorek; Langer, Robert M., Arpad Gerster and Max Thorek Contributions to American Surgery," *Journal of Investigative Surgery*, Vol. 22, Issue 3 (2009), pp. 162-166.

Walter Robert Tkach (1917-1989), b. LaBelle, PA; physician, surgeon, Air Force Major General, White House physician
Bio: "Major General Walter Robert Tkach," in: U.S. Air force. See - http://www.af.mil/About-Us/Biographies/Display/Article/105421/

major-general-walter-robert-tkach/; "Walter Tkach, 72; Served as the Doctor To Three Presidents," the *New York Times*, Nvember, 1989.

30. Urologists

Benjamin Berger (1884-1968), b. Hrabovec, Slovakia; physician, dermatologist, urologist, NYC
Bio: *Who's Who in American Jewry*. New York: Jewish Biographical Bureau, 1926, Vol. 1., p. 45; "Berger, Benjamin," in: *Who's Who in the East*, 1930.

Joseph M. Jakšy (1900-1991), b. Bratislava, Slovakia; urologist, New York University, NYC
Bio: "Joseph Jaksy, 91; Helped Rescue Jews," *The New York Times*, January 23, 1991; "Jakšy, Jozef," in: Pejskar 4, pp. 66-67; "Jakšy, Joseph," in: *SVU Directory* 4.

Patrik Luzny (ca 1986-), a Slovak American; physician, urologist, practicing in Logan, UT. He is affiliated s affiliated with Behavioral Health Access Center-DRMC in St. George, as well as Logan Regional Hospital in Logan.
Bio: "Dr. Patrik Luzny, MD," in: CareDash. See - https://www.caredash.com/doctors/patrik-luzny-md-logan-ut

Peter Zvara (1962-), b. Slovakia; physician, urologist; research fellow at University of California, San Francisco (1992-93), McGill University, Montreal (1993-95), University of Toronto (1995-96); associate professor, University of Vermont (2014); professor of experimental surgery, Syddansk Universitet, Odense (s. 2015).
Bio: "Peter Zvara," in: SDU. See - http://findresearcher.sdu.dk/portal/en/persons/peter-zvara(8b972a43-3503-41e2-b94f-ce5d36233b9a)/cv.html?id=121050826

F. Physical Sciences

1. Astronomers

Gustav Bakos (1918-1991), b. Trnava, Czech.; astronomer; first astronomer appointed at the Physics Department of the University of Waterloo (Ontario), Canada, professor
Bio: "Bakos, Gustav," in: *Science*, 15; "Gustav Bakos," American Astronomical Society. See - https://aas.org/obituaries/gustav-bakos-1918-1991

Ivan A. Getting (1912-2003), b. New York, NY, of Slovak ancestry; astrophysicist, and electrical engineer, founding president of the Aerospace Corporation (1960-1977)
Bio: "Getting, Ivan Alexander," in: *SVU Directory* 8; "Ivan A. Getting," in: Wikipedia. See - https://en.wikipedia.org/wiki/Ivan_A._Getting; "Getting, Ivan Alexander," in: *American Science, 14.*

Ivan Pauliny-Toth (1935-), b. Bratislava, Czech.; radio astronomer, assst. scientist, National Radio Astron. Observatory, Green Bank, WV (s. 1964)
Bio: "Pauliny-Toth, Ivan," in: *American Science*, 11

Milan R. Stefánik (1880-1919), b. Košariská, Slovakia; astronomer in France, who undertook observations in Brazil and an assignment in Ecuador, about which a book was subsequently published. During the first World War, Stefanik became a General in the French army and close associate of Masaryk in the founding of the Czechoslovak Republic.
Bio: Milan Rastislav Štefánik," in: Wikipedia. See - https://en.wikipedia.org/wiki/Milan_Rastislav_ Štefánik

Peter Vereš (1982-), b. Slovakia; astronomer; Caltech Postdoctoral Scholar; Jet Propulsion Laboratory/NASA, Pasadena, CA (2015-17); astronomer, Harvard-Smithsonian Center for Astrophysics, Cambridge, MA (s. 2017)
Bio: "Peter Veres, Ph.D.," In: CfA. See - https://www.cfa.harvard.edu/~pveres/

2. Chemists

Laszlo Ambrus (1934-), b. Topoľčany, Slovakia; chemist, with Cutter Lab, Berkeley, CA

Ivan Juius Andrasik (1938-2010); b. Rožnava, Czech; research chemist and supervisor of the Research Analytical Lab at the DL Institute in Laurel, MD
Bio: "Ivan Andrasik Obituary," *Maryland Gazette*, December 1, 2010.

Steven James Assony (1920-2006), b. Czech.; organic chemist, head of Tech. Serv., CPR Division, Upjohn Co., Lakewood, CA (s. 1970)
Bio: "Assony, Steven James," in: *American Science*, 10

William M. Banick, Jr. (1956 -2009), b. Dunmore, PA, of Slovak descent; analytical chemist, with the American Cyanamid Co.
Bio: "William M. Banick Jr. Obituary," *Scranton Times*, Nov. 14, 2009.

Andrew Beelik (1924-), b. Nižné Valice, Czech.; organic chemist, ITT, Rayonier, Inc., Shelton, WA
Bio: "Beelik, Andrew," in: *American Science*, 14

Emanuel Theodore Böhm (1909-1990), b. Vrútky, Slovakia; chemist, director of research at Hoffman Beverage Co., Newark (1952-71); director of beverage research at Refined Syrups and Sugars, Yonkers, NY (1971-74)
Bio: "Böhm, Emanuel Theodore," in: *Who's Who in the East*, 18; "Emanuel Böhm," in: Wikipedia. See - https://sk.wikipedia.org/wiki/ Emanuel_Böhm

Erwin Buncel (1931-), b. Prešov, Czech., organic chemist, professor of chemistry, Queen's University, Kingston, Ont., Canada
Bio: "Buncel, Erwin." In: *American Science*, 10; "Dr. Erwin Buncel, Professor Emeritus," in: Queen's University. See - http://faculty.chem.queensu.ca/people/faculty/buncel/; "Curriculum vitae: Dr. Erwin Buncel," in: Queen's University. See - http://faculty.chem.queensu.ca/people/faculty/buncel/Buncel%20CV.pdf

Paul Davidovis (1935-), b. Moldava, Czech.; chemical physicist, professor of chemistry Boston College, Chestnut, Hill, MA
Bio: "Davidovits, Paul," in: *American Science, 14*; "Paul Davidovits," in: *Encyclopedia,* Vol. 2, pp.1600-1601; "Paul Davidovits," in: Wikipedia. See - https://de.wikipedia.org/wiki/Paul_Davidovits

John Fabianek (1922-), b. Pribeta, Czech.; biochemist, professor of chemistry at New York Institute of Technology, New York, NY
Bio: "Fabianek, John," in: *American Science, 14;* "Fabianek, John S.," in: *Who's Who in the East,* 15

Bela M. Fabuss (1924-2013), b. Piešťany, Czech.; chemical engineer, physical chemist, research group, Monsanto Research Corp., Everett, MA
Bio: "Fabuss, Bela," in: *American Science,* 11

Harry H. Fall (1920-2004), b. Lučenec, Czech.; physical organic chemist, sr. research chemist with General Tire & Rubber Co., president of the American Chemical Society
Bio: "Fall, Harry H.," in: *American Science,* 10, "Dr. Harry H. Fall," *Akron Beacon journal,* March 21, 2004.

Vojtech Fried (1921-2000), b. Ložín, Czech.; physical chemist, Brooklyn College, Brooklyn, NY
Bio: "Fried, Vojtech," in: *SVU Directory,* 7; "Fried, Vojtech." In: *Who's Who in the East,* 12; "Deaths: Fried, Vojtech," *The New York Times,* October 10, 2000; "Fried, Vojtech," in: *American Science, 14*

Ivan Furda (1938-), b. Trnava, Czech.; organic chemist, food chemist, General Mills, Minneapolis, MN
Bio: "Furda, Ivan," in: *SVU Directory* 8

Neil Victor Hakala (1917-d.), b. South Range, MI; chemist, with Exon Research Eng. Co., Florham Park, NJ
Bio: "Hakala, Neil Victor," in" Science 9

Theodore Tibor Herskovitz (1928-), b. Košice, Czech.; physical chemist, professor of chemistry, Fordham University, New York, NY
Bio: "Herskovits, Theodore Tibor," in: *American Science, 14*

Oscar Keller (1908-d), b. Prešov, Slovakia; chemist, senior chemist with Upjohn Co., MI (1939-40), with Hoffmann La Roche, Inc., Nutley, NJ (s. 1940)
Bio: "Keller, Oscar." In: *American American Science,*10

Pavol Kovac (1938-), b. Martin, Czech.; in US s. 1981; chemist; head of Carbohydrate Section, Lab. of Bioorganic Chemistry, NIH, Bethesda, MD (s. 1983)
Bio: "Pavol Kovac," in: ResearchGate. See - https://www.researchgate.net/profile/Pavol_Kovac

Louis Laufer (1912-), b. Medzilaborce, Slovakia; chief research chemist, Schwarz Bioresearch Inc., Orangeburg, NY (s. 1959)
Bio: "Laufer, Louis," in: *American Science,* 11

Jan Matejovic (ca 1970-), Slovak American; medicinal chemist, academic associate, University of Ontario Institute of Technology, Toronto, Canada (s. 2011)
Bio: "Jan Matejovic," in: LinkedIn. See - https://www.linkedin.com/in/jan-matejovic/

Zoltan Mendel (1924-2003), b. Prešov, Czech.; textile chemist, senior research chemist at E.I du Pont de Nemours & Co., Wilmington, DE (s. 1972).
Bio: "Mandel, Zoltan," in: *American Science, 14*

Otto Meresz (1932-), b. Rimavská Sobota, Czech.; environmental chemist, with Ontario Ministry of the Environment (s. 1974)
Bio: "Meresz, Otto," in: *American Science, 14*

Francis Onuska (1935-), b. Humenné, Czech.; analytical chemist, organic chemist, scientist
with National Water Research Institute, Burlington, Ont., Canada
Bio: "Onuska, Francis Ivan," in: *American Science, 14*

Albert Alan Pavlic (1916-2010), b. Racine, WI; organic chemist, with E. I. du Pont de Nemours & Co., Wilmington, DE
Bio: "Pavlic, Albert Alan," in: *American Science, 9*

John C. Polanyi (orig. Pollacsek) (1929-), b. Berlin, Ger., of Slovak ancestry, Canadian chemist, recipient of the Nobel Prize in chemistry
Bio: "John Polanyi," in: Wikipedia. See - https://en.wikipedia.org/wiki/John_Polanyi

Milan Andrew Rolik (1926-2008), b. Akron, OH; research chemist, General Tire
Bio: "Milan Andrew Rolik," in: Find a Grave. See - https://www.findagrave.com/memorial/185311259/milan-andrew-rolik

Michael J. Sienko (1923-1983), b. Bloomfield, NJ; chemist, professor of chemistry, Cornell University, Ithaca, NY (s. 1958)
Bio: "Michael J. Sienko," in: Commons.Cornelll. See - https://ecommons.cornell.edu/bitstream/handle/1813/18684/Sienko_Michell_J_1983.pdf;sequence=2; Sienko, Michael J.," in: *Who's Who in America*, 41.

Frank Šipoš (1926-), b. Lučenec, Czech.; organic chemist, specializing in peptide chemistry, sr. research investigator, Squibb Institute of Medical Research, New Brunswick, NJ (s. 1970)
Bio: "Šipoš, Frank," in: *SVU Directory* 2; "Šipoš, Frank," in: *American Science*, 10

John Godfrey Šurák (1909-1969), b. Brezová pod Bradlom, Slovakia; chemist, associate professor with Marquette University, Milwaukee, WI (s. 1956).
Bio: "Surak, John Godfrey," in: *American Science*, 11

Ivan Tkáč (1954-), b. Bratislava, Czech.; physical chemist, asst. professor in dept. of radiology, University of Minnesota, Minneapolis
Bio: "Tkáč, Ivan," in: *SVU Directory* 8; "Ivan Tkac," in: CMRR. See - http://www.cmrr.umn.edu/facultystaff/ivan/

Edward Joseph Tomcik (1919-), b. Cleveland, OH, of Slovak parents; chemist with manufacturing department of Searle & Co., Niles, IL
Bio: Tomcik, Edward Joseph," in: *American Science* 9

Andrew Stephen Tomcufcik (1921-2005), b. Czech.; organic chemist, inventor, group leader, t with American Cyanamid Co., Lederle Labs., Pearl River, NY (s. 1955)
Bio: "Tomcufcik, Andrew Stephen," in: *American Science, 11*

Cyprian Tomecko (1890-d.), b. Payer, PA, of Slovak parents; R.C. priest, O.S.B., professor of chemistry, founder and head of the chemistry program at St. Procopius College
Bio: "Tomecko, Cyprian," in: *American Science, 5*

Aladar Tvarenko (1929-), b. Galanta, Czech.; chemist, research chemist with Res. Center, ESB, Inc., Yardley, PA (1958-63), research staff, Research Center of Western Electric Co., Princeton, NJ (s. 1966)
Bio: "Tvarenko, Aladar," in: *Who's Who in the East, 14*

Thomas Michael Valega (1937-2014), b. Linden, NJ, of Slovak descent; organic chemist, science administrator at NIH, Bethesda, MD
Bio: "Valega, Thomas Michael," in: *SVU Directory* 8; "Thomas M. Valega, chemist, NIH grants official," *The Washington Post*, February 20, 2014.

John Wein (1921-), b. Kežmarok, Czech.; organic chemist, biochemist with Hope Medical Center, Duarte, CA (s. 1962)
Bio: "Wein, John," in: American Science, 11

3. Physicists

Emil 'Mike' Banas (1921-2015), b. East Chicago, of Slovak parents; physicist, research physicist with Amoco Oil Co. in Whiting, IL and Naperville, IL
Bio: "Banas, Emil 'Mike,'" in: *Who's Who in the Midwest*, 17; "Obituary: Emil "Mike" Banas, 93, of Pullman," *Moscow-Pullman Daily News*, September 29, 2015.

Jeno Michael Barnothy (1904-1996), b. Bratislava, Slovakia; physicist, astrophysicist, pioneer of cosmic ray research professor at Barat College, Lake Forest, IL (1948-53), then in Evanston, IL
Bio: Fenyves, Ervin J., "Jeno M. Barnothy," *Bulletin of the American Astronomical Society*, 29, No. 4 (1997), pp. 1467-1468; "Barnothy, Jeno M.," Biographical Encyclopedia of Astronomers. Springer, 2007, Vol. 1, p. 99.

George Feher (1924-2017), b. Bratislava, Czech.; physicist and biophysicist
Bio: "George G Feher 1924-2017," in: LaJolla Light Obituaries. See: http://www.legacy.com/obituaries/lajollalight/obituary.aspx?n=&pid= 187592684&referrer=0&preview=True; "Feher, George," in: Educators, p. 6; "George Feher," in: Wikipedia. See: https://en.wikipedia.org/wiki/ George_Feher; "Feher, George," in: *American Science*, 10.

Leslie Lawrence Foldy (1919-2001), b. Sabinov, Czech.; theoretical physicist, professor of physics at Case Western Reserve University (s. 1966)
Bio: "Foldy, Leslie Lawrence," in: American Science, 14; "Leslie Lawrence Foldy," in: Wikipedia. See - https://en.wikipedia.org/wiki/ Leslie_Lawrance_Foldy; "Foldy, Leslie Lawrence," in: *Who's Who in America*, 41.

Miroslav Grmela (1939-), b. Trnava, Czech.; theoretical and mathematical physicist, Polytechnique Montréal (s. 1981)
Bio: "Grmela, Miroslav," in: *Encyclopedia*, Vol. 2, pp. 1690-1691; "Grmela, Miroslav," in: *American Science, 14*

Joel Louis Lebowitz (1930-), b. Tačeva, Czech.; mathematical physicist, professor, dept. of physics, Yeshiva University, New York, NY, professor of pathology, Rutgers University (s. 1977), NAS member
Bio: "Lebowitz, Joel Louis," in: *American Science* 11; "Joel Lebowitz, in: Wikipedia. See - https://en.wikipedia.org/wiki/Joel_Lebowitz; "Lebowitz, Joel Louis," in: *Who's Who in America*, 41, "Lebowitz, Joel Louis," in: *Who's Who in the East*, 14.

Louis Kossuth Oppitz (1878-1938), b. Košice, Slovakia; physicist, specializing in optics; professor of physics at Mc Kendre College (s. 1930)
Bio: "Oppitz, Louis Kossuth," in: *American Science*, 5; "Oppitz, Louis Kossuth," in: *Leaders in Education*

Douglas Osheroff (1945-), b. Aberdeen, WA, of Slovak ancestry; physicist, recipient of the Nobel Prize
Bio: "Douglas Osheroff," in Wikipedia. See - https://en.wikipedia.org/wiki/ Douglas_Osheroff

Hugh David Politzer (1949-), b. New York, NY, of Czechoslovak parents; theoretical physicist, Nobel Prize recipient in physics for the discovery of asymptotic freedom in quantum chromodynamics
Bio: "Hugh David Politzer," in: Wikipedia. See - https://en.wikipedia.org/wiki/Hugh_David_Politzer

Stephen Pribil (1919-), b. Bratislava, Czech.; physicist, professor, State University of New York, Brockport, NY
Bio: "Pribil, Stephen," in: *SVU Directory* 8, "Pribil, Stephen," in: *American Science, 14*

Veronika Ariana Rabi (1945-), b. Michalovce, Czech; physicist, specializing in energy conversion, with Argonne National Lab., IL (1977-81); project manager, Electric Power Research institute, Palo Alto, CA (s. 1981-)
Bio: "Rabi, Veronika Ariana," in: *Science, 15*

Marcel Schein (1902-1960), b. Trstená, Slovakia; physicist, professor of physics, University of Chicago (s. 1946)
Bio: "Marcel Schein," in Wikipedia. See - https://en.wikipedia.org/wiki/Marcel_Schein; "Schein, Marcel," in: *American Science*, 5; "Schein, Marcel," in: *Who's Who in America*, 28; "Obituary: Prof. Marcel Schein," *Nature* 186 (1960), pp. 355-356.

Leo Szilard (orig. Spitz) (1898-1964), b. Budapest, Hungary, of Slovak father; physicist
Bio: "Leo Szilard," in: Wikipedia. See - https://en.wikipedia.org/wiki/Leo_Szilard; "Leo Szilard," in: Atomic Heritage Foundation. See - https://www.atomicheritage.org/profile/leo-szilard; Zund, Joseph D., "Szilard, Leo," in: National Biography, Vol. 21, pp. 238-239.

Edward Teller (1908-2003), b. Budapest, of Slovak ancestry; theoretical physicist, father of the hydrogen bomb
Bio: "Edward Teller," in: Wikipedia. See - https://en.wikipedia.org/wiki/Edward_Teller; Blumberg, Stanley A., and Louis G. Panos, *Edward Teller: Giant of the Golden Age of Physics; a Biography. New York:* Scribner's, 1990; Hargittai, Istvan, *Judging Edward Teller: A Closer Look at One of the Most Influential Scientists of the Twentieth Century.* Amherst, NY: Prometheus, 2010.

4. Mathematicians

John J. Bartko (1937-), b. Massillon, Ohio, of Slovak descent; mathematical statistician, National Institute of Mental Health, Bethesda, MD
Bio: "John J. Bartko," in: Virginia Tech. Hall of Distinction. See - https://www.science.vt.edu/about/Alumni/hallofdistinctionmain/johnbartko.html; "Bartko, John, J." in: *SVU Directory* 8; "Bartko, John Jaroslav," in: *American Science*, 14.

Hilda Geiringer (1893-1973), b. Vienna, of Slovak ancestry; mathematician, professor, Wheaton College
Bio: "Hilda Geiringer," in: Wikipedia. See - https://en.wikipedia.org/wiki/Hilda_Geiringer

Joseph Albert Hratz (1908-1999), b. Malý Šariš, Slovakia; mathematician, associate professor of mathematics, St. Ambrose College, Davenport, IA
Bio: "Hratz, Joseph Albert," in: *American Science* 10

Rosella Kanarik (1909-2014), b. Bardejov, Slovakia; in US s. 1913; mathematician. She was the first woman to receive a Ph.D from the University of Pittsburgh. She taught math at USC, Bancroft Jr. Hi, and Los Angeles City College. She ended her career as a Counselor at LACC. After retiring, she tutored hundreds of students, and she refused to take a penny for her time.
Bio: "Rosella Kanarik," in: *Los Angeles Times*, April 22, 2014; "Kanarik, Rosella," in: *Pioneering Women in American Mathematics: The Pre-1940 PhD's*. By Judy Green and Jeanne LaDuke. Providence, RI: AMS, 2009, pp. 215-215.

Anton Kotzig (1919-1991), b. Kočovce, Czech.; a Slovak–Canadian mathematician, expert in statistics, combinatorics and graph theory.
Bio: "Anton Kotzig," in: Wikipedia. See - https://en.wikipedia.org/wiki/Anton_Kotzig

Vojtech Ličko (1932-), b. Banská Štiavnica, Czech.; biomathematician, modeler, analyst of biological dynamic phenomena, professor, University of California, San Francisco, CA
Bio: "Ličko, Vojtech," in: *SVU Directory* 8; "Licko, Vojtech," in: *Educators*, p. 6; "Licko, Vojtech," in: *American Science, 14*

Paschal Michael Mino (1911-1972), b. Mestisko, Slovakia; R.C. priest, professor of mathematics and electronics, St. Francis College, Loretta, PA
Bio: "Mino, Paschal Michael," in: *American Science*, 11

Charles Roth (1939-), b. Huncovce, Czech.; applied mathematician, assoc. professor of mathematics, McGill University, Montreal (s. 1970)
Bio: "Roth, Charles," in: *American Science, 14*

G. EARTH SCIENCES

1. Geologists

Bela Csejtey, Jr. (1934-2012), b. Myjava, Slovakia; geologist, with USGS, first in Antarctica, then in Alaska. The US Board on Geographic Names recognized his distinguished service in Antarctica by naming a mountain in the Geologists' Range Mount Csejtey in his honor.
Bio "Bela Csejtey," in Mike Diggles Home Page. See - http://www.diggles. com/denalifault/Bela_Csejtey.pdf

Tibor Gasparik (1950-), b. Levice, Slovakia; in US s. 1976; experimental petrologist, associate professor, dept. of geosciences, SUNY, Stony Brook (s. 1989).

Angelo Heilprin (1852-1907), b. Nové Mesto pod Šiatrom, Slovakia; n American geologist, paleontologist, naturalist, and explorer. He is mostly known for the part he took into the Peary expedition to Greenland of 1891–1892 and for his observations and photographs of the 1902 eruption of Montagne Pelée in Martinique.
Bio: "Angelo Heilprin," in: Wikipedia. See - https://en.wikipedia.org/wiki/ Angelo_Heilprin

Peter P. Hudec (1934-), b. Nitra, Czech.; engineering and environmental geologist, University of Windsor, Ont., Canada
Bio: "Peter P. Hudec," in: *SVU Directory 9*; his Website. See - http://web2. uwindsor.ca/courses/earth_science/hudec/peter_p.htm

Miriam Kastner (1935-), b. Bratislava, Czech.; oceanographer and geochemist, professor at Scripps Institution of Oceanography, University of California, San Diego
Bio: "Miriam Kastner," in; Wikipedia. See - https://en.wikipedia.org/wiki/Miriam_Kastner; "Kastner, Miriam," in: *Educators,* p. 4, "Kastner, Miriam," in: *American Science, 14*

Tibor Klobusický (1911-d.), b. Prešov, Slovakia; geologist, mining engineer, consultant, Spokane, WA
Bio: "Klobusicky, Tibor," in: *American Science,* 11, "Klobusicky, Tibor," in" in: *Who's Who in the West,* 9

Paul Krutak (1934-2016), b. Pueblo, CO, of Slovak descent; an eminent American micropaleontologist; a Professor of Geology at Eastern New Mexico University, Ball State University, and the University of Nebraska-Lincoln. After leaving the University of Nebraska in 1982, Krutak worked as a consulting geologist for ARCO Oil Company, primarily in Lafayette, Louisiana, with some time spent on the North Slope in Alaska.
Bio: "Paul Krutak," in: Wikipedia. See - https://en.wikipedia.org/wiki/Paul_Krutak

Emil Makovicky (1940-), b. Bratislava, Czech.; geologist, mineralogist, crystallographer; received doctorate from McGill University, Montreal (1970); research geologist with Yale University (1970-72); with Geological Institute of University of Copenhagen (s. 1972), as professor of minerology (s. 1995)
Bio: "Emil Makovicky," in: Wikipedia. See - https://de.wikipedia.org/wiki/Emil_Makovicky

John Nábelek (1952-), b. Prague, Czech.; geologist, and geophysicist, Oregon State Univerrsity, Corvallis; applied and theoretical seismologist.
Bio: "Nábĕlek, Jan Ludvik," in: *SVU Directory* 8; "John Nabelek," in: Oregon State University - directory of People. See - http://ceoas.oregonstate.edu/profile/nabelek/

Peter Nábelek (1955-), b. Prague, Czech; geologist, geochemist, petrologist, University of Missouri, Columbia; studies igneous and metamorphic processes in the lithosphere using geochemistry and computer simulations.
Bio: Nábělek, Peter Igor," in: *SVU Directory* 8; "Peter Nabelek," in: University of Missouri - Geological sciences. See - https://geology.missouri.edu/people/nabelek

Ján Veizer (1941-), b. Pobedim, Czech.; geologist; Distinguished University Professor of Earth Sciences at the University of Ottawa. He is an award-winning isotope geochemist; his research interests have included the use of chemical and isotopic techniques in determining Earth's climatic and environmental history. Recipient of many awards.
Bio: "Jan Veizer," in; Wikipedia. See - https://en.wikipedia.org/wiki/Jan_Veizer

Barry Voight (1937-), b. US, of Slovak descent; brother of actor Jon Voight; American geologist, volcanologist, author, and engineer. After earning his Ph.D. at Columbia University, Voight worked as a professor of geology at several universities, including Pennsylvania State University, where he taught from 1964 until his retirement in 2005. Voight's publications on landslides and avalanches and other mass movements attracted the attention of Rocky Crandell of the United States Geological Survey (USGS), who asked him to look at a growing bulge on the Mount St. Helens volcano in the state of Washington. Voight foresaw the collapse of the mountain's north flank as well as a powerful eruption. His predictions came true when St. Helens erupted in May 1980; Voight was then hired by the USGS to investigate the debris avalanche that initiated the eruption. After his work at Mount St. Helens brought him international recognition, Voight continued researching and guiding monitoring efforts at several active volcanoes throughout his career, including Nevado del Ruiz in Colombia, Mount Merapi in Indonesia, and Soufrière Hills, a volcano on the Caribbean island of Montserrat.
Bio: "Barry Voight," in: Wikipedia. See - https://en.wikipedia.org/wiki/Barry_Voight

Paul M. Yaniga (1950-2012), b. Houlton, MA, of Slovak ancestry; geologist, hydrologist, business executive; co-founder of Groundwater Technology, Inc.,

a multi-national environmental consulting and remediation, etc., Kenneth Square, PA
Bio: "Yaniga," Paul Milan," in *SVU Directory* 8; "Paul Yaniga Obituary," West Chester *The Daily Local*, April 20, 2012.

2. Hydrologists

Shlomo P. Neuman (1938-), b. Žilina, Czech.; professor of hydrology and water resources, University of Arizona, Tucson
Bio: "Neuman, Shlomo Peter," in: Educators, p. 2; "Shlomo P. Neuman," in: Wikipedia. See - https://de.wikipedia.org/wiki/Shlomo_P._Neuman; "Shlomo P. Neuman: A Brief Autobiography," in: *Ground Water*, 46, No. 1 (January-February 2008), pp. 164-169, "Neuman, Shlomo Peter," in: *American Science, 14.*

3. Meteorologists

William Kaciak (1921-2007), b. Varin, Czech.; meteorologist, oceanographer, president of Weather Routing, Inc., New York, NY. (s. 1960)
Bio: "Kaciak, William" in: *American Science* 11; "William Kaciak," in: poststar. com. See- https://poststar.com/lifestyles/announcements/obituaries/william-kaciak/article_68ec9691-6b50-5a41-b8cd-cd1701948c5a.html

H. ENGINEERING

1. Acoustical Engineers

Igor Vojtech Nabelek (1924-2012), b. Banská Bystrica, of Moravian father; acoustical engineer, with University of Tennessee, Knoxville
Bio: Nabelek, Igor Vojtech," in: *SVU Directory*; "Igor Vojtech Nabelek," in: Highland Memorial Parks Obituaries. See - http://www.tributes.com/obituary/show/igor-nabelek-93246136

2. Aeronautical Engineers

Luboš Brieda (ca. 1981), b. Banská Bystrica, Czech.; aerospace and mechanical engineer; senior engineer, ERC Inc., Air Force Research Lab.,

Edwards, CA (2005-08); president, Particle In Cell Consulting LLC, Falls Church, VA (s. 2008); residing in Falls Church, VA.

Bio: "Lubos Brieda's Personal Site". See - http://www.iamlubos.com/me/ resume brieda.pdf; "Lubos Brieda," in: LinkedIn. See - https://www.linkedin. com/in/lubosbrieda/

Arnold Polak (1927-), b. Michalovce, Czech; aerospace engineer, professor of aerospace engineering and engineering mechanics, University of Cincinnati, OH

Bio: "Polak, Arnold," in: *SVU Directory* 8; "Arnold Polak," in: ase & em / emeriti. See - http://www.ase.uc.edu/~tmel/people/info/polak.htm, "Polak, Arnold," in: *American Science, 14*

Eugene Stolarik (1946-1989), b. Žilina, Czech.; aerospace engineer, associate professor of aerospace engineering and mechanics, University of Minnesota, Minneapolis

Bio: "Stolarik, Eugene," in: *American Science, 14*; "Eugene Stolarik Bio." See - https://conservancy.umn.edu/bitstream/handle/11299/196665/Eugene%20 Stolarik%20Bio.pdf?sequence=1&isAllowed=y; "Stolarik, Eugene," in: *Educators,* p. 27 entomologists

3. Agricultural Engineers

Pavol Blaho (1903-1987,), b. Skalica, Slovakia; agricultural engineer, politician, residing in Elmhurst, NY

Bio: "Blaho, Pavol," in: *SVU Directory* 5; "Blaho, Pavel," in: *Panorama,* p. 190; "Blaho, Pavel," in: *Czechoslovakia Past and Present,* Vol. 2, p. 1803.

Stephen Papánek (1901-1997), b. Brezová pod Bradlom. Slovakia; agricultural engineer, politician, agrobusinessman, residing in Lincolnwood, IL

Bio: "Papanek, Stephen," in: *SVU Directory* 7; "Papánek, Stephen," in: *Panorama* pp. 116-117; "Papánek, Ján," in: *Czechoslovakia Past and Present,* Vol. 2, pp. 1824-1825.

4. Bioengineers

Arnošt Froněk (1923-), b. Topoľčany; physiologist, professor of surgery and professor of bioengineering, University of California School of Medicine, San Diego
Bio: "Froněk, Arnošt," in: *Encyclopedia*, Vol. 2, pp. 1561-52; "Fronek, Arnost," in: *American Science, 14*.

5. Chemical Engineers

Ladislav Boor (1895-d.), b. Skalica, Slovakia; chemical engineer, with US Army Q.M.C., Philadelphia (s. 1946)
Bio: "Boor, Ladislav," in: *Who's Who in the East*, 10.

Jana Furda (1940-), b. Gottwaldov, Czech.; chemical engineer; research chemist, Technicon corp., Tarrytown, NY
Bio: "Furda, Jana," in: *SVU Directory*, 9

Michael Mickey Garay (1927-), b. Svodín, Czech.; project manager, American Cyanamid, Wayne, NJ (s. 1974)
Bio: *Who's Who in the East*, 15.

Imrich Klein (1928-1995), b. Košice, Czech.; chemical engineer, specializing in plastics, president of Scientific Process & Research, Inc., Highland Park, NJ
Bio: "Klein, Imrich," in: American Science, 14

Jiří Erik Kresta (1934-2003), b. Košice, Czech.; chemical engineer, polymer chemist, res. prof. of polymer science, dept. of chemistry and chemical engineering, Univ. of Detroit (s. 1971).
Bio: "Jiří Kresta," in: *Encyclopedia*, Vol. 2, p. 1622, p. 180; "Kresta, Jiri Erik," in: *American Science, 14*.

Eugen Singer (1926-d.), b. Levoča, Czech.; chemical engineer, Toronto
Bio: "Singer, Eugen," in: SVU Directory 8

Thomas Škrovanek (ca 1956-), b. Czech., chemical engineer with Shell, Houston, TX, IT, global portfolio manager of process control, automation

and optimization software; currently independent advanced process control consultant, residing in Philadelphia
Bio: "Thomas Skrovanek," in: LinkedIn. See - https://www.linkedin.com/in/taskrovanek/

6. Civil Engineers

Peter O. Belansky (1933-), b. Košice, Czech.; civil structural engineer, EBASCO, Norcross, GA
Bio: "Belansky, Peter O.," in: *SVU Directory* 8

Jerry George Capka (1922-1978), b. Middletown, PA, of Slovak descent; civil engineer; with US Army. In 1961-64, he was the area engineer for the US Engineer Group in Turkey, where he received the Legion of Merit. After retiring in 1969, he joined Kaiser Engineers where he was based in London, where he responsible for project development in Europe, Africa and the Middle East. He then went to Seoul and established Korea-Kaiser Engineering Company, Ltd.
US Army Lieutenant Colonel, recipient of Legion of Merit for action during Vietnam War (1965).
Bio: "Col. Jerry George Capka," in: Find a Grave. See - https://www.findagrave.com/memorial/125817730/jerry-george-capka

John Galandak (1915-), b. Chicago, of Slovak descent; civil engineer, partner and vice president, Alexander Potter assoc., environmental consulting engineers, NYC (s. 1963), assistant professor of hydraulic and sanitary engineering, Newark College Engineering (1963-67)
Bio: "Galandak, John," in: *Who's Who in the East*, 15

Béla Gerster (1850-1923), b. Košice, Slovakia; civil engineer, canal architect, s designer of the Panama Canal
Bio: "Béla Gerster, in: Wikipedia. See - https://en.wikipedia.org/wiki/Béla_Gerster;

Frank Heger (1930-1997), b. Dolné Orešany, Czech.; structural engineer, a vanguard of the engineering industry; associate professor at MIT (1955-63); co-founder of Simpson Gumpertz & Heger Inc. (SGH).
Bio: Bell, Glenn R., "Frank Heger," Structure magazine. See - https://www.structuremag.org/?p=1556

Joseph Francis Kuchar (1884-), b. Slovakia; civil engineer, with Morgan Engineering Co., Dayton, OH
Bio: "Kuchar, Joseph Francis," in: *Who's Who in Engineering*, Vol. 6

Magdalena Maria Majevsky (1941-), b. Trnava, Czech.; civil engineer, district engineer, Ontario Ministry of Transportation, Downsview, Ont., Canada
Bio: "Majevsky, Magdalena Maria," in: *SVU Directory* 8

Nicholas Masika (1931-), b. Košice, Czech.; structural engineer, Ottawa, Ont., Canada
Bio: "Masika, Nicholas," in: *SVU Directory* 8

Dennis S. Tarnay (1932-2016), b. Spišská Nová Ves, Czech; civil engineer, Federal Power Commission, Washington, DC
Bio: "Tarnay, Dennis S," in: *SVU Directory* 8; "Dennis S. Tarnay," *Washington Post,* February 2, 2016.

Ivan M. Viest, (1922-2012), b. Bratislava, Czech; civil engineer, structural engineer, Bethlehem Steel Corp., Bethlehem PA (s. 1967)
Bio: "Viest, Ivan M.," in: *SVU Directory* 8; "In Memoriam: Dr. Ivan Viest," in: Georgia Tech Coll. Engineering. See - https://ce.gatech.edu/node/5964; "Viest, Ivan," in: *American Science,* 11; Fisher, John W., "Ivan M. Viest," The National Academy Press - Memorial Tributes 18 (2014). See - https://www.nap.edu/read/18959/chapter/62; "Viest, Ivan M.," in: *American Science,* 11; "Viest, Ivan Mikulas," in: *Who's Who in America,* 42

7. Computer Scientists and Engineers

Růžena Bajcsy (1933-), b. Bratislava, Slovakia; computer scientist, specializing in robotics, professor of computer science, University of Pennsylvania, Philadelphia
Bio: "Růžena Bajcsy," in: Wikipedia. See - https://en.wikipedia.org/wiki/Ruzena_Bajcsy; "Bajcsy, Růžena," in: SVU *Directory* 8, "Bajcsy, Růžena," in: *American Science*, 15; *SVU Directory*, 9

George Albert Bekey (1928-), b. Bratislava, Czech., computer scientist, professor, University of Southern California, Los Angeles
Bio: "Bekey, George Albert," in: *SVU Directory*; "Bekey, George A.," in: Wikipedia. See - ttps://en.wikipedia.org/wiki/George_A._Bekey; "Bekey, George Albert," in: *American Science*, 14; "Bekey, George Albert," in: *Who's Who in America*, 41

Petra Cross (ca 1980-), b. Slovakia; computer scientist; senior software engineer, Google, San Francisco, CA (s. 20005). In her some 11 years at Google, Petra Cross has worked on Search, Gmail frontend, and her current project is Android Pay.
Bio: "Petra Cross," in: LinkedIn. See - https://www.linkedin.com/in/petra-cross-7b24823/

Karel Čulík (1926-2002), b. Skalica, Czech.; professor of computer science, Wayne State University. Detroit
Bio: "Čulík, Karel," in: *SVU Directory* 8; "Karel Čulík," in: Math MUNI. See - https://web.math.muni.cz/biografie/karel_culik.html

Gideon Frieder (1937-), b. Zvolen, Czech.; assoc. professor of computer science, State University of New York in Buffalo, NY
Bio: "Frieder, Gideon," in: *American Science, 14*; "Gideon Frieder," in: US Holocaust Memorial Museum. See - https://www.ushmm.org/remember/office-of-survivor-affairs/survivor-volunteer/gideon-frieder

Jan Gecsei, Slovak Canadian; Holocaust survivor; electrical engineer, computer scientist; with IBM Corp in San Jose, CA (1973-74); professor of computer science, University of Montreal.
Bio: "Jan Gecsei," in: J.UCS. See - http://www.jucs.org/jucs_articles_by_author/Gecsei_Jan/BusinessCard

Igor Jurisica (1967-), b. Martin, Czech.; computer scientist, integrative computational biologist, professor at University of Toronto
Bio: "Igor Jurisica," in: Wikipedia. See - https://en.wikipedia.org/wiki/Igor_Jurisica;
Igor Jurisica," in: Medical Biophysics University of Toronto. See - http://medbio.utoronto.ca/faculty/jurisica.html; "Igor Jurisica," in: Prabook. See - https://prabook.com/web/igor.jurisica/3571497

Kamil Marcinka (1958-), b. Bratislava, Czech.; computer scientist, system analyst with Chevron Information Technology Co. (1986-2002; senior systems analyst with eDataTech (2004-09); senior systems analyst with Naval Postgraduate School (s. 2009).
Bio: "Marcinka, Kamil," in: *SVU Directory* 7; "Kamil Marcinka, in: LinkedIn. See - https://www.linkedin.com/in/kamil-marcinka-a503a78/

John Lukas Pituch (1953-), b. Paludzka, Czech.; computer scientist, engineer with Lockheed, Sunnyvale, CA
Bio: Pituch, John Lukáš," in: *SVU Directory* 8"

Štefan Šurka (1954-), b. Bratislava, Czech.; electrical and computer engineer, principal software engineer, system designer and technologist, lately with EBSCO Information Services
Bio: "Šurka, Štefan." In: SVU Directory 8; "Stefan Surka," in: LinkedIn. See - https://www.linkedin.com/in/stefan-surka-bb9a7338/

Miroslav Valach (1926-), b. Hnúšťa, Czech.; computer scientist, professor of information and computer science with Georgia Tech. (1969-74), research director with Karsten Mfg. Corp. (1974-80), with Friday Corp. (s. 1980)
Bio: "Valach, Miroslav," in: *SVU Directory* 3; "Miroslav Valach," in: *Encyclopedia*, Vol. 2, p. 1781.

8. Electrical and Electronic Engineers

Orestes Baycura (1923-2002), b. Ladimirová, Czech.; electrical engineer, associate professor, Naval Postgraduate School, Monterey, CA
Bio: "Baycura, Orestes," in: *American Science, 14*; "Orestes Methodius Baycura," in: *Encyclopedia,* Vol. 2, p. 1826.

Igor Bazovsky (1914-2000), Lučenec, Slovakia; electrical engineer; in US s. 1957; Research engineer Boeing, Seattle (1957-59), manager reliability engineering United Control Corporation (1959-62); systems reliability manager Litton Industries, Woodland Hills, California (1963-66), Director science and consultant division Genge Industries, Inc., Sherman Oaks (1966-69); president, chief scientist Igor Bazovsky & Associates, Inc. (s. 1969).
Bio: Igor Bazovsky," in: Prabook. See - https://prabook.com/web/igor.
bazovsky/3689280

Igor Bazovsky, Jr. (1942-), b. Bratislava, Czech.; electrical engineer, with Igor Bazovsky and Assoc., Inc., Sherman Oaks, CA
Bio: "Bazovsky, Igor, Jr." *SVU Directory* 3

John Stephen Bolen (1933-2014), b. Bethlehem, PA, of Slovak descent; electronic engineer; with Hughes Aircraft Co., Orange, County in electronics in anti-electronic warfare systems
Bio: "John Stephen Bolen," in: *Orange County Register,* May 3, 2014

Michael J. Doslak (1945-2002), b. Lorain, OH, of Slovak descent; electrical and biomedical engineer, assistant professor of electrical engineering, University of Nebraska-Lincoln (1980-88)
Bio: "Michael J. Doslak, 56, Electrical Engineering Professor," in: LorainCounty.com. See -

Edward A. Erdelyi (1909-1980), b. Hlohovec, Slovakia; electrical engineer; professor, University of Colorado, Boulder
Bio: "Erdelyi, Edward A.," in: Educators, p. 7; "Edward Alexander Erdelyi," in: *Encyclopedia,* Vol. 2, p. 1832; "Erdelyi, Edward A.," in: *American Science, 14*

Milan P. Getting (1902-1990), electrical engineer, Pittsburgh, PA
Bio: "Getting, Milan P.," in: *SVU Directory* 6

Thomas Hornák (1924-), b. Bratislava, Czech.; electrical engineer, inventor, principal scientist with Hewlett Packard Labs., Palo Alto, CA (s. 1992)
Bio: "Hornák, Thomas," in: *Encyclopedia*, Vol. 2, pp. 1835-36, "Hornak, Thomas," in: *American Science, 14.*

John Jarem (1921-), b. Jarembina, Czech.; electrical engineer, professor of electrical engineering, Drexel University, Philadelphia PA (s. 1964); with University of Alabama, Huntsville (s. 1987)
Bio: "Jarem, John," in: *American Science, 14;* "Dr. John H Jarem Biography," in: UAH Engineering Faculty and Staff. See - https://www.uah.edu/eng/departments/ece/people/faculty-staff/john-jarem

Edward S. Kolesar, Jr. (1950-2009), b. Canton, O0 H, of Slovak descent; electrical engineer; he taught at Air Force Institute of Technology (AFIT) (for 8 years), before accepting the newly established Montecrief Professor of Engineering chair at the Texas Christian University
Bio: "Edward Steven Kolesar, Jr.," *Fraternally Yours*, Vol.96, No. 5 (February 2010), p. 17.

Alexander Eugene Martens (1923-), b. Banská Štiavnica, Czech.; electrical engineer, department head, Electronics Research & Development, Bausch & Lomb, Inc. Rochester, NY (s. 1960)
Bio: "Martens, Alexander Eugene," in: *American Science, 11*

Jaromir Matula (1923-1980), b. Bratislava, Czech.; electrical engineer

Eugene Mittelmann (1903), b. Bratislava, Slovakia; industrial electronics engineer, consulting engineer, Chicago, IL
Bio: "Mittelmann, Eugene," in: *American Science, 14, Who's Who in Commerce and Industry*, Vol. 14, p. 916.

John M. Nosko, b. Brezová, Slovakia; electrical engineer, consulting engineer, residing in Chicago
Bio: "Nosko, John M.," in: Droba, pp. 162-163.

Anton Jozef Rozsypal (1935-), b. Bratislava, of Czech parents; electrical engineer, professor, department of Linguistics, University of Alberta, Edmonton, Canada
Bio: "Rozsypal, Anton Jozef," in: Encyclopedia, Vol. 2, pp. 1785-86.

Ambroz Karol Škrovánek (1928-), b. Senné, Czech.; electronic engineer, Harvey Hubell Inc, Herndon, VA
Bio: Škrovánek, Ambroz Karol," in: *SVU Directory* 8; NCSML Oral Histories. See - https://www.ncsml.org/exhibits/ambroz-skrovanek/

Rudolph Steckl (1929-), b. Bratislava, Czech.; electronic engineer, semiconductor components manufacturing executive; dev. engineer, DuPont Co. (1957-610; Motorola, Inc., Phoenix, AZ (s. 1961), manager, electronic materials group (s. 1977)
Bio: "Steckl, Rudolph," in: *Who's Who in Finance and Industry,* 21

9. Environmental Engineers

Eugen Singer (1926-2013), b. Levoča, Slovakia; Ing., CSc., Vysoká škola chemicko-technologická Prague; environmental engineer, specializing in monitoring and instrumentation for air pollution
Bio: "Singer, Eugen," in: *SVU Directory* 8; "Eugen Singer," in: Heritage Funeral Centre. See -
http://www.heritagefuneralcentre.ca/book-of-memories/1644731/singer-eugen/obituary.php

10. Industrial Engineers

Daniel John Kisha (1937-2016), b. Johnstown, PA, of Slovak descent; chemical engineer, industrial engineer; president of Kisha Engineering, Inc., Pensacola, FL; previously employed by Exxon, Fluor and James Chemical Engineering; residing in Johnstown, PA, president of Slovak Import Company
Bio: "Kisha, Daniel John," in: SVU *Directory* 8; "Slovak Import Company," See - https://www.manta.com/c/mvrxms9/slovak-import-company; "Daniel john Kisha," *The Tribune Democrat,* December 20, 2016.

11. Materials Science Engineers

Ivan Odler (1930-2005); b. Bratislava, Czech; materials science engineer; with the Clarkson Technological University, Potsdam, NY, Westvaco Research Center, Charleston, SC and Grace Co., Cambridge, MA; in the year 1975 he moved to Germany and joined the Technical University Clausthal-Zellerfeld, where he was appointed Professor of Materials Science and director of the Institute of Nonmetallic Materials in 1976.
Bio: "Obituary: Professor Ing. Dr. Ivan Odler," See - https://www.chempap. org/file_access.php?file=595a371.pdf

Jan Peter Skalný (1935-), b. Bratislava, Czech.; chemical engineer, industrial research manager, associate director of Martin Marietta Labs and construction materials research director for W. R. Grace & Co.; presently president of Materials Service Life, specializing in service life prediction of concrete-based infrastructure; now residing in Florida
Bio: "Skalny, Jan Peter," in: *SVU Directory*, 8

Edward Snajdr (1938-2005), b. Edwardsville, IL, of Czech and Slovak descent; ceramic engineer; with Vesuvius and its predecessor companies (s. 1974).
Bio: "Edward Snajdr," in: *Edwardsville Intelligencer*, Sept. 12-13, 2005

12. Mechanical Engineers

Bohumil Albrecht (1921-), b. Teplička, Czech.; professor of mechanical engineering, University of New Mexico
Bio: "Albrecht, Bohumil," in: *Science* 14

Egon Alex DeZubay (1921-), b. Bratislava, Czech.; mechanical engineer, sr research engineer, Thermodyn. and Combust., Westinghouse Research Labs (s. 1952)
Bio "De Zubay, Egon Alex," in: *American Science, 9*

Peter Durenec (1937-1996), b. Trenčianske Teplice, Czech.; mechanical engineer, Silver Spring, MD
Bio: "Durenec, Petr," in: *SVU Directory*, 3

František L. Eisinger (1927-2010), b. Bratislava, Czech.; mechanical engineer, Foster Wheeeler Corporation, Clinton, NJ
Bio: "Eisinger, František," in: *SVU Directory* 8, "In Memoriam: Frantisek L. Eisinger (1927-2010), *J. Pressure Vessel Technol* 135, No. 3 (May 21, 2013), p. 1.

Peter Andras Engel (1935-), b. Košice, Czech.; engineer specializing in applied mechanics and tribology, research engineer of material sciences, Endicott Lab., IBM Corp., Endicott, NY
Bio: "Engel, Peter Andras," in: *American Science, 14*

Thomas Grossman (1948-), b. Michalovce, Czech.; mechanical engineer, mechanical chemical engineer with Ebasco Services, NYC (1972-84); chief mechanical engineer, US Postal Svc,- northern, NYC (1984-88);
Bio: "Grossman, Thomas," in: *Who's Who in the East*, 17; "Grossman, Thomas," in: Prabook. See - https://prabook.com/web/thomas.grossman/825819

Edward George Keshock (1935-), b. Campbell, OH, of Slovak descent; mechanical engineer, professor, Cleveland State University, Cleveland, OH
Bio: "Keshock, Edward George," in: *SVU Directory* 8; "In Memoriam: Dr. Edward Keshock," in: Friends of Slovakia. See - http://www.friendsofslovakia. org/fos/news/newst125.htm; "In Memoriam: Dr. Edward Keshock," in: cleveland.com. See - http://blog.cleveland.com/mosaic/2010/12/ in_memoriam_dr_edward_keshock.html

Emory Lakatos (1905-1986), b. Lučenec, Slovakia; mechanical engineer
Bio: "Lakatos, Emory," in: *Science*

Rudolf Glenn Minarik (1907-1993), b. Cleveland, OH; mechanical engineer, professor of mechanical engineering, Syracuse University (1943-45), president of The Integral Engineering Services Co. (s. 1947)
Bio: "Minarik, Rudolf Glenn," in: *Who's Who in the Midwest*, 1

John Jakob Nosko (1922-2005), b. Gary, IN, of Slovak descent; mechanical engineer, with Bemnix Energy Controls Division (37 years)
Bio: "John Jakob Nosko," in: Kaniewski Funeral Homes, Inc. See - https:// www.kaniewski.com/notices/John-Jakob-Nosko

Egon Orowan (1902-1989), b. Budapest, of Slovak father; in US. S. 1950; mechanical engineer, metallurgist, inventor; professor of mechanical engineering, Massachusetts Institute of Technology (MIT), NAS member.
Bio: "Egon Orowan, 87, Engineering Professor," *The New York Times*, August 5, 1989; Egon Orowan," in: Wikipedia. See - https://en.wikipedia.org/wiki/Egon_Orowan

Robert Pudmericky (1961-), b. Bratislava, Czech.; mechanical engineer, with Maryland Department of the Environment, Baltimore, MD
Bio: "Pudmericky, Robert," in *SVU Directory* 8

Emanuel A. Salma (1908-1989), b. US, of Slovak descent; mechanical engineer, Associate Dean of the College of Engineering and Science at New York University
Bio: "Skriba, Emanuel A.," in: *Panorama*, p. 274; "Emanuel A. Salma, Educator, 81," *The New York Times*, January 28, 1989.

Louis S. Skriba (1896-d.), b. Oslany, Slovakia; mechanical engineer, with Western Electric Company, Chicago
Bio: "Skriba, Louis S.," in: Droba, pp. 163-164

Rudolph A. Skriba (1894-1960), b. Simnovany, Slovakia; mechanical engineer, head of engineering dept. of F. J. Little Co., Chicago
Bio: "Skriba, Rudolph A.," in: Droba, p. 164, "Rudolph Anthony Skriba," in: Find A Grave. See - https://www.findagrave.com/memorial/152164089/rudolph-anthony-skriba

John Slezák (1896-1986), b. Stará Tura, Slovakia; Colonel, mechanical engineer, chairman of the board, Kable Printing Co., Mt. Morris, IL
Bio: "Slezák, John," in: *SVU Directory* 5; "Slezak, John," in: *Who's who in America*, 28; "John Slezak," in: Wikipedia. See - https://en.wikipedia.org/wiki/John_Slezak

Jerry J. Taborek (1922-), b. Czech.; mechanical engineer, develop. Engineer, Phillips Petroleum Co., Bartlesville, OK (s. 1956)
Bio: "Taborek, Jerry," in: *American Science*, 11.

Julius M. Werner (1897-d.), b. Tisovec, Slovakia; mechanical engineer, associate professor, Syracuse University (s. 1959)
Bio: "Werner, Julius M." in: *American Science*, 10

Ivan Frank Zarobsky (1892-1953), b. Pittsburgh, PA; mechanical engineer, professor and head of mechanical engineering, University of Toledo (s. 1921)
Bio: "Zarobsky, Ivan Frank," in: *Who's Who in America*, 28

13. Metallurgical Engineers

Peter Filip (1960-), b. Pravotice, Czech.; physical metallurgist, professor, Dept. of Mechanical Engineering and Energy Processes, Southern Illinois University, Carbondale, IL. His research includes: relationship between the structure and properties of metals, ceramics, composite materials, pioneering work in the development and optimization of brake linings, and smart implant materials.
Bio: "Filip, Peter" in: *SVU Directory* 8; "Peter Filip," in: Southern Illinois University. See - https://engineering.siu.edu/me/faculty-staff/faculty/filip.php

John Janos (1933-2016), b. Lakewood, OH, probably of Slovak descent; metallurgical engineer, with US Steel (for 42 years), starting in the American Steel and Wire plant in Cleveland, OH, senior service metallurgist in the Midwest, working in Chicago, St. Louis and Minneapolis.
Bio: "John Janos," *The Plain Dealer*, October 24-30, 2015.

Gary Judd (1942-), b. Humenné, Czech.; metallurgical engineer, professor, Rensselaer Polytechnic Institute (s. 1976), Dean of the faculty (1994-1997), Provost, Troy, NY
Bio: "Judd, Gary," in: *American Science, 14*

14. Mining Engineers

Ervín Podrabinský (1931-), b. Jasina, Czech.; mining engineer, Standard Metals Corp., Silverton, CO
Bio: "Podrabinský, Ervín," in *SVU Directory*

15. Nuclear Engineers

Lenka Kollar (ca 1987-), b. Slovakia; nuclear engineer; turned into a public communication professional; director of business strategy at NUScale Power, Washington, DC
Bio: "Lenka Kollar," in: LinkedIn. See - https://www.linkedin.com/in/lenkakollar/

Harold Ujc (ca 1933-), b. Slovakia; nuclear engineer; senior design specialist, Ontario Hydro (now. OPG) (1981-93).
Bio: "Harold Ujc." In: LinkedIn. See - https://www.linkedin.com/in/harold-ujc-m-eng-p-eng-144801a/?originalSubdomain=ca

16. Systems and Reliability Engineers

Igor Bazovsky (1914-2000), b. Lučenec, Slovakia; electrical engineer, research engineer, Boeing, Seattle (1957-59), manager, reliability engineering, United Control Corporation (1959-62), president, chief scientist, Igor Bazovsky & Associates (s. 1969)
Bio: "Bazovsky, Igor," in: *Who's Who in the West*, 11; "Igor Bazovsky," in: Prabook. See - https://prabook.com/web/igor.bazovsky/3689280

17. Mastering Engineers

Vlado Meller (1947-), b. Humenné, Czech.; an audio mastering engineer, currently mastering at Vlado Meller Mastering in Charleston, South Carolina. Vlado masters across multiple genres of music, with credits on rock, hip-hop, pop, jazz, metal, dance, opera, Broadway, and classical albums. Over his 43-year career, Vlado has worked on many hit records and has worked with such artists as: Beastie Boys, Andrea Bocelli, Johnny Cash, Charlotte Church, Celine Dion, Duran Duran, Kenny G, Kenny Loggins, Julio Iglesias, Michael Jackson, Lil Wayne, Limp Bizkit, Linkin Park, Paul McCartney, Metallica, George Michael, Oasis, Pink Floyd, Public Enemy, Rage Against The Machine, Red Hot Chili Peppers, Shakira, Barbra Streisand, System Of A Down, A Tribe Called Quest, Weezer, Kanye West, Jack White, Samey and many more.[2] Vlado currently holds the position of senior mastering engineer at Vlado Meller Mastering in Charleston, South Carolina. He has won two Grammy awards.

Bio: "Vlado Meller," in: Wikipedia. See - https://en.wikipedia.org/wiki/ Vlado_Meller

H. Inventions

Štefan Banič (1870-1941), b. Smolenice, Slovakia; Slovak American inventor of early parachute-like device, which he donated to the US army, but was not used
Bio: "Štefan Banič," in: Wikipedia. See - https://en.wikipedia.org/wiki/ Štefan_Banič

Itzhak Bentov (1923-1979), b. Humenné, Slovakia; amateur inventor, mystic, author
Bio: "Itzhak Bentov," in: Wikipedia. See - https://en.wikipedia.org/wiki/ Itzhak_Bentov

John Dopyera (orig. Dopjera) (1893-1988), b. Šaštín-Stráže, Slovakia; inventor of a new Dobro resonator guitar
Bio: "John Dopyera," in: Wikipedia. See - https://en.wikipedia.org/wiki/ John_Dopyera

Ivan A. Getting (1912-2003), b. New York, NY, of Slovak ancestry; electrical engineer, one of the developers of the Global Positioning System (GPSP)
Bio: "Ivan A. Getting," in: Wikipedia. See - https://en.wikipedia.org/wiki/ Ivan_A._Getting; "Getting, Ivan A.," in: *Who's Who in the West*, 11

John J. Hanacek (1902-2003, b. Ružomberok, Slovakia; instrument designer, biological science dept., University of Chicago
Bio: "John J. Hanacek Obituary," *Chicago Tribune*, May 11-12, 2002.

Jozef Murgaš (1864-1929), b. Tajov, Slovakia; inventor, pioneer wireless communicator
Bio: Palickar, Stephen J., *Rev. Joseph Murgas, Priest-Scientist: His Musical Wireless and the First Radio: Biography.* New York, 1950. 164 p.; Palickar, Stephen J., *A Pictorial Biography of Rev. Joseph Murgas, Pioneer Inventor in the Field of Wireless Telegraphy and Radio.* Wilkes-Barre, PA: Murgas Memorial Foundation, 1953. 83p.

Thomas G. Polanyi (1918-2007), b. of Slovak grandfather; in US s. 1943; physicist, inventor, residing in Bolkon, MA. He patented a carbon dioxide surgical laser system. The system which includes a surgical microscope in operative rigid connection with a stereo laser endoscope, the microscope/ endoscope assembly being freely positionable, and a CO laser device fixedly mounted with respect to the assembly and capable of operating under virtually any angular orientation of the microscope/endoscope assembly which may be necessary to accommodate a surgeon or other person who may be operating the system and performing surgery upon a patient.
Bio: "Thomas G. Polanyi," in: MA Obituary and Death Notice Archives. See -http://www.genlookups.com/ma/webbbs_config.pl/noframes/read/606

Bohumil Vančo (1907-1990), b. Madunice, Slovakia; studied film and psychology; in 1949 immigrated to Brazil and resided in Sao Paulo; in 1964 he moved to the US. Worked in optics and photography, areas in which he received several patents for his inventions. Inventor of stereoscopy.
Bio: "Vančo, Bohumil," in: CESA Project. See - http://www.cesa-project.eu/ svk/slovnik/authors/bohumil-vanco

Howard Lawrence Weinberger (1927-2009), b. New York, NT, of Slovak descent; inventor; developer of missile systems and communication satellites for Hughes Aircraft. Sailed with Fairwind Yacht Club in Marina del Rey, and, an avid cycler, took many bicycle trips in the U.S. and overseas.
Bio: "Howard Lawrence Weinberger," *Los Angeles Times*, December 23-27, 2009.

I. EXPLORATION, ADVENTURE, REVOLUTION, ESPIONAGE

1. Explorers

George F. Kosco (1908-2008), Harrisburg, PA, of Slovak descent; Captain, US Navy; chief aerologist and chief scientist of US Navy Operation Highjump (1946-47); visited North and South Pole with Admiral R. E. Byrd; Kosco Glacier is named in his honor
Bio: "Deluge," in: *Sea Cobra*. By Buckner F. Melton, Jr. Guilford, CT: The Lyons Press, 2007, pp. 91-144.

Alexander Liška (1883-1941), b. Yugoslavia, of Czech father and Slovak mother, raised in Zamarovce, Slovakia; traveler, explorer, physician, geologist, gold-digger.
Bio: Kopanic, Michael J., "Slovaks in Alaska? Alexander Liska's Life," Jednota, Sept. 23, 2015.

2. Astronauts

Robert J. Cenker (1948-), b. Uniontown, Pa, of Slovak descent; an American aerospace and electrical engineer, aerospace systems consultant, and former astronaut. n January 1986, Cenker was a crew member on the twenty-fourth mission of NASA's Space Shuttle program, the seventh flight of Space Shuttle Columbia, designated as mission STS-61-C. Cenker served as a Payload Specialist,[a] representing RCA Astro-Electronics. This mission was the final flight before the Challenger disaster, which caused the Space Shuttle program to be suspended until 1988, and impacted NASA's Payload Specialist program for even longer. s a result, Cenker's mission was called "The End of Innocence" for the Shuttle program. Following the completion of his Shuttle mission, Cenker returned to work in the commercial aerospace field.
Bio: "Robert J. Cenker," in: Wikipedia. See - https://en.wikipedia.org/wiki/ Robert_J._Cenker

Eugene Cernan (1934-2017), b. Chicago, IL, of Slovak father and Czech mother; astronaut, naval aviator, electrical engineer, aeronautical engineer, and fighter pilot
Bio: "Eugene Cernan," in: Wikipedia. See - https://en.wikipedia.org/wiki/ Eugene_Cernan; "Cernan, Eugene A.," in: *Who's Who in America*, 41

Michael Fincke (1967-), b. Pittsburgh, PA, of Slovak ancestry; astronaut
Bio: "Michael Fincke," in: Wikipedia. See - https://en.wikipedia.org/wiki/ Michael_Fincke

3. Aviators

Nadia Marcinko (1986-), b. Kosice, Czech.; a 'Global Girl' ; FAA-certified commercial rated pilot and flight instructor, holding a Single (land & sea)

Multi-engine (land) instrument rating and Gulfstream C/G-IV & C/G-1159-type rating certificate.
Bio: "Nadia Marcinko," in: Wikipedia. See - https://en.wikipedia.org/wiki/Nadia_Marcinko

Mira Slovak (1929-2014), b. Cifer, Slovakia; a daring pilot, Cold Ware defector, stunt flyer, Hydro racer
Bio: Chawkins, Steve, "Mira Slovak dies at 84; Cold War defector flew to freedom and fame," *Los Angeles Times,* June 21, 2014. See - http://www.latimes.com/local/ obituaries/la-me-mira-slovak-20140622-story.html; Yardley, William, "Mira Slovak, a Daring Pilot Who Won Freedom, Then Races, Dies at 84," *The New York Times,* June 29, 2014. See - https://www.nytimes.com/2014/06/29/us/mira-slovak-a-daring-pilot-who-won-freedomthen-races-dies-at-84.html; The Incredible Story of Mira Slovak, The Flying Czech," in Return of Kings. See - http://www.returnofkings.com/46600/the-incredible-story-of-mira-slovak-the-flying-czech; Mira Slovak Obituary," in: Hydroplane and Raceboat Museum. See - https://thunderboats.ning.com/profiles/blogs/mira-slovak-obituary

4. Forty-Eighter Revolutionaries

Péter Pál Dobozy (1832-1919), location of his birth uncertain but could be Slovak ancestry; soldier in Hungarian revolution of 1848; in US s. 1861; Civil War veteran. After the Civil War, resided in Missouri as a farmer.
Bio: "Dobozy Péter Pál," in: Wikipedia. See - https://hu.wikipedia.org/wiki/Dobozy_ Péter_Pál

František Samuel Figuli (1825--1880), b. Klenovec, Slovakia; adventurer, traveler, writer, participant in the 1848 Revolution, fought in the Civil War, owned a plantation in Virginia, later joined an exploratory expedition to the North Pole.
Bio: "František Samuel Figuli," in: Wikipedia. See - https://sk.wikipedia.org/wiki/Figuli; https://www.tyzden.sk/casopis/12878/slovaci-ktori-bojovali-za-lincolna/

Cornelius Fornet (1818-1894), b. Stráže pod Tatrami, Slovakia; engineer; soldier in Hungarian war of 1848; in US s. 1849; participated in Civil War

with the rank of Major of Engineers. Due to injuries, he then returned to Hungary, where he became government official
Bio: "Fornet Kornel," in : Wikipedia. See - https://hu.wikipedia.org/wiki/ Fornet Kornél Wikipedia; See - https://hu.wikipedia.org/wiki/Fornet Kornél

Andrew Gálfy-Gállik (1818-1883), b. Brzotín, Slovakia; merchant in Košice; officer during the 1848 revolution; came to America, settling in Cincinnati, OH; in 1862, enlisted in the 58th Ohio Infantry Regiment, in which he was appointed major. After being captured, he was exchanged and then served on the gunboat 'Mound City. After the War, he studied medicine and then practiced in Boston, then in Cincinnati and finally in Kansas City. In 1881, he returned to Košice.
Bio: "Gálfy-Gállik, Andrew, in: Lincoln's Hungarian Heroes, p. 55; "Gallik, András, Gálfy," in: Arcanum. See - https://www.arcanum.hu/en/online-kiadvanyok/Lexikonok-magyar-eletrajzi-lexikon-7428D/g-gy-757D7/ gallik-andras-galfy-7585C/

Anthony (Antal) Gerster (1825-1897), b. Košice, Slovakia; uncle of Dr. Arpad G. Gerster; civil engineer; military officer in the 1848 Revolution in Hungary; in US s. 1852; served in the Civil War as an officer of the engineer corps under General John C. Frémont with General Alexander Asboth and later served under the Generals Rosecrans and Grant. He died in California in 1897.
Bio: "Gerster Antal," in: Wikipedia. See: https://hu.wikipedia.org/wiki/ Gerster_Antal; Gerster Anthony," in: *Lincoln's Hungarian Heroes*, p. 55.

Adolph Huebsch (1830-1884), b. Liptovský Svätý Mikuláš, Slovakia; officer in in the Hungarian Revolutionary Army
Bio: Rechcigl, Miloslav, Jr., "Adolph Huebsch," in: *Beyond the Sea of Beer*, p. 45.

Philip Korn, bookseller from Bratislava; Captain in the Hungarian Revolutionary Army, managed to escape to US
Bio: Rechcigl, Miloslav, Jr., "Adolph Huebsch," in: *Beyond the Sea of Beer*, p. 46.

Lajos Kossuth (in Slovak: Ludevít Košút), b. 1802-1894), b. Monok, of Slovak descent; a Hungarian nobleman, lawyer, politician, statesman, a revolutionary; in US s. 1851; he later returned to Europe.
Bio: "Lajos Kossuth," in: Wikipedia. See - https://en.wikipedia.org/wiki/Lajos_Kossuth

Joseph Majthenyi, b. Nitra, Slovakia; member of the landed gentry and prominent politician, a member of upper chamber of Hungarian parliament. Having taken part in the War of Independence, he was forced to flee to America. He and his family settled in New Buda, Iowa, but soon moved to Davenport.
Bio: See writeup about his son -"Theodore Majthenyi," in: *The Bracken Rangers: Company K, 28ᵗʰ Regiment, 1ˢᵗ Indiana Cavalry*. By Robert Allan Stevens. 2ⁿᵈ ed. Miami-Los Angeles: Three Stars Press, 2011, pp. 83-85.

Richard Marcinko (1940-), b. Lansford, PA, of Slovak grandfather; US Navy SEAL commander and Vietnam War veteran; the first commanding officer of SEAL Team Six and Red Cell
Bio: "Richard Marcinko," in: Wikipedia. See - https://en.wikipedia.org/wiki/Richard_Marcinko

Joseph Nemeth (1816-1889), b. Lošonec, Slovakia; professional soldier in the 4ᵗʰ Cavalry Regiment in the Imperial Army with the rank of 1ˢᵗ Lieutenant. At the outbreak of the Hungarian War of Independence, deserted with some 500 hussars and returned to Hungary. He volunteered in one militia regiments and was mustered as 1ˢᵗ Lieutenant, later elevated to a Captain in the 62ⁿᵈ Honved Battalion. He participated in more than two dozen engagements and was wounded several times, until he was discharged in July 1849. After the surrender of the Hungarian revolutionary forces, he fled to Turkey. In 1851 arrived in the US.
Bio: Vida, pp. 277-278.

Emeric (Imre) Radnich (1824-1903); b. Selice, Slovakia; railroad engineer. When the Hungarian War for independence started, he enlisted as lieutenant, first at the 3ʳᵈ, then at the 2ⁿᵈ Sapper Battalion. In July he was promoted to 1ˢᵗ Lieutenant and in August he was, not only, transferred to the Sapper Battalion in Komárno, but further elevated to the rank of Captain. After the collapse of the Hungarian cause, the Austrian government granted him a safe conduct and he escaped first to Hamburg, then to Britain. Along with the Újhazy family he soon set sail for America, arriving in NYC in December 1849. He then was farming in Prairie, AR. Soon after, he then joined Narciso Lopez's expedition to Cuba, but the enterprise turned out to be a huge fiasco. The Spanish defeated the small army and Radnich was sentenced to imprisonment a hard labor at Ceuta, North Africa. At the intervention of his brother John, at the legation of the US in Madrid, the Queen of Spain granted him a pardon. After his return to the US, he settled down in New Buda, Iowa, working as an engineer. After the Compromise of 1867, he returned to Hungary, where he had prominent career. He became inspector of the Hungarian State Railways and then director of the Railway Gyor-Sopron-Ebenfurt.

Bio: "Radnich Imre," in: Wikipedia. See - https://hu.wikipedia.org/wiki/Radnich_Imre

Stephen Radnich (1828-1912), b. Egreš, Slovakia; took part in the Hungarian War of Independence, as an officer. Some sources claim that he served in a cavalry unit under General Bem, whereas others refer to him as an artillery lieutenant. After the surrender of the revolutionary army, he left the country, first he moved to Britain and finally immigrated to the US in 1850.

Bio: Vida, p. 289

Johann Theodore (Tivadar) Rombauer (1803-1855), b. Levoča, Slovakia; metallurgical engineer and entrepreneur who played significant role in the development of metal industry in Hungary; the founder of the iron works at Rimamurány-Salgótarján (near Slovak border); and the leading personality of arms supply in the Revolution. After the capitulation at Vilagos in 1848, Rombauer had to flee disguised as a poor journeyman. He traveled to Hamburg through Austria, to England, finally immigrating to America. He got involved there with mining and foundry. He even made a proposal for President Washington regarding gold mining in California but was refused. After his tour to South America, where he met many of his countrymen, he returned and settled in Iowa, near Davenport. Be became co-editor of the German-language newspaper *Der Demokrat,* but a few years later died; he was only fifty-two years old. His wife, Bertha, who also participated in the War of Independence, as a nurse, followed him to the US in 1850. They had eleven children, many of whom excelled professionally. Upon his death in 1855, the family moved to St. Louis, Missouri, a burgeoning city offering plenty of opportunities to immigrants. Several of his sons participated in the Hungarian Revolution and, in the US, they took part in the Civil War. Bio: Koudela, Pál, A Hungarian War Hero, Factory Founder and Refugee in the United States - Tidvar Rombauer," *Hungarian Studies*, 30, Issue 1 (2016), pp. 3-16;. "Rombauer Tivadar," in: Wikipedia. See - https://hu.wikipedia. org/wiki/Rombauer Tivadar; "Theodore Rombauer," in: Find A Grave. See - https://www.findagrave.com/memorial/28109163/theodore-rombauer

Richard Rombauer (1831-1848), b. Szeleszto, of Slovak-born father; doing battle for liberation, as the 2nd oldest son, a soldier in the Hungarian revolutionary army of 1848, severely wounded at the disastrous battle of Vizakna, died of his wounds, and rests in an unknown grave. He was only eighteen years old.
Bio: "Rombauer Richárd," in: Wikipedia. See https://hu.wikipedia.org/wiki/ Rombauer_ Richárd; "Richard Gottfried Rombauer," in: Find A Grave. See - https://www.findagrave.com/memorial/137031808

Robert Julius Rombauer (1830-1925), b. Mukačevo, of Slovak father (from Levoča). After finishing the Lutheran HS in Bratislava, moved to Vienna in 1848 and as a freshman in the Polytechnic joined the Legion of the Academy and later entered the army as a Lieutenant in artillery. After the fall of the Revolution, enlisted in the Austrian army as a private, but in 1850, freed by ransom, immigrated to America with his mother.
Bio: "Rombauer Gyula Robert," in: Wikipedia. See - https://hu.wikipedia. org/wiki/Rombauer_ Gyula_Róbert

Roderick Rombauer (1833-1924), b. Szeleszto, of Slovak father; fought in the Hungarian War of Independence with his three brothers. He immigrated with mother and six siblings from Hamburg to New York in September 1851.
Bio: "Roderick Emil Rombauer," in: find A Grave. See - https://www. findagrave.com/memorial/95173680; "Rombauer E. Roderick," in: Wikipedia. See - https://hu.wikipedia.org/wiki/Rombauer_E._Roderick

Matthias Ernest Rozsafy (orig. Ruzicska) (1828-1893), b. Komárno, Slovakia, presumably of Czech origin; a pioneer journalist. As a twenty-year old, took part in the 1848 revolution, during which he almost lost his life. When the Revolution failed, he got involved in planning a new insurrection, during which he was captured, and sentenced to death. Fortunately, he succeeded to escape, garbed in woman's clothing. Eventually he got to London, and in 1850 moved to America. There he took part in the Civil Artillery Regiment;

was mustered out as a Major by brevet. After the War, he lived in New York, and later moved to Washington, DC, where he had a government position and later had his own patent bureau. He died in Washington and was buried in Arlington National Cemetery.

Bio: "Rozsafy Matthias Ernest," in: Lincoln Hungarian Heroes, pp. 77-79.

Károly Semsey (1830-1911); b. Kračúnovce, Slovakia; officer in revolution of 1848, with the rank of captain; in US s. 1859; veteran of Civil War with the rank Major of the 45th New York Volunteer Infantry Regiment. After the War, worked in the Customs Office and then in the immigration service.

Bio: "Semsey, Karoly," in: Wikipedia. See - https://hu.wikipedia.org/wiki/ Semsey_ Károly; "Semsey, Charles," in: *Lincoln's Hungarian Heroes*, p. 81; "Charles S3emsey," in: Vesvary Collection Newspaper. See - http://vasvary. sk-szeged.hu/newsletter/04jun/beszedits.html

Benjamin Szold (1829-1902); b. Zemianske Sady, Slovakia; future rabbi; for his participation in the Revolution of 1848 was expelled from Vienna where he studied

Bio: "Benjamin Szøld," in: Wikipedia. See - https://en.wikipedia.org/wiki/ Benjamin_Szold; Zola, Gary F., "Szold, Benjamin," in: *National Biography*, Vol. 21, pp. 240-241.

Laszlo Újházy (1795-1870), b. Budimír, Slovakia; son of a landowner of the lesser nobility; one of the defenders of Komárno fortress, the last stronghold of the Hungarian army in the fall of 1849. In exchange for the fortress, soldiers were granted amnesty and they wished also a passport for emigration. Újházy belonged to the first group of Hungarian refugees who arrived in New York in December1849.

Bio: "Ujhazy, Laszlo," in: Wikipedia. See - https://hu.wikipedia.org/wiki/ Újházy_László

3. Adventurers - Daredevils - Spies

a. General

Raska, Jan, "Allies Abroad, Enemy Aliens at Home: Czechs, Slovaks, and the Canadian 'Enemy Aliens' Registration Issue (1938-1942)," Canadian

Ethnic Studies Association Nineteenth Biennial Conference, Hotel Fort Garry, Winnipeg, Manitoba, Canada, September 28, 2007.

Raska, Jan, "Forging States of Dissent: Czech Émigrés, Communist Spies, and Canadian >State Security, 1945-1968," International Conference: Secret Weapon or Victims of the Cold War? Central and Eastern European Political Émigrés, Institute of National Remembrance, Lublin, Poland, November 13, 2008.

Raska, Jan, "Masking 'Undesirable' Entry, Subverting Integration: Czechoslovakia's Émigrés, Espionage, and Canadian State Security, 1945-1968," Canadian Association of Slavists Annual Meeting 2009, Carleton University, Ottawa, Ontario, Canada, May 23, 2009.

Raska, Jan, "Spies, Lies, and Diplomatic Ties: Czechoslovakia's Postwar Emigres, Communist Spies, and Canadian Citizenship and State Security, 1945-1968," Sixteenth Annual International Tri-University History Conference, University of Guelph, Ontario, Canada, February 27, 2010).

b. Individuals

Móric Benyovszky (Benovský) (1746-1786), b. Vrbové, Slovakia; Count, soldier of fortune, globetrotter.

Bio: Tybor, Martina, "The Slovak Presence in America up to 18990," in: *Slovaks in America. A Bicentennial Study.* Middletown, PA: The Slovak League of America, 1978, p.p. 7-8; *Memoirs and Travels of Mauritius Augustus Count de Benyowsky. Magnate of the Kingdom of Hungary and Poland.* London, 1789-90; "Beňovský, Móric," in: *Slovenský biografický slovník.* Martin: Matica slovenská, 1996, Vol. 1, pp. 220-221; Čulen, Konstantin, "The Beňovský. Brothers in America," in: *History of Slovaks in America.* Minneapolis, MN: CGSI, 2003, p. 17; "The Slovakian King of Madagascar – Móric Benyovszky," An Illustrated History of Slavic Misery. By John bills. See - https://anillustratedhistoryofslavicmisery.wordpress.com/2016/09/16/the-slovakian-king-of-madagascar/.

John Stephen Bugas (known as Jack Bugas) (1908-1982), b. Rock Springs, WY, of Slovak parents; businessman, cattle rancher, FBI agent. Bugas rose quickly through the ranks of the FBI. By 1938 J. Edgar Hoover appointed him head of the FBI's Detroit office, a strategically very important position as at the time Michigan counted "heavily in the national defense plans. Bugas established a reputation as a "man with unlimited patience and efficiency" in

his work on "notorious kidnapping, espionage, bank robbery and other major cases." At the FBI he most notably led the quashing of two Nazi spy rings (including German Countess Grace Buchanan-Dineen, whom Bugas 'turned' to a double agent) and personally captured Public Enemy Number One Tom Robinson at gunpoint. Most of all, Bugas made a notable record when he "kept sabotage in war plants at 0." Bugas was known in the bureau as an 'agent's agent-in-charge,' a man all like to work for' (the highest compliment in the service), always leading his men personally on important cases.
Bio: "John Bugas," in: Alchetron. The Free Social Encyclopedia. See - https:// alchetron.com/John-Bugas

František Samuel Figuli (1825--1880), b. adventurer, traveler, writer, participant in the 1848 Revolution, fought in the Civil War, owned a plantation in Virginia, later joined an exploratory expedition to the North Pole
Bio: "František Samuel Figuli," in: Wikipedia. See - https:// sk.wikipedia.org/wiki/Figuli; https://www.tyzden.sk/casopis/12878/ slovaci-ktori-bojovali-za-lincolna/

Eugene Fodor (1905-1991), b. Levice, Slovakia; writer and publisher of travel literature; secret spy. During the second world war, he served at the office of strategic services (OSS), which was located in Europe. A multilingual and wide-ranging knowledge-based knowledge has taken him to a service in the us army intelligence service. He participated in the liberation of Prague and Pilsen for which he was also decorated. During the cold war, he served as a CIA agent in Vienna and Budapest. Many of the writers of Fodor guides were secret embassies in favor of the us.
Bio: Italie, Leanne, "Eugene Fodor Feted as the Spy who Loved Travel," in: NBC News.com. See - http://www.nbcnews.com/id/42215999/ns/travel-news/t/eugene-fodor-feted-spy-who-loved-travel/#.W4n1b-j0k2x

Maria Gulovich (1921-2009), b. Litmanová, Czech.; trained as schoolteacher, a member of the underground resistance during World War II, aiding agents of OSS and British intelligence escape the Nazi-occupied territory
Bio: Warnes, Kathy, "Maria Gulovich Liu Joined the Czech Resistance, Won the bronze star and became an American citizen," in: https:windowstoworldhstory weebly.com; "Maria Gulovich Liu," in: Wikipedia. See - https://en.wikipedia. org/wiki/Maria_Gulovich_Liu

Andrew Jelik (ca 1730-1783), b. Baja, Bačka region of Serbia; adventurer. His anonymous biographer did not document his sources, but based his story on Jelík's own oral account, so facts are difficult to verify. He traveled around Europe, escaped military service, but was finally caught in Rotterdam and impressed on a ship to the Far East. He survived an Atlantic storm and washed ashore to England. Hired as a tailor, he sailed on a Dutch ship to America and returned to Europe via Portugal. On his way to Venice, pirates captured him, and he was sold as a slave to a wealthy Turk. After escaping following a beating, he earned his keep as a tailor and traveled to India and China, where he joined the Dutch military for a short time. Moving to Java, he married and English colonist, but was drafted again and escaped to a desert island. After over a year, he became wealthy in Batavia, but returned to Europe after his wife's passing, left his daughter in England, and died in Budapest.

Bio: Tybor, Martina, "The Slovak Presence in America up to 1890," in: Slovaks in America. A Bicentennial Study. Middletown, PA: The Slovak League of America, 1978, pp.4-5; Čulen, Konstantin, "The Adventurous Journey of Andrej Jelik," in: History of Slovaks in America. Minneapolis, MN: CGSI, 2003, pp. 16-17' "Andreas Jelik." See - https://www.pitt.edu/~votruba/qsonhist/celebrities/andreasjelkyandrejjelik.html

Karel Koecher (1934-), b. Bratislava; in US s. 1965; a mole known to have penetrated the CIA.

Bio: "Karl Koecher," in: Wikipedia. See - https://en.wikipedia.org/wiki/Karl Koecher "How a Czech 'super-spy' infiltrated the CIA," in: The Guardian, June 30, 2016. See - https://www.theguardian.com/world/2016/jun/30/how-a-czecin: FBI Stories. See -h-super-spy-infiltrated-cia-karel-koecher'; "Fascinating tale of CIA mole Karel Koecher," in: FBI Studies, See - https://fbistudies.com/2015/12/03/fascinating-tale-of-cia-mole-karel-koecher/; Cates, Ellan, "FBI to spy: Czech mate," in: UPI Archives. See - https://www.upi.com/Archives/1984/11/27/FBI-to-spy-Czech-mate/7494470379600/

Franz Sakalsky (1865-?), b. Solivar pri Prešove; traveler and adventurer; came to America as a 17-year old bricklayer. He traveled all over America and also British Columbia in Canada. It took him 12 years to finally settle in Portland, Oregon. He founded a small Slovak colony.

Bio: "Franz Sakalsky," in: Američania slovenského pôvodu. See - https://www.facebook.com/AmericansofSlovakorigin17/?tn-str=k*F

Mira Slovak (1929-2014), b. Cifer, Slovakia; a daring pilot, Cold Ware defector, stunt flyer, Hydro racer

Bio: Chawkins, Steve, "Mira Slovak dies at 84; Cold War defector flew to freedom and fame," *Los Angeles Times,* June 21, 2014. See - http://www.latimes. com/local/obituaries/la-me-mira-slovak-20140622-story.html; Yardley, William, "Mira Slovak, a Daring Pilot Who Won Freedom, Then Races, Dies at 84," *The New York Times,* June 29, 2014. See - https://www.nytimes. com/2014/06/29/us/mira-slovak-a-daring-pilot-who-won-freedomthen-races-dies-at-84.html; The Incredible Story of Mira Slovak, The Flying Czech," in Return of Kings. See - http://www.returnofkings.com/46600/the-incredible-story-of-mira-slovak-the-flying-czech; Mira Slovak Obituary," in: Hydroplane and Raceboat Museum. See - https://thunderboats.ning.com/profiles/blogs/mira-slovak-obituary

XII. Organizations

A. GENERAL SURVEYS

"Cleveland /Slovak /Organizations," in: Slovak Institute. See - http://www.slovakinstitute.com/Organizations.htm

Čulen, Konstantin, "The Beginnings of Slovak Organizations," in: Čulen, pp. 75- 83.

"Czech Republic & Slovakia - Societies & Groups," in: Cyndi's List. See - https://www.cyndislist.com/czech/societies/

"Czechoslovak-American Organizations," in: Consulate General of the Czech Republic in Chicago. See - ttps://www.mzv.cz/chicago/en/culture_events/cz_us_community/czechoslovak_american_organizations/index.html

Husek, Stephanie O., "Slovak American Fraternal, Cultural, and Civic Organizations to 1914," in: *Slovaks in America: A Bicentennial Study*. Middletown, Pa.: Slovak League of America, 1978, pp. 23-38.

"Social Organizations and Forces," in: Miller, pp. 82-86.

Stein, Howard F., "An Ethnohistory of Slovak-American Religious and Fraternal Associations: A Study in Cultural Meaning, Group Identity, and Social Institutions," *Slovakia* 29, No. 53-54 (1980-1981), pp. 53-101.

Stolarik, M. Mark, "A Place for Everyone: Slovak Fraternal- Benefit Societies," in: *Self-Help in Urban America: Patterns of Minority Economic Development*. Edited by Scott Cummings. Port Washington, N.Y.: Kennikat Press, 1980, pp. 130-141.

"Toronto Slovak Organizations," in: *Kanadský Slovak*. See - https://www.kanadskyslovak.ca/index.php/toronto/toronto-slovak-organizations/86-toronto-slovak-organizations

B. FRATERNAL & BENEVOLENT

1. Surveys

Čulen, Konštantín, "Support Organizations and Societies," in: Čulen, pp. 145-156.

Alexander, June Granatir. "Ethnic Fraternalism and Working-Class Activism: The Expanding Role of Slovak Fraternal Organizations in the United States During the Interwar Years," *Etnicni Fraternalizem v Priseljenskich Dezelach*. Edited by Matjaţ Klemenčič, Pedagoška Fakulteta Univerze v Mariboru, 1996, pp. 161–70.

Kopanic, Michael J., The Beginnings of Slovak Fraternal Societies in the U.S.A." Posted on academia.edu. See - https://www. academia.edu/37286528/The_Beginnings_of_Slovak_Fraternal_ Societies_in_the_USA_edited_2018_01_29_18_13_31_UTC_.doc

Stolarik, M. Mark, Slovak Fraternal-Benefit Societies in Pennsylvania," *Pennsylvania Folklife*, 44 No. 2 (1994-95), pp. 78-83.

Tanzone, Daniel F., *Fraternalism and the Slovak Immigrant*. Cleveland, OH, 1978. Reprint from the journal Furdek. In 1978. 13p.

Zahorska, Michaela, "The First Slovak-American Fraternal Organizations and Press," *Communications*, Vol. 14, No. 1 ((2012), pp. pp. 69-78.

2. Individual Organizations

Canadian Czech Slovak Benevolent Association Inc. (CCSBA), Winnipeg
Website: "Canadian Czech Slovak Benevolent Association Inc." See - http:// mb.211.ca/agencies/canadian-czech-slovak-benevolent-association-inc/

Czech-Slovak Protective Society (CSPS), St. Louis, MO
"Czech-Slovak Protective Society," in: Wikipedia. See - https://en.wikipedia. org/wiki/Czech-Slovak_Protective_Society

First Catholic Slovak Ladies Association (FCSL), Beachwood, OH
Official Website: "First Catholic Slovak Ladies Association." See - http:// www.fcsla.org/; "First Catholic Ladies Association," in: *Slovaks in America. A Bicentennial Study*, pp. 10-168.

First Catholic Slovak Union of the USA and Canada (FCU), Independence, OH
Official Website: "First Catholic Slovak Union." See - https://www.fcsu. com/; "First Catholic Slovak Union (Jednota) of the US and Canada," in: *Slovaks in America. A Bicentennial Study*, pp. 169-195.

The First Hungarian-Slovak Sick Benefit Society, New York (founded 1886).

The Ladies Pennsylvania Slovak Catholic Union (LPSCU), Wilkes-Barre, PA
Official Website: "Ladies Pennsylvania Slovak Catholic Union (LPSCU)."
See - http://www.lpscu.org/ The Ladies Pennsylvania Slovak Catholic
Union," in: *Slovaks in America. A Bicentennial Study*, pp. 201-208.

National Slovak Society of the United States of America (NSSUS), McMurray,
PA
Official Website: "National Slovak Society." See - http://nsslife.org/
Baumgarten, R. Vladimir & Joseph Stefka, *The National Slovak Society: 100 Year
History, 1890-1990*. Pittsburgh: National Slovak Society, 1990.

Pennsylvania Slovak Catholic Union (PSCC), Pittston, PA (established 1893
"Pennsylvania Slovak Catholic Union," in: *Slovaks in America. A Bicentennial
Study*, pp. 197-200.
Records. See - http://fliphtml5.com/umov/ovue/basic

Presbyterian Beneficial Union, Pennsylvania
Website : Slovak- Historical Society of Pennsylvania. See - http://www2.hsp.
org/collections/Balch%20manuscript_guide/html/slovak.html

United Lutheran Society (ULS), Ligonier, PA;
Website: http://www.insuranceagentsnearyou.com/United-Lutheran-
Society/Ligonier/PA/74405.html

Živena Beneficial Society, Pittsburgh, PA
Website: https://pabusinessdb.com/biz/ligonier/zivena-beneficial-
society/604095
"1891-1941 Zivena Beneficial Society of the U.S.A.: 50th Anniversary. Slavia
Print Company, 1941. 416p.; "Zivena Beneficial Society," in: *Slovaks in America.
A Bicentennial Study*, p. 196
Commemoration of Fifty Years of Loyal Service to the Women in America. Cleveland,
1942. 222p.

C. Religious

Czechoslovak Baptist Convention of USA and Canada (CZSKBC)
Official Website: http://czskbc.org/

Vojta, Vaclav, *Czechoslovak Baptists*. Czechoslovak Baptist Convention of America and Canada, 1941. 280p.

Dominican Sisters Congregation of St. Rose of Lima, Oxford, MI
Website: https://cmswr.org/community/dominican-sisters-congregation of-st-rose-of-lima/; "Dominican Sisters of St. Rose of Lima," in: *Slovaks in America*. A Bicentennial Study, pp.265-266.

The Passionists
"The Passionists and Slovak Americans," in: Slovaks in America. A Bicentennial Study, pp. 267-270.

Sisters of SS. Cyril and Methodius, Danville, PA
"Sisters of SS. Cyril and Methodius (Danville, PA), in: *Slovaks in America*. A Bicentennial Study, pp. 235-248.

Slovak Catholic Federation of America (SCF), Wilkes-Barre, PA
Official Website: "Slovak Catholic Federation" See - http://www. slovakcatholicfederation.org/.
"The Slovak Catholic Federation," in: *Slovaks in America. A Bicentennial Study*, pp. 223- 234;
Tanzone, Daniel R., "The Slovak Catholic Federation." See - http://www. slovakcatholicfederation.org/docs/scfhistory14.pdf

Slovak Franciscan Fathers, Pittsburgh, PA
"Development and History of the Little Portion of St. Francis Fraternity." See - http://littleportionofstfrancis.com/history.php
Portasik, Richard A., *Slovak Franciscans in America*: History of Most Holy Savior Commissariat, Pittsburgh, PA. Franciscan Fathers, 1966.
Portasik, Richard A., Slovak Franciscan Fathers," in: *Slovaks in America*. A Bicentennial Study, pp. 271-276.
Slovak Franciscans in America: History of the Holy Savior Vice Province Part II, 1967-1997, Pittsburgh, PA: Franciscan Friars, 1998.

United Lutheran Society, Ligonier, PA
Official Website: "United Lutheran Society." See - https://www.facebook. com/pages/United-Lutheran-Society/415345172004863

The Vincentian Sisters of Charity, Bedford, OH
"The Vincentian Sisters of Charity, Bedford, OH," in: *Slovaks in America. A Bicentennial Study*, pp. 262-264.
"Vincentian Sisters of Charity," See - http://museumofdivinestatues.com/queen-of-heaven-vincentian-sisters.html

The Vicentian Sisters of Charity, Pittsburgh, PA
"The Vincentian Sisters of Charity, Pittsburgh, PA," in: *Slovaks in America. A Bicentennial Study*, pp. 255-261.
"Vincentian Sisters of Charity," in: Wikipedia. See - https://en.wikipedia.org/wiki/Vincentian_Sisters_of_Charity

Society for the History of Czechoslovak Jews, New York, NY
Official Website: "Society for the History of Czechoslovak Jews." See - http://www.shcsj.org/
"Descriptive Summary" and "Historical Note," in: Archives of the Society for the History of Czechoslovak Jews." See - http://digifindingaids.cjh.org/?pID=2956147

D. HERITAGE

American Slovak Club, Lorain, OH
Official Website: "American Slovak Club." See - http://www.americanslovakclub.com

American Slovak Cultural Association of the Mahoning Valley, Youngstown, OH
Website : http://www.americanslovak.org and https://www.facebook.com/American-Slovak-Cultural-Association-of-the-Mahoning-Valley

American Slovak Sokol Camp, Broadview Heights, OH,
Website: https://www.facebook.com/events/272491643233611/

Czech and Slovak Association, Inc., Boston, MA
Official Website: http://www.czskboston.org/

Czech and Slovak Heritage Foundation (CSHA), Baltimore, MD
Official Website: Czech and Slovak Heritage Foundation." See - http://www.panix.com/~czslha/

St. Paul Czech And Slovak Folk Dancers, MN
Official Website: "St. Paul Czech And Slovak Folk Dancers." See - http://www.tancuj.org/info.html

The Slovak- American Cultural Center, New York, NY
Official Website: "Slovak-American Cultural Center." See - http://slovakamericancc.wixsite.com/slovakamericancc

Slovak American Cultural Society of the Midwest (SACSM), Naperville, IL

Slovak Educational Club, Windber, PA
Website: https://www.facebook.com/Slovak-Educational-Club-207961089278614/

Slovak Heritage Association of the Laurel Highlands, Johnstown, PA
Official Website: "Slovak Heritage Association of the Laurel Highlands." See - https://shalh.org

Slovak Heritage Association of San Diego, San Diego, CA

Slovak Heritage Foundation of Windsor-Essex County, Tecumseh, Ont., Canada
Website: https://www.canadahelps.org/en/charities/slovak-heritage-foundation-of-windsor-essex-county/

Slovak Heritage and Folklore Society International, Rochester, NY
Official Website: http://archive.is/GyMax

Slovak Heritage & Folklore Society of North America,
Official Website: "Slovak Heritage & Folklore Society of North America," See - http://www.iarelative.com/shfsinfo.htm

Slovak Heritage Society of Greater Cleveland, Cleveland, OH (founded 1995)
Website: https://www.guidestar.org/profile/34-0348709

Slovak Heritage Society of Northeast PA (N.E.P.A)), Wilkes-Barre, PA
Official Website: http://www.shsnepa.org/

Slovak League of America Heritage Foundation (SLAHF)

Slovak National Alliance, Bridgeview, IL
Website: https://www.facebook.com/Slovak-National-Alliance-274320205
968606/

Virginia Czech/Slovak Heritage Society
Official Website Site: "Virginia CzechSlovak Heritage Society." See - http://
www.virginiaczechslovak.org/index.html

Western Pennsylvania Cultural Association (WPSCA), Pittsburgh, PA
Official Website: "Western Pennsylvania Slovak Cultural Association," See -
http://www.wpsca.org/http://www.wpsca.org

Wisconsin Slovak Historical Society, Cudahy, WI
Official Website: "Wisconsin Slovak Historical Society." See - http://www.
wisconsinslovakhistoricalsociety.org/

E. Public Affairs & Political

American Czech and Slovak Association, Washington, DC
Official Website: "American Czech and Slovak Association," See - https://
en.wikipedia.org/wiki/American_Czech_and_Slovak_Association

Canadian Slovak League
"History of the Canadian Slovak League," in: Kanadský Slovák. See - https://
www.kanadskyslovak.ca/index.php/csl/history-of-csl
Sutherland, Anthony X. *The Canadian Slovak League: A History, 1932-1982.*
Toronto, Ont.: Canadian Slovak League, 1984. 208p.

Cleveland-Bratislava Sister Cities, Inc. (founded in 1990)
Official Website: http://www.cleveland.com/mosai/
Facebook: https://www.facebook.com/search/top/?q=Cleveland-
Bratislava%20Sister%20Cities

Council of Free Czechoslovakia
Raška, Francis Dostál, *Fighting Communism from Afar: The Council of Free Czechoslovakia.* Bloomington, IN: East European monographs, 2008. 229p.

Council of the Solidarity of Czechs and Slovaks

Czechoslovak National Council
"Czechoslovak National Council of America," in: *Panorama.* Cicero, IL: Czechoslovak National Council of America, 1960, pp. 10-132.

Czechoslovak National Council of Women in Exile
"Czechoslovak National Council of Women in Exile," in: Panorama. Cicero, IL: Czechoslovak National Council of America, 1960, p. 183.

Czech & Slovak Solidarity Council, Appleton, WI
Website: "Czech & Slovak Solidarity Council." See - https://www.manta.com/c/mtt46y3/czech-slovak-solidarity-council

Czech and Slovak Solidarity Council -- New York, NY

Friends of Slovakia, Washington, DC
Official Website: "Friends of Slovakia." See - http://www.friendsofslovakia.org/fos/
"Friends of Slovakia," in: Wikipedia. See - http://www.friendsofslovakia.org/wordpress/

Slovak American Business and Innovation Council (SABIC), Washington, DC
Website: http://www.sabicdc.org/

Slovak League of America (founded 1907)
Čulen, Konstantine, "Beginnings of the Slovak League of America," Slovakia, 40 (1967), pp. 18-29.
Hrobak, Philip A., "50 Years of the Slovak League of America," *Slovakia,*7, No. 2 (June 1957), pp. 10-18.
Kocur, Jan, *A Story of Slovak Pride, American Patriotism, and the Golden Age of the Slovak League of America.* Modra Publishing, 2009. 286p.
Mikuš, Joseph A., "The Slovak League of America: A Historical Survey," in: *Slovaks in America: A Bicentennial Study,* pp. 39-56.

Pauco, Jozef, *60 Years of the Slovak League of America*. Middletown, PA: Jednota Press, 1967. 146p.

Sidor, Karol, "The Slovak League of America and the Slovak Nation's Struggle for Autonomy,"
Slovakia 17, 40, 1967, 29-62.

Stolarik, M. Mark, "The Slovak League of America and the Canadian League in the Struggle for the Selfdetermination of the Nation, 1907-1992," *Slovakia*, 39, 72 & 73, 2007, 7-35.

Slovak World Congress, Toronto, Ont., Canada
Website: "Slovak World Congress (SWC), in: Open Yearbook. See - https:// uia.org/s/or/en/1100003445
"Slovak World Congress," in: WorldCat Identities.

Youngstown-Spišská Nová Ves Sister Cities Program, Youngstown, OH (founded 1991)
Official Website: Slovak E American Rolehttp://www.youngstown sistercities.com/about.html

F. CULTURAL

American Czech-Slovak Cultural Club, North Miami, Florida
Official Website: "American Czech-Slovak Cultural Club". See - http:// acscc.org/
Facebook: https://www.facebook.com/profile.php?id=100008205853144

American Slovak Cultural Association of the Mahoning Valley, Youngstown, Ohio Area
Official Website - http://www.americanslovak.org
Facebook - https://www.facebook.com/American-Slovak-Cultural-Association-of-the-Mahoning-Valley-152703974765429/

Cleveland Slovak Cultural Garden, Rockefeller Park, Cleveland, OH
Website: http://www.culturalgardens.org/

Czech and Slovak Cultural Center of Minnesota, St. Paul, MN
Official Website - "Czech and Slovak cultural Center of Minnesota."
See - https://www.facebook.com/Czech-and-Slovak-Cultural-Center-of-Minnesota-326536374832/

Czech and Slovak Cultural Center, New York, NY
Official Website: "Czech and Slovak Cultural Center." See - http://czechslovakculturalcenter.org/

Czech and Slovak Society of Indiana, Indianapolis, IN
Official Website: http://www.czechandslovakin.org

John Kollar Literary and Library Society, Pittsburgh, PA (founded 1913)
Official website: https://kollarclub.weebly.com
Facebook: https://www.facebook.com/kollarCLUB/
"Pittsburgh's Kollar Club," *Pittsburgh Post-Gazette*, July 31, 2001. See - https://newsinteractive.post-gazette.com/thedigs/2013/07/31/pittsburghs-kollar-club/

Limbora Slovak Folk Ensemble, New York, NY
Official Website: "Slovak Folk Ensee." See - http://www.limbora.szm.com/en.htm;
"Limbora Slovak Folk Ensemble," in *Slovaks in America*. A Bicentennial Study, pp. 408-409;
"Limbora Slovak Folk Ensemble 2016 - 40th Anniversary - New York," in: Folklorfest.sk. See - http://www.folklorfest.sk/4738-limbora-slovak-folk-ensemble-2016-40th-anniversary/

Slovak Alliance of Greater Bridgeport, Connecticut
Website: https://www.orgcouncil.com/ein/237445213
"Slovak Alliance of Greater Bridgeport, Connecticut," in: Slovaks in America. A Bicentennial Study, pp, 411-412,

Slovak American Association of California
"Slovak American Association of California," in: *Slovaks in America*. A Bicentennial Study, pp. 413-415.

Slovak-American Cultural Center (S-ACC), New York, NY
Official Website: "Slovak-American Cultural Center." See - http://
slovakamericancc.wixsite.com/slovakamericancc

Slovak American Cultural Society of the Midwest, Naperville, IL

The Slovak-American International Cultural Foundation, Inc., Wauconda, IL

Slovak American Society of Lackawanna and Susquehanna Counties
"Slovak American Society of Lackawanna and Susquehanna Counties," in:
Slovaks in America. A Bicentennial Study, pp. p. 421.

Slovak American Society of Washington, D.C., Washington, DC
Official Website: "Slovak American Society of Washington D.C." See - http://
dcslovaks.org/

Vansova Ladies Guild, Broadview Heights, OH
Archivist: Emily Uhrin

Western Pennsylvania Slovak Cultural Association (WPSCA), Pittsburgh, PA
Official Website: "Western Pennsylvania Slovak Cultural Association." See -
http://www.wpsca.org/

H. SOCIAL CLUBS

American Slovak Club, Lorain, OH
Website: "American Slovak Club." See - http://www.americanslovakclub.com/

American-Slovak Zemplin Social Club, Lakewood, OH
Website: https://www.fcsu.com/wp-content/uploads/2016/02/77th-
anniversary-flyer.pdf; "Zemplin Club of Parma, OH," in: *Slovaks in America*.
A Bicentennial Study, p. 425.

California Czech and Slovak Club, Castro Valley, CA
Website: http://members.tripod.com/h_javora/ccsc.htm

California Czech and Slovak Club, San Mateo, CA
Website: "California Czech and Slovak Club." See - https://www.smc-connect.org/locations/california-czech-and-slovak-club

Czech and Slovak Club, Kansas City, MO
Website: "Czech and Slovak Club." See - https://csclubkc.wordpress.com/contact-us/

Parma American Slovak Club, Parma, OH
Website: "Parma American Slovak Club Inc in Parma, Ohio (OH)," See - http://www.nonprofitfacts.com/OH/Parma-American-Slovak-Club-Inc.html
"Parma American Slovak Club," in: *Slovaks in America*. A Bicentennial Study, p. 410.

Pitt Slav Club (orig. Pitt Student Slovak Club), University of Pittsburgh, Pittsburg, PA
Official Website: https://pitt2.campuslabs.com/engage/organization/slovakclub
Facebook: https://www.facebook.com/pg/pittstudentslovakclub/posts/?ref=notif

Slovak American Citizens Social Club, Braddock, PA
Website: https://www.facebook.com/pages/Slovak-American-Social-Citizens-Club/121122427900021

Slovak American Club of Greater New York
"Slovak American Club of Greater New York," in: *Slovaks in America*, A Bicentennial Study, pp. 426-420.

Slovak Club, Gary, IN
Website: https://www.flickr.com/photos/kimjohnsonimages/5743893113

Slovak Club, Inc., Merriville, IN
Website. https://slovakclub.business.site/

Slovak Club, New Castle, PA
"Slovak Club Celebrating 100 Years," *New Castle News*, October 15, 2016.

Slovak Social Club of East Pittsburgh, East Pittsburgh, PA
Website: https://www.guidestar.org/profile/25-0801450

H. - SCHOLARLY & SCIENTIFIC

Czechoslovak Society of Arts and Sciences (SVU)
Official Website - "Czechoslovak Society of Arts and Sciences (SVU)." See - https://www.svu2000.org/
"Czechoslovak Society of Arts and Sciences," in: Wikipedia. See - https://en.wikipedia.org/wiki/Czechoslovak_Society_of_Arts_and_Sciences
Rechcigl, Miloslav, Jr., *On Behalf of their Homeland: Fifty Years of SVU*. Boulder, CO: East European Monographs, 2008p. 700p.

Czechoslovak Studies Association
Websites: http://www.public.iastate.edu/~zarecor/CSA/welcome.htm; https://www.historians.org/about-aha-and-membership/affiliated-societies/czechoslovak-studies-association

Slovak Institute, Cleveland
Official Website: "Slovak Institute and Research Library," See - www.slovakinstitute.com
Paučo, Joseph, "Twenty Years of the Slovak Institute in Cleveland," *Slovakia* 23, No. 46 (1973), pp. 16-23.

Slovak Studies Association (SSA), Lisle, IL
Official Website: http://www.slovakstudies.org
Stein, Howard, F., Some Anthropological Reflections: Inaugural Meeting of Slovak Studies Association," *Jednota*, 26, December 1979.

Slovak Writers and Artists Association (SWAA), Cleveland, OH
Website: https://uia.org/s/or/en/1100028183

I. PHYSICAL EDUCATIONAL

The First Slovak Wreath of the Free Eagle, Bridgeport, CT
Website: https://discover.hsp.org/Record/ead-3563/Description

"The First Slovak Wreath of the Free Eagle," in: *Slovaks in America. A Bicentennial Study*, pp. 221-222.

Slovak Athletic Association, Berwyn, IL
"Slovak Athletic Association to celebrate 90 year," in: My Suburban Life, December 2, 2014. See - https://www.mysuburbanlife.com/2014/12/02/slovak-athletic-association-to-celebrate-90-years/anh6fa5/

Slovak Gymnastic Union of Sokol of the U.S.A., East Orange, NJ
Bednar, Karol, "The Slovak Gymnastic Union Sokol in the U.S.A.," in: *Panorama: A Historical Review of Czechs and Slovaks in the United States of America.* Cicero, IL: Czechoslovak National Council of America, 1970, pp. 144-52. Fiftieth Anniversary of the Slovak Gymnastic Union Sokol in U.S.A., 1896-1946. Perth Amboy, NJ, 1947. 81p.

Slovak Catholic Sokol, Passaic, NJ
Official Website: http://www.slovakcatholicsokol.org/
The Slovak Catholic Sokol Story: Recalling a Century of Fraternal Progress. Compiled and edited by Daniel F. Tanzone. Passaic, NJ: Slovak Catholic Sokol. 2006. 181p.; "The Slovak Catholic Sokol," in: *Slovaks in America. A Bicentennial Study*, pp. 209-22

J. CHARITABLE & RELIEF & PHILANTHROPIC

American fund for Czech and Slovak Leadership Studies (successor to the American Fund for Czechoslovak Refugees)
Website: http://www.afcsls.org/

American Fund for Czechoslovak Refugees, New York, NY
Website: http://www.afcsls.org/documents/afcr.pdf
"The American Fund for Czechoslovak Refugees," in: *Panorama: A Historical Review of Czechs and Slovaks in the United States of America.* Cicero, IL: Czechoslovak National Council of America, 1970, pp. 101-103.

American Fund for Czechoslovak Relief (AFCR), New York, NY (formerly American Fund for Czechoslovak Refugees)
Website: http://archiv.krajane.net/societyDetail.view?id=370

Slovak American Charitable Association, Zion, IL (a healthcare provider)
Website: https://healthprovidersdata.com/hipaa/codes/NPI-1114903754-slovak-american-charitable-association
"Slovak American Charitable Association," in: *Panorama*. Cicero, IL: Czechoslovak National Council of America, 1970, p. 153.

Slovak American Foundation
Official Website: http://www.slovakamericanfoundation.org/
"Introducing Mary MacPherson, the President and CEO of the Slovak-American Foundation," in: Slovak Startup. See - https://slovakstartup.com/2017/01/08/mary-macpherson-slovak-american-foundation/

Slovak Relief Fund (SRF), Washington, DC
Website: http://www.nonprofitfacts.com/DC/Slovak-Relief-Fund-Inc.html

K. Genealogical

1. General

"Czech Republic & Slovakia » Societies & Groups," in: Cyndi's List. See: https://www.cyndislist.com/czech/societies/

2. Individual Societies

Czechoslovak Area Genealogy Club of Southern California, Santa Ana, CA
Official Website: "Czechoslovak Genealogy Club of Southern California." See - http://cagc-ca.org/

Czechoslovak Genealogical Society International, Inc. (CGSI), St. Paul, MN
Official Website: "Czechoslovak Genealogical Society International." See - https://www.cgsi.org/

Czech & Slovak American Genealogy Society of Illinois
Official Website: "Czech & Slovak American Genealogy Society of Illinois." See - http://www.csagsi.org/

Czech & Slovak Genealogical Society of Arizona (CSGSA), Phoenix, AZ
Official Website: https://www.acronymfinder.com/Czech-and-Slovak-Genealogical-Society-of-Arizona-(Phoenix%2C-AZ)-(CSGSA).html

East European Genealogical Society, Winnipeg, MB, Canada
Official Website: "East European Genealogical Society." See - https://eegsociety.org/Home.aspx

Federation of East European Family History Societies (FEEFHS), Seattle, AW - renamed to: Foundation for East European Family History Studies
Official Website: http://feefhs.org/

Slovak Genealogical Research Center, Chino, CA
Website: http://feefhs.org/resource/slovakia-genealogical-research-center

So. California Czech & Slovak Genealogy and Social Meetup, Los Angeles, CA.
Website: https://www.meetup.com/So-Calif-American-Czech-Slovak-Genealogy-Social-Meet-Up/?_cookie-check=Xxco9Mh_roA8CQXm

L. HOBBY AND RECREATIONAL

Czechoslovak Collectors Guild International (CCGI), Kansas City, MO

First Czechoslovak Garden Club of America, Berwyn, IL

First Czechoslovak Philatelic Club of North America (FCPCNA), Berwyn, IL

Society for Czechoslovak Philately (SCP), Woodbury, NJ
Website: http://www.csphilately.net/

XIII. Political Relations of Slovak Americans and the Bilateral Relations between Slovakia and America

A. Slovak-American Contacts with and Attitude toward the Homeland

Braxátor, František, "Slovaks Abroad and Their Relationship to Czecho-Slovakia," in: *Slovakia in the 19th and 20th Centuries*. Proc. of the Conference on Slovakia. Toronto: Slovak World Congress, 1973, pp. 343-350.

Ference, Gregory C., *Sixteen Months of Indecision: Slovak American Viewpoints toward Compatriots and the Homeland from 1914 to 1915 as Viewed by the Slovak Language Press*. Selinsgrove, PA: Susquehanna University.

"Slovaks Reconnect with their Heritage," *Pittsburgh Post-Gazette*, May 20, 2001

B. Relations between Slovaks and Czechs in America

Cude, Michael Robert, Transatlantic Perspectives on the Slovak Question, 1914-1948. A Ph.D. Thesis, University of Colorado, 2012.

Dérer, Ivan, *The Unity of the Czechs and Slovaks: Has the Pittsburgh Declaration Been Carried Out?* Prague: Orbis, 1938.

Mamatey, Albert, *The Czecho-Slovaks: Who are They?* Pittsburgh: Slovak League, 1919.

Mamatey, Victor S., "The Czecho-Slovak Agreement of Pittsburgh (May 30, 1918) Revisited," *Kosmas. Journal of Czechoslovak and Central European Studies* 2, No, 2 (Winter 1983), pp. 41-81.

Pichlík, Karel, "Relationships between Czechs and Slovaks in the United States during the First World War," *Nebraska History* 74 (1993), pp. 189-194.

Pittsburgh Agreement," in: Wikipedia. See - https://en.wikipedia.org/wiki/Pittsburgh_Agreement

Slovak Catholic Federation of America, *The Slovaks and the Pittsburgh Pact*. Slovak Catholic Federation of America, 1934.

C. Slovak American Role in the Founding of Czechoslovakia

Cude, Michael, "The Imagined Exiles: Slovak Americans and the Slovak Question during the First Czechoslovak Republic," *Studia Hisorica Gednensis*, Vol. 5 (2014), pp. 287-305.

Derer, Ivan, *The Unity of Czechs and Slovaks. Has the Pittsburgh Declaration been Carried out?* Prague: Orbis Pub. Co., 1938. 38p.

Dubovický, Ivan. "The Role of Czechs and Slovaks in America in the Founding of Independent Czechoslovakia," in: *Birth of Czechoslovakia*, The: Seminar on the Founding of the Independent Czechoslovak State. Edited by Sharon L. Wolchik and Ivan Dubovický. Prague, 1999, pp. 37-62.

Garver, Bruce," Americans of Czech and Slovak Ancestry in the History of Czechoslovakia", *Czechoslovak and Central European Journal* 11, No. 2 (Winter 1993), pp. 1-14.

Getting, Milan, *American Slovaks and the Evolution of the Czechoslovak Concept during the Years 1914-1918.* Getting-Cibula Family Reunion Trust, 1993. 330 p.

Mamatey, Victor S., Building Czechoslovakia in America, 1914-1918. Washington, DC: SVU Press, 1976. 17p.

Stolarik, M. Mark, *The Role of American Slovaks in the Creation of Czecho-Slovakia, 1914-1918.* Rome: Slovak Institute, 1968. 82 p.

Paučo, Joseph, "American Slovaks and the Beginnings of Czecho-Slovakia," in: Slovakia, 16, 39, 1966, 63-75.

Pergler, Charles, *America in the Struggle for Czechoslovakia.* Philadelphia: Dorrance & Co., 1926. 110p.

Pichlik, Karel, "Relationships between Czechs and Slovaks during the First World War," *Nebraska History* 74, No. 3 & 4 (Fall /Winter 1993), pp. 189-194.

Slovak Action Committee. Slovak National Council in London, Slovak League of America, Canadian Slovak League, Memorandum: Presented to the Peace Conference Concerning the Rationality of Existence of Czecho-Slovakia. Paris: 1946.

Stolarik, M. Mark, *The Role of American Slovaks in the Creation of Czecho-Slovakia, 1914-1918.* Cleveland: Slovak Institute, 1968

D. American Aid to Czechoslovakia

"American Relief for Czechoslovakia," in: *Panorama:* A Historical Review of Czechs and Slovaks in the United States. Cicero, IL: Czechoslovak National Council of America, 1970, pp. [96-98.

Andic, Vojtech E., "The Way Americans Helped Czechoslovakia," in: *Panorama:* A Historical Review of Czechs and Slovaks in the United States of America. Cicero, IL: Czechoslovak National Council of America, 1970, pp. 90-92.

Selsam, J. Paul, "The United States and the Funding of the Czechoslovak Republic," *Social Studies* 40 (October 1949), pp. 259-263.

E. Slovak-US and US-Slovak Contacts and Relations

Cude, Michael Robert, Transatlantic Perspectives on the Slovak Question, 1914-1948. Ph.D. Dissertation in history, University of Colorado, 2012. 359p.

Cude, Michael R., "Wilsonian National Self-determination and the Slovak Question during the Founding of Czechoslovakia, 1918-1921," *Diplomatic History*, Vol. 40, Issue 1 (January 2016), pp. 155–180.

Kovtun, Jiří, *Masaryk and America: Testimony of a Relationship.* Ann Arbor: University of Michigan Library, 1988. 100p.

Lubek, Sister M., Foreign Relations between the United states and Czech-Slovakia, 1920-1960. M.A. Thesis, De Paul University, Chicago, 1964. 150p.

Mamatey, Victor S., *The United States and East Central Europe, 1914-1918: A Study in Wilsonian Diplomacy and Propaganda.* Princeton: Princeton University, Press, 1957. 431 p.

Mamatey, Victor S., "The Slovaks and Carpatho-Ruthenians", in: O'Grady, Joseph P., Ed., *The Immigrants' Influence on Wilson's Peace Policies.* Lexington, KY: University of Kentucky Press, 1967, pp. 224-249.

Mamatey, Victor S., "Masaryk and Wilson: A Contribution to the Study of their Relationship," in: *T. G. Masaryk (1850-1937).* New York: St. Martin's Press, 1989, Vol. 2, pp. 186-197.

Partl, Václav, "American Influence on Political Thought in Czechoslovakia," *American Political Science Review* 17 (1923), pp. 448-452.

"Slovak-United States Relations: Optimism for the Future," in: Council of American Ambassadors. See - https://www.americanambassadors. org/publications/ambassadors-review/fall-2003/slovak-united-states-relations-optimism-for-the-future

"Slovakia - United States Relations," in: Wikipedia. See - https://en.wikipedia. org/wiki/Slovakia%E2%80%93United_States_relations

Svoboda, George Josef, "Wilson and Masaryk: The Origin and Background of their Diplomacy," *Czechoslovak and Central European Journal* 8, No. 1 /2 (Summer / Winter 1989), pp. 54-67.

Unterberger, Batty Miller," President Wilson, Professor Masaryk, and the Birth of Czechoslovakia," *Kosmas* 17, No. 2 (Spring 2006), pp. 1-19.

F. SLOVAK-CANADIAN AND CANADIAN-SLOVAK CONTACTS AND RELATIONS

"Canada-Slovakia Relations," in: Wikipedia. See - http://www. canadainternational.gc.ca/austria-autriche/bilateral_relations_bilaterales/ canada-slov.aspx?lang=eng

"Canada-Slovakia Relations," in: Government of Canada. See - http://www. canadainternational.gc.ca/austria-autriche/bilateral_relations_bilaterales/ canada-slov.aspx?lang=eng

G. SLOVAK- LATIN AMERICAN AND LATIN AMERICAN-SLOVAK CONTACTS AND RELATIONS

Lenghar, J, "Intercultural Communication in International Economic Relations - The Experience of Slovakia with Latin America," in: *Megatrend Review*, 3, No. 2 (2006), pp. 111-137.

Lenghardtová, Jana and Jana Paľková, "Perceptions of Latin America and their Reflections at the University of Economics in Bratislava," *Economic Review*, 43, No. 2 (2024), pp. 121-140.

"Mexico–Slovakia Relations," in: Wikipedia. See - https://en.wikipedia.org/ wiki/Mexico%E2%80%93Slovakia_relations

"Mexico and Slovakia Strengthen Ties of Friendship and Cooperation," in: gob.mx. See - https://www.gob.mx/presidencia/prensa/mexico-and-slovakia-strengthen-ties-of-friendship-and-cooperation?idiom=en

Opatrný, J., "Czechoslovak-Latin American Relations 1945-1989: The Broather Context," *Central European Journal of International and Security Studies*, No. 2013 (2013, pp. 12-37.

Pochmanová, Iva. Československo-chilské a československo-argentinské vztahy v letech 1945-1975 v československé diplomatické korespondenci. Disertační práce, SIAS FF UK, 2005.

XIV. Genealogy

A. GENEALOGY GUIDES AND PERIODICALS

1. Guides

Alzo, Lisa A., *The Family Tree. Polish, Czech and Slovak Genealogy Guide: How to Trace Your Family Tree in Eastern Europe.* Family Tree Books, 2016. 240p.

Baxter, Angus, "Czechoslovakia," in: *In Search of your European Roots.* Baltimore: Genealogical Publishing, Co., Inc., 1986, pp. 53-64.

Kona, William, *Slovak Genealogy.* Wilmette, IL: K & K House, 1988. 150p.

Miller, Olga K. *Genealogical Research for Czech and Slovak Americans.* Detroit: Gale Research, 1978. 187p.

Rechcigl, Miloslav, Jr., *Czech and Slovak Genealogy. A Bibliography of Publications in English and Guide to Other Information Resources.* Rockville, MD: The Author, 1999.

Rechcigl, Miloslav, Jr., *Czechoslovak Genealogy Sites on the Internet.* Rockville, MD: SVU, 1999.74p.

Schlyter, Daniel M. *A Handbook of Czechoslovak Genealogical Research.* Buffalo Grove, Ill.: Genun Publishers, c1985. 131p.

Schlyter, Daniel M., "Czechoslovak Research and Use of Gazetteers," in: *The Genealogical Helper* 33, No.1 (January-February 1977), pp. 9-15.

"Slovak Genealogy," in: Slovakia.org. See - http://www.slovakia.org/society-geneology.htm

"Slovak Genealogy Toolkit," in: Family Tree. See - https://www.familytreemagazine.com/premium/slovak-genealogy-toolkit/

Slovak Pride: Family Names & Ancestral Villages. Rochester, NY: Slovak Heritage & Folklore Society International, 1996.

"Slovakia Resources," in: FEEFHS. See - http://feefhs.org/resource/slovakia

"Three Ways to Search for Slovak Ancestors," in: Legacy News. See - http://news.legacyfamilytree.com/legacy_news/2016/09/three-ways-to-search-for-slovak-ancestors.html

Wellauer, Maralyn A., *Tracing Your Czech and Slovak Roots.* Milwaukee, WI, 1980. 77p.

Wheeler, Glenn E., Genealogical and Local History of Ličartovce, Prešov, Slovakia. Published by the Author in 2013. See - https://sites.google.com/site/licartovcegen/home

2. Periodicals

East European Genealogist. Published by East European Genealogical Society, Inc. (EEGS). Quarterly. 1991-. Vol. 1-.

FEEFHS Newsletter. Published by Federation of East European Family History Societies (FEEFHS). Quarterly. 1987-. Vol. 1-.

FEEFHS Quarterly: a journal of central & east European genealogical studies

FEEFHS Journal: a publication of Central and East European genealogical studies

Kořeny (Roots). Journal of the Czech & Slovak American Genealogical Society of Illinois Quarterly. Chicago, IL, 1997-. Vol. 1-

Naše Rodina (Our Family). Newsletter of the Czechoslovak Genealogical Society. A quarterly. St. Paul, MN, 1989-. Vol. 1-.

Včera a Dnes (Yesterday and Today), Journal of Arizona Czechoslovak Genealogical Society. Quarterly, 1997-. Vol. 1-.

3. Gazetteers

Gardiner, Duncan B., *German Towns in Slovakia and Upper Hungary: A Genealogical Gazetteer.* Family Historian, 1991. 118p.

Hornack, Joseph J., SLRP Database, SLRP Ancestral Tree Slovakia Roots, Independence, OH: The Author, 1996. The database lists villages of surnames and villages/towns.

"List of Slovakia: All Villages," in: Genealogy Slovakia. See - https://www.cisarik.com/0_former_Saros_Saris_county.html

Schlyter, Daniel M., "Czechoslovak Research and Use of Gazetteers," in: *The Genealogical Helper,* 33, No. 1 (January-February 1977), pp. 9-15.

Slovak Pride Database. 25,000 Surnames and Villages. See - http://slovakpride.homestead.com/

4. Surnames

Czechoslovak Surname Records. St. Paul, MN: CGS, 1989-1995. Vol. 1-6.
A Dictionary of Lemko Surnames. See - http://lemko.org/genealogy/
krasowskii/namesUS.html
Slovak Pride Database. 25,000 Surnames and Villages. See - http://
slovakpride.homestead.com/
"Slovak Surname Location Reference Project," in: FEEFHS. See - http://
feefhs.org/resource/slovakia-surnames

B. SOURCES OF VITAL DATA

"Data Collections," in: Slovakia Online Genealogy Records. See - https://
www.familysearch.org/wiki/en/Slovakia_Online_Genealogy_Records
"Slovakia -Data Collections," in: ancestry. See - https://search.ancestry.com/
Places/Europe/Slovakia/Default.aspx

C. FAMILY HISTORIES AND GENEALOGIES

1. Listings of Family Histories

Rechcigl, Miloslav, Jr., "Family Histories and Genealogies," in his: *Czech and Slovak Genealogy. A Bibliography of Publications in English and Guide to Other Information Resources.* Rockville, MD: SVU, 1996.
Rechcigl, Miloslav, Jr., "Selected Personal Home Pages," in his *Czechoslovak Genealogy Sites on the internet.* 2nd ed. Rockville, MD: SVU, 20001, pp. 27-38.
"Slovak Home Pages," in: Eastern Slovakia - Slovak and Carpatho-Rusyn Genealogy Research Pages. See - http://www.iarelative.com/slovaki1.htm

2. Individual Families

BACA

A Humble Beginning: My Life. By John Baca. Saline, MI: Allegra Print Imaging, 2011.

BETTELHEIM

"The Bettelheim Genealogy and Family Tree Page," in: Surname Finder. See - https://www.genealogytoday.com/surname/finder.mv?Surname=Bettelheim

CEBULA - see KOPCHAK

DEMBITZ

"The Dembitz Genealogy and Family Tree Page," in: Surname finder. See - www.genealogytoday.com/surname/finder.mv?Surname=Dembitz
"Siegmund Dembitz Family Tree," in: Geneanet. See - https://gw.geneanet.org/alanguggenheim?lang=en&n=dembitz&oc=0&p=sigmund
"Siegmund Dembitz MD," in: WikiTree. See - https://www.wikitree.com/wiki/Dembitz-3

DUDA

"Duda Genealogy," in: Wiki Tree. See - https://www.wikitree.com/genealogy/Duda
"Our Legacy," in: DUDA. See - http://www.duda.com/about-duda/our-legacy
"The Duda Family," in: Orlando Memory. See - http://orlandomemory.info/memory/organization/duda-family

FRANKFURTER

"Frankfurter Genealogy," in: WikiTree. See - https://www.wikitree.com/genealogy/FRANKFURTER

GALAYDA - see KOPCHAK

GURKA

A Gurka/Tomo/Hechko/Tomko Family History. By Barbara Gurka Clark, with Conrad Terrill. The Author, 2009.

HECHKO - See GURKA

HUDAK

"Hudak Genealogy," in: WikiTree. See - https://www.wikitree.com/genealogy/HUDAK

"The Hudak Genealogy and Family Tree Page," in: surname Finder. See - https://www.genealogytoday.com/surname/finder.mv?Surname=Hudak

KACSENYAK

"Kacsenyak Family of Slovakia and the US. By Linda Stufflebean," in: Empty Branches on the Family Tree. See - https://emptybranchesonthefamilytree.com/2018/03/kacsenyak-family-of-slovakia-and-the-u-s/

KLUVANEK

Rodokmeň rodiny Kluvánkovej. See - http://www.kluvanek.com/rodokmen/priezviska.htm

KONA

Kona, Martha Mistina, *Kona-Mistina family in the United States of America*, Wilmette, IL. The Author, 1995.

KOPCHAK

"Index to Kopchak / Macala / Galayda / Cebula Families." See - http://www.iarelative.com/alpha2.htm

KOWAL

John Kowal's Family history Blog. See - https://kowalfamilyhistory.wordpress.com/2011/09/28/a-breakthrough-on-the-slovak-branch-of-the-family-tree/

KOZACHIK

"The Kozachik Genealogy and Family Tree Page," in: Surname Finder. See - https://www.genealogytoday.com/surname/finder.mv?Surname=Kozachik

KRISKO

The Barely Branching Krisko Family Tree. See - http://vricko.com/index. php/2016/12/10/barely-branching-krisko-family-tree/

KRUPITZER

"Genealógia rodiny Krupitzerovcov," in: Vacilando. See - http://www. vacilando.org/article/genealogia-rodiny-krupitzerovcov
The Krupitzer Family of Metzenseifen. By Duncan Gardiner. Lakewood, OH: The Family Historian, 1990.

LANGSAM

"Langsam/Miller/Spira/Ekstein Genealogy." See - https://www.ics.uci. edu/~dan/genealogy/Miller/langsam.htm

LAUDER

"Josephine Esther MENTZER Estée LAUDER," in: Geneanet. See - https://gw.geneanet.org/garric?lang=en&n=mentzer&oc=0&p= josephine+esther
"Leonard Lauder – Family, Family Tree," in: CelebFamily. See - https://www. celebfamily.com/entrepreneur/leonard-lauder.html

LEFKOWITZ

"Lefkowitz Genealogy," in: Wiki Tree. See - https://www.wikitree.com/ genealogy/lefkowitz

MACALA - see KOPCHAK

MARCZINKO - see SIVAK

MILLER

"Miller Genealogy," See - https://www.ics.uci.edu/~dan/genealogy/Miller/ homemilr.htm#YY

MISTINA - *see* KONA

PALKA

"The Palka Genealogy and Family Tree Page," in: Surname Finder. See - https://www.genealogytoday.com/surname/finder.mv?Surname=Palka

REISENAUER - see RYBNIKÁR

ROMBAUER

"A Piece of Late Modern Age History of Hungary through the Rombauer Family Tree." By Pal Koudela. In: *Prague Papers on the History of International Relations*, Vol. 1 (2015), pp. 28-45.
"A Piece of Migration History through the Rombauer Family Tree." By Pál Koudela. In: Prague *Papers on the History of International Relations*, Vol. 2 (2016), pp. 46-70. Published by Charles University, Faculty of Arts.
"Rombauer Genealogy," in: Wiki Tree. See - https://www.wikitree.com/genealogy/rombauer

RYBNIKÁR

Rodokmen rodiny Rybnikárovej, Františka Reisenauera a jeho detí Olgy a Františka. By Martin Ambruš. The Author, 2018. See - http://zahoraci.huncokari.sk/rodokmen-rodiny-rybnikarovej-frantiska-reisenauera-a-jeho-deti-olgy-a-frantiska/

SIVAK

From Slovakia to the United States: A history of Sivak-Marczinko families. By Kathy Smierciak. The Author, 1998.

STEINER

Between the Old and the New: The Story of the Steiner Family in Pressburg. By Martin Trančík. Bratislava: Albert Marenčín Vydavatelstvo PT, 2006, c1995.

ŠTÚR

Rodokmen a osudy rodiny Štúrovcov. By Martin Ambruš.

Bratislava: Tatran, 1988. 185 p.

SZOLD

"The Szold Genealogy and Family Tree Page," in: Surname Finder. See - https://www.genealogytoday.com/surname/finder.mv?Surname=Szold

TOMKO - see GURKA

WASSILAK

History and Genealogy of the Wassilak Family. By Leighto Wassilak.
"The Wassilak Genealogy and Family Tree Page," in: Surname Finder. See - https://www.genealogytoday.com/surname/finder.mv?Surname=Wassilak

WILCOX

"Slovaks in Youngstown: One Family's Story," in Steel Valley Voices. See - http://steelvalleyvoices.ysu.edu/resources/collections/slovaks/slovaks-in-youngstown-one-familys-story/

D. FAMILY TREES ON GENI

Note: The family trees frequently contain extensive biographical information

Albrecht, Paul, virologist
Altmann, Alexander, Orthodox Jewish scholar, rabbi, philosopher
Barkan, Adolf, ophthalmologist
Bartók, Béla, pianist, composer, ethnomusicologist
Benyovszky, Emánuel, Count
Benyovszky, Maurice, Count, soldier of fortune, globetrotter
Berger, Oscar, caricaturist, cartoonist
Bettelheim, Aaron Siegfried, rabbi, Hebraist
Bettelheim, Bruno, clinical psychologist, psychoanalyst
Bettelheim, Sidonia Cyd, resident directress of Emanu El Sisterhood, NYC
Bettelheim, Felix Albert, physician and surgeon of Panama

Bihari, Joseph, co-founder of Modern Records, the Los Angeles-based record company

Boffa, Michelle Elizabeth (Striker), clinical psychologist, psychotherapist

Bondy-Charvat, Richard, landscape architect

Bongiovi, John Francis (Jon Bon Jovi), singer, songwriter, record producer, actor

Boor, Ladislav Michal, Lutheran minister, pastor

Boreanaz, David Patrick, American actor, TV producer and director

Branca, Ralph Theodore Joseph, American professional baseball pitcher

Bunzl, Walter Henry, manufacturer, Atlanta, GA

Cernan, Eugene Andrew, astronaut, last person to walk on the Moon

Curtis, Tony, film actor

Daddario, Alexandra Anna, American actress

Dembitz, Arthur Aaron, instructor of Hebrew, Gratz College

Dembitz, Lewis Naftali, lawyer, legal scholar

Dembitz, Nanette, lawyer, New York Judge

Dembitz, Siegmund, pioneer physician

Derschowitz, Zvi, rabbi

Ditko, Stephen J., comic book artist

Dohnányi, Ernst, pianist, composer, conductor

Dudik, Duane A., attorney, Pleasant Hills, PA

Fleischhakcer, Desider, pharmaceutical chemist, biochemist

Foyta, István Kálmán, business executive

Frankfurter, Felix, Associate Justice of the US Supreme Court

Gardiner, Duncan, certified genealogist

Gajdusek, Daniel Carleton, medical researcher, recipient of the Nobel Prize in physiology or medicine

Galos, George, accountant, club officer, Chicago

Gardini, Etelka (Gerster), opera singer, soprano

Gelley, Zacharia, rev (rabbi), of the Khal Adas Jeshurun (KAJ) *kehillah* of Washington Heights, NY

Getting, Ivan Alexander, physicist, electrical engineer, co-inventor of GPS

Gilinsky, Jack, singer

Gleiman, Lubomir, philosopher

Goldberger, Henry R., rabbi, Erie, PA

Goldberger, Joseph, physician, epidemiologist

Goldberger, Joseph Herman, public health officer, ophthalmologist

Haven Voight, James, actor

Hepburn, Audrey, actress, model, dancer, humanitarian
Hexner, Ervin Paul, economist, International Monetary Fund, Washington, DC
Hitschmann (Link), Irene, psychiatrist
Honochick, Jim, American Leagues umpire
Huebsch, Adolph, rabbi
Huebsch, Benjamin W., publisher, NYC
Jazsi (Moskovitz), Amália, writer, painter, graphic artist
Jászi (Jakubovits), Oszkár, historian, sociologist, politician
Joseffy, Rafael, pianist, composer, conductor, teacher
Kalanick, Travis, a co-founder of the peer-to-peer file sharing company Red Swoosh and the transportation network company Uber.
Kerney, Alexander (orig. Kornhauser), business executive, Toronto, Canada
Klein, Imrich, chemical engineer, NJ
Klein, Philipp Hillel (HaKohen), rabbi, "Moes of Hungary"
Kocak, Matej, soldier, recipient of Medal of Honor
Kohut, Rebekah (Bettelheim), communal worker
Kojis, Ferdinand George, physician, internist, NYC
Kolarik Josef, Lutheran minister
Kolarik, Josef Milan, Lutheran minister
Kovacs, Ernest Edward, American comedian, actor and writer
Kovály, Heda Margolius (Bloch), Holocaust survivor, writer, translator
Kovály, Pavel, Holocaust survivor; professor of philosophy, Northeastern University
Kozlay, Eugene A., Brigadier General, Union Army
Kraus, Lili Mandl, pianist
Kurková, Karolina, model and actress
Lefkowitz, David, rabbi
Lefkowitz, David, Jr., rabbi
Lehár, Franz Christian, composer of operettas
Lilienthal, David Eli, attorney, head of TVA and then of Atomic Energy Commission
Loebl (Lőbl), Eugen (Janci), economist
Lorre, Peter Laszlo (Löwenstein), actor
Low-Beer, Bertram, radiologist, professor, University of California, San Francisco
Madarasz, Louis T., calligrapher

Marian, Joseph, wood technologist, University of California
Massarik, Fred, professor of management, UCLA
Mendlowitz, Shraga Feivel Mendlowitz, Orthodox rabbi, Brooklyn, NY
Munk, Peter Meir Abraham, industrial tycoon, investor, philanthropist, Canada
Newfield, Morris, rabbi
Newman, Paul Leonard, movie star
Orowan, Egon, mechanical engineer, metallurgist
Pásztory, Ditta, pianist
Pauliny-Toth, Ivan, radio astronomer
Pereles, Nathan, pioneer Jewish grocery merchant in Milwaukee, attorney
Pereles, Thomas Jefferson, attorney, Milwaukee
Polanyi (orig. Pollacsek), John C., Canadian chemist, recipient of the Nobel Prize in chemistry
Polanyi (orig. Pollacsek), Károly (Karl) economist, sociologist, philosopher
Polier, Justine (née Wise), jurist
Politzer, Alan, physician, surgeon, New York, NY
Politzer, Hugh David, theoretical physicist, recipient of the Nobel Prize in physics
Reiner, Frederick 'Fritz' Martin, composer, conductor
Reinhardt, Max (Goldmann), theater director
Rich, Richard H. (orig. Rosenheim), merchant and business executive, president of Rich's Inc., Atlanta, GA
Rich, Morris (Mauritius Reich), the founder of the Rich's Department Store chain, Atlanta, GA
Roberts, John Glover, Jr., lawyer, Chief Justice of the US
Rombauer, Emil Roderick, 1848 revolutionary, US Civil War veteran; lawyer, judge
Rombauer, Gyula Róbert, US Civil War veteran
Rombauer, Johann Theodore (Tivadar), engineer, industrialist, entrepreneur, supplier of arms to 1848 revolutionaries
Rombauer, Rafael Guidó, US Civil War veteran
Rombauer, Roland Theodore, 1848 revolutionary, US Civil War veteran
Roth, Feri, violinist
Rovnianek, Peter Pavol, journalist, writer; founder of Slovaktown, AR
• **Schoenberg, Arnold,** outstanding innovative composer
Sekerak, Richard John, physician, otolaryngologist, Bridgeport, CT
Selleck, Thomas 'Tom' William, American actor and film producer

Serly, Tibor, violist, violinist, composer, teacher, NYC
Sonneschein, Solomon Hirsch, rabbi
Staub, Allen Alexander, conglomerate executive, Wichita, KS
Staub, Barry Alan, Wichita, KS
Staub, Milton, corporate executive, Columbus, OH
Steinerman, Debora, lawyer, an activist
Steinitz, Wilhelm, chess master, World Chess Champion
Striker, Laura Matild (Polányi - Pollacsek), historian, feminist prolific non-fiction writer
Striker, Michael S., patent lawyer, NYC
Sychak, Bret Michael, singer, songwriter
Szell, George, conductor, composer
Szilard (orig. Spitz), Leo, physicist, inventor
Szold, Benjamin, rabbi and scholar
Szold, Henrietta, Zionist leader and founder of Hadassah
Ujhazi, Ladislaus, founder of New Buda, Iowa
Urich, Robert Michael, film, TV, and stage actor, TV producer
Ventura, Jesse, professional wrestler, politician, Governor of Minnesota
Voight, Angelina Jolie, actress, filmmaker, humanitarian
Voight, Jonathan Vincent, American actor
Weinberger, Howard Lawrence, inventor
Weinberger, Jacob, lawyer, Federal judge
Wilde, Cornelius Louis (orig. Weisz),
Wise, Aaron, rabbi
Wise, Stephen Samuel, Reform rabbi, Zionist
Zahorsky, John, physician, St. Louis
Zathureczky, Ede, violin virtuoso and pedagogue
Zemplinsky, Alexander von, composer, conductor, teacher

ABBREVIATIONS TO FREQUENT REFERENCES

American Scholars - *Directory of American Scholars*

Beyond the Sea of Beer - *Beyond the Sea of Beer.* History of Immigration of Bohemians and Czechs to the New World and their Contributions. By Miloslav Rechcigl, Jr. Bloomington, IN: AuthorHouse, 2017.

Catholic Who's Who - *The American Catholic Who's Who.* Grosse Pointe, MI: Walter Romig.

Čulen - *History of Slovaks in America.* By Konštantín Čulen. Minneapolis: Czechoslovak Genealogical Society International, 2007. 438p.

Czechoslovak Contribution - *The Czechoslovak Contribution to World Culture.* Edited by Miloslav Rechcigl, Jr. The Hague-London-Paris: Mouton & Co., 1964.

Czechoslovakia Past and Present - *Czechoslovakia Past and Present.* Edited by Miloslav Rechcigl, Jr. The Hague-Paris: Mouton, 1968. 2 Vols.

Droba - *Czech and Slovak Leaders in Metropolitan Chicago.* By Daniel D. Droba. Chicago: The Slavonic Club of the University of Chicago, 1934. 307p.

Educators - *Educators with Czechoslovak Roots.* A US and Canadian Faculty Roster. By Miloslav Rechcigl, Jr. Washington, DC: SVU Press, 1980. 122p.

Encyclopedia - *Encyclopedia of Bohemian and Czech-American Biography.* By Miloslav Rechcigl, Jr. Bloomington, IN: AuthorHouse, 2017. 3 Vols. 2538p.

Krajsa - *Slovaks in America. Bicentennial Study.* Edited by Joseph C. Krajsa et. al. The Slovak League of America, 1978. 494p.

Lincoln's Hungarian Heroes - *Lincoln's Hungarian Heroes: The Participation of Hungarians in the Civil War, 1861-1865.* By Edmund Vasvary. Washington, DC.: Hungarian Reformed Federation of America, 1939. 171p.

Miller - *The Czecho-Slovaks in America.* By Kenneth Dexter Miller. New York: George H. Doran, 1922. 196p.

National Biography - *American National Biography.* Edited by John A. Garraty and Mark C. Carnes New York: Oxford University Press, 1999.

Panorama - *Panorama.* A Historical Review of Czechs and Slovaks in the United States of America. Cicero, IL: Czechoslovak National Council of America,1970. 328p.

Pejskar - *Poslední pocta.* Památník na zemřelé československé exulanty…. By Jožka Pejskar. Konfrontace, 1982, 1985, 1989, 1994. Vol. 1-4.

American Science - *American Men (and Women) of Sciences.*

Social Sciences - *Social and Behavioral Sciences*

SVU Directory - *Biographical Directory of the Members of the Czechoslovak Society of Arts and Sciences.* Compiled and edited by Eva Rechcigl and Miloslav Rechcigl, Jr. New York, and later,
Washington, DC: SVU Press, 1966, 1968, 1972, 1983, 1988, 1992, 2003. 1-8 editions

Vida - *The True Cause of Freedom: The Kossuth Emigration ad the Hungarians: Participation in American Civil War.* By Istvan Kornel Vida. See - https://dea. lib.unideb.hu/dea/bitstream/handle/2437/33398/vida_istvan_dissertation. pdf?sequence=5&isAllowed=y

OTHER ABBREVIATIONS AND ACRONYMS

Academia.edu - American social networking website for academics to share papers

AFC - Average Fixed Cost

AFCR - American Fund for Czechoslovak Relief, NYC

AFIT - Air Force Institute of Technology

AFL - American Federation of Labor

AHA - American Historical Association

AHL - American Hockey League

AK - Alaska

AR - Arkansas

ASA - American Softball Association

ASCAP - American Society of Composers, Authors & Publishers

AZ - Arizona

Bapst Library - (Boston College Library)

BC - British Columbia (Canada)

BVM - Sisters of Charity of the Blessed Virgin Mary (religious order)

CA - California

CARA - Center for Applied Research in the Apostolate (Georgetown University)

CBS - Columbia Broadcasting System

CDA - Chargé d'affaires

CEO - Chief Executive Officer

CGSI - Czechoslovak Genealogical Society International

CHL - Canadian Hockey League

CIO - Congress of Industrial Organizations (Federation of Unions)

CNN - Cable News Network

Co. - Company, County

CO - Colorado

CSGSA - Czech and Slovak Genealogical Society of Arizona, Phoenix, AZ

CSPS - Czech-Slovak Protective Society

CSsR - Congregatio Sanctissimi Redemptoris (the Redemtorists)

CT - Connecticut

CUNY - The City University of New York

Czech. - Czechoslovakia

DACVIM - Diplomate of the American College of Veterinary Internal Medicine

DC - District of Columbia

DE - Delaware

DIY Network - a Canadian English-language Category BH specialty channel

Doximity - online social networking service for US clinicians

DPM - Doctor of Podiatric Medicine

DVM - Doctor of Veterinary Medicine

Ed. - Editor, Edited

Ethnicelebs - Celebrity ethnicity popular website

FACS - Fellow of American College of Surgeons

FCCP - Fellow of the College of Chest Physicians

EU - European Union

FAA - Federal Aviation Administration

Family Search - genealogy organization operated by the Church of Jesus Christ of Latter Saints

FBI - Federal Bureau of Investigation

FCSLA - First Catholic Slovak Ladies Association

FCSU - First Catholic Slovak Union (insurance)

FCU - First Catholic Slovak Union of the USA and Canada

FEEFHS - Foundation for East European Family History Studies

Find A Grave - a website allowing search and add to an online database of cemetery records

FIU - Florida International University, Miami, FL

FL - Florida

fl. - floruit (flourished) - denotes a date or period during which a person was known to have been alive or active

GA - Georgia

GATT - General Agreement on Tariffs and Trade

Geneanet - an international genealogy database

GENi - Genealogy Database

GPO - Government Printing Office

GPS - Global Positioning System

HBO - Home Box Office (an American premium cable and satellite TV network

Healthgrades - US company that provides information about physicians, hospitals and health care providers

HI - Hawaii

HS - High School

IA - Iowa

IAO - International Association of Orthodontics

ID - Idaho

IHRC - Immigration History Research Center (University of Minnesota)

IL - Illinois

ILGWU - The International Ladies' Garment Workers' Union

IMDb - Internet Movie Database (an online database of world films, TV programs, videos, etc.)

IN - Indiana

ISF - International Softball Association

ITF - International Tennis Federation

Jr. - Junior

KS - Kansas

KY - Kentucky

LA - Louisiana

LIC - Literárne informačné centrum

LinkedIn - a social networking website for people in professional jobs.

LLC - Limited Liability Company

LLP - Limited Liability Partnership

MA - a Master of Arts

MD - Maryland

ME - Maine

MFA - Master of fine Arts

MI - Michigan

MIT - Massachusetts Institute of Technology

MLB - Major League Baseball

MN - Minnesota

MPH - Master of Public Health

MS - Manuscript

MS - Mississippi

Msgr. - Monsignor

MT - Montana

MUNI - Masaryk University, Brno

NASA - National Aeronautics and Space Administration

NATO - North Atlantic Treaty Organization

Navy SEAL - Sea Air and Land (a Naval Special Warfare Unit)

NBA - National; Basketball Association

NC - North Carolina

NCI - National Cancer Institute (NIH)

NCSML - National Czech & Slovak Museum & Library

ND - North Dakota

NE - Nebraska

née - originally or formerly called

NFL - National Football League

NH - New Hampshire

NHL - National Hockey League

NIH - National Institutes of Health, Bethesda, MD

NJ - New Jersey

No. - Number

NPR - National Public Radio

nr. - near

NSSUS - National Slovak Society of the United States of America

NY - New York

NYC - New York City

OD - Doctor of Optometry

O.F.M. - Order of Friars Minor (Franciscans)

O.F.M.C - Order of Friars Minor Conventual

OH - Ohio

OK -Oklahoma

OMC - Order of Merciful Christ (Religious Order)

Ont. - Ontario (Canada)

OR - Oregon

O.S.B. - Order of Saint Benedict

PA - Pennsylvania

PBS - Public Broadcasting Service

pp. - pages

PQ - Province of Quebec

PR - Puerto Rico

Prabook - Biographical encyclopedia of individuals at community or any professional field

ProZ.com - a membership-based website targeting freelance translators

QC - Quebec

R.C. - Roman Catholic

ResearchGate - a social networking site for scientists and researchers to share papers

Rev. - Reverend

RFE - Radio Free Europe

RI - Rhode Island

Rt. Rev. - Right Reverend

s. - since

S-ACC - Slovak-American Cultural Center, NYC

SC - South Carolina

SCF - Slovak Catholic Federation of America

SCP - Society of Czechoslovak Philately

SCRIBD - a digital library, e-book and audiobook subscription service, including million titles

SD - South Dakota

SDU - Syddansk Universitet (Denmark)

SELC - Slovak Evangelical Lutheran Church

Sharecare - a health and wellness engagement platform

S.J. - Society of Jesus (Jesuits)

SLAHF - Slovak League of America Heritage Foundation

SLRP - Surname Location Reference Project

Sr. - Senior

SRF - Slovak Relief Fund

S.S. - Saints

SSA - Slovak Studies Association

SS.CM - Servants of the Holy Heart of Mary

St. - Saint

STD - Sacred Theology Degree

STL - Licentiate in Sacred Theology (SJ)

SUNY - State University of New York

supt. - superintendent

Surname finder - genealogy surname finder

SVU - Czechoslovak Society of Arts and Sciences

SWAA - Slovak Writers and Artists Association

TGFC - The Golden Flashes Club

TGMG - Tampa General Hospital, Florida

TN - Tennessee

Top.NPI.com - Nation's leading doctors' and physician's directory

T.O.R. - Tertius Fratrum Regularis S. Francisci (Brothers of Penance)

TWUA - Textile Workers Union of America

TX - Texas

UAH - University of Alabama - Huntsville, AL
UCLA - University of California - Los Angeles
UCSF - University of California - San Francisco
UGCCWA - United Gas Coke and Chemical Workers of America
ULS United Lutheran Society
UN - United Nations
UMWA - United Mine Workers of America
UNCW - University of North Carolina, WUS - United States
USA - United States of America
USDA - US Department of Agriculture
UPWA - United Packinghouse Workers of America
USGS - US Geological Survey
USN - US Navy
UT - Utah
VA - Virginia
Vol. - Volume
VT - Vermont
VW - Volkswagen
WA - Washington
WebMD - American online publisher of news relating to human health and well-being
WHL - Western Hockey League
WI - Wisconsin
Wikipedia - The Free Encyclopedia
WikiTree - a free, shared social networking genealogy website
WIX - Website Builder
WPSCA - Western Pennsylvania Slovak Cultural Association, Pittsburgh, PA
WQED - Virtual and very high frequency digital TV channel (PBS)
WTA - Women's Tennis Association
WV - West Virginia
WWI - World War I
WY - Wyoming

Printed in the United States
By Bookmasters